GENERAL JOSEPH E. JOHNSTON, C.S.A.

A Different Valor

GENERAL JOSEPH E. JOHNSTON, C.S.A.

A Different Valor

By
Gilbert E. Govan
and
James W. Livingwood

This edition published in 1995 by SMITHMARK Publishers Inc.,
16 East 32nd Street, New York, NY 10016

SMITHMARK books are available for bulk purchase for sales
promotion and premium use. For details write or call the
manager of special sales, SMITHMARK Publishers Inc.,
16 East 32nd Street, New York, NY 10016; (212) 532-6600.

This edition published by special arrangement with
W.S. Konecky Associates, Inc., 156 5th Avenue, New York, NY 10010.

ISBN: 0-8317-2442-0

Printed in the United States of America

10 9 8 7 6 5 4 3 2 1

CONTENTS

The authors acknowledge with thanks the permission graciously granted to them to quote material from books, periodicals and letters, as follows:

From *A Southern Girl in '61*, by Louise Wigfall Wright. Copyrighted 1905 by Doubleday & Co., Inc.

From three letters from Joseph E. Johnston and eight letters from Louis T. Wigfall, reproduced by permission of The Huntington Library, San Marino, Calif.

From *A Diary from Dixie*, by Mary Boykin Chesnut. Copyright 1905, by D. Appleton & Co. Reprinted by permission of the publishers, Appleton-Century-Crofts, Inc.

From *A Diary from Dixie*, by Mary Boykin Chesnut (1949), ed. by Ben Ames Williams, Houghton Mifflin Co.

From *General Kirby Smith*, by A. H. Noll (1907), University Press of Sewanee, Tenn.

From *Leonidas Polk*, Bishop and General, by W. M. Polk (1915), Longmans, Green & Co., Inc.

From *General Edmund Kirby Smith, C.S.A.*, by J. H. Parks (1954), and *With Beauregard in Mexico*, by P. G. T. Beauregard (1956), Louisiana State University Press.

From "The Correspondence of Robert Toombs, Alexander H. Stephens and Howell Cobb," ed. by U. B. Phillips, *The Annual Report of the American Historical Association for the Year 1911*.

From *Yours Till Death: Civil War Letters of John W. Cotton* (1951), and *The Civil War Diary of General Josiah Gorgas* (1947), University of Alabama Press.

From *Jefferson Davis, Constitutionalist: Letters, Papers and Speeches*, ed. by Dunbar Rowland (1923), Department of Archives and History, State of Mississippi.

From *A Son's Recollections of His Father*, by W. W. Mackall (1930), E. P. Dutton and Co.

From *The Railroads of the Confederacy*, by R. C. Black III (1952); *Two Soldiers: The Campaign Diaries of Thomas J. Key, C.S.A., and Robert J. Campbell, U.S.A.*, by W. A. Cate (1938); *I Rode with Stonewall*, by H. K. Douglas (1940); *Stephen R. Mallory: Confederate Navy Chief*, by J. T. Durkin (1954); *James Longstreet*, by H. J. Eckenrode and B. Conrad (1936); *Joseph E. Brown and the Confederacy*, by L. B. Hill (1939); and *Pemberton, Defender of Vicksburg*, by J. C. Pemberton (1942); University of North Carolina Press.

LIST OF MAPS

GENERAL JOSEPH E. JOHNSTON, C.S.A.

A Different Valor

CHAPTER I

THE MAKING OF A SOLDIER

On Monday morning April 22, 1861, Brigadier General Joseph E. Johnston, Quartermaster General of the United States Army, walked briskly along familiar Washington streets. His manner concealed the strain he had suffered for the past few days just as his pace denied his fifty-four years. Many of the thoroughfares along which he passed had a strange deserted appearance, some shops were closed and houses vacant, but the soldier didn't notice his surroundings as he made his way to the office of the Secretary of War. In his pocket he carried a letter which was the most important one he had ever written, and he was intent on its early delivery.

In the privacy of his home he had pondered long before making his decision. On Friday he knew definitely that his native state of Virginia had reacted to the guns of Fort Sumter by seceding from the Union. The next day he penned his letter, but the gravity of its contents along with unfinished official business preoccupied his entire week end. Meanwhile, the city had been feverish with fear and tension as residents realized they were virtually ringed by rebellion, and guests departed before an effort might be made to capture the capitol.

Before entering the office of the Secretary, Johnston was joined by the Adjutant General who had agreed to accompany him. Simon

Cameron had been in office for such a short time that he was scarcely accustomed to the formal salutes of the visitors who soon stood erectly before him. Johnston handed him the letter which the Secretary read carefully.

Sir: With feelings of deep regret I respectfully tender the resignation of my commission in the army of the United States. The feelings which impel me to this act are, I believe, understood by the Honorable Secretary of War. I hope that long service, with some labor, hardship, danger, and loss of blood, may give me claim to ask the early consideration of this communication.

Most respectfully, your obedient servant,

J. E. Johnston, Quartermaster General.[1]

The Secretary was not surprised by the content of the letter. Strangely enough the administration thought there was nothing unusual in such resignations. Just two days before, Colonel Robert E. Lee had taken that step. Now, another of the most experienced and highly considered officers presented his. With all these things in mind Secretary Cameron expressed his sincere regret that Johnston thought it necessary and requested the Adjutant General prepare the proper orders immediately.

Joseph E. Johnston was the grandson of Peter Johnston, who emigrated from Scotland in 1727 to Virginia. A successful merchant, the elder Johnston moved from his first location on the James River to the Piedmont section of the colony shortly after the French and Indian War. His younger son, also named Peter, when only seventeen joined the legion of Light-Horse Harry Lee for the campaign in the Carolinas and served with it during the rest of the Revolution with such distinction that he became a favorite of his commander. This association laid the foundation for a friendship between the Johnston and Lee families which became even closer with the sons of the two Revolutionary soldiers.

In 1788 the younger Peter Johnston married Mary Wood, a niece of the fiery Virginia patriot, Patrick Henry, and the two made their home at the family farm in Prince Edward County, which Peter inherited at the death of his father. He developed an interest in politics and was a member of the State Assembly for thirteen terms, twice being chosen speaker of the House of Delegates. Prominent in the debates in which the issues of States' rights first occurred, he stood with the majority in denying the Federal government the authority claimed in the Alien and Sedition Laws. A few years later he served on the commission which settled the boundary dispute between Tennessee and Virginia, and in 1811 he became a judge of the Virginia General Court.

The birth of the eighth son of Peter and Mary Johnston occurred February 3, 1807, at Cherry Grove. They gave him the name Joseph Eggleston, for the captain under whom Peter served in the Revolution. When the boy was four years old, the family moved to Panicello—the name of their new home near Abingdon, a location more convenient for Peter to serve the southwest Virginia circuit. There the young Virginian grew up, playing typical games with friends about the countryside. Judge Johnston was an ardent huntsman and his sons naturally followed his interest. A number of the veterans of the Battle of King's Mountain lived in the area and excited the youthful interest of the boys by stories of their adventures. Emulating these heroes, the boys organized themselves into armies with young Joe as one of the leaders. With such a background of outdoor activity he became a fine horseman and a good marksman. It contributed also to a hardy constitution which enabled him to withstand the rigors of military campaigns and to recover from the number of wounds which he received as a soldier.

Joe did not grow up a young savage, running wild about the neighborhood. His father had the family's traditional interest in education and his mother was a cultured woman as capable of instructing her children in the classics and inspiring them with a love of reading and learning as she was of managing her large household. On cold nights the family gathered around the fire to listen as one of the older brothers read. It was then that Joe first made his acquaintance with the novels of Sir Walter Scott, for which he retained an affection through all his life.

Mrs. Johnston gave the boy his earliest teaching, after which he attended the Abingdon Academy, which his father had helped to establish some years before. He did good work there and showed interest in the classics particularly. Even so his inclination continued to be toward the military. His father early recognized this trait and consequently gave him the sword he had carried through the Revolution. Through a political friend Judge Johnston worked to secure Joe an appointment to West Point, which President Adams made February 21, 1825, when Joseph was eighteen years old. In the roster of cadets from Virginia the name of Robert E. Lee, the son of Judge Johnston's Revolutionary leader, immediately precedes that of Joseph.

In June of that year the two young Virginians successfully passed the examinations to become members of an entering class of 105 cadets. Although Lee was slightly older the two soon became fast friends. Years later Johnston wrote of this relationship:

We had the same intimate associates, who thought, as I did, that no other youth or man so united the qualities that win warm friendship and command high respect. For he was full of sympathy and kindness, genial and fond of gay conversation, and even of fun, that made him the most agreeable of companions, while his correctness of demeanor and language and attention to all duties, personal and official, and a dignity as much a part of himself as the elegance of his person, gave him a superiority that every one acknowledged in his heart. He was the only one of all the men I have known who could laugh at the faults and follies of his friends in such a manner as to make them ashamed without touching their affection for him, and to confirm their respect and sense of his superiority.[2]

In the four years of Johnston's experience at West Point he was associated with a number of cadets who played a part also in the great trial of the Confederacy. Three of them—Albert Sidney Johnston, as well as Lee and Joseph—were among the first five nominations as full generals. Two were in Richmond as heads of bureaus—Abraham C. Myers as Quartermaster General and L. B. Northrop as Commissary General. Of the others, Leonidas Polk and Theophilus H. Holmes held commissions as lieutenant generals. In all, twelve achieved the rank of brigadier general or above. Although some of them won temporary prominence in the early months of the war, none of the cadets attending West Point the same four years as Johnston reached permanent positions of importance in the Federal Army in the Confederate War.

In addition to those who achieved military prominence in the Confederacy a cadet from Mississippi in the class of 1828 became its president. During their period together at West Point Johnston and Jefferson Davis were but casual acquaintances. The occasionally encountered story that the two had an altercation over a girl cannot be substantiated from a contemporary source and seems a complete fabrication. "The Colonel," as his intimates called Johnston, and Lee did not join in the escapades which more than once created trouble for Davis with the authorities.[3]

Johnston had to work against one major handicap in order to maintain his scholastic average. For a period of time an eye affection totally prohibited any night study, but neither this trouble nor the Spartan existence the cadets led prevented him from maintaining his early interest in books. French, astronomy, military history and biography were his favorite subjects and continued to be through his whole life. On July 1, 1829, when he graduated and was commissioned a second lieutenant in the Fourth Artillery, he ranked thirteenth in a class of forty-six, while his friend Lee stood second.

His first assignment was to garrison duty at Fort Columbus, New York. For the next seven years he served at posts up and down the Atlantic coast and in some of the final phases of the removal of eastern Indians. Two of his assignments forecast the threatening clouds which were gathering for the future. One was at Fort Monroe at the time of the Nat Turner slave uprising, and the other at Charleston Harbor during the Nullification crisis.[4]

The experience at Fort Monroe was a happy one. The trouble among the slaves developed no serious proportions and he found Lee stationed there. The two immediately resumed their West Point intimacy and enjoyed the social activities of the garrison together. But the second of these assignments gave the appearance of being crucial. Under the leadership of John C. Calhoun, South Carolina adopted the Ordinance of Nullification in a bold stand to assert States' rights. Johnston was among the troops whom the national government sent quickly to the scene to reinforce the garrison at Charleston. At the same time three of his brothers, who lived in Columbia, were drilling with the state's minutemen, while another brother in the United States Congress was a vigorous supporter of the States' rights position.

When the South Carolina difficulties subsided, Johnston was reassigned to Fort Monroe, where Lee was still stationed. In one letter to a mutual friend Lee remarked that "The Colonel" was "in some danger of being caught by a pair of black eyes," but the affair was apparently of only passing duration. Early in 1834 the artillery school was broken up and the officers and batteries ordered to different stations. But Lee and Johnston soon found themselves to-

gether again in Washington, with Lee as assistant to the Chief of
Engineers and Johnston on topographical duty. Johnston lived at
Mrs. Ulrich's boardinghouse, where a number of prominent political
and military men resided. When duty prevented Lee from returning
to his home in Arlington, he usually joined their "mess."[5]

Though he was still officially assigned to duty with the Topographical Engineers an outbreak of the Seminole Indians in Florida
took Lieutenant Johnston to that area. Major General Winfield
Scott, who commanded the troops, selected Johnston as one of his
aides. It was not the young officer's first experience with Indian
difficulties, as he was among the troops sent to the Black Hawk War,
although he saw no action, and for a time in 1833-1834, was stationed in the Creek Nation.

The Florida theater was one of the wildest and least known sections of the American frontier. The Seminoles were expert guerrilla
fighters and had the advantage of swamp and forest tangle, which
concealed their movements and camps. The climate also handicapped the troops, who were limited to operations in the winter
months.

Nothing noteworthy was accomplished in the campaign, which
was late in starting and resulted in no important engagement. When
in July Scott was recalled, a storm of protest, official and public,
consequently swept the country and led to a court of inquiry. Johnston had been close to Scott and is mentioned in the general's
testimony. The inquiry was an unusual experience for the younger
man, and in it he gained firsthand knowledge of the type of dissension which could break about the head of any army leader.

General Thomas S. Jesup, who succeeded Scott in Florida, was
more successful, and with the surrender to him in the spring of 1837
of a number of the prominent Indian leaders, the war seemed to be
over. Although gratified by his promotion to first lieutenant in July
1836, Johnston felt that with the end of the war he should resign.
The department accepted his resignation May 31, 1837, whereupon
he entered the profession of civil engineering. In September, though,
hostilities again broke out in Florida, and he immediately volunteered his services.

Secretary of War Poinsett appointed him Adjutant and Topographical Engineer, without military rank, with a heterogeneous
party of civilians, soldiers and sailors under Lieutenant L. M. Powell

of the Navy. Under orders they explored the coasts and rivers of South Florida in co-operation with the Army to recommend sites for depots and forts. On January 15, 1838, the small detachment of which Johnston was a part encountered a band of Indians near the head of the Jupiter inlet of the Indian River. In the ensuing engagement every officer received incapacitating wounds. When the commander fell, a contemporary account reads, "Mr. Johnson [sic] took command. . . . ; and the coolness, courage, and judgment he displayed at the most critical and trying emergency was the theme of praise with every one who beheld him." In this engagement, Johnston did not escape unscathed. His clothing was pocked with bullet holes, and he carried a scar on his forehead from a slight wound for the rest of his life.[6]

This second experience in Florida reawakened his military ambition, and he secured his reappointment in the Army as a first lieutenant in the Corps of Topographical Engineers on July 7, 1838. On the same day he received the rank of brevet captain "for gallantry on several occasions in the war against the Florida Indians." Because he was out of service for so short a time, and possibly for his performance in emergency, he lost none of his seniority as an officer.

With all the variety of interesting assignments this period of his life had greatest importance for the ambitious engineering officer because of its personal aspects. While engaged in coastal survey he lost his heart to Lydia McLane of Baltimore. He had known her brother, Robert, also a West Point graduate, in the Florida war, and the two served together as engineers along the Canadian border. The result of their association was lifelong, devoted friendship and the meeting of Joseph and Lydia. The McLanes were a prominent family of Delaware. The father of Robert and Lydia, Louis McLane, had served in both houses of Congress, as minister to England, and in Jackson's Cabinet. In 1837 he became president of the Baltimore and Ohio Railroad and moved to Baltimore, where the family lived when Joseph courted Lydia. They were married there July 10, 1845.

Lydia was never noted as a beauty, but she fascinated both men and women by her graceful charm and delightful, endearing wit. It was a happy marriage, with the two brought closer together by being childless. In the first years that void was somewhat filled by an orphan nephew of Joseph, Preston Johnston, who had but recently graduated from West Point. In the series of letters he wrote to this beloved nephew, for whom he described his feeling as that of a father and brother mixed, Johnston revealed himself far more frankly than he usually did. He advised the younger man while at the military academy on the choice of profession, both within the Army and without, should peace prove a block to promotion. He counseled on studies and on development in other ways: "Read the Greek authors in English, & if you have time the Latins in the original."[7]

In this period of purely engineering duty for Johnston, war between the United States and Mexico precipitated him again into military action. When he heard of this new development, he applied for active service. Quickly, orders came for him to go to the Brazos, a few miles to the north of the point where the Rio Grande enters the Gulf of Mexico. It was one of the places where ships and men met to prepare for the movement on Veracruz.

Here, Johnston found himself once more with Captain Lee, and they occupied the same cabin on the general's ship as it made its way down the coast. The expedition arrived at Veracruz on March 5 and by nightfall a vast fleet of around seventy ships anchored in the harbor. The next day, Scott with his general officers and technical staffs reconnoitered the coast close by to seek a landing place. In doing so they came under fire from the batteries of a fort, which led to criticism from Lieutenant George Gordon Meade: "This operation I considered very foolish; for, having on board all the general officers of the army, one shot, hitting the vessel and disabling it, would have left us a floating target to the enemy, and might have been the means of breaking the expedition." Such a fortuitous catastrophe might have had a great effect upon future military history, as in the party were Lee, Johnston, Beauregard, G. W. Smith, McClellan and Meade.[8]

The leaders determined upon Sacrificio, a few miles down the coast, as the landing place. Across the water the town lay, surrounded by walls and crowned by an irregular skyline of church domes and castle towers. Offshore the collection of vessels defied description.

In late afternoon a signal gun started the first wave of craft ashore. As the men splashed onto the beach and pushed for the dunes beyond, the boats returned to the ships for a second party. By ten o'clock that night about 10,000 men were on Mexican soil.

Scott selected April 8 as the day for the advance to begin. Mexico City was the ultimate objective, but between Veracruz and that point lay much difficult country and the gathering armies of Santa Anna. The day after the invasion began Johnston transferred from the Topographical Engineers to a regiment of *voltigeurs,* troops who were trained as expert skirmishers and in Scott's army wore gray uniforms, instead of the traditional blue. As lieutenant colonel, he led his regiment on a reconnaissance well in advance of the army as it moved into the mountains over the road Cortez had followed more than 300 years before. Johnston's determination to secure as accurate information as possible about the works defending the pass through the mountain of Cerro Gordo led him to venture too close, with the result that he was twice wounded by musket fire.

Incapacitated by his wounds he spent the next week in a "spacious reed house," where a fellow Virginian, Dabney H. Maury, wounded also at Cerro Gordo, furnished comradeship. But an acquaintance of Maury, who requested that he be moved to the same house, soon created an unpleasant situation.

The partitions of the rooms were of reeds, wattled together, so that conversations could be heard from one room to the other. John Phoenix Derby was an incessant talker and uttered a stream of coarse wit, to the great disgust of Joe Johnston, who endured it in silence, till one day he heard Derby order his servant to capture a kid out of a flock of goats passing our door, when he broke out, "If you dare to do that, I'll have you court-martialed and cashiered or shot!"

After Scott had cleared Santa Anna out of the way and established possession of the town of Jalapa, he had the wounded men brought there by litter. It was "a lovely little town, on the slope of the mountain, looking down toward the sea, some ninety miles away." Maury continued to visit Johnston, whose nephew, Preston Johnston, then a lieutenant of artillery, cared for him. The army in this period remained at the town of Puebla, while its leaders tried to arrange peace with the Mexicans. When the negotiations failed Scott resumed the march toward the capital city.[9]

Johnston, who had recovered from his wounds, resumed his place with his regiment in time to take part in the series of engagements at Padierna, Contreras and Churubusco on August 19-20, just outside of Mexico City. In one of these attacks his nephew was killed. Lee, who had been standing close by the young artilleryman when he fell, met Johnston early the next morning. The latter had just heard of his nephew's death. Both men recorded the meeting. Lee said that Johnston's "frame [was] shrunk and shivered in agony." Johnston always remembered the feeling Lee displayed. After the war of 1861-1865, he wrote:

I saw strong evidence of the sympathy of his nature the morning after the first engagement of our troops in the Valley of Mexico. I had lost a cherished relative in that action, known to General Lee only as my relative. Meeting me, he suddenly saw in my face the effect of that loss, burst into tears, and expressed his deep sympathy as tenderly in words as his lovely wife would have done.[10]

But a few actions remained before the occupation of Mexico City. The first, Molino Del Rey, occurred on September 8, and the second and more important, the storming of Chapultepec, five days later. Johnston led his *voltigeurs* with distinction in both. In his report General Gideon J. Pillow, the division commander, referred to the work of the "very gallant and accomplished Lieutenant-Colonel Johnston" who "received three wounds, but they were all slight, and did not at all arrest his daring and onward movements." For his "gallant and meritorious conduct," he received the rank of brevet colonel. General Scott is reported to have said, "Johnston is a great soldier, but he has an unfortunate knack of getting himself shot in nearly every engagement." [11]

The Mexican capital city fell to the Americans on September 14. From that day on Johnston's duties consisted of routine matters, except when he took charge of the parties bringing supplies and replacement troops over the guerrilla-infested road from Veracruz. In this period of comparative quiet he joined with the other officers in organizing the Aztec Club, "to perpetuate the memories of their Mexican service." This society was a bond between men who later fought on opposite sides in fratricidal war. Some of them after 1865 attempted to use it as a means to re-establish old friendships.[12]

Johnston's regiment was mustered out of service in the summer of 1848. As a consequence there was some doubt about his status, but a special act by Congress, July 19, 1848, reinstated him in his rank as a captain in the Topographical Engineers.

In the early years after the close of the Mexican War Johnston surveyed boundaries and worked on the improvement of rivers. On one of these assignments in Texas he was again associated with Maury. In traveling through an extraordinary canyon Maury asked his friend "how he explained the power of that little stream to make a way for itself through the great mountain barrier," expecting some profound geological solution. The reply was, "I presume the Power that could make the stream could make a way for the stream to pass, sir." This incident not only contains an implication of a steadfast religious belief but also, in Maury's expectation of a "profound geological solution," evidence of Johnston's intellectual interest which was known throughout the Army.[13]

Johnston's career took a new direction in 1855 when he transferred from the Topographical Engineers to the Cavalry. Because of the territorial expansion of the country and a new wave of westward migration, which disturbed the Indians of the Plains, Congress increased the size of the Army by two regiments of cavalry and two of infantry. When Johnston learned of the new plans, he asked Adjutant General Samuel Cooper for consideration for promotion. Johnston's distinguished record in the Mexican War and his quarter of a century of service won him a commission as lieutenant colonel of the First Cavalry, of which E. V. Sumner was colonel. At the same time, Albert Sidney Johnston and Robert E. Lee became, respectively, colonel and lieutenant colonel of the Second Cavalry.[14]

After the Mexican War, because of their different assignments, Johnston and Lee rather lost touch with each other, and according to Johnston grew more formal in their relationship.[15] But Joe found spirits of kindred interest in a group of younger officers. They were all West Pointers with whom on one duty or another he had been in friendly association. Closest of them, apparently, was George B. McClellan, who was nineteen years younger, and whom he addressed as "Beloved Mc." Johnston's letters to him are frank and intimate, and display the playful humor which he used with those close to him. "We are just fairly settled," he wrote from Jefferson Barracks. " 'The Madame' has exhausted the pleasures of fixing up—& I am in hourly fear of a taking up of carpets & moving of furniture—for the sake of renewing the enjoyment of fixing."

When McClellan was on a tour of Europe as a member of a commission to observe latest military developments, Johnston wrote: "Had your musings on the subject of female Sardinians & assimilation of allowances anything to do with the determination to hurry to Constantinople?" He requested that the traveler perform certain errands for him. "If you meet with a good sword for fighting with, get it for me," he wrote, and he asked that good books on cavalry tactics, except for those written in Russian or German, be sent to him.

A common professional interest runs consistently through the letters. Both Johnston and McClellan were intent upon the improvement of the cavalry service and equipment. When McClellan returned from his observation tour in Europe, Johnston asked that he stay in Washington long enough to influence the improvement of the service. "The old infantry notion exists here," he wrote, "that to make a decent appearance on dress parade is the only object in instruction." The men were not even taught to ride, he complained. "Fancy 120 boobies who never straddled a horse, starting on an expedition of nearly two thousand miles—with the chance of getting into an occasional skirmish with the best horsemen in the world."

From his point of view there were other limitations on that expedition in addition to the poorly prepared soldiers. He found no interesting people in the party:

. . . but on the contrary I had such an infliction for one month as never was imposed upon Christian man. An infernal member of Congress, because the getter up of the appropriation for running this line, took it into his head that he had a claim on the party employed upon it—thinking, probably, that we were all beholden to him for offices. Such an impudent bore never before came out of Yankeedom. Of course, I had him in my tent. Not to do things by halves he brought a nephew with him.[16]

McClellan had tendered his resignation from the service some months earlier, and the Secretary of War accepted it, effective January 15, 1857. Johnston expressed keen disappointment as soon as he heard the news. In a letter, which was written from Jefferson Barracks January 2, he lamented his young friend's decision.

It has overturned a great many castles-in-the-air on the subject of professional daily talks—reading—fencing—marches & camp fire talks —chases of Buffalo wolves & Indians—there is no one left in the regiment or army to take your place. I wish I was young enough to resign too.[17]

The positive way that Johnston expressed himself about needed reforms and his resentment over the limitations placed upon securing them by "old fogyism" did not endear him to his more conservative colleagues, one of whom accused him of "injurious and malicious practice." [18] This and the isolation of the frontier posts caused a

paucity of acceptable social relationships. Consequently the Johnstons welcomed a transfer to the nation's capital in 1858. Mrs.
Johnston was extremely pleased. Washington was close to her home
in Baltimore. Both offered opportunities for the play of her natural
social interest, and the prominence of her family, particularly that of
her father, opened every door to her. She and two close friends of
equal vivacity attracted wide attention. "In Washington, before
I knew any of them except by sight," Mrs. James Chesnut, the
famed Confederate diarist, recorded, "Mrs. Davis, Mrs. Emory and
Mrs. Johnston were always together, inseparable friends; and the trio
were pointed out as the cleverest women in the United States."[19]

While on detached duty at Washington Johnston served on a
board of cavalry officers which met for the purpose of selecting
uniform equipment for their branch of the service. Among other
recommendations, they decided upon McClellan's design for a saddle, which Johnston actively supported. Even this success and greater
opportunity for cultural interests afforded by Washington did not
still Johnston's criticism. "Old Fogyism is in the ascendant," he
wrote McClellan.[20] Nor did his ambition abate. This last had been
noted as early as 1846 by his friend Lee, who wrote to a classmate:
"Joe Johnston is playing Ajt. Gen'l in Florida to his heart's content.
His plan is good, he is working for promotion. I hope he will
succeed." When Secretary of War John B. Floyd, who was a cousin
by marriage of Johnston, brought the latter to Washington for several important assignments, Lee again spoke of Johnston's fortunes,
this time as affected by favoritism. He complained that "in proportion to his [Johnston's] services he has been advanced beyond anyone
in the army. . . ."[21]

One phase, which may be related to Johnston's ambition, offers a
mystery. Beginning in 1857, letters passed among Johnston, McClellan, Gustavus W. Smith, and possibly others of the younger group
of officers, with whom Johnston had established close friendship,
about some activity in Latin America. The time was close to that of
the Walker filibustering expedition, but though there are some references to interest in Cuba and other areas, it is apparent that this
group had eyes on Mexico. Relations between that country and the
United States, despite the victory of the latter in the war of ten years
before, remained in a complicated state, caused by turmoil in Mexican domestic politics and unabated desire of the Americans for further concessions.

In 1859 when Mexico was again beset by civil war, Johnston made
an official visit to Veracruz. He wrote McClellan about it, saying
that the object of his trip was then unknown, even to him. While
there, however, he "had some faint hope of founding a Spanish
castle upon the basis of last year. I shall write to you from Vera Cruz
whatever I can learn from party leaders & conditions of affairs
generally." There is another interesting juxtaposition of events here
to cloud further the historical vision. Robert McLane, Lydia Johnston's brother, reached Vera Cruz on April 1 as minister to Mexico
from the United States, with power to recognize or not the newly
established Juarez regime. One week later Johnston wrote his letter
to McClellan from Vera Cruz. Yet neither Johnston nor McLane ever
said anything about his brother-in-law in relation to this visit.

Johnston's chief content in his letters to McClellan was about the
project they had previously discussed. He wrote:

> I am already convinced that there is no chance for anything like
> our schemes of last year. The leaders, both civil and military, are too
> jealous of us to adopt any such course—they had rather run the risk
> of being overthrown by the opposite party of their countrymen, than
> that of being supplanted in the control of their own party by us . . .
> Our castles in the air, my dear Mc, are blown away. You'll have to
> consent to becoming a rich civilian, instead of member of a small
> but select party of maintainers of human liberty. There is at present
> no escape from Civil Engineering for you in this direction. Apropos
> of that profession, what was it you once wrote me of railroad making
> in this country? I should like vastly to join you in making a few
> $1000 in a short time—leave of absence could now be had without
> difficulty, & there is no military service of any interest at present—nor
> pleasant garrison life.

Though McLane remained in Vera Cruz and continued his efforts
to secure concessions for the United States, the plan of Johnston and
his friends, "our respectable quartette," as he termed them, had to
be given up. So Johnston wrote to his "beloved Mc," while on his
way home, before the end of the month. In the letter he revealed the
reason for his trip and expressed a hope for the future.

> I didn't tell you the ostensible object of my going to Mexico be-
> cause it was a very small one. To me, it served merely as an excuse.
> It was to look at some military routes which our dept. wanted to get
> the use of & right to protect. I am going back to Washington in the
> hope that some better scheme may be gotten up for my employment

in that country, & no scheme of the kind will be worth much to one that doesn't embrace the four.[22]

Shortly after Johnston returned to the national capital, he received an assignment to go to New Mexico as acting inspecting general. While in the West he also resumed his old service for a short time as Topographical Engineer. Officially he was still on detached service at Washington, when Quartermaster General Thomas S. Jesup died June 10, 1860. Jesup was a fellow Virginian under whom Johnston had served in the Seminole War. Jesup's chief service, though, was as head of the Quartermaster Department, a position which he held for all the years after 1818. Upon his death, Secretary of War Floyd asked Major General Scott, the commanding officer of the Army, to suggest a successor. Scott sought safety in numbers and recommended four candidates for the much sought office: Albert Sidney Johnston, Joseph E. Johnston, Robert E. Lee and Charles F. Smith.

There accounts begin to conflict. Robert M. Hughes, Johnston's great-nephew and biographer, says that the selection narrowed down to the two Johnstons, who were not related. Jefferson Davis, then chairman of the Senate Military Affairs Committee, supported A. S. Johnston, and Floyd, J. E. Johnston. Davis, however, in a letter written in 1878, says that his support won the appointment for J. E. Johnston. The nomination, he claimed, "met serious opposition and . . . all my power and influence were required to prevent its rejection." But the Senate record shows that the vote on confirmation, which was by the wide margin of 31 to 3, came on June 28, 1860, the day after the committee presented its report. The comparative ease of the victory evidenced by these facts appears to refute Davis' claim.[23]

In his new position Johnston's rank was that of brigadier general, staff. When his friends heard of the appointment they hastened to congratulate him. Lee wrote, with a magnanimous interest, in view of the fact that this promotion elevated Johnston for the first time above him in rank:

My dear General: I am delighted at accosting you by your present title, and feel my heart exult within me at your high position. I hope the old State may always be able to furnish worthy successors to the first chief of your new department; and that in your administration the country and army will have cause to rejoice that it has fallen upon you. Please present my cordial congratulations to Mrs. J., and say that I fear, now that she will have you constantly with her, she will never want to see me again. May happiness and prosperity always attend you. . . .[24]

To G. W. Smith and Mansfield Lovell, two of his younger intimates, Johnston wrote an acknowledgment of their congratulations in the customary spirit of his correspondence with members of that group. "I have received with great satisfaction your 'hearty congratulations at my success!' Why it should gratify me I can't say. For what you tell me was as well known before as after reading your letter." Apparently with reference to their onetime Mexican plans, he said, "Filibustees are doing better, I think, than Filibustering." Then in an aside to Smith, he adds the cryptic note, "I'll tell Davis nothing about Wood d—m him. (D—m Wood, you understand)." This effort to distinguish between Davis and Wood would seem to imply that Johnston feared his friends would incorrectly associate his "d—m" (this is, incidentally, the strongest word used by Johnston in his correspondence and is rarely found). It is possible that the feeling between these two men, Johnston and Davis, which was to have such a grave effect upon the history of the Confederacy, had developed by this time.[25]

The office of the Quartermaster General was in the War Department building, a brick structure which stood close by the White House and near the Johnston home on H Street. Forty officers administered the department under Johnston, the duties being "to insure an ample and efficient system of supply, to give the utmost facility and effect to the improvements and operations of the Army, and to enforce a strict accountability on the part of all officers and agents charged with monies and supplies." These responsibilities brought Johnston into an era of interest for certain Southern leaders who contemplated secession. As the crisis grew between the sections, especially after the election of Abraham Lincoln, both he and Floyd received requests from officials for the Southern states for assistance in the purchase of materials of war. This was not so unwarranted as it might appear. At the time the administration of President Buchanan had taken no positive position on the issues. Secession, many people believed, was a constitutional right which would not lead to war. The provision of means of defense for the states did not carry the implication of treachery which afterward came to be attributed to it. Johnston, inasmuch as munitions fell within the province of the Ordnance office, had no direct connection with such sales. However, on one occasion, he endorsed the filling of the request of the Governor of Georgia, Joseph E. Brown, for "two knapsacks, $5.56; two haversacks 78 cents; and two canteens and straps, 92 cents." These things, he said, could be furnished with no inconvenience to the department.[26]

War was not inevitable in the minds of many participants in the events of the period. On December 11, the Senate passed a resolution which called for economies in the military establishment. When the Secretary of War asked Johnston what suggestions he had for the Quartermaster's department, he wrote, "As our troops are now stationed and employed, the estimate for the next fiscal year made in this office includes, I think, nothing which can be dispensed with or reduced." Matters though, continued to move with increased rapidity. On December 20, South Carolina seceded, to be followed by other states of the Deep South. Despite all this and the resignation of fellow officers and civilian employees of the government Johnston remained aloof.[27]

On March 15, 1861, Secretary of War Leroy P. Walker of the newly established Confederate States of America notified Johnston of his appointment as a brigadier general. No reply to the offer is on record, so it is not known whether or not he received it. Although no definite date can be given to it, sometime in this period General Scott, in addition to his better known appeal to Lee, attempted to persuade Johnston not to join the Confederacy. Scott was also a Virginian by birth, but his long service in the Army held him faithful to the Union. This interview was reported by Mrs. Johnston to Mrs. Chesnut.

General Scott also spoke to Mrs. Johnston. "Get him to stay with us. We will never disturb him in any way." "My husband cannot stay in an army which is about to invade his native country." "Then let him leave our army, but do not let him join theirs." She answered: "This is all very well, but how is Joe Johnston to live? He has no private fortune, or no profession but that of arms."[28]

The convention which considered the question of an Ordinance of Secession for Virginia met at Richmond February 13, and proceeded slowly to debate the issues. Delegations arrived from the states which had seceded and attempted to persuade the Virginians to follow their example. The sentiment, though, was divided. As late as April 4 a resolution to offer to the people of the state an ordinance to secede was defeated 88 to 45. The news of Fort Sumter, where Southern troops fired upon a Federal garrison on April 12, created great excitement in Richmond. When, two days later, President Lincoln sent his call for troops to the governors, the issue was decided. Governor Letcher interpreted it as the inauguration of war against the South. The convention followed the trend of the times and passed the ordinance, which the people were to vote upon May 23.

The Virginians in Washington, whether proponents of secession or not, watched anxiously the proceedings of the Richmond convention. On April 16 that body went into secret session and in consequence issued no immediate official comment upon its action. By the nineteenth Washington newspaper accounts left no doubt what the result of its deliberation had been. Informed observers, particularly those in positions of authority, realized that the issue was decided in the Old Dominion, even though the vote of the people was necessary to ratify the ordinance. The geographical position of Virginia with relation to the national capital made it imperative that defensive measures be not delayed. The convention recommended to Governor Letcher that volunteers be sought for the state's defense, particularly among the Virginians who were serving as officers in the Army and Navy of the United States. The governor immediately appointed a committee led by Judge John Robertson of one of the state circuit courts to visit Washington and call upon such prominent officers as Scott, Lee and Johnston.

Like most American military leaders Johnston was never an active participant in politics but observed these developments with careful interest. When the news came of the action of the Virginia convention he felt bound by it. His wife remained unconvinced of the wisdom of his decision, which for her meant "leaving . . . home & family & all," and she particularly distrusted Jefferson Davis: ". . . he hates you, he has power & he will ruin you," she told her husband. But Johnston remained adamant, replying to her, "He can't, I don't care, my country," and on the next day, April 20, wrote his resignation. He used the week end to get the affairs of his office in order, and when Judge Robertson called to see him on Sunday he refused to discuss the idea of serving in the Virginia forces "while holding a commission from the United States." Informally, he assured Governor Letcher's emissary that "his sword would never be drawn against his native state." The next day, April 22, he left home for his official visit to Secretary of War Cameron, carrying his resignation from the United States Army.[29]

CHAPTER II

INTO THE CONFEDERACY

On Tuesday morning, April 23, the Johnstons left Washington for Richmond. When they closed the door upon their home, they not only severed many happy associations but they left behind all their property except for a few clothes they carried and his personal arms. On their shelves remained his precious books, and in their places still sat the bric-a-brac and other mementos Lydia Johnston had collected. Under his arm, as they proceeded to Alexandria to take the train south, the General held tightly his most precious physical possession, his father's Revolutionary sword.

The trip from Washington to Richmond in 1861 was a long one under the best of conditions, but to the Johnstons it seemed interminable. Accidents extended the slow schedule, and it was not until the sun first showed itself above the hilly horizon of Richmond on Thursday morning April 25 that the two weary travelers detrained. They had missed the great excitement of the celebration of Virginia's secession the preceding Friday, and of the fear which raised its head on Sunday, "Pawnee Sunday" as the Richmonders called it. On that day reports rapidly circulated that the *Pawnee*, a Federal sloop of war, was on its way up the James River to bombard the city. By the time the Johnstons arrived, such thrilling matters had subsided, although still the subject of conversation on every hand.

Robert E. Lee had resigned from the United States Army April 20 and arrived in Richmond four days later. Governor Letcher commissioned him a major general and made him commander-in-chief of the Virginia military and naval forces. As soon as Johnston reached Richmond, he called upon Lee, who recommended that Letcher make him a major general. The governor issued the commission at once, whereupon Lee assigned his old friend the duty of organizing and instructing the troops who were already gathering in and around Richmond.

Major General Johnston entered upon his duties vigorously. He was fifty-four years old, but carried himself erect and was capable of great physical and mental activity. His hair had grayed with his years and had receded to accentuate his naturally high forehead. His somewhat florid complexion contrasted with the gray of his eyes and was almost lost in the side whiskers, which he habitually wore, and to which he at times added a mustache and tuft of beard. Slightly built, he was well proportioned, weighing about 150 pounds, and being, according to various observers, between five feet, seven inches and five feet, nine inches in height. One of his associates said of him that "while his grave handsome face, & bright eye, telling of intellectual power and cultivation, were frequently lighted up by a flashing, sunny smile, which betrayed, in spite of an habitual expression of firmness & austerity, a genial nature & a ready appreciation of humor." He did everything with a will, and disliked "to be beaten even at a game of billiards."

Reticent to an extreme, he remained aloof, generally, although he easily won the confidence of his associates, most of whom were devoted to him. Johnston "has the qualities which attract men to him," James Chesnut, Jr., said to a group of friends in Columbia. "That is a gift of the Gods." He was calm and deliberate, spoke in a low tone and was very courteous, yet positive in command, "brave and impetuous in action." Disciplined in his taste and habits, with a fine mind and a retentive memory, he had the reputation among his fellow professionals of being the best-read soldier in America and an excellent strategist.

However, like any other man he had his weaknesses. At times he was moody, and one of his close associates, who admired him greatly, said he "was critical, controversial and sometimes irritable by nature. . . ." As was true of most Southerners of his station, he was highly sensitive about personal honor and dignity.

Within two weeks of his arrival in Richmond, Johnston was startled by the action of the Virginia government which reduced his rank from that of major general to brigadier general, because of the belief that public policy required the appointment of only one man to the higher rank. Lee, because of his earlier arrival, was left in that place, but he and Johnston were shortly invited to come to Montgomery by the Confederate government, which wished to secure information about the situation in Virginia. Lee replied that he was too busy and Johnston was ill. But in an effort to secure co-ordination, President Davis appointed Lee to the command of the Confederate troops in Virginia on May 10, although at the time he held only his rank as an officer of the state troops.

Johnston had more and more come to realize that the war would be directed not by the separate states but by the united government. As a consequence, when he recovered, he departed for Montgomery. Exactly when he left Richmond or arrived in Montgomery is not recorded, but he was in that city on May 15.[1]

In his conferences with government officials Johnston renewed some old acquaintanceships and made some new ones. The most important of them was Jefferson Davis. Then fifty-three years old, slender, tall, Davis suffered frequently from illness. Generally courteous, he had an imperious, positive manner. Consultation with him was likely to be more of an exposition of his views than an effort to secure a general opinion. He was easily offended and could not tolerate criticism. With his friends he was genial and interesting; but with those whom he considered his enemies he was sarcastic and controversial. The weight of his office already showed in his appearance. "The expression of his face is anxious," wrote the correspondent of the *London Times* on May 9, 1861, "he has a very haggard, careworn, and pain-drawn look though no trace of anything but the utmost confidence and the greatest decision could be detected in his conversation."[2]

Davis had just completed the task of steering through the Confederate Provisional Congress the final acts for a military establishment. Army relationships were confused and complex because of the time lapse between the secession of individual states and the creation of the Confederate government, and the necessity to hurry the transition from peace to possible war. The individual states organized troops early, and one of the first actions of the new Congress in February was the passage of legislation authorizing a Provisional Army, which could take over the state forces. Wide discretionary powers were granted to the President, both in regard to its size and its command.

A few days later the Congress also established a Regular Army, which it limited to a few regiments and four brigadier generals, the highest ranking officers. An amendment to this law increased the number of brigadiers to five. In this amendment a section specifically stated a pledge to officers who resigned their commissions in the United States Army:

That in all cases of officers who have resigned, or who may within six months tender their resignation from the Army of the United States, and who have been or may be appointed to original vacancies of the Army of the Confederacy, the commissions issued shall bear one and the same date, so that the relative rank of officers of each grade shall be determined by their former commissions in the U. S. Army, held anterior to the secession of these Confederate States from the United States.

On May 14 another amendment passed the Congress, which raised the rank of the brigadiers to that of full general. The only other change in this portion of the act restricted the President's appointing power as follows: "Appointments to the rank of general, after the Army is organized, shall be by selection from the army."[3]

While in Montgomery Johnston received his commission as brigadier general in the Regular Army. He was the first field commander to receive this rank as Lee had declined to transfer from the Virginia forces. Unofficially Johnston knew of the action of Congress, elevating brigadiers to full generals, and could expect automatic promotion to that status as soon as the law became effective.

In their conferences Davis and Johnston met with Secretary of War Leroy P. Walker, an Alabamian, who had no previous experience in government, and the three professional soldiers who held appointments to important staff positions. The first of these, Brigadier General Samuel Cooper, a native of New Jersey, was Adjutant General in Washington when Johnston was Quartermaster General. He was a close friend of Davis, who, upon his resignation from the

United States Army, appointed him Inspector and Adjutant General of the Army of the Confederate States. Lucius B. Northrop, a South Carolinian, also a close friend of the President, studied medicine after graduating from West Point, and was practicing medicine in Charleston when his state seceded. Davis made him a colonel and Commissary General. Abraham C. Myers, another South Carolinian, who had long experience in the quartermaster's department of the Federal Army, became Acting Quartermaster General with the rank of lieutenant colonel.[4]

The military problems which formed the chief subjects of the conferences were huge. At few places in the Southern states was there any industry which could be turned to war purposes. The long coastal area, from the Potomac to the Rio Grande, was past the ability of the Confederate Army to defend and no navy was in being to assist it. A great river, which with its tributaries penetrated the long land frontier into the heart of the country, made defense even more complicated. Through much of the middle of the area there were mountains which separated one portion of the country from another. They could not be used as a first line of defense as that would have abandoned much important territory. Food supply was more than adequate in a predominant rural region, which had only ten cities of a population of 10,000 or more in 1860, but the transportation network of railroads and rivers left much to be desired. Strategically, these problems were complicated by the philosophy upon which the new government was built, that of States' rights. This meant that state governors and legislators held a virtual veto over national action. It made necessary also a geographical consideration in the distribution of troops which plagued the government throughout the whole of its existence.

In numbers the Confederacy was far inferior to the Union. Counting all which eventually came into the new government, eleven states stood against the twenty-three which remained in the old. A population of less than nine million Southerners, of whom three and a half million were Negro slaves, pitted themselves against more than twenty-two million Northerners. This disproportion is even greater when it is recalled that most of the Southern mountain areas remained loyal to the Union, or at best were lukewarm in their allegiance to the Confederacy. However, the spirit of the people generally refused to recognize any such handicaps. Inspired by a spontaneous faith in the righteousness of their cause and a patriotic belief in their destiny, Southerners spoke and acted as though the war would be short and easily won. Both Johnston and Davis took a more realistic view of the circumstances. They made their plans cautiously, not impetuously, but at the same time they wished to nourish and preserve the ardor of the people.

On May 15 Adjutant General Cooper ordered Johnston to proceed to Harper's Ferry, Virginia, and take command there. Harper's Ferry stands at the junction of the Shenandoah and Potomac rivers, where the Baltimore and Ohio Railroad crossed the Potomac on its way westward. It was important not only because it commanded this rail line where it entered Virginia but also because of its supposed strategic position with relation to the traditional route southward from Pennsylvania through the Shenandoah Valley. The Potomac, itself, separated Virginia from Maryland, and in these critical early days, both the Union and the Confederacy tried to avoid any action which might endanger relations with this border region.

In addition to its geographical and political importance Harper's Ferry was also the site of a United States Arsenal, where small arms were manufactured and stored. It was the latter fact which caused Virginians immediately upon secession of their state to organize an expedition to seize it. Early in the morning of April 18 volunteer troops descended upon it, to find that its small Union garrison had fired the arsenal and fled. The fire was only partially successful. None of the machinery was damaged and but few of the arms burned. Most of the finished rifles and muskets, however, were lost to the troops, as they were picked up and carried away by the people of the area. A small garrison of Virginia troops remained in the town, and on April 27 Governor Letcher and General Lee ordered Colonel Thomas J. Jackson to take command.

On May 23 Johnston completed his long journey from Montgomery, after stopping for a day at his old home at Abingdon and again at Lynchburg. At the latter place in accordance with his orders he attempted to secure troops to add to the force at Harper's Ferry. But consultation with Colonel Edmund Kirby Smith, who was in command, revealed that none remained at that training center as all had been earlier dispatched in response to orders from Lee. This bearded, slightly bald soldier, whose spectacles gave him a scholarly appearance, Johnston chose for his Acting Adjutant General.[5]

Within a few hours of Johnston's arrival at Harper's Ferry, Jackson, who had been under him in the training program at Richmond less than a month before, called upon him. The two had a friendly conversation, but Johnston waited until the next morning to execute his orders formally. Johnston was an officer of the Confederate Army; Jackson's commission was in the Virginia service, and he had heard nothing previously about being superseded in command. As a consequence he explained, "Until I receive further instructions from Governor Letcher or General Lee, I do not feel at liberty to transfer my command to another. . . ." But before orders came directing him to do so, Jackson received an endorsement which revealed Richmond's knowledge of Johnston's instructions from Jefferson Davis. Without further hesitation Jackson turned over the command.[6]

Although Johnston found only 8,000 troops at Harper's Ferry he was fortunate in one respect. To assist him in confronting his troublous problems he had several officers who were to prove themselves among the most capable in the Confederacy: Colonel A. P. Hill, Lieutenant Colonel J. E. B. Stuart, Major W. H. C. Whiting, and Colonel W. N. Pendleton, as well as Kirby Smith and Jackson. All with the exception of Pendleton, who had been at West Point with Johnston, were young or relatively so. Only Kirby Smith and Whiting, from Florida and Mississippi, respectively, were not Virginians. At Harper's Ferry, Hill and Jackson were infantry commanders; Stuart, in charge of the single cavalry regiment; Pendleton, who had given up his post as Episcopal rector at Lexington, Virginia, to enter the Confederate service, in command of the artillery. Kirby Smith and Whiting, both of whom became infantry commanders, were on Johnston's staff.

As the training program proceeded at Harper's Ferry, changes occurred in the Army and the location of the Confederate capital. Limitations which were a consequence of overcrowding and a lack of transportation and communication facilities forced the recognition that Montgomery was not the proper place for the capital of the new nation. The belief that the war would largely be fought in Virginia was also important in causing the change to Richmond.

On May 29 President Davis arrived to establish official headquarters in the new capital. As his party proceeded from the railroad station to the Spotswood Hotel, which the President chose as the temporary executive residence, cheering crowds lined the streets and showered bouquets of flowers upon them. Mrs. Davis found a greater field for her social interest in Richmond than Montgomery had afforded. At the Spotswood she was soon the center of a gay group, which included Mrs. Johnston, her crony of the days in Washington, Mrs. Chesnut, Mrs. Louis T. Wigfall, whose husband was an aide to the President, and the wives of the other political and military leaders. They gathered to gossip and took long carriage rides together. All of it was somewhat disturbing to Richmond society, which found itself on the outside of this important social group.[7]

Less than two weeks after the arrival of the government in Richmond, Governor Letcher officially transferred the Virginia army to the Confederacy. Although it would seem that this would have the effect of overcoming some of the difficulties of command communication, Johnston reported on June 29 to Adjutant General Cooper that he had received no official advice as to when or how the transfer of the contingent of Virginia troops in his army was to be effected. This confusion extended to others also. After the incorporation of all the Virginia troops into the Confederate Provisional Army, Lee seems to have misunderstood his status, apparently not knowing that with the absorption his commission as brigadier general in the Confederate Regular Army became effective. Johnston, who had been corresponding from Harper's Ferry with Lee as the titular commander of all the forces in Virginia, began to address Cooper on official business, and continued to do so even though Lee frequently wrote to him about such matters. The Confederate government did not, it seems, make any official statement about the command or precedence of rank.[8]

In this period of training and organization of the Confederate troops the Union authorities had also been busy. An army under Major General Robert Patterson, a veteran of the War of 1812, gathered at Chambersburg, Pennsylvania, approximately sixty miles north of Harper's Ferry. According to the best information Johnston could secure, Patterson was busily engaged in training and preparing for an offensive move. Meanwhile, to the west, Union forces began activities in the mountain area of Virginia.

The mixed loyalties in the border section between the stronghold of Unionism and the center of the secession interests put Johnston's army at Harper's Ferry in the middle of the growing tension. The political division within the state was also noticeable among the Virginia troops under Johnston. Many members of the companies from the Unionist regions refused to accept service with the Confederacy, when the vote of the people of the state took it into that government. As quickly as they could, they deserted the camps and returned home. Immediately armed details went to arrest them and bring them back. In this almost mass mutiny, according to D. H. Strother, the *Harper's* correspondent, Johnston conducted himself admirably. The journalist wrote:

> In short, his judicious management of a power, not yet secured by the habits of military discipline and continually disrupted by adverse opinion, marked him as a man of uncommon ability, and one likely to be dangerous to the Government against which he had taken arms."[9]

Confronted by armies to the north and west in the midst of a populace which was divided in its allegiance, Johnston was disturbed about his situation. When Davis at Montgomery gave him his assignment to command at Harper's Ferry, he emphasized both the importance of the place and its strength, opinions which Lee confirmed when Johnston discussed the situation with him at Richmond. As soon as Johnston reached Harper's Ferry, he investigated its military potentialities with his engineer officer, Major Whiting. He was surprised to find that it could be easily turned, could not be held against an equal or superior force and did not command the way from Pennsylvania into Virginia. He called the attention of the authorities in Richmond to these facts. Lee agreed with him about the weakness of the position, but hoped he could be given sufficient force to hold. Later Lee remarked that the loss of Harper's Ferry would be a terrific shock to public opinion, but Johnston replied that the loss of the garrison, should it be bottled up and captured, would be as great a shock and a graver military disaster. Thus at Harper's Ferry there is laid down one of the fundamental differences over military principle between Johnston and the higher command in Richmond. Johnston understood that fortresses had been superseded in modern war, that armies for their own protection had to maintain their freedom of movement and should not bottle themselves up within walls, however high.[10]

On June 7 Lee, who was then assisting the Confederate War

Department in its efforts to take over and organize operations in Virginia, was in the anomalous position, apparently, of being an officer only of the state's troops. He wrote Johnston that Davis placed "great value upon our retention of the command of the Shenandoah Valley and the position at Harper's Ferry." Thus he reiterated the previous orders to Johnston but went on to say "Precise instructions cannot be given you." He hoped that by exercise of "discretion and judgment" the commander at Harper's Ferry could insure his safety. From Johnston's point of view this told him exactly nothing. Did it mean he was to hold Harper's Ferry as a post of observation or a fortress, or was he to wait until attacked and withdraw? Or was he free to do what he considered necessary, move to a more tenable and better located position at once?

His repeated requests for more specific or clarified orders apparently piqued Adjutant General Cooper. On June 13 the latter wrote that Richmond placed full confidence in Johnston's "sound judgment and soldierly qualifications," but as he was apparently reluctant to use them, the high command would assume authority. He wrote:

As you seem to desire . . . that the responsibility of your retirement should be assumed here, and as no reluctance is felt to bear any burden which the public interests should require, you will consider yourself authorized, whenever the position of the enemy shall convince you that he is about to turn your position and thus deprive the country of the use of yourself and the troops under your command, to destroy everything at Harper's Ferry . . . and retire upon the railroad towards Winchester. . . .

This aroused Johnston's indignation and immediately he replied:

I know myself to be a careless writer, and will not, therefore, pretend to have expressed clearly the opinions I wished to have put before the Government. I am confident, however, that nothing in my correspondence with my military superiors makes me obnoxious to the charge of desiring that the responsibility of my official acts should be borne by any other than myself.

He displayed the truth of this contention when he retired from Harper's Ferry before he received Cooper's communication or wrote his reply to it. In the last paragraph of his letter, Johnston called the attention of the Adjutant General to his communication of the day before. "I had the honor yesterday," he said, "to report to the

President the removal of the troops from Harper's Ferry and other matters authorized in your letter just received."[11]

How to explain this misunderstanding is possibly more difficult now than then, inasmuch as confusion has been compounded by postwar writings. The people at Richmond unquestionably thought they had been explicit in their directions. Johnston was equally sure that they had failed to make his responsibilities clear. It is possible that the conflict can be charged, at least in part, to the difficulties of corresponding without an opportunity for personal consultation, as Johnston suggested. On the other hand, it may have been because of temperamental weaknesses in Johnston, as some of his adversaries later charged. A more intelligent interpretation might be that military necessity demanded here and elsewhere in Johnston's mind, clear-cut, unmistakable directions, which put responsibility wholly on the shoulders of the field commander, after laying down certain general objectives which the high command expected him to achieve. This was anticipating too much of Davis, whose interpretation of his own ability was that of a first-rate soldier, and who sooner or later desired to direct all operations. Another assumption is possible, although it includes an even greater amount of subjectivity. Had Johnston's experience with Davis before 1861 been of the sort that instilled distrust and suspicion in him? In other words, did he fear that the apparent flexibility in his orders concealed an opportunity for the government to escape all accountability in case of adversity?

While these exchanges of correspondence occurred, the cavalry under Stuart and the equally dashing Ashby kept watch over the Potomac, that visible, traditional division between the North and South. On June 10 Patterson began moving south from Chambersburg. A few days later Johnston learned from local sources that another Federal army from out of the west was advancing on the village of Romney, some sixty miles west of Harper's Ferry. This expedition was the advance part of the army led by Johnston's old friend, "Beloved Mc" McClellan. These twin thrusts at the Confederate communications compelled Johnston to take immediate action. Although his army numbered only about 7,000 effectives, he detached two regiments under Colonel A. P. Hill to move toward Romney in an effort to keep the Federals from entering the Shenandoah Valley from that direction.[12]

The pressure which was felt because of Patterson's movement

convinced Johnston that he should evacuate Harper's Ferry at once. The mechanics hastened to remove the last of the machinery from the armory. The subsistence and quartermaster officers sent their stores to Winchester, about thirty-five miles to the southwest. Details labored to load the trunkfuls of personal belongings of every description, which the men had brought from home, on railroad cars for the move to the new point of concentration. Finally Major Whiting and his crew of engineers destroyed the bridges over the Potomac, tore up the railroad and damaged the public buildings which might be of use to the enemy.

On June 15 the troops moved out, leaving behind them a "scene of filthy desolation." When intelligence came that Patterson had crossed the Potomac and was moving toward Martinsburg, Johnston changed his plans and routed his troops to oppose this thrust, rather than to Winchester. The next morning while awaiting scouts who knew the roads, a courier from Richmond arrived with Cooper's order which authorized the evacuation of Harper's Ferry. As soon as the guides arrived the army moved by way of Smithfield to Bunker Hill, which lay across the main turnpike from Martinsburg to Winchester, over which Patterson was supposedly moving.

The troops on this, their first long march, moved slowly and deliberately; rests were long and the stream of men seemed to crawl. The hot, dry weather caused clouds of dust to hover over them, without their realization that this symbol of marching men would accompany them for four long years. Some of them were "as ragged and tattered as Falstaff's crew." The artillery horses were largely untrained farm animals, while the caissons were improvised by fastening ammunition chests upon country wagons. Each regiment had a train of Negro servants. The cavalry, by contrast, according to Strother, who saw the procession pass, "was admirably mounted, and better equipped . . . than any other arm. It was composed almost entirely of volunteers from the rural gentry and independent landlords of the country, who furnished their own horses, arms and accoutrements."

From the same source there is a description of the commander.

General Johnston himself appeared in plain citizen's dress, with common round hat, his deportment and manner altogether as unostentatious as his dress. His person seemed to be rather under the medium size, erect, vigorous, with a military whisker and a handsome face. It required no imagination, however, to see through this unimposing exterior the leading attributes which the world characterizes as soldierly.[13]

On Sunday afternoon the Confederates reached Bunker Hill. The next morning Johnston placed the troops in line of battle to await Patterson. The men were fired up for what they believed might prove to be their only action in the war. In the meantime Patterson encountered difficulties. His intelligence reports led him to believe that Johnston was much stronger than he was, and General Scott, who feared an attack upon Washington, had requested troops from him. These facts caused the Union general to give up his offensive plans. He took the troops back across the Potomac and decided to wait upon developments. With no enemy to confront Johnston withdrew to Winchester, which brought some complaints from his men, who were most anxious for a fight.[14]

CHAPTER III

FIRST MANASSAS

Johnston's Army of the Shenandoah was in a highly strategic spot at Winchester. It could guard against a Union advance from the Potomac by way of Williamsport and Martinsburg as well as thrusts originating in the Romney area to the west. It was also in readier access to the Confederate army near Manassas Junction.

A. P. Hill, who found no enemy troops at Romney, rejoined Johnston at Winchester after destroying the railroad bridge at New Creek, where the B. & O. made one of its crossings of the Potomac. Even such a slight adventure won high acclaim at that time and Colonel John C. Vaughan, who carried out the mission, came back a hero with the colors of the small force of Federals that he routed before burning the structure.

New units continued to join the Army of the Shenandoah, which on June 30 numbered a total of 10,654 present for duty. Johnston reorganized it in four brigades with the First Virginia Cavalry under Stuart and an unbrigaded regiment of infantry in addition. He chose four of his best officers for the commands: Jackson for the First, which was to win undying fame as the Stonewall Brigade; Francis S. Bartow for the Second; Barnard E. Bee for the Third; and

Arnold Elzey for the Fourth. He recommended the officers for promotion to rank equal to their responsibilities.[1]

On July 2 Patterson again forded the Potomac at Williamsport and took up his march toward Winchester. Stuart immediately advised Johnston and Jackson. The latter, in accordance with his orders, attempted to find if the movement was in force, and placed his troops across the line of advance at Falling Water. Jackson soon discovered, in an action in which his fellow Virginian and West Pointer, Colonel George H. Thomas, commanded the Federals, that the enemy was too strong for the number of troops he had, so he retired to Darkesville about six miles south of Martinsburg. Johnston on receiving word of what was taking place put the main body of the army in movement toward Darkesville, where it joined Jackson on the morning of the third and formed a line of battle to receive the attack of the Union forces.

But Patterson decided to remain at Martinsburg to bring up supplies and requested additional troops. He overestimated Johnston's number and respected his opponent's ability.[2] According to his engineer officer his position at Martinsburg was dangerously exposed. General Scott, at Washington, still hoped for an attack by Patterson, to whom he sent reinforcements and urgent messages to move.

Johnston stayed in position at Darkesville for four days, hoping for a Federal advance against him. When it did not occur, he returned to Winchester. The only excitement for the men of both armies was the celebration of the Fourth of July. Kirby Smith, writing from camp that day, said: "We are drawn up in position within hearing of Patterson's army, the booming of whose guns has been ringing the national salute into our ears. Powder is too scarce a commodity to waste in such festivities, but our bands have played 'Dixie' from one end of the line to the other."[3]

The withdrawal to Winchester created dissatisfaction among both the troops and the public. Mrs. Chesnut reports the "horrified" feeling of the people in Richmond, and the troops were disappointed that they were given no opportunity to display their superiority to the enemy. Johnston, however, believed that he was at too great a disadvantage to attempt to attack superior numbers "in a town so defensible as Martinsburg, with its solid buildings and inclosures of masonry. . . ." In this opinion he was upheld by Davis, who wrote him: "The anxiety of the reckless and the short-sighted policy of the selfish may urge you to fight when your judgment decides otherwise. The responsibility is great." Davis reminded him that he should "follow the dictates of your own good judgment and true patriotism."[4]

The problems of the Confederates were largely repeated among the Union forces confronting them. Some of the Southerners' supply difficulties were more pressing, but the Federals experienced compensating troubles. One was the fact that the troops had enlisted for only three months, and the time approached for them to be released. Almost to a man they announced their intention to perform no duty after their term of enlistment expired.

Scott's original idea was that Patterson should undertake an offensive move in the Shenandoah Valley, something which that commander hesitated to do. Then Scott, worried by what might happen in front of Washington, wanted Patterson merely to keep Johnston occupied, without risking a major engagement, while stronger forces assembled near the capital. For one reason or another Patterson did nothing until July 15, when he moved no farther south than Bunker Hill.

The only other Federal force which had possibilities of putting pressure upon Johnston at Winchester was that under McClellan. After its movement to and away from Romney in mid-June, this army, though successful in a campaign which excited the Northern people and won prestige for its commander, created no problem for the Army of the Shenandoah. On July 13 it did reoccupy Romney, but its main movements pointed farther south in the direction of Staunton.

In the meantime a new commander, Brigadier General Pierre G. T. Beauregard, had assumed charge at Manassas on June 1 and had opened communication with Johnston, who was then at Harper's Ferry, about their common problems. As the telegraph lines from Richmond to Harper's Ferry ran through Washington, they used couriers to transport their messages. Both were in advanced positions, where if attacked in force they would have difficulty defending themselves. Both lacked trained troops, arms, ammunition and other equipment. Richmond was so busy with the details of organization that there was no over-all military command, so the co-ordination of the two armies fell upon the two generals.[5]

The strategic importance of Manassas Junction was obvious. There

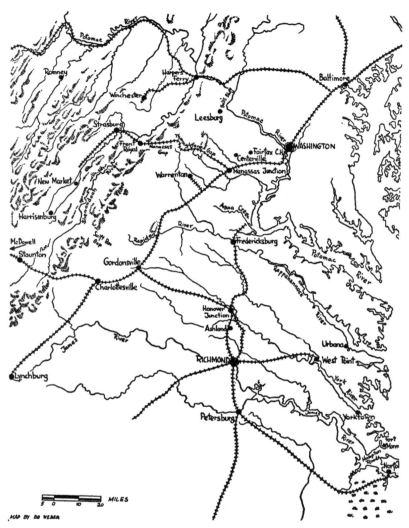

THE VIRGINIA THEATER

the principal north-south railroad of Virginia met one which ran
west into the Shenandoah Valley. As early as May 6 Lee placed
Virginia troops there to defend it, and from that time it had held
a major part of Southern attention.[6] Should either Johnston's army

in the Shenandoah or Beauregard's at Manassas be attacked, the Manassas Gap Rail Road would be the best means for rapid concentration. So long as Federal armies remained in front of Johnston and Beauregard, it was imperative to have this important way open. Manassas also stood directly on the railroad between Washington and Richmond, about thirty miles from the Federal capital.

Johnston apparently understood the implications of this situation better than Beauregard. The latter proposed to Richmond and to Johnston several schemes for uniting to take the offensive. All were rejected by the government. Johnston, however, realized that the Confederate weaknesses required that they conserve resources for purposes of defense, at least at that time. Sooner or later he expected a Federal offensive movement, not against himself, but against the army at Manassas.

The commander of the Army of the Shenandoah had to restrain his eager men and officers from premature battle. "If we are beaten here," he advised Cooper, "General Beauregard's left will be very insecure." He had to be certain that Patterson did not venture southeastwardly and block the main communication corridor between his army and that of Beauregard. Johnston desired to give the impression that he was preparing a defensive position at Winchester, which he did by felling trees to protect his retirement from Darkesville and by building works at the base. Finally, he had to calculate to the last possible moment the time for moving to join the Confederate Army of the Potomac at Manassas, in order to prevent Patterson from paralleling his movement and bringing about a Union consolidation. This enlarged view of the activity in the Valley was difficult to grasp and perfect because of military uncertainties and questionable performance of green troops. But Patterson tended to play into Johnston's hands, and his movements revealed that he was making but a series of feints.[7]

When Patterson moved on July 17, he went from Bunker Hill to Smithfield, rather than in the direction of Winchester. Smithfield was off to his left, and Johnston interpreted his intention as having one of two possibilities. It "created the impression," he wrote in his report, "that he intended to attack us on the south, or was merely holding us in check while General Beauregard could be attacked at Manassas. . . . " That interpretation seemed to be confirmed, when on the same day he received from Beauregard a telegram, which read: "War Department has ordered you to join me; do so immediately, if possible, and we will crush the enemy." But Johnston had received no direct word from Richmond. Possibly he remembered Beauregard's plans for an offensive movement. Before committing himself, consequently, he asked for further information. "Is the enemy upon you in force?" he wired Beauregard.[8]

Before he heard from Beauregard Johnston had the answer to his question. About 1:00 A.M. on July 18, he received a message from Cooper at Richmond:

> General Beauregard is attacked. To strike the enemy a decisive blow, a junction of all your effective force will be needed. If practicable, make the movement, sending your sick and baggage to Culpeper Court-House, either by railroad or by Warrenton. In all the arrangements, exercise your discretion.

Within half an hour he again heard from Beauregard, who emphasized the urgent need for his immediate co-operation.[9]

The same night the Union army moving toward Manassas was camped along the Warrenton Turnpike in the neighborhood of Fairfax Court-House, after a six-mile march from Alexandria. Its approximately 35,000 men were a heterogeneous array, some with little or no training, under Major General Irvin McDowell. His government had pressed McDowell to make this advance because of political as well as military expediency. Many weeks had passed since the expiration of the date Lincoln had given in his proclamation for the chastisement of the seceding states. Public opinion chafed over the delay.

Beauregard's intelligence service, which reached directly into the Federal capital, informed him at once that McDowell had begun his advance. He immediately flashed the news to Richmond, and Cooper passed it on to Johnston at Winchester. While the Union forces rested around Fairfax Court-House, the Confederates at Richmond, Winchester and Manassas were busy with their preparations to meet the enemy thrust.

When Johnston received the message of the attack on Beauregard, he summoned his brigade commanders for a conference and announced to them his decision to march to the assistance of Beauregard as quickly as possible, unless Patterson made a move to prevent it. Whether for precautionary reasons or not Johnston apparently informed no one else of his intentions. There appears to have been no

further communication with Beauregard after the telegraphic exchange on the seventeenth. He did write on the morning of the
eighteenth, telling Cooper, "Unless [Patterson] prevents it, we shall
move toward General Beauregard today." But the Adjutant General
was without this information the next day, when he advised Beauregard, "We have no intelligence from General Johnston." Johnston's
dislike of official correspondence and reluctance to reveal information
was a major weakness of his temperament and his silence at this
period is unexplainable otherwise.[10]

The pressing problem for the commander of the Army of the
Shenandoah was the determination of Patterson's intentions. He
ordered Stuart to make a close reconnaissance to see what the Federal
commander had in mind. It was possibly late in the morning before
Johnston had word from his cavalry that Patterson up until nine
o'clock had given no sign of advancing. New instructions went to
Stuart to screen the movement of the army until night, and then to
follow it by way of Ashby's Gap through the Blue Ridge. Johnston
decided to leave the sick where they were at Winchester, since they
numbered some 1,700 and he lacked the transportation to take them
to Culpeper Court-House.

Shortly after leaving Winchester the column halted, and officers
read to the assembled companies the ringing challenge of the order
from Johnston: "Our gallant army under General Beauregard is now
being attacked by overwhelming numbers. The commanding general
hopes that his army will step out like men, and make a forced march
to save the country." The words brought new life to the troops. "At
this stirring appeal," Jackson wrote to his wife, "the soldiers rent the
air with shouts of joy, and all was eagerness and animation. . . . "[11]

Johnston spent the night with the advance of the army at Paris,
where he had the first word from Beauregard since the telegram of
the day before. A member of the latter's staff arrived with a specific
plan of co-operation. Beauregard wanted Johnston not to come to
Manassas Junction but to go by way of Aldie to Centerville and fall
upon the right rear of the Federal army. At the same time the Confederates at Manassas would attack McDowell's army from the front.
Johnston wisely rejected the plan as impracticable, since it required
greater co-ordination than could be expected from inexperienced
troops, and in his opinion the earlier the accomplishment of the
junction of the two armies, the better.[12]

Major Whiting brought word that enough engines and cars were available at Piedmont to transport all the infantry to Manassas Junction within twenty-four hours. Couriers carried orders to the cavalry and artillery commanders to make their way by road across the country. Johnston urged Jackson to entrain as quickly as possible. His troops were under way by daylight and reached the railroad by six in the morning. They ate a hasty breakfast before climbing on the cars, which they did in time to arrive at their destination by four o'clock on the afternoon of Friday 19.

The other brigades had not kept pace with Jackson. Bartow's troops were in the lead, and two of his regiments entrained only an hour before Jackson arrived at Manassas Junction. An unforeseen contingency or series of them then interfered to hinder the rapid accomplishment of the movement. The facilities of the Manassas Gap Rail Road proved incapable of such an intensive use, but the principal failure was that of men. The engineers and trainmen were no better prepared for the strenuous duties of wartime service than were the soldiers. At any rate having worked long hours, they refused to do more without a night's rest, and halted the movement until the morning of the twentieth.

On Saturday morning Johnston decided to go forward himself, as he realized that it was time for him to be at the point of concentration. A portion of Bee's brigade crammed the cars, but about three-fifths of the army, according to the commander's estimate, still remained along the tracks at Piedmont. Before leaving, Johnston placed Kirby Smith in charge of the forwarding of these troops. About noon the commander's train arrived at Manassas Junction. The first thing he did was to effect a temporary organization under Bee of the separate units of that officer's and Bartow's brigades which had arrived. Then he hurried to a conference with Beauregard, even though he was physically exhausted. He had had no opportunity to rest since receiving the telegram from Richmond early on Thursday morning the eighteenth.[13]

When he arrived at Manassas, Johnston had the rank of full general. He had expected it ever since his visit to Montgomery, although he had not been notified "in the usual way" by the War Department, nor, so far as he knew, had it been published to the Army. Puzzled by this circumstance, he wired Davis for clarification "to prevent the possibility of a doubt of the relative rank of General Beauregard and

myself in the mind of the former." The reply which he received was
a clear answer to his query:

You are a general in the Confederate army, possessed of the power
attaching to that rank. You will know how to make the exact knowledge of Brigadier-General Beauregard, as well of the ground as of
the troops and preparations, avail for the success of the object in
which you co-operate. The zeal of both assures me of harmonious
action.

The issue of command settled, Johnston proceeded to explain to
Beauregard his interpretation of the general circumstances. He still
feared what Patterson might do; already he might be on his way to
join McDowell. Whatever the Confederates undertook had to be
done at once.[14]

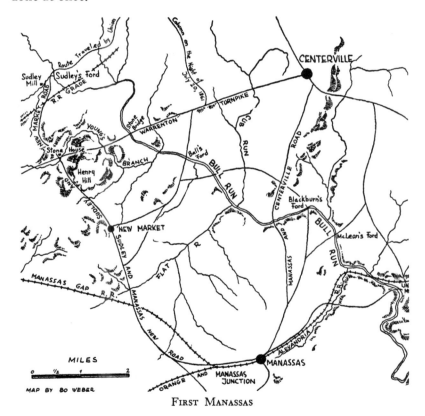

FIRST MANASSAS

Beauregard informed Johnston that his army consisted of seven brigades, in addition to one under the command of General Theophilus H. Holmes and some unattached cavalry and artillery. They were distributed along Bull Run from the Stone Bridge on the left to the railroad crossing at Union Mills on the right. As the distance, seven miles, was too long for the line to be held continuously, the troops were placed where they commanded the fords and bridges on the stream, with the greatest strength near the center at Blackburn's and Mitchell's fords. The center of the line was approximately three miles north of Manassas and the same distance south of Centerville.

Beauregard also told Johnston that the Federals had attacked his position at Blackburn's Ford on the eighteenth, but had been unsuccessful. The Confederates there were under the command of Brigadier General James Longstreet. Since that attack, however, a disturbing lull had descended upon the whole front. Beauregard agreed with Johnston that it was possible that McDowell waited the arrival of Patterson and that immediate action was vital. He had a plan prepared for such a move, an offensive against McDowell at Centerville to begin early the next morning. Johnston accepted the proposal; then leaving Beauregard to prepare the battle orders, he turned in to secure some badly needed rest.

Nothing had been heard from Kirby Smith or the men he was to hurry forward from Piedmont, but while Johnston slept, about one o'clock the morning of the twenty-first, the artillery and cavalry of the Army of the Shenandoah began to arrive. They had been on the way by road since late of the eighteenth.

While the artillery was unharnessing and preparing their bivouac, other men were waking in another part of Virginia not many miles away. In the vicinity of Centerville McDowell's troops fell into formation about 2:30 A.M. for their march on the Confederate positions. The Federal commander after the failure at Blackburn's Ford gave up the thought of a direct attack. He was also convinced that a move around the Confederate right was too difficult. He sent engineers, consequently, to try to find a way by which he could circle the left of the Manassas line. They reported that a road was open, so in spite of green troops and a ten-mile march, which would have to start before daylight, he ordered the advance for early Sunday morning, July 21.

At the Confederate headquarters staff officers had been busy most of the night preparing the orders to carry out Beauregard's offensive plan. When they were completed Johnston was awakened to read and sign them, which he did just as day was dawning. He was surprised and vexed by the length of time which had been used in the writing of the orders; nor were they the same as those he and Beauregard had discussed. They were not clear, contained many organizational difficulties and required a second order to set them into execution. No time remained to correct such shortcomings, so he signed and gave them to couriers for delivery to the unit commanders.[15]

The obscurity of the Confederate orders, which might have had unfortunate results, was rendered of no consequence by the discovery about five o'clock of the Federal movement down the Warrenton Turnpike. The Confederates then assumed that an enemy attack would be directed against the extreme left of their line at the Stone Bridge, so the command to launch the offensive toward Centerville was never given. Beauregard issued new orders, this time for a diversion only, and preparations went forward for a defense against the newly discovered Federal threat.

Because the firing, which started around six o'clock in the vicinity of the Stone Bridge, seemed to indicate that the battle had been joined, Johnston and Beauregard, accompanied by their staffs, left their headquarters at Manassas and rode to a hill near Mitchell's Ford to observe developments. Beauregard was still reluctant to give up the idea of an offensive, and another set of orders for such a move was prepared and sent to the brigade commanders on the Confederate right. The inexperienced staff and couriers could not cope with the rapidly developing circumstances. The messenger who carried the most important order, that to the general whose brigade was to lead the way, failed to deliver it, or to report his failure at headquarters, with the result that no movement occurred.

In the meantime the troops at the Stone Bridge had been under sporadic artillery fire. Their commander, Colonel Nathan G. Evans, a West Pointer, proved himself foresighted, bold and courageous. From the failure of the Federals to attempt to press with their infantry across the barricaded bridge, Evans decided that the movement along the Warrenton Turnpike must be a feint to cover an attack at another point on the line. This opinion was shortly confirmed, when a picket whom he had posted at the Sudley Springs Ford, about two miles northwest of the bridge, reported that a large party of Federal troops had crossed there and was proceeding in a direction which would shortly place them in Evans' rear.

Almost at the same time Evans received a wig-wag message from Captain Edward P. Alexander, Beauregard's chief signal officer, that he had observed the Federal movement. A Georgian, Alexander had been out of West Point two years when, in 1859, with Assistant Surgeon O. A. Myer, he developed the system of wig-wag signaling, which he now put into use for the first time in battle. Having informed Evans, Alexander advised Beauregard of the Federal movement, but Evans, entirely of his own volition and only notifying the brigade commander on his right, changed the position of the major portion of his troops to one upon a small ridge to his left rear, which commanded the road over which the Federals were marching. This move by Evans was a risky gamble but a necessary one. He could leave only a few companies to protect the bridge, where they confronted a whole Federal division.[16]

Evans was right in his interpretation that the Federal movement against his position at the Stone Bridge was a feint. The main effort, according to McDowell's plan of battle, was to cross Bull Run upstream and get into the Confederate rear by circling the left flank. From Captain Alexander's signal post most of the area which separated Evans and the advancing Federals was visible. From Sudley Springs Ford a road ran southward to the Warrenton Turnpike, about one and one-half miles distant. This junction point, in turn, was something more than a mile from the Stone Bridge. Because of the meanderings of Bull Run, the distance from the bridge to the ford had best be calculated on an air line, which closed the triangular section and was approximately two miles long. Within this area, where most of the morning's action developed, the ground was broken and wooded. The ridge on which Evans placed his troops and waited for the Union attack slightly flanked, from within the triangle, the road from Sudley Springs Ford.

While Evans was getting into position, Captain Alexander spotted another movement in the far distance. The baking July sun was blazing brightly, when on the horizon a great column of dust rose to meet the sky. It was in the direction from which General Patterson would come, if he planned to join McDowell. Alexander chose to be his own messenger with such vital news, and rode hard to carry it to the commanding generals, who were still on the hill near Mitchell's ford, approximately five miles from Evans' position. The effect of Alexander's information increased the feeling of apprehension in the minds of the Confederate commanders. They feared it signified the approach of Patterson, whose arrival would give the Federals an over-whelming superiority in numbers. Their attention quickly turned to a nearer danger, when the sound of firing and the sight of rising dust signified the opening of fighting on the left. Alexander observed Johnston's anxiety and obvious desire to go to the threatened sector, but the two commanding generals awaited evidence of the Con-federate advance on the right, a movement they still expected, not knowing the courier's failure to deliver the order to initiate it.[17]

Evans' troops had remained in their new position for more than an hour, while they awaited the appearance of the Federal column of which they had been warned. McDowell's men moved slowly and cautiously. Nor was their slowness their only handicap. The road down which they marched from Sudley Springs Ford offered good opportunity for the easy deployment of troops against Evans' posi-tion. But when they reached that point, in place of taking advantage of it to attack the small Confederate force with all or a major part of theirs, they opened the fight with a single regiment. Even later they did not bring into concerted action a combination of units, but continued to bring up individual regiments for isolated attacks. Even a regiment, though, outnumbered Evans' force, and the repeated assaults began to tell on him.[18]

Under this severe pressure, with riflemen often but one hundred yards apart, and the smoke and dust of battle falling over them, Evans' men—new to combat, as were almost all those engaged—began to waver. As the action developed, Bee with his brigade of the Army of the Shenandoah moved from his position in reserve toward the firing without awaiting orders. Evans, realizing his plight, sent an appeal to Bee to come to his rescue. The latter moved at once to strengthen the right of Evans' line.

The increase of fire which was a consequence of the entry of these new troops into the fighting caught the attention of Johnston and Beauregard at their field headquarters on Lookout Hill. Johnston's anxiety about the situation on the left mounted with the minutes. To allay it in part, Beauregard sent a staff officer to that sector with couriers, by whom he was to send messages every ten minutes. But Johnston was not satisfied with reports. He wanted to see for himself what was taking place, and was convinced that the hour of importance had passed for the area which he and Beauregard had been watching all morning.

Suddenly a more telling blast of battle noises reached their ears. Although uninformed as to its origin, which was a new surge of fighting to the right and rear of Bee's position by Federal troops who had crossed Bull Run at a near-by secluded ford, its volume left no doubt as to its importance. "All paused for a moment and listened," Alexander wrote. "Then Johnston said, 'The battle is there! I am going.' Walking rapidly to his horse, he mounted and set off at a gallop, followed by his own staff, as fast as they could get their horses." [19]

Beauregard remained but a moment to send orders to some of the brigade commanders of the center and right to move troops at once to the scene of action, and then rode rapidly to catch up with Johnston. Shortly the generals began to encounter stragglers. Startled by their appearance in such numbers, the commanders wondered if they were too late. Had the Federal strategem been entirely successful? Was the day lost? They spurred their horses up the slope and to the elevation beyond, eager to reach some point from which they could determine the battle pattern. Minutes later they came to the level top of Henry House Hill. Here, they had their first view of the fighting, obscured by smoke and dust.

This height stood just south of the Warrenton Turnpike and Young's Branch, a winding tributary of Bull Run. The slopes toward the turnpike were gentle with slight ravines and offered but little obstacle to mounting troops. Its top was a plateau about 200 yards wide where open fields blended with woods in a typical rural landscape.

Here the scene was one of almost indescribable confusion, and the generals with their staffs worked steadily to achieve order. Amid the noise of artillery fire and the explosion of Federal shells, Johnston and Beauregard found one fresh brigade in line. It was that of General Jackson. He had chosen his position well, near the eastern edge of the plateau over which the Federals would advance.

Johnston found one regiment at order arms but out of position. He soon learned that all of its field officers had been lost. He quickly moved it into line and appointed a temporary commander for it. From other fragmentary units he organized a battalion and placed his ordnance officer in command of it. Thus under fire, order was gradually restored, and the Confederates, numbering some 6,000, stood in a strong position ready to receive McDowell's next move.

When Johnston and Beauregard were satisfied that all that could be done had been done, the latter requested that Johnston retire to a safer spot to direct the battle and that he be given the responsibility of command at the immediate front. Johnston had never quit a battle because of danger, and agreed with great reluctance to Beauregard's suggestion. He established his headquarters at the Lewis house, known as Portici, about a mile to the rear.[20]

The battle then became a race between the commanders to see who could bring up reinforcements quicker and place them in a more effective position, as well as a bitter contention between the men engaged upon the field. McDowell, who had come up to take personal charge of the Federal troops, had between ten and eleven thousand men to assault the Confederate position, and a large number of reserves who had not been engaged and were dangerously close. About two o'clock he ordered the assault to begin. The Union troops moved across the turnpike and the branch, then up the slopes of Henry House Hill. As their line tended to extend to the west and south, Johnston interpreted McDowell's intention as an effort to get between the Confederates and their base at Manassas Junction.

He immediately sent orders to hurry forward some of the brigades which were still in their original positions on the center and right of the morning line. Every man possible was needed for the left of the Henry House Hill front to stop the Federal turning movement. In the midst of this effort he received a new report that a supposed Federal army was approaching from the northwest. This reawakened old fears of Patterson, so he immediately alerted the remaining brigades at the fords along the right of the original line to hold themselves in readiness to move at a moment's notice to meet any new attack.

Fighting on the plateau became fierce as soon as the Federals reached the top. The infantry surged back and forth. Units melted away. Men charged to the front or ran to the rear on impulse. Beauregard rode back and forth behind the line, exhorting all to do their utmost, and had his horse shot under him. The battle was still touch and go. McDowell's men kept coming forward for the attack as the contest surged back and forth. Johnston, in turn, continued to send reinforcements for the left of the Confederate position. Shortly after three o'clock, he was overjoyed with the arrival of General Kirby Smith with three regiments.

When Johnston left Kirby Smith at Piedmont on Saturday morning, it was with the hope that the latter could reach Manassas Junction before any fighting started. But Kirby Smith encountered repeated difficulties in his efforts to transport the remaining portion of the Army of the Shenandoah. The men and equipment of the Manassas Gap Rail Road continued to be unequal to the strain of such a concentrated necessity. Finally, Sunday morning, after the soldiers had been on the cars all night, waiting for the track to be cleared, trains began to move, with Kirby Smith himself on the first of them.

They moved slowly and a collision further delayed some of them. In one instance an engine gave out of water and the troops had to scoop up a new supply with shovels. The commanders feared that the enemy might be in position to attack the trains, and once they got the men off the cars to form a battle line. As they neared their destination the noise of the fighting greeted their ears. They arrived at Manassas Junction about two o'clock, "when the excitement was at its height. . . ."[21]

At a hurried conference Johnston explained the situation to Kirby Smith. The left was the critical portion of the line, and he ordered the newly arrived commander to move there as quickly as possible and attack the enemy in the flank. Almost immediately Johnston met one of Beauregard's brigades, under Colonel Jubal A. Early, hurrying to the fighting. He directed Early also to move quickly to the left. This gave the Confederates virtually two fresh brigades to throw upon the Federal right flank. As they moved forward under cover of the woods, Beauregard ordered a general advance along the line. Although the Union troops had also been reinforced during the afternoon's fighting, their superiority of numbers did not counterbalance the strong Confederate position and the effectiveness of the Confederate command. Many of the Federal soldiers had been up since the middle of the preceding night. They had marched good distances and for the major part of the day had been the attacking force. The conflict had been long, hard and bitter for green troops. With the final onslaught on their front and flank, they decided that the day was lost.[22]

With the battle over, the day's duties were not done for Johnston.

He apparently took time to look at his watch, as he noted the hour the Federals broke as 4:40. He sent instructions to two of the brigades, which had held the fords along the original Confederate line all day without becoming engaged, to cross Bull Run and pursue the fleeing enemy. Several reasons have been given for the failure of these fresh troops to make the day even more conclusive. The only positive thing is that they did little more than hasten the retreat, if they had any effect at all. Another report came in that a Federal force was approaching Manassas Junction. Beauregard and Johnston immediately conferred about this new problem and determined on a movement to meet it. Fortunately it proved to be another case of mistaking a friendly for an enemy unit, something which had plagued the Confederate commanders several times during the day.

Fear of defeat had given way to the exultation of victory, when Jefferson Davis rode up to Johnston. He had arrived at Manassas Junction from Richmond to find it surrounded by men "bearing the usual evidence of those who leave the field of battle under panic." He secured horses for himself and his aide, and rode with fearful anticipation toward the field. When he reached Johnston, he inquired anxiously as to the day's outcome. Johnston immediately allayed his fears by replying "that we had won the battle."[23]

CHAPTER IV

THE GENERAL'S RANK

The bright July sun gave way to night before Davis and Johnston rode up to the army headquarters at Manassas. Off to Richmond went the President's exultant message of accomplishment in the first great battle of the war: "We have won a glorious though dear-bought victory. Night closed on the enemy in full flight and closely pursued." The elixir of victory stimulated all, but all were also very tired and each left for history conflicting accounts of what took place.

It was apparently after the arrival of Beauregard that Davis heard that there had been a false report of Union activity after the army of McDowell had fled the field. Then two staff members brought word that an officer had just reported that he had been all the way to Centerville and had found that village bulging with abandoned equipment and deserted by the enemy. This information gave new impetus to the discussion. Immediate pursuit seemed imperative. Possibly in deference to each other, all of the principals hesitated to issue the command. Finally Colonel Thomas Jordan, who was Beauregard's chief of staff and had guided Davis to the field, turned to the President and asked if he would dictate it.

As Jordan began to write, someone recalled that their informant about the circumstances at Centerville was known as "Crazy" Hill.

They all knew him or of him from old army days. Should his report be accepted? Then, in some way, the discovery was made that Hill had not been to Centerville, but had seen discarded equipment on the blocked bridge over Cub Run. This led to new discussion. The result was that the President gave no order for pursuit but, he always insisted, agreed to one which called for a follow-up next morning. Beauregard, who issued the order, maintained it was "for the purpose of making a reconnaissance—of affording assistance to our wounded, and of collecting 'all the arms, ammunition, and abandoned stores, subsistence and baggage.' " Johnston, writing in 1874, simply said that no pursuit order was given. Thus, the famed night meeting after Manassas went down in history, as the weary men, who were later to spend many hours in futile dispute over the conference, left it to prepare for the events of a new day.[1]

Before dawn rain began to fall over the Manassas area. Pursuit became less practicable as streams rose, fields grew sodden and roads were made difficult for travel. Activities were restricted chiefly to the collection of the wounded and of material, which was either thrown away by the retreating Federals or left in their camps. The searching parties brought in a total of twenty-eight pieces of artillery, 4,500 muskets, and almost a half million cartridges. These were a great boon to the sadly hampered ordnance department and caused Johnston to write the President on July 24, somewhat jubilantly, "We hope to show you an efficient artillery soon—Northern material and Southern personnel."[2]

All during the night of the twenty-first lanterns and torches flickered on the field as some sought friends among the wounded and killed, and others went about their official or self-imposed task of assisting the suffering. The dull rainy dawn of the twenty-second disclosed the litter of haste, confusion and destruction which was everywhere. Huge windrows of dead men and horses marked those spots where the fighting had been fiercest. In all, 481 Federals and 387 Confederates died at Manassas, while 1,011 Northerners and 1,582 Confederates were wounded. Also, 1,216 Federals were missing.[3]

Because McDowell seized the initiative, the battle had been fought contrary to the Confederate plan. This caused Johnston's Army of the Shenandoah to sustain the heavy Southern losses, more than two thirds the total. General Bee and Colonel Bartow were among the killed; General Kirby Smith was severely and Colonel Jackson slightly wounded.

Sad as these losses were, the heaviest handicap for the moment was the extreme confusion among the troops. "Regiments seemed to have lost their colonels, colonels their regiments," wrote Colonel Richard Taylor. "Men of all arms and all commands were mixed in the wildest way." In addition to this disorder, which Johnston compared to that of the Federals, the general had other reasons for opposing pursuit. Supplies and ammunition were wanting, and the troops were raw, unaccustomed to marching. In addition, he knew Washington to be protected by the mile-wide Potomac, patrolled by "vessels of war" and fortifications manned by 50,000 troops, half of whom had not been at Manassas.[4]

At the time, there was little argument. Some men like Jackson were disappointed that no effort to follow up the victory occurred, but others felt very much as Davis did when he wrote Beauregard on August 4:

Under the circumstances of our Army, and in the absence of the knowledge since acquired—if, indeed the statements be true—it would have been extremely hazardous to have done more than was performed. You will not fail to remember that, so far from knowing that the enemy was routed, a large part of our forces was moved by you in the night of the twenty-first to repel a supposed attack upon our right, and the next day's operations did not fully reveal what has since been reported of the enemy's panic. Enough was done for glory, and the measure of duty was full. Let us rather show the untaught that their desires are unreasonable than, by driveling on possibilities, recently developed, give form and substance to the criticisms, always easy to those who judge by the event.[5]

On the day after the battle Johnston recommended Beauregard to Davis for promotion, which the latter said he had already made. At breakfast, there must have been a pleasant scene when the President handed a letter to Beauregard which told him that he was a full general in the Regular Army, a rank equal to that of Johnston. Beauregard also received new laurels from the public, which interpreted Manassas as his victory and thought the Confederate force there his army. The hero of Fort Sumter thus reached new heights, the zenith of his fame.

An appreciative letter from Lee pleased Johnston who received acclaim as word of the victory spread through the country. Editorials of praise and public expressions of thanks for the victory were frequent, and shortly the Confederate Senate passed a resolution of appreciation for both the commanders. Davis could not recognize Johnston by further promotion, but instead offered him the command of the Confederate troops in West Virginia—an assignment later given to Lee—with a promise of reinforcements. This opportunity Johnston declined, as he believed the Federals would launch another offensive before fall in the area where he was, "if the Northern people persist in their mad scheme of subjugation."[6]

Praise for the participants, pleasant though it was, was not the major consequence of the victory at Manassas. That was the fact that it preserved the chance of the Confederacy to endure. Had it gone the other way, the defeat might have precipitated the immediate collapse of the Southern government. Most credit for the accomplishment must go to the soldiers and subordinate officers, whose courage and strength in battle were impressive. Some should be assigned to the Federals, who helped in a number of ways to bring on their own defeat. Among them was Patterson, whom Johnston, with great skill and intelligence, deceived so badly that the Federal continued to inform his superiors in Washington two days after the Confederate departure from Winchester that "the enemy has stolen no march on me. I have kept him actively employed." [7]

In the battle itself Johnston played no spectacular role. It was he, however, who first realized the exposed position on the left, and then when the firing grew heavy, understood that the battle would take place in that area and insisted upon going there. In the afternoon the skill with which he placed reinforcements and extended the Confederate line showed his unusual military acumen and ability.

The battle and its attendant movements have a significance which extends past Johnston or all the Confederates and Federals who were engaged. It brought to warfare two elements which were virtually new, and another which had been so little tested previously as for all practical purposes to be considered new. For the first time the telegraph and railroads became major factors in war. The first made possible the rapid communication which enabled the authorities at Richmond and Johnston to know of Beauregard's danger almost as quickly as he himself was convinced of it. The Federals used the telegraph to advise McDowell and the railroad to transport both supplies and reinforcements from Washington to the army. The more dramatic use of either, though, was the movement of the Army of the Shenandoah by the Manassas Gap Rail Road for immediate co-operation with Beauregard's force already on the battlefield.

Although the experience was vexing in some aspects and not wholly satisfactory to Johnston, the fate of the whole Confederacy rested possibly, July 20 and 21, on the locomotives, cars and the parallel strips of iron between Piedmont and Manassas Junction. Thus a new flexibility and rapidity in both communication and the movement of troops and material were introduced to the old science of warfare.

Less tangible but no less potent was the fact that the peoples who supported both armies held democratic political principles. Public opinion, informed or uninformed, based upon reality or imagined circumstances, demanded the consideration of politicians and generals, alike. It was most difficult for the professional soldier to make the necessary adjustment. As a technician, he wished to have a free hand to use his army in the best way to achieve results. That forced, at times, an apparent disregard of immediate consequences to achieve an ultimate goal. A strategic retreat or a failure to undertake an offensive may be interpreted by historians as the proper procedure, but contemporaries seldom have a historical perspective.

Both these failures, as they were interpreted at the time, were to be charged to Johnston, but the immediate problem after Manassas contained even larger implications. It was to hold down the elated Southerners, who saw in the single victory the accomplishment of everything for which they had gone to war. The news of Davis' victory message and the generals' proclamation to their troops, which ended with the ringing words, "and thus the Northern hosts were driven from Virginia," spread rapidly. This overoptimism produced a lethargy among the people of the South and had an equally demoralizing effect upon the troops.

As no effort was made to achieve the complete results of the Manassas victory, occasional rumblings of discontent were heard. Some people went so far as to charge the President with responsibility. They knew his great military interest and expected him to go to the front to take command when large operations occurred. He had gone to Manassas, as expected. He must have assumed the prerogative of commander-in-chief when there. If the Confederates had failed to follow up the victory, it should be charged to him. Already opposition to Davis was growing, and his opponents were actively engaged in spreading the charge that he had hindered the pursuit. The statements of Northern officials and press fed this dissatisfaction when they related how exposed and undefended Washington actually was after Manassas.

As time passed without further operations, the accusations of responsibility increased. Finally the President felt it necessary to call upon Johnston for a statement as to whether or not he had "obstructed the pursuit of the enemy after the victory at Manassas," as the charges, if allowed to go unanswered, could have the effect "to create distrust, to excite disappointment, and must embarrass the administration in its further efforts to reinforce the armies of the Potomac, and generally, to provide for the public defense."

Although misunderstanding of an entirely different nature troubled relations between Davis and Johnston by this time, the latter's reply was immediately forthcoming and unequivocally cleared the President of responsibility. So, if public opinion still sought an individual upon whom to place the blame, its obvious target was the general.[8]

Because of the conviction that the next major Federal offensive, whenever it was attempted, would be directed again toward Richmond by way of Manassas, Johnston and the Army of the Shenandoah remained in that area. This proposed a problem of organization, which Johnston and Beauregard adjusted by keeping the two armies, that of the Shenandoah and of the Potomac, intact as separate corps in a combined force, with Beauregard still in charge of his old command and Johnston over his but with the additional responsibility of the over-all command. With this accomplished and such disagreeable tasks as the burial of the dead completed, Johnston moved the army to positions nearer Washington. The main body went into camp about Centerville and Fairfax Court-House, with outposts pushed closer to the Potomac at Leesburg and Vienna. Headquarters continued to be at Manassas.[9]

As the troops moved to their new stations, some of them continued to pick up materials of all descriptions, which had been abandoned by the Federal army in its flight. These fortunate ones "lived on the enemy in the most luxurious style" for a while. It lasted but a short time, and the less favored were in difficulty from the first. Appeals for food and transport were filed at Richmond almost before the debris of the battle was cleared up. When no help was forthcoming, Beauregard wrote to two members of Congress who had served briefly on his staff as volunteers. His communications were read to Congress in a secret session, but the news quickly spread, with the result that Commissary General Northrop was subjected to much criticism.[10]

Johnston wrote directly to Davis, deploring the shortage of subsistence, and stated that they "never had a supply for more than two days, sometimes none." Again he wrote on August 23, complaining that rations were neither regular nor full. Johnston, along with all the commanders of the armies of the Confederacy in the war, found great fault with the conduct of the Commissary General's department. Colonel Northrop had good intentions but his judgment was questionable and his ability limited. But he had a consistent supporter in the President: the greater the criticism of Northrop, the stancher Davis' defense of him.

At this time shortly after Manassas, Northrop insisted that all subsistence supplies had to come from Richmond. This was to Johnston ridiculous, but all complaints were unavailing. The result was that the army continued to exist on something of a hand-to-mouth basis, while the army's supply officer lost his post, unfairly in Johnston's opinion, as "He had no other part in [the complaints] than furnishing, at my orders, information from his office for my use in the correspondence."[11]

Although the food problem was of major proportions, it was no more important than finding a way to create real soldiers out of the elated participants in the recent victory. It was essential that the army be stripped down to fighting weight before a new Union force made a challenge to battle. In confidence, Johnston disclosed to the President the state of affairs on August 3:

> It must be confessed . . . that this victory disorganized our volunteers as utterly as a defeat could do in an army of regulars. Everybody, officers and privates, seemed to think that he had fulfilled all his obligations to country—& that before attending to any further call of duty, it was his privilege to look after his friends, procure trophies, or amuse himself. It was several days after you left us before the regiments who really fought could be reassembled.[12]

With such problems of army administration pressing upon him Johnston soon found himself involved with a much larger and more fundamental issue with the President himself. Johnston's request of Davis for clarification of his rank while on the way to Manassas was the first evidence of this difficulty which rankled through the whole history of the Confederacy. Primarily Johnston's reason was to avoid any conflict in authority between himself and Beauregard in the conduct of the coming battle. When he received the President's message that he was a full general, his natural assumption was that Davis had acted according to the law, under which Johnston held the ranking position in the army under the President.

Three days after the battle of Manassas the confusion of rank and command created its first crisis, when Dabney Maury presented himself to Johnston with an order from Lee, appointing him Johnston's adjutant general. When Johnston read the message, according to Maury's description of the scene, he exclaimed: "This is an outrage! I rank General Lee, and he has no right to order officers into my army." After the angered general regained his composure, he put his arm around the shoulder of Maury, who was his long-time friend, and assured him that he would rather have him for his adjutant general than any other officer in the army. He could not, though, allow such an infringement of his authority.[13]

The incident was not closed. On the same day, July 24, Johnston wrote Cooper that Maury had reported. However, he continued, "I had already selected Major Rhett for the position in question, who had entered upon its duties, and can admit the power of no officer of the Army to annul my order on the subject; nor can I admit the claim of any officer to the command of 'the forces,' being myself the ranking General of the Confederate Army." Five days later, he wrote again on the same general subject:

I had the honor to write you on the 24th instant on the subject of my rank compared with that of other officers of the Confederate Army. Since then I have received daily orders purporting to come from the "Head Quarters of the Forces," some of them in relation to the internal affairs of this army.

Such orders I cannot regard, because they are illegal.

Permit me to suggest that orders should come from your office.

Apparently, the officials at Richmond ignored these communications, but Davis indorsed each of the letters, "Insubordinate."[14]

Several things should be noted about these letters. They are curt and to the point. With full knowledge of the law Johnston considered himself to be the ranking general of the Army. It seems difficult to charge any failure here to him. Neither Lee's rank nor any listing of seniority had been published, although for some time Lee had been using the grade of general after his signature. Lee's position, for all Johnston apparently knew, was as anomalous as it appeared earlier to Lee himself. After the move of the government to Richmond, no communication of Lee's authority was made to the army. Finally in his second letter Johnston pointedly reflected on the procedural weakness of the Confederate high command.[15]

So matters rested until early September. For some reason Davis waited until August 31 to send to the Congress for confirmation his nominations for the rank of general under the act of May 16. In violation of the stipulation in the law he assigned different dates for the appointments to become effective, but the Congress made no objection. First on the list was Adjutant and Inspector General Cooper, to rank from May 16. Next was Albert Sidney Johnston, to rank from May 30. Third was Lee, to rank from June 14. Fourth was Joseph E. Johnston, to rank from July 4. Last was Beauregard, to rank from the day of the battle of Manassas.[16]

The startling news that he was fourth, not first, among the generals of the Confederacy was not received by Johnston until the second week in September. Shocked by what he interpreted to be a grave personal injustice, he sat down at once and wrote a long, indignant letter of protest to the President. After finishing it he laid it aside for further consideration. Two days later he sent it unchanged.

I will not affect to disguise the surprise and mortification produced in my mind by the action taken in this matter by the President and by Congress. I beg to state further, with the most profound respect for both branches of the Government, that I am deeply impressed with the conviction that these proceedings are in violation of my rights as an officer, of the plighted faith of the Confederacy, and of the Constitution and laws of the land. Such being my views, lest my silence be deemed significant of acquiescence, it is a duty as well as a right on my part at once to enter my earnest protest against the wrong which I conceive had been done me. I now and here declare my claim that, notwithstanding these nominations made by the President, and their confirmation by Congress, I still rightfully hold the rank of first general in the Armies of the Southern Confederacy.

He next gave an historical summary of the appointments—his own and others—to the various grades of general, and the Congressional acts under which the War Department had made the assignments. The conclusion was obvious: he stood first among the officers of that rank, followed by Cooper, Albert Sidney Johnston, Lee and Beauregard, in that order of seniority. ". . . I little thought," he continued, "that one of the acts of [the] Government would be to ignore me as its officer by trampling upon its own solemn legislative and executive action." If he were a general at all, he had been one since the act of May 16, not merely since July 4, the date of the nomination.

The effect of the course pursued is this: It transfers me from the position of first rank to that of fourth. The relative rank of the others among themselves, is unaltered. It is plain, then, that this is a blow aimed at me only. It reduces my rank in the grade I hold. This has never been done heretofore in the regular service in America but by the sentence of a court-martial, as a punishment and a disgrace for some military offense. It seems to tarnish my fair fame as a soldier and as a man, earned by more than thirty years of laborious and perilous service. I had but this—the scar of many wounds, all honestly taken in my front and in the front of battle, and my father's Revolutionary sword. It was delivered to me from his venerated hand without a stain of dishonor. Its blade is still unblemished as when it passed from his hand to mine. I drew it in war not for rank or fame, but to defend the sacred soil, the homes and hearths, the women and children; aye, and the men of my mother Virginia, my native South. It may hereafter be the sword of a general, leading armies, or of a private volunteer, but while I live and have an arm to wield it it shall never be sheathed until the freedom, independence, and full rights of the South are achieved. When that is done, it may well be a matter of small concern to the Government, to Congress, or to the country, what my rank or lot may be. I shall be satisfied if my country stands among the powers of the world free, powerful, and victorious, and that I, a general, a lieutenant or a volunteer soldier, have borne my part in the glorious strife and contributed to the final blessed consummation. What has the aspect of a studied indignity offered me? My noble associate in the battle has his preferment connected with the victory won by our common toils and dangers. His commission bears the date of the 21st of July, but care seems to be taken to exclude the idea that I had any part in winning our triumph. My commission is made to bear such a date that my once inferiors in the service of the United States and the Confederate States shall be above me; but it must not be dated as of the 21st of July, nor be suggestive of the victory of Manassas. I return to my first position. I repeat, my right to my rank as general is established by the act of Congress of the 14th of March, 1861, and the 16th of May, 1861, and not by the nomination and confirmation of the 31st of August, 1861. To deprive me of that rank it was necessary of Congress to repeal those laws. That could be done by express legislative act alone. It was not done, it could not be done by a mere vote in secret session upon a list of nominations. If the action against which I have protested be legal, it is not for me to question the expediency of degrading one who has served laboriously from the commencement of the war on this frontier and borne a prominent part in the one great event of that war, for the benefit of persons neither of whom has yet struck a blow for the Confederacy.[17]

Davis, angered by the letter, wasted neither time nor words in replying. On the fourteenth of September he wrote: "I have just received and read your letter of the 12th instant. Its language is, as you say, unusual; its arguments and statements utterly one-sided, and its insinuations as unfounded as they are unbecoming."[18]

With this letter, the correspondence between the two on the subject closed. Johnston in the *Narrative* wrote: "It is said that it irritated him greatly, and that his irritation was freely expressed. This animosity against me that he is known to have entertained ever since was attributed, by my acquaintances in public life, in Richmond at the time, to this letter." Davis after the war stated his reasons for the selections and his wife in her biography of him reiterated them. In neither instance is the explanation satisfactory. Usually in such circumstances Davis was legalistic in his approach. This time he ignored the law and based his reasoning upon a distinction between the rank of line and staff officers in the United States Army. Johnston's grade as brigadier general, in the staff position of quartermaster general, did not entitle him to the command of troops in the field. The highest rank in that capacity was that of lieutenant colonel. Therefore as line officers Albert Sidney Johnston, who held the grade of colonel, brevet brigadier general, and Lee, who was a colonel, at the time of their resignations, ranked him. But this argument fails to explain Cooper's rank as senior of the generals. In the old service this officer never held line rank above the grade of captain. His place as the Adjutant General of the United States Army, which he held at the time of his resignation, carried the staff rank of colonel. The fact that Davis nominated him for first place among the Confederate generals without staff designation invalidated the argument about staff and line distinction.[19]

Robert M. Hughes, in his biography of Johnston, assigns an entirely different explanation. He believed that the delay in the nominations and their order should be attributed to Davis' friendship for Albert Sidney Johnston. The latter had been a close friend of Davis since school days. He had not resigned his commission in the United States Army until early May. He was stationed in California, and as he feared to come through Union territory because Washington had issued orders to intercept him, he made his way over the long route by Mexico. Davis according to Hughes waited for definite news of his safe arrival in the Confederacy before sending the nominations of the generals to the Senate.[20]

Hughes in drawing this conclusion disregarded two important

statements in Johnston's letter. "It is plain, then, that this blow is aimed at me alone," he wrote; and again, "What has the aspect of a studied indignity offered me?" These signify incontrovertibly Johnston's belief that Davis' action was intended to embarrass him, as Mrs. Johnston had predicted at the time her husband resigned from the old service. Neither principal ever indicated what the motive might have been. Could it have been a consequence of a grudge because of the rumored fight in the long-before days at West Point? The fact of the fight itself has not been proved, and college fracases seldom are remembered so long. Could it be that Davis saw in this circumstance an opportunity to repay Johnston for his victory in 1860 over Albert Sidney Johnston for the post of Quartermaster General of the United States Army? It is possible. Davis, in his explanation to Mrs. Davis, somewhat strangely introduces the irrelevant argument that he supported Joseph E. Johnston at that time. The facts seem to indicate otherwise. Why associate the two things together, unless in some way Davis had been affected by the first in his actions in the second?

There is a third suppositional reason which may have intensified the earlier feeling of Davis. Mrs. Davis and Mrs. Johnston, who had been extremely close friends, began in this summer of 1861 in Richmond to grow apart. It may have been as a consequence of a social rivalry which developed between them. It may have been that a gossip repeated to the one a chance, unfortunate remark of the other. Mrs. Chesnut, who caught almost every nuance of social Richmond reported it on August 8, 1861: "Mrs. Sam Jones . . . said that Mrs. Pickens had confided to someone that Mrs. Wigfall described Mrs. Davis to her as a coarse western woman. At first Mrs. Joe Johnston called Mrs. Davis 'a western belle'; but when the quarrel between Johnston and the President broke out, Mrs. Johnston took back the 'belle' and substituted 'woman.' "

There is a difficulty proposed by this entry in Mrs. Chesnut's famous diary. At this time, August 8, nothing significant enough to be termed "the quarrel" had occurred between Davis and Johnston. It may be that the whole entry is incorrectly dated (Mrs. Chesnut, as is true of all diarists, sometimes caught up with events by writing later, rather than at the time). It is possible that the social break between Mrs. Davis and Mrs. Johnston antedated the difficulty between their husbands, and that Mrs. Chesnut, seeking a reason, later inserted her explanation. Whether this growing antagonism between the wives was a consequence of the feeling between the husbands or contributed to it, no one can say. It is true that many Southerners felt that Mrs. Davis had an undue influence upon her husband. It is also known that the President could bitterly resent an innocent slight of his wife. But whether Mrs. Davis, angered by Mrs. Johnston, played a part in this puzzling "studied indignity," which was visited by her husband upon Mrs. Johnston's can now be only a matter of interesting speculation.[21]

Johnston, many have thought, should have ignored the whole matter, or, at most, have written a short, dignified protest. He was the subordinate and should have accepted the decision of his superior. But he did not conceive his duty in that manner. He did not write a public protest, but one intended for the eyes of the President only. When Jackson, early in 1862, felt that an action of the War Department infringed upon him so deeply that he was forced to resign, Johnston wrote what should be interpreted as his motives in this incident which concerned himself: "Let us dispassionately reason with the Government on this subject of command," he wrote Jackson. The fact that he continued to be completely courteous in his relations with Davis seems to indicate that once he had said his say, he planned to ignore the matter.[22]

Although Johnston may have tried to forget it for a time, the fact is he couldn't completely do so. The quarrel cut too deeply for that. Both he and Davis were highly sensitive, and a matter of honor was involved. On the surface they were polite to each other, but the undercurrent of feelings is easily apprehended in Davis' letters. After this time in closing them to Johnston, he is no longer "Your friend," but only, conventionally and coolly, "Very respectfully yours." [23]

The rumblings of the dispute could not be kept within official circles. Less than a month later an officer of Johnston's army wrote to a friend stationed at Charleston. He pointedly reviewed Johnston's trials, and wondered if his commander's experience would illustrate "the way our new Government proposes to reward their officers for hard fought battles, and victories they are pleased to call glorious." Whatever reason lay behind Davis' action, the ultimate effect upon the Confederacy was calamitous.[24]

CHAPTER V

"PROVOKINGLY NEAR WASHINGTON"

In the summer and fall succeeding the Battle of Manassas, the Federal authorities busied themselves with changes of command and army reorganization. The defeat which they had suffered was a terrific shock to the North, where people were just as convinced of the invincibility of their forces as the Southerners were of theirs. The victory added to the feeling of Southern superiority and in some ways hindered efficiency by creating a wave of complacency; the humiliating defeat caused the North to buckle down in preparation for a hard struggle, in which its greater resources could be brought to bear.

Hardly had the panic-stricken soldiers reached Washington, before a call went to Johnston's "beloved Mc," George B. McClellan, to come at once from West Virginia to Washington. Before the end of the week he took over McDowell's command. As by magic the atmosphere at Washington changed. The new commander, vigorous, attractive and ambitious, worked day and night to inspire officials, troops and the public. At the request of President Lincoln he prepared a general plan of operations, the first consideration of grand strategy by anyone on either side. He displayed his unusual talents for the organization and training of troops in the rapidly expanding army, and within a month Lincoln gave him command of the Army of the Potomac. Before the fall was over, he succeeded Scott as general-in-chief of all the Federal armies.

From the Northern newspapers the Confederates secured intelligence of the growing number of Union troops and the intensified training program. To prevent any possibility of a surprise movement by the enemy, Johnston's army near the end of August pushed forward to new outposts just outside the southwestern boundary of the District of Columbia and within sight of the unfinished dome of the capitol. From high points along the line, communication was possible with friends within the city, and signal officers devised schemes of various sorts to accomplish this purpose.

Johnston was not at all confident about the army's advanced position. "I confess," he wrote Beauregard, "that I do not like the present arrangement in front, at Munson's and Mason's hills. In authorizing their occupation I did not mean to have such posts—posts of such magnitude—established, and now nothing but reluctance to withdraw—to go backward—prevents me from abandoning them." He believed the whole line to be "deceptive," because of its length and an exposed right flank. He had noted the great effort of the Federals to concentrate around Washington and wrote to Davis that he believed that should the North begin active operations it would be against his army from the Union capital. His opinion of McClellan confirmed it and caused him to think that such a movement would not be long delayed. He pertinently asked the President if the Confederacy should not also concentrate all the "disposable troops in Virginia" and recommended a complete reorganization of his army.

This frontier . . . should have but one commander, district lines should be abolished—our organization perfected—the divisions to be tactical instead of geographical—corps, divisions, brigades, etc. Such organization would relieve the supreme commander of everything like drudgery—and leave him to bestow his mind upon grand operations alone. Let me beg you to think of this—& to send the troops & the major generals, some of whom can be found here—& the commander-in-chief.[1]

Within his own command, Johnston was especially concerned with getting together a group of capable officers and securing promotions for those who had shown distinctive qualities of leadership. When he learned that his good friend William W. Mackall had resigned his commission in the United States Army, Johnston wrote, "I would give my right arm if they would send you to me as a major-general." He also sought to secure two other old army friends, G. W. Smith and Mansfield Lovell, who, he explained, "have not come forward, because not belonging to seceded States, they didn't know how they would be received." Continuing his search Johnston asked for Colonels Earl Van Dorn and W. H. T. Walker, who he heard were in Richmond. From the ranks of his own army he secured the promotion of "Jeb" Stuart to brigadier general. In his endorsement Johnston called Stuart "a rare man, wonderfully endowed by nature with the qualities for an officer of light cavalry. Calm, firm, acute, active, and enterprising, I know of no one more competent than he to estimate the occurrences before him at their true value. If you add to this army a real brigade of cavalry, you can find no better brigadier-general to command it." [2]

Johnston and Beauregard both hoped for offensive operations in September. Their army was high in morale with the "Advanced Forces" in sight of Washington without serious opposition. But such a movement would require reinforcements. Johnston sought additional men in his letter to Davis on September 3, and asked that they be sent from an unassigned force, which he heard was gathered at Richmond. Davis soon informed him that no such body of men was stationed at the capital. He added that he believed the size and spirit of the Federal army had declined considerably "since the date of your glorious victory. . . ." The President believed that the decision to initiate an engagement that fall rested with the Confederates. Although Johnston did not agree with Davis' estimate of Federal numbers or morale, he was interested to see that the President had also been considering a movement against the enemy. [3]

Later in the month Johnston explained that he had moved to the advanced position as quickly as the restoration of the railroad made it possible to supply the army, and that in addition to observation his men would "be ready to turn the enemy's position and advance into Maryland whenever the strength of this army would justify it." The time had come for a decision, he continued, about a full offensive. In conclusion he asked that either the President or the Secretary of War, or someone representing them, come to his headquarters to confer on that momentous question. [4]

Johnston addressed his communication to Secretary of War Judah P. Benjamin who had succeeded Walker in that important post on September 17. Benjamin informed Johnston that it was difficult to determine if Richmond could furnish the "further means" the army commander felt necessary "to assume the active offensive." "We have not in the Department," the Secretary stated, "a single return from your army of the quantity of ammunition, artillery, means of transportation, or sick in camp or in hospital, to enable us to form a judgment of what your necessities may be." But the issue Johnston proposed was too vital to wait on belated reports, so Benjamin had "earnestly requested" the President to visit Johnston for a conference.[5]

Davis met with Johnston, Beauregard and G. W. Smith around October 1. The principal discussion centered on the question of whether the army could be strengthened sufficiently to launch an offensive. According to G. W. Smith, who wrote a memorandum on January 31, 1862, of the conversations at the council:

It was clearly stated, and agreed to, that the military force of the Confederate States was at the highest point it could attain without arms from abroad—that the portion of this particular army present for duty was in the finest fighting condition—that if kept inactive it must retrograde immensely in every respect during the winter, the effect of which was foreseen and dreaded by us all. The enemy were daily increasing in numbers, arms, discipline and efficiency. We looked forward to a sad state of things at the opening of a Spring campaign.

The generals desired additional men to cross the Potomac. Their argument rested on the principle of concentration of forces at the one point and the conviction that victory there, in front of Washington and against the main Federal army, could have the effect of "saving all." In reply to a query from Davis as to the number required, Smith placed his estimate at 50,000, while Johnston and Beauregard thought it should be 60,000. All must be "seasoned" troops.

The President's discouraging reply was that "no reinforcements could be furnished to this army of the character asked for." Arms were not available for new troops. He had been disappointed by not getting shipments from abroad, nor did he know that such shipments would come, and the development of arms manufacture in the Confederacy had been of little significance. More important was his decision that he could not draw arms and trained troops from other sectors. As he pointed out, "the whole country was demanding protection at his hands, and praying for arms and troops for defense." In place of a general offensive Davis suggested "certain partial operations," such as raids against outlying positions. By small successes, he argued, the troops would be encouraged, as would "the people of the Confederate States generally." [6]

The proposals of the generals called for reinforcements from points in the South which were not directly threatened. They believed that the ability of the Confederacy to carry the war forward would be arrested by the utilization of troops then scattered over the whole South. Their ideas called for concentration at a point from which a vigorous campaign could be launched against the major enemy force, or a proper defensive arrangement could be completed to oppose an enemy thrust. Fundamentally this had been Johnston's position when he advocated the evacuation of Harper's Ferry. It was the army which was important, not the holding of a certain geographical point or area. The latter could be retaken, when circumstances were proper for it, but only if the army remained in being. Throughout the war this was Johnston's constant position, one from which he never wavered.

Davis, on the other hand, at the Fairfax council vetoed the idea of concentration. Instead and strangely in view of the agreement among the conferees that inactivity during the winter would have a harmful effect upon the troops, he proposed a defensive policy. "I repeat," he wrote to Johnston on September 8, "that we cannot afford to fight without a reasonable assurance of victory or a necessity so imperious as to overrule our general policy. We have no second line of defense, and cannot now provide one. The cause of the Confederacy is staked upon your army, and the natural impatience of the soldier must be curbed by the devotion of the patriot." [7]

Actually Davis was in a difficult position. As President he was under constant demands from governors and private citizens. Possibly because of this pressure, or, it may be, because of his own desire to retain geographic territory, Davis' policy was the attempted defense of all Southern soil. Certainly, it was a more popular strategic conception than concentration, as it gave more people a feeling of security. This attempt to present the appearance of resistance on all frontiers was, however, deceptive of true strength as was to be well shown when the Federals began to apply pressure at chosen areas later. Although it may have been designed to assist in winning foreign recognition in 1861, that was no justification for holding to it. Certainly it would have been difficult for Davis to bring a public unschooled in military strategy to accept the theory of concentration, but that was, after all, one of the responsibilities of the civil administration. By not doing so but continuing the easier policy of the geographical distribution of troops, Davis failed to face one of the genuinely large issues of the Confederate effort.

A less important factor from a general point of view, but one of much consequence to his own army, was the reorganization Johnston asked for in the latter part of the summer. After somewhat protracted negotiations the Richmond authorities agreed to the creation of four divisions with commanders to rank as major generals, with Jackson, Longstreet, Van Dorn and G. W. Smith appointed to the posts. At the time the army was divided into two corps, actually a continuation of the arrangement under which the Battle of Manassas had been fought, with Beauregard in command of one and Johnston the other, as well as in over-all command of both. The organization had never been officially recognized, though Beauregard's letters and returns, in particular, gave repeated evidence of it, with no expression of disapproval from the War Department. The Secretary of War did advise a correspondent that he was incorrect in assuming that the army had two corps, but neither Johnston nor Beauregard was so informed. Finally, on October 17 the Secretary wrote a letter to Beauregard in which he stated that that general was "second in command of the whole Army of the Potomac, and not first in command of half the army." Three days later, the President confirmed this opinion. However, this peculiar circumstance was made even more anomalous by the continuance of the department and the President to address Beauregard directly, as though he were an independent commander.[8]

In addition to this loose and unorthodox structure of command, which had evolved in the Confederate Army of the Potomac, another matter of somewhat the same sort grew into importance because of similar misunderstandings. In early June the War Department assigned Brigadier General T. H. Holmes to the command of the area around Fredericksburg, with outposts on the Lower Potomac at such points as the mouth of the Aquia Creek and Evansport. Although Holmes co-operated in the Battle of Manassas as part of Beauregard's army he returned to his independent command afterward. Thus these troops, which totaled only 6,135 officers and men, were separated from the larger force, although in the same general geographical area.

It was to correct such loose command structure that Johnston made his suggestion for the abolishment of district lines and co-ordination of units under a single commander in late August and early September. Not until seven weeks later, on October 22, did the War Department finally move to effect a general reorganization. It established the Department of Northern Virginia with three subsidiary districts: the Potomac, Aquia and Valley. Johnston was given over-all command. Beauregard was in charge of the Potomac District, which ran from the Blue Ridge in the west to Powell's River in the east. Holmes retained command of the Aquia area, which included the region between Powell's River and the mouth of the Potomac, and the counties on either side of the Rappahannock as far west as Fredericksburg, where his headquarters remained.[9]

The great change in this order was that it sent Jackson to the command of the Shenandoah Valley District. Whatever regret Johnston may have felt over losing the immediate services of Jackson was compensated by the relief of having so capable a commander in the troublesome Valley area. There were, however, two points in the reorganization order with which he differed. The first was relatively easy of adjustment. It placed all the cavalry of the Army under Van Dorn, a division commander. When Johnston pointed out the obvious fact that the cavalry should be at the disposal of the Army, not a unit commander, Richmond corrected the blunder. The other was more fundamental and created long controversy. One section of the order called for organization of troops on state lines. Each brigade was to be made up of regiments and commanded by a brigadier general from the same state. This would require changing troops and commanders around regardless of how well they worked together. The breaking up of effective organizations hardly seemed wise; particularly in the face of an enemy who might be daily preparing an attack. For both reasons Johnston hesitated to order the changes necessary, but Richmond continued to be insistent that it be done.[10]

In some respects the reorganization plan proved less than effective. Jackson apparently understood his position clearly and worked through the Department of Northern Virginia properly, as did Holmes in the Aquia District, although at times the latter complained that he did not receive sufficient instructions. The place of principal difficulty was the area in which, because of its obvious importance, the Department commander chose to place his headquarters. Johnston's presence with Beauregard's troops caused the Louisianian to continue in the shadowy role of a subordinate. This would have been true even had Johnston officially turned the command of the Potomac District over to him, which he did not do. Beauregard, though the district commander, consequently continued to use the earlier unofficial designation, "Headquarters, First Corps, Army of the Potomac," as the explanation of his command, and again Richmond apparently ignored it.[11]

To add to these problems Beauregard found himself involved in a difficulty with the President over his report of the Battle of Manassas, in which Davis made his usual quibbling objections to bits of phraseology and to the inclusion in it of a proposed plan of action prior to the battle. Troubled by his position, near the year's end Beauregard wrote to Davis, "Please state definitely what I am to command, if I do not command a corps, in consequence of latter being unauthorized." To this request he received no reply, and the situation continued until on January 26, 1862, he was ordered to Kentucky.[12]

Davis' decision against an offensive movement at the Fairfax conference caused the army to remain stalemated along its Potomac line. Since that portion of the army near Washington was in an exposed position and one which was not easily defended, Johnston pondered its withdrawal. Some skirmishing had taken place along this part of the front, but the only outstanding action occurred when Stuart, with his cavalry and about 800 infantry, drove an enemy force from Lewinsville in great confusion. This small success did not stay Johnston's apprehension over McClellan's growing power, which with some threatening Federal movements near Harper's Ferry caused him to withdraw the army on October 19. He then took up a line "of triangular shape, with Centreville as the salient, one side running to Union Mills and the other to the Stone Bridge, with outposts of regiments three or four miles forward in all directions, and cavalry pickets as far in advance as Fairfax Court-House."

From that position he watched the wide area from the Blue Ridge to the Chesapeake Bay tidelands with an army which, as he repeatedly pointed out, was no stronger than at Manassas. Engineers prepared defenses and to cover the weakness in artillery, "rough wooden imitations of guns were made, and kept near the embrasures.[13]

Despite all shortcomings the Confederates hoped that McClellan would press forward, as the anxiety of waiting for a possible Federal blow kept them in nervous tension. On October 21 a Union force did precipitate action near Leesburg on the upper Potomac. In an uncoordinated demonstration this force crossed the river at Ball's Bluff. They were trapped by the Confederates and an engagement followed. In addition to the steep bank the attacking soldiers had the river to their rear and not enough boats to carry them back. The failure at Ball's Bluff lingered in the Northern spotlight, while it gave the Southerners fresh enthusiasm for action.[14]

Back in Centerville Johnston lived in a tent on a lot near a church, where the recently married Kirby Smith rejoined him late in October as division commander. The army commander had worse equipment than a private, Kirby Smith wrote his bride, and slept on the ground, wrapped in the same blankets he had used at Winchester. "I tell you now," he continued, "that he is too much of a Diogenes for me, that I can no longer keep him company in his contempt for the necessaries of life, that I am now a married man with too much at stake." To Kirby Smith, Johnston was a "true patriot, sensitive and retiring, and with an abnegation of self which ignores all personal grievances and slights in his great sense of duty & devotion to his country." [15]

After Ball's Bluff, the Confederates were fearful that McClellan would not attack that year, but rumors kept hope alive that he would. As long as Johnston felt that military operations were possible, he held his army ready. This brought on criticism from even such loyal subordinates as Kirby Smith, who complained about the cold and the miserable conditions of his troops in mid-December. He wrote to his wife that Johnston, "firm & decided, almost to obstinacy and impracticability," refused to move into winter quarters. The reason was that he feared that the "Northern people are waiting to disturb us as soon as we have become comfortable for the winter." Finally when conditions seemed to preclude any possibility of action, the commander allowed the troops to prepare their living arrangements for the winter months.

Actually Johnston had been concerned since early fall about the matter of winter quarters for the men of his army. In the first week of October he wrote Richmond about the construction of huts. Arrangements dragged out over the weeks. Misunderstandings interfered and nothing was done. When operations were no longer feasible because of the winter conditions, the army had to build its own shelters from materials improvised where it was.

For men and officers life in winter quarters was boring. They drilled, had snowball fights, read, sang and gossiped. Cock fighting proved a great interest: "Such was the mania for roosters that the camp sounded like a poultry show, or a mammoth farm yard." Card playing was almost universal, with stakes increased when the players received word that the government planned to provide pay and clothing allowances. A mythical fellow, Bolivar Ward, put in his appearance, to be used by practical jokers to welcome rookies, and was found almost as frequently as his later counterpart, Kilroy.[16]

At Army headquarters by contrast, such relaxation was less possible. There attention continued to be concentrated upon probable activities of the enemy and plans for the future. At the end of the year rumors were abroad that the Union would give up the war, but Johnston wrote them off as without foundation. On Christmas Eve he stated his analysis, "All branches of the Northern Gov't & all classes of the people are too fully committed to back out without utter disgrace." Such a belief required that his vigilance be constant, as, should a general Federal move occur, he could oppose it only with an inferiority in men and guns.[17]

CHAPTER VI

TROUBLES WITH THE WAR OFFICE

The morale of the troops in the Department of Northern Virginia was generally good in the fall of 1861. They still were completely optimistic about their ability to meet the foe. But at the same time the long periods of quiet on the field permitted misgivings about internal affairs and personalities to crop up. Sometimes they were the product of men who were chronic complainers; sometimes the result of injured honor. Again there was basis of reality in what was said. The citizens' army did not qualify its views but asserted for itself the complete freedom from censorship that existed in the Confederacy. Its members wrote freely to people in all walks of life about both governmental and military matters. One officer, in a letter to his friend Vice President Alexander H. Stephens, as early as October said: "The temper of the army is not good. The troops widely feel the unjust oppression and partial hand that is laid up on them. . . . " In another letter to Stephens the last day of December he was more specific: "Mr. Davis and the peculiar people he trusts have given cause for every gentleman in the army to mutiny. . . . " [1]

Such an expression of discontent undoubtedly reflected the vexing relations between the army command and the government at Rich-

mond. After the passage of letters between Johnston and Davis over
the matter of seniority of rank, relations between the two seemed
as before. But the new personality who entered the picture in mid-
September as Secretary of War quickly began to agitate old issues
and create new personal and official problems. Secretary Walker
left his post without having developed either its functions or its
prestige, but the new holder of the office, Judah P. Benjamin, immediately undertook to do the one and insist upon the other.

Although he had no military experience, his great assurance caused
him to have no hesitancy about injecting his views into any issue,
however technical. His comments were facile and calculated; his
rebukes, belittling and stinging. A lawyer by training, he took a
legalistic approach to any question, even though it required that he
disregard the realities of the military situation. When a difference
arose between Benjamin and a commander, Davis consistently
supported the Secretary of War, who was no less loyal to the
President.

Almost as quickly as Benjamin took office, differences began to
agitate relations between the command in the field and the War
Office. Johnston exasperatedly expressed the situation, "The Secretary
of War will probably establish his headquarters within this department soon." When Benjamin learned that the General had done
nothing toward the accomplishment of the state organization of
troops he issued peremptory orders assigning Mississippi regiments
to two brigades, under Generals W. H. C. Whiting and Richard
Griffith, both also from the state. Johnston immediately objected as
it would require the withdrawal from the field for almost a week of
at least nine regiments. The troops were scattered and accustomed to
their present assignments. "The execution of [the order] would work
a complete revolution in the organization of the army," the commander insisted. If the army attacked while the change was in
progress, disaster might well result.[2]

Benjamin, writing for the President, replied three days later that
Davis "adheres to his order, and expects you to execute it." Again
Johnston protested and emphasized the danger of his position, the
length of his line and the comparative weakness of his force. "I hope
the President will favorably consider my appeal," he wrote, "earnestly
and respectfully renewed, for a continuance of the discretion he has

vested in me, merely to the time of executing the orders in question." [3]

In addition to his letters, Johnston sent General Richard Taylor, a brother of Davis' first wife, to the President in an effort to strengthen the presentation of his point of view. Some years later, Taylor recalled:

My mission met with no success; but in discharging it, I was made aware of the estrangement growing up between these eminent persons, which subsequently became "the spring of woes unnumbered." An earnest effort made by me to remove the cloud, then "no greater than a man's hand," failed; though the elevation of character of the two men, which made them listen to my appeals, justified hope. [4]

About this time General Whiting entered the controversy by informing Richmond that he did not wish the command of a Mississippi brigade. His letter, according to military procedure, went to Richmond after passing through Johnston's hands. It is not printed in the *Official Records* but is marked "not found." Whiting, however, wrote a fellow officer his reasons for not taking the position: he wanted to keep the troops he had, they were used to him, and he was used to them; in his opinion the attempt to group by states was a "policy as suicidal as foolish." Already it had been responsible for an effort to persuade two of his colonels to transfer. "If they persist in Richmond," he insisted, "they will be guilty of inconceivable folly. . . . For one, I am not disposed to submit for one moment to any system which is devised solely for the advancement of log-rolling, humbugging politicians—and I will not do it." [5]

Benjamin's letter to Johnston of December 27 displayed unmistakable evidence of the indignation Whiting's letter created in Richmond. "The President has read with grave displeasure," he wrote, "the very insubordinate letter of General Whiting, in which he indulges in presumptuous censure of the orders of his commander-in-chief, and tenders unasked advice to his superiors in command." In place of preferring charges the Secretary merely stated that he had no other brigade for Whiting and withdrew his commission as brigadier general in the Provincial Army. This meant that Whiting reverted to his status as a major of engineers.

In concluding his letter, Benjamin advised Johnston, "the President requests me to say that he trusts you will hereafter decline to forward to him communications of your subordinates having so obvious a tendency to excite a mutinous and disorganizing spirit of the Army." [6]

Whatever reservations Johnston may have had about the refusal of the administration to listen to the objections of experienced soldiers to an impractical program, he answered Benjamin on January 1, 1862, with disarming restraint:

I beg to be allowed to intercede in this case, partly because this officer's services as a brigadier-general are very important to this army, and partly because I also share the wrong. I am confident that he has in his heart neither insubordination nor disrespect. Had I returned the letter to him, pointing out the objectionable language in it, it would, I doubt not, have been promptly corrected. I regret very much that in my carelessness it was not done. No one is less disposed than I to be instrumental in putting before the President a paper offensive in its character.[7]

Despite all the argument about this incident and the supposed removal of Whiting, he continued in command of his brigade. Johnston, in compliance with the directive, asked for a successor, but he never received one. Whiting did withdraw his letter for "modification," but even that was apparently never made.[8]

Richmond continued to press Johnston to reorganize his army, and he, to express his inability to carry out the policy. In mid-January he changed his reasons for postponement. "Could the President see the condition of the country at this season, and that of our means of transportation," he said, "I am sure he would regard these changes as physically impossible now." All the teams and wagons were busy transporting provisions and fuel. None was available in the area and the Quartermaster's Department was hard put to keep supplies at hand. The horses, in particular, were consequently in "wretched condition." [9]

The paramount problem which confronted the directors of Confederate policy was the effort to induce the re-enlistment of the twelve-month volunteers, whose terms began to expire in early spring. Johnston estimated that they composed about two-thirds of his army. Anticipating the difficulty he wrote Adjutant General Cooper on the first of December and suggested that the term of re-enlistment be for the duration of the war. He recommended that furloughs be granted as an inducement but dependent on the "enemy's course during the winter." Another suggestion was that training camps be established for recruits, whose term should also be for the period of the war." [10]

The Congress in an effort to care for the situation on December 11 passed the Bounty and Furlough Act, which the War Department published to the Army on January 1 in a general order. The writer of this law, which Jeb Stuart described to his wife as the "most outrageous abortion of a bill ever heard of," could scarcely have done the Confederacy a greater injury. It granted a bounty of fifty dollars and a furlough for sixty days to every veteran who re-enlisted for a total of three years or for the duration of the war; at the same time the bounty was paid to all new volunteers for three years or the duration. The re-enlisted veteran could select a new branch of service if he wished or could quit his old company to join another in the same branch. After the reorganization was effected the men could elect company and regimental officers without regard to previous selections. After the initial elections all vacancies above the grade of second lieutenant, who could still be chosen by popular vote, would be filled by promotion from the officers of the unit in which the vacancy occurred. [11]

The law was obviously prepared to persuade the enlistment of the soldiers without regard for its effect upon morale or administration. The provision for the election of company and regimental officers not only meant that good disciplinarians might be endangered by their efficiency but also provided the opportunity for an ambitious man to solicit soldiers from a number of companies and thus assure his elevation to an officer's place. The law contained no protection of army or subordinate commanders about either the time furloughs were granted or the number of men to whom they might be given at any one time, as Secretary of War Benjamin had complete authority. [12]

When Richmond tried to place the new law in operation, misunderstandings arose on every turn. Only Beauregard of the commanders in Northern Virginia received the order to execute the new procedures. Johnston protested and inquired of Benjamin about the administration of the act. Benjamin in his reply seemed to give responsibility to Johnston, whom he advised "to go to the extreme verge of prudence in tempting your twelve-months' men by liberal furloughs. . . . " [13]

But the issue was not so easily disposed of, as Johnston pointed out in his reply when he protested about Benjamin's habit of

granting leaves of absence, furloughs, discharges, and acceptances of resignations upon applications made directly to yourself, the officers concerned having had no hearing, and detailing in the same way mechanics and other soldiers to labor for contractors, ordering troops into the departments without informing me of the fact, and from it without consulting me, and moving companies from point to point within it. Two of these companies were at Manassas, having been selected to man some of the heavy batteries there. They had been well instructed in that service, and of course were impractical as infantry. The companies that take their places will for weeks be worth less as artillery than they as infantry. If as general, I cannot command such matters, our heavy guns will prove a useless expense.

I have been informed that you have already granted furloughs to four entire companies, three belonging to the same regiment, but have received but one of the orders. They are, it is said, re-enlisting as artillery. We thus lose good infantry and gain artillery having no other advantage over recruits than that of being inured to camp life. This increases the difficulty of inducing the re-enlistment of infantry as such. You will readily perceive that while you are granting furloughs on such a scale at Richmond I cannot safely grant them at all.

To execute these orders consistently and advisedly there must be a system. If the War Department continues to grant these furloughs without reference to the plans determined on here, confusion and disorganizing collisions must be the result.

Johnston then introduced a somewhat different circumstance by remarking upon an order he had just received from Richmond, which detailed a single private soldier for a working party. "I hazard nothing in saying," he stated, "that in time of war a Secretary of War never before made such a detail."

He emphasized that he was not writing because of "mere official propriety," or in a "spirit of captiousness." The consequences of Richmond's actions were "weighing heavily" upon the Army. Subordinate officers attributed responsibility to him for "changes which . . . are made without their wishes and in opposition to their plans." He closed by saying to Benjamin that it was necessary to "secure concert of action between us," so he asked that the Secretary of War extend confidence to him "in those matters of minor detail which legitimately belong to my position. . . ." [14]

On March 1 Johnston took his problem with the Secretary of War directly to the President, to whom he appealed as a "trained soldier" to protect "the discipline and organization of the army." He said that he had remonstrated with the honorable Secretary, "but to no avail." [15]

Davis agreed in his reply that "some imposition" had been practiced upon Johnston, but Benjamin had told him that no furloughs or leaves had been granted to soldiers of Johnston's army "for a month past." The President assured Johnston that he would uphold the commander's authority and that the Secretary of War had no "desire to interfere with the discipline and organization of your troops." However, Davis continued, Benjamin had objections about Johnston of consequence equal to the latter's about him. The Secretary had told the President "that his orders are not executed, and I regret that he was able to present to me many instances to justify that complaint, which were in nowise the invasion of your prerogatives as a commander in the field." [16]

Apparently this last referred to the failure of Johnston to effect the organization of brigades by states. There his only recourse was the negative one of doing nothing. In the instance of furloughs and re-enlistments he decided upon aggressive action. On February 4 he announced the order governing it to his troops. After complimenting them on their past deeds and unselfish patriotism, he appealed to their future service.

The enemies of your country, as well as your friends, are watching your action with deep, intense, tremulous interest. Such is your position that you can act no obscure part. Your decision, be it for honor or dishonor, will be written down in history. You cannot, will not, draw back at this solemn crisis of our struggle, when all that is heroic in the land is engaged, and all that is precious hangs trembling in the balance.[17]

Nothing was said in this spirited appeal to the patriotism of the soldiers about bounties or furloughs, but in his order placing the re-enlistment program into effect in the Department of Northern Virginia, Johnston said that furloughs would be granted at a rate of twenty per cent of the men present. Fortunately the desire to transfer from the infantry to the artillery began to take care of itself, as the Ordnance Department could not furnish the necessary equipment for any additional batteries.[18]

Nothing in all that long dreary winter of discord and difficulty contained more possibility of ultimate damage to the Confederacy than a different problem which confronted Johnston in early February. Again, it was precipitated by an effort of the Secretary of War to infringe upon the prerogatives of a field commander, this time Stonewall Jackson, who had planned a winter campaign in the Valley. General W. W. Loring's brigade was a part of Jackson's troops and some of the men grew indignant about their treatment while at Romney. Stories of their difficulties mushroomed into exaggerated tales of cruelty and irresponsibility on the part of Jackson. One of Loring's colonels protested their lot to a politician in Richmond, while a round-robin letter was signed by eleven officers, endorsed by Loring and sent to Jackson.

Before Jackson forwarded this communication with his disapproval endorsed upon it, Benjamin, apparently alert to the echoes of the trouble in Richmond, wrote Johnston to investigate the "condition of the army in the Valley District," and report if anything should be done to restore its "efficiency, said to be seriously impaired." Although somewhat puzzled by the circumstances, three days later, January 29, Johnston replied, "Without being entirely certain that I understand the precise object of apprehension in the Valley District, I have dispatched the acting inspector general of the department to see and report without delay the conditions of Major-General Jackson's troops." [19]

Without waiting for this report or even consulting Johnston, the Richmond authorities decided to move quickly of their own volition. On the thirtieth Benjamin wrote Jackson curtly to order Loring from Romney to Winchester immediately. He gave as his reason that the Federals were about to cut Loring off in his exposed position. Jackson did not wait. On the thirty-first he replied, sending his letter, according to military courtesy, to Johnston to forward to Richmond. He announced that the order had been "promptly complied with," and added: "With such interference in my command, I cannot expect to be of much service in the field, and accordingly respectfully request to be ordered to report for duty to the Superintendent of the

Virginia Military Institute at Lexington. . . . Should this application not be granted, I respectfully request that the President will accept my resignation from the Army." [20]

Though quickly done, Jackson's action was not hasty or ill-considered. When a friend made an effort to persuade him not to send the letter of resignation, the general was adamant. The friend argued that the government must have acted upon "misinformation." "Certainly they have," Jackson replied; "but they must be taught not to act so hastily without a full knowledge of the facts. I can teach them this lesson by my resignation, and the country will be no loser by it. If I fail to do so, an irreparable loss may hereafter be sustained, when the lesson might have to be taught by a Lee or Johnston." [21]

Johnston held up Jackson's letter of resignation, although he forwarded a second communication, which the Valley commander had written. In it Jackson denied that Loring's troops were in danger of being cut off, and recommended that Johnston countermand Benjamin's order and hold Loring at Romney. Johnston's endorsement on this letter was short and to the point: "Respectfully referred to the Secretary of War, whose orders I cannot countermand." [22]

He hoped to do something, though, about Jackson's resignation. No one better understood Jackson's position than he did. He had known the interference of Richmond in both large and small matters, but he was eager as usual to recommend that country be placed above self. Resignation, though comfortable to the individual, was not the way for a man of ability. He wrote Jackson:

Under ordinary circumstances, a due sense of one's dignity, as well as care for professional character and official rights, would demand such a course as yours, but the character of this war, the great energy exhibited by the Government of the United States, the danger in which our very existence as an independent people lies, requires sacrifices from us all who have been educated soldiers.

He pointed out that the affront by Richmond was as much of an indignity to him as to Jackson.

I received my information of the order of which you have such cause to complain from your letter. Is not that as great an official wrong to me as the order itself to you? Let us dispassionately reason with the Government on this subject of command, and if we fail to influence its practice, then ask to be relieved from positions the authority of which is exercised by the War Department, while the responsibilities are left to us.

He told Jackson that he had not forwarded the letter of resignation, as he wished "to make this appeal to your patriotism, not merely from warm feelings of personal regard, but from the official opinion which makes me regard you as necessary to the service of the country in your present position." [23]

Two days later, February 5, Johnston wrote Davis and again called attention pointedly to Benjamin's methods. He did not mention Jackson's resignation, which he still held, hoping that Jackson would withdraw it, even though it might have proved a most potent argument for him. He told Davis that Benjamin had not consulted him before sending the order, nor had the Secretary addressed it through the department headquarters as was customary military usage. Johnston wrote:

> On a former occasion I ventured to appeal to your excellency against such exercise of military command by the Secretary of War. Permit me now to suggest the separation of the Valley District from my command, on the ground that it is necessary for the public interest. A collision of the authority of the honorable Secretary of War with mine might occur at a critical moment. In such event disaster would be inevitable. The responsibility of the command has been imposed upon me. Your excellency's known sense of justice will not hold me to the responsibility while the corresponding control is not in my hands. Let me assure your excellency that I am prompted in this matter by no love of privilege of position or of official right as such, but by a firm belief that under the circumstances what I propose is necessary to the safety of our troops and cause.[24]

In closing Johnston urged Davis to visit the army and added, "The highest benefit would be your assuming the command." By such a statement in that context the General seems to have meant that as the President wished to issue orders without regard to usual military procedure he should take over full responsibility. Benjamin confirmed this point of view when in a letter written February 3 he told Johnston that the orders to Loring were sent at Davis' direction. The Secretary included some new directions for movements in the Valley but insisted in something of a placating tone that they were but suggestions. But Johnston was in no forgiving mood. He replied that he regretted that Benjamin had not referred the original order to him. "Let me suggest," he added, "that, having broken up the dispositions of the military command, you give whatever other orders may be necessary." [25]

Johnston held Jackson's letter until February 7, when, having had no answer to his appeal to the Valley commander, he sent it on to Richmond with this endorsement: "Respectfully forwarded, with great regret. I don't know how the loss of this efficient officer can be supplied. . . . " Fortunately, other influential men were also at work to save Jackson for the Confederacy. Jackson finally agreed to withdraw his resignation, but Richmond had the final word. Jackson had preferred charges against Loring on a number of counts for his and his troops' conduct. Not only was no action taken on them but Loring was promoted to major general on February 15, and his troops were transferred from Jackson's command.

Johnston's role in this controversy was chiefly his effort to retain Jackson. Davis characteristically placed an entirely different interpretation upon it. He ignored Johnston's intentions in regard to Jackson in his letter of February 14, and again placed responsibility upon the department commander for the Secretary's actions. He said:

> While I admit the propriety in all cases of transmitting orders through you to those under your command, it is not surprising that the Secretary of War should, in a case requiring prompt action, have departed from this usual method, in view of the fact that he had failed more than once in having his instructions carried out when forwarded to you in the proper manner.

He chose an unfortunate example to point out—that which had just transpired in the Valley—inasmuch as the record hardly fits his contentions. He said that Johnston himself had been ordered to go to Romney on an investigation. He thus ignored Johnston's acknowledgment, in which the army commander stated that the order was not clear, but he was nevertheless sending his acting inspector general to Winchester to look into the condition of Jackson's troops. Neither Loring nor Romney was mentioned in Benjamin's order. Had the Secretary been as exercised as Davis indicated, it would seem that in place of direct intervention, which jumped over the authority of both Jackson and Johnston, he would have clarified his original order and specifically directed that Johnston go to Romney.

Two other factors should be noted in this instance. First, Johnston had implicit confidence in Jackson. Second, Benjamin did not wait even to discover what the result of the investigation by Johnston's inspector might be. His order to Jackson to move Loring's troops from Romney was dated January 30, the day after Johnston wrote his acknowledgment of the order he received. It seems from the record that Benjamin acted with more haste than discretion, and that the original order was carelessly prepared.[26]

Although the commander in the Valley had been saved for the Department of Northern Virginia, Johnston was not so fortunate generally. On February 16 he wrote the President that he had lost by reassignment Beauregard, Van Dorn and five brigadier generals, although he had repeatedly asked that additional general officers be sent to him. In addition he had heard rumors that G. W. Smith was to go. In a letter three days later Davis denied that Smith would be transferred, but in the meantime Johnston had discovered that the error had been one of initials. On the fifteenth the War Department ordered Major General E. Kirby Smith to report to Richmond for a new assignment.[27]

On February 19, just three days before his scheduled inauguration as the permanent President of the Confederacy, Davis wrote that he was anxious to see Johnston. The next morning the general was in Richmond and met with the President and his Cabinet. No record of their deliberations was preserved, but the two principals in later years recorded their memory of what occurred. Contradictions and variations as usual were the result.

Johnston said that the discussion was about the withdrawal of the army from its position at Centerville and Manassas to one which was less exposed. He agreed that such a retirement was necessary before McClellan moved against them, but at the same time he pointed out that it could be done only at the cost of suffering to the men and heavy loss of material and personal baggage, because of the miserable roads and winter weather. He thought it might be well, therefore, to postpone the change of position for some time. The meeting lasted from ten in the morning until nearly sunset, and ended without definite orders having been given, "but with the understanding on my part," Johnston stated, "that the army was to fall back as soon as practicable." [28]

The President later argued that Johnston maintained that his Potomac line was untenable, but that he had no proposal for a new one, as he did not know the topography of the area to his rear. "This confession was a great shock to my confidence in him," Davis wrote, and "was inexplicable on any other theory than that he had neglected the primary duty of a commander." Johnston reiterated that the line, by contrast, offered a good opportunity to initiate an advance, if the army could be reinforced sufficiently to undertake an offensive movement. The decision, consequently, according to Davis, was that Johnston "should mobilize his army by sending to the rear all heavy guns and all surplus supplies and baggage, so as to be able to advance or retreat as occasion might require." In his book about the war Davis says nothing of this meeting, but leaves the impression that his first knowledge even of an intention by Johnston to retreat came when he had the report that such a move was in progress. [29]

Thus the meeting ended. If Johnston neglected the "primary duty of a commander," the President made no move to relieve him of command, nor did he apparently take the precaution to give him written instructions as to what to do. Twice before the end of the month Johnston referred in letters to Davis to "your plans" and the "movement you have ordered," apparently alluding to the retirement of the army, but the orders must have been oral. The door was again wide open for misunderstanding. [30]

If Davis was shocked at Johnston's failure to inform himself about terrain, the general, in turn, became gravely apprehensive immediately after the meeting in Richmond about the government's inability to protect information. He understood that the subject which was discussed there was one of strictest confidence, but when he reached his hotel a young officer asked him if he had heard "that the cabinet had been discussing that day the question of withdrawing the army from the line then occupied."

On his way back to headquarters the following day he met an acquaintance on the train, a man who was "too deaf to hear conversation not intended for his ears." He also volunteered the same information. Johnston immediately reported to Davis these leaks of supposed confidential knowledge, which made him certain of "indiscretion" on the part of someone who had been present at the secret deliberations. His official reticence undoubtedly became stronger as a consequence of these episodes.[31]

Politically the administration was under considerable attack, although the opposition was not organized and views varied radically. Much of it centered upon the Cabinet and particularly the Secretary of War. Troops in the field were aware of the dispute between Benjamin and the generals, and public opinion, nervous under the military reverses, was not slow about placing the responsibility for them upon the Secretary's shoulders. In Congress some members echoed the public sentiment. Among the leaders was Representative Henry S. Foote of Tennessee, who blamed Benjamin for all the disasters of the day and went so far as to move the abolition of the office of Secretary of War, even though he called Benjamin a "mere clerk . . . acting uniformly under the direction of his executive chief." [32]

According to Foote, Johnston played an important part in forestalling the reappointment of Benjamin as Secretary of War in Davis' permanent Cabinet. The congressman tells of a dinner party in Richmond at which he, some twenty other members of the houses of Congress, Johnston and others were present. Benjamin's administration became a topic of conversation, and one guest directly asked Johnston "whether he thought it even *possible* that the Confederate cause could succeed with Mr. Benjamin as war minister." Johnston paused before answering, and then responded with an emphatic "negative," an opinion which was cited in both houses of Congress and "was in the end fatal to Benjamin's hopes of remaining in the Department of War." It also had the result, Foote said, of adding to the feeling of both Davis and Benjamin against Johnston.[33]

Jones, the war clerk, heard the story, but drew a more positive conclusion as to its effect upon Johnston. He wrote in his *Diary* that when Benjamin heard it, which he would, sooner or later, "Joseph E. Johnston is a doomed fly. . . . " [34]

Davis met all objections to Benjamin with stubborn resistance but shifted him to Secretary of State, and appointed George Wythe Randolph Secretary of War. Johnston's observation on the departure of Benjamin from the War Department was that it "enabled the military officers to re-establish the discipline of the army. . . . " [35]

Further to placate dissatisfaction Davis brought Lee back to Rich-

mond on March 13. Congress had indicated a desire for Lee's appointment as Secretary of War when it passed an act which protected
an officer against loss of rank if he were appointed to that position.
Davis did not accept the idea. Then Congress adopted a measure
which provided for the President to nominate a commanding general,
one who could take personal command of any army in the field when
it was needed. Davis vetoed this act, on the basis of unconstitutionality
as it infringed upon the President's position as commander-in-chief.
At the same time he brought Lee from his assignment to improve the
coastal defenses of South Carolina and Georgia for "duty at the seat
of government," where "under the direction of the President," Lee
would supervise the "conduct of military operations in the armies of the
Confederacy." By these actions Davis disclosed his obvious intention to
continue to make all decisions of consequence, as in his new position
Lee held only the power to suggest, despite his rank. The situation was
similar to his earlier experience in Richmond and he confessed that
he could not see "either advantage or pleasure" in his duties.[36]

At the end of February the Department of Northern Virginia had
an effective total present of 47,617 men, of whom 5,400 were
in the Valley under Jackson and 6,000 with Holmes in the Aquia
District. As no general had been appointed to Beauregard's place,
Johnston himself was in command of the Potomac area, with
approximately 36,000 men. His division commanders were G. W.
Smith, Longstreet and two others recently appointed, Major General
Richard S. Ewell and Brigadier General Jubal A. Early. Stuart still
commanded the cavalry and Pendleton the artillery.

At three important outposts on the Potomac Johnston had
stationed sizable bodies of troops. At Leesburg, about twenty-five
miles above Washington and near the Potomac, Brigadier General
Daniel H. Hill commanded 2,500 men. At Dumfries, about the
same distance below Washington along the Potomac as Leesburg
was above, Whiting had his brigade of 7,600. The third was at
Evansport, where Brigadier General Samuel G. French was stationed
with his brigade.[37]

Dumfries and Evansport were part of the Confederate right, which
Johnston always interpreted as dangerously vulnerable to a Federal
turning movement. Even before Manassas, the Confederates had
occupied positions along the Potomac in this area and below,
and had placed fortifications in strategic spots. They removed buoys

and other channel markers from the river and brought heavy guns from Norfolk in the late summer and fall to assist in blocking traffic. McClellan did not have the naval strength to clear the stream; he had to use the army to do that, if it were done. If, either by direct attack or by a flanking movement, he could force Johnston to fall back from his Centerville line, the Confederates would have to give up their positions along the Potomac. The Federals would then be able to use the river freely. When Lincoln in late January issued his order which called for a forward movement of the army by Washington's Birthday, McClellan's plan was to move against this portion of the Confederate position.

CHAPTER VII

CENTERVILLE TO YORKTOWN

When Johnston returned to Centerville after his meeting with the President he began to plan the retirement of the army. Federal activity on his flanks made him realize that the enemy would not spare him much time. "We may indeed have to start before we are ready," he wrote Whiting on February 28.[1]

His major concern in planning the movement was over transportation. The troops had accumulated a huge amount of baggage, a trunk to a volunteer as Johnston described it. He had tried to keep no more than fifteen days' rations at Manassas, but the Commissary General's department had ignored his requests and in addition had placed a "very extensive" meat-packing plant at Thoroughfare Gap, despite its exposed position and his protests. To add a further handicap for a quick withdrawal, several of the states had gathered stocks of provisions and clothing under their agents at Manassas.[2]

The roads of Virginia were in bad condition from the winter rains and snows. Even a well-mounted man could travel but little more than two miles an hour over them. Johnston feared that he could not save the artillery in advanced positions under such conditions. But his principal efforts were to secure the efficient operation of the single track railroad, the Orange & Alexandria, upon which he had to depend to move the mass of baggage and supplies before the retirement of the troops could start. As in the instance of the transfer of his army from Winchester to Manassas over the Manassas Gap Rail Road the civilian management and employees controlled the operation of the trains. None of them appreciated the urgent need for haste, and cars and engines which they repeatedly promised failed to appear.

Despite the urgent military necessity and Johnston's complaints to Richmond of the "wretched mismanagement" of the railroad, nothing of any consequence occurred. It is possible that the service was as good as should have been expected. The road was a single track with few "turnouts" or sidings. The cars were small and the engines could draw but few of them at a time. All joined to create probably an insurmountable handicap for a quick evacuation. But it never occurred to the government to take over the railroad as a military measure, or for improved efficiency, or to give Johnston the authority to do so temporarily. The truth is that the Confederacy failed to develop any adequate policy for the use of its railroads, possibly because of an unwillingness even under the stress of war to invade the property rights of citizens.

The result was that the railroad from Manassas continued to operate inefficiently from Johnston's point of view. In an effort to improve the situation he wrote the President on March 3 that the removal of army stores and other materials "goes on with painful slowness." He warned that a "large quantity. . . . must be sacrificed or your instructions not observed," but then stated that he would "adhere to them as closely as possible." [3]

Davis forwarded Johnston's communication to Quartermaster General Myers to see if he could intervene to secure more engines and cars to assist in the evacuation. Myers' reply left little hope, not because of a shortage of rolling stock but because of the incapacity of the road itself. "From the reports of conductors," Myers told Davis, "I am inclined to think that there are too many trains now on that road; they are not able to pass each other on the turnouts. Some engines have been thirty-six hours making the trip from Manassas to Gordonsville." [4]

On February 28 the President wrote and agreed with Johnston about the circumstances of his army. He fully recognized the weakness of Johnston's position and the isolation of his army from supporting troops for the defense of Richmond. Davis wrote:

Two questions therefore press upon us for solution. First how can your army best serve to prevent the advance of the enemy while the want of force compels you to stand on the defensive? Second, what disposition can you and should you make to enable you most promptly to co-operate with other columns, in the event of disaster to their forces or to yours, and of consequent danger to the capitol? . . . As has been my custom, I have only sought to present general purposes and views. I rely upon your special knowledge and high ability to effect whatever is practicable in this our hour of need. The military paradox, that impossibilities must be rendered possible, had never better occasion for its application.

Thus Davis stated his agreement with Johnston's position without reservation, although he chose to deny it later.[5]

The letter from the President confirmed the sense of urgency which Johnston felt, although he hoped that a movement by McClellan might make retirement unnecessary. Should he attack and the Confederates defeat him, "we might move at leisure," Johnston told Whiting. Otherwise the retirement, a "measure of the Government," could not be changed, and the general carefully devised plans for it. He advised his subordinates of them and enjoined secrecy upon them. All would move but Jackson, who would continue to hold his position.[6]

On March 7 Johnston sent the order for the retirement to begin. The troops along the Potomac moved first, to be followed on the ninth by those from the Manassas-Centerville area. The original plan called for these to start earlier, but the amount of supplies which still remained at Manassas caused them to be held up. By the evening of the ninth, however, the troops were on their way to the points of concentration on the south bank of the Rappahannock and at Fredericksburg.[7]

While the main army, at long last stripped to condition for active field campaigning, moved to forestall possible enemy plans, Stuart and his cavalry stayed at Manassas to complete the destruction of the abandoned storehouses and supplies. Included in the supplies were four days' rations for the men and a similar amount of grain for the horses, which Johnston reported, "by a singular blunder, was put there just in time to be destroyed." [8]

At Evansport General French detailed demolition crews to spike the heavy guns or to throw them in the Potomac, and to burn whatever else was at hand. In some instances they were apparently unsuccessful, and the Federals who took possession after their departure reported, "Everything left behind indicates that they left hastily and in great confusion." At the Thoroughfare meat-packing establishment all the buildings were burned except for the smokehouses, which were too close to privately owned property and were consequently torn down. Some of the meat was distributed to the people of the area and the rest was burned with the buildings.[9]

By March 11 all the infantry and artillery from Manassas had crossed the Rappahannock, and Johnston had set up his head-quarters at the Rappahannock Station. Those posted along the lower Potomac joined the forces of Holmes in and around Fredericksburg. On the thirteenth Johnston reported on the movement to Davis, and added:

A reserve of ammunition and subsistence kept at Culpeper Court-House is to be removed before the army marches farther. The management of this railroad is so wretched that it is impossible to guess when the removal of these stores will be completed. When it has been I shall cross the Rapidan and take such position as you may think best in connection with those of other troops. By proper management of the railroad it seems to me that from the neighborhood of Gordonsville 20,000, or even 30,000 men might be thrown into Richmond on a single day.[10]

The President's reply was critical in tone. Although Johnston's letter indicated that other communications had been sent, none had reached him. That on the thirteenth was the first official word he had received. He had heard of the destruction of property, "indicating precipitate retreat," but "was at a loss to believe it," as he had no knowledge of a cause for such a sudden move. Until that time, he continued, "I was as much in the dark as to your purposes, condition, and necessities as at the time of our conversation on the subject about a month since." Davis' criticism was possibly further justified in his mind by the message he had sent Johnston on the tenth: "Further assurance given to me this day that you shall be promptly and adequately re-enforced, so as to enable you to maintain your position and resume first policy when the roads will permit."[11]

If Davis believed that the promise of reinforcements could have caused Johnston to hold his position, the facts do not justify it. He sent the message on the tenth, by which time the movement was sufficiently advanced to be difficult to recall. No recruits were at hand, only "assurance" that they would be. A soldier in the field can hardly build upon such a promise. The War Department had asked, and Governor Letcher later gave, permission for the Confederate generals to call out the Virginia militia wherever need existed. But that would take time to accomplish, and Johnston's problems were immediately pressing, or seemed to be. In addition, such troops would be both untrained and unarmed, as the Confederacy had no equipment at Richmond at the time.[12]

All had agreed in late February that the Manassas-Centerville line should be given up, both because it was untenable and because the troops should be closer to Richmond so they might co-operate in the defense of the capital against threatened attacks from the south and east. But by the time he wrote in mid-March, either Davis had changed his mind or circumstances were different. "The question of throwing troops into Richmond is contingent upon reverses in the West and Southeast. The immediate necessity for such a movement is not anticipated." [13]

Davis' interpretation of the events grew more unrealistic as the years passed. In his later writings he ignored both the conference with Johnston and the correspondence about the plan to withdraw and the difficulty of carrying it out. As early as February 1865 he stated that Johnston "surprised" the government by his "hasty retreat without giving notice of an intention to do so." In a letter to Northrop in 1878 he said that Johnston "fled, though no man pursued." In his discussion in *Rise and Fall* Davis based a portion of his argument upon the testimony of General Early, who remarked, in an account he wrote after the war, upon the large amount of stores and baggage burned at Manassas. Davis quoted Early's belief "that all might have been carried off if the railroads had been energetically operated," but said nothing about the Army's having to rely upon the civilian operation of the road. Nor did he include Early's total conclusions about the retirement, although they follow in Early's narrative:

The movement back from the line of Bull Run was in itself a very wise one in a strategic point of view, if it was not one of absolute necessity, but the loss of stores was very much to be regretted. I do not pretend to attach censure to anyone of our officials for this loss, especially to General Johnston. I know that he was exceedingly anxious to get off all the stores and made extraordinary exertions to accomplish that object.[14]

Others who were present and wrote later about the retirement felt much as Early did about the movement itself and were not critical otherwise. E. P. Alexander thought the loss of stores not too great and said, "When all is considered the movement was eminently successful as it was judicious." Richard Taylor remarked, "The movement was executed with the quiet precision characteristic of Johnston, unrivaled as a master of logistics." The "English Combatant" published his book in 1864 and may have been carried away by enthusiasm for the cause. "This great retreat," he said, "was undoubtedly a feat of the originator; but the exact schedule of movements, route, time of junction, transportation, and a thousand other points were calculated and fulfilled with so much nicety" as to demand admiration.[15]

With the retirement accomplished Johnston's attention concentrated upon the effective arrangement of his army to meet the campaign against Richmond which he expected from McClellan as quickly as weather conditions made it possible. From his analysis of the geography it would come by one of four routes. Of them only that through Manassas had been sufficiently well covered by the winter-quarters position. The others lay farther to the east: one by land through Fredericksburg and the other two by the Potomac and Chesapeake Bay with embarkation either on the lower Rappahannock or at Fort Monroe. To cover all these probabilities the Rappahannock line was not entirely satisfactory, so within a week Johnston planned another move, to a line behind the Rapidan. Closer to Richmond, it removed the opportunity for the Federals to get easily between him and the capital. He left Ewell's infantry and Stuart's cavalry at the Rappahannock in an advanced position, while the troops at Fredericksburg remained there. All the rest moved to the new Rapidan line.[16]

In their new grouping the units were close enough to support one another and could move quickly to oppose any major Federal thrust. But the retirement accomplished an accompanying important result in that it upset McClellan's plans. For some time the Federal commander had attempted to convince Lincoln of the wisdom of using a water rather than an overland route toward Richmond. On the very eve of Johnston's move to new positions McClellan finally won his point. He received permission to carry his men by transport to the town of Urbana on the lower Rappahannock, where the army could disembark. There, he would be within fifty miles of the Confederate capital and in the rear of Johnston's Manassas-Centerville line. But with Johnston's army behind the Rapidan, this movement lost all of its value. This forced the preparation of a new plan, a matter which was complicated by the fact that McClellan had begun to lose the confidence of both the public and the political leaders by his inaction and repeated delays. Lincoln relieved him of command of the Armies of the United States on March 11 but left him in charge of the Army of the Potomac.

In the meanwhile, the move to the Rapidan had not solved all the Confederate problems. To discuss them, Davis, Lee and Johnston met at Johnston's headquarters on March 22. Earlier that month, the Federal movement against New Bern started a clamor for help from North Carolina, whereupon the War Department ordered first French and then Longstreet to that state. Johnston protested vigorously against the transfer of Longstreet, not only because of his ability, which the army commander praised highly, but because G. W. Smith's health was apparently uncertain. Richmond agreed to the retention of Longstreet in the Army of Northern Virginia, as it had come to be called, and at Gordonsville, the conferees decided upon Holmes, a native of the state, for the North Carolina command. To replace him at Fredericksburg, Johnston immediately appointed Smith.[17]

The need to determine upon a location for Johnston's army was more important than these details. An inspection of the position at Fredericksburg disclosed that the force there was not strong enough to defend it. Davis still had hope that the reinforcements, about which he had informed Johnston on March 10, would be forthcoming. These sanguine expectations and the inability to ascertain at that time the intentions of the enemy caused the decision to leave the army where it was, as from its position it could cover Richmond and protect the Virginia Central railroad, then the only rail connection between the capital and the Shenandoah Valley.[18]

Although ties with Jackson were difficult to maintain, because of his geographical isolation in the Valley, he and Johnston kept in frequent communication. Shortly after the retirement of the main army from Manassas, Jackson withdrew reluctantly from Winchester under Federal pressure. After he had fallen back about forty miles to Mount Jackson, between Strasburg and Newmarket, he discovered that the Federals were moving troops from the Valley toward Manassas. This was exactly what Johnston had warned him to prevent, so in what was to become typical fashion, he moved thirty-six miles in a day and a half to Kernstown, where from reports there was a small enemy force. The Federals, whose numbers scouts had under-estimated, won the day at Kernstown, but the results were virtually as important to the Confederates as a victory. Washington assumed from his boldness that Jackson had received reinforcements, and immediately halted the movement of troops from the Valley. Thus, Johnston's foresight and Jackson's ability as a field commander com-bined to give the first evidence of the Confederate strategy which had the effect of neutralizing a large portion of the Federal superiority of numbers in that critical period.[19]

To the east and southeast of Richmond two relatively small Con-federate forces, each acting under independent command, guarded the water approaches to the capital. At Yorktown Brigadier General John B. Magruder commanded 12,000 men. The other of these in-dependent Confederate commands was at Norfolk. There Major General Benjamin Huger had some 13,000 troops to protect the city and the near-by Navy Yard at Gosport, where the Federal frigate *Merrimac*, which the Confederates had raised and rechristened the *Virginia*, was stationed. With her sides heavily protected by iron the *Virginia*, though a revolutionary example of marine construction, was "as unmanageable as a water-logged vessel." On March 8 she won a great victory over the Federal wooden ships but the next day fought a drawn engagement with the odd-looking *Monitor*. These renowned contests sent the *Virginia* back to her base for re-pair, but with her prestige and role confirmed. As the *Monitor* was the bulldog to protect the Union fleet in Chesapeake Bay, the *Virginia* was the floating barrier to the James River, which was navi-gable all the way to Richmond and too broad in its lower reaches to be defended by land batteries.[20]

In the co-ordination of these various forces, Davis had the assist-ance of one new and one old hand in the War Department. George W. Randolph had taken Benjamin's place as Secretary of War, while Lee had assumed again the post of military adviser to the President. As they concentrated upon their complicated tasks, they were startled by news of thunderbolt proportions on March 24. From the lower James and York rivers telegrams brought word of a considerable Union force in that area. Huger said that more than twenty steamers had come down Chesapeake Bay and that men were disembarking at Old Point Comfort near Fort Monroe. Magruder reported that the enemy force then facing him had jumped to 35,000, and asked for 10,000 reinforcements from Johnston's army at once.[21]

Other information soon confirmed these first messages, but while they all described the size of the enemy's army as "immense," all the informants failed to answer the more important question, the objective against which it planned to move. The next day Lee dispatched by special messenger to Johnston an urgent communication about developments. At the request of the President he inquired the number of men Johnston could send to reinforce Magruder's Army of the Peninsula or that of Huger at Norfolk. He explained that they were not sure in Richmond whether the troops at Old Point Comfort were a part of McClellan's army or not, but suspected they were. The important thing was that Johnston should organize his force so that a part of it could be spared to come to Richmond, where it would be ready to move to the point of Union attack, while the rest held the line of the Rapidan.[22]

In reply Johnston proposed that he leave but a skeleton force at the Rapidan and take 25,000 men to Richmond, when it became necessary. Instead he received an order on March 27 to send 10,000 men. He selected 7,500 from those in the positions along the Rapidan and 2,500 from Fredericksburg, but in advising Richmond of his action, he protested against piecemeal reinforcement. He said that a line of outposts could mask the move and continued, "The division of the troops of this department made by the telegram of this afternoon leaves on this line a force too weak to oppose an invasion, and furnishes to the threatened point a reinforcement too small to command success." Before sending the letter Johnston added a postscript, in which he restated his fundamental belief: "We cannot win without concentration." [23]

The difficulty in Richmond was that no one could be sure where the point of concentration should be. Johnston created further confusion there by enclosing with his letter reports of subordinates which indicated considerable enemy activity on his front. Lee pointed out to him that the call for his co-operation was a consequence of the belief that the enemy "could not advance" in his area. The reports he sent seemed to point to the reverse. His army was the only protection for the important rail connection with Tennessee. Possibly it should remain where it was. The President, Lee said, was willing to assume responsibility for any movement, but Johnston's knowledge of the circumstances at the Rapidan front was greater. If Johnston were doubtful about what to do, the President encouraged him "to a full conference at this place, where the latest intelligence is collected." [24]

The fluid situation created opportunity for a great amount of confusion. Again confronted with the necessity to move supplies, Johnston asked Richmond for advice. "It is necessary to move public property from Gordonsville," he wired Randolph. "The commissary-general forbids our sending it to Richmond. Where shall it go?" When Johnston needed to be in constant communication with Richmond, he found the wire service unreliable. "I attempted last night," he wrote on April 4 from Fredericksburg, "to give the President by telegraph the information I found here, but the operator reported that he was unable to communicate with Richmond, the office there being closed apparently." He reported that Early's division, which had been ordered to Richmond March 28, was on its way, but that another brigade was being held because of enemy activity on his front.[25]

Up to that time McClellan's objective was still unknown. His hesitancy kept the Confederates off balance, but it also occasioned additional reproaches for him from the Union politicians and public. But he moved 121,500 men, and tremendous amounts of equipment from Washington to Fort Monroe, where he arrived himself on April 2, expeditiously and to the confusion of the Confederates. On the fourth he telegraphed Stanton, "I expect to fight tomorrow . . . ." But on that same day Washington stepped in further to divest him of authority, when Lincoln, troubled by Jackson's movements in the Valley, informed him that the force left for the purpose was too small to protect the capital. The President, consequently, changed the geographical limits to remove McDowell from McClellan's control and at the same time placed Banks in a similar independent command in the Shenandoah.[26]

On April 4 Lee advised Johnston that the Federal forces were advancing in the Peninsula, thus disclosing their intention to move against Richmond. Although not certain earlier about McClellan's objective or what might occur on Johnston's front, the Confederate authorities had gradually moved troops from the Rapidan-Fredericks-

burg position until the divisions of Early, D. H. Hill and Whiting were
in the Peninsula. This left three with Johnston, those of Ewell, Longstreet and D. R. Jones, who received G. W. Smith's command when
that officer was given charge at Fredericksburg. This was the sort of
dispersal Johnston feared, but Confederate weakness forced it until
McClellan's intention was clear. As soon as that was seen new orders
were immediately issued to combat it. Longstreet and Jones moved at
once to the Peninsula but Ewell remained where he was with instructions to co-operate with Jackson, if necessity arose.[27]

When Johnston reached Richmond he reported to the President,
who told him that his command included the further responsibility

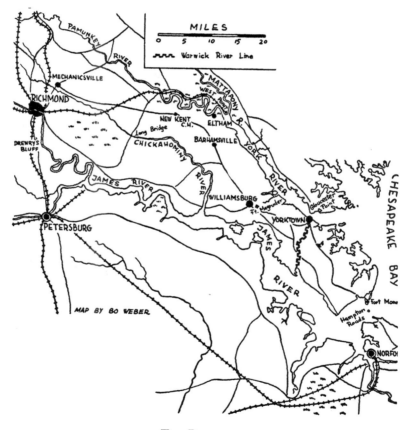

THE PENINSULA

of the Yorktown-Norfolk areas. After his visit he set out for an inspection of Magruder's positions in the Peninsula. Once past the Chickahominy River, the Peninsula narrowed to comparatively small proportions. In that area the country was generally wooded with frequent small clearings on the higher ground. Tidal creeks, with their indefinite, soggy margins of salt marsh, ate, at times, far into the center of the narrow strip of land between the two rivers, the York and the James. The latter, which was to the south, was broad and sluggish, and offered a water avenue all the way to Richmond for light-draft vessels. The York, on the north, was formed by the junction of the Pamunkey and the Mattapony at West Point, and was navigable for its whole length. A railroad ran from West Point thirty-eight miles to Richmond. Down toward the water end of the Peninsula, land batteries at Yorktown and Gloucester Point, directly across the river, commanded the York, but the flank along the James was open to enemy movement, except for the protection of the *Virginia*. Control of both rivers was necessary, or the army would find itself in a trap.

If the river flanks held and sufficient troops could be secured, a line at Yorktown might be tenable. There Johnston met Magruder and carefully investigated the fortifications which he had constructed. Even then work still continued, as the Peninsula commander tried to strengthen his line, which the Union forces tested on April 5, only to settle down to siege operations. Magruder's early requests for help had been only partly granted, as Lee wished to be sure of McClellan's intentions before he committed troops. At the time of Johnston's visit the Confederates numbered 31,500, some of whom were in garrisons at Yorktown and Gloucester Point, while 23,000 manned the fourteen-mile line across the Peninsula.[28]

The Warwick River line, on which the Confederates worked and watched, for a large part followed the tidewater stream, which rises near Yorktown and flows across the Peninsula into the James. Magruder had built dams along its course and created pools of sufficient depth to retard an enemy advance. On the high ground a line of field works stretched from the water barrier to and around the gullies near Yorktown. At places these were constructed directly on top of the old British works of the Revolution. At Yorktown, as well as at Gloucester Point across the York, batteries were in position to guard that all-important channel.[29]

From his examination Johnston believed that the Warwick River line was untenable and of use only for a delaying action. Though a great deal of effort had gone into it, the construction had been under the supervision of engineers who were inexperienced in war. Though McClellan might try for a break-through between the dammed-up pools and Yorktown because of his superiority in artillery the fundamental weakness was the readily turned flanks by the use of the rivers. By such a maneuver McClellan could place a force in the rear of the Confederates anywhere along the Peninsula and nullify any advantage the terrain offered otherwise.[30]

Magruder had chosen one other spot in which to construct works—near the old colonial town of Williamsburg, a little more than ten miles from Yorktown. There he used the natural barrier of two streams, one of which ran to the James and the other to the York. On the high ground between them he constructed a major defense point, Fort Magruder, and about a dozen scattered redoubts and other earthworks. In front of the position the Confederates felled trees to open a line of fire and dug rifle pits.[31]

Convinced by his examination that the Peninsula offered great handicaps to successful defense, Johnston hastened back to Richmond. On the next morning, April 14, he was in Davis' office when the President arrived. He at once summarized his observations. He suggested.that instead of a defensive campaign in the Peninsula, all the troops possible from Georgia, North and South Carolina be brought to Richmond to join with those in Virginia in an offensive movement against McClellan's army at the proper moment. He pointed out the length of the Warwick River-Yorktown line and the lack of the man power necessary to hold it. He remarked on the weak point between the flooded areas and Yorktown and pointed out that the inundated sections protected the Federals as much as the Confederates. He emphasized McClellan's advantage in artillery; the Federal naval and rifled cannon could far outdistance the Confederate smoothbores. With their aid the Union commander could smash the defense lines at Yorktown and Gloucester Point and open the York River. Thus a trap could be sprung on the Southern army, if Federal transports carried troops to the rear of the Confederate line and landed them between it and Richmond. By contrast an army committed to an offensive near Richmond would gain a surprise, inasmuch as the Federals looked only for defensive action. They could be caught also with long-extended communications, far from any base. Such a Confederate victory could end the war, while one in the Peninsula, in which Johnston placed small faith, could be little more than a local triumph.

The President was gravely concerned by the discouraging report on the situation in the Peninsula, but before making any decision in such a crucial matter, he wished to consult with Randolph and Lee. At Johnston's suggestion he also asked G. W. Smith and Longstreet to attend the meeting. Johnston had long highly regarded Smith, while in the preceding months he had steadily placed more and more responsibility on Longstreet.

Later in the morning the two representatives of the civil government gathered with the four generals. In the short time before the meeting started Smith wrote a memorandum which he gave to Johnston. After reading it Johnston handed it to Davis and said that he agreed with the opinions in it. Davis read it aloud and it became the basis of the early discussion. Smith made two suggestions, both of which required the assembling of Confederate forces and an offensive movement. The first called for the abandonment of the Peninsula and Norfolk and a concentration near Richmond, which was Johnston's suggestion in the earlier conversation with Davis. When McClellan was sufficiently away from his gunboats and his base at Fort Monroe, the Confederates could attack and whip him. The other plan was to garrison Richmond with enough troops to withstand a siege by McClellan, while the rest of the army struck out offensively beyond the Potomac. It was Smith's idea that they might even go so far as Philadelphia and New York before McClellan could capture the Confederate capital.

Johnston, in stating his opinion, reviewed the circumstances as he had presented them to the President. The most that could be gained from sending a major force into the Peninsula was a few weeks' time. It would be bought with a high price in men because of the unhealthy swamps, the bad water, and the difficulty of operating in the low tidelands. Furthermore, if the Confederates forced the Federals back from the Yorktown-Warwick River line, they could not achieve full victory, as the enemy could retire to the protection of Fort Monroe. But Johnston's main emphasis was on the fundamental weakness of the Peninsula to flank attack.

The policy advocated by Johnston was one which called for the retention of the force then in the Peninsula. He believed that it could hold McClellan until the Federals were ready to open against the batteries at Yorktown and Gloucester Point and another Confederate army had concentrated in the vicinity of Richmond. He emphasized that this force was to be an attacking army and not one assembled for the defense of the capital. Furthermore, if his plan were accepted and followed, it would be McClellan's army which would suffer most from the camp diseases contracted in the tidal swamps.

In the early phases of the long discussion the President took little part. Secretary of War Randolph, who had served as an officer of the United States Navy as well as in the Confederate Army, opposed any plan for giving up the Peninsula without a fight, as it meant the evacuation of Norfolk and the loss of Gosport Navy Yard, where Confederate ships were on the ways and the *Virginia* had her base. If Norfolk were given up, the Confederacy would lose its only hope of developing any naval power.

Lee supported Randolph's views. He stated that they could not bring any large number of reinforcements from other areas to Richmond. Not only did Lee argue against the suggested concentration but he believed that the Peninsula held strong positions for defense, where McClellan's army could be held. Strangely he showed no concern, apparently, over the possibility of a flanking movement by McClellan, although he had singled out this serious danger in a communication to Magruder less than a week before.

It is difficult to understand Lee's position at the conference. It is possible that he hoped to gain time by the defense of the Peninsula for the completion of the army reorganization. That process continued, even in those critical days, because of re-enlistments and Virginia's establishment of virtual conscription, with the consequent formation of new companies, regiments, brigades, and the election of new officers. Another reason for delaying the action was the Confederate conscription law, which was then pending in the Congress and passed two days later. Although it could bring no men directly into service in time to be of immediate help, it did hold the men then in the Army, regardless of the date of the expiration of their term of enlistment.

Whatever Lee's reasoning, he and Randolph upheld the defense of the Peninsula against Johnston and Smith. Longstreet, new to such a deliberative session and offended by a curt interruption by Davis when he did attempt to say anything, offered no opinion. The

President at first listened to the others and said little, but as the meeting continued through the afternoon and evening, he began to show a disposition to accept the views of Lee and Randolph. Finally he announced about midnight that the Peninsula should be defended and Norfolk held as long as possible. Thus, for the second time, the President committed the Army of Northern Virginia to a defensive role.

Johnston was still unconvinced. "The belief that events on the Peninsula would soon compel the Confederate Government to adopt my method of opposing the Federal army reconciled me somewhat to the necessity of obeying the President's order," he wrote later.[32]

CHAPTER VIII

IN THE PENINSULA

With the meeting over Johnston went at once to his new command post at Yorktown, where an army of 53,000 awaited him. The two forces faced each other less than half a mile apart. Johnston concluded that he had best finish the field works which Magruder had started and continue to clear roads through the thick forest. The pick and ax had become as indispensable in warfare as the rifle or musket. Along swamp and highland soldiers stacked their arms to pick up tools. On April 22 Johnston wrote Lee: "Labor enough has been expended here to make a very strong position. . . ." About the same time Magruder reported that his men were so exhausted from their work on and their exposure in the trenches that they would be ineffective in action, unless they could secure rest by being relieved.[1]

Hill informed Johnston that he had withdrawn his Negro labor force from the outer works and would try to use them to relieve his men. The use of slave labor was not new in the Confederate Army, but it was a constant source of issue between army commander and slaveowner over contract or impressment. In January Benjamin stated a policy to Magruder, under which the latter should contract for slaves outside the district under his command and impress them within it. With the landing of McClellan's army at Fort Monroe the

114

pressure on the Confederates in the Peninsula to complete and to strengthen the field works in the area increased. Magruder asked Richmond to help by sending him 1,000 additional slaves, as he did not have the time to secure them in the neighboring counties. Lee replied that it was inadvisable in his judgment to place slaves so close to the enemy's line. "It would be unsafe, and in the event of an engagement they would be much in the way." Instead of slaves Lee suggested that the troops do the work.

Undaunted Magruder turned to the people of the Peninsula and across the James. In a proclamation of April 11 he called upon them for "one negro man, with his ax or spade, to be furnished at once by each proprietor. Without the most liberal assistance in axes, spades, and hands to work, we cannot hope to succeed, and the Northern army will be in possession of your farm in a few days." [2]

The pomp and circumstance of 1861 were no longer evident in either army; war had settled everywhere to the serious business it was. In the Peninsula it was more than generally trying. The extraordinarily heavy rains made the flat, low country sodden, and the trenches stood deep in water which drained into rather than out of them. The men who were crowded into them in great numbers could only sit or crouch, as the parapets were too low for them to stand erect and be protected from the sharpshooter, and the water kept them from lying down.

Night attacks, or more accurately, night alarms added to these difficulties. Incredible darkness hung over the swamps in the cloudy, rainy weather, and seemed to give added volume to the roar of the artillery and the crack of lesser arms, as they sounded and echoed with fiendish implications along the line. It was on such a night that a working party of several hundred slaves stampeded and swept back a part of the infantry support. On another occasion a detachment of soldiers gave way completely under the mental strain. The relieving party said that they found "some of these poor lads . . . sobbing in their broken sleep, like a crying child just before it sinks to rest. It was really pathetic. The men actually had to be supported to the ambulances sent down to bring them away." [3]

Clothing, too, illustrated the transition which had taken place in Confederate army life. There was no accumulation of trunks at Yorktown as there had been at Manassas. Instead, the only clothes were those being worn, and they were "perforated in all manners of places . . . and had known no soap as it was a commodity that had

ceased to exist." If his stay at Yorktown had been a little longer, the
English Combatant recorded, "I might have exclaimed with Falstaff:
'There is but half a shirt in my whole company.' " A persistent
tribulation was the soldier's most constant enemy, the "gray-back." [4]

Food was generally short in quantity and unappetizing in quality.
Flour and bacon were regularly doled out in half rations, one soldier
reported, but coffee, fresh meat, molasses, salt, bread and crackers
were luxuries of almost forgotten memory. The English Combatant
heard no complaints among the men, although he expressed some
personal misgivings in his report that his comrades "fried the abomin-
able bacon for its fat, which they mixed with their flour, and this
with water was the chief food of all for many weeks." [5]

Although in the midst of an active campaign against an enemy
who was superior to him in numbers and equipment, Johnston again
confronted the old trying problems of reorganizing his army. The
men whose twelve months of service was up had not responded as
had been hoped to the Furlough and Bounty law, so, to keep
its armies in the field, the Confederate government turned to the ex-
periment, novel in America, of conscription, which became law April
16. Johnston had to provide the companies and regiments with the
opportunity to hold elections for officers, and to bring troops from
the same state together in brigades. All this had to be done within
forty days of the passage of the law. Thus, in the very face of the
enemy, would-be officers contended for positions of command. [6]

D. H. Hill complained that the remodeling of his division had
disrupted matters to the extent that "I scarcely know my officers by
name." But the total consequences were far more serious, as Johnston
displayed. "The troops, in addition to the lax discipline of volunteers,
are partially discontented at the conscription act and demoralized
by their recent elections," he wrote Lee. In the same letter he said,
"Stragglers cover the country, and Richmond is no doubt filled with
the absent without leave." Because of its effect on morale and discipline, he apparently did not allow a complete reshuffling of his army.
Such reasons were ignored by Davis, who reminded Johnston of his
neglect in failing to brigade together the troops from the same state.
The President wrote:

While some have expressed surprise at my patience when orders to
you were not observed, I have at least hoped that you would recognize the desire to aid and sustain you, and that it would produce the

corresponding action on your part. The reasons formerly offered have one after another disappeared, and I hope you will as you can, proceed to organize your troops as heretofore instructed. . . . [7]

Despite the statement of Davis the important reason for not reorganizing the army remained: the presence of the enemy. Although McClellan held off committing the Federals to any movement of size, except for a reconnaissance in force on April 16, the day before Johnston took command in the Peninsula, small skirmishes frequently occurred. But he had decided to rely upon artillery and engineering rather than infantry to break the Confederate position, which all his observers reported as very strong. Along the Federal lines troops worked night and day to prepare emplacements for the heavy-siege guns and mortars, which men and animals struggled to move over the muddy roads from the rear. On April 8 McClellan reported to Washington, "The roads are horrid, and we have the devil's own time about supplies." He called for more men, more Parrott guns, more time. He wished to blow the enemy line apart when all was ready. He received Franklin's division as a reinforcement on April 22, and kept it on board transports in preparation for an attack upon Gloucester Point. Johnston knew McClellan well and relied on his cautious thoroughness which would work to delay him. Lincoln soon arrived at a similar conclusion and chided his general to act. Public opinion was growing restive in the North over the repeated delays, but McClellan's plans had not matured, and his intelligence agent, Allen Pinkerton, continued to haunt him with exaggerated reports of Confederate man power. Pinkerton even said that the number of rations which were issued in a day confirmed his statistics.[8]

The Confederate troops in the Yorktown line knew little about rations and less about statistics; Johnston, though, knew that he was in an unhappy position. He complained that the telegraph service with Richmond was often disrupted, and requested that messages be duplicated by steamer. He asked that the bridges in his rear over the Chickahominy be repaired. On the twenty-fourth he suggested to Lee that if he were forced to withdraw from Yorktown, "it would be a great convenience to have a few day's provisions in wagons, which could meet the army on any road we might take." [9]

As early as April 21, Lee wrote asking that Johnston be forthright in expressing his views, so that he might "lay them before the President." Two days later he wrote again: ". . . should there be reason, in your opinion, for a withdrawal from the Peninsula, I beg you will state them [sic], with your recommendation, that I may submit them to the President. You can best judge of the difficulties before you and know the interests involved in the question." It was apparent from these communications, so close to the date of the Richmond conference, that Lee's mind was not closed about the advantages or disadvantages of fighting on the Peninsula, and that his convictions may not have been as positive at the conference as they have been represented, or that he had changed them.[10]

It would appear from a letter to Johnston from Louis T. Wigfall, Senator from Texas, that the latter might be the proper conclusion. Wigfall, who had commanded a brigade in Johnston's army before he took his seat in the Senate on February 18, 1862, was also interested in presenting Johnston's point of view in Richmond. He had supported the department commander's idea of concentration for an offensive in the fall of 1861, and tried to get Davis to abandon the defense of the southern seacoast to assemble all possible troops in the vicinity of Richmond. He advised Johnston that he still had some hope that it might be done before it was too late. "I would have been down to see you before," he wrote, "but hoped by staying here to be able to infuse red blood into this inanimate body of a government of ours. . . . Lee and Randolph are both now for active operations, agree that it is better to flog the Devil than the Quaker Congress." [11]

On the twenty-seventh Johnston reported to Richmond that McClellan's preparations were apparently nearing completion, and that his attack upon the lines at Yorktown with a great artillery concentration might occur any time. The Federals had gathered a large number of vessels with which they could pass up the York and turn his flank as soon as the land attack started. He warned Richmond, and at the same time Huger, that such an effort by McClellan would necessitate the abandonment of the Peninsula, and that troops at Norfolk should be prepared to evacuate and move to Richmond "with the utmost promptness." Remembering, possibly, his bitter experience after Centerville and Manassas, he added, "As little public property as possible should be left to the enemy." [12]

Again, two days later, he issued a warning of events to come. He feared that McClellan was waiting only for the arrival of ironclads to run the James. With water transport the Federal commander could move his army three days quicker than the Confederates could march overland. "The fight for Yorktown," Johnston wrote Lee, "as

I said in Richmond, must be one of artillery, in which we cannot win." The best that could be done in that event was to hold out for a few hours; even a few days' delay would be insignificant. He thought it best to retire at once and to put the army in the best position possible to defend Richmond.[13]

The reasoning Johnston followed seems obvious. It would be far easier to move before the enemy expected it than to wait and retreat under the pressure of an army which had been victorious in its assault. Huger, however, saw only the difficulty of a hurried retirement. He promptly reported to Richmond that an early move would be impossible, and that he thought it would be better to stay and fight as long as he could. Lee's reply was both tactful and practical. Norfolk was in no immediate danger, so Huger could plan and effect his withdrawal "with discretion, judgment and energy," but he should not waste time.[14]

Johnston's conviction continued to grow that the Confederates had no chance against McClellan's superiority in artillery and men, so long as the Federal general could choose the "mode of warfare." In an effort to overcome the disadvantage, he wrote Lee and again suggested for the President's consideration a plan for an invasion of the North. He, with the combined armies of the east, would cross the Potomac, while Beauregard led those of the west across the Ohio. Davis rejected the plan as impracticable at the time, although he agreed about the "benefits to be gained by taking the offensive." As a consequence, Johnston turned to the only alternative—a retreat up the Peninsula with the hope that he might in some way catch the Federal army off balance.[15]

As plans matured for the evacuation of the lines at Yorktown, he was startled by a letter from Davis, which had been written May 1 and told him that arrangements for the evacuation of Norfolk had begun. But the President went on to say: "Your announcement today that you will withdraw tomorrow takes us by surprise, and must involve enormous losses, including unfinished gunboats. Will the safety of your army allow more time?" Actually Johnston had told Richmond on April 27 that the evacuation was imminent in a letter which was delivered within ten hours. He might well have wondered, upon receiving Davis' letter, as at Manassas, how much delay would be necessary. But the situation was more dangerous and complicated than the earlier one. Here he was confronted by a superior, better equipped force which might at any moment get around his

flank and bottle him in the lower Peninsula. Any amount of delay
might mean the loss of his army, and that could not be balanced by the
saving of all the public property in the area.[16]

As though the major problem of the extrication was not enough,
numerous other difficulties arose, both with Richmond and in the
army. On May 1 Davis sent Johnston a second letter, one which
contained the startling suggestion that either Smith or Longstreet,
the two chief subordinates of Johnston's army be sent to Richmond
to command the troops between Washington and Richmond. On
the same day Lee requested an engineer and a portion of the important Negro labor force. As a final vexing matter Johnston
discovered on May 3, just when the need for quick communication
was most pressing, that the telegraph line to Richmond no longer
functioned, "as the superintendent took away the operator from
Williamsburg." [17]

On Saturday night, May 3, after last minute complications had
caused a delay of hours, the army began its retirement. The men had
no large accumulations of baggage this time, no trunks to burn.
Masked by heavy artillery fire the troops moved out of the trenches,
which they left intact, with only the heavy naval guns still in place.
Some dummies, stuffed with old clothes and labeled with "highly
complimentary" placards addressed to the Yankees, also were left.
The roads were extremely heavy because of the recent rains, as Longstreet and Magruder took the one along the southern side of the
Peninsula toward Williamsburg, and Smith and Hill made their way
along the one on the northern side from Yorktown. Stuart's cavalrymen dismounted and took over temporarily the posts of the pickets
along the line, while artillery detachments kept the heavy guns roar-
ing. Johnston rode in the rear of the retiring infantry, where he
would receive quickly any reports from Stuart.[18]

Left behind by the Confederates in the Yorktown-Warwick River
lines were fifty-six guns, practically all of which the Federals reported
in good condition. They found, too, large amounts of ammunition
and supplies, although Major R. G. Cole, Confederate subsistence
officer, maintained there was little loss in his department. It may be
that some of Pinkerton's agents were present to make this tabulation
for McClellan. Again as in the retirement from Manassas Johnston's
timing was more remarkable than he anticipated, as McClellan
planned his big opening effort for May 6. On the day before, his chief

of artillery reported that when Johnston retired all the Federal batteries but two were in position and they would have been ready in six hours for action. He estimated that had the Confederates remained, such an artillery attack could have been launched as to force their surrender or retirement the next day.[19]

Although few of the Confederates knew how Johnston frustrated McClellan's planned demonstration of power, the men who made the march up the Peninsula were glad to be out of the trenches. McClellan's pickets did not discover that the Southerners had left the lines before Yorktown until daylight the next morning. Immediately the Federal commander started his cavalry in pursuit and later ordered infantry to follow. With the York River opened by the abandonment of the Confederate positions, Union gunboats moved up it, reconnoitering in preparation for its use by transports.

Details of Union soldiers explored the Confederate lines, where they reported to McClellan, they found mines. One week after the news reached Washington, Johnston read of the circumstances in the New York *Herald*. He started an inquiry to find who placed the mines and by what authority. Brigadier General Gabriel J. Rains admitted that he had prepared and planted these innovations in the war, but he denied their employment about wells, springs and other such places, as McClellan reported. The Confederates felt about mines much as the Federal commander did and vetoed their further use.[20]

By noontime on May 4 the Confederate divisions converged upon the road junction just south of Williamsburg, where the two roads from Yorktown came together. All of the more than fifty thousand men under Johnston were forced upon the single dirt road, which snaked past the redoubts and rifle pits of the Magruder line and on into the village. It was a tired, dirty, hungry army which finally found temporary bivouac in the environs of the town.

Johnston had continued to ride with the rear of the column, to receive any messages from Stuart, whose troops still masked the retiring army. Such contact was vital. Although Johnston feared that McClellan would use the York River to get in his rear by landing troops in the vicinity of West Point, his primary concern was that the Federals might try to press his retreat. The march had been slow, and the stop at Williamsburg was planned as a temporary one, to allow the men to rest and eat. Magruder's division, then under D. R. Jones, as "Prince John" was ill, was to lead the column, when the march was resumed on the afternoon of the fourth. Its route lay along the road to New Kent Court-House, until it reached the small community of Burnt Ordinary, about ten miles up the Peninsula from Williamsburg. There it was to turn off the road toward Richmond. G. W. Smith's division was second in the line of march, but was to continue on the New Kent Court-House road, where it would be close to possible landing places of a Federal flanking force along the upper reaches of the York. A. P. Hill's division would be next in line, with Longstreet covering the rear in conjunction with Stuart.[21]

Before the leading troops could start their march from Williamsburg, reports from Stuart said that the Federals were driving him. Johnston immediately moved to the cavalry's assistance, by himself leading a brigade to one of the positions in the Magruder line, although he had no definite knowledge of the size of the Federal attacking force. Finding that one brigade was not enough, and meeting General Lafayette McLaws, he directed that officer to take his brigade and two batteries and move to the action where he should take command.[22]

After some minor skirmishing the pursuers lost both their aggressiveness and one piece of artillery, so the Federal threat apparently vanished with the coming of darkness. McLaws' men were relieved and proceeded to take their place with Magruder's leading division in the column of march. Two brigades from Longstreet's division moved to take the position left in the defensive line before Williamsburg. Without knowing what lurked in the swamps and thickets before them, they posted pickets along the line for their vigil in renewed heavy rain through the long black night.

The action outside of Williamsburg on May 5, like so many in the war, was not by choice of the commander of either army. McClellan had remained at Yorktown to superintend the embarkation of troops for his move up the York River around the left flank of the Confederates. Johnston was with the advance units of his column, hurrying to protect against that move. Longstreet, as has been said, was in command of the Confederate rear, while Major General E. V. Sumner, the colonel of the First Cavalry when Johnston was its lieutenant colonel, commanded the Federal advance column of all the available cavalry, four infantry divisions and four batteries of artillery. Both Johnston and McClellan assumed that any fighting at Williamsburg would be skirmishing in a Confederate delaying action.

In a misty drizzle, dawn broke on that May morning to the sound of skirmishers' fire. Added to the crack of rifles and muskets, the heavy sound of artillery shortly displayed a widening of the front and an increase of action. The pickets along the Confederate line soon found the weight of the Federals too much for them to handle and fell back to the line Magruder had prepared. They asked Longstreet for assistance, which he shortly sent. Though the firing at this point still continued to be heavy, Johnston decided that nothing more than a Federal demonstration was in prospect and moved on from Williamsburg.[23]

As though to belie Johnston's analysis of the situation, the Federals opened new attacks upon the Confederate positions, and Longstreet sent additional brigades from Williamsburg to strengthen his line. Soon he brought all the rest of his division into position. The Union forces were persistent in their efforts, and though their left was held in check, their maneuvers on the right—the Confederate left—began to develop a threat to the entire line. Longstreet, sensing the danger, sent to D. H. Hill for a brigade from his division with which to meet it.

The men chosen by Hill for this reinforcement were those of General "Jube" Early, who had delivered the final, clinching blow at Manassas. Shortly, Hill received orders to countermarch his entire division to Longstreet's assistance, and Johnston, too, returned when he learned of the increased pressure of the Federals. He left the direction of the fighting on Longstreet's hands and watched the action with intense interest. One of his aides reported that, though under fire, he sat his famous charger, Sam Patch, "as calm as a May morning," which it was.[24]

What happened next is lost amid the confusion of the scene which echoes its way through history in the battle reports and the later writing of the participants. Underbrush and trees joined to assist in producing a difficult tactical situation. Some units came under heavy fire which pinned them down, while others ranged out of position to accomplish nothing. The Federals were caught in the process of adjusting their lines, and ensuing disorder among them was quelled only by the retirement of the Confederates after heavy loss to their original position. After this attack the day closed as it began, with the sputter and crack of musket and rifle fire, and the roar of the field pieces, all gradually dying out.

This affair at Williamsburg was long acclaimed by both sides as a victory, but it had for neither results which compensated for the losses. On the Confederate right and center affairs had gone well for them, while on the left results left a heritage of divided victory. The reports disclose Union losses of 2,283, and a Confederate total of 1,560, both including killed, wounded and missing.

The comparative importance of the action at Williamsburg dwindled fast in the ensuing summer. At the time, however, it was an affair of magnitude. McClellan could claim it as a victory as the Confederates continued their retirement, even though his losses were heavy. Johnston could claim success also, as he properly interpreted the engagement as a delaying action, which had no real effect upon his planned movement. But coupled with the retirement from York-town, it caused some expression of dissatisfaction among Southerners, who hoped that every fight would end with their army master of the field. It was strange that the Confederate commanders were apparently unacquainted with the full extent of the line Magruder had prepared. However, the Williamsburg action gave evidence of Johnston's willingness to turn and fight. From that point on, the Federal commander moved with even greater caution, refusing to disturb the Confederate rear guard. For the soldiers themselves, Williamsburg proved a good training ground. Many of them learned for the first time what the actual turmoil of battle was like: knowledge they could never acquire from rehearsal for it in drills and on parade.

On the morning after the battle the Confederate divisions resumed the march up the Peninsula toward Richmond. During the night the wounded, both Federal and Confederate, were gathered and placed where they could be given care. Because of the lack of transport, Johnston had to leave them there, and ordered surgeons to go to their assistance.[25]

Through the heavy mud, the Confederates moved steadily along, with Johnston encouraging them. He had given orders at Williams-burg "that any gun caisson, quartermaster, or commissary wagon which might become set in the mud so as to impede the line of march must be destroyed at once." The orders said nothing about guns, but when one weak team mired up over the axles of the wheels of the 12-pound Napoleon it was drawing, and even the help of the drivers was unable to dislodge it, a young lieutenant was on the verge of abandoning it. Just then the commanding general rode up with his staff and asked what the trouble was. When told, he said it was not necessary to leave the gun. " 'Let me see what I can do.' Whereupon he leaped from his horse, waded out in the mire, seized one of the wheel spokes, covered as it was with mud, and called out, 'Now, boys, altogether!' The effect was magical, and the next moment the gun jumped clear of the mudhole. After that our battery used to swear by 'Old Joe.' " [26]

By late afternoon on May 6 the advanced divisions under Magruder and Smith had completed their marches. The latter, eighteen miles from Williamsburg at Barhamsville, had orders to remain there until the rear divisions could consolidate with him. Concentration was necessary, Johnston believed, because of the possibility of the flank movement along the York, the movement he so consistently dreaded and annoyingly referred to in his letters to Davis. The York, with its many landings and connecting roads, closely paralleled his line of march. To protect the army against any surprise from that quarter, he had cavalry patrols along the river's banks, to report at once the sight of enemy transports.

Their vigil was not long maintained. McClellan gathered at Yorktown a strange flotilla of barges, schooners, steamers, ironclads and "canal-boats fastened together in pairs, decked over so as to serve as wharves." Early on the morning of May 6 the armada moved out through the narrows at Yorktown and up the river. By midafternoon the lead vessels were at Eltham's Landing, just across the river at West Point. There the Federals were squarely on Smith's flank, but no sooner had they arrived than they were conscious of the fact that they were under observation by the enemy. They were ignorant of the topography of the area and of the number of troops the Confederates could throw against them. So they worked feverishly all evening to get guns and men ashore and to prepare defensive positions.[27]

Confederate couriers immediately carried word to Johnston and Smith of the Federal landing. Johnston prepared countermeasures at once by ordering Magruder's division to Barhamsville and by placing Smith in command over both that division and his own. He also ordered Longstreet and Hill to hurry forward, so as to be within supporting distance. Meanwhile, Smith had decided that an effort to oppose the landing would be unwise, because of the unfavorable terrain to an attacking force and the protection the fire of the Federal gunboats would give their troops. But before the march of the army, then concentrated at Barhamsville, could be resumed, the Federal forces at Eltham's Landing had to be neutralized in some way. Smith assigned that task to Whiting, with instructions to drive the enemy out of the protecting woods, and, if possible, to place artillery where its fire could reach both the Landing and the transports.[28]

The Confederates quickly went to work. They drove the enemy skirmish line back easily, but the Federals took shelter behind a high bluff along the river, where the Confederate fire could not reach them, while the gunboats and transports were out of range of the Confederate artillery. Nevertheless, the brief action accomplished its purpose, to hold the Federal flanking threat until the army was secure in its march. Johnston reported to Lee: "The want of provision and of any mode of obtaining it here, still more the dearth of forage, makes it impossible to wait to attack [the enemy] while landing. The sight of the iron-clad boats makes me apprehensive for Richmond, too, so I move on. . . . " [29]

In two columns the army resumed its march. Fear for the York River flank vanished under the skill of the generalship of Smith and Whiting, and the poor, unaggressive handling of his opportunity by the Union commander. Johnston had successfully extracted his force from the exposed lower Peninsula. He was pleased by Longstreet's conduct of the engagement at Williamsburg and by the judgment of Smith at Barhamsville. He urged that Whiting be promoted for the "very handsome style" with which he had dislodged the enemy at Eltham's Landing, and recommended promotion also for Colonel Wade Hampton, who with Brigadier General John B. Hood had an important part in that affair.[30]

Hampton and his legion had been under Johnston since they joined him on the field at Manassas. Although not a professional soldier, Hampton was singled out early by Johnston as a leader of courage and judgment. In February he recommended the promotion of the South Carolina planter and assigned him a brigade command. In addition he presented him with a sword, which Hampton apparently took to be a loan and accepted by saying, "I shall try to return it untarnished. It is a beautiful one, and I trust it may do good service whilst in my hands." After Eltham's Landing, Hampton received wide acclaim, and Johnston pressed hard for his promotion.[31]

John B. Hood, the blond giant of thirty years who was a comparative newcomer to Johnston's army, also won praise for his conduct at the Landing. A West Pointer, this young Kentuckian joined the Confederacy early, but as his state did not secede, he decided to make his residence in Texas and fought under that state's banner. Well trained, his men displayed the results of his efforts, and he led them in action with daring. At Eltham's Landing this element of boldness was apparently somewhat disturbing to Johnston, who did not wish to provoke a major engagement. After listening to him, Johnston said: "General Hood, have you given an illustration of the Texas idea of feeling an enemy gently and falling back? What would your Texans have done, sir, if I had ordered them to charge and drive back the enemy?" The brigade commander interpreted his men's attitude by replying, "I suppose, General, they would have driven them into the river, and tried to swim out and capture their gunboats." With no evidence of reprimand, Johnston smilingly concluded the conversation by saying, "Teach your Texans that the first duty of a soldier is literally to obey orders." [32]

Upon leaving Barhamsville, Smith led his and Magruder's divisions up the New Kent Road. Longstreet and Hill followed the one which led toward the Long Bridge over the Chickahominy where they halted and took positions. The men were glad of the opportunity to rest after their weary days of combatting the mud. But again torrential rains wet them through and forced some of them to seek higher ground. The divisions of Smith and Magruder passed through New Kent Court-House and on to the Baltimore Cross Roads, nineteen miles from Barhamsville, and encamped there. [33]

By then the picture on the other flank of the Peninsula, that of the James River, had changed. With the evacuation of the Yorktown line, it was necessary also to quit Norfolk and Gosport Navy Yard. To prepare for the move, Davis sent both Secretary of War Randolph and Secretary of the Navy Mallory to the scene. Shortly after they arrived, Huger received Johnston's order to leave Norfolk at once. But the Secretaries authorized Huger to delay the movement while he with their assistance removed as much of the guns, munitions, other equipment and supplies as possible. Finally on May 9 the Confederates moved out toward Petersburg, where they would be in position to join Johnston's army. The next day a delegation of the residents surrendered Norfolk to the Federals. [34]

The abandonment of Norfolk brought the end of the *Virginia.* Deprived of a base in the area, she had either to run the Federal fleet, which its strength precluded, or to escape up the James, which pilots assured her commander could be done, if she could be lightened to draw no more than eighteen feet. Everything but shot and powder was removed from the ship, which rode so high in the water that her unarmored, below-the-water-line areas were exposed. This brought her within the limits set by the pilots, but they refused to make the voyage. There was no alternative but to destroy the vessel, after which the crew marched away toward safety.[35]

When McClellan received the news of the destruction of the *Virginia*, he asked immediately that gunboats proceed up the James "as far as possible." Early on the morning of May 15, four days later, a flotilla, which included the *Monitor*, steamed up the river and chased the few Confederate patrol boats before it. It was the sort of expedition the Confederates had long feared and were busily engaged in preparing for at Drewry's Bluff. There the James narrows to approximately a mile, with high cliffs along the south side, on which the last protective batteries before Richmond were located. Construction workers mingled with soldiers, as they hurried to finish a near-by pontoon bridge and a line of obstructions across the river. Pile drivers hammered huge logs into the bottom of the stream, while from barges workmen tumbled stones about them. The heavy guns on the cliffs commanded a narrow channel, which was left for navigation. On the day of the Federal attack upon the position at the Bluff, Lee wrote encouraging those in charge of the construction to use all vigor and energy to complete it.[36]

The engagement between the Federal naval vessels and the Confederate land batteries lasted for about four hours before the ships withdrew. But they left behind the fear that they would come again, and emphasized Johnston's realization that he had to draw closer to Richmond, so he would be prepared to cope with Federal movements up either the James or the York. He therefore moved the army across the Chickahominy on May 15, and sent a regiment of infantry to Drewry's Bluff, where its rifle fire from the height of the cliffs would be effective against exposed naval personnel on the decks of the ships. Two days later the Army of Northern Virginia encamped within three miles of the capital, as the first position they took on the south bank of the river proved unfavorable.[37]

Johnston's relief upon reaching Richmond was expressed in a statement to his aide, Colonel E. J. Harvie: "The folly of sending this army down the Peninsula is only equalled by our good fortune in getting away from there." More than good fortune was necessary. Greatly outnumbered as the Confederates were by the Federals, Johnston's ability to anticipate his opponents and to maneuver enabled him to bring the army virtually untouched to Richmond.

CHAPTER IX

HELP FROM THE VALLEY

As Johnston's army backed closer and closer to Richmond, McClellan followed somewhat leisurely. Now rain and mud favored the Confederates, and good days came to be called "Union weather." Richmond had responded to events that spring with about the same range of emotion that a barometer displays. In a frenzy of concern the voice of public criticism grew loud. Davis became a target of those who opposed conscription and talked of despotism. A Charleston newspaper editor went so far as to say, "Jeff Davis now treats all men as if they were idiotic insects." The Congress, too, was denounced as dilatory about helpful legislation, and was attacked for adjourning in late April, as if to escape the dangers of McClellan's approaching army.

The people of Richmond scarcely knew which way to turn. Would Johnston fight in defense of the capital? Could he stop McClellan if he did? Why was the railroad bridge being planked for wheeled traffic, if retreat were not planned? These and hundreds of other questions were on the residents' lips. As early as May 6, the provost marshal at Petersburg was told to burn or otherwise destroy the cotton and tobacco which was stored there and not to allow it to fall into the hands of the enemy. Precautions were taken to safeguard the archives by preparing them for immediate shipment from the capital, and officials were warned to move them from the rear of the buildings, "to avoid panic or excitement in the city." The treasury's reserve of gold was packed and a special train made ready to carry it away. New commissary depots were set up at various points and plans devised for the removal to them, in the event the city fell, of the stores then housed in Richmond. The presidents of the Virginia Central and the Richmond, Fredricksburg & Petersburg railroads were told to prepare to send rolling stock and other operating materials south, "and should the danger become imminent, you will remove it without waiting for further instructions." [1]

Wagons gathered up personal belongings of the many families who quit the city, leaving deserted homes, which in themselves, under the crowded conditions, seemed symbols of despair. An Episcopal clergyman privately administered the rite of baptism to the President, just before the latter placed Mrs. Davis and their children on the train for the safety of Raleigh. On May 14 Secretary Randolph had to step in for the second time to keep the railroads open for military traffic. "In the present state of affairs," he said "I think it would be wholly unjustifiable to impede the transportation of troops and munitions of war for the purpose of facilitating the removal of private property."[2]

Near Richmond the two largest armies ever gathered on the American continent up to that time faced each other. They were, however, but the main units in the over-all forces engaged in Virginia. It was to the other portions of his widely scattered command that Johnston's mind began to turn, as the troops immediately under him slowly worked their way out of the dangerous Peninsula. For some time he had been out of touch with Jackson and Ewell. The first had remained in the Valley and the second had been left on the Rappahannock, when the rest of the Army of Northern Virginia moved to Yorktown. Johnston did not even know that troops from North Carolina, called the "Army of the North" by Davis, were stationed in the vicinity of Gordonsville and Fredericksburg, until he received an order from the President to send one of his major generals, either Longstreet or G. W. Smith, to take command of them. He had no specific information of the movements of Huger or of the evacuation of Norfolk.

As quickly as circumstances allowed, after reaching the Chickahominy, Johnston began to correspond with Lee about the disposition of the other units. His tone was tart and critical, somewhat similar to that he had used in his letters to Benjamin, not that which would be ordinarily used to a classmate and long-time friend. Although he had requested some of his subordinates to communicate with him through the Adjutant General's office in Richmond, he had received only indirect, scattered reports. To Lee he grumbled: "I have had in the Peninsula no means of obtaining direct information from the other departments of my command nor has the Government furnished it." On learning that Richmond had countermanded his order to one of his subordinate commanders, he asked for no explanations but displayed his indignation by stating: "My authority does not extend beyond the troops immediately around me. I request therefore to be relieved of merely nominal geographical command. The service will gain thereby the unity of command, which is essential to war." His isolation, the poor communication services, and the casual way with which Richmond reported official matters combined to whet his irascibility.[3]

In his replies Lee was typically diplomatic and informative. He briefed Johnston on developments and assured him that his command had in no way been changed. He did use the opportunity to call to Johnston's attention the fact that the latter had not "requested information relating to the other departments of your command to be furnished by any other means than the usual course of the mails," which, he had assumed, Johnston's subordinates had used for direct communication with him.[4]

The military situation in Virginia which confronted the Confederates was a desperate one and called for the most skillful co-ordination. Not only did the troops of McClellan threaten the capital, but other growing armies loomed forebodingly near. At Fredericksburg, dangerously close to Johnston's flank and to Richmond, McDowell had some 40,000 men. Johnston had left only a small force there to watch the enemy when he moved into the Peninsula. To them the government had added 9,000 men under the command of Brigadier General J. R. Anderson. Another small force under Brigadier General L. O'B. Branch had been placed at Gordonsville. It was these troops to whom Davis referred as the "Army of the North."

In the Valley of the Shenandoah large, hostile forces under the politician-soldier, Major General Nathaniel P. Banks, crowded down upon Jackson's little army of around 9,000 men. When Johnston left the Rapidan, Jackson had about completed reorganizing and refitting his force after the battle at Kernstown. Johnston instructed Jackson to use his troops to hold Banks' attention in the Valley. The primary purpose was to prevent the reinforcement of either McDowell or McClellan by Banks. If Jackson could drive the Union army north of the Potomac, the result would be achieved, but he should not allow them to penetrate as far south as Staunton through which the railroad passed to Tennessee. To assist him to achieve these results, Jackson had the authority to call upon Ewell, whom Johnston had left on the Rappahannock. If Jackson could entice Banks to follow him into the Blue Ridge, Johnston suggested that the two Confederate forces could combine for a battle near the crest of the mountains. Johnston made plain that he offered nothing but general instructions, as "the question of attacking the enemy in front of you is one which must be decided on the ground." [5]

Thus the Federals held two points of heavy pressure on the flanks of the Confederate line in Northern Virginia, and Jackson in the Valley and Anderson before Fredericksburg had to counter them with inferior forces. Ewell's role was that of a sort of floating reserve, one which might be drawn in any direction. As Johnston's attention concentrated upon operations in the Peninsula, Lee began to co-ordinate those in the other areas. In his correspondence with Ewell and Jackson he advocated the same general policies which Johnston had authorized and also left virtually complete discretion about carrying them out in Jackson's hands. But Jackson felt some limitations, because of Johnston's directives, and called upon Lee to enlarge them so that he might bring Ewell into the Valley, where the two of them could combine against Banks. [6]

While Johnston was deep in the difficulties of his withdrawal from the Peninsula, Jackson made a lightning stroke against the Federals west of Staunton. To keep an eye on Banks, Jackson brought Ewell into the Blue Ridge theater at Swift Run Gap. This was the situation when Johnston emerged from the blanket of silence which enveloped the lower Peninsula. Worried that Jackson had moved so far from Banks' army, Johnston wrote on May 12 that the Valley commander should resume his attention to his original assignment.

Your troops with those of Ewell may be able to take the offensive. That of course depends upon the force of the enemy of which I have no information nor indeed of your numbers. If the enemy is so strong as to make it imprudent to attack, you should endeavor to prevent his leaving the Valley by your positions. Should he move toward Fredericksburg before you return to the neighborhood of Harrisonburg, you and Gen. Ewell should make the corresponding movement as rapidly as possible reporting to me frequently that I may modify your instructions if necessary.[7]

Although in these communications Johnston reasserted his command over the Valley theater, his orders, which now were enlarged to permit an offensive, continued to allow Jackson complete latitude of tactical execution. But strategically they were wedded to the entire situation in Virginia.

On May 13 Ewell reported to Jackson that the Federals in the Valley had begun to move back. Although he did not know their destination, Ewell feared that they might be on the way to Fredericksburg and suggested, in line with his instructions from Lee, that he should return to Gordonsville. There, he would be in a better position to co-operate against the two-pronged threat against Richmond, from whose defense no troops should be kept, "except for the strongest reasons." Jackson solved his dilemma by ordering him to move down the Valley after Banks. Ewell immediately called upon the supporting force under Branch at Gordonsville to join him, and advised its commander not to encumber his march with unnecessary equipment, as "The road to glory cannot be followed with much baggage." But contradictory orders within a short time again began to come in from all sides to disturb the bald, enthusiastic Ewell.[8]

By the sixteenth Lee in Richmond knew that the Federals had fallen back to Strasburg, from which point they had put the railroad in running order to Alexandria. He feared that their intention might be to transfer troops by rail from the Valley to Washington and from there by water either to Fredericksburg or the Peninsula. Stating again the principle laid down by Johnston that the Federals in the Valley should be held there, he suggested that Jackson strike speedily to prevent a movement by them to the east. Lee thought that, if successful, Jackson might be able to drive Banks down the Valley and across the Potomac. But, like Johnston, he urged caution upon the doughty Jackson. The latter, he said, should not lose sight, in any demonstration he might make, "that it may become necessary for you to come to the support of General Johnston," and that he should be in constant readiness to do so.[9]

Jackson and his men had come out of the mountains into the Valley proper by this time, and on the sixteenth the pious commander rested, in accordance with the President's decree which established that day as one of fasting and prayer. On the seventeenth he briefed Johnston about the situation. Banks, he heard, was fortifying Strasburg, while a portion of his force, about 6,000 men, had crossed the Blue Ridge and were moving east. Ewell, as a consequence of his original orders from Johnston, planned to go east also as a counter to the Union movement. The loss of Ewell's support would prevent an attack on Banks, as Jackson had planned, but, Jackson continued, he intended to keep up his march toward Banks until he got "within striking distance" of the Federal commander unless Johnston ordered him also to cross the Blue Ridge to the east.[10]

Johnston replied the same day but addressed his communication to Ewell, whom he instructed to send it on to Jackson after reading it. He opposed the idea of attacking fortified positions at Strasburg, as he feared that Jackson might be pinned down in an action there by a portion of Banks' force, while the rest would hasten to reinforce McClellan or McDowell. He suggested instead that Jackson keep Banks under observation while Ewell continued to move to the east. "We want troops here; none, therefore, must be kept away, unless employing a greatly superior force of the enemy." He told Ewell also to keep in touch with Anderson, near Fredericksburg, as he might need help.[11]

Here one begins to run into difficulties with the exchange of communications among the four: Johnston, just outside Richmond, Lee, in the capital, Jackson, in the Valley, and Ewell, on its rim. Some of the messages have been lost, and it is not possible to tell how much time elapsed between writing and their delivery. Jackson endorsed, without date, the above communication from Johnston to Ewell, telling the latter to hold up his movement to the east until Richmond could answer a telegram he had sent. The only telegram that seems to bear on the matter from Jackson to Lee around this time in the *Official Records* was dated May 20, and no answer to it is found. So an exact chronology of events and the communications possibly creates an incorrect impression.

Ewell was torn between his instructions from Johnston to move back toward the Rapidan, if there was a Federal movement eastward from the Valley, and the opportunity to co-operate with Jackson in a campaign in the Valley itself. Even though he still wondered if Jackson were in his right mind, he determined to ride to him to discuss the situation. He reached Jackson's headquarters at Mount Solon Sunday, May 18. There, he reviewed for the Valley commander the conflicting orders he had received. If he followed his original orders, Jackson had to give up his plans. "Then," the latter exclaimed, "Providence denies me the privilege of striking a decisive blow for my country; and I must be satisfied with the humble task of hiding my little army about these mountains to watch a superior force." [12]

Ewell boldly offered a possibility. Jackson was his immediate commander and he would follow his orders, even if they contradicted those he had from Johnston and Lee. Jackson's latest instructions from Lee, though they warned him to be prepared to move at once to the assistance of Johnston, left room for his initiative otherwise. Jackson agreed and prepared an order for Ewell which the latter could use to justify his actions if called on to do so. In addition, the two planned the details of the attack which matured into the famed Valley Campaign. [13]

In the meantime, Johnston had written two communications to Ewell on May 18, in both of which he again granted discretion to the field commander. In the first of them he said:

The object you have to accomplish is the prevention of the junction of General Bank's troops with those of General McDowell. Should it now be too late to prevent that by attacking, you have only to adopt the alternative expressed in my note of May 13th—making the corresponding movement. I cannot provide for modifications of the case, but having full confidence in the judgment and the courage of both the division commanders, rely upon them to conform to circumstances without fear for the result.

Later that day, after receiving an inquiry from Lee whether Ewell should continue to move eastward, Johnston wrote Ewell that it was impossible for him to determine the proper course on the information he had. "The whole question is," he pointed out, "whether or not General Jackson and yourself are too late to attack Banks. If so the march eastward should be made. If not (supposing your strength sufficient) the attack." [14]

In the Valley plans were maturing into action. On the twentieth, as already stated, Jackson ordered Ewell to suspend his eastward movement. On the same day Ewell was jarred by a message from Branch, who had started his march to join in the campaign against Banks. Branch reported that a courier from Johnston had overtaken him with orders for his return to Gordonsville. Johnston's two communications of the eighteenth were still not at hand apparently, and the two generals in the Valley thought that their commander was forcing them to take the wrong steps, even though he had constantly insisted that the initiative had to rest with them. It was then that Jackson decided to send his telegram of the twentieth to Lee. From his camp near New Market, he urgently expressed a wish to undertake aggressive action. "I am of the opinion," he said, "that an attempt should be made to defeat Banks, but under instructions just received from General Johnston I do not feel at liberty to make an attack. Please answer by telegraph at once." [15]

It is this message for which there is no reply, but from the fact that Jackson moved immediately, it is evident that he received permission. It is only conjecture to say that it was given by Lee alone, or by Lee with the approval of Davis, or by Lee after consultation with Johnston, or that the two messages written by Johnston on the eighteenth came to hand shortly after Jackson sent his telegram. There was sufficient answer to allow Jackson to proceed with the attack. However it may have happened, once the way was cleared, Jackson, behind a veil of silence, began his dramatic march. Down the Valley pike to Harrisonburg moved the men of Stonewall and on to New Market. There they turned right and crossed the Massanutten Mountains into the Luray Valley. Behind the mountains they met Ewell's command which augmented their numbers to 17,000. On the twenty-third they suddenly appeared at Front Royal and drove the Federals from the field.

Jackson then turned toward Banks at Strasburg, but the latter soon decided to retire down the Valley to Winchester, almost seventy miles away. Despite the distance, Jackson was there by the twenty-fifth, mystifying the enemy by his tactics and the speed of his movements. Here, where he had had his winter quarters, he brought his forces up in a flank attack and flushed Banks again into the open. Back, back, the Federals went in growing disorder, to the Potomac and beyond. The Confederates captured great stocks of Federal supplies and munitions, and wagon trains filled the roads to the south, to carry them away. Only a lack of more transport and the failure of some cavalry at Winchester prevented an even greater harvest, Jackson emphasized in his report. After moving as far as Harper's Ferry to be sure that the enemy had left the Valley, Jackson resumed his position at Winchester. The opening phase of the Valley campaign—that which affected the fortunes of Johnston's effort—had been won.

The success of the Valley Campaign was that of Jackson and those under him. It was their interpretation of orders, their skillful planning and maneuvering, their insensibility to toil and fatigue which defeated Banks, and not the plans of Lee and Johnston. Even in the North recognition of Jackson was quickly forthcoming. As a correspondent to the New York *Times* wrote: "One thing is certain, Jackson is equally eminent as a strategist and tactician. He handles his army like a whip, making it crack in out of the way corners where you scarcely thought the lash would reach." [16]

Some credit, though, must go to Johnston. From their earliest association he understood Jackson's ability. Throughout the period from May eighth to the twentieth, though he cautioned the Valley commander to consider his activity as an integral part of the whole campaign in Virginia, he consistently emphasized the use of Jackson's discretion as the one on the ground and acquainted with the situation. One of Johnston's staff, writing in 1911, said, "In command of all the troops in Virginia, and realizing the strategic importance on the Valley and value of Stonewall Jackson, it was Johnston's order to this mighty warrior to guard that gate, which led to the ever memorial [sic] Valley campaigns." [17]

General George Gordon Meade, writing to his wife from the Peninsula, stated it fully. He asked if she had read the instructions Johnston had sent Jackson before the Valley Campaign. Apparently a copy had been captured and published earlier that month in the newspapers. He wrote:

I hope you have, for they most singularly confirm my expressed views of the object of Jackson's raid. Johnston tells him that anything he can do, either to prevent reinforcements reaching McClellan or to withdraw any portion of his force, will be of inestimable service; suggests his attacking either McDowell or Banks—whichever he thinks most practicable—and says it is reported McDowell is about advancing on Richmond, which he, Johnston, thinks extremely probable. You see how completely Jackson succeeded in carrying out these, by paralyzing McDowell's force of 40,000 men, through the stupidity of the authorities at Washington becoming alarmed and sending

McDowell on a wild-goose chase after a wily foe who never intended
to be caught in a trap, and was prepared to back out so soon as his
plans proved successful. I must do McDowell the justice to say that
he saw this himself, but no protest on his part could shake the strategy
of the War Department.[18]

Meade had astutely put his finger on the great consequences of
Jackson's campaign. Far more important than victories gained, supplies captured, Federal casualties or Banks' flight, was the effect on
the Union high command. Fear that so many troops had been removed from Washington's defense as to make it vulnerable to attack
mounted to hysteria as the details of Jackson's successes became
known. Since President Lincoln and Secretary of War Stanton had
dissolved McClellan's over-all command in Virginia, they alone
co-ordinated Union movements. Now their reasoning lost all perspective, although the rout at Manassas the year before and the
ensuing danger to the capital formed a historical basis for what they
did. To thwart the fast-moving, unpredictable Jackson, they called
off McDowell's movement toward Richmond and shifted his troops
from Fredericksburg to the assistance of the Federals in the Valley
and the protection of the capital. Thus, at virtually the height of
Johnston's fears for his left flank and for Richmond's seeming plight,
Washington intervened to neutralize thousands of Federal troops.[19]

Johnston immediately paid tribute to the "brilliant success" of the
Valley commanders and their troops in a General Order, which he
issued May 29. In a letter to Jackson himself, he said: "I congratulate
you upon your new victories and new titles to the thanks of the
country and of the army." [20]

In the period when Jackson was hurrying from one corner of the
Valley to another and befuddling his men as well as the enemy,
Johnston brought his army closer to Richmond. Shortly after it
reached the north bank of the Chickahominy, Davis and Lee rode
to Johnston's headquarters to discuss his "plans and expectations."
Their talk was so extensive as to cause an overnight stay at camp. As
usual, no records were kept. Davis said, writing years later, that he
and Lee agreed that they were unable "to draw from it any more
definite purpose than that the policy was to improve [the army's]
position as far as practicable, and wait for the enemy to leave his
gunboats, so that an opportunity might be offered to meet him on
the land." [21]

Johnston, in the postwar clash of words, challenged this conclusion. He said, "I explained that I had fallen back that far to clear my left flank of the navigable water [of the York River], and so avoid having it turned; that as we were too weak to assume the offensive, and as the position I then held was an excellent one, I intended to await the Federal attack there." He also pointed out that Davis must have been satisfied at the time, for three days later the President wrote, "If the enemy proceed as heretofore indicated, your position and policy, as you stated it in our last interview, seems to me to require no modification." [22]

Johnston, who was always reluctant to make specific commitments about military plans, was uncommunicative with Davis. "I did not consult the President as commander of the army," he wrote Senator Wigfall, "because it seemed to me that to do so would be to transfer my responsibilities to his shoulders. I could not consult him without adopting the course he might advise, so that to ask his advice would have been, in my opinion, to ask him to command for me." [23]

Although he does not mention it, Johnston might also have been influenced by his knowledge of the way news had leaked from Richmond sources before his winter retirement. There is also another possibility, one in which feelings and attitudes had no part. As a military leader, Johnston wished to keep his position fluid, so he would be able to take advantage of blunders made by his opponents or any opportunity which circumstances created. In his judgment a fixed plan was not essential, but secrecy was.

That flexibility was the better method of operating was shortly demonstrated, when the Federals threatened Richmond by the James River approach and Johnston changed his position to meet it. He drew back across the Chickahominy to the very limits of the city itself. His line formed a semicircle, from the northern suburbs, where McDowell could be met should he move toward Richmond, to the James River on the south, across from Drewry's Bluff, to guard that way of entry to the capital. The main portion of the army still confronted McClellan to the east.

With the army thus disposed to meet Federal threats from the three obvious directions, Davis sent his aide, Colonel Custis Lee, eldest son of General Lee, with a letter to Johnston. In it the President discussed the situation. Since the repulse of the Federal gunboats two days before—May 15—he said that the spirit in Richmond

had greatly improved. "There is much manifestation of a determination," he wrote, "that the ancient and honored capital of Virginia,
now the seat of the Confederate Government, shall not fall into the
hands of the enemy. Many say rather let it be a heap of rubbish. To
you," Davis said as though to emphasize it, "it is needless to say that
the defense must be made outside of the city. The question is, where
and how?" In his final paragraph, the President said that his intention
was not to direct but only to suggest, and that Colonel Lee would
bear to him "any information and reply" that Johnston might send.[24]

Johnston apparently gave young Lee no specific information, and
the next day the latter's father wrote and invited the department
commander, inasmuch as he was "so convenient to the city," to meet
with the President in his office for a conference about plans. Again
on the twenty-first Lee wrote that Davis desired the "programme of
operations which you propose." He also evidenced an understanding
of Johnston's position when he added that "your plan of operations,
dependent upon circumstances perhaps yet to be developed, may not
be so easily explained, nor may it be prudent to commit it to paper."
He suggested again that a meeting in Richmond might be a better
method than writing.[25]

CHAPTER X

FAIR OAKS AND SEVEN PINES

As May began to draw to a close, Johnston's soldiers were grouped just outside of Richmond to the north and east. This proximity to the city's comforts made the never-ending tasks of the field close to the enemy disagreeable, particularly picket and outpost duty along the Chickahominy. The river flowed southeastwardly to the James and formed a moat between the main bodies of the two armies. In its upper reaches it passed approximately four miles north of Richmond, where Meadow Bridge served roads to Ashland and Hanover Court-House. Due east of the city, about twelve miles away at Bottom's Bridge, the road to Williamsburg crossed it. The roads to the bridges made two sides of a rough triangle with the stream as the third. Some seventeen miles of waterfront separated the two bridges, and several other road and railroad structures crossed the river within the sector.

Along the margins of the stream and in the adjoining low spots, bogs and swamps were lush with vegetation. As well-defined banks did not mark the course of the Chickahominy, the swampland ebbed and flowed with the height of the stream, which in turn reflected the runoff of rain from the neighboring countryside. In the unusually rainy spring of 1862 the river ran almost constantly full to overflowing.

Across the stream, men from Pennsylvania and New England maintained an equally lonely vigil and struggle with the elements. On the twentieth Federal advance troops reached the Chickahominy and skirmishing became a daily activity between the armies. Three days later General Erasmus D. Keyes' corps crossed the river at Bottom's Bridge, and that of General Samuel P. Heintzelman followed shortly after. Johnston did not seriously contest the crossing. The corps under generals Fitz John Porter, Edwin V. Sumner and William B. Franklin remained on the other side of the river. On May 27 one of Keyes' divisions under General Silas Casey reached Seven Pines, where the Williamsburg Road crossed the Nine Mile Road, which also led to Richmond. There, the Federals were so close to the Confederate capital that McClellan wrote Lincoln he hoped soon to be within shelling distance of the city.[1]

On the other side of the Chickahominy McClellan moved some of his troops to positions where they might establish easier contact with McDowell, who was then in the neighborhood of Fredericksburg. On May 17 Washington had ordered McDowell, upon the arrival of reinforcements then moving toward him, to co-operate with McClellan in the latter's campaign against Richmond. Although McDowell had approximately 40,000 men and McClellan over 100,000, both proceeded with extreme caution possibly because of Pinkerton's reports on the size of Johnston's army. Nevertheless, McClellan was positive of the outcome of any engagement with the troops under his old friend. The only reason for failure to achieve victory would be Johnston's refusal to fight.[2]

Whatever the result might be McClellan's hope for a fight before Richmond was to be realized. The commitment of the Confederate army to the defensive in the Peninsula insured that. The only question was where it would be. The army still suffered under handicaps, although Davis under Johnston's requests had finally promoted A. P. Hill and Lafayette McLaws to major general to fill those needed places. The principal difficulty was that the army with inferior numbers faced the possibility of simultaneous attack from north and east by the armies of the two Mc's. Under such conditions it was necessary for Johnston's tactical moves to be expedient in nature. He could plan only in relation to daily developments and could not foresee himself his next move, let alone console the President with a plan specific in nature and fixed in purpose. Davis was as disturbed about

Johnston's intention as McClellan was. On the twenty-second he and Lee rode out along the front in the vicinity of Mechanicsville, across the Chickahominy to the north of Richmond, where they found an artillery action in progress. Davis was dissatisfied with what he saw and the next day wrote Johnston a critical report of his experience.[3]

On May 24 one of Johnston's brigades fought a sharp skirmish with the Federals about ten miles from Richmond, between Seven Pines and Bottom's Bridge. Johnston, however, still chose not to press the action to larger proportions, as he preferred to draw the enemy farther from the Chickahominy and the supporting corps beyond. On the same day Federal cavalry drove the Confederates out of Mechanicsville. This caused Johnston anxiety, as the extension of the Federal right could readily separate the forces near Richmond from those to the north under Generals Branch and Anderson. Already the Confederate commander had ordered these two subordinates to draw closer to the main army, while at the same time he advised Huger to move from Petersburg to Drewry's Bluff, where he should be prepared to cross the river to take part in a general engagement, should one occur.[4]

Johnston visited Richmond on the same day but again did not disclose his intentions. Davis, exasperated by his reticence, discussed the circumstances with Lee. The latter agreed, according to Davis' postwar account, that the Federals should be attacked north of the Chickahominy before they could institute siege operations against Richmond. Lee also thought that Johnston should advise the President of his plans, and requested, "Let me go and see him, and defer this discussion until I return." When Lee came back from the interview with the field commander, he had good news, Davis said; Johnston planned to attack McClellan on the coming Thursday on the north side of the river.[5]

Davis must have grown confused in his memory of the chronology of events. Johnston did plan a battle for the twenty-ninth, but it was a consequence of information received on the twenty-seventh that McDowell was marching south, something he could not have foreseen at the time Lee is supposed to have visited him. The news was alarming and pointed to the union of the Federal forces. Johnston advised G. W. Smith, "We must get ready to fight." Smith rode at once to army headquarters where he received oral battle instructions. Johnston assigned him to the command of the left wing, which was to initiate the attack by striking the Federals on the north side of the Chickahominy, as they were in better position to co-operate with McDowell. The plans for the remaining portion of Johnston's army are obscure, lost in contradictory memories of what took place. It is possible that a simultaneous assault was planned against the two Federal corps south of the river. But before any attack could be undertaken, new information canceled it. When the generals met for final consultation on the night of the twenty-eighth, to discuss the next day's probabilities, word came from Stuart that McDowell was countermarching, and the immediate pressure from the north was consequently relaxed.

Apparently, the majority of the generals still approved the attack upon the Union right, but Smith began to point to the difficulties which would confront him. During the long discussion which ensued, the merits and limitations of the action were approached from every angle. Johnston wearied of the argument and moved aside from the group. Longstreet followed him and insisted that the attack should be made as scheduled, but Johnston was downcast and said that he had selected the wrong officer for the work. He feared that the plan would fail because of Smith's attitude and decided that it would be best to cancel it. As in similar situations to come, Johnston was unwilling to overrule the objections of a reluctant subordinate.[6]

Whether or not Johnston informed the authorities in Richmond of the decision to fight and the later one to call the engagement off, the record does not show. Davis in the *Rise and Fall* says that he expected a battle on May 29, and after hurrying through some work at his office, rode out to the field, but found only troops dispersed in the woods and nothing of moment occurring. In this account, written years later, he says that he was again dissatisfied with Johnston, but there is no contemporary evidence of it.[7]

If, as he states, he thought a battle was in prospect and rode to watch it, without knowing it had been called off, it is possible that the long meeting of the generals, which lasted until late in the night, was responsible for Johnston's failure to inform the President that he had changed his plans. Other important decisions also pressed upon the army commander. Although he had knowledge of Jackson's success in the Valley by this time, he had no information as to its effect on the enemy. The behavior of McDowell was consequently more confusing. Johnston did not know that the report he had received was but partially correct. The Federals observed were only a reconnoitering party of cavalry moving south from Fredericksburg. Meanwhile, McDowell had slipped away with half his force, to join the Federals in the Shenandoah Valley.

As late as Friday, May 23, with Lincoln present at his headquarters, McDowell was perfecting plans to march against Richmond. Wagon trains were ready to roll on Sunday morning. Soldiers were preparing rations for five days, and all was activity. Lincoln, however, advised his general to make "a good ready," and postpone the movement for one day. On Saturday all this was changed. Late that day Lincoln, who had returned to Washington, ordered McDowell to suspend the march against Richmond and instead to move as rapidly as possible to the Valley. Although the Federal general objected strenuously he began the new movement at once. Thus the dramatic work of Jackson intervened to prevent overwhelming force being thrown in a pincers movement against Johnston.[8]

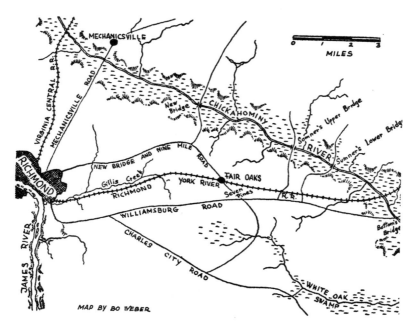

SEVEN PINES AND FAIR OAKS

May 30 was a day of decision for Johnston, although the men in the ranks noted nothing unusual about the morning other than the fact that the rain had ceased, at least temporarily. D. H. Hill about noon reported what he had learned from another reconnaissance. The enemy was between Seven Pines and Richmond and was constructing works: one to the west of Seven Pines, another at that point and the third between it and Bottom's Bridge. The reconnoitering party had not been able to determine the anchor point of the enemy's left flank. With this information and the knowledge that Keyes and Heintzelman were separated from the rest of McClellan's army by the Chickahominy, then at a higher level than had been known in twenty years, Johnston decided to fight. He knew that Huger was close enough to participate and would increase the Confederate numbers to approximately 63,000. He also had the encouragement of a friendly message from Lee, who offered his services in any capacity.[9]

During the afternoon Johnston and Longstreet had a long discussion, in which the former explained his plans for the battle. The design conformed to the location of the roads which led from Richmond to the area occupied by Keyes' and Heintzelman's corps. Starting from the northeast suburb of the capital, the Nine Mile Road ran about six miles east to a fork with the New Bridge Road. The latter wound northward to the Chickahominy, while the former turned southeastward through Fair Oaks, where it crossed the York River Rail Road, to Seven Pines, which was approximately nine miles from Richmond by this route. South of the Nine Mile Road, the Williamsburg Road, which began in the southeast corner of the city, extended due east to its junction with the Nine Mile Road at Seven Pines, a distance by this way of only seven miles. It continued to the Chickahominy and crossed the river by Bottom's Bridge. On this road approximately two and a half miles east of Richmond the Charles City Road branched off. The area between the two for several miles was high enough for easy movement in normal weather, but as one neared the river the White Oak Swamp fingered up to make going difficult.

Johnston's plan was simple and offered a minimum of possibility for confusion. Huger was to follow the Charles City Road, where he would form the Confederate right. D. H. Hill was in the center with the responsibility of opening the attack by moving down the Williamsburg Road against the Federal positions constructed by Casey.

Longstreet should go down the Nine Mile Road which would bring him into action against the Federal right. Smith was to follow Longstreet until he reached the junction of the Nine Mile and New Bridge roads, where he would be able to resist any effort of the Federal corps on the north of the Chickahominy to cross to the assistance of Heintzelman and Keyes. A. P. Hill and Magruder were to remain in position along the river to protect against other attempted Federal crossings.[10]

Johnston assigned Longstreet to the tactical command of the action, although he was not the senior major general present. None of the division commanders had led men in a major action, but Longstreet had commanded well at Williamsburg. As Johnston and Longstreet continued to discuss details another severe storm broke overhead. Thunder and lightning shook the heavens and heavy rains fell on the already saturated land. At the first lull in the storm Longstreet departed for his own headquarters. His orders for the morrow were all oral, and no information exists to indicate whether they were formally summarized or were informally arrived at in the course of the talk.

Johnston informed D. H. Hill of the plans for an attack the following morning and that Longstreet would have tactical command of the engagement. Later Hill received specific instructions of his role from Longstreet who said that Hill was to lead the attack but was not to move until Huger was in position on his right.

It was not until 8:40 that night that Johnston wrote orders for Huger. He instructed him to move his division at daybreak to the Charles City Road from his bivouac just outside Richmond. There he was to relieve a brigade of D. H. Hill's division. He was to protect the Confederate right and to "Be ready, if an action should be begun on your left, to fall upon the enemy's left flank." Huger was not informed of the over-all plan of attack, or of the fact that Longstreet was to command all troops at the scene of action.

At 9:15 Johnston wrote Smith and told him that "If nothing prevents we will fall upon the enemy in front of Major General Hill . . . early in the morning—as early as practicable." Smith was to lead his men to the junction of the Nine Mile and New Bridge roads. Johnston also sent a copy of the order to Whiting, who would command in the event of Smith's absence. Johnston did not indicate Smith's mission when he arrived at his designated position, and failed to inform his subordinate of the complete battle plan. The divisions of A. P. Hill and Magruder still stood along the Chicka-hominy on the left of the army. Thus the commander left affairs for the morning.[11]

Long before May 31 dawned, Confederate troops were in motion, on their way to the positions Johnston had assigned to them. Although some of the soldiers wondered if it were possible to fight a battle under such miserable weather conditions, their commander planned to bring twenty-three of his twenty-seven brigades to bear against two of the five corps of McClellan's army. "The heavens were supercharged with clouds," but the rain held up. Streams small and large tore out of their banks to add to the swampy lowlands and made even more troublesome the efforts of the soldiers, particularly those who had to go across country, rather than along the roads.

Among the first of the Confederates to move was Smith's division under the command of Whiting. Smith himself arrived at Johnston's headquarters as day was breaking and reported that the division was on its way. At the same time he said that he had left A. P. Hill in charge of affairs on the extreme left. Thus Smith, having removed himself from both division and wing command, had no direct re-sponsibilities in the battle but was available in case of emergency.

Whiting reached the Richmond end of the Nine Mile Road early in the morning, only to find his way blocked by some of Longstreet's men. As Johnston had told him nothing which would explain this traffic entanglement, Whiting wrote the army commander for in-structions, and received the reply that Longstreet was to precede him, Johnston's assumption being that Longstreet would move down the Nine Mile Road.

While Whiting nervously waited, Longstreet's men broke camp and loaded wagons, as though they were merely engaged in a routine march, not preparations for a crucial engagement. In exasperation Whiting finally sought the assistance of Smith to get the hindering troops out of his way. Smith went to Johnston to secure information as to Longstreet's whereabouts, realizing that the division commander might be necessary to hasten his subordinates. Johnston said that Longstreet should be somewhere on the Nine Mile Road, directing the movement of his troops; if not there, he was probably over on the Williamsburg Road. Smith immediately sent one of his staff officers, whose account of his experiences is an important document in the history of these involved events, to search for Longstreet.

In the meantime Huger had started his troops from the outskirts of Richmond to their battle positions on the Charles City Road. Earlier that morning, Johnston had changed his instructions. The army commander wrote:

I fear that in my note of last evening, of which there is no copy, I was too positive on the subject of your attacking the enemy's left flank. It will, of course, be necessary for you to know what force is before you first. I hope to be able to have that ascertained for you by cavalry. As our main force will be on your left, it will be necessary for your progress to the front to conform at first to that of General Hill. If you find no strong body in your front, it will be well to aid General Hill; but then a strong reserve should be retained to cover our right.

Again Johnston failed to tell Huger that Longstreet was to be in tactical command.[12]

Huger had the same experience as Whiting; soon after they began to move, his men encountered troops in their path. For some reason Longstreet, in place of following the comparatively easy and obvious way down the Nine Mile Road, as Johnston had directed, decided to cut across the country just east of Richmond and go down the Williamsburg Road.

Huger's men encountered those of Longstreet at the crossing of Gillies Creek, which formed a sort of arc around the eastward side of Richmond to the James. It, like all the other streams in the area, was greatly swollen. Even so one of the officers who was present maintained that the troops could have forded it in column of fours with the water coming no higher than their waists. But Longstreet's officers decided to construct a makeshift bridge. They placed a wagon in the stream, anchored it and put planks on it. In single file the soldiers began to cross. As they did, Huger's advance units reached the stream, but on the basis of "first come, first served," and the fact that they had laid the "bridge," the men of Longstreet insisted on precedence. Apparently no one had the foresight to place a second wagon or to attempt the fording of the creek.

At another point the two major generals, themselves, had a different sort of conflict. Amid the nervous tension of the hour they met at D. H. Hill's headquarters on the Williamsburg Road. Huger immediately asked if Longstreet knew who was the senior officer. After some discussion, which is variously reported, Huger accepted

Longstreet's claim to command, and from that time on subordinated his movement to Longstreet's decisions.

Back at Johnston's headquarters in the meantime, a courier reported that Smith's staff officer, Captain Beckham, had been unable to find Longstreet on the Nine Mile Road and was consequently riding across to the Williamsburg Road to see if he could be there. Johnston was apparently startled by this message, as Captain Beckham further said that there was no sign of Longstreet's troops on the Nine Mile Road. Unable to accept this the army commander sent one of his own aides to search for Longstreet and his troops. This messenger carried instructions to Longstreet, if he had misunderstood his orders and moved by the Williamsburg Road, to take three brigades to the other road, unless the movement would cause too much delay in the attack. At the same time Johnston told Whiting to stay where he was until Longstreet was found.

Sometime after Johnston's aide departed (he did not return but, constantly expecting to encounter Longstreet's men, mistakenly rode straight into the Federal lines near Fair Oaks and alerted those troops to their possible danger), a report came from Captain Beckham that he had found Longstreet and his division, although the latter was not where Johnston had planned for it to be. Instead those troops and their commander were on the Williamsburg Road at the junction with the Charles City Road, where, having forced Huger's division to wait while they crossed Gillies Creek, they in turn waited as the other troops marched over the makeshift bridge and across the muddy fields to file down the Charles City Road toward the positions they should have taken several hours earlier. For some still unexplained reason Longstreet had changed Johnston's simple, direct use of the area's roads into an involved series of movements over difficult terrain.

By then it was obvious why the attack had been delayed: the various elements were not in position for it. Johnston, when he heard where Longstreet's troops were, could only offer one explanation, that Longstreet had misunderstood his orders. An observer reported that Johnston said that he wished the troops were back in their camps. But it was too late to call the engagement off, and despite the delay, there was still hope that it could be fought to a successful conclusion. Orders consequently went to Whiting where he had halted early that morning, to resume his march toward the junction of the Nine Mile and the New Bridge Road.

As the plan called for Hill to initiate the action of the Williamsburg Road, nothing could be done until the signal guns for the start of the battle were heard. At Johnston's headquarters men sat or walked uneasily about, listening constantly for the sound of firing from the south. Lee arrived from Richmond and joined the tense group. The minutes slowly passed, while Johnston, Lee and Smith anxiously awaited the noise of Hill's guns. Finally around two o'clock Smith suggested that he send another aide to discover the reason for the further delay.

Curiously enough, an aide-de-camp of Lee, who had never heard firing in battle until that day, said that he and others on one side of the house in which Johnston had his headquarters, had heard the fire of muskets for some time before it was noted on the opposite side, where the generals were. They made no mention of what they heard because they did not know that the commanding officers were awaiting that very sound. It was not until three o'clock that the roar of cannon informed everyone that an action had commenced, but even then Johnston interpreted it as only an artillery duel. Apparently so many mishaps in one day had convinced him that nothing of real consequence could then occur.

Over on the Williamsburg Road where Smith's hard-riding aide found Longstreet around ten o'clock in the morning, confusion had continued to delay the opening of the engagement. Here in a comparatively small area near the junction of the Charles City and Williamsburg roads, three divisions had to pass because of Longstreet's failure to follow the original plan. First, Hill moved down the Williamsburg Road and arranged his command to start the attack. Then, while Longstreet's troops, who had held them up at Gillies Creek, watched from the side of the road, the men of Huger's division began their march to their assigned positions. As though to give them strength, Longstreet detached half of his division, under the command of Brigadier General Cadmus M. Wilcox, to join them.

The use of these troops that day by Longstreet might well form a scene in a comic opera were not the whole background so serious and tragic. Their work consisted of marching and countermarching to conform to Longstreet's orders and bearing up under the frustration thus created. Originally Huger was directed to a "designated point" on the Charles City Road, where he should await further orders, while Wilcox was to keep abreast of the firing on the Williamsburg

Road. But, as Wilcox displayed in his report on Seven Pines, that was just the start.

> I was . . . ordered to move with three brigades . . . on the Charles City road in rear of a part of Huger's division . . . as a support to these troops; this order was soon modified and my three brigades ordered to precede Huger's two. Having passed Huger's brigades, the march was continued but for a short time, when orders were again received, and this time to counter-march to the Williamsburg road and follow on in the rear of the troops then advancing. The brigades had retraced their steps near 1 mile, and orders were again given to face about and march down the Charles City road, and to keep abreast of the firing then heard raging furiously off to our left front, and known to be on the Williamsburg road.
>
> Again orders were received in writing to move across to the Williamsburg road, following country roads and paths through woods and fields, a guide being furnished to conduct the command. The intervening distance between the two roads was low and flat, and in many places covered with water and at one point waist-deep. The march was of necessity very slow.[13]

Longstreet's apparent inability to decide how he would use the three brigades under Wilcox and the two from Huger's division was but another evidence of his failure in the execution of Johnston's plan. Moreover he ordered another of his brigades to cover the York River Rail Road, even though the whole left of the Confederate army was in that direction. This arrangement left but two brigades of his division to support Hill in the actual assault upon the Federals. In other words out of a possible thirteen brigades—six of his, four of Hill's and three of Huger's—which could have been brought into action against the enemy, Longstreet decided to launch the vital effort with but six!

Actually Hill sent his men forward before Longstreet's brigades came up and before some of his own men reached their positions. After waiting impatiently all morning to start the engagement, which was supposed to open at eight o'clock, the fiery North Carolinian gave his signal at about 1:00 P.M. At that time one of his brigades under Brigadier General Robert Emmett Rodes was struggling to get into the attacking line. Rodes had waited on the Charles City Road to be relieved by Huger. Then, after a false start because of an incorrect order, Rodes put his men in motion to reach his place on Hill's right. He soon discovered the march was more easily ordered than

made. Fighting the mud of the fields, the undergrowth in the thick
woods, and the water and swamps in the low places, the troops pro-
gressed slowly, despite Hill's frequent messages to hurry. A bridge
across White Oak Swamp was out, and the "men had to wade in
water waistdeep and a huge number were entirely submerged." Only
Rodes' skirmishers—the Sixth Alabama, under the energetic young
Georgian, Colonel John B. Gordon—were in position when Hill fired
the signal gun, which sent the Confederates forward to open the
battle.

The Federals were not caught by surprise. As early as eleven o'clock in
the morning their advanced units had noted the massing of the Confederates on the Williamsburg Road. Before that the capture of
Johnston's aide warned them that something was in the wind. Even
so the first wave of Hill's attacking division shortly overran the first
Union line. The Federal left flank was easily turned, although Casey
had constructed a redoubt in that direction. Hill's right eagerly swept
past it, and the threat of encirclement caused Casey's green troops
to give up. The frontal blow along the Williamsburg Road was
equally successful. The Confederates soon had possession of both the
Federal advanced works, where they captured eight guns and Casey's
camp with all its equipment and supplies.

The Union troops did not rally until they reached the second line
at Seven Pines, where Casey had constructed another abatis on the
edge of the woods. They received the support of fresh troops there,
and organized a counterattack. But the Confederates kept the pressure on them and met the charge with even fiercer fire. As one Union
general reported: "Volley after volley was given and received. An
order was given to charge, but 100 yards brought us into such close
proximity with the enemy that a sheet of fire was blazing in our faces.
. . . So close were the contending forces, that our men in many
instances whilst at a charge poured their fire into the breasts of the
enemy within a few feet from the points of their bayonets." [14]

For some reason the brigade on the extreme right of the Confederate line was unable to keep pace, so Gordon and the other men
of Rodes bore the brunt of this portion of the fighting. Fortunately
a reserve brigade, one from Longstreet's division, came up and filled
the gap. In the meantime the left of Hill's line had picked up the
forward movement. Using a combination of frontal and flank attacks,
despite the courageous stands the Federals made when they reached

their prepared positions, the Confederate left swept its opponents back.

On the Nine Mile Road action had also followed delay. Shortly before four o'clock Smith's aide returned with the news that the troops on the right were heavily engaged. Soon a courier arrived with a communication in which Longstreet reported that he had "beaten the enemy after several hours severe fighting; that he was disappointed in not receiving assistance upon his left, and, although it was now nearly too late, that an attack by the Nine-miles road upon the right flank and rear of the enemy would probably yet enable him to drive them into the Chickahominy before dark." [15]

Johnston wasted no time in recriminations about Longstreet, who had he followed orders would have been in exactly the important place he asked someone else to assume, but told Smith to order Whiting to move toward the fighting while Smith himself should hurry up other brigades. Johnston mounted and spurred his horse away in the direction of Seven Pines. The urgency of Longstreet's request for an attack against the Federal right flank brought to mind possibly the close of the Battle of Manassas, then almost a year away. There Johnston on the field directed the movements of the reinforcements against the Federal flank with the result that the Union troops suddenly abandoned the fight. Now within the hour there might be a similar favorable chance. Unfortunately he departed from headquarters to realize this possible opportunity just as Davis arrived. The President, members of his Cabinet and other officials of the Government were on the battlefield, eager to know the results and to lend a hand if needed. Since Johnston rode off as Davis approached from a different direction, he possibly did not see the President. Some observers later ascribed Johnston's hasty departure to a desire to avoid Davis, but the reason as given seems far more logical.

The success of the Confederate attack down the Williamsburg Road caused the isolation from the main Federal force of some regiments which had been placed on the York River Rail Road at Fair Oaks in the morning. For reasons of safety those troops drew off to the north toward the Chickahominy and sent word to Sumner, who commanded the nearest Federal corps on the other side of the river. This tough old army man had been advised by McClellan early in the afternoon that he should hold himself in readiness to move at once to the assistance of the Union forces south of the river.

Sumner prepared at once for the crossing. He marched his men to the Chickahominy and awaited orders. His engineers had built two bridges over the stream, but its swollen flow threatened their use. Portions of the center section of the lower one were gone and a foot or more of water swirled over the floor. Despite these handicaps, when the order to cross came, some of the men used it, but most of them had to march to the second. Even when on the south side their troubles were not over, as they found themselves in the Chickahominy swamps. They often had to wade waist deep in the mire and water. The horses were almost helpless, as they sank in the deceiving ponds and endless mud. Nevertheless, the persistent soldiers struggled on toward the sound of the firing.

Johnston realized how much of a handicap the swollen Chickahominy and its swamps would be to troops who attempted to cross them. In fact he thought they would combine to hold off the Federal troops on the north side of the river until the engagement on the south side was decided. When he and Whiting rode with the troops down the Nine Mile Road, no one expected to encounter any danger on the left, the flank toward the river. As the marching column drew near Fair Oaks, though, a battery opened fire upon them from their left rear. It was a part of the Federal force which had been at Fair Oaks. Smith, who was behind Johnston and Whiting, turned one of the Confederate brigades toward the battery. From this beginning the action mushroomed.

Though it was growing late in the afternoon, each side brought about 9,000 men into action. Purely unplanned, the encounter was both fortunate and unfortunate for each side. Had Sumner's troops been allowed to proceed unhindered to the south, they could have come into action with stunning surprise on the left and rear of Longstreet's attacking force, which was already heavily involved in its front. Had the Federals under Sumner not engaged when and where they did, the Confederates Johnston was leading to the field could have hit the Union forces in front of Longstreet on their flank with devastating result. As it was, the two groups tangled in what, because of its separation from the other, was in effect a second battle in the same general area.

Johnston, who had got as far as Fair Oaks, remained there with Whiting for a while, but as the fighting grew in intensity, he rode closer to it. Before long he realized that the conclusion could not be accomplished that day, so he sent staff officers to advise the regiments to sleep in their positions on the field and to renew the contest in the morning. As twilight began to close upon the scene, he was hit by a musketball in his right shoulder. Within a few moments, a fragment of shell struck him in the breast and knocked him from his horse, unconscious.

Only two members of his staff were present when he was wounded, but one of the couriers, Drury L. Armistead, picked the wounded General up and carried him to a spot protected from the enemy's direct fire. Quickly an excited group gathered. Some of them helped to carry him to a still safer place farther back. There they put him on the ground, while they sought a stretcher to take him from the field. Within a few minutes President Davis came up and expressed concern over the misfortune. As Davis dismounted and walked over to Johnston, the latter regained consciousness: ". . . he opened his eyes," the President said, "smiled, and gave me his hand, said he did not know how seriously he was hurt, but feared a fragment of shell had injured his spine."

Within a few minutes Johnston discovered that he did not have his sword and pistols. "That sword," he exclaimed, "was the one worn by my father in the Revolutionary war, and I would not lose it for $10,000; will not someone please go back and get it and the pistols for me." Several immediately volunteered to do so, among them Armistead. Although the spot was then under heavy enemy fire, the courier found the sword and pistols where Johnston had been wounded. He hurried back to the general who presented one of the pistols to him.[16]

G. W. Smith, the ranking general after Johnston, assumed command of the army. He was directing troop movements, some distance away in the woods, when he received word of the serious wounding of his friend and superior. Shortly after, Davis and Lee met him, and Smith told them all he knew of what had happened in that day's fighting, including his conversation with Johnston about Longstreet's misunderstanding of his orders. He knew nothing of the late developments on Longstreet's front and found that neither Davis nor Lee could give him any information. During the night the new commander made strenuous efforts to realign his troops to close the gap between the two wings of the army. He planned to change the direction of the attack from the east to the north, with Longstreet again leading it. But on Sunday, June 1, only indecisive fighting occurred.

That morning Davis issued an order in which he appointed Lee to the command of the Army of Northern Virginia. He then rode again to the battlefield, where at Smith's headquarters he told that officer what he had done. Lee reached the field about 2:00 P.M. and took charge. After a conference with Smith and Longstreet, he decided to break off the engagement and to return the troops to the positions they had held before it started. The Battle of Seven Pines, with casualties of 6,134 killed and wounded for the Confederates, and 5,031 for the Federals, was over.[17]

CHAPTER XI

DEPARTURE FROM VIRGINIA

All the night of May 31 and the next day a stream of ambulances and carriages brought the seriously wounded from the battlefield to Richmond. People were appalled by the number of casualties but most alarming was the fact that Johnston was among them. President Davis offered to take the General to his home, but the wounded officer's staff secured a house in one of the capital's suburbs, Church Hill. There, Mrs. Johnston joined them.[1]

The doctors soon discovered that the General's more serious wound had caused the fracture of several ribs, an injury which led to "an obstinate adhesion of the lungs to the side, and a constant tendency to pleurisy." The treatments, from a more modern point of view, were as dreadful as the wound itself, as they consisted of "bleedings, blisterings and depletions of the system." [2]

At first no public announcement of the wounding of Johnston was made, but on June 4 the Richmond *Examiner* said that it was no longer a military secret. In an editorial which expressed the hope that Lee would prove a "competent successor," the editor gave most of the attention to Johnston.

He is the only commander on either side in this contest that has yet proven, beyond all question, a capacity to manoeuvre a large army in the presence of one yet larger; to march it, fight it, or not fight it, at will, and while so doing, to baffle the plans of the ablest opponents in every instance. Time may yet produce another, but no living man in America is yet ascertained to possess a military knowledge so profound, or a decision of character so remarkable. He is one of those who can take responsibility; who is never a nose of wax; and who can hold out with the solidity of a rock against all foolish projects formed for him by others.

Pleasing as this public acknowledgment of his ability was to him, Johnston found greater satisfaction in the large number of personal expressions of sympathy and affection, among them one from Lee. Addressed to Mrs. Johnston from his camp "Near Richmond, June 2, 1862," it read:

I am so grieved at the general's wound, on his account, yours, and the country's. I heard of it on the field, but he was carried from it before I could get to him. . . . You must soon cure him. In the meantime the President has thought it necessary that I should take his place. I wish I was able, or that his mantle had fallen on an abler man. Remember me kindly to him, and tell him he has my sincere sympathy.[3]

Johnston realized that his army would be well led in his period of incapacity. He recognized Lee's merits and abilities even to the one he failed to have himself, that of getting along with Davis. When reinforcements began to reach the Army of Northern Virginia in June, a friend reported the fact to Johnston. Immediately, in spite of his pain, he responded and expressed his pleasure: "Then, my wound was fortunate; it is the concentration which I earnestly recommended, but had not the influence to effect. Lee has made them do for him what they would not do for me." [4]

In this comment there is reflection of Johnston's chief handicap as an army commander. His failure to achieve the wholehearted support of Davis was responsible for the major part of his difficulties. Apparently, people discussed it at the time, and Jones, the war clerk, wrote that Johnston "has had his day." But Davis himself privately confided to his wife: "I wish he were able to take the field. Despite the critics, who know military affairs by instinct, he is a good soldier, never brags of what he did do, and could at this time render most valuable service." [5]

While Johnston remained impatient in his confinement, Lee prepared to break the cordon McClellan had created before Richmond. The new commander ordered Jackson to march to Richmond from the Shenandoah, to attack the Federal right. The other divisions would then join to sweep McClellan from the Peninsula. Again simple and effective plans did not insure able execution. On the twenty-sixth of June the Confederates launched their initial assault in the great and bloody series of battles called the Seven Days'.

Like all Richmond, Johnston could hardly await the outcome. Mechanicsville, Gaines Mill, Savage Station, Frayser's Farm, Malvern Hill: each day the reports told of Confederate initiative. But the puritanical Jackson was not so effective as he had been when operating alone in the Valley. Nor did the work of other subordinate commanders and the staff prove any more creditable under Lee than with Johnston at Seven Pines. But the Federals, defeated, withdrew from the Peninsula and Richmond was freed from immediate military pressure.

From far away in the West the result of the Seven Days' fighting won an expression from Thomas Jordan to his former chief, Beauregard, of what may well have been Johnston's thought also. "What fate or fortune," he wrote, "could be harder than that of General Joe Johnston to have commanded such an army up to the very eve of such a campaign, and when his army was ripe for great deeds, to lose the command in a petty affair; and how fortunate of the most fortunate is General Lee?" [6]

While recovering, Johnston worked on his report of Seven Pines, and already there was evidence that another verbal war was in prospect. Longstreet had placed heavy blame in his official account on Huger and ignored his own responsibility for the change in Johnston's plans. When G. W. Smith wrote his report he included reflections upon Longstreet's conduct. But Johnston returned it to Smith with a request for certain deletions in those sections where Smith discussed "two subjects which I never intended to make known, which I have mentioned to no one but yourself, and mentioned to you as I have been in the habit of doing everything of interest in the military way. I refer to the mention of the misunderstanding between Longstreet and myself in regard to the direction of his division, and that of his note to me, received about 4 o'clock, complaining of my slowness, which note I showed you. As it seems to me that both of these matters concern Longstreet and myself alone,

I have no hesitation in asking you to strike them out of your report, as they in no manner concern your operations." [7]

Smith made the changes in his report, which, with Longstreet's, Johnston used to prepare his own. In it he overlooked the blunders of Longstreet entirely but praised him, along with Smith and D. H. Hill, and was critical only of Huger. This aroused the elderly Huger who protested to both Davis and Johnston about the injustice done him. He asked for a court of inquiry which he was confident would clear him. But Johnston refused to prefer charges and Davis failed to order a court, although he did promise to convene one when the "state of the service" permitted. This time never came so Huger continued under the accusation of failure. [8]

Johnston's role in this episode is impossible to justify. He based his report upon those of his direct subordinates; if Huger believed Longstreet had done him an injustice, then any appeal should be directed to that officer. Johnston's motives may have been attributable to loyalty. Huger had been an integral part of the Army of Northern Virginia for but a few days when Seven Pines was fought, whereas Longstreet had served with it since Manassas. At any rate, it remained for G. W. Smith, writing at a much later date about the errors of Seven Pines, to do justice to Huger and to place Longstreet's participation in the engagement under serious question. [9]

By fall the Johnstons were comfortably located on Grace Street with the family of Louis T. Wigfall, Senator from Texas. The 46-year-old politician was a native of South Carolina but had moved to Texas in 1848. After serving as a member of the state legislature he became United States Senator in 1859 and was among those who urged secession and the organization of the Confederacy. He had drawn wide attention by the dramatic part he played at Fort Sumter. The Wigfalls were regarded as among the most pleasant of Richmond's wartime families, although one which spoke with "exceptional frankness . . . both on public and social affairs." The two young daughters, Louise, or Luly as she was familiarly called, and Mary Frances, kept the spirit of the house bright and youthful, in which they were joined by their brother, Halsey, when he was home on leave. [10]

Mrs. Johnston and Mrs. Wigfall had been prominent in Washington society before secession, and assumed a similar leadership in Richmond. They were frequently in the company of Mrs. Davis, with

whom in the early months of the war they were on closest terms. But
as factions developed in other areas of the Confederacy, animosities
also grew within the coterie of the First Lady. As criticism became
more open and differences widened, reports were that Mrs. Johnston
developed "a little court of her own," one which was antagonistic to
the President's wife. Whether it was because of social ambitions,
tensions of a desperate day, personality differences, or reflection of
husbands' attitudes, gradually Mrs. Johnston and Mrs. Wigfall
moved apart from Mrs. Davis and her group.[11]

Johnston was relatively inactive until November when he began
to ride horseback. "My other occupation," he wrote, "is blistering
myself, to which habit hasn't yet reconciled me." Lee had watched
his friend's progress with interest but had been unable to see him
because of active campaigning. On November 11 Lee wrote regretting that they had been unable to confer about the "condition of
this army and its operation for the winter. I wish you were again able
to take the field, for I do not think it could be in abler hands than
yours." Lee obviously considered himself as acting as a substitute
until such time as Johnston could again assume command.[12]

But official Richmond had other plans, as Johnston found out
when two days after the date of Lee's letter he reported to the War
Department for duty. For some time requests had come to Davis
from civilians and soldiers that he assign Johnston to the West. In
October when the Richmond authorities summoned General Braxton Bragg to report in person on his campaign in Kentucky, he took
the opportunity to ask that Johnston be given the "whole command
in the Southwest with plenary powers." Possibly because Johnston
had not then reported for duty, Richmond did not accede to Bragg's
request. But Bragg, according to his account, did not give up the
effort. He sent one of his division commanders, Bishop-General
Leonidas Polk, to the capital to emphasize the request. Polk gave a
different story. After reporting to the President, whom he knew well,
on the Kentucky campaign, Polk said that the generals of Bragg's
army had lost confidence in their commander. When Davis asked
for his recommendation of a successor, Polk suggested Johnston.[13]

These calls for Johnston from the West reflected the misfortunes
and the disappointments which had pursued the Confederates there
since the start of the war. Neither A. S. Johnston nor Beauregard nor
Bragg, who had succeeded each other in that order, had been able to

withstand the Federal assaults. In the fall of 1862 the situation, particularly that along the Mississippi, became sufficiently acute for Davis to create a new department, that of Mississippi and East Louisiana, with the hope of assisting it. He assigned Major General John C. Pemberton, whose Northern birth and limited field experience made him a poor choice in the minds of many, to the command, which Pemberton assumed in mid-October.

The troops under Pemberton were widely scattered over a large district and consisted of "not more than 25,000." When Johnston reported to the War Department for duty and received the news of his assignment to the command in the West the Secretary of War conferred with him on the problems which were involved. Johnston proposed that General T. H. Holmes, then in command west of the Mississippi, should transfer troops to Pemberton so that the latter could oppose the Federals on more equal terms. Randolph replied that he had sent such orders to Holmes more than two weeks before, and read them to his visitor.[14]

As Randolph finished reading to Johnston the orders sent Pemberton, he turned with a smile to a letter from Davis, which he also read aloud. The President had apparently not seen the order to Holmes before November 12, but as soon as he read it, he wrote to the Secretary in objection. He said:

I regret to notice that in your letter to General Holmes of October 27th . . . you suggest the propriety of his crossing the Mississippi and assuming command on the east side of the river. His presence on the west side is not less necessary now than heretofore, and will probably soon be more so. The co-operation designed by me was in co-intelligent action on both sides of the river of such detachments of troops as circumstances might require and withdrawal of the commander for the Trans-Mississippi Department for temporary duty elsewhere might have a disastrous effect, and was not contemplated by me.

Two days later Randolph submitted his resignation, which Davis promptly accepted and appointed the studious James A. Seddon, an able politician but without experience in military affairs, to the position. According to Jones, the war clerk, Randolph's hasty decision, of which Jones disapproved, produced a "profound sensation" in Richmond.[15]

Undoubtedly the quick changes in the War Department between

the time Johnston reported for duty, November 13, and his receipt of his orders, the twenty-fourth, were responsible for the delay. The assignment was to the large geographical area between the Blue Ridge Mountains and the Mississippi River. He was to establish his headquarters at Chattanooga unless for reasons of communication he preferred another location. The orders pertinently read that he should "repair in person to any part of said command whenever his presence may, for the time, be necessary or desirable." [16]

In Davis' interpretation, "This arrangement made of several departments . . . was intended to secure the fullest co-operation of the troops in those departments, and at the same time to avoid delay by putting each commander in direct correspondence with the War Office." It seems a strange military procedure. Orders and reports could pass back and forth between Richmond and subordinates without the knowledge of the district commander, who bore responsibility for over-all supervision. Johnston apparently was not informed of this phase of his assignment, from which confusion would seem inevitable. The careful delineation of the territory placed under him was evidence that Richmond expected a strict observance of its boundaries, but by using such indefinite markings as natural features instead of the established state lines the authorities left room for additional misunderstanding. More than once Johnston had to ask for clarification to be sure that he did not overstep and bring upon himself the ever-ready reproaches of the legalistic High Command.[17]

As soon as Seddon took office Johnston talked with him and suggested as he had to Randolph the use of troops from the Trans-Mississippi Department to assist at Vicksburg. But to Johnston's surprise the orders he received on the twenty-fourth contained nothing about that threatened spot on the Mississippi or the needed co-operation of the troops on both sides of the river. Instead the orders were very general and did not give him field command.[18]

Johnston acknowledged the orders immediately and reiterated his recommendation to unite the troops east and west of the Mississippi against the enemy. Again as he remarked the "suggestion was not adopted, not noticed." Despite misgivings about the practicability of his new assignment he made his plans for an early departure. He assembled his staff with Colonel Benjamin S. Ewell as adjutant general. This scholarly soldier, who after graduation from West Point gave up the military for a life of college teaching and administration, relieved Johnston of the task of keeping records and writing letters.[19]

Friends gave the General a breakfast before he left Richmond. It is reported that one purpose was to bring about a reconciliation between two of his prominent political friends, Senator Henry S. Foote of Tennessee and Senator William L. Yancey of Alabama. After an unusually bountiful meal, "rare in those days," and congenial merriment, Yancey called for fresh glasses of champagne and proposed a toast: "Gentlemen, let us drink to the only man who can save the Confederacy—General Joseph E. Johnston!" The room rang with applause. As the others, after drinking, seated themselves, Johnston rose with his glass in his hand. He turned to Yancey and said with serious mien: "Mr. Yancey, the man you describe is now in the field, in the person of General Robert E. Lee. I will drink to his health!"

Undismayed Yancey quickly countered by saying: "I can only reply to you, sir, as the speaker of the house of Burgesses did to General Washington:—'Your modesty is only equalled by your valor.'" So the party ended, with all sounding the praises of the General. But all through it he had remained taciturn and preoccupied, as though his thoughts were held by consideration of the largely unknown problems which his new assignment contained.[20]

The Johnstons left Richmond Saturday, November 29. At the stations as they passed people gathered and greeted the General with "hearty good will," Mrs. Johnston wrote Mrs. Wigfall, "music and bouquets, as you foretold. . . . [They] called upon him for speeches and offered him all they had, 'from a team of well broke mules' down to 'every red copper cent I own he may have it,' said one in his enthusiasm." [21]

At long last, after five days of tiresome journeying, the Johnstons arrived at Chattanooga, which was to be his headquarters, early on the morning of December 4. After he rested briefly the General issued his order in which he took command of the department.[22]

CHAPTER XII

A GEOGRAPHICAL COMMAND

Johnston found little time to observe the facets of Chattanooga life, but he missed the old associations in Virginia. "How can I eat, sleep, or rest in peace," he grieved to Jeb Stuart, "without you upon the outposts?" The "halcyon days" of all his service were those with the Army of the Potomac. From the start he was apprehensive about the situation in the West. "Nobody ever assumed a command under more unfavorable circumstances," he wrote to Wigfall. "If Rosecranz had disposed our troops himself, their disposition could not have been more unfavorable to us." But if he was despondent, his coming gave a lift to others. "I am indeed rejoiced that Joe Johnston is to take command in the West," Kirby Smith, who commanded in East Tennessee, wrote his wife. "I can serve under and with him in earnestness of purpose and devotion of heart." [1]

The problems the General had foreseen as soon as he received the orders which assigned him to a geographical command immediately confronted him. On arrival in Chattanooga he found a telegram from Cooper in which the Adjutant General said that Pemberton had fallen back in the direction of Vicksburg under pressure from the Federals. Cooper also said that he had "peremptorily" ordered Holmes to reinforce Pemberton and urged Johnston to send troops from Bragg as those from Holmes might be too late. Cooper's expla-

166

nation of the circumstances hardly made sense and Johnston pointed
out as quickly as he could that if Pemberton had retired toward
Vicksburg he had moved closer to Holmes and away from Bragg. To
be sure that was the situation, Johnston asked Pemberton to send
information about the positions of his troops and advised him to
urge Holmes to hurry the reinforcements. But the truth is that
Cooper had sent no such order to Holmes as he described. He had
done no more than to ask the Trans-Mississippi commander if he
could send help to Pemberton.[2]

With his official duties attended to, Johnston wrote his gloomy
letter to Wigfall. After describing the situation he appealed to the
Texan to help in securing prompt action from Holmes by seeing
Secretary Seddon and explaining the necessity. Wigfall complied by
writing Seddon as soon as he received Johnston's letter. He conveyed
the General's analysis and added his support to the request for
Holmes' celerity by insisting that the government should ignore

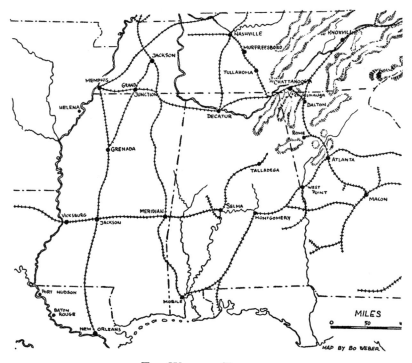

THE WESTERN THEATER

political desires in moving troops. He reminded Seddon that he had earlier advocated bringing all Confederates from Arkansas and Texas to assist Bragg against Buell.

Wigfall stated that he had never met a Texan who disagreed with him about it. "I mention this," he told Seddon, "to show that those who oppose the concentration of our troops . . . on political grounds, are mistaken as to public opinion. Our people are full of good sense and patriotism, and they will not refuse the means necessary to secure success." The Senator then stated his earnest hope "that the last battle has been fought by us with inferior numbers. Whenever the enemy divides, concentrate and crush. . . . "[3]

On the day after his arrival at Chattanooga Johnston hastened by train to Murfreesboro, where he hoped to learn at first hand the truth about the condition and problems of Bragg's command, which then numbered about 42,000. There the Army of Tennessee faced the Union Army of the Cumberland under Major General William S. Rosecrans. The Federals numbered, according to the estimate sent Cooper by Johnston, around 65,000 men, with an additional 35,000 at various places along the railroad between Nashville and Louisville and at other points in Kentucky. Because of the Federal superiority in numbers, Johnston stated, it would be dangerous to attempt to reinforce Pemberton from Tennessee, and if as the President said the assistance was needed quickly, the position of the Army of Tennessee would prevent it. "The movement to join General Pemberton would, by any route, require at least a month," Johnston pointed out. "To send a strong force would be to give up Tennessee, and would, the principal officers think here, disorganize this army. Rosecrans could then move into Virginia, or join Grant before our troops could reach Pemberton's position, for the Tennessee is no obstacle to him."[4]

Johnston sought information from the officers about the condition of the Army of Tennessee, its morale and in particular its feeling toward its commanding general. He was handicapped somewhat in that attacks of illness, a consequence of his wounds, incapacitated him at times. Before he could complete his inspection he received an unexpected summons to meet the President in Chattanooga, where Davis arrived on December 10. It was the latter's first extensive journey out of Richmond since the start of the war, a fact which had led to some feeling among soldiers and civilians that the government did not appreciate properly the importance of the West.[5]

Although the Johnstons had but three rooms in a cottage which they shared with others, they invited the President to stay with them. He declined, but did come for coffee; it was the "real Rio," Mrs. Johnston wrote Mrs. Wigfall, and then exclaimed over the hardships of a day when she would think such coffee "good and fine." Claiming the saddest heart in all Chattanooga, she confided her despondency: ". . . how ill and weary I feel in this desolate land & how dreary it all looks, & how little prospect there is of my poor husband doing ought than lose his army, truly a forlorn hope it is. . . . "[6]

The next morning the Presidential party left for Murfreesboro where for two days Davis reviewed troops and talked with commanders. He found that Bragg like Johnston was against sending men from Tennessee to Mississippi, but Davis' mind was made up. The troops on the west side of the Mississippi would remain where they were, while reinforcements for Pemberton would go from Tennessee. The President, in Bragg's words, was "inexorable and reduced me to the defensive, or as he expressed it, 'Fight if you can, and fall back beyond the Tennessee.' "[7]

In a letter to Seddon, Davis said that he found Bragg's army "in fine spirits and well supplied," and the enemy with no indication of anything but defensive action. Nothing he saw caused him to change his opinion that Middle Tennessee had no importance other than as a source of supplies, so he directed Johnston to send some 9,000 infantry and artillery from Bragg's army to Pemberton at once. Although convinced that the movement was unwise, Johnston had no volition in the matter and issued the orders on the President's return to his headquarters.[8]

Davis' stay at Chattanooga was made anxious by news that a battle was imminent at Fredericksburg, but its favorable outcome relieved him. More permanently disturbing was word from prominent Mississippians that the situation there was critical. The people seemed "to have sunk . . . in listless despondency. The spirit of enlistment is thrice dead," one reported. Only Davis' presence could inspire a revival, it was claimed.[9]

As Davis listened to and read these discouraging reports, Johnston made preparations to accompany the President on his visit of inspection to Mississippi. Again he wrote his friend Wigfall. From Davis he had discovered that the Secretary of War had "not carried our sion left to him, Holmes decided that he was unable to send the point & reinforced Pemberton with Holmes' troops." With the deci-

troops. That threw the responsibility back upon Johnston. "This has blown away some tall castles-in-the-air. I have been dreaming of crushing Grant with Holmes' & Pemberton's troops, & with the latter, Bragg & Kirby Smith marching to the Ohio. Our troops beyond the Mississippi seem to be living in great tranquility." [10]

Johnston explained to Wigfall his objections to his geographical command. Bad at best, as he had pointed out, it was particularly so as arranged.

Mississippi and Arkansas should have been united to form it. Not this state & Mississippi—which are divided by (to us) an impassable river & impracticable country. The troops in Middle Tennessee could reach Fredericksburg much sooner than Mississippi. Then General Holmes' communications depend upon our possession of the Mississippi. It is certainly his business to at least assist in the maintenance of his communications. . . ."

The reference to Fredericksburg was a natural one, as the battle there had just occurred under circumstances very favorable to the Confederacy. It led Johnston to comment in an envious fashion uncommonly found in his letters: "What luck some people have. Nobody will ever come to attack me in such a place." [11]

Davis and Johnston left Chattanooga for Vicksburg late on the afternoon of December 16 on the long tedious journey by way of Atlanta, Montgomery, Mobile and Jackson. On their arrival at the Mississippi river town they spent two days inspecting land and water defenses. Some distance north of the city, where the Yazoo with its swampy bayous joined the Mississippi, a series of irregular hills, tortuous ridges and bluffs, which rose some 200 feet above the stream, offered natural strongholds. After a test of strength by Union craft in July 1862 was turned back, the Confederates began the construction of additional defensive works to guard against an attack by land. Haines' Bluff on the Yazoo, about twelve miles north of Vicksburg, and Warrenton, about half that distance to the south, were fortified as the anchor positions of the line. These intricate preparations immediately aroused Johnston's interest as an engineer, but as at Yorktown he was critical of what had been done. The result, he pointed out, "was an immense intrenched camp, requiring an army to hold it . . . instead of a fort requiring only a small garrison." The batteries along the river were "planned to prevent the bombardment of the

town, instead of to close the navigation of the river to the enemy."
The heavy guns were scattered along the stream in such a way that
their fire could not be concentrated against a ship. To strengthen the
defenses Davis promptly wired the Secretary of War to send additional heavy guns and long-range field pieces.[12]

While at Vicksburg Johnston secured for Davis information on
the military resources and necessities in Mississippi. Vicksburg, alone,
needed at least eight more regiments, a total of around 5,000 men,
while Fort Hudson, the second Confederate strong point, about 300
miles by river and 130 miles by land to the south, should have as
many or slightly more. Both garrisons would then consist of 11,000
to 12,000 men. The army in the field numbered 21,000, but to hold
Grant and other possible Federal threats, particularly one from the
South, at least 40,000 men were needed. For these reinforcements,
in addition to the 9,000 men from Tennessee, rumor had it that an
equal number had started from the Trans-Mississippi command.
That left the need for an additional 8,000 to 10,000. As no more
could safely be taken from Bragg, Johnston suggested that Davis
order Holmes to send them. "Our great object," he stressed again,
"is to hold the Mississippi." As a consequence, he thought it would
be unwise to reinforce Pemberton temporarily with troops from
Holmes: "I firmly believe . . . that our true system of warfare would
be to concentrate the forces of the two departments," he wrote to the
President, "on this side of the Mississippi, beat the enemy here, and
then reconquer the country beyond it, which he might have gained
in the meantime." [13]

At Vicksburg, as at Harper's Ferry, Johnston opposed the idea of
placing a large body of troops where they could be rendered ineffective by siege and be in danger, not only of losing the place they
occupied, but their own potentialities by capture. His idea was to
place in Vicksburg and Port Hudson only as many men as were
necessary to defend them, while the army in the field should be
strong enough to assist by maneuver and to attack the enemy, if needs
be, and thus relieve the garrisons.[14]

Davis accepted the idea of the cardinal importance of the Mississippi to the Confederate cause and emphasized it in a letter to
Holmes. At the same time he still refrained from ordering the Trans-
Mississippi commander to co-operate with Johnston but left full
discretionary power in Holmes' hands. Davis showed this letter to

Johnston before sending it to Holmes. The General must have been pleased by the early paragraphs, which sounded as though he had convinced Davis of the value of concentration. The last sections, of course, contradicted the earlier impression.[15]

After their stay in Vicksburg Davis and his party journeyed approximately 150 miles north to Grenada, where Pemberton's main force faced the Federals under Grant. There, all was astir, as the army labored to construct works to oppose a Union effort to cross the Yalobusha River. But Johnston again was critical of the engineers. This line, as was true of the one at Vicksburg, was too extensive to be manned by the available troops. His pessimism was not allayed in his discussions of the situation with Davis and Pemberton. The latter had displayed in his communications that he doubted the ability of his army to hold against the superior numbers of the enemy, and in the conversations at Grenada differed widely with the department commander about the best way to make his smaller force effective.[16]

On Christmas Davis and Johnston returned to Jackson, and addressed a meeting of citizens and the State Legislature. The President used the opportunity to attempt to arouse all to assist the army achieve a victory, and then prepared to depart for Richmond. Before he left, Johnston, who had become more convinced by his examination of the situation in Tennessee and Mississippi that his command over both areas was impracticable, explained his objections, and asked to be transferred from a "position so little to my taste." [17]

Davis was not convinced by Johnston's arguments. Richmond was too far from the Tennessee and Mississippi theaters to supervise them as closely as he thought necessary. Someone with higher authority than the army commanders should be at hand "to transfer troops from one army to the other in an emergency." This was exactly the type of nominal duty Johnston did not desire; furthermore his frank expression about the impracticability of the command proved that he was not the man for the assignment.[18]

While Johnston was still in Jackson, word came on December 27 that the Federals under Grant were retiring. A spectacular Confederate cavalry raid on the Union base at Holly Springs forced the Northerners' withdrawal and had the further effect of causing an accompanying effort closer to Vicksburg to fail. While Grant held attention at the Yalobusha his associate Sherman moved from Memphis down river in a heterogeneous armada of rivercraft. The plan was for co-operation with Grant, but the latter's withdrawal caused Sherman to undertake alone the assault on the Confederate position at Haines' Bluff. The result was a bloody repulse by the Southerners under Pemberton, who had hurried to the threatened spot. For his part in this phase of the campaign, Johnston told Cooper that Pemberton "deserves high credit." [19]

Although the Federal retirement and defeat relieved the immediate anxiety of the Confederates, Johnston still emphasized to the President the need for additional men and asked if the victory at Fredericksburg would not allow Lee to send troops from the Army of Northern Virginia. There was still the danger that the Federals would unite to invest Vicksburg, and demands over the department were such that troops could not be spared from one point to aid another. Actual experience tended to increase rather than to lessen Johnston's worry about his command. When he wished to use the cavalry under Forrest, Roddy and Van Dorn, he could not locate the first two, who were under the command of Bragg, while Van Dorn was in Mobile, a long distance from where he was needed. The transfer of the troops under General Stevenson from Tennessee to Mississippi confirmed Johnston's fears about the practicability of attempting such movements. Two of the brigades, having started their journey to Vicksburg on December 18, arrived in time to take part in the repulse of Sherman's attack on the twenty-eighth and twenty-ninth. But the rest of the division required more than three weeks to complete the trip, and the wagons, which went by road, did not arrive for a month. [20]

Even before he made his inspection trip with Davis to Mississippi, Johnston apparently planned to move his headquarters from Chattanooga to that area of his command. On December 27, writing from Jackson, he told Ewell: "I intended that headquarters should move after the troops [Stevenson's]. Either you or Colonel Lamar should remain until the crisis is over near Murfreesborough." Mrs. Johnston was so confident of the move that, after spending Christmas Day packing, she wrote Mrs. Wigfall: "This change of headquarters leads me to think that some change has been made in the General's command by the great 'commander-in-chief.' " Even though Jackson might prove pleasanter than she had found Chattanooga, she was suspicious of Davis' intentions toward her husband. [21]

She made her journey as planned but headquarters remained at Chattanooga. The "crisis" at Murfreesboro, instead of getting better, grew worse, when General Rosecrans struck at Bragg, weakened by the departure of Stevenson for Mississippi. On open ground, where flanks could not be securely anchored, just northwest of Murfreesboro, the two armies met on the last day of the year. All day the bloody contest echoed along Stone's River, with the advantage going to the Confederates. Bragg, believing that the Federals would retire the next day, telegraphed Richmond, "God has granted us a happy New Year." Johnston, after hearing the news, immediately sent his congratulations to the commander of the Army of Tennessee and urged him to press the enemy "vigorously." [22]

But Rosecrans did not retire. For a day and a half the two forces faced each other before Bragg launched an attack against the left of the regrouped Union army. The Confederates found themselves under a galling artillery fire from their flank and finally fell back, with approximately 2,000 comrades left as casualties on the field as the result of one hour's action. On the night of January 3 Bragg withdrew to Tullahoma, thirty-five miles to the south of Murfreesboro, and went into winter quarters there.[23]

As late as January 6 Johnston had no news from Bragg in Middle Tennessee, and on that day he informed Davis that he had indirect reports that the Army of Tennessee had fallen back. He used this fact to impress again upon the President the awkwardness of his situation: ". . . the impossibility of my knowing the condition of things in Tennessee shows that I cannot direct both parts of my command at once." The evidence in this instance was incontrovertible, so Davis could only reply, "The difficulty arising from the separation of troops of your command is realized but cannot be avoided." [24]

CHAPTER XIII

DIFFICULTIES IN TENNESSEE

The Johnstons found themselves far more pleasantly situated at Jackson than they had been in Chattanooga. In place of the restricted quarters which were all they could secure in the Tennessee community, they had a comfortable country house, which the owner insisted that they use. The General's staff lived with them and made a "mess" of twelve who enjoyed a "very merry social time."

In a long newsy letter to Mrs. Wigfall, Mrs. Johnston disclosed how bitter the enmity among the members of the onetime close social circle in Richmond had become: "The people here have a great horror of Mrs. D. & abuse her in the most unusual terms." A visitor who had called upon her in Chattanooga "left upon [her] mind that she was a spy for the D. family." All of this was "*entre nous.*"

As for the General she reported that he "looked unusually well & is reserving his strength." But, she continued, "It is hard on him to feel himself laid aside." She had tried to console him as best she could. "I tell him to be patient and watch with hope. . . . " [1]

In the latter part of January Johnston went to Mobile to inspect his defenses. Shortly after he arrived, he received a message from the President, telling him to proceed "with the least delay" to Bragg's headquarters at Tullahoma. On the way he would find at Chattanooga a letter which would explain the reasons for the order.[2]

175

Whatever Johnston's curiosity about the message, it was not satisfied at Chattanooga, for no communication from Richmond awaited him there. He did receive a disquieting telegram from Pemberton who was at Vicksburg. "Enemy in full force again opposite the city," Pemberton reported, "with indications of attempting to force his way below." What the future might hold, Pemberton could not say, but papers captured from a Federal colonel said that Vicksburg "must be taken." [3]

Johnston immediately sent news of the developments in Mississippi to Richmond and said that he was still in Chattanooga awaiting the letter of explanation. At the same time he advised Pemberton to disregard a previous order to send four regiments to Meridian and to bring supporting troops closer to Vicksburg. Then, his official duties done, he wrote a long letter to Wigfall in which he requested the Texan's help and advice. As he had received no reply to a query as to whether troops were available to reinforce Bragg, he asked Wigfall to see Seddon and explain that the situation in Middle Tennessee was critical. Pemberton had no troops to spare and himself needed help because of the new Federal efforts. Johnston again remarked upon the failure of the government to accept his advice and to bring troops from the Trans-Mississippi to assist east of the river. The President still thought that troops could be exchanged between Tennessee and Mississippi to take care of emergencies, but that was obviously impracticable when both armies needed help.

The situation also showed that the President's position about an over-all commander was wrong, particularly the suggestion that Johnston could command either army in emergency. Each had its own commander whom he could not feel justified in supplanting at will, yet he realized that the country might well hold him responsible for whatever happened in his wide geographical territory. As Jordan had earlier written Beauregard, Johnston bemoaned that wounds received in battle had caused his removal from an important command and had placed him where he could expect no accomplishment. It was possible that Davis assumed the post to be a consequential one, but if so he misunderstood what the situation between Tennessee and Mississippi was. In closing Johnston made another appeal for Wigfall to help him to escape from his then nominal command, although he doubted that the Senator had the kind of cunning diplomacy which would be required. [4]

The Senator went quickly to work for within two weeks Secretary of War Seddon, who, Wigfall constantly emphasized, was Johnston's friend, wrote the General a letter which he said was a personal, not an official communication. In it he tried to make clear that the intention in Richmond was to give Johnston an important command. He had been chosen as the general of the "largest experience and greatest ability . . . to have over it something of the same guiding direction and control as was exercised nearer the Capital by the Department and the President." They expected that he would take charge when and where needed, and the Secretary expressed disappointment that he had not done so at Vicksburg and even more over his failure to direct the "great operations around Murfreesborough." Seddon asked Johnston to accept that interpretation of his assignment, but if he couldn't, the Secretary suggested that he take over the command of the Army of Tennessee and use Bragg as "an organizer and administrator" under him. If that were not agreeable, he suggested that Johnston supplant Bragg and let the department use that officer in some other capacity. The letter, which was consistently friendly in tone, closed with the request that Johnston state frankly his preferences in the matter.[5]

From Johnston's point of view the practicability of these suggestions was well displayed in Seddon's statement of disappointment that he had not commanded in the engagements near Vicksburg and at Murfreesboro. In order to have done so he would have had to be in both places at the same time. But he had other reasons for disliking the assignment. He had been brought up in an older tradition and did not comprehend fully the influence the new methods in communication and transportation, as well as the increased size of armies, could have on the conduct of war. This is not to say that the authorities at Richmond did understand it; obviously, their plans were more expedient than anything else. Even had the importance of these new methods been realized, the lack of experience, the inability to keep them in adequate operating condition and popular resistance to centralized control would have reduced to a minimum their usefulness in Johnston's huge command area. But in any circumstances, Johnston had no desire to be a desk general, an administrator. His idea of a commander's post was at the head of an active army. As Mrs. Johnston told Mrs. Wigfall: "He cares nought for comfort & would rather have a blanket under a tree for his bed with the hope of a fight on the morrow. . . . He wants to have an army with the right and force to command it, which he has not here." [6]

Had Johnston known the reason, when he wrote Wigfall January 26, why Davis had ordered him to Bragg's headquarters he might have been further troubled. On the next day the President telegraphed him to proceed from Chattanooga, even though the instructions were still delayed. When they finally reached him three days later, he was at Tullahoma with Bragg. In his letter Davis said there was new evidence of a "want of confidence" in their commander among the subordinate generals of the Army of Tennessee. Although his own belief in Bragg was unshaken, he realized that if it were true that Bragg's officers and men distrusted him, "a disaster may result which, but for this cause, would have been avoided." As a consequence, the President wanted Johnston to investigate and if necessary to take the command.[7]

The retirement after the Battle of Murfreesboro caused a great deal of unfavorable comment, not only in the press of the Confederacy, but among people in various walks of life. It awoke new echoes of all the old stories of dissension and dissatisfaction. Bragg, not the first to attempt to excuse his own shortcomings by accusations against others, blamed the unfavorable opinions on the "malicious falsehoods of a lying correspondent" and "private letters from some vile scamps who write under the lash of my rigid discipline" (later he changed to the generals as the cause). He consequently decided to controvert quickly the harmful impression before it became widespread. A week after the retirement, he wrote letters to his corps and division commanders, in which he stated the situation and asked their help.[8]

Up to that point Bragg was on sound ground, but he failed to stop there and opened the way, although he said without this intention, for the generals to express freely their opinion of him as a commander. He apparently thought that he had to act fast, as he continued: "General [E. Kirby] Smith has been called to Richmond, it is supposed with a view to supersede me. I shall retire without a regret if I find that I have lost the good opinion of my generals, upon whom I have ever relied as upon a foundation of rock." [9]

Replies were in Bragg's hands before Davis asked Johnston to make an investigation, and according to the information which had reached the President were "indicative of a lack of confidence, such as is essential to success. Why General Bragg should have invited [the army's] judgment upon him, is to me unexplained; it manifests, however, a condition of things which seems to me to require your presence." [10]

The information Davis had received was correct. All the generals except Polk, who was on leave for a visit to his family, replied quickly to Bragg's inquiry. They acknowledged that the retirement from Murfreesboro did not originate with Bragg, but they then proceeded to take the opportunity their commander's invitation afforded to be candid with him as to his ability as a leader.[11]

Polk went further: he wrote to Davis and for the second time advised the President to replace Bragg with Johnston, who, he said, "will cure all discontent and inspire the army with new life and confidence." Polk's endorsement of him as Bragg's successor was exactly what Johnston had feared when he undertook the investigation which Davis ordered. Conscientious to a fault and determined never to offend his sense of personal integrity, he could not bring himself to take Bragg's command on the basis of his own derogatory report. For similar reasons he could not execute his original orders, which gave him the authority at will to supplant Bragg in the command of the army. Nor was he convinced of Bragg's failure. Actually he wrote Wigfall, "Bragg has done wonders, I think—no body of troops has done more in proportion to numbers in the same time." [12]

Johnston sent a preliminary report to Davis on February 3 and said that as best he could discover the feeling against Bragg was declining. "I am very glad to find that your confidence in General Bragg is unshaken," he said. "My own is confirmed by his recent operations, which, in my opinion, evince great vigor and skill. It would be very unfortunate to remove him at this juncture, when he has just earned, if not won, the gratitude of the country."

At the end of his report Johnston ventured a word of advice, and in it displayed the reasons for his own reluctance. "I respectfully suggest," he said, "that should it . . . appear to you necessary to remove General Bragg, no one in this army or engaged in this investigation ought to be his successor." [13]

Johnston's final report to Davis, dated February 12, confirmed his earlier one. In the interim, he had seen the whole of Bragg's army. "Its appearance is very encouraging, and gives evidence of General Bragg's capacity to command," he wrote. It was stronger in numbers than before Murfreesboro, because the "general's vigorous system" had brought back to duty many absentees, and in no way was its ability to defeat Rosecrans impaired. Although some of the general officers insisted that there was a lack of confidence in the commander, Johnston pointed out that its operations in Middle Tennessee had been "conducted admirably . . . evincing skill in the commander and courage in the troops, which fully entitle them to the thanks of the Government." Johnston emphasized his embarrassment, should he be asked to take Bragg's place. "I am sure that you will agree with me that the part I have borne in this investigation would render it inconsistent with my personal honor to occupy that position." [14]

As soon as his final report on the investigation was on its way to Richmond, Johnston left Tullahoma. But the authorities at the capital were not so well satisfied with the situation as he apparently was. Davis, in acknowledging the reports on February 19, said that he was pleased with Johnston's commendation of Bragg and the optimistic account of conditions in the army. But he was, obviously, still concerned about the wisdom of keeping Bragg in Tennessee, inasmuch as there could be no doubt as to the feeling among the "superior officers" about his "fitness to command."

The problem of a successor to Bragg was doubly difficult, the President said, because of the confidence he had in the general's "ability and zeal." Nor had Johnston helped the situation by his recommendations. Davis wrote:

You limit the selection to a new man, and, in terms very embarrassing to me, object to being yourself the immediate commander. I have felt the importance of keeping you free to pass from army to army in your department, so as to be present wherever most needed, and to command in person wherever present. When you went to Tullahoma, I consider your arrival placed you for as long a period as you should remain there in the immediate command of that army, and that your judgment would determine the duration of your stay. You have borne no part in the investigation of the statements made in relation to the command of General Bragg other than that which seems to me appropriate to your position of commanding general of all the forces of the department. The removal of General Bragg would only affect you in so far as it deprived you of his services, and might restrain your freedom of movement by requiring more of your attention to that army. Therefore, I do not think that your personal honor is involved, as you could have nothing to gain by the removal of General Bragg. You shall not be urged by me to any course which would wound your sensibility or views of professional propriety, though you will perceive how small is the field of selection if a new man is to be sought whose rank is superior to that of the lieutenant-generals now in Tennessee. I will expect to hear further from you on this subject.[15]

In his reply Johnston made no effort to explain further to Davis his position about succeeding Bragg permanently. Even his friends had difficulty understanding that. To him command in the field was superior to any administrative post, so though he held the higher rank, Bragg held the more important assignment. Should he receive Bragg's command as a consequence of his investigation, "it would be reasonable to suppose that I had recommended a vacancy for my own benefit." Like Davis, Secretary Seddon could not understand so scrupulous an attitude. He had asked Johnston in his letter of February 3 for a candid statement of the General's preference in the matter, and was not satisfied with the reply. On March 3 Seddon wrote:

I appreciate the nobility of spirit which constrained you to be less explicit than I would have wished on the subject of what would be most agreeable to you in respect to your command in the West, but have, at the same time, not been able to escape some embarrassment and uncertainty, in deciding, in consequence, on what line of action I should direct my counsels and actions here.

He suggested that Johnston take the command and keep Bragg as an assistant for "his efficient capacities as an organizer and disciplinarian." [16]

From Johnston's point of view, it doubtless seemed queer that neither Davis nor Seddon apparently considered that it was their function to order him to perform the duty which they urged him to undertake at his own initiative. Their failure to do so was doubly difficult to understand after he made his own position so patently clear. Another confusion may have resulted when Seddon, despite his expressions of respect, dismissed Johnston's testimony that the effectiveness of Bragg's army had not been impaired by the controversy. Because of the confusion it would seem that Seddon would have visited Tullahoma in this period of relative quiet of all fronts, or would have called Johnston to Richmond for a full discussion of the problem. Neither of these, though, was apparently even considered.

Wigfall urged Johnston to state his wishes about the command, and he would try to explain them to Seddon. In his first letter after his arrival at Tullahoma for the Bragg investigation, Johnston insisted to the Texan again that Bragg had "commanded ably in Tennessee," and that the Congress should adopt a vote of thanks for the work of the Army of Tennessee at Murfreesboro. In somewhat franker terms than he had written the President, Johnston said that his duties actually were only those of an "inspector general." [17]

In his reply of February 27, Wigfall implored Johnston to be frank with him. Both Davis and Seddon, he said, interpreted Johnston's letters to mean that he did not want the command of Bragg's army. If he would only say that he did, the Texan believed Richmond would order the appointment at once. But if that was not the desire of Johnston, he should say what he did want and Wigfall would work to secure it. On the next day Wigfall wrote again, and unimpressed by Johnston's praise of Bragg said that he was "pressing Seddon" to replace Bragg with Longstreet. Should the appointment go to Johnston, he warned the General against keeping Bragg in any capacity. "You have now the confidence of the whole Army as well as the country. Retain it," wrote the Texan. To hold to Bragg would impair it. In closing Wigfall suggested that paroled prisoners be gathered in a division under General John B. Hood, should Johnston accept the command. "Hood," he said, "is very anxious to serve under you." [18]

Wigfall's two letters reached Johnston the same day and stimulated the General to write revealing replies in which he stressed the strategic importance of Middle Tennessee, and the dilemma of his own position. Should Middle Tennessee fall, East Tennessee would follow, opening the way to Virginia or Atlanta as the enemy chose. Richmond did not comprehend this fully and chose to give first attention to the Army of Northern Virginia. It was not so easy to state his desires about his own position. He would not ask for the removal of a brother officer if he would benefit himself; only if Richmond ordered him to do so would he replace Bragg. But that was not his real wish. If the President and Secretary of War really thought the Western command the most important post in the Confederacy, Lee should have it. Then "with great propriety," Johnston could return to the duty "where the Yankee missiles found me."

He was reluctant to make any such statement even to so close a friend as Wigfall. "My only official wish," he told the Texan, "is to render service, my only ambition as to place, to have one in which I may be useful. For more than three months I have been doing next to nothing. If there was anything for me to do, not knowing it. I don't want to remain so. Anything else would be better." [19]

CHAPTER XIV

TO REPLACE BRAGG

The only one in the group concerned who seemed to be pleased by Johnston's visit to Tullahoma and his reports was Braxton Bragg. To Colonel Ewell of Johnston's staff, forgetting his earlier charge against a journalist, he wrote that the "only dissatisfaction that ever existed was fomented by a few disappointed generals, who supposed they could cover their own tracks and rise on my downfall. They have failed, mainly owing to the discrimination and the just conception of your noble chief, who saw at a glance the whole bearing." To General Mackall, Bragg wrote similarly and added that Johnston had said, "when I told him I should call for him in case of a prospect for battle, 'I will come most cheerfully and serve on your staff, but not as commander.' " [1]

Despite the pressure of the responsibilities of his command, Johnston was his usual friendly and gracious self with the residents of Chattanooga. A writer in the Chattanooga *Rebel*, who in an earlier issue called the General a "game cock," said:

Speaking of pleasant things—peace, spring and independence—leads me to speak of Gen. Jo. Johnston. Do you know that very gallant but equally agreeable man? If not, call upon him. You will find him most accessible and if disengaged from the press of official business that must demand the larger share of his time, disposed to talk with you in a way, which will send you off, feeling better of yourself and him than when you came. He is one of those men for whom you cannot resist a personal impulse of kindness. Easy himself, he has the happy faculty of all men of good heart and graceful address of putting those with whom he is thrown also at ease. . . . General Johnston is only awe-inspiring on the battlefield. At all events, in the private relations of life, he is eminently graceful and gracious, setting an example of true worth to affectation, which might be studied to advantage by some of the many apostles of cant and assumption in the military service of the Confederate States.[2]

Chattanoogans were unwilling to allow this pleasing comment by their newspaper to be their only recognition of the General. They quickly planned a "soiree dansante" in his honor. Unfortunately the "press of official business" interfered, as Johnston had to leave town before the affair occurred, on his way to visit with Pemberton's army. His first stop was Mobile, where a large crowd gathered and called for him to make an appearance as the hero of Manassas. When he came out he said that the hero of Manassas (Beauregard) was at Charleston. Not dismayed the gathering sent up cheers for the hero of Seven Pines, but with characteristic modesty Johnston said: "Gentlemen, no one man was ever the hero of Seven Pines. In that bloody battle there were many heroes under our flag, and the very noblest of them were from Alabama." This reference to the work of the Sixth Alabama sent the crowd into a frenzy of cheering, during which Johnston bowed, called good night and left.[3]

The two commanders at the First Manassas were interestingly associated in another incident on that trip to Mobile, when Johnston met the widely read Southern novelist, Augusta Jane Evans. In a letter to Beauregard she reported that their friendship had proved an immediate "open sesame" to Johnston's interest. "He is surely a noble magnanimous soul . . ." she said; "a stranger to the miserable weakness of envy." By implication she contrasted Johnston's spirit with the "Presidential Jealousy," about which people muttered angrily. "Mr. Davis seems to have learned but one rule of government: that laid down by Machiavelli in the celebrated sophistical dictum; 'the dissensions of great men contribute to the welfare of the state.'"[4]

Johnston was not to complete his trip to Mississippi, for while he was in Mobile, Davis and Seddon ordered him to take over Bragg's command. Johnston replied immediately on March 12 that he would obey as quickly as possible, but he hoped "that that most meritorious officer's removal is but temporary, and the Government will adopt no course which might be regarded by the public as evidence of want of confidence in his generalship." He requested the Secretary of War to send a copy of the order to Bragg.[5]

A week later he was at Tullahoma, where he learned that Mrs. Bragg was critically ill of typhoid fever. Because of Bragg's great concern about her, Johnston advised Seddon that he would not then order Bragg to Richmond. He told the Secretary that the country was becoming open for military movements and "should the enemy advance, General Bragg will be indispensable here." At the same time he proceeded to execute the portion of the order under which he was to take command of the army, but sensitive to Bragg's worried circumstances he issued no official statement of the change.[6]

Among the officers and men at Tullahoma Johnston quickly won admiration and affection. In part it was a consequence of his feeling for them. After a review which was held for him early in February, he said that "he had never seen men he would rather trust." For those who came in association with him it was for closer reasons. "I found General Johnston a charming man," reported Dr. Charles Todd Quintard, who served the Army of Tennessee as both surgeon and chaplain. "He was of perfectly simple manners, of easy and graceful carriage and a good conversationalist."[7]

General Polk again determined to take direct action in the effort to achieve Bragg's removal. On March 30, he wrote Davis a letter marked "Private," in which he recommended that Bragg be transferred to the post of Inspector General where his talents for organization and discipline would be of great service. Then the way would be open for the assignment of Johnston to command of the Army of Tennessee, "a measure which would give universal satisfaction to officers and men." Polk disagreed with the general opinion that Johnston wished to keep Bragg in command. "I think," he said with proper insight into Johnston's character, "the case would be more properly stated by saying that he does not wish to be, or seem to be, the cause of his removal. I have conversed with him on the subject, and he feels a delicacy, as I understand it, in touching the case of a man to whose command he might succeed in event of his being removed from it."

Should Johnston not feel capable of continuing his duties over the whole western area, while commanding in Tennessee, Polk continued, the President should give Pemberton full responsibility in Mississippi, with both men reporting directly to Richmond. "Whether General J. is the best man for the place or not is not the question. The army and the West believe so, and both would be satisfied with the appointment, and I believe it is the best that could be made." [8]

Davis was no more inclined to take Polk's advice than before, but he was assisted this time by Johnston's incapacity to serve actively. A recurrence of illness, a consequence of his wounds, caused him to write the President on April 10 that he was under medical care and that Bragg's presence in Tullahoma was a necessity. He suggested that if the situation required a conference between the Richmond authorities and Bragg, an officer be sent from the War Department for that purpose. [9]

Polk's suggestions were in part offset by the official report which Colonel W. Preston Johnston, aide to the President, prepared on April 15. He was well pleased with what he saw and in his report bore out in almost every detail all that the General had previously said. To the President he wrote:

This army is in a high state of efficiency, well clad and armed, and marked with every evidence of good discipline, high courage, and capacity for endurance. There is vast improvement in this army since I inspected it last June at Tupelo; and while great credit is due the high soldierly qualities of the eminent officers by whom he is surrounded, much is also due to the peculiar talents for organization of the commander, General Bragg, and to his laborious attention to the details of his command. This is not an opinion, but the testimony of all with whom I came in contact. [10]

Colonel Johnston reported that the army had been increased to 49,447 effectives, of whom 15,616 were cavalry. This was a consequence of efforts of both Generals Johnston and Bragg. General Johnston had recommended the abolishment of both sick leaves and furloughs. Bragg directed his efforts to the control of other absentees, which he accomplished in part by reserving permission to grant leaves and furloughs to his own headquarters. He also undertook to prevent transfers to the cavalry by making that service less attractive. [11]

A directive of Adjutant and Inspector General Cooper of January 8, 1863, made it possible for Bragg to tap a new important source of man power. Under it field commanders had the authority to detail officers and men to the areas where their regiments had been raised in an effort to secure volunteers, even among men who were liable to conscription. Bragg immediately ordered Brigadier General Gideon J. Pillow, Johnston's old division commander in the Mexican War, "to the supervision of the gathering of conscripts, securing volunteers, and arresting stragglers for the regiments in this department," something of an extension of Cooper's directive.[12]

Preston Johnston noted in his report that both Generals Johnston and Bragg credited the growth of the Army of Tennessee to Pillow's "energy and vigorous system." But the War Department was not convinced by the arguments and ordered Pillow to stop recruiting and closed his bureau because of the methods he used.[13]

The most vital and alarming problem of the Army of Tennessee noted by Colonel Johnston was subsistence. He reported that Bragg's men lived "from hand to mouth" and relied upon reserves. Major J. F. Cummings, of the Atlanta office of the General Purchasing Commissary, was even more gloomy in a report which the President's aide passed on to Richmond. "It is evident," Cummings said, "to all in authority (those who have investigated the question of subsistence) that our battle against want and starvation is greater than against our enemies; hence I think no stone should be left unturned in this great struggle for subsistence, for, without subsistence, all must admit our Government to be a failure." [14]

Such problems were nothing new to Johnston or any other commander of the Confederacy. In the West in the early months of 1863 the problems were both different and worse than those he had experienced in Virginia. Then Northrop had insisted upon taking all supplies into Richmond and issuing them from that point to the army, even though agents had collected them in the country the army occupied. By contrast, in Middle Tennessee during the winter of 1862-1863, the army drew its supplies from the territory it held, its subsistence agents frequently competing for the same supplies against those who worked for Northrop out of Richmond. The result was unending difficulty with Northrop holding to his system, commanders struggling to secure supplies and the soldiers the victims.[15]

While Johnston's health as well as his orders held him closely to

Tullahoma, developments in other areas of his command were constant reminders of the impracticability of administering such a large area in the way Richmond expected. In the Department of East Tennessee, with headquarters at Knoxville, four commanders followed each other in quick succession at Richmond's orders between mid-January and mid-May. Each faced exactly the same problems. They had only 10,000 men with whom to guard a territory which one described as but a "mere frontier, with a railroad line of 200 miles or more in extent, parallel to which is the enemy's line of occupation, from which by many routes he can assail us . . . " It was an area in which Federal sentiment was strong, and Johnston, who realized his subordinates' difficulties, said that the Confederate force was scarcely large enough to control the Unionists.[16]

The situation at Mobile was not an urgent one, and the problem there was largely a consequence of its location and its place in the chain of command. Richmond changed its designation from district to the Department of the Gulf under Johnston's jurisdiction in early 1863, but its commander still did not report to Johnston. Instead he was responsible to Bragg, although there were "no immediate military relations" between them, and despite the more essential association with Mississippi had only an indirect official contact with Pemberton. The complex, anomalous command situation was made plain by General Simon B. Buckner when transferred from Mobile to Knoxville. He recommended to the Secretary of War as a remedy that the Department of the Gulf be placed under Johnston's direct command as were the other three departments.[17]

The problem in the Department of Mississippi and Eastern Louisiana was again a different one. To Colonel Preston Johnston at Tullahoma, General Johnston reiterated all his old arguments about his command but was most emphatic about a new one. He bitterly complained, Colonel Johnston wrote the President, that "he receives no intelligence from General Pemberton, who ignores his authority, is mortified at his command over him, and receives his suggestions with coldness or opposition." General Johnston had fears about the effectiveness of Pemberton's command and wished, the colonel added, that a "speedy and thorough inspection" be undertaken.[18]

It is possible that Pemberton's attitude was in part a consequence of his misunderstanding of Johnston's status at the time. More than once he referred to matters affecting the relations between the army

in Mississippi and that in Tennessee as though the latter was Johnston's sole command. The communications Johnston did receive
from Pemberton were generally in the direct words of scouts, or
about details which were not evaluated or assimilated into the tactical
plans of the department commander in such a way as to give Johnston, so far from the scene, a necessary orientation. He was often at
a loss about the dispositions Pemberton made to counter the Federals and was consequently even more than usually hesitant about
making specific recommendations. Richmond frequently complained
also of a want of information from Vicksburg and requested a clarification of messages which were confused in transmittal. Yet no one
there seems to have understood that Johnston had the same trouble.[19]

All in all Pemberton's position was as uncomfortable as that of
Bragg. Like Bragg he had the loyal support of the President but little
else. Mrs. Johnston remarked upon his failure to win the backing of
the people in a letter to Mrs. Wigfall on March 16. "There is a very
strong feeling here against Pemberton," she said. "No one trusts him
or has confidence in him. . . . Pemberton's opinion of himself is
charming, if the country only had half as good a one, it would be
well for all of us." [20]

All through the early months of 1863, Pemberton's primary purpose was to contain the enemy, who he reported on January 24 had
returned to the Vicksburg area, although this time on the western
side of the Mississippi. The Federals had resumed work on a canal,
which would enable them to escape one of the great bends of the
river and to avoid the guns of Vicksburg. Johnston, who was then on
his way to Tullahoma for his first investigation of Bragg's difficulties
with his subordinates, asked Pemberton what he believed the enemy's
designs to be. Pemberton, whose force of about 40,000 men was
scattered over his department, replied, "unless the enemy designs
landing below Vicksburg and a protracted investment, perhaps first
capturing Port Hudson, I can see no purpose in his arrangements." [21]

At the time Grant was himself not sure of the exact details of his intentions with his gathering host. Fortunately for him the Federal high
command in Washington had greater flexibility than Johnston's superiors in Richmond. Lincoln and Halleck saw in January that a
single commander was necessary for a successful campaign in the
Mississippi Valley, and on the twenty-first issued orders that gave
Grant "control of both banks of the river." The tenacious Union

commander began at once to test all opportunities and by a series of feints kept his Confederate opponents on edge. He was not sure that any of them included a feasible plan, but he wanted to keep Northern opinion satisfied and his men busy even as he kept the Confederates off balance. He held the men to the task of digging the canal until early March when floods swept the area, destroyed equipment and demonstrated that the project was then impracticable.[22]

On February 2 a Federal naval vessel ran the Vicksburg batteries and established itself in the stretch between that point and Port Hudson, where it created havoc among the Confederates until they captured it. Then in mid-March, Farragut sailed his flagship upstream past the Port Hudson batteries, to give again Federal naval strength in that portion of the river, so Grant could plan with some degree of confidence on a crossing below Vicksburg.

Pemberton was not idle in the face of the Federal activities. He armored steamboats with cotton bales and sent them into the Yazoo to oppose the enemy. He collected supplies to care for the expected siege, and called for more arms, artillery and ammunition. He feared that Grant might successfully accomplish his canal project, and felt forced to disperse some of his too few batteries to fortify Grand Gulf, which was opposite the lower end of it. He felt open to almost any Federal activity because of his lack of cavalry and called upon Johnston for such units, particularly the return of Van Dorn and his command. Johnston disappointed him when he replied on March 23 that "Van Dorn's cavalry is absolutely necessary to enable General Bragg to hold the best part of the country from which he draws supplies."

Johnston was not unsympathetic with Pemberton's plight and complimented him on his operations against Grant. "Your activity and vigor in the defense of the Mississippi must have secured for you the confidence of the people of the State; that of the Government you have previously won." But at the same time Johnston as over-all commander still held to the idea that assistance for Pemberton should come from across the Mississippi River.[23]

Grant's maneuvering was deceptive and frustrating to the Confederates, whose scouts in early April began to report that he was retiring up the Mississippi. On the third Pemberton suggested that it possibly meant that the Federals were on their way to reinforce Rosecrans before Bragg. Johnston immediately advised Pemberton that if this information proved to be correct he should send the troops under Stevenson or a similar number to assist Bragg. Even with them the combination of Grant and Rosecrans might force Bragg from his position in Middle Tennessee. To prepare for such an emergency Johnston asked Pemberton to establish depots of supplies where they would be available if it became "necessary or expedient for this army to cross the Tennessee near the Muscle Shoals to move into Northern Mississippi and West Tennessee." [24]

The only alternative was adequate reinforcements for Bragg. On April 6 Johnston wrote to Cooper and on the tenth to Davis, explaining the circumstances. Rosecrans without Grant had about double the number of Bragg's army and occupied a fortified position. To attack him in a preventive effort before the arrival of troops from Mississippi "would be madness." Seddon in a despairing communication explained the circumstances to Lee, saying that it was "very important" to reinforce Bragg, but he was unable to find any troops with whom to do it unless they could be safely sent from Northern Virginia. Lee in reply voiced objections similar to those of Johnston to sending men from Tennessee to Mississippi. "The most natural way to re-inforce General Johnston," Lee wrote Seddon, "would seem to be to transfer a portion of the troops from this department . . . but it is not so easy for us to change troops from one department to another as it is for the enemy, and if we rely upon that method we may be always too late." In his opinion a better way to help would be for him to undertake an offensive into Maryland.[25]

Pemberton, who felt assured that Grant's men were on their way to Rosecrans, complied with Johnston's order to send men "as fast as transportation can be furnished." But as the movement got under way, reports came of renewed Union activity on the Mississippi. At first Pemberton was not convinced and as late as April 15 reported that he was "satisfied that a large portion of Grant's army is re-inforcing Rosecrans." The next day he changed his mind, reduced the number of troops to be sent to Tennessee to two brigades, and informed Johnston that the latest information indicated that "no large part of Grant's army will be sent away." One day later he informed both Cooper and Johnston that he could send no more men and that "those on the way to General Johnston ought to come back." Johnston immediately agreed and moved to intercept the troops and to return them to Mississippi.[26]

On the day that Pemberton realized that the recall of the troops was necessary, messages poured into his headquarters at Jackson from Vicksburg. They reported that in the preceding night, a Federal flotilla had run the gantlet of the Vicksburg batteries. Thus the first phase of Grant's final effort against Vicksburg was successfully accomplished. With Federal craft in command of the river between Vicksburg and Port Hudson, Grant could choose the spot to ferry his troops to the eastern side of the Mississippi beyond the southern flank of the principal Confederate strong point.

As these activities went forward, Sherman remained upstream, where on April 27 he created a diversion by attacking Haines' Bluff. But blue-clad troops had some time before begun to make their way southward over the land route of forty miles on the other side of the river. Undisturbed by the Confederates of the Trans-Mississippi command, whose attention was held by a Federal expedition from Louisiana under Banks, they waded the swamps and bridged the bayous in their slow progression. As they could not carry with them sufficient supplies for a reserve, six more steamboats and a dozen barges attempted to slip by Vicksburg on the night of April 22. Again the Federal effort proved successful, as five of the steamers and about half the barges with their valuable cargoes made their way past the Confederate batteries.

Pemberton immediately reported these grave developments to Johnston and to Richmond. He sent a dispatch which included a reminder of part of his dilemma: "There are so many points to be defended at this time—Vicksburg, Grand Gulf, Port Hudson, Snyder's Mill and Fort Pemberton—that I have only twenty-eight guns at Vicksburg." He sought the co-operation of Kirby Smith, who had replaced Holmes in the command of the Trans-Mississippi Department, but before any steps to combat Grant's movements could be taken, attention was drawn to another Mississippi area. The very day that Porter's fleet tied up below Vicksburg, Colonel Benjamin H. Grierson with his command of Federal cavalry set out on his famous raid. Grierson swept by Pemberton's weak cavalry, tore up rail lines, burned Confederate workshops and warehouses, and moved so fast that Pemberton could not keep up with his whereabouts, much less delay or stop his progress.

The Confederate general had so few cavalrymen that he was forced to use infantry in his effort to pursue Grierson. He called upon Richmond for assistance and upon Governor Pettus to impress civilians and farm animals to form a protective force for supply depots. On April 26 he advised Johnston in Tullahoma that he could not prevent such raids as that of Grierson without more cavalry. By that time the Army of Tennessee had similar difficulties as Streight's raid deep behind its lines into Alabama and Georgia required the attention of Forrest, while Wheeler and Morgan were set the task of protecting the army's flanks. Johnston did tell Pemberton that he had directed the cavalry at Mobile to operate upon the enemy's rear in Northern Mississippi, but the Confederate weakness in numbers prevented any conclusive action. On May 2 Grierson reined up in Baton Rouge, having ridden from Tennessee in fifteen days. There, he was safe in Union territory, as the Federals controlled the area around New Orleans.[27]

On April 28 Pemberton received the disturbing news that Union troops were demonstrating in large force at Hard Times on the west side of the river across from Grand Gulf, which was approximately twenty-five miles south of Vicksburg overland and fifty by water. Pemberton could not transport his troops over the Mississippi to combat the Federals and there were no signs that the Confederates of the Trans-Mississippi area would be of assistance. The Southern commander moved quickly to establish a battery of five heavy guns at Grand Gulf, but they soon came under the attack of Porter's gunboats. At this crucial moment Pemberton at Jackson found himself out of telegraphic communication with Grand Gulf and guessed it signified Grant's successful crossing of the river. He nervously wired Johnston and Richmond and again asked anxiously for assistance.[28]

While Porter banged away at Grand Gulf, Grant watched from a chair which was lashed to the railing of a tug. On transports 10,000 Federal troops huddled and awaited the signal to cross, but Grant again shifted his plans. He decided that Grand Gulf would prove too difficult a landing site, and ordered a move downstream that night. "By the time it was light," he wrote later, "the enemy saw our whole fleet, iron-clads, gunboats, river steamers and barges, quietly moving down the river three miles below them, black or rather blue, with National troops." Quickly the Union soldiers began to disembark at Bruinsburg, about ten miles south of Grand Gulf.

Pemberton sent the word of the landing of the Federals on the east side of the river to Davis and Johnston as quickly as he could. He

told the President that the success of the enemy in crossing the river
forced a change in the "character of defense." Telegrams hurried
along the wires. Seddon promised "heavy" reinforcements from
Beauregard at Charleston, and Davis said that Johnston was trying
to send some cavalry assistance from Southern Alabama. Pemberton
again asked Kirby Smith for help, this time suggesting that he do
something against Grant on the west side of the river, but that officer was occupied with a threat from the enemy army operating out
of Louisiana.[29]

Although Pemberton's message to Johnston was not explicit, inasmuch as it said only that the "enemy can cross all his army," Johnston immediately advised the Mississippi commander: "If Grant's
army lands on this side of the river, the safety of Mississippi depends
on beating it. For that object you should unite your whole force."
On the next day he advised Pemberton that he had ordered cavalry
to operate in Mississippi and again stated his advice of the day before: "If Grant crosses, unite all your troops to beat him. Success will
win back what was abandoned to win it."[30]

Johnston displayed in these messages the need to concentrate to
oppose the enemy, and Pemberton, seemingly convinced, wrote
Governor Pettus on May 3 that to beat Grant he had to bring his
army together. But he failed to make sufficient effort to accomplish
the purpose and years later wrote that the advice of Johnston came
too late. Possibly a better reason is found in his stated conviction
that he would have been a traitor had he abandoned Vicksburg to
oppose the Federals.[31]

Grant moved 20,000 men across the Mississippi on the night of
April 30. The way then lay open to Port Hudson in the south, to
Jackson to the east, and to Vicksburg to the north. The Federal
commander chose to move first the short distance to Grand Gulf to
refit and to concentrate his forces. At the time he intended to operate
first against Port Hudson in co-operation with Banks, but discovering
that this would necessitate some delay, he decided upon another
plan—to cut loose from his base, defeat the Confederates in detail if
possible and thus gain control of Vicksburg. It was a bold conception,
and having determined upon it, Grant moved quickly. He gathered
all sorts of wagons for transport, brought in farm animals from the
surrounding area, and assembled all the troops he could, including
those of Sherman whose diversionary effort at Haines' Bluff was no
longer necessary. On May 7 Grant cut loose from his base at Grand

Gulf and moved columns toward Jackson and Edwards Station, on the railroad between Jackson and Vicksburg.[32]

Meanwhile Pemberton continued to call for assistance. Still without word from the Confederates on the other side of the river, he sent Kirby Smith another plea to move against Grant's communication lines. Johnston, who had earlier promised Pemberton supporting cavalry operations, found that developments in Tennessee prevented. The President, who was ill through much of this period, informed the harassed commander in Mississippi that Beauregard, in place of the requested 10,000 troops, could send only 5,000, and weakly commented, "I hope he may change his views." This was cold comfort to Pemberton, who emphasized to Seddon that 5,000 were far too few. "The stake is a great one," he said. "I can see nothing so important." On his own part he continued to accumulate supplies in Vicksburg, where he moved his headquarters from Jackson.[33]

Johnston at Tullahoma anxiously awaited information from Pemberton. When it came, cipher difficulties prevented its full translation, but as best he could determine, Johnston agreed with the arrangements: "Disposition of troops, as far as understood, judicious," he telegraphed Pemberton; "can be readily concentrated against Grant's army." But Pemberton had no such intention. On the following day, he wrote to Kirby Smith: "Vicksburg, and consequently the navigation of the Mississippi River, is the vital point indispensable to be held. Nothing can be done which might jeopardize it." [34]

Pemberton's conclusions were in part sound, but his efforts to make his force effective were not. He ignored Johnston's directives to concentrate, by which he could have remained in contact with Grant to take advantage of any Federal tactical blunder. There was no evidence that he might expect reinforcements or any other material help from west of the river, and by moving to Vicksburg he made it more difficult for the assistance which was on the way from the east to reach him. Davis added to his conviction that Vicksburg and the Mississippi were his primary responsibilities by his message of May 7. In it the President said that the enemy troops would be compelled, for want of other sources for the transportation of supplies, "to seek a junction with their fleet after a few days' absence from it." But from Pemberton's point of view, the important content was, "To hold both Vicksburg and Port Hudson is necessary to a connection with Trans-Mississippi."[35]

Both Pemberton and Johnston knew that Davis' strategic concep-

tion called for a defense at all points, but Johnston had learned by
bitter experience of its impossibility. On the very day, May 7, of
Davis' message to Pemberton, Johnston stated his disagreement with
the policy of the President in a letter to his brother Beverley. He
wrote:

Here (which includes Mississippi) things begin to look gloomy.
We are too much outnumbered everywhere. Burnside may go thro'
E. Tennessee to the Ga. railroad. The enemy is fortified in front of
Bragg, who for that reason can't attack. Mississippi is invaded by an
army, 50 per cent greater than ours & our general (don't mention it)
can't comprehend that by attempting to defend at all valuable points
at once he exposes his troops to being beaten everywhere. I have
urged him to concentrate to fight Grant, with no hope that he will
regard a suggestion of mine, & at this distance one can't give orders.[36]

Why Pemberton should have interpreted what seems an obvious
statement of fact by Davis, "To hold both Vicksburg and Port Hudson is necessary to a connection with Trans-Mississippi," as an absolute order not to give up either point, one cannot now understand,
unless implicit in it there is a policy already stated. That he did so
interpret it is displayed in his immediate telegram to Major General
Franklin Gardner, in command of the troops at Port Hudson: "Return with 2,000 troops at Port Hudson and hold it to the last. President says both places must be held." [37]

On May 8 Governor Pettus telegraphed Davis: "Hour of trial is on
us. We look to you for assistance. Let it be speedy." On the same day
the editors of the Jackson *Mississippian* sent the President a long
communication: "The people within this department—soldiers and
citizens—do not repose the confidence in the capacity and loyalty of
General Pemberton which is so important at this junction. Whether
justly or not, we are certain three-fourths of the people in army and
out doubt him." [38]

Either these or similar messages started a typical stream of Richmond rumors about affairs in Mississippi, most of which had but
little more foundation than the turmoil of that faraway area. Members of the government responded to the appeals in various ways.
When Seddon sought the aid of Lee, the commander of the Army of
Northern Virginia refrained again from a commitment of men and
instead presented reasons why the suggested movement was impracticable. Strangely, in view of his failure to accept Johnston's similar

reasoning, Davis endorsed Lee's dispatch: "The answer of General Lee was such as I should have anticipated, and in which I concur." His reply to the editors of the *Mississippian* sounds as though he had accepted another of Johnston's arguments to which he had earlier given no indication of listening. "Your despatch is the more painful because there is no remedy," he wrote. "Time does not permit the change you propose, if there was no other reason; but you will see that a new man would have everything to learn when immediate action was required." He refused to leave even the implication of agreement with the accusations against Pemberton. "The distrust surprises me and is surely unjust. Try to correct it, for our country's sake." [39]

The situation in Mississippi was too insistent to be dismissed. Somewhere troops for reinforcements and a "new man" for the command had to be found. On May 9 the Secretary of War telegraphed Johnston to proceed at once to Mississippi and to take "chief command of the forces, giving to those in the field, as far as practicable, the encouragement and benefit of your personal direction," and to take "3,000 good troops" with him from the Army of Tennessee. Johnston had been ill for more than a month although both he and his doctor thought he was "improving slowly." As he told Wigfall, "I will decline no position . . . —however small—unless one inconsistent with my honor." That evening he replied to Seddon, "I shall go immediately, although unfit for field service." Bragg should have felt relief at his departure, but in a typical, disgruntled comment, he told Quintard, "Doctor, he was kept here to watch me too long." [40]

CHAPTER XV

OFF TO MISSISSIPPI

Accompanied by his personal physician Johnston left Tullahoma early on May 10. At a small way station just before reaching Jackson he received a message from Pemberton, who gave specific details about the enemy, then moving in heavy force toward Edwards Station, a point about halfway between Jackson and Vicksburg. Edwards, Pemberton stated, "will be the field of battle if I can carry forward sufficient force, leaving troops enough to secure the safety of [Vicksburg]."

At the Mississippi capital Johnston found everything in turmoil. An enemy force of around 25,000 was "looking toward" the city, and only two brigades of 6,000 Confederates were at hand to oppose it, with about twice that number on the way as reinforcements. As night enveloped the city in the midst of a heavy rain Johnston advised Richmond of the situation: "I arrived this evening finding the enemy's force between this place and General Pemberton, cutting off communication. I am too late."

But with no semblance of a defeated attitude he moved to make the best disposition he could of the scattered Confederate troops. He emphasized to Pemberton the opportunity to defeat the enemy in detail before Grant could effect a consolidation. If practicable Pemberton should strike the Federals at Clinton. "Time is all important," Johnston stressed. To insure delivery he sent three copies of the message by as many couriers.[1]

As a rainy dawn broke new intelligence came that the enemy was on the move toward Jackson from both Raymond and Clinton. Johnston immediately sent his two brigades, one down each road, to hold up the progress of the advancing Federals, while he gave orders to prepare for the evacuation of the capital. The townspeople abandoned business establishments and attempted to save personal belongings. Details loaded available railroad cars and other conveyances. All the trains but one, which Johnston held to accompany the troops, moved to the east across Pearl River.

West of the town Confederate pickets engaged the advancing Federals, but after a brief holding action the defending brigades retired into Jackson. Before the threat of the enemy Johnston withdrew northward for about seven miles. All day Johnston awaited word from Pemberton but to no avail. That night the Confederate commander again addressed his subordinate. He informed Pemberton of the day's events and asked, if Grant depended on the Mississippi, "Can you not cut him off from it, and above all, should he be compelled to retreat, beat him?" The experience of the past day or so had made Johnston more emphatic that dispersal was not an effective way to meet the enemy's superior force. "As soon as re-enforcements are all up," he wrote, "they must be united to the rest of the army. I am anxious to see a force assembled that may be able to inflict a heavy blow upon the enemy." To do that the whole army must be brought together. "If prisoners tell the truth, the forces at Jackson must be half of Grant's army. It would decide the campaign to beat it, which can be done only by concentrating, especially when the remainder of the eastern troops arrive. . . ." [2]

Circumstances intervened to make all Johnston's plans ineffectual. Pemberton received the message late in the afternoon of the sixteenth, two days after it was written, when it was impossible for him to follow instructions to move toward Jackson. Nor could an effort to cut Grant's supply lines with the Mississippi prove effectual, as the resourceful Union commander was not dependent on them.

As the three Federal corps under Sherman, McClernand and McPherson moved up the state from Grand Gulf, Pemberton had made no effort to concentrate against them. Leaving the scattered forces

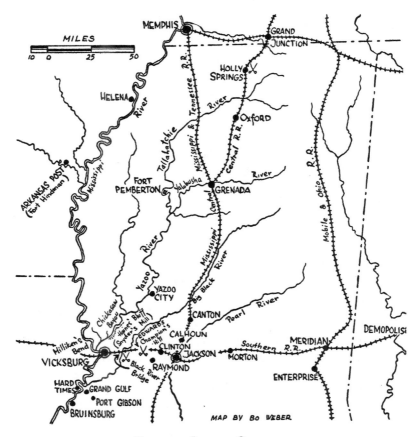

VICKSBURG-JACKSON CAMPAIGN

still in the Vicksburg area, he led about 18,000 men to Edwards. But
on the night of May 12 events caused Grant to change his plan.
When McPherson reached Raymond he encountered the Confederates, whom he drove toward Jackson. The easy victory convinced
Grant that he need fear no further about his communications so he
decided to turn toward Jackson. There he would stand between Pemberton and the expected reinforcements from the east and handicap
the arrival of Johnston who "was hourly expected [there] to take
command in person." [3]

After taking Jackson on the fourteenth Grant received unexpected help when one of the couriers, whom Johnston had sent with his first message to Pemberton, delivered it instead to McPherson. With that knowledge of Johnston's plan Grant moved at once to counter it by concentrating the troops of McPherson and McClernand at the little town of Bolton on the railroad east of Edwards. Sherman remained at Jackson to destroy what he could of value. He put detachments at work to burn manufacturing plants, the arsenal, and to damage the railroads. All accomplished their purpose effectively, particularly in the destruction of the bridge over the Pearl River which prevented from then on the movement of valuable railroad equipment from Mississippi to the east.[4]

Pemberton received Johnston's order to move against Clinton early on the morning of the fourteenth. He immediately replied, telling Johnston that he would "move at once with whole available force, about 16,000. . . . " He left approximately 10,000 Confederates and two brigades of Mississippi militia to protect Vicksburg and the crossings of the Big Black. "In directing this move," Pemberton said, "I do not think you fully comprehend the position that Vicksburg will be left. . . . "[5]

It was Pemberton who misunderstood, not only the plight of Vicksburg but the whole situation. In order to save the important river town his outnumbered army had to be kept mobile. It had to meet the Federals under more favorable circumstances than siege offered. One seemed present in the separation of the Federal forces, and had Pemberton moved promptly he would have found but one Federal division at Clinton. But he saw no further than the immediate physical possession of Vicksburg. By leaving forces to protect the river crossing at Big Black Bridge he disclosed either his intention to disregard Johnston's order or his misunderstanding of his superior's design. All the difficulties of his task rose to disturb him. If he moved as Johnston directed the enemy might slip behind him and take Vicksburg. He would then lose all for which he had contended.

The result was that he changed his mind and called a council of his general officers. He explained Johnston's order to them and countered it with his own views "strongly expressed as unfavorable to any advance which would separate me farther from Vicksburg which was my base." A majority of the generals approved the execution of Johnston's order, but a few thought that a better plan might be an attempt to cut the enemy's supply line, not realizing Grant was operating unconventionally without one. Pemberton's decision was to ignore the order of his superior and the will of the majority. He decided to operate to the south against Grant's supposed communications.[6]

To this blunder of disobedience, Pemberton added another, dilatoriness. Johnston had urged upon him the value of celerity of movement, but it was not until 5:30 P.M., after a long day of conference and indecision, that he finally got off another message, one which told Johnston of his new determination. It signified a further delay of about twelve hours. "I shall move as early tomorrow as practicable," he wrote, " . . . to cut enemy's communications and force him to attack me, as I do not consider my force sufficient to justify an attack on enemy in position or to attempt to cut my way to Jackson." [7]

This second message reached Johnston early the next day, May 15, before he received the first. It contained no mention of his orders and signified only that opportunity had slipped through his hands. Instead of the two armies being on the move toward a junction, they were proceeding in opposite directions. He immediately wrote Pemberton to that effect. "Our being compelled to leave Jackson makes your plan impracticable. The only mode by which we can unite is by your moving directly to Clinton, informing me, that we may move to that point with about 6,000." [8]

Still in the neighborhood of Edwards, Pemberton continued to display a reluctance to make any real movement away from Vicksburg. When the courier delivered Johnston's message of the fifteenth to him on the sixteenth, about thirty-six hours after he had written of his determination to attack Grant's communications, his army had moved a total of four miles. When he read Johnston's instructions to go to Clinton, he ordered a countermarch by way of Edwards and wrote Johnston that he would follow instructions. He detailed his route so that the two armies could make a junction, but in a postscript added an ominous note: "Heavy skirmishing is now going on in my front." [9]

The troops with whom Pemberton's men were engaged were the vanguard of Grant's gathering army. Although the Federal commander had maneuvered his forces with precision and daring, they were not in position to prevent Pemberton's carrying out the march he had outlined to Johnston. But instead of proceeding with a strong rear guard, Pemberton chose to make a stand along a small stream, Baker's Creek, and on Champion's Hill, a prominent knoll somewhat to the east of Edwards. There he waited for several hours for Grant's attack. On the wooded, irregular slopes, fighting continued for much of the afternoon of the sixteenth. The Union troops outnumbered the Confederates and finally a portion of the Southern line broke. In the retreat which followed, Loring's division was cut off from the main force and marched around the union flank toward Jackson. Pemberton with his depleted ranks retired westward to the Big Black Bridge, which the first division reached about 1:00 A.M. on the seventeenth. There the Confederates bivouacked for the night, having lost some 3,800 casualties and much of their artillery.

As Pemberton's troops fought this desperate, undesired action, Johnston anxiously waited at Calhoun, about fifteen miles north of Jackson. A reconnoitering party of cavalry discovered that Sherman, after destroying its major facilities, had evacuated Jackson. It was not until evening that Johnston received the message in which Pemberton stated his agreement to accomplish the junction of their forces. At 7:00 P.M. Johnston wrote again. He advised Pemberton that the enemy had given up Jackson and had moved out the road toward Clinton. "It was a matter of great anxiety to me to add this little force to your army," he wrote, "but the enemy being exactly between us, and consultation by correspondence so slow, it is difficult to arrange a meeting. I will take the route you suggest . . . if I understand it." [10]

While he waited at Calhoun for word from Pemberton, Johnston used the opportunity to urge forward the reinforcements from the east. Johnston evidenced determination to improve the situation in communications to Cooper and Seddon. He reported on the events of the previous three days and the difficulties he had encountered, and stated his intention to join Pemberton.[11]

Johnston then set out with his small command from Calhoun in the direction which from Pemberton's information would bring the two forces together. By late afternoon he had covered fifteen miles as the troops cautiously moved through the countryside. As their bivouac fires began to blaze, Johnston received a message from Pemberton, who had written it that morning and in it gave the events of the past few days. He said that he had received Johnston's order of the fourteenth to advance toward Clinton but had not obeyed it. "I deemed the movement very hazardous, preferring to remain in

position behind the Big Black and near to Vicksburg." After thus
disclosing the motive which dominated all his actions Pemberton
described the engagement at Champion's Hill and Baker's Creek.
But he was not sure of his position on the Big Black. "There are so
many points by which I can be flanked that I fear I shall be compelled to withdraw. If so, the position at Snyder's Mill [Haines' Bluff]
will also be untenable. . . . I have about sixty days' rations in
Vicksburg and at Snyder's." He concluded his message by saying,
ironically in view of what had happened, "I respectfully await your
instructions." [12]

From other sources Johnston soon had information that Pemberton
had quit his Big Black position. The Confederates destroyed the
bridge, but Pemberton still feared that Grant might move around
his flank to beat him to Vicksburg, and ordered an immediate retreat into its defenses. Johnston, still hopeful that he might save the
situation and unite the two Confederate forces, pointed to the obvious when he acknowledged receipt of Pemberton's dispatch of the
morning. He wrote:

> If Haynes' Bluff is untenable, Vicksburg is of no value, and cannot
> be held. If, therefore, you are invested in Vicksburg, you must ulti-
> mately surrender. Under such circumstances, instead of losing both
> troops and place, we must, if possible, save the troops. If it is not
> too late, evacuate Vicksburg and its dependencies, and march to
> the northeast.[13]

Johnston started his troops on the eighteenth to effect the junction,
but as he prepared to mount his horse a courier delivered to him a
second dispatch dated May 17 from Pemberton. This one was from
Vicksburg and contained the details of the action at the Big Black,
in which the Confederates "were forced from their positions, owing
to the demoralization consequent upon the retreat of yesterday."
The army was then in the entrenchments at Vicksburg and Pemberton hoped it could be speedily reinforced. He reported that he
had evacuated Snyder's Mill and had lost touch with Loring's division. Then as though to display again his consistent desire to avoid
battle in the open he said, "I greatly regret that I felt compelled to
make the advance beyond Big Black, which has proved so disastrous
in its results." His regrets were properly directed at himself, as he
was east of the Big Black, when Johnston arrived in Mississippi.[14]

Johnston telegraphed Richmond of developments and reported that he had intended personally to join Pemberton but it was then "impracticable and would be useless." He regretted that his physical condition had prevented the forced ride to Pemberton's troops "at any time after my arrival in Jackson." But he still refused to admit that the situation was hopeless. He planned to unite all available men and asked that reinforcements be hurried to him.[15]

Johnston proceeded on the march to the northwest still hopeful that he could accomplish something, but a courier met him on May 19 with a communication from Pemberton which confirmed his worst fears. Pemberton had written it the day before and in it discussed his actions and reasoning after receiving the order to evacuate Vicksburg. For the second time within a week in the face of his superior's orders he called a council of his subordinates and "asked the free expression of their opinions as to the practicability of carrying them out. The opinion was unanimously expressed that it was impossible to withdraw the army from this position with such *morale* and material as to be of further service to the Confederacy. . . . I still conceive it to be the most important point in the Confederacy."[16]

One portion of Johnston's problem was thus solved. He no longer needed to apprehend what Pemberton might do. Although Federal gunboats had demonstrated their ability to pass up and down the Mississippi, Pemberton chose to believe that Vicksburg still dominated the river. Despite Johnston's urgent pleas that troops were more important as a mobile force than shut up under siege, Pemberton had allowed them to be trapped. His great comfort was his belief that he acted as Davis would have him.

If Pemberton wished to rely upon the efforts of others to relieve the situation, Johnston was willing to assume his share of the responsibility. He told the commander in Vicksburg to hold out and that he was doing all he could "to gather a force which may attempt to relieve you." One portion of it could be troops under Major General Franklin Gardner, more than one hundred miles to the south at Port Hudson. Johnston ordered Gardner to march at once toward Jackson with all his munitions and field pieces. As the need for the movement of his own troops toward the northwest no longer existed, Johnston took them back to Canton, where he directed the reinforcements from the east to meet him.[17]

Grant also allowed no time to escape. His subordinates worked as a team with dispatch and ingenuity. Within a day his ingenious engineers spanned the Big Black with three bridges and by eight o'clock the morning of the eighteenth were crossing the stream. Early the next day, the Federals had completely invested Vicksburg.

At Canton some of the expected reinforcements began to join Johnston's little army. With them was a young Britisher, Lieutenant Colonel Arthur James Lyon Fremantle, who was touring the Confederacy. He offered Johnston a welcome relief from military problems. They discussed everything from historical personages to the immediate campaign. The soldier-writer was primarily interested in the personality and ability of the man he visited and recorded his impressions in his journal. Johnston, he noted, had a "calm, deliberate, and confident manner." He was very affable but had the "power of keeping people at a distance when he chooses, and his officers evidently stand in great awe of him." He possessed the "entire confidence of all the officers and soldiers under him," which confirmed an opinion Fremantle had earlier discovered in conversations with the civilian population as he traveled through the region. Some of the officers said that his reputation was inferior to that of no other Confederate general as a military leader.

Before he left Mississippi, Fremantle saw another side of Johnston, one which had won the admiration of the men of the artillery battery in the Peninsula campaign, when the general removed his coat to assist in moving a gun. With Fremantle and a member of his staff, Johnston left Canton on a locomotive to go to Jackson. On a stop to refuel, Johnston did not stand on his prerogative as a commanding general but worked so hard "as to cause his Seven Pines wound to give him pain." When a few miles before they reached Jackson, they discovered that the Federals had destroyed the track and they had to walk, he set out with a will and took the cloaks of all three, as Fremantle carried his saddlebags and the staff officer, the visitor's knapsack.[18]

In Jackson before farewells ended the pleasant interlude of Fremantle's visit, Johnston received the good news that more reinforcements were at hand. The increase in numbers was welcome but it did not solve the General's problems. His force was still too small to move against Grant with any chance of success, and was deficient in artillery and transport. Loring, after his escape from Baker's Creek, was even without such simple implements as cooking utensils. In fact, the new troops accentuated the shortages. The only accumulations of stores were in Vicksburg and Port Hudson. Wagons, horses, harness, rations, ammunition, all had to be collected from sources which were already overtaxed.[19]

But the primary problem was Vicksburg, where Pemberton too needed aid. On May 20 he wrote that he required musket caps and said, "An army will be necessary to relieve Vicksburg, and that quickly. Will it not be sent? Please let me hear from you if possible." The next day he repeated these imperative needs in four separate messages.[20]

Gardner too appealed for help from faraway Port Hudson on the twenty-first, a message Johnston received two days later. In it Gardner reported that a Union force from Louisiana was in his front and he needed reinforcements. Johnston repeated the order he had sent on the nineteenth to give up Port Hudson as of no value with Vicksburg under siege, and told Gardner: "You cannot be re-enforced. Do not allow yourself to be invested. At every risk save the troops, and, if practical, move in this direction." Here again disobedience of orders had been fatal, as by the time the courier bearing the second order reached the neighborhood of Port Hudson the Federals had placed it under tight siege and he could not deliver it.[21]

Only from Richmond could assistance come, so Johnston turned to Davis. The President first advised the army commander to do all possible in Mississippi and requested help from Governor Pettus. But Pettus with better knowledge of the desperate situation replied that militia and small bodies of reinforcements would be of little if any value. The new troops had to be strong enough to fight their way into Vicksburg. Davis called upon the army commanders for help, but only Bragg promised to send troops and he could spare but few. Beauregard had been unable to comply with all the first request because of the protests of the population in his area. Lee again recommended that he be strengthened for an aggressive move across the Potomac instead of sending men to Johnston, and the administration accepted his suggestion, with all hoping that the situation far away in Mississippi might be relieved.

But hopes could not answer Johnston's pressing need. Exclusive of the garrisons at Port Hudson and Vicksburg he had but 23,000 men to concentrate in Mississippi. Opposed to them Grant had 60,000. But Pemberton's "tenacity" gave Johnston confidence, and he told the President, "If the army can be organized and well commanded, we shall win."

Davis was pleased by Johnston's praise of Pemberton but began an argument about the number of reinforcements dispatched to Mississippi. He told Johnston that Richmond's figures totaled 34,000 instead of 23,000. The Secretary of War took up the issue and Johnston replied that all the Richmond figures were too large, "in reference to Beauregard nearly ten to six." The matter died hard and brought no evidence of the needed help. Seddon quenched hope when he concluded, "You must rely upon what you have and the irregular forces Mississippi can afford." [22]

As the Confederate commander worked in every way he could to secure an effective force with which to threaten the Federals, Grant drew an ever tighter ring of batteries and entrenchments around Vicksburg. The line was fifteen miles long and because Johnston stood as a threat to its rear, a second one was built, faced toward Jackson. Without request from Grant, Washington hurried reinforcements forward. Assistance came also from across the Mississippi, when Major General John M. Schofield, who had taken command in Missouri where things were quiet, decided that his only practical course was "to send all available forces to assist in the capture of Vicksburg and the opening of the Mississippi to the Gulf." Sherman gave the Federal evaluation of the circumstances in a letter to his wife. "We must work smart," he said, "as Joe Johnston is collecting the shattered forces, those we beat at Jackson and Champion Hill, and may get reinforcements from Bragg and Charleston and come pouncing down on our rear. The enemy in Vicksburg must expect aid from that quarter, else they would not fight with such desperation." [23]

CHAPTER XVI

JOHNSTON, PEMBERTON AND GRANT

As Grant tightened his hold on Vicksburg, Johnston's problems grew daily more difficult. The disparity between his and the Federal forces ever widened. Pemberton had warned that no effort to relieve the besieged town should be attempted without at least 30,000 to 35,000 men. Where they could be secured quickly enough was the paramount question.

Everyone, whether of official or private capacity, had ideas as to what should be done. Mississippians were desperate and insisted to Davis that he put all else aside and devote the full effort of the Confederacy to saving their state. Friends wrote Johnston and expressed full confidence in his ability to conquer the enemy. These opinions disturbed him more than they pleased him. He could see little hope unless Richmond sent him help, or the Federals made a serious mistake in generalship.[1]

Some with more knowledge of the actual circumstances wrote to sympathize with him and to warn him. Bragg said from Middle Tennessee:

I feel most acutely for you, general, in the position in which you find yourself. Great ends to be secured, high expectations formed, and most inadequate means furnished. How we can now see the folly of last spring's operations in diverting you from your aims. The men who were the real authors of that suicidal course will never be known for the harm they have done. They sit quietly and enjoy the exemption from responsibility, only awaiting another opportunity to criticise you or anybody else, and wisely say, "I told you so." God grant you what I almost fear to hope for—success. But whatever the result, general, I bear witness you are not responsible for the dangers brought upon us.[2]

Others were dubious about what Johnston might accomplish. Gorgas wrote in his diary that the country would never forgive the General if he allowed Vicksburg to fall without a struggle. Gorgas expressed the attitude which was already beginning to spread among the supporters of the administration. Wigfall wrote a former colleague in the Congress that he had no doubt that should disaster occur in Mississippi an effort to place full responsibility on Johnston would ensue. To the General himself Wigfall said that some of the Richmond newspapers, anticipating the possible loss of Vicksburg, had begun to charge him with the whole failure. "Let me warn you against Pemberton," Wigfall continued. "The moment he was whipped at Edward's Station he wrote to the President that he had made the fight against his judgment and under positive orders from you. The President will sustain Pemberton at your expense if possible. He must do so to sustain himself in placing an entirely untried man in command of so important an army. . . . Seddon is a fair man and your friend but will not quarrel with the President." The Texan hoped that Johnston would not protect Pemberton as he had Bragg, or assume any responsibility which was not justly his.[3]

Seddon showed the correctness of Wigfall's interpretation of his feeling when he wrote Johnston that though his lack of military knowledge and his removal from the actual scene prevented his giving useful advice, he assured the General of his "full appreciation and confidence, and cheer myself . . . by unabated reliance on your zeal, fertility of resources, and generalship." Later he was to forget his reluctance to offer military advice and attempt to inspire Johnston to abandon realistic caution and undertake a heroic attempt to assault the Federal might. "Rely upon it, the eyes and hopes of the whole Confederacy are upon you, with the full hope that you will act and with the sentiment that it were better to fail nobly daring than through prudence even to be inactive."[4]

Johnston in reply to Seddon's first letter expressed gratitude for the Secretary's expression of feeling but remarked that campaigns were not won by confidence in commanders. If Richmond had done all it could to build up his army, he would do his best with what he had, but victory under the circumstances was practically beyond hope. This brought from Seddon an inquiry about additional reinforcements from Bragg. "You as commandant of the department have power so to order, if you, in view of the whole case, so determine." [5]

The suggestion startled Johnston, who felt that he had been too long away from Tennessee to judge the situation there, where the Federals had forced Bragg out of his Tullahoma line. Johnston still held to the opinion that the decision to move troops from one active theater to another was more than a military one as it involved the possible abandonment of states. The responsibility for such a political choice necessarily rested with the government. But the most important revelation in the Secretary's message of June 8 was the statement that Johnston still commanded the whole department. In his reply the General expressed his surprise: "I have not considered myself commanding in Tennessee since assignment here, and should not have felt authorized to take troops from that department after having been informed by the Executive that no more could be spared." [6]

Johnston may have thought the matter was settled by this exchange of correspondence, but he did not count upon the literal-minded Davis. Promptly the President asked Johnston for the source of his belief that his command had been changed. In placating terms the General acknowledged that it was an assumption based on the letters of Davis of May 28 and Seddon, whom he included in the term, Executive, of June 5. The President was not satisfied with the explanation and refused to relinquish the argument. Instead he began to plan a comprehensive reply by a study of all correspondence between Richmond and Johnston from the time the General was ordered to Mississippi. But even while holding Johnston's attention to arguments which might well have rested until the campaign was decided, the President corresponded with commanders in Tennessee about the removal of that state from Johnston's command area. In a strange confession to Bragg on June 17 he said that as long as Johnston's attention was absorbed by Mississippi the existing command arrangement was unworkable. Despite it all no change occurred. [7]

Grant gave Johnston no relief while Richmond argued, nor did Davis' support of Pemberton physically aid the besieged. As the sultry days of June settled over Mississippi, couriers who tried to keep up contact between the two Confederate commanders found their path ever more difficult. Deliveries if made were sometimes five to seven days late, and no continuity of effort was possible. All suggestions and appeals for the help of Trans-Mississippi troops brought no results for want of communication, management and execution. But the basic tenor of the dispatches was clear: Pemberton's calls for relief grew more urgent, while Johnston's replies repeated that he did not have the force to dislodge Grant. Johnston offered to try to save the garrison with an effort which required "exact co-operation" from Pemberton, but the invested general distorted the plan to a diversion by Johnston during which the besieged troops could escape in a different direction.[8]

On June 23 Pemberton made a new proposal to Johnston, a plan of ridiculous aspect, to persuade Grant to allow the Confederates to walk out of Vicksburg scot-free. Pemberton naïvely said that Johnston could better undertake the negotiations. "You could make the showing of my ability and strength to still hold out for several weeks longer, which, together with his impression regarding your strength, might operate upon him to comply with your terms." Memories of Bragg's letter and Wigfall's warning undoubtedly occurred to Johnston as he read the fanciful appeal. But in his reply, which failed to get through, he merely said that all undertakings with Grant regarding the besieged army had to be made by Pemberton.[9]

Davis still ignored the need to make a choice among the geographical areas, the defense of which forced the division of the Confederate army into units inferior in strength to those they faced. But he continued to make efforts within that strategical concept to strengthen Johnston. He again asked Bragg and Beauregard if they could spare men for the purpose, but both felt they could not safely do so.[10]

On June 25 Johnston's army numbered 31,226 officers and men "present for duty." Of these 11,137 were in Mississippi under Pemberton's command when Johnston arrived from Tullahoma. Only 20,089 after all the correspondence and claims were reinforcements from other areas. Gathered in divisions under the command of Breckinridge, French, Loring and Walker, with a smaller unit of cavalry under W. H. Jackson, the little army, which was delayed past the dates Johnston hoped to make his move, marched westward toward the Big Black on the morning of June 29. In addition to the other equipment it carried food and wagons for the Vicksburg troops, and a floating bridge. The next day was the first anniversary of the Battle of Seven Pines. To Johnston even that dark day of blundering misfortune must have seemed bright by contrast with his experience in Mississippi.[11]

The divisions of French, Loring and Walker bivouacked between Brownsville and the Big Black north of the railroad on the evening of July 1. Breckinridge was some six miles to the south near Edwards, while Jackson's cavalry sought possible crossing places. For three long hot days infantry and cavalry reconnoitered the area and confirmed the evidence of scouts. The Federals had felled trees to block the roads while strong bodies of troops guarded the river. The Confederates found that the Federals had constructed a line of fieldworks which extended from the railroad to the Yazoo. From these observations and reports Johnston decided that it was impossible for him to move upon the enemy from the north as he originally planned and turned to attempt a way south of the railroad which some officers said was not so strongly protected.[12]

In Vicksburg civilians and soldiers alike watched anxiously for a sign of a relieving army. All were so convinced of the justness of their cause that they could not believe that it would fail. This was so evident in the townspeople's letters which the Federals intercepted that Grant wrote Sherman June 25, "Their principal faith seems to be in Providence and Joe Johnston." To alleviate circumstances somewhat Pemberton suggested the use of mule meat as an addition to their ration and was pleased by its reception. Its use must not have been widespread as within a few days an "Appeal for Help," signed "Many Soldiers," went to him. They said that they could not continue to fight on "one biscuit and a small bit of bacon" as their daily ration. "If you cannot feed us," the petition read, "you had better surrender us, horrible as the idea is, than suffer this noble army to disgrace themselves by desertion." [13]

As Johnston pondered what he should attempt to do, still without word from Pemberton since the message in which he suggested that Johnston treat with Grant, a courier reached his headquarters from the Vicksburg commander but without dispatches as he had feared capture and destroyed them. All that he knew was the date they bore,

June 28. Johnston did secure from him pertinent information about the worsening conditions among the besieged garrison and immediately wrote Pemberton that it was necessary

to create a diversion, and thus enable you to cut your way out, if the time has come for you to do this. Of that time I cannot judge; you must, as it depends upon your condition. I hope to attack the enemy in your front about the 7th, and your co-operation will be necessary. The manner and the proper point for you to bring the garrison out must be determined by you from your superior knowledge of the ground and distribution of the enemy's forces. Our firing will show you where we are engaged. If Vicksburg cannot be saved, the garrison must.[14]

Quiet enveloped Johnston's camps on July 4. No sound of artillery from Vicksburg broke the ominous stillness to remind listeners of the danger, fear and death to be found in the besieged town. Occasionally patrols encountered each other near or crossing the Big Black and the rattle of musketry echoed sharply and as quickly died. The main body of Johnston's army waited for the fateful order to resume its march toward Grant's circle of steel. General French says that it came the next day, but the army did not execute it because of the news from Vicksburg. On Sunday, July 5, word arrived that Pemberton had surrendered the day before.[15]

With the loss of the Mississippi fortress the reason for the Confederates' position near the Big Black no longer existed. To remain there might prove suicidal, as Grant could turn the whole weight of his force against them. Johnston quickly ordered a retreat to guard the vital rail center of Jackson. In the hot, dry weather the army marched along roads which were ankle-deep in dust. Wherever they observed water they polluted it by leading animals into it and killing them. Many small streams and ponds had dried up and they hoped that the acute shortage of water might prove a major hindrance to the Federal advance.[16]

As soon as the troops reached Jackson, Johnston placed them in the trenches to await the coming of the Federals, whom he expected to make an immediate assault because of the difficulty of supplying themselves with water. Pemberton had prepared the lines earlier that year, but the engineers had extended them to protect the flanks better after the first Union campaign in May. Johnston and French considered them "miserably located" and but slight obstacles to a vigorous assault. They ran from a position somewhat east of the Canton road on the north around the west side of Jackson and ended a short distance from the Pearl River on the southeast. Here Johnston's army stood in preparation for Sherman's expected attack.[17]

Johnston's order to move to Jackson was none too quickly given. Grant and Sherman had never left him out of their minds or plans. On July 3 when Grant told his subordinate of the possible surrender of Vicksburg the next day he added that when it happened Sherman should "drive Johnston from the Mississippi Central Railroad, destroy bridges as far as Granada [sic] with your cavalry, and do the enemy all the harm possible. You can make all your own arrangements and have all the troops of my command, except one corps. . . ."[18]

Grant's order to do the "enemy all the harm possible" contained a new Federal intention, one which went further than damage to the opposing army itself. Halleck had written Grant on March 31 that all hope for reconciliation between North and South had vanished and the Federal policy for conducting the war had consequently changed. In a letter to one of Grant's subordinates on May 13 Halleck explained the new policy as one of attrition: "We must live upon the enemy's country as much as possible, and destroy his supplies," the Union General-in-chief wrote. "This is cruel warfare, but the enemy has brought it upon himself." Except for the first brief foray against Jackson, the army was too busy with its immediate task to carry out Halleck's instructions, but as Grant's order to Sherman displayed, with the capture of Vicksburg the time had come to make a more intensive effort to accomplish it. Thus the Union forces initiated the realistic methods of modern, industrialized warfare and recognized that the people behind an army are as potent a morale and fighting factor as the army itself.[19]

The angular Sherman turned all his superabundant energy toward the accomplishment of his new assignment. Stand-by orders for a rapid, light march against Johnston and toward Jackson went out July 3, the same day as Grant's order to him. When definite news came of Vicksburg's surrender, Sherman wrote, "Already are my orders out to give one big huzza and sling the knapsack for new fields." Although somewhat more delayed than the commander expected by the double celebration of the victory and the Fourth, Sherman's army of approximately 50,000 men appeared before the Confederate lines at Jackson early on the morning of July 9.[20]

Instead of the attack the Confederates awaited, Sherman entrenched his men, constructed battery emplacements and made obvious preparations for a siege. From the surrounding hills he had a commanding position within easy artillery range of the Mississippi capital. He discovered that the civilian population had evacuated the place so he felt no compunction about making it "pretty hot to live in." At times there was spirited skirmishing between the two armies, but as soon as he could, the Federal commander ordered that the cannon of four batteries fire every five minutes day and night. Grant pressed his subordinate to action and offered more men. "I will send everything but one brigade and the convalescents," he said. But Sherman was well pleased with things as they were. He was satisfied that Johnston would receive no reinforcements and told Grant: "I think we are doing well out here, but won't brag till Johnston clears out. . . . If he moves across Pearl River and makes good speed, I will let him go. By a flag of truce today I sent him our newspapers . . . that, with our cannon tonight will disturb his slumbers." [21]

Sherman's early application of psychological warfare through the news stories in the papers and the noise of his cannon were not the only things which disturbed Johnston's sleep those hot July nights in Jackson. He had the disagreeable task of informing Richmond about the tragic climax at Vicksburg and the following events. An early report went in from one of his staff on July 5, and on the seventh Johnston gave more details, basing his account on information from an officer who left the surrendered town the day after its fall. The Federals would parole the garrison and allow their return to the Confederate lines with the officers retaining their sidearms and personal luggage. He also reported his own retirement to Jackson. [22]

On the next day Johnston repeated this information in a message to the Secretary of War and added that Pemberton had asked for supplies for 22,000 men to be collected at Jackson. The problem of this unarmed, paroled force created a number of questions which Johnston addressed to Cooper. "What shall be done with the men?" he asked. "They cannot remain in this department without great injury to us from deficiency of supplying them. Shall they go to their homes until discharged, or be distributed in regiments in their respective States? Can they be exchanged immediately for prisoners taken in the recent great Confederate victory?" [23]

There was nothing of irony in the last question. Such was the quality of communication that his belief in a victory by Lee at Gettysburg was but an indication of faulty information. He wished to arouse no further antagonism in Richmond than necessary, but he had no hesitancy where his own circumstances were involved. Davis continued to insist on an explanation of Johnston's interpretation of the status of his command, so on the fifth the General again attempted to clarify it:

The orders of the War Department transferring three separate bodies of troops from General Bragg's army to this, two of them without my knowledge and all of them without consulting me, would have convinced me had I doubted. These orders of the War Department expressed its judgment of the number of troops to be transferred from Tennessee. I could no more control this judgment by increasing the number than by forbidding the transfer. I regret very much that an impression which seemed to me to be natural should be regarded by you as a strange error.[24]

Davis had no time for argument then about this communication, although he refused to drop the matter. "The mistakes it contains will be noticed by letter," he said in reply to Johnston's effort to be tactful. He devoted his principal attention to the loss of Vicksburg and its garrison, and ignored every phase but one. The President said nothing about the inferiority in numbers or the inability to achieve co-operation with Pemberton. His telegram contained only bitter reproaches for Johnston himself. "Painfully anxious as to the result," he said, "I have remained without information from you as to any plans proposed or attempted to raise the siege. Equally uninformed as to your plans in relation to Port Hudson, I have to request such information in relation thereto as the Government has a right to expect from one of its commanding generals in the field." [25]

This communication was all too reminiscent of those of May 1862, when debate grew heated about plans to halt McClellan in the Peninsula. Johnston might well have wondered what merit there could be in a paper plan when necessity forced him by his weakness to seek some mistake by an opponent, who had every advantage of strength and equipment. All he did was to call attention to what is obvious from an examination of the correspondence. As Sherman drew closely up to the entrenched lines of Jackson with an army about double his in size on July 9, the Confederate commander telegraphed the President:

I have never meant to fail in the duty of reporting to the Executive whatever might interest it in my command. I informed the Secretary of War that my force was much too weak to attempt to raise the siege of Vicksburg, and that to attempt to relieve Port Hudson would be to give up Mississippi, as it would involve the loss of this point, and that the want of adequate means of transportation kept me inactive until the end of June. I then moved toward Vicksburg to attempt to extricate the garrison, but could not devise a plan until after reconnoitering, for which I was too late. Without General Pemberton's co-operation, any attempt might have resulted in disaster. The slowness and difficulty of communication rendered co-operation next to impossible.[26]

The Richmond authorities sought from Johnston the number of each rank surrendered at Vicksburg so they might arrange a speedy exchange. Later, Seddon asked that only "serviceable" men be included as the Confederacy held too few Federal prisoners to waste any in exchange for wounded or ill Southerners. Pemberton wanted instructions. His was the difficult task of holding the paroled men against the temptation to wander home or to desert. He thought a furlough for thirty days might have a good effect and requested permission to grant it. Johnston passed the suggestion on to Richmond and advised Pemberton to march his charges south of the railroad to Enterprise, near Meridian. Davis liked neither the destination named in Johnston's order nor the idea of the furlough. He changed the first to Demopolis, Alabama, and attempted to persuade Pemberton that he could hold the men by an appeal to their patriotism. A discouraging reply brought reluctantly from the President the authority for Pemberton to grant the furloughs at his discretion. Pemberton attempted to combine the President's idea with his own. He gave blanket authorization for furloughs and at the same time appealed to the patriotism of the soldiers for their prompt return to duty.[27]

While the correspondence among Richmond, Johnston and Pemberton was in progress, Pemberton reported to Johnston as Grant had instructed him. Johnston and his staff were sitting "on a cleared knoll" in the moonlight the hot night of July 13, according to one account. Discussion naturally developed about the siege and the efforts to relieve it. Pemberton remarked after learning the strength of Johnston's army that "it would have been folly to attack Grant with double the number," and one of his staff added that Grant's entrenched force "could have repulsed 100,000 men." The next morning Pemberton left to join his paroled army in its march across Mississippi.[28]

Whatever Johnston's feelings about Pemberton's attitude may have been he had no time to dwell upon them. His real problems continued to press upon him too greatly for that. "The importance of your position is apparent," Davis wrote him typically on July 11, "and you will not fail to employ all available means to insure success. I have too little knowledge of your circumstances to be more definite, and have exhausted my power to aid you." The President again attempted to enlist the assistance of Governor Pettus, who he hoped could rally the citizens of Mississippi to the desperate cause. In asking the state's executive about prospects, Davis also inquired about public opinion and said that he thought the Vicksburg garrison had done "its full duty." [29]

Assistance from Pettus, as Johnston knew from experience, was but another of Davis' forlorn hopes. A joint call from the governor and himself had brought only 176 men to the army. Johnston said no more, but French in his diary was much more critical of Pettus who, he said, "goes over the river at night to prevent being captured. He believes the main object of [Sherman's] expedition is to capture him." [30]

Sherman continued to exert pressure upon the Confederates at Jackson. He extended his lines to the Pearl River, while his skirmishers and artillery kept up a continuous fire. Johnston tried to distribute his force to defend the city, but he was gloomy about the prospects. Word came on the twelfth that Port Hudson had surrendered four days earlier, and Johnston informed Richmond that he feared he would also have to give up Jackson. The poorly planned works, the lack of supplies and the failure to receive assistance, all combined to make it impossible for him to withstand a siege.[31]

Johnston heard that a Federal force had moved north to turn his right flank and get in his rear, but he was more exercised by reports from his scouts on the fourteenth that heavy replenishments of artillery ammunition were on the way to Sherman. The Federal tactics were all too obvious. Sherman planned to use his overwhelming superiority in artillery to beat the Confederates into submission or, by reaching around them, to cut them off. Either required the abandonment of Jackson, but Johnston first attempted to intercept the ammunition train with his cavalry. He advised Richmond of the developments, that Sherman instead of attacking had started siege operations. "It would be madness to attack him," Johnston said. "In the beginning it might have been done, but I thought then that lack of water would compel him to attack us." [32]

When Johnston learned on the afternoon of July 16 that the cavalry had failed to arrest the movement of the ammunition to Sherman he realized that he had to give up Jackson. Because he feared that conclusion Congressman Ethelbert Barksdale, a close friend of the President, telegraphed Davis from Jackson: "Enemy are intrenching around our lines. Unless immediately otherwise directed, result may be easily conjectured." But Johnston again had no mind for heroics or for losing an army to the enemy by siege. He informed the President, "The enemy being strongly re-enforced, and able when he pleases to cut me off, I shall abandon this place, which it is impossible for us to hold." At the same time he asked Bragg, who had retired to Chattanooga from his Middle Tennessee position, to send if possible a large force of cavalry into Northeast Mississippi to protect against enemy raiding parties there and in Alabama. [33]

That night Johnston's men slipped away from Sherman. His orders were clear, specific and concise. He sent all army property and the sick and wounded eastward. Troops moved artillery by hand from the forward positions before limbering up so as to preserve the quiet and not provoke the curiosity of the Federals. Noiselessly brigade after brigade made their way safely out of the lines and away from Jackson without betraying their departure to the Union pickets. A few Confederates who slept heavily from weariness awoke the next morning to find their comrades gone. When later in the day they caught up with the army they brought the report that the evacuation had been successful, for when they left Jackson the Federals were still unaware of it. To the army the cost had not been high: 76 killed, 504 wounded and 24 missing. But the latter total grew greatly by deserters and stragglers on the long hot march, first to Brandon and then to Morton, about thirty-five miles east of Jackson. [34]

Johnston had gone but Sherman wasted no regrets. Instead of following the Confederates, he set about accomplishing Grant's orders to "destroy the Great Central Railroad north and south, and damage the enemy as much as possible." Already he had made a good start with the destruction of locomotive cars, shops and equipment as well as the rail line at Clinton, Brookhaven and other points. Sherman remained at Jackson but a few days, which he used to do more damage, particularly on the railroad, where he burned cars, equipment and ties, and twisted rails into distorted semblances of their former usefulness. He completed the task of removing at Jackson all war potentialities and left it well qualified for its later, desolate name, "Chimneyville." [35]

The Confederates might have saved some of this valuable equipment had Johnston been able to take it to safety across the Pearl River. Unfortunately the bridge over the stream remained in disrepair. The Federals had destroyed it in their first occupation of Jackson in May. When the Confederates returned to the city, the civilian authorities, who retained the responsibility for the railroad's operation, went to work to rebuild it but had not completed the task when Sherman's army arrived for the second time. As he could not carry the locomotives and cars to safety, Johnston ordered the destruction of some of them; Sherman wrecked others. The consequence was to create bitter criticism of Johnston by his enemies who charged the responsibility wholly to him. [36]

Grant's operations in Mississippi, free as they largely were of tactical and strategic errors, pointed up examples for both Union and Confederate armies to follow. In part his success was attributable to Washington, which had begun to learn the lessons that war demands trust and a flexibility of command and authority. Richmond, confronted as it was by greater problems, made no comparable advances in either understanding or administration. The only Southern accomplishment in Mississippi was Johnston's avoidance of the traps which the Federals laid for him. He exercised judgment throughout the campaign and refused to rush into rash positions, even though he early realized that the government wished to place him between it and its responsibility for the outcome. The extreme conservatism with which he used his relatively small army won him no new fame. What the result might have been had Pemberton obeyed his first order and moved to attack the Federal forces in detail, no one can say. [37]

Because of the failure in Mississippi—of the details of which few were informed—Johnston became the target for criticism, the scapegoat which the Confederate government so desperately needed in the dark days of July 1863. The defeat of Lee in Pennsylvania; the retreat of Bragg from Middle Tennessee; the loss of the great Mississippi; all combined to chronicle disaster. Events told visibly upon the Secretary of War, who the Rebel War Clerk said "looks today like a galvanized corpse which has been buried two months. The circles around his eyes are absolutely black." They could also be noted in the President's increased sensitivity and temper. "He is bitter against Johnston, as I judge from a single remark," Chief of Ordnance Gorgas confided to his diary. "When I said that Vicksburg fell, apparently, from want of provisions, he remarked: 'Yes, from want of provisions inside, and a general outside who wouldn't fight.' " [38]

CHAPTER XVII

PRESIDENTIAL REPRIMAND AND
REAPPOINTMENT TO COMMAND

As Johnston led his army east from Jackson, he received information that Tennessee was no longer part of his command. It is possible to interpret this order as a rebuke for the General's failure to save Vicksburg, but the acute situation in Mississippi and Bragg's long retreat to Chattanooga made obviously true Johnston's argument that to control such widely separated areas was impracticable. His new command consisted of the territory between the Georgia-Alabama line and the Mississippi River, from the Tennessee River to the Gulf of Mexico.

Johnston seemed to be in the shadows of the war and had little hope of commanding again in an important capacity. His small force could do no more than observe Grant and Sherman. "My purpose is to hold as much of the country as I can and to retire farther only when compelled to do so," he told Davis. Morale was at a low ebb among all elements. The Mississippi rail system was a chaotic tangle as a result of Sherman's application of sledge and fire. Moreover it led to a show of selfish interest which caused disputes between owners and government.[1]

Bureaucratic control of man power proved troublesome. As early as June 28, Johnston advised Seddon that conscription, which the bureau in Richmond administered, worked ineffectively in the three states—Alabama, Mississippi and Tennessee—of his district command and suggested that the War Department delegate to him the responsibilities. Richmond accepted the recommendation and assigned Pillow again to the task under him. Pillow established his headquarters in Georgia, outside the area of his activity, and went to work, expressing the hope that he would not a second time encounter conflict with the Richmond authorities.[2]

Pillow's hopes were no deterrent on his aggressive methods, which for a second time created trouble. Seddon explained that Pillow's conduct of the conscription law contained "graver difficulties" than generals in the field realized. "You look at it naturally with the almost exclusive view to the speedy recruitment of your army," the Secretary of War wrote Johnston, "and for that essential end do not hesitate with more haste and less formality of examination and allowance of exemptions than are allowed by law." Richmond had to keep legal procedures in mind and complaints about Pillow's actions, which some compared to that of a "press gang," were constant, even though he had achieved success by them.[3]

Pillow's enthusiasm shortly began to accentuate his difficulties with Richmond. He asked for more troops to bring in men and recommended the extension of his system over the entire Confederacy. But despite his obvious success Seddon continued to question his methods. In late September the Secretary emphasized that the right of reviewing appeals rested in the War Department. The exasperated Pillow wrote for Johnston's attention that this action made him only the "nominal superintendent, while in fact the business of the bureau is drawn to the War Office." When Seddon soon after ordered that he report to Richmond, Pillow informed Johnston that though his efforts were "daily adding 500 men to the different armies," the interference of the department in Richmond made it impossible for him to continue in his post.[4]

The unhappiness in the Confederacy over the fall of Vicksburg manifested itself in many ways. Some Mississippians who a few weeks before had asserted their positive allegiance to the Southern cause turned to the Federals in expedient capitulation. Adherents of the administration followed the President's lead and heaped a variety of animadversions on Johnston, whose supporters were no less critical of Davis and Pemberton.

As for the General himself he remained unaffected. He had long prepared himself for what might come. He knew that when he gave the order for Pemberton to evacuate Vicksburg, it would if obeyed ruin him with the government and the people. He might never be able successfully to vindicate his action, he told a Confederate official. He said in conclusion, "I was satisfied that the Confederacy could do without General Johnston, while I did not believe it could do without the veteran army under General Pemberton. . . ." [5]

It was a consistently held attitude, which he voiced particularly in letters to his wife. "Consciousness of doing my best manfully & loyally is worth a thousand times more than the favor of Governments & crowds," he emphasized. "For neither of the two last will I ever strive." He implored her to control her feelings and not to allow any idea of his "ruin [to] obtrude itself into your beloved heart." He had no fear but that eventually the country would "accord me the only reputation I have ever coveted—that of a brave, & honorable soldier, & disinterested Patriot." Her love was his "only strong hope. My life depends upon it. So love me & pray for me, for your prayers are worth a thousand times more than mine." [6]

Mrs. Johnston could not bring herself to be as tolerant as her "dear old soldier." From Montgomery she confided in Mrs. Wigfall: "I wish I could feel as indifferent to blame as he does but I can't. The idea of the country blaming him for his misfortunes keeps me disturbed." Nor were her feelings toward the "Royal Family," as she called the Davises, helped when her husband received a long letter in mid-July from the President. [7]

As the summer sun grew hotter in Richmond, Davis waxed even more bitter. Wigfall wrote Senator Clay of Alabama that the criticism of Lee after Gettysburg had created increased resentment in the President, who was denouncing Johnston

in the most violent manner . . . & attributing the fall of Vicksburg to him & to him alone, regretting that he had been sent to the West & accusing himself of weakness in yielding to outside influence etc. His opinion of Johnston had undergone no change. His utter want of capacity he had always known etc. Has it ever occurred to you that Davis' mind is becoming unsettled? No sane man would act as he is doing. I fear that his bad health & bad temper are undermining his reason & that the foundation is already sapped. God knows what is to become of us with such a man at the head of the government.[8]

The editor of the *Examiner* did not hesitate to speak openly and ironically on July 10 about rumors which were heard around Richmond. "No one here is yet acquainted with the circumstances which attended and preceded the fall of Vicksburg," he wrote, "but the blame is Johnston's. He did it—Who can suppose, even for a moment, that the fortunate, victorious, heaven-born Pemberton could have done the wrong?" [9]

Editor Pollard was possibly acquainted with the Richmond gossip that Davis was preparing a long, critical letter to Johnston. In faraway Charleston Beauregard heard of a "bill of accusation" as early as July 1, but it was not until July 15 that Davis was sufficiently satisfied with his accumulation of material to sit down and write it formally. In detail he examined the orders and letters between Richmond and Johnston to restate his insistence that no change had occurred in the extent of Johnston's command after Seddon had sent him to Mississippi in May. He insisted that Johnston still retained command over Bragg as well as Pemberton. In his conclusion Davis granted that circumstances had made his argument an academic one, but he could not leave Johnston's effort at an explanation unanswered.

Now that Vicksburg has disastrously fallen this subject would present no pressing demand for attention, and its examination would have been postponed to a future period, had not your despatch of the 5th inst. with its persistent repetition of statements which I had informed you were erroneous, and without adducing a single fact to sustain them, induced me to terminate the matter by a review of all the facts. The original mistakes in your telegram of 12th of June would gladly have been overlooked as accidental, if acknowledged when pointed out. The perseverance with which they have been insisted on has not permitted me to pass them by as a mere oversight, or by refraining from an answer to admit the justice of the statements.[10]

An officer traveled from the capital with the document and handed it to Johnston at Mobile where he joined Mrs. Johnston for a few happy but troubled days. Upon returning to Montgomery she wrote a startlingly frank and revealing letter to Mrs. Wigfall, whom she told that she had seen her "ain, ain dearie" for the first time in several months. "I think my old soldier shines brighter when clouds are blackest above him," she said. "Certainly I found myself continually thinking when with him, there is sure something grand in your character." She explained that he was looking well and was in "tolerable spirits, as cheerful as if Jeff was throwing rose leaves at him, instead of nettles and thorns." [11]

She then told Mrs. Wigfall about the communication from Davis, "a letter of 15 pages of such insults as only a coward or a woman could write. I wish it could be published along with his pious proclamations." As she thought about it, it seemed difficult to believe. "Imagine," she exclaimed to her friend, "in times like these a President writing 15 pages of rebuke to an officer commanding an army. . . . " When she finished reading it, she "implored" her husband to resign. It was impossible, she said, "for him to aid the cause when Mr. D. has those feelings." But her efforts were of no avail. "The Gen. says," she wrote, " 'No indignity from Davis could drive him from the service. He is not serving him, but a people who have never been anything but kind to him.' "

"I feel now nothing can make me forgive either of [the Davises]," she wrote. "When I looked at my dear old husband's gray head & careworn face & felt how many of those tokens of trouble that man and woman planted there, I could almost have asked God to punish them." But her chief anger was directed at the President. "It is not this war that has broken up my home & almost my heart but the vengeance of one wicked man. . . ." Yet it was not unexpected to her; for when her husband was making his plans to leave Washington, she reminded him that he would have to work with Davis: ". . . he hates you, he has power & will ruin you—and the same old reply, 'he can't, I don't care, my country.' " Mrs. Johnston feared Mrs. Wigfall would think her "no patriot," but she was nearly frantic. "These things make me so unhappy," she said, "that sometimes I am almost wild & have no one I can express myself to. You have made me feel that not in pleasant hours but in trial you are ever ready to hear me." [12]

At his headquarters in Morton, where he returned when he completed his inspection of the defenses at Mobile, Johnston discussed Davis' letter with his staff. Colonel Ewell reports that the General was "so disgusted" that he was inclined "to give up the fight," and it was only after the members of his "military family" argued with him that Johnston wrote a reply. Dated August 8, it was, Johnston said, the longest letter he ever wrote. Completely documented and reasonable in tone it answered even some of the minor allegations in Davis' longer communication and thereby caused Davis to charge that Johnston had introduced extraneous matters into the argument. At the start Johnston asked the President "to reconsider" his charges, particularly that of misapprehending the order which sent him to Mississippi. It had "no practical results" upon the exercise of his "military functions" and had even been corrected by the Secretary of War before it was noted by Davis. "Had I received a copy of your orders of May 22d, directing General Bragg to send troops from his army to Mississippi, my error would have been corrected then; but it was not sent to me, and I have its evidence for the first time in your letter." As for the "repetition and persistence," with which Davis charged that he had tried to maintain his position, Johnston pointed out that all his communications were in response to messages he received, answers which were "dictated by the respect" he owed the Executive.

One of Davis' major points rested on the fact that Johnston while at Tullahoma ordered cavalry from Mississippi to Tennessee, an obvious attempt to draw the parallel that Johnston had not interpreted his assignment to Tullahoma as removing his authority over Mississippi. Johnston either did not see or avoided the fundamental weakness of Davis' contention. The President had objected at the time to the movement from Mississippi to Tennessee. Why assume that a movement from Tennessee to Mississippi would not be equally objectionable? Instead of this argument Johnston explained his action in terms of the military situation and went on to analyze at length the weaknesses of his geographical command and to deny the President's charge that he had "abandoned" his duties.[13]

When Johnston wrote to Wigfall about the exchange of letters, he explained that it was partly because of Mrs. Johnston, "who apprehends that the whole power of the government is preparing to overwhelm me." He confessed that he could not comprehend "how, when the army north of the Potomac was in so doubtful a position & the fragment here in Mississippi was invested in Jackson, the head of the government could find time to write such a letter on such a subject." He pointed out to Wigfall that Davis' argument and the tone of his letter combined "to prove ill feeling towards me—for which certainly I have given no cause."[14]

The unfortunate relations between the President and one of the important military leaders could not be kept quiet. In fact, knowledge of their differences was so widely prevalent that Colonel Harvie of Johnston's staff ventured to call upon the President's brother to use his influence to keep them from "leading to results injurious to the service and prejudicial in the last degree to the vital interest of the Republic. . . . " Already the issue had reached the press and was being argued "with too much warmth" by others. Harvie felt justified in doing his best to secure an adjustment of the difficulties, not only for patriotic reasons but because of his personal regard for both men. If the two but thoroughly understood each other, Harvie suggested, there "would be no reason for the unhappy feelings" which according to rumor existed. He assured Colonel Davis that in all his close association with Johnston "I have never heard one word escape his lips savoring of any want of personal regard for the President. On the contrary he has repeatedly expressed anxiety that their relations should be kind and cordial." If the President had heard the opposite, it came from "mischief-makers and meddlers—I may add calumniators." [15]

What happened to this effort to adjust the difference between the two is unknown. It had grown to far larger proportions than "the cloud, then 'no greater than a man's hand,' " which General Richard Taylor had seen in the fall of 1861, when on a mission of similar reconciliation. Not only had the President determined to make no effort to establish better relations with Johnston but he actively began to throw his support to those who assumed the position of Johnston's enemies. First among them was Pemberton, who saw the best opportunity to clear his own responsibility for Vicksburg in an aggressive effort to place the blame on Johnston.[16]

A letter which Davis read in several newspapers gave new impetus to his anxiety about Pemberton's ability to clear himself of responsibility for the outcome in Mississippi. A member of Johnston's staff had written it to a friend who had allowed others to see it. Johnston minimized its importance, but Davis used it to urge Pemberton to write a full report promptly. Pemberton agreed but asked the President if he didn't think that he should request a court of inquiry. Davis replied that he had ordered the court and hoped that it would "develop the real causes of events and give to the public the means of doing justice to the actor." [17]

It was not until August 17 that Johnston learned of the court of inquiry, although the orders called for it to convene in Montgomery on the fifteenth or as soon thereafter as possible. At his request Richmond authorized his presence and assigned his command for the period to Lieutenant General Hardee. The General had no fear about the decision as the facts were so overwhelmingly in his favor although he had no doubt but that the intention in calling the court was "to find something in my conduct" which would give an opportunity for criticism.[18]

The government changed the arrangements for convening the court, and it was not until September 2 that Johnston left Mississippi for Atlanta, where the hearing would be held. But when he arrived in the Georgia city he found that Richmond had called off the proceedings. Troubled, he wrote Wigfall that he was greatly disappointed by the indefinite adjournment. "I cannot, in any other way, show the position I have occupied—& how completely my military opinions were disregarded in relation to what was called my command. I am particularly anxious to bring out the President's letter of July 15th . . . & one received yesterday. . . . "[19]

The letter Johnston had just received was the President's reply to the General's defense against the long "bill of indictment." In it Davis held tenaciously to all his earlier contentions and stated that Johnston had brought in extraneous arguments in the attempt to build his case. Although he magnanimously wrote, "I cheerfully accept your admission of your 'misapprehension,' " and thus ignored that Johnston had said as much to Seddon before Davis took up the issue, the President chidingly remarked that he hoped "it may have been unattended with any ill consequence, as you assure me it affected your military course in no way." [20]

This letter angered Johnston who called it the "coolest piece of impudence I ever read," but other matters diverted his attention. He had just read in a newspaper that Pemberton, contrary to usual military custom, had filed his report direct with Richmond. In addition he learned of some articles in the *Richmond Sentinel* which he sensed were based on information from the War Department. He wrote immediately to Cooper for a copy of Pemberton's report and renewed his request for it as necessary to the preparation of his own when it was not forthcoming. He asked Wigfall to send him copies of the *Sentinel* as he wished to practice a "little retaliation" for the treatment Davis had shown him after the press had carried the letter written by one of his staff. For that Davis had written him two letters with the intention of making him "very uncomfortable. I want to take the same ground—& appeal to him for protection against his organ and the War Dept." [21]

Wigfall furnished the articles and confirmed Johnston's belief of the source of the information. He had also learned of Pemberton's report from Seddon and insisted that Johnston in his should answer in detail the charges Pemberton made. Failure to do so would be unfair to himself and those who upheld him. As to calling off the court of inquiry Wigfall was not surprised. "You probably explained too clearly the strength of your case & in its strength is [Davis'] weakness. Davis will not willingly let the world know that the troops were removed from Bragg's Army before the battle of Murfreesboro against your advice & by his order & that your advice was not followed as to the union of Holmes & Pemberton." [22]

Wigfall's interpretation of the reason for the suspension of the court was not entirely correct as military affairs in Tennessee had reached such a crisis as to make the hearing impracticable. As early as August 1 Richmond had asked Bragg if he could not turn from his long retreat to Chattanooga and attack Rosecrans, if most of Johnston's army could join him. Bragg rejected the suggestion and explained his decision to Johnston:

To "fight the enemy" is a very simple operation when you have the means and can get at him. But with less than half his strength and a very large river and 50 to 100 miles of rugged, sterile mountain, destitute even of vegetation, between you and him, with our limited commissariat, the simple fighting would be a refreshing recreation. This being the only conclusion at which I can arrive, the defensive seems to be our only alternative and that is a sad one. [23]

Within a few weeks Bragg called for help from Johnston to withstand Rosecrans' forward movement. Johnston carefully requested Richmond's approval for the transfer and received orders to aid the Army of Tennessee "as far as you are able." At once he informed Bragg that he was sending two divisions although it would leave him with only 8,700 infantry to man his whole department. Bragg soon called for more and Johnston complied with two additional brigades but he emphasized that these and the earlier units were on loan and should be returned as quickly as need permitted. [24]

Johnston was hopeful about the outcome in Tennessee as he observed that the War Department seemed finally to have accepted the principles of concentration for which he had long contended. In the quiet which followed Gettysburg, Richmond ordered Longstreet with a major part of his corps to Bragg. Thus troops from Virginia as well as Mississippi were on their way to join the Army of Tennessee for battle. Johnston was not so optimistic about his own future: "The temper exhibited toward me," he wrote Wigfall, "makes it very unlikely that I shall ever again occupy an important position." [25]

When word came that Bragg had defeated Rosecrans in the bloody contest along Chickamauga Creek, Johnston wired congratulations. He was pleased as this turn of Confederate events appeared to justify his confidence in Bragg and underscored the value of concentration. But Bragg let all realization of complete victory slip through his hands by besieging the Union army in Chattanooga instead of instigating an aggressive pursuit. With the example of Vicksburg fresh before them, Washington immediately sent orders for Hooker in Virginia and Sherman in Mississippi to move to Chattanooga.

When Johnston received word of Sherman's movement, he planned what cavalry opposition he could and secured the approval of Richmond to raid in Bragg's department. The troops were given two objectives, to hinder the Federal advance to Chattanooga and to interrupt railroad communications. One unit almost secured fame by encountering the train on which Sherman himself rode, but the Federal general escaped capture. The main party in Sherman's words "settled down like a swarm of bees" to tear up the track as fast as the Northerners could restore it. Although these efforts upset the Union schedule by creating delay troops got through and the Federal build-up of strength continued. [26]

Bragg's inactivity after Chickamauga led to a revival of his difficulty with his subordinates, which this time brought Davis himself for an investigation. Pemberton traveled with the President who had hopes of finding a place for him with the Army of Tennessee. Although Bragg was agreeable the temper of the army was different. Davis wisely did not press the case for Pemberton and called a meeting of the generals to discuss the more important reason for his visit. He asked each to give his opinion about the army commander who was also present. One by one they stated the conviction that

Bragg "could be of better service elsewhere. . . . " On the next day the President met privately with Longstreet and offered him the command of the army, but Lee's corps commander felt forced to decline. Instead he recommended that Johnston receive the responsibility. The "suggestion of that name," Longstreet said, "only served to increase [Davis'] displeasure, and his severe rebuke." Emotions ran high and Longstreet offered his resignation, but Davis would not hear of it. As the sun disappeared behind Lookout Mountain the conference ended. "The President walked as far as the gate," Longstreet noted, "gave me his hand in his usual warm grasp, and dismissed me with his gracious smile; but a bitter look lurking about its margin . . . admonished me that clouds were gathering about head-quarters of the First Corps even faster than those that told the doom of the Southern cause." [27]

Longstreet was not alone in his desire to have Johnston in command. Bragg's chief of staff, Brigadier General W. W. Mackall, watched developments closely and repeatedly reported opinion in the army to his wife. "If Mr. D. would send [Johnston] here, his presence here would be worth ten thousand men to this army, but [Davis] won't see with his eyes. With an empire at stake and the happiness of the whole people, he will indulge like a spoiled child his prejudices," he wrote shortly after Chickamauga. As Mackall gloomily foresaw, the President decided to retain Bragg and, shortly after, left for a tour of Alabama and Mississippi.[28]

By contrast with the weighty decisions the Vicksburg campaign had demanded Johnston's duties consisted of unimportant if vexing details. He and Mrs. Johnston lived at Meridian in "almost a peace establishment," as he described it to Wigfall, and Mrs. Johnston wrote the Senator's wife that existence was simple and happy in their "little cabin." She even had time to talk about clothes and an opportunity to secure them. Her conscience bothered her a bit about it, but she excused herself by believing that "little frivolities help us to bear the ills that are." Such agreeable life proved of short duration, for the General as though frustrated by his narrow duties decided to move his headquarters and residence to Brandon, nearer to the enemy. Mrs. Johnston explained that he "imagines he will smell powder there," but regardless she would go with him happy to be in his company.[29]

In this relatively quiet period the General prepared his report on operations in Mississippi from the time of his arrival, May 13, until the evacuation of Jackson, July 16. He dated it November 1 and did not send it to the War Department until three weeks later. He described fully his movements, orders and relations with Pemberton and concluded his report with a direct reply to the report of his subordinate. He pointed out that his orders to concentrate and to attack Grant upon the Federals' crossing of the Mississippi were "neglected" and that others were "disobeyed." He denied that his instructions compelled Pemberton to make the disastrous move east of the Big Black, as Pemberton said. Johnston stated:

> Before I reached Jackson and the order was given, General Pemberton made his first advance beyond (east of) the Big Black to Edwards Depot. After the receipt of the order, in violation of it, he made his second and last advance from that point to the field of Baker's Creek. He further claims that this order caused the subversion of his "mature plans." I do not know what these plans were, but am startled to find "mature plans" given up for a movement in violation of my orders, rejected by the majority of his council of war, and disapproved (as he states) by himself.

Never before had Johnston so bluntly charged a subordinate with failure, but Pemberton's endeavor to evade responsibility exasperated him so that he made it as emphatic as he could.

> It is a new military principle that, when an officer disobeys a positive order of his superior, that superior becomes responsible for any measure his subordinate may choose to substitute for that ordered; but had the battle of Baker's Creek not been fought, General Pemberton's belief that Vicksburg was his base rendered his ruin inevitable. . . . His disasters were due not merely to his entangling himself with the advancing columns of a superior and unobserved enemy, but to his evident determination to be besieged in Vicksburg, instead of maneuvering to prevent a siege.

Johnston apologized at the end of his report for the amount of detail and the "animadversions upon the conduct of General Pemberton," but the latter's report and his method of filing it required that it be answered. Johnston had no other recourse but "to show that in his short campaign General Pemberton made not a single move in obedience to my orders and regarded none of my instructions, and, finally, did not embrace the only opportunity to save his army—that given by my order to abandon Vicksburg." [30]

Before the bearer of Johnston's report had reached Richmond, the War Department began to receive alarming messages from Bragg about the situation at Chattanooga. Although the Confederate position along Missionary Ridge and the sides of Lookout Mountain seemed impregnable, faulty tactical arrangements and heavy Federal concentration overcame the natural advantages. On November 23, 24 and 25, Grant, Thomas, Sherman and Hooker convincingly defeated Bragg's army and made of Chickamauga a barren victory. Bragg saw no fault in his own conduct; it rested with the men. As he confided to Johnston, the loss in artillery was "very heavy . . . in men, very small. The disastrous panic is inexplicable." Understandable or not, the defeat left Bragg but one course. Davis had sustained him over the objections of his subordinates too short a time before. With morale at its lowest ebb, he put the army in motion toward Dalton, Georgia, where, removed from its powerful, victorious foe, it might have time to replenish and recuperate for another struggle. Then, on November 29, Bragg requested to be relieved of his command.[31]

Even Davis realized that hope of holding Bragg longer in charge of the Army of Tennessee was gone, so Richmond the next day ordered Hardee to assume the post, as the "officer next in rank and now present for duty." Bragg advised Johnston of developments on December 2, the day he relinquished the command. The enemy gave up the pursuit at Ringgold, about eighteen miles southeast of Chattanooga, he reported, and then in strange contradiction of his earlier statements said, "We are in good condition, with plenty of artillery." He was optimistic about the future, which was "pregnant with great events, but I believe our destiny is safe with prompt and united action." [32]

Bragg's retirement from command met with little disapproval, but it came too late to relieve Davis. On November 25 before the news of the debacle at Chattanooga was known, War Clerk Jones noted: "To us it *seems* as if Bragg has been in a fog ever since the battle of the 20th of September. . . . If disaster ensues, the government will suffer the terrible consequences, for it assumed the responsibility of retaining him in command when the whole country (as the press says) demanded his removal." On the next day he recorded rumors of dissension in the Cabinet a majority of whose members favored Bragg's removal.[33]

The resignation of Bragg quieted any developing Cabinet crisis, although the fact of his failure after all the warnings about his incompetency was another confirmation of the growing belief that the President was incapable of judging the capacity of his subordinates. As a consequence, the choice of Bragg's replacement became a matter of great interest. When Hardee as the senior general officer present succeeded to the command he protested to Cooper that he accepted it only as a temporary assignment. Davis offered the post to Lee, who declined consideration unless the intention was to make it his permanent command.[34]

By this time discussion had become general about a leader for the Army of Tennessee, and opinion gradually centered upon Johnston. Throughout the West enthusiasm for him never flagged, and Mrs. Chesnut noted that her husband reported to the President "that every honest man he saw out West thought well of Johnston." She added that "whether advancing or retreating, [he] is magnetic . . . and draws the good will of those by whom he is surrounded." But he had no such fortune with Davis. As a close friend of the Davis family, she doubtless knew the President's feeling, but she had no way to secure similarly accurate knowledge of the attitude of Johnston. Yet she went on to say that the General's "hatred of Jeff Davis amounts to a religion. With him it colors all things. . . . " A reading of Johnston's extant private correspondence does not bear her out. It contains evidence of Johnston's resentment but nothing of the bitterness she described.[35]

Officers in the Western command confirmed Chesnut's findings about Johnston's popularity. Mackall reported it to Johnston himself and Polk wrote again to the President that "General Joe Johnston is the person to whom you should offer that command." On the same day that Polk wrote his letter to Davis, the Congress listened to a message from the President. He included mention of the recent failures at Chattanooga, which he charged to a lack of valor on the part of the troops. This was too much for Representative Foote of Tennessee, who not only took issue with the President's charge but accused him of responsibility for the defeat. It was not cowardice on the part of the Army of Tennessee which lost the battle of Missionary Ridge but the "gross misconduct" of the President, who kept his favorites in important positions and practiced "partialities and prejudices, which, if persisted in longer, will prove fatal to our cause." [36]

Foote then turned to the more disputed question of Vicksburg, and introduced a resolution to examine the causes of the disaster there. It called for all orders and correspondence between the government and Johnston for May, June and July. Johnston saw a notice of its passage in a newspaper and immediately wrote Wigfall that the period covered by the requested correspondence was insufficient. The campaign for Vicksburg actually began in December 1862 and his connection with it started as soon as Richmond sent him to the West. A complete collection and publication of the correspondence would justify him entirely "in the opinions of all thinking men." [37]

Determined to keep the fire of his attack alive Foote introduced a new resolution that the President be requested to displace all commanders who did not possess the confidence of the army and the people. In supporting it he turned to other phases of the military administration: "But why," he asked, "is Johnston not appointed? Why is not Beauregard? Why is [the Army of Tennessee] left so long without a permanent commander? . . . The country is tired of the delay and every moment becomes more and more perilous." [38]

The administration found a ready defender in another Tennessee Congressman, William G. Swan, who read into the record the order under which Johnston went to the West. He used the old argument that Johnston had authority to supplant Bragg as commander of the Army of Tennessee and quoted extracts from Johnston's letters to the President as the reason for the retention of Bragg. Foote welcomed the intervention of Swan, and congratulated the President upon finding a champion. He "rejoiced to meet the issue now propounded," but its use puzzled him, as "ungenerous and unmanly," as it was obviously based upon "*garbled* extracts" from Johnston's correspondence.[39]

Wigfall was, of course, busy in Johnston's behalf. He met with Seddon and other friends in the Secretary's room. In writing of this meeting to Johnston Wigfall said ironically that he sat quiet until called upon

because I did not approve, my opinion being that you should not be sent unless they wish disaster. Desiring success . . . it would be better to send Pemberton who would be supported and sustained by the President & who might in spite of his incompetency not prevent a victory. I was satisfied that if you were sent every effort would be made to produce your defeat." [40]

Wigfall was not alone in suspecting that Davis, should he appoint Johnston, would attempt to place difficulties in the General's way. Beauregard expressed a similar opinion to Congressman Miles of South Carolina. "I think gross injustice is done by the administration and its entourage to General Johnston," Beauregard wrote. "They have never given him an opportunity to show his true metal; they have tied a leaden weight to his feet, and then told him to see what he could do in a deep, rapid stream!" After remarking that they had tried the same scheme with him Beauregard concluded by asking "who in the world can accomplish anything, either for himself or the country, in despite of Government power and influence?" [41]

Although Seddon was somewhat disappointed by what he called Johnston's "absence of enterprise" in the Mississippi campaign, he advocated Johnston's appointment. At the Cabinet meeting in which the important matter of the commander of the Army of Tennessee was decided, Seddon proposed Johnston but met with opposition, particularly from Benjamin. The then Secretary of State said that when he was Secretary of War he had found in Johnston "tendencies to defensive strategy and a lack of knowledge of the environment. . . . " Davis and some of the other members agreed with Benjamin, but as the discussion continued no general received sufficient support for the appointment. Gradually the sentiment of the meeting turned to Johnston, until according to Seddon's account a majority of the Cabinet recommended him, and the "President after doubt and with misgiving to the end, chose him, and not as due exaltation on this score, but as the best on the whole to be obtained." [42]

Seddon gave no credit for the appointment to Lee, but others were sure of his place in it. Mrs. Chesnut stated briefly, "General Lee had this done," and Wigfall emphasized Lee's part in winning Davis' reluctant approval. "Genl. Lee came to Richmond at once &—you were appointed," he wrote Johnston. "You owe your appointment to Genl. Lee & doubtless fully appreciate his kindness."

The President advised Johnston on December 16 of his new

responsibility and told him that he would find his instructions at the headquarters of the Army of Tennessee. Johnston was in the field on an inspection tour. He hastened home, turned the command of the Army of Mississippi over to Polk as directed, and arranged his affairs preparatory to the move. Mrs. Johnston was torn between regret and pleasure. She realized that the task meant a resumption of active campaigning and separation, but at the same time she rejoiced that her husband's punishment was over and that the efforts of his friends had "untied his hands." On December 22 Johnston entrained for North Georgia.[43]

The last months of 1863 had been a time of growing disillusionment within the Confederacy and a dark period in the career of Johnston. The voice of public dissatisfaction with the course of affairs grew louder and louder, and Davis afforded the dissidents a rallying point by his treatment of Johnston. Johnston was aware of it and had grave concern about it. Wigfall repeatedly assured him that those who supported him were his friends and not just the President's enemies. Mrs. Chesnut interpreted their interest differently. At the end of 1863 she said that there were "politicians and men with no stomach for fighting, who find it easier to cuss Jeff Davis and stay at home than to go to the front with a musket. They are the kind who came out almost as soon as they went into the war, dissatisfied with the way things were managed. Joe Johnston is their polar star, their redeemer."[44]

Committed as wholeheartedly and uncritically as she was to the support of Davis, Mrs. Chesnut had no idea as to the real reasons behind the dissatisfaction or how widespread it was. She made no distinction between constructive effort and carping criticism. But her principal failure was in her inability to understand that if Johnston's name had become a rallying point for Davis' opposition, the responsibility rested with the President not Johnston.

CHAPTER XVIII

DALTON REALITIES AND
RICHMOND VIEWS

On the way from Mississippi to North Georgia Johnston noted the improved facilities at Atlanta. Since summer engineers had been at work on the defenses of the town to make it an "admirable base," upon which the Army of Tennessee at Dalton depended. From it to the Army the state-owned Western & Atlantic was the only rail route, and as quickly as possible the General stepped aboard one of its trains for the last stage of his tedious, inconvenient journey. On the morning of December 27 he assumed command of a dispirited army of around 42,000.[1]

Dalton like Atlanta and Chattanooga was a rail center, although of much smaller proportions. There the Western & Atlantic turned northwestwardly to penetrate the parallel ridges which interrupted the landscape toward Chattanooga and gave it the rough appearance of a gigantic washboard. About four miles from Dalton the rugged, difficult Rocky Face Ridge forced the railway, wagon road and the small stream, which gave the pass its name, close together in Mill Creek Gap under the crags of the unromantically designated Buzzard Roost. Beyond another small valley the W. & A. passed through a tunnel and here at the village of Tunnel Hill, seven miles from Dalton, the Confederates' advanced units held their positions with their pickets thrown out a few miles to Taylor's Ridge. Past that point was unoccupied territory for a dozen miles beyond which Union divisions were scattered over the countryside in localities ranging out to thirty or more miles from Chattanooga. The screening ridges ran generally from northeast to southwest, across country which was sparsely populated, for only a generation before the Cherokee Indians possessed the area. Its rugged topography made it difficult country in which to sustain or maneuver an army.

From Dalton a second railroad reached more directly northward into the valley of East Tennessee, but it offered no use to the Confederates as it soon entered territory controlled by the Federals. Far up in East Tennessee at Morristown, about 150 miles from the army in Dalton and separated from it by the Union forces, was Longstreet's corps, but Johnston did not know definitely whether or not he could count it part of his Army of Tennessee.[2]

At Dalton the General found heartwarming letters from a number of friends in either military or political circles, all of whom offered their congratulations on the new appointment and belief that he would accomplish success in it. One from Jeb Stuart brought nostalgic memories of the Army of Northern Virginia while that from Bragg, who was particularly cordial in his expression of loyalty to both the General and the Army of Tennessee, was most pleasing also because of earlier associations. The letter from Wigfall contained a typical warning against the President, who "had at last been forced to do [Johnston] justice . . . " but the Senator still doubted Davis' intentions and urged the General to stay in touch with his friends in Richmond, who would always stand behind him.[3]

From Davis and Seddon there were official communications, which in a number of details differed greatly from each other. The Secretary of War feared that the army "may have been by recent events somewhat disheartened and deprived of ordnance and material," but trusted that the General would be able "to inspire hope and reestablish confidence." Johnston could count on no help from Richmond but must depend on himself and what assistance Polk could give from Mississippi. While Seddon devoted most of his letter to the need for attention to administrative detail, Davis informed Johnston about the condition of the army at Dalton. The President based his comments on the report of one of his aides, and stated that the army had not suffered seriously at Missionary Ridge. In fact, he told the General, "the effective condition of your command . . . is a matter of much congratulation. . . . " Davis not only differed with Seddon on this but contradicted the Secretary when he added, "I assure you that nothing shall be wanting on the part of the Government to aid you in your effort to regain possession of the territory from which we have been driven." Both the President and Seddon hoped that Johnston could soon begin active operations although neither offered any suggestions of a strategic or tactical nature. Davis did ask the General to write him "fully and freely" about a plan of action so that the assistance of the government could be properly organized.[4]

These letters puzzled Johnston because of their contradictory contents. Seddon's was on such elementary matters as appeared unnecessary to discuss, while that of the President ignored even previously accepted facts about the army's condition and morale. Coming on top of Wigfall's warning, it caused the General to believe that it had no "military object." But he replied seriously to both Davis and Seddon, and explained the truth about the army's condition. As to plans, he told Davis:

To assume the offensive from this point we must move either into Middle or East Tennessee. To the first the obstacles are: Chattanooga, now a fortress, the Tennessee River, the rugged desert of the Cumberland Mountains, and an army outnumbering ours more than two to one. The second would leave the way into Georgia open. We have neither subsistence nor field transportation enough for either march.

Bragg in the preceding fall had been unable to move against the Federals, when he had the support of Longstreet's troops, and the enemy had not received the addition of Sherman's corps. As conditions existed, Johnston concluded, his only hope was to repulse a Federal attack and then to undertake an offensive. But that required that his army should receive reinforcements.[5]

The General went to work at once to create an effective fighting force of the army by a rigorous training program. He published instructions for the "government of the troops," which he ordered to be read weekly to each company. He reminded officers that "assiduous attention" to even the slightest task was a "sacred duty resting upon them" and that the "test of their fidelity" was in the discipline and effectiveness of their troops. Failure would bring the "censure of their own consciences" and that of their countrymen, not only for the period of the war but to the "very end of life." [6]

In an effort to secure increased numbers as well as efficiency and morale, Johnston gave a general pardon to all men who were absent without leave if they returned to the ranks. He also installed a furlough system by which every man in the army could go home for a visit. He made some changes in the reorganization of the army which Bragg had ordered before the battle of Missionary Ridge and in doing so returned Cheatham's old division to his command. It was a fortunate move, one which "created unbounded enthusiasm" among the men. With Cheatham and a band leading them they marched to Johnston's headquarters and called for the army commander. The exuberant Cheatham presented him in an informal manner which was most effective in its results. "Placing his hand upon the bare head of the chief of the army, he patted it two or three times. Looking at the men he said: 'Boys, this is Old Joe.' " [7]

Daily the troops watched Old Joe as he rode his horse at a gallop through the camps, stopping to speak to individuals and groups. "He passed through the ranks of the common soldiers, shaking hands with everyone he met," wrote Sam Watkins, a private soldier himself. "He was loved, respected, admired; yea, almost worshipped by his troops." The feeling was a mutual one. Johnston emphasized to the President that whatever the shortcomings of numbers, equipment and material in the Army of Tennessee, he had "no doubt of the spirit of the soldiers" and "full confidence in their courage." He still held reservations about some of his general officers, whom he wrote Wigfall he would "distribute . . . over the Confederacy," if he were Davis, because of their "factious" spirit and "electioneering" efforts. [8]

Davis was determined to follow his own wishes about the assignment of officers. The General suggested several appointments but was successful in only the instance of Mackall for the important post of chief of staff. Although he had a different man in mind for the vacant corps commander's place, Johnston was pleased when Davis assigned John B. Hood to it. The General remembered Hood's service in the Peninsula, since which time Hood had won more commendation for his work at Gettysburg, where he lost the use of an arm, and at Chickamauga, where he sacrificed a leg. Despite his physical handicaps Johnston welcomed Hood as a stanch, aggressive fighter. He remembered also Wigfall's assurance of Hood's admiration and desire to be assigned to command under him. All caused the General to telegraph Hood as soon as he heard the news, "We want you much." [9]

Ever present were the perplexing Confederate logistic problems: where to secure material and how to transport it. Rifles, bayonets, blankets and shoes were wanting. Food came irregularly and Johnston received warning from supply officers to expect difficulty in getting rations, as the area was fast approaching the exhaustion point. When Seddon said that the General was responsible for procuring food, Johnston reminded the Secretary that he had little authority in the matter. By the system instituted the year before responsibility was in the hands of officers who represented the subsistence and transportation departments in Richmond, and he had no control over them. "I refer to this in no spirit of discontent," he insisted, "but to beg you to consider if the responsibility . . . ought not to rest upon the general, instead of being divided among a number of officers who have not been thought by the Government competent to the duties of high military grade." [10]

Inadequate transportation further complicated these pressing difficulties. The army at Dalton was dependent on the W. & A., which proved no more effective for military purposes than privately owned companies. Before Johnston took command Joseph E. Brown, the peppery Governor of Georgia, had engaged in heated words with field commanders and Richmond authorities over its use. Johnston soon found that it could not keep up deliveries because of mismanagement. He asked Davis for an investigation and the improvement of operation. Argument between the President and the Governor seemed to indicate an impasse and left many features of the problem unanswered. There was some improvement of service by the end of January although there was still no night operation and trains took thirty-six hours for each trip from Atlanta to Dalton or return. [11]

The most important of all shortages continued to be that of men, and the necessity to increase the strength of the army seemed to require the institution of radical means. Although tentative suggestions to use Negroes had previously been made, no one previously had worked out so carefully reasoned an argument to enlist them as General Pat Cleburne, able division leader, presented to a meeting of the general officers at Dalton one week after Johnston's arrival. The idea so incensed one of the group that he requested Johnston to send a copy of it to Davis. Johnston refused, as he thought it both a confidential and a political matter. A copy did reach the President, who promptly disapproved it but informed Johnston of his pleasure that the General had neither approved the idea nor thought it proper to send it on to Richmond.[12]

The practical question of the use of slaves as a source of potential man power still remained, and from the meeting of January 2 Johnston evolved a more realistic suggestion. After the group had dispersed he wrote the President a summary of the idea. It offered the best plan in his opinion to increase quickly the size of the Army of Tennessee: to substitute Negroes "for all soldiers on detached or daily duty, as well as company cooks, pioneers, and laborers for engineer service." The result would be the freeing of 10,000 to 12,-000 men for fighting in even such a relatively small army as that at Dalton. He recognized that new legislation was necessary and asked for its enactment. Johnston also urged Wigfall to support the measure and asked him to enlist the help of others in the Congress. The need for haste was obvious. "The plan is simple and quick," he explained. "It puts soldier & negro each in his appropriate place—the one to fight, the other to work." [13]

A bill authorizing the use of free Negroes and up to 20,000 slaves was approved February 17 by the Congress, and within a month Cooper explained the new act and its administration in a general order. It placed responsibility for enrolling and assigning free Negroes in the Bureau of Conscription, but jurisdiction over slaves continued as in the past. Commanding officers could impress them but only after consultation with the state authorities. When Johnston requested Negroes to carry out the purpose of his recommendation officials of the Bureau of Conscription advised him that they would send the free Negroes who were available but that was all. The result was that the Army of Tennessee could not count on the help for which Johnston had hoped when he made his suggestion.[14]

As the Army of Tennessee trained and reorganized, the Mississippi-

Mobile theater drew attention again. Polk, then in command in that area, interpreted a Union move through Jackson in early February as the opening of a campaign to take Mobile. Davis advised Johnston to keep in touch with Polk and to do anything he could to help, "either by sending him re-enforcements or joining him with what force you can." The President thought it would be well to meet the Federals before they reached the coast and established a base.[15]

Johnston immediately sought information from Polk about the numbers and positions of the two forces, and especially inquired if any troops had moved from the Chattanooga area to join the Federal thrust. Excitement grew as messages flew back and forth among Dalton, Richmond, Mississippi and Mobile, and the enemy drove farther into Confederate territory. Johnston, caught in the middle, attempted to explain that he could not hold at Dalton and at the same time help in other areas. Davis replied that he had no contemplation of surrendering Dalton, but unless the enemy gave more evidence of aggressive action there than dispatches indicated Johnston should send enough infantry to Polk to accomplish the defeat of the Federal attacking columns. Such a great misunderstanding of the situation brought a new, more detailed explanation from Johnston. Sherman had 35,000 men and Polk 8,000. To send sufficient troops from Dalton for the purpose would be to open the way to Atlanta. The movement could not be made quickly enough to prevent the enemy's taking advantage of it. Johnston added that he was anxious to do all that he could but wished to make the true state of affairs clear.[16]

But Davis was not deterred by anything Johnston said. He peremptorily ordered that Hardee with three divisions, about half the infantry at Dalton, move to Polk's assistance. In acknowledging the order Johnston asked if he could have help from Beauregard while Hardee and the troops were away. Davis realized that something should be done so he ordered Longstreet to return the Army of Tennessee's cavalry then serving with him, but he only requested Beauregard "if possible" to send troops to Dalton. Beauregard, whose department included South Carolina, the Georgia coast and Florida, feared too much a Federal movement against Jacksonville and so advised Davis.[17]

Johnston based his apprehension about weakening Dalton on knowledge not only of Grant and Sherman but of Union capabilities and resources. From experience and observation the General had begun to realize that the North could mount major action in more than one area at the same time, while Richmond felt sure that a Federal campaign in one place precluded activity elsewhere. Davis informed Johnston that to destroy Sherman would prove the "most immediate and important method of relieving you." Helpful as it might be to be rid of Sherman in Mississippi, there would remain the powerful army under Thomas, before which Johnston feared to weaken his command. The order to send Hardee away was too reminiscent of that which Davis gave over Johnston's protest to send troops to Mississippi from the Army of Tennessee in December 1862, just before the battle at Murfreesboro.[18]

Nor was Johnston wrong in his estimate of the situation. Before Sherman began his movement in Mississippi the Federal commanders near Chattanooga received orders from Grant to be ready for an advance. Thomas was to be particularly watchful of Longstreet in East Tennessee and should take command himself if needs be to force Longstreet out of the state. At the same time other troops should make a demonstration toward Dalton. But Thomas had learned that some Confederate brigades had left Dalton for Mobile. He did not know that these were two Bragg had borrowed from Johnston the preceding fall and which Richmond had just ordered to be returned. The movement aroused his curiosity, and he suggested to Grant that if he could secure forage for a ten days' expedition the time might be more propitious for a strong demonstration against Johnston unless Longstreet should by some action force attention to East Tennessee.[19]

Longstreet continued to hold Grant's interest above Dalton, and in the second week of February he directed Thomas to join with the Army of the Ohio at Knoxville under the command of Major General John Schofield, "to drive Longstreet out of East Tennessee." But on the receipt of new information Grant revoked the order and because preparations were complete accepted Thomas' recommendation to make a "formidable reconnaissance" toward Dalton. He expressed the hope that Thomas might catch the Confederates off balance and take Dalton "as a step toward a spring campaign." The change of direction delayed the Federals just long enough for Johnston to receive the orders to send Hardee to help Polk. Thus unknown to themselves the Union commanders initiated this movement at a moment of great weakness for Johnston.[20]

On the night of the twenty-second Johnston heard from scouts of

the Federal advance and gathered his scant troops as best he could
to meet it. The next day Davis advised him that Hardee was too late
to help in Mississippi and would return. This was welcome news
but might well have brought from Johnston the comment that it
confirmed his original misgivings which the move against him
emphasized. Actually Sherman had accomplished his purpose,
to destroy Meridian.[21]

When Thomas approached Tunnel Hill February 23, only
Wheeler's cavalry stood in his way as the infantry division which
had held that position was somewhere on the road to Mobile.
Johnston placed some of his remaining infantry at Mill Creek Gap
to withstand Federal attack should it develop. For the next two
days the armies skirmished over the ridges and valleys of the rugged
North Georgia country, but in only one area, Dug Gap, a short
distance southwest of Dalton, did the Federals threaten to make
their way through Rocky Face Ridge. Johnston heard of this danger
as he rode up to headquarters after a day in the saddle. Fortunately
the first of Hardee's men had just returned and Johnston sent them
from the train to the endangered spot with orders to drive the enemy
away in the morning. But Thomas assumed that the Confederates
outnumbered him and decided on a general withdrawal, having
accomplished but little more than the discovery of the strength of
the Southerners' position at Buzzard Roost. Johnston was satisfied
with the action of the soldiers who capably defended Dalton but
was disturbed by the artillery officers, who "exhibited a childish
eagerness to discharge their pieces." [22]

In the midst of the excitement attending Thomas' threat
Lieutenant General John B. Hood made his long expected appearance and brought with him as an aide young Lieutenant Halsey Wigfall, son of the Senator. To his surprise Hood discovered that Johnston
considered the position at Dalton weak and feared that if Thomas
pushed sufficiently hard the Confederates would have to retire
south of the Oostenaula River. Hood without stopping to analyze
the situation interpreted this as willingness by Johnston to withdraw before the need actually arose. He had come ready to demand
aggressive action in accordance with Davis' wish, and offered the plan
upon which Richmond had settled. It called for uniting the troops of
Polk and Longstreet with those at Dalton for a march into Tennessee. Richmond promised every assistance, and had Lee's endorsement

of the plan. But Johnston, according to Hood, had only objections and thought he should have the troops to use as opportunity best afforded.[23]

On the same day as Hood's arrival at Dalton, Davis appointed Bragg as his military adviser. This caused Johnston to hope that because of their previous cordial relations and Bragg's knowledge of the problems facing the Army of Tennessee he would have a more understanding hearing in Richmond. In a letter to Bragg of February 27 Johnston, referring to the two letters of instructions from Davis and Seddon received two months earlier, asked if Richmond still wanted him to undertake a forward movement. The task was huge and delay dangerous, so he urged immediate action.[24]

Bragg assured Johnston that Richmond did expect an offensive and that the General was "to have all things in readiness at the earliest practicable moment for the movement indicated." Bragg reiterated Seddon's statement of late December that Johnston would have to rely largely on his own efforts as only such reinforcements could be sent "as the exigencies of the service elsewhere will permit." In addition he informed Johnston that the artillery chief he had requested was more necessary in another place. Three days later Bragg reaffirmed his instructions for prompt attention to preparations for aggressive action. But he was vague in detail and revealed none of the knowledge of conditions in the West for which Johnston had hoped. "The enemy.is not prepared for us," Bragg wrote, "and if we can strike him a blow before he recovers success is almost certain. The plan which is proposed has long been my favorite, and I trust our efforts may give you the means to accomplish what I have ardently desired but never had the ability to undertake." [25]

Such replies were of no help to Johnston. There was the contradiction about possible support and no particulars of the plan he was to execute, but only the delusion that the enemy was unprepared and in the process of recovering from something. Certainly it was not from the series of battles around Chattanooga in the previous November.

Hood's presence offered Johnston comfort, "indeed the only one in a military way," the General wrote Wigfall. The two dined together frequently and the younger man found his superior "cordial and kind." Johnston gave the Texan command of the Second Corps of the army with Hindman, Stevenson and Stewart as division commanders. Hardee remained in charge of the First with Bate, Cheatham, Cleburne and Walker under him. On the surface all relations between Johnston and Hood appeared cordial and beneficial to the army. But Hood had a hidden purpose. Acting either as a self-appointed agent or according to prearranged plan, as seems indicated by his apology in a letter for not having written sooner, he soon began a clandestine correspondence with Davis, Seddon and Bragg about affairs at Dalton.[26]

On March 7 Hood wrote Davis a letter which he said was in "furtherance of General Johnston's wishes," when after the war Hood tried to explain this correspondence. He reported the army as "well clothed, well fed" and in spirit "anxious for battle." Transportation was in the "greatest possible quantity required" and in excellent shape. All that was needed was the addition of a few artillery horses to "place this army in fine condition." While he believed that 10,000 to 15,000 more troops were necessary to advance into Tennessee, other than Longstreet's corps might be unnecessary, unless Richmond wished to accomplish the destruction of the Union army. In that event he suggested that Polk should join them. That would give Johnston 60,000 to 70,000 men, a force Hood believed strong enough "to defeat and destroy all the Federals on this side of the Ohio River." The enemy, he insisted, was "weak, and we are strong." The Confederates should consequently "march to the front as soon as possible." He assured the President that he was "eager for us to take the initiative, but fear we will not do so unless our army is increased." [27]

Three days later Hood wrote in a similar way to Bragg. He emphasized the need for reinforcements and the likelihood of a loss of more territory in Georgia if they were not forthcoming. He said accurately that Johnston had about 40,000 men but underestimated the enemy's strength as approximately 50,000. On the same day he wrote Seddon and assured him, "I am an earnest friend to the President and am ever willing to express to him my ideas in regard to the approaching campaign." [28]

Everyone it seemed had plans. Beauregard suggested a grandiose scheme for driving to the Ohio. Longstreet wished to unite with Lee for a campaign into Kentucky. Before this idea could be thoroughly explored, Longstreet received a partial outline of Richmond's plan for himself and Johnston through a subordinate just returned from the capital. As Davis wished the two commanders to confer on it, Longstreet wrote Johnston what he knew of the proposal. It called for a junction of their forces between Chattanooga and Knoxville and a move into Middle Tennessee. Longstreet said that it looked uninviting to him and would appear more so to Johnston. His most serious objection to it was that the enemy might slip behind Johnston, fortify strongly and thus force both Confederate armies to disperse in the mountains. Even so he agreed to undertake the movement if Johnston could meet him promptly "with subsistence and forage for my army." [29]

Johnston, who had difficulty gathering more stores than were necessary to fill the day-to-day needs of his army, was startled by the idea that he could find enough to take care of both his and Longstreet's troops in a long campaign away from the railroad. But he said nothing of it when on March 12 he asked Bragg if the communication of March 4, in which Bragg had said to be ready "for the movement indicated," referred to some particular operation. If so he had no word of it from Richmond and needed information about it and the number of troops so that he might make proper preparations. But should Sherman join Thomas, Richmond would have to send reinforcements just to hold Dalton much less to undertake an aggressive move. [30]

In writing Longstreet Johnston emphasized that though he wished to execute zealously any order from the President the proposed operation was impracticable from any point of view. The enemy stood squarely between them and could strike either of them in detail before they could possibly unite. As to the amount of supplies necessary it was a "greater undertaking . . . than anything yet accomplished" by the quartermaster and subsistence departments. Their best chance as he had told the President was to strike a counterblow when the enemy advanced. [31]

Johnston and Longstreet in the midst of the area could not forget something Richmond never seemed to comprehend (although Bragg should have): that the section of East Tennessee through which the army would have to move was sparsely settled and at best poor in agricultural products. It was a largely unmapped region of ridges and mountains whose thin soil produced little more than was necessary to keep alive the people who lived there. A section of high annual rainfall, most of which fell in the winter and spring months, it was crisscrossed by rivers and smaller streams which in February, March and April made travel across it difficult even for individuals. What it might have proved for an army with the huge wagon train necessary for the proposed movement can only be conjectured. From any realistic consideration Johnston's evaluation of the operation as impracticable seems proper.

Unknown to Johnston, Longstreet was then on his way to Richmond to meet Lee. As the government had invited proposals from Longstreet, Lee suggested that he offer the scheme for the invasion of Kentucky, but Longstreet felt that he was in Davis' bad graces and urged Lee to present it instead. On the morning of March 14 Lee met with Davis for that purpose, but later in the day, he took Longstreet with him for a conference which included Seddon and Bragg. They discussed the war in the West in great detail and analyzed the possibilities of the campaign into Kentucky. But the generals quickly saw that Davis had given his approval to the plan devised by Bragg, and it held attention for the remainder of the meeting. Longstreet asked if anyone knew Johnston's opinion and someone reported that he objected to it. Only two days before Johnston had asked Bragg if there were a plan and it was not until March 18 that Bragg's letter explaining it reached Dalton by courier. But if Richmond had no direct knowledge Hood's letters were at hand with their interpretation of Johnston's attitude. Lee wanted to know if Johnston "had maturely considered the matter." Longstreet thought that he had and continued "that the objections of the officer who was to conduct the campaign were, of themselves, reasons for overruling it."

There the discussion began to wander, but Lee brought it back to the pertinent matter when he asked if there were other arguments against the plan. Longstreet recalled Bragg's objections in his report on the battle of Chickamauga. He had rejected a similar plan,

reported it "visionary"; said that it would leave his rear open to the enemy, and alluded to the country through which the march was proposed as 'affording no subsistence to men or animals.' This at harvest season, too! the enemy demoralized by the late battle, and the Confederates in the vigor of success! Now, after a winter of foraging by the Union armies, the country could not be so plethoric of supplies as to support us, while an active army was on each flank, better prepared to dispute our march.[32]

None of this had any effect upon Bragg and Davis, who held to the suggested plan, and the conference broke up with everyone agreed that "we should take the initiative," as Longstreet advised Johnston. But it was not until March 18 that Johnston, whose duty it was to execute the operation, received his first detailed knowledge of it.

Fundamentally the plan was the same as that communicated by Longstreet to Johnston. The point named for the junction of the units was Kingston on the Tennessee River, from where the Confederates could move, according to the optimistic authors of the plan, by a "very practicable and easy route" across the mountains. By a rapid march Johnston might capture Nashville or by getting in its rear "compel a retrograde movement of the enemy's main force," possibly to the "line of the Cumberland." To accomplish it, Bragg said that 75,000 troops "will be available if nothing shall occur to divert them." [33]

In Johnston's view the plan was totally unrealistic. Grant was at Nashville and Sherman at Memphis with every indication that the Federal intention was a major move against him at Dalton. To meet the inevitable attack he needed all the troops Bragg had enumerated for the offensive program. There was no need to wait to bring them to Dalton until the completion of all arrangements, as Bragg proposed. With the proper efforts it was just as easy to feed them at Dalton as where they were. Johnston's idea was to be prepared for any emergency, but should the intention be to move into Middle Tennessee "at all hazards," the General said that Rome and Gadsden offered many advantages over the suggested advance by Kingston.[34]

Johnston's carefully reasoned objections to the plan left little in it which could be salvaged, but Bragg's reply of March 21 contained no intimation that he once had a similar opinion nor any comment on Johnston's alternate plans. Instead it was curt and hostile, and advised Johnston that only for an advance could he expect any additional troops. Johnston immediately answered that he had accepted the idea of an offensive for which he was then preparing and differed only about the details. He had attempted to point out that the Federals might not wait for Confederate initiative and it would be well to be ready at Dalton to meet an enemy advance.[35]

Richmond gave no indication of understanding the problems confronting Johnston despite his efforts to convey them, but did

order Brigadier General W. N. Pendleton, who had served with
Johnston in Virginia, to make an inspection of the artillery at
Dalton. Bragg had proposed Pendleton as chief of artillery for the
Army of Tennessee, but Lee, whom Pendleton served in that
capacity, objected, and Richmond sent Brigadier General Francis
A. Shoup instead. By the end of March Pendleton was back in Richmond with his report in which he said that Johnston had only 111
pieces of artillery. Of them fifteen were six-pounders, which in
Pendleton's opinion were worse than useless as they could accomplish nothing even against the "long range muskets of the enemy."
He called the twelve-pound howitzers of which the army had twenty-
seven "scarcely more valuable" and strongly recommended haste in
correcting the deficiencies.[36]

Pendleton's report, which he gave in person at a meeting with
Davis, Seddon, Bragg and Cooper, bore out all of Johnston's contentions. The morale of the troops had impressed him greatly, he
told the group who listened to him carefully. He reported the same
opinion to Lee, who, pleased by Pendleton's description, wrote Davis
about it. But Lee was made unsure about the proposed campaign
by other phases of Pendleton's conversation. Scarcity of supplies, Lee
told the President, he could understand, but he could not "properly
estimate" difficulties which arose "from the features of the country,
the strength or position of the enemy." Only the commander who
was responsible for the movement could properly judge those things
in Lee's opinion. But the group in Richmond were unimpressed by
Pendleton's report and decided to send him back to Dalton to persuade Johnston of the need for an immediate offensive by him "to
distract the enemy's plans and prevent more troops being massed"
in front of Lee.[37]

The situation at Dalton at the end of March contained little to
create a feeling of fair prospects for an offensive campaign. Johnston
had an aggregate of around 55,000 troops—45,000 infantry, 7,000
cavalry, 3,000 artillery—in front of approximately 90,000 Federals,
gathered in camps for thirty to forty miles around Chattanooga.
Transport was still far below the amount necessary to undertake an
advance and efforts to improve it had been discouraging. Richmond
sent Lieutenant Colonel Cole, inspector general of field transportation, to assist in making it better, but the first message Cole received
from one of his agents said: "I have only time to write a few lines

to prevent General Johnston from expecting what I have no idea he will get. I really do not believe that in sixty days 1,000 mules can be obtained from all sources in this district." [38]

Cole was exercised about much that he found. No one at Dalton, whether the quartermaster officers who bore the responsibility or the commanding general, had accurate knowledge of the amount of transportation on hand or necessary to carry on a campaign. After ten days he informed Richmond that at least 900 additional wagons and teams had to be secured for the amount of supplies needed for an advance. He planned to scour Alabama and Georgia for horses and mules, but North Carolina would have to help if the government planned for the army to move. Again a report from one of Richmond's official inspectors disproved the optimistic statements of Hood.[39]

None of it seemed to help Johnston, who expressed discouragement to Wigfall. "I fear that the government does not intend to strengthen the army," he wrote. Nothing had been done up to then and from appearances things would grow worse rather than better. Grant's arrival in Virginia, of which he had heard, would "turn the eyes of our authorities too strongly in that direction to let them see in this." [40]

Grant's departure did not mean security at Dalton. An experienced successor for command in the West was at hand. The Federals had found their team in Grant and Sherman and, as Johnston had earlier warned Richmond, planned to mount war in increasing pressure on the two fronts. In an effort to clear up any misunderstanding he decided to send Colonel B. S. Ewell of his staff to talk to Davis. Ewell was to explain that Johnston accepted the general principle of offensive action and differed only with the specific plan suggested. He was also to appeal for reinforcements, as a necessity either for an advance or to hold the enemy, should the Federals move first.

Ewell explained Johnston's ideas to Bragg who accepted all of them but pessimistically said that because of new pressures in Virginia and North Carolina help could be sent to Dalton only if Johnston were willing to initiate an offensive. Reinforcements of 15,000 men could then go to him, and Ewell should be prepared to give the President a categorical answer at their meeting the next day. Ewell, who didn't feel authorized to commit Johnston so com-

pletely, wired Johnston for the reply and to inform the General
of the departure of Longstreet from Tennessee. But failing to receive
word in time, Ewell gave Davis a "decided affirmative answer." The
President seemed interested as Ewell reported the conditions at
Dalton, but with the misunderstanding in Richmond of Federal
capabilities he desired that Johnston fight, not only to defeat the
enemy in his front but also to ease pressure on the Army of Northern
Virginia.[41]

While Ewell labored in Richmond to achieve an understanding of
Johnston's role, the General listened courteously to Pendleton as on
his second mission to Dalton he presented Richmond's proposal. No
one appreciated more than Johnston the need for some sort of
action, but the plan was based on incorrect estimates of the enemy's
strength and a misapprehension of other phases of the situation.
Wheeler, who was present at most of the discussion, agreed with
Johnston's conclusions. "In view of the facts exhibited and reasons
urged," Pendleton said in the memorandum he prepared for Richmond, "I did not feel justified in pertinaciously advocating the
particular movement into Tennessee, and could not but admit that
the mode of attack preferred by General Johnston might, on the
whole, prove most proper." Information gathered from a variety of
sources showed that Richmond had underestimated the strength
of the enemy's army in front of Dalton and the reports of Wheeler's
scouts displayed that the Federals were preparing for a great effort.
To combat it Pendleton emphasized the wisdom of getting ready
quickly for the most telling blow possible against them.[42]

Despite the accumulation of testimony from its own investigators
to support Johnston Richmond listened more attentively to anyone
who would offer opposing statements. Hood was ready and willing
to furnish them. On April 3 and again on April 13, the day before
Pendleton's arrival at Dalton, Hood wrote to Bragg letters which
said that only Johnston stood in the way of a successful advance by
the Army of Tennessee. Hood said that he had talked to Hardee,
who though aware of the difficulties was willing "to do anything that
is thought best for our general good." As to his own opinion, Hood
stated without reservation, "When we are to be in a better condition
to drive the enemy from our country I am not able to comprehend." [43]

In his concluding paragraph Hood suggested that as McPherson's Federal corps had moved from Mississippi the Confederates under Polk might join the Army of Tennessee, not to strengthen it for its own use but to enable it to "be in condition to re-enforce General Lee in case it should be necessary." Bragg thought the suggestion sufficiently important to ask Polk to send a division to Dalton, "if not essential for immediate operations." But the bishop-general thought it imprudent to make the transfer and Bragg was not insistent. Seated in his office in Richmond, the new military adviser to the President drew his own conclusions from the reports that he received. He interpreted that of Pendleton as evidence that Johnston had so long delayed his advance as to enable the enemy "to make combinations which render it now inexpedient, if not impracticable. . . . " He refused to accept the figures of Union strength, 103,000, given by Pendleton; at most it amounted to no more than 70,000, he wrote Davis, and of that only 60,000 faced Johnston.[44]

Bragg and the others in Virginia still failed to comprehend that Johnston had not delayed an advance into Middle Tennessee out of perverseness or dilatoriness. Neither terrain and distance nor the Federal strength and leadership lent themselves to the creation of another Jackson Valley campaign. Instead all could too easily combine to create disaster for the Army of Tennessee and thereby the Confederacy. Impetuosity in Georgia and Tennessee was the way to destruction. But to the impatient strategists in Richmond Johnston's repeated calls for additional men and equipment together with his critical analysis of suggested operations seemed a lack of enterprise and zeal. Actually they were but displays of the same military judgment which caused the General in late April to write Wigfall: "The U. S. have the means of collecting two great armies— here & in Virginia. Our government thinks they can raise but one, that of course in Virginia." [45]

In the midst of all his problems and labors Johnston was perplexed at indications of a new upsurge of old issues. He hoped that time and present necessities might quiet the Vicksburg controversy, but at the end of April he expressed surprise in a letter to Wigfall that the government still attacked him on the subject in the newspapers and sought the Senator's advice about the publication of an answer. At the end of April the General again wrote Wigfall, this time to be sure that he had the truth about a new attack from the government. "I learn that it is given out," Johnston said, "that it has been proposed to me to take the offensive with a large army & that I refused. Don't believe any such story." He then gave Wigfall in pretty much the same terms he had repeatedly written Richmond what the situation at Dalton actually was. "It would have been much easier to take the offensive (excuse such frequent use of that expression) in Va. than here," he said further. "For our army there is larger than this & the U. S. Army of the Cumberland was far stronger than that of the Potomac. . . . " [46]

Pride in the feeling for him among the soldiers to a degree allayed Johnston's anxiety about the attitude of the government. "If this army thought of me & felt towards me as some of our high civil functionaries do it would be necessary for me to leave the military service," he told Wigfall, "but thank heaven, it is my true friend." The feeling was a reciprocal one as he had written Whiting more than a month before that he would "freely meet odds of three to two," so much better had the spirit of the army become. He was not alone in discerning it. Generals and privates, visitors and those stationed at Dalton, all were conscious of the excellent morale. Mackall spoke of the improvement in his letters and so did a young captain of Wheeler's cavalry, who told his bride of a few weeks, "I doubt whether a volunteer army could be more perfect in its organization than the Army of Tennessee. General Johnston seems to have infused a new spirit into the whole mass, and out of chaos brought order and beauty." [47]

Sam Watkins of "Company Aytch" who never hesitated to express the disdain he and his comrades held for incompetent officers wrote in wonder of the army under Johnston: "A new era had dawned; a new epoch had been dated. . . . [General Johnston] restored the soldier's pride; he brought the manhood back to the private's bosom. . . . The revolution was complete. He was loved, respected, admired; yea, almost worshipped by his troops." But he insisted upon discipline and efficiency. When he was himself challenged one day he complimented the soldier, which caused the officer of the guard to contrast the conduct of the "Old General" with that of "little colonels and majors," who became very indignant, even angry under such circumstances. The officer's conclusions were that a "great man is an humble man, and does not look with contempt upon his inferiors in rank, whatsoever the rank may be." [48]

About the middle of April scouts' reports began to point to serious business. From headquarters orders went out for all wives to leave and for soldiers to send all surplus baggage to the rear. Alerts to hold everything in readiness for an immediate move came April 29 and rumors soon followed that the Yankees had their haversacks loaded with three days' rations, to the soldiers a sure sign of marching and fighting. The growing activity among the Federals was under the personal direction of General Sherman. On April 4 Grant instructed him, "It is my design, if the enemy keeps quiet and allows me to take the initiative in the spring campaign, to work all parts of the army together and somewhat toward a common center." There were to be no more individual wars in Virginia, in North Carolina, in Tennessee-Georgia, but all to be brought together in one great strategic scheme. Grant did not detail specifically how Sherman should conduct the part assigned to him, but his role was unmistakable: "to move against Johnston's army, to break it up and to get into the interior of the enemy's country as far as you can, inflicting all the damage you can against their war resources." [49]

Sherman planned to concentrate at least 100,000 men against the Army of Tennessee. But he was not satisfied with men alone. He stressed organization, flexibility and speed in his preparations to meet staggering logistical problems. Everything had to move to the front over a single railroad from Nashville but that was under strict military control with all private traffic stopped. Troops marched, except in special circumstances, so supplies could use all available trains without hindrance. Thousands of cattle moved overland from Nashville to pens erected near the army. Before the end of April Quartermaster General Montgomery Meigs had gathered at Nashville enough food to care for 200,000 men for four months and sufficient grain to sustain 50,000 animals for the rest of the year. [50]

Sherman overlooked nothing. He regulated field transportation strictly, allowing but one wagon and one ambulance to each regiment, while each company officer had a mule on which to pack his belongings. Similar restrictions reached to headquarters where Sherman set an example for all. "Soldiering as we have been doing in the past two years with such trains and impediments is a farce," he said. He organized a railroad repair crew of 2,000 men to be sure that no delay in its operation would occur, and made careful preparations to take care of the telegraph by providing a light wagon train to carry wire and other equipment. The men assigned to it were to string telegraph lines on trees from his headquarters to those of his subordinate commanders so he could be in constant touch with them. To avoid any unnecessary confusion in a virtually unmapped region "of mountain, forest, ravine and river," he ordered each division commander to detail a topographical officer, who received instruments and gathered information from scouting and reconnaissance reports for the engineer corps to use in making maps.[51]

Warehouses in Nashville and Chattanooga, packed with paraphernalia of war from the factories of the North, waited the calls upon them. Even a government-built and operated rolling mill stood by the Tennessee River at Chattanooga ready to re-roll twisted railroad iron. Sherman himself had all the confidence he once had lacked. "I'm going to move on Joe Johnston the day Grant telegraphs me he is going to hit Bobby Lee," he told one of his quartermasters, "and if you don't have my army supplied, we'll eat your mules up, sir—eat your mules up!" On April 29 Sherman telegraphed Grant from Chattanooga, "I am here." Anticipating modern war Grant had set D-day for May 5, when Virginia and Georgia were simultaneously to hear the opening thunder of Union guns.[52]

In the little junction town of North Georgia, surrounded by ridges, Johnston awaited what the future might bring. He had received few additional troops despite all that Richmond had promised. His supplies were sufficient to his daily needs, but his transport remained inadequate for a move away from the railroad. Where Sherman's army stood as the epitome of Federal efficiency, power and material resources, that of Johnston represented Confederate delay and weakness. But leader and men had courage, intelligence and resourcefulness and were ready to match all against their adversaries.

CHAPTER XIX

"A BIG INDIAN WAR"

The "grass of May" showed green in the scattered pasture lands and along the roads of North Georgia with the weather just right for campaigning. Rocky Face Ridge was crowned with Confederate fieldworks whose occupants kept alert watch for Federals in the direction of Chattanooga. John Cotton reported that he and his comrades were "well fortified betwixt tunnelhill and dalton." Mill Creek, arching north along the ridge and east through it, was a moat, dammed for the purpose at all railroad culverts. Fallen trees blocked the roads in the directions from which Sherman might come and working parties strengthened the positions at Buzzard Roost and Dug Gap. Details hastened to finish the improvement of roads to enable the army to move quickly, and over in Rome, a little less than forty miles to the southwest, groups labored to complete fortifications. Eighteen miles to the south, soldiers who grumbled about their assignment so far from the possible fighting front guarded the bridges across the Oostenaula River and prepared a defensive position at Resaca. Constant rumors stirred the indescribable feeling that action was imminent but initiative necessarily rested with the Federals.[1]

On May 2 Sherman telegraphed to Grant, "we will be on time." Soon after, the tide of blue-clad men began to flow across the state line into North Georgia. Schofield's Army of the Ohio moved south from Knoxville along the railroad, past Cleveland to the little village of Red Clay. Thomas with the Army of the Cumberland concentrated in the neighborhood of Ringgold, while McPherson and his Army of the Tennessee continued the march toward their appointed place south of the previous fall's battlefield of Chickamauga.[2]

As scouts reported their evidence of the gathering host of Union troops, Johnston repeated his urgent appeals for help but Bragg remained unconvinced. On May 2 he suggested that as his information represented the movement of large bodies of Federal troops to Virginia the activity in front of Dalton must be a deceptive demonstration. But two days later Johnston emphasized the reality of the enemy concentration. "I urge you," he told Bragg, "to send Loring's division and Reynolds' brigade at once to Rome, and put them at my disposal till the enemy can be met." This time Bragg assented and ordered the troops as Johnston requested. But Cooper at the same time, acting under instructions from the President, sent somewhat different orders to Polk, in which he advised that general to move with Loring's division "and any other available force at your command, to Rome, Georgia, and there unite with General Johnston to meet the enemy." The bishop-general immediately promised full co-operation and started the first troops toward Dalton.[3]

To meet the massed throng of the enemy until Polk could bring up his troops, Johnston had approximately 45,000 men ready for action. On May 5 he placed them in defensive positions along the rugged ridges and in the gaps. Hardee was on the left with his men posted high on Rocky Face; Hood held the right, where the line bent down to the east of Dalton. Wheeler's horsemen covered the flanks, guarded the gaps through Taylor's Ridge and watched for the advance of the enemy. Martin's cavalry, which had been near Cartersville recuperating after its return from Longstreet, moved up to Rome. Cantey's brigade, the first of Polk's troops, had reached Rome and Johnston ordered it to move at once by train to Resaca. Urgent requests went to other of Polk's units to hasten their journey by road and rail.[4]

The campaign actually began on May 2 when Federal cavalry drove Confederate units back upon Tunnel Hill from Ringgold Gap, but then things quieted down while Sherman waited for the time to start the business seriously. On May 5 skirmishing began between the two forces and continued through the next day as the Union leaders felt their way for a favorable position. Sherman pushed past Tunnel Hill on the seventh and in the afternoon formed his line, which he adapted to that of the Confederates along Rocky Face Ridge and then to the east to cover the road which ran from Dalton to Cleveland. Johnston could watch the gathering Federals from the heights of Rocky Face and realized that a great battle impended. But he had better news than usual. Not only had the first of Polk's troops reached Resaca, where he assigned them to watch "all routes leading from Lafayette to Resaca or Oostenaula on your left," but Polk himself was on the way. The bishop was a doughty fighter and his

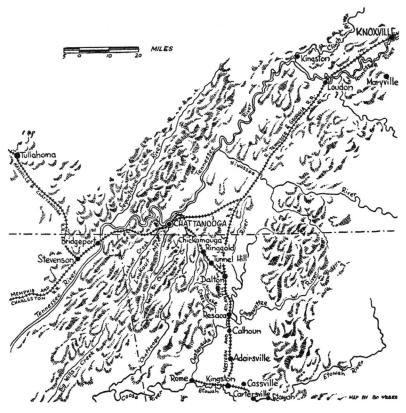

DALTON-ATLANTA CAMPAIGN, FIRST PHASE

arrival would afford the opportunity to reorganize the army in three corps as Johnston had long desired.[5]

Action flared up on the eighth as Thomas drove the Confederate cavalry behind Rocky Face and sent men into action both at its north end and at Mill Creek Gap. By noontime Johnston began to get fragmentary evidence of Federal movements off to his left. From Resaca came the news that scouts had observed the enemy around Villanow. This brought to mind immediately the situation to the west where Wheeler's men supposedly held Taylor's Ridge with a picket line. A report from Hood also indicated action in that direction. Messages to Wheeler followed fast upon one another as Johnston and his subordinate commanders attempted to discover exactly what the Federals planned. The cavalry which Johnston had said from the first was too few in number to perform the necessary tasks of observation and protection, spread even thinner as its requirements extended in a huge arc from Resaca to Taylor's Ridge to Rocky Face Ridge and beyond. Early on the morning of the ninth Johnston gave Wheeler the task of discovering "whether the force that can be seen from different points of Rocky Face" was the enemy's whole army, and then asked him also to observe any movement by the Federals against Dalton from the direction of Resaca, with particular emphasis upon the passages through Rocky Face south of Dug Gap.[6]

Later in the day calls again went to Wheeler from headquarters for careful observation of the gaps through Rocky Face between Dalton and Resaca. The latter place was in no danger itself, the message stated, as 4,000 men were there to defend it. But the Confederate command feared the enemy might slip through in that direction, from which reports continued to contain sufficient warning for Johnston himself to ride southward to observe developments. He hurried reinforcements to Cantey upon whom he impressed the importance of holding the bridges, while he promised aid should the troops at Resaca find themselves under attack by a large enemy force. He interpreted Sherman's intention to be a major battle at Dalton so he advised Cantey to be prepared at any time to move to join the main army.[7]

Sherman too was anxious about developments in the same area. Fighting on Rocky Face "against precipices and mountain gaps," as well as men, had gone on all day to keep Johnston's army busy, he told Halleck. But his principal interest centered upon McPherson's

Army of the Tennessee then in the process of moving across country to reach the Confederate rear at Resaca via Snake Creek Gap. Thomas had reported this route to Sherman and urged that he be allowed to use it with his Army of the Cumberland, but Sherman decided on McPherson. He ordered McPherson to move from the west through a gap in Taylor's Ridge into Snake Creek Gap and on to Resaca. His hope was that McPherson could reach the railroad unobserved, tear it up to interrupt Johnston's communications, and be in readiness to pounce on the Confederate flank should Johnston retreat southward.[8]

McPherson moved into the Gap on May 8, having encountered no opposition after sweeping aside a small cavalry detail the day before at Taylor's Ridge. When this news reached Sherman, he could hardly contain himself. "I've got Joe Johnston dead," he shouted and the dishes on the table rattled from his pounding. The next day the Federals proceeded still unopposed through the forest along the single road until they encountered a Confederate cavalry brigade hurrying too late to defend the Gap. About a mile from Resaca they observed fortified positions from which the Confederates, whom the Federals estimated as in "considerable force," opened artillery fire. This opposition and the failure to find a feasible way to the railroad caused McPherson to retire to the Gap to await developments.[9]

Johnston's information about the movements of McPherson's men did not come directly from the cavalry he had stationed at Taylor's Ridge. A similar outpost in Dug Gap early in the morning of the eighth reported an advance of Federal troops west of Rocky Face as did Cantey from Resaca, but the messages were not complete enough to reveal the enemy's design. As far as Johnston knew Snake Creek Gap was secure until Cantey advised him on the night of the ninth of the action west of Resaca earlier in the day. But if a mistake occurred about that gap good fortune rested with the Confederates otherwise. Had Cantey not arrived McPherson would have found Resaca so weakly guarded that he could easily have closed Sherman's trap for the Army of Tennessee.[10]

Snake Creek Gap is five to six miles long and has come to be the crucial point in all discussions of this phase of the Dalton-Atlanta campaign. It has been inaccurately described as an extremely narrow pass which could be easily defended by a small detachment with proper works. Actually it is only relatively narrow and the ridges on either side have gradual slopes which attackers could easily climb and descend to get in the rear of the defenders. It was heavily wooded at the time and the trees concealed the truth about the topography. Johnston had far too few men to defend adequately all the gaps through which the Federals might make their way in the rugged country around Dalton, and this one would have required a large portion of his force to hold against the weight of McPherson's army. From a practical point of view the chief defense against its use was to delay with cavalry the advance through the gap, to erect at Resaca works which were strong enough to protect the railroad and river crossing for at least a day, and to construct good military roads from Dalton so the army could move quickly to escape a threat against its flank and rear.[11]

For this arrangement to be effective Johnston had to depend upon the alert co-operation of the cavalry. On May 5 he had reminded Wheeler to keep Taylor's Ridge covered, and repeatedly in the intervening days he requested information as to Federal movements in the valley between Rocky Face and Taylor's Ridge. That he knew of the possibility of a Federal movement through the valleys to the west of Dalton is shown by Mackall's prediction after Thomas' threat in February that the enemy the next time "would try and go past" Dalton. In his report General Cleburne remarked upon the failure to resist McPherson in Snake Creek Gap and said, "Certainly the commanding general never could have failed to appreciate its importance." He added that Mackall explained it as a "flagrant disobedience of orders." Neither Cleburne nor Mackall said who was at fault, and Johnston typically refrained from any criticism of subordinates or any mention of disobedience of orders. The evidence points to the cavalry as the source of failure, but beyond that nothing can be said.[12]

To meet McPherson's dangerous threat Johnston immediately ordered Hood with three divisions to Resaca. The next day Hood found that the Federals had withdrawn into Snake Creek Gap. Johnston who was still in the process of forming his opinion of his opponent interpreted the movement as a feint to draw attention from the main point of Sherman's interest, battle closer to Dalton. He recalled Hood but instructed him to post Cleburne's and Walker's divisions at Tilton, a village about halfway between Dalton and Resaca. This weakening of the Confederate right gave some concern to Hardee who, however, conceded to Wheeler that he couldn't "decide what the Yankees are endeavoring to accomplish" because of the relative quiet along his positions on Rocky Face. Johnston's apprehensions extended over a greater area. He was troubled by the possibility that McPherson might turn on Rome, where Polk's troops reached the railroad which carried them to join the Army of Tennessee. He also suggested to Polk and S. D. Lee, whom Polk had left in command in Mississippi, that Forrest be sent to Middle Tennessee for an attack upon Sherman's communications.[13]

Sherman was greatly disappointed when couriers arrived the night of the ninth to tell him that McPherson had failed to cut the railroad in Johnston's rear. But he would not give up. He was still resolved to save his men from the "terrible door of death that Johnston had prepared for them in Buzzard Roost." He planned a feint on that strong Confederate position and then, using Rocky Face Ridge for a cover, to move the army through Snake Creek Gap to Resaca except for the cavalry and a single corps, whom he would leave in front of the enemy at Dalton. He believed that Johnston did not have the strength to detach troops to interfere, but to be sure he instructed McPherson to hold against any attacking force "and I will get to you." [14]

Sherman underestimated his enemy. By 7:30 on the morning of the eleventh Johnston ordered Wheeler to investigate the position of the Federals to discover where their left rested and "whether they are in motion for the Oostenaula." Suspecting that they were, he told Polk to proceed to Resaca and to take command there, and asked Atlanta for railroad cars to hasten troop movements from Rome. From every vantage point scouts examined the countryside in an effort to uncover Sherman's intention. By the time Polk arrived on the afternoon of the eleventh it was evident to everyone that the Federal commander was "moving everything" toward and probably down Snake Creek Gap.[15]

On the arrival of Polk at Resaca Hood returned to his corps. The two generals rode together to Dalton, where Polk reported that he was on hand and with him the remaining regiments of Loring's division. After an exchange of greetings and a briefing conference Polk rode with Hood to the latter's headquarters. On the way from Resaca the badly crippled, thirty-two-year-old general confided that he wished to be baptized. The general was always glad to resume the clerical functions of the bishop. Along toward midnight after turning the furnishings of the simple room into the proper setting, Hood, supported by his crutches and with his staff officers to act as witnesses, presented himself in the dim light of a lonely candle to the Bishop of Louisiana.[16]

At midday on May 12 Johnston reported to Richmond that the Federal army was in motion toward Calhoun or some point on the Oostenaula. "I will follow the movement," he said in conclusion. Sherman had failed to pin the Confederates but used his superior numbers to force them from their position. "The Yankees had got breeches hold on us," Sam Watkins said, and retirement, which started at 1:00 A.M., was the only safe procedure.[17]

The Federal troops at Dalton had orders to press ahead after Johnston, who, General Howard reported, had effected "one of his clean retreats." Sherman himself had gone with the greater portion of the army through Snake Creek Gap, but the long march over the narrow roads took more time than he anticipated. By noon he had reached the comparatively open ground, where skirmishing was in progress, to the west of Resaca along a small stream, Camp Creek. He planned to fight that afternoon for the railroad and advised Washington, "All is working well and as fast as possible." He had the news about Spotsylvania and said, "Let us keep the ball rolling." [18]

Skirmishers of Loring's division held up Sherman's advance until the troops of Hardee and Hood could arrive. The position Johnston had chosen was a ridge west of Resaca. Polk was on the left with his flank resting on the Oostenaula, Hardee in the center and Hood on the right with his line bent back to the east across the railroad and his flank on a tributary of the river. The two streams close upon his rear were the chief weakness of the position Johnston chose.[19]

The skirmishing in which the two forces briskly engaged on the thirteenth was but a preliminary symptom of the fury of the coming day. Federals who had scrambled through thicket and thorn and had cursed the rocky ledges along the way struggled to get themselves and their artillery into position over the roadless, broken country. Confederates who had marched south from Dalton the previous night and had then worked on the fortifications were weary but ready as the clear, warm May day found them well entrenched. All signs pointed to a great collision, the first true test of strength of the campaign.

Action started on the flanks: on the left where Polk guarded the bridges close in his rear across the Oostenaula, and around on the right where Hood held against lesser assaults. Fighting grew fiercer in Polk's sector as the Federal commander built up his right in the effort to drive the Confederates from the possession of the important bridges, but the bishop-general in an old hunting shirt and a slouch hat unconcernedly went about his task of directing operations despite the heavy fire which roared like a tornado about the countryside.

Johnston as usual was in the center of action, exposing himself repeatedly to the fire of the enemy sharpshooters and causing members of his staff to worry about his safety. He wore a "light or mole-colored hat, with a black feather in it," when Company Aytch marched by him, and was listening intently to the firing. The men saw him and there was "one little cheer" to start; then the "very ground seems to shake with cheers. Old Joe smiles as blandly as a modest maid, raises his hat in acknowledgment, makes a polite bow, and rides toward the firing." [20]

Believing that the Federals were crowding their forces to the right, Johnston sought confirmation from the cavalry. Upon finding it to be true, he ordered Hood to assault the enemy left. Hood made a slight change of front to his left and smashed at the Federals with encouraging success about 6:00 P.M. Darkness shortly halted the action, but the results created enough optimism for Johnston to instruct Hood to resume the attack in the morning. The plan was to hold the enemy right and to combine with Hood enough of Hardee's and Polk's troops to defeat the left. [21]

Fitful firing by outposts disturbed the efforts of the men to sleep, but Johnston had little time even to try to rest that night. After dusk he rode from Hood's front over to the rear of Polk's line which he found the Federals had pushed back from its original position to one sufficiently close to the bridges for them to be reached by enemy artillery fire. More disturbing was the report by the cavalry that Union units had crossed the Oostenaula on a pontoon bridge down river and threatened the railroad and the Confederate rear. This required a change of plans. Johnston instructed Walker to move at once to the reported point of the Federal crossing and counter-manded the order to Hood to resume the fight in the morning. Instead he told Hood to withdraw to the position he held before his attack. To be sure of an unobstructed way over the Oostenaula in the event he had to move hurriedly to meet a Federal thrust at his rear Johnston ordered the engineers to place a pontoon bridge a mile above the threatened permanent structures and to build a road to it.[22]

Next morning Sherman again concentrated on the enemy left as skirmishing mounted at times to the proportions of a battle. Johnston awaited full details about the Federal movement to his left rear, and in the afternoon messages from Walker indicated that the early reports of a crossing of the Oostenaula were wrong. He then decided to resume the attack by Hood, part of whose force under Stevenson had already returned to the advanced positions of the previous day, with a battery of four guns even farther to the front. When the battery opened prematurely upon the enemy the Federals replied so effectively that the Confederates had to abandon the guns, which stood sullenly mute between the lines. As Hood prepared to renew the assault, word came that the Federal threat against the rear was true. Enemy troops had already crossed the Oostenaula. Again Johnston countermanded the attack by Hood, but Stewart's division, failing to receive word in time, suffered heavy casualties before it could be recalled.[23]

One thing Johnston felt sure about and he so advised Richmond: Sherman had sent none of his troops to Grant. The Federal commander was too intent upon pressing his advantage against the Army of Tennessee. Johnston did not have the men to detach a sufficient number to oppose the enemy who threatened his rear and at the same time hold the position at Resaca, so he called his corps and division commanders for a conference to arrange a line of retreat and schedules. About dark the generals began to gather at headquarters, where each received his instructions. Hood was to use the pontoon bridge which the engineers had placed the night before, while Polk and Hardee were to cross by the railroad and common or trestle bridge, which were at Polk's rear in the fighting. About midnight the Union army was aroused by the firing of muskets and other small arms by Confederate units, who masked their withdrawal in that fashion.[24]

In the night the lightly equipped army made its way southward over parallel roads, as Johnston again made a successful escape from Sherman. Some said that not even an old wheel was left behind. Rear guards took up the pontoon bridge and placed the materials on wagons for use another place. Others burned the railroad bridge. Only the one for wagons was left undamaged in the confusion of the growing day. The weary men found the country much more open south of Resaca and traveling was easier than over the rough ridges to the north.[25]

The army halted just south of Calhoun in a valley where the routes of the column converged. Here most of the men rested for fifteen to eighteen hours while the rear guard kept up steady skirmishing to hold up the pressing Federals. Johnston had decided upon a slow withdrawal before the enemy in the hope that Sherman might blunder or that the great numbers of his army might bog down on the rough country roads. Johnston still had hope that expirations of enlistments in June would decrease Sherman's ranks. Principally he sought a valley which was narrow enough to afford him an advantageous position with his flanks protected and the enemy forced to approach unable to use their superiority in numbers.[26]

He believed that such a position was available near Calhoun but reconnaissance revealed none. So, early on the morning of the seventeenth, the Confederates again took up the march, this time toward Adairsville, about eight miles farther to the south. The men were in good spirits and joked about the "stirring fellow," Sherman, who kept them alert and their time occupied. At Adairsville, Polk's cavalry joined them, a division of about 3,700 troopers under Major General W. H. Jackson. General French was still at Rome where he resisted attacking enemy cavalry and hurried as rapidly as possible arriving infantry units to Kingston. Johnston urged French repeatedly to make all possible haste to join the retiring army, even though it meant giving up Rome with its factories and iron foundry. Officers scoured the countryside in search of a good field of battle for the Confederates, but the reports were unfailingly discouraging. On the night of the seventeenth as the generals assembled for a conference at Adairsville, Johnston received word from S. D. Lee that Forrest would start on the twentieth with around 3,500 picked men and two batteries for an attack upon Sherman's communications. The strength of the Army of Tennessee was nearing its greatest possible potential and discussion naturally turned to the question of attack. Hardee wanted to stand where they were, but Hood seemed anxious to continue the retirement beyond the Etowah River. Johnston however had a different plan, which he proceeded to explain.[27]

Two roads led southward from Adairsville. One followed the railroad slightly to the southwest to Kingston, while the other ran somewhat east of south to Cassville. A third road connected Kingston and Cassville and thus closed a triangle. Johnston saw the possibility that Sherman might divide his forces at Adairsville to utilize and to cover both roads, and if the Confederates could mass their strength at one point they would catch the Federals at a disadvantage. He ordered Polk and Hood to march directly to Cassville, while Hardee, who had the rear position should act the decoy and take the road to Kingston. When he reached that point he was to march at once to join the other corps at Cassville. Reconnaissances displayed that should the Federals fall into the trap, eight or nine miles of crooked, narrow country roads would separate the two sections of the enemy.[28]

After deciding the matters affecting the movements of the army Hood, Hardee and Polk went to Johnston's tent to fulfill a request Mrs. Johnston had made of the bishop-general. Two days before she had written him:

You are never too much occupied, I well know, to pause to perform a good deed, and will, I am sure, even whilst leading your soldiers on to victory, lead my soldier nearer to God. General Johnston has never been baptized. It is the dearest wish of my heart that he should be, and that you should perform the ceremony would be a great gratification to me. I have written to him on the subject, and am sure he only waits your leisure. I rejoice that you are near him in these trying times. May God crown all your efforts with success, and spare your life for your country and friends.[29]

For the second time since reaching the Army of Tennessee, Bishop Polk put aside his military status to assume that of his episcopal position. He improvised an altar and the service was even more than usually impressive with the participants in uniform and the background of distant firing. When it was over, the little assemblage dispersed and "went to bed, as we call it, laying down on the floor and jumping up every few moments to read one dispatch and write another," Mackall wrote his wife. Everything, rest included, had to be subordinated to preparations for the morrow, when good and bad news came to hand. For one good omen French arrived with his division which quickly assumed its place with the rest of Polk's troops. But S. D. Lee advised that Federal threats out of Memphis had forced him to call off Forrest's movement against Sherman's extended supply line. This was somewhat balanced by the encouraging news of heavy Federal losses in Virginia. Johnston himself felt confident of the direction of events, but there were some among the officers who feared Sherman would continue by maneuver to draw them south of the Etowah and then hurry reinforcements to Grant.[30]

Since leaving Dalton both armies had been either fighting or marching. The Confederate rear guard of cavalry and supporting infantry stopped frequently to drive back the advanced troops of the Federals, whom Sherman had started in their pursuit early on the morning after Johnston left Resaca. Whenever crowded the Southerners hit hard and when the confusion of the march occasionally isolated units they fought with unexcelled spirit. Sherman's confident Midwesterners pressed constantly on their heels. Superior in numbers the Federals were superior in every material resource. The railroad was quickly placed in operation to the Oostenaula to care for the huge demands of active campaigning. Everything combined to give Sherman the feeling that all was well. "Our difficulties will increase beyond the Etowah," he wrote Halleck from Resaca, and ignoring the fact that his maneuver which threatened the Confederate rear pulled Johnston from his position continued, "but if Johnston will not fight us behind such works as we find here, I will fight him on any open ground he may stand at."[31]

The Federals swept through the countryside with Schofield's Army of the Ohio on the left, Thomas' Army of the Cumberland, the largest of the three, in the center and McPherson's Army of the Tennessee on the right. As they marched onward, Sherman interpreted the Confederate quandary to Halleck in this way: ·

Johnston will be compelled to fight on this side of the Etowah, or be forced to divide his army, or give up either Rome or Allatoona. If he attempts to hold both, I will break the line at Kingston. If he concentrates at Kingston, I will break his railroads right and left, and fight him square in front. My belief is he will abandon Kingston and Rome, and retire on Allatoona, beyond the Etowah, in which case I will fix up my roads to Kingston, and then determine in what manner to advance beyond the Etowah . . . I know we must have one or more bloody battles, such as have characterized Grant's terrific struggles.[32]

In his analyzing of Johnston's possible plans Sherman overlooked the move the Southern commander chose. When he reached Adairsville and discovered that the Confederate route clearly led to Kingston, Sherman was perplexed but he directed his columns toward the same spot except for the division he had sent from Resaca to Rome. By this line of march McPherson and Thomas moved to the southwest, away from the Confederates gathering at Cassville, while Schofield's line of march carried him almost squarely across the front of Johnston's position. By that night, May 18, Sherman was confident that he had correctly interpreted his adversary's intention, but he expressed his puzzlement in a communication to Schofield. He said:

All signs continue of Johnston's having retreated to Kingston, but why should he lead to Kingston, if he designs to cover his trains to Cartersville, I do not see. But it is possible he has sent to Allatoona all he can by cars, and his wagons are escaping south of the Etowah by the bridge and fords near Kingston. In any hypothesis our plan is right. All of General Thomas' command will follow his trail straight, let it lead to the fords or toward Allatoona. You must shape your course to support General Hooker and strike the line of railway to your left. As soon as you can march in the morning get up to General Hooker and act according to development. If we can bring Johnston to battle this side of the Etowah we must do it, even at the hazard of beginning the battle with but a part of our forces.[33]

Sherman misjudged his man but he had his troops so in hand that he could make a quick re-adjustment. As Hardee led the Federals astray toward Kingston, Johnston made his preparations to take advantage of the separation of the Federal army. He realized that the timing had to be accurately planned as the greatest distance between the two portions of Sherman's force would be only seven miles. Hood was to push forward to the east of the road from Adairsville to Cassville and then to turn upon the left flank of the Union column while Polk hit it in front. Hardee was to continue his march from Kingston and to take position on the army's left.[34]

Johnston's big moment seemed at hand when the curious history of May 19 began to unfold. A stirring battle order was read to all. "Old Joe" assured his soldiers that their rear was at last secure from the enemy. "You will now turn and march to meet his advancing columns. Fully confiding in the conduct of the officers, the courage of the soldiers, I lead you to battle," he said. Veterans like Sam Watkins and George Guild cheered the reading of the order and reported that they never saw their comrades happier or surer of victory. Hood and Polk started their move as soon as the cavalry reported that the Federal column approached Kingston. As was frequently true of him, Johnston wrote no battle orders but rode with the corps commanders to get them started to their positions and then returned to his headquarters. About 10:20 he sent General Mackall to Hood to inform him that Hardee reported a heavy advance upon his position. Hood was "to make quick work" and not to commit himself to "too wide a movement." [35]

On reaching Hood Mackall was startled to find that the corps instead of moving to the attack was falling back to form a defensive line. Hood explained his failure to carry out his orders by the reported discovery of Union troops east of him on his flank and rear, and asked Mackall if he had not seen them. Mackall said that he had not, but word was already on its way to headquarters. When the messenger arrived with the news that the enemy was "in heavy force close to Hood on the Canton road," Johnston immediately expressed his disbelief in the report, as the cavalry had found no Federals in the area. But when he looked at a map he said that if the report were true Hood could do nothing but fall back. [36]

At headquarters Johnston had to rely upon information from the field commanders, and Hood passed on this report without verification or investigation. Closer observation would have disclosed, as Hood's own report later stated, that the enemy was not in "heavy force" but was a unit of McCook's cavalry, certainly not large enough to hold up Hood's entire corps or to cause its commander to assume responsibility for setting aside the plans for the day's attack. But by the time he discovered that Hood had incorrectly interpreted the situation, Johnston realized that it was too late to regroup to assume the offensive and instead sent orders to his subordinates to take up a defensive position. [37]

With Polk and Mackall accompanying him Johnston rode to examine a position along a wooded ridge just outside of Cassville to the east and south. From its top the generals saw that it commanded "a broad, open, elevated valley" in its front and Johnston termed the location the "best that I saw occupied during the war." From the sound of the firing the Confederate commander believed that an attack by the Federals was imminent so he hurried the army into place to receive it. The line still ran with Hood on the right, Polk in the center, and Hardee on the left. No sooner were the troops in position than Federal artillery began to thunder away at them. Sherman heard of Johnston's concentration for battle and rode rapidly across the gravelly plateau between the Kingston and Cassville roads to reach the scene. Soon orders were out for all Union forces to move to Cassville for the expected fight on the next day.[38]

As Johnston rode the line that afternoon General Shoup, the commander of the army's artillery, pointed out a sector near the junction of Polk's right and Hood's left which Federal batteries could enfilade from a position on an opposite ridge. Johnston did not feel the danger to be alarming but told Shoup to instruct the officer in command there to construct defensive works and if necessary to protect his men by moving to some near-by ravines. After supper he went to a council of the lieutenant generals, completely confident of what the next day would bring.[39]

Hardee was not present for the opening of the conference, at which Hood, acting as chief spokesman, insisted that his and Polk's portion of the line was untenable, with Polk supporting him but less insistently. The Federal batteries could easily enfilade their lines and they urged a withdrawal south of the Etowah. Johnston attempted to give them faith in the position but after a long discussion yielded to their opinion, "in the belief that the confidence of the commanders of two of the three corps of the army, of their inability to resist the enemy, would inevitably be communicated to their troops, and produce that inability." When General Hardee arrived and heard of the decision he remonstrated against it, but he could not overcome the fears of the other two corps commanders.[40]

The decision was one of enormous consequences. Such soldiers as Sergeant John W. Hagan who held that the army "must make a Stand Soon" had cheered the battle orders in the morning. They were perplexed and amazed by the change of events. Johnston was himself tremendously disappointed. Through the whole of the arduous campaign he had held the hope that Sherman might blunder and create an opportunity to meet the Federals on something like equal terms. Now when a favorable circumstance had occurred he had not only lost his chance by a subordinate's error of judgment but through the insistence of the same man and another he had felt it necessary to give up an equally favorable opportunity to withstand the enemy's assault. The next day in explanation he wrote the President: " . . . yesterday having ordered a general attack, while the officer charged with the lead was advancing he was deceived by a false report that a heavy column of the enemy had turned our right and was close upon him, and took a defensive position. When the mistake was discovered it was too late to resume the movement." [41]

Johnston undoubtedly realized that the situation contained danger as well as disappointment for him. "This retreat will damage the General in public estimation till we best the foe—trusting in God, I think we will," Mackall said in a letter. "I was so sure the other day that I could not restrain my tears when I found we could not strike." Mackall kept to himself his feeling or beliefs about responsibility for the failure, but a young relative of his, Lieutenant Thomas B. Mackall, who was also a member of Johnston's headquarters staff and who kept a most informing journal for the period, was more blunt in assessing the cause of the retirement. In the secret pages of his diary he wrote, "One lieutenant-general talks about attack and not giving ground, publicly, and quietly urges retreat." [42]

Johnston made no further explanation of the unfortunate events of the nineteenth or responsibility for them. But Hood apparently wished to risk no misunderstanding of his position and dispatched his own emissary with a letter to the President on May 21. "Colonel Brewster has been with us since we left Dalton," Hood told Davis, "and can give you an account of the operations of this army since the enemy made their appearance in our immediate front. He leaves for Richmond today and I think it would be well for you to have a conversation with him in relation to our affairs etc. etc." [43]

Nothing is known of the report Brewster made to the President, but it is obvious that Hood's version of events was its basis. That was the impression left by Brewster in a conversation he had with Mrs. Chesnut on June 24. "He said Joe Johnston was kept from fighting at Dalton by lack of a plan. 'Hood and Polk wanted to fight, but he resisted their council. All this delay is breaking Hood's heart. So much retreating would demoralize even General Lee's army.'" Mrs. Chesnut expressed her agreement and stated bitterly, the "Joe Johnston disaffection is eating into the very vitals of our distracted country." [44]

But what Mrs. Chesnut and her group may have considered disaffection and voluntary retreats had an entirely different aspect for those with the Army of Tennessee. No one knew the truth about the situation better than Mackall who early in June wrote his wife:

Of course, the friends of the President will now try to show that Johnston has done exactly like Bragg [in the retreat from Middle Tennessee], but the army sees that it is not so. We came back step by step, never out of sound of the enemy's guns and have hit them many hard blows. I do not think that we have destroyed less than fifteen thousand of them perhaps more. . . . Governor Harris of Tennessee, who is with this army and a very shrewd, earnest man, thinks all the army is satisfied that it could not have been better managed; but there are always nervous people, who want quick victory and are ready to join in anything the President may say. Johnston has much to contend with. It is unjust to put a man at the head of an army and then try to destroy his capacity for usefulness by expressing fears and distrust. . . .[45]

For the better part of three weeks the two armies had been marching and countermarching, skirmishing and engaging in occasional heavier action. Both were consequently glad of the opportunity to enjoy a little rest. Johnston placed his men in temporary camps a few miles south of the Etowah River at Allatoona, where a spur of the Southern Appalachians provided a natural stronghold directly on the railroad, while Sherman refitted and collected supplies for a new push south from Kingston. The theater of coming operations was certain to be between the Etowah and the Chattahoochee rivers. The heights of Allatoona, Pine, Lost and Kennesaw mountains dominated the area close to the Western & Atlantic railroad but to the westward gave way to a rough, hilly terrain, cut by muddy streams and eroded gullies, and generally covered with forest and undergrowth right up to the canebrakes which edged the streams. About halfway between the two rivers was Marietta, where Johnston located his headquarters.

Both commanders knew the topography of the section. Johnston had seen it many times from his car window, as he rode the train along the Western & Atlantic, and Sherman as a young lieutenant had ridden widely through it. Each had watched eagerly every move made by the other, intent upon learning all possible about the mental processes and the methods of his opponent. Each had demonstrated masterful handling of his forces and hoped to find in the territory ahead some geographical feature which could be used to advantage to trick his opponent into a fateful error of judgment or maneuver. Amid the dense undergrowth where marching by compasses was frequently necessary, disaster lurked for the unwary.

While his army used the welcome opportunity for rest at Allatoona Johnston explained the cause of the retirement to the President. He had "earnestly sought an opportunity to strike the enemy," he said in his communication of May 21, but the "direction of the railroad to this point" had enabled Sherman by consistently extending his right to force the Confederates back. Then "by fortifying the moment he halted" the Federal commander "made an assault upon his superior forces too hazardous." But despite the long retrograde movement the Confederates had lost few men by straggling and desertion.[46]

At Allatoona Johnston received word from Richmond that a brigade of infantry and a regiment of cavalry were on their way to

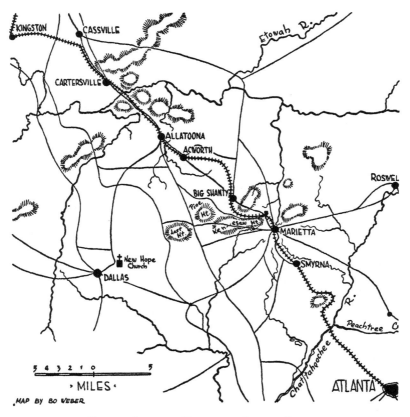

DALTON-ATLANTA CAMPAIGN, SECOND PHASE

him, but with that welcome news there was an accompanying discouraging report that these were the last the government could send. In informing him of this Bragg said that in Richmond, "from the high condition in which your army is reported, we confidently rely on a brilliant success." In Georgia closer to events Governor Brown knew that men as well as optimism were necessary. On May 28 he addressed a resounding proclamation to the people of Georgia. Ten days before he had asked the civil and military officials of the state to accept their responsibilities in the growing emergency. Now he called "all who are able for service, and can be possibly spared from home, to hasten to the field till the great battle is fought. . . . The destiny of our posterity for ages to come may hang upon the results of the next few days. . . . Rally to the rescue, and till the danger is past let the watchword of every patriot be, 'To arms, and to the front'; and the vandal hordes will soon be driven back." [47]

While the Confederates rested and refitted at Allatoona the Federals at Kingston made ready to cross the Etowah, which Sherman called the "Rubicon of Georgia." By the twentieth engines and cars brought trainloads of supplies, and troops loaded wagons in preparation for a period of campaigning away from their valuable logistical ally, the railroad. With two bridges and good fords across the Etowah south of Kingston Sherman decided to cut straight across country to Dallas, south and west of Johnston at Allatoona. Everything had to be done with caution now that he was so far within the state, but he declared that he would be "in motion like a vast hive of bees, and [expected] to swarm along the Chattahoochee in five days." [48]

At Allatoona the Confederates had an advantageous interior position which made them closer to any point in the general area toward which Sherman might choose to march. In order to watch for any indication of the Federal commander's intention and to do what damage it might to unsuspecting enemy trains Johnston ordered the cavalry to ride the countryside. Almost as soon as the Union troops began to cross the Etowah Johnston had word of it and set his gray-clad troops also in motion along the hot, dusty roads. He instructed Wheeler to go as far north as Cassville to find out if all Sherman's army had left the railroad to march through the country to the west. On the twenty-fifth the two forces drew near each other in the rough, wooded country between Dallas and New Hope Church.[49]

Skirmishing started early, but the main fighting occurred late in the afternoon when Hooker's Federal corps fiercely assaulted the Confederate right under Hood at New Hope Church. Hooker formed his men so deeply that their front corresponded to that held by the single division of Stewart, and for about two hours they attacked without lull or pause. Overhead a dark, angry-looking cloud gathered. Giant claps of thunder added their share to the man-made commotion and lightning flashed simultaneously with the cannon. Men who were wet with sweat found themselves further drenched with rain as they huddled behind tree trunks or rocks and scrambled through the thickets. The Confederate commander in his report said, "No more persistent attack or determined resistance was anywhere made," while the Federal ordinary soldiers changed the name of the church to "Hell Hole." [50]

The following night was dark as pitch and the rain continued to fall in torrents. Foot soldiers, horsemen, artillery and wagon trains on both sides jammed in bewildered masses as they used the hours of darkness to shift to new positions. "All was hurry and confusion and nearly everyone swearing at the top of his voice," wrote one Kentucky Federal in his diary. Sherman worked his front toward the east and next morning to prevent the overlapping of his line Johnston transferred Polk to Hood's right. There was little action for two days as both armies put weapons aside to throw up entrenchments. Men were by then expert at digging ditches and earthworks braced with timbers entirely changed the character of the fighting. Out in front of the line men on outpost duty dug rifle pits in which two could find cover. As Sherman put it, "Both sides [were] duly cautious in the obscurity of the ambushed country." [51]

With the two armies so close to each other and the effort of the commanders to match maneuver with maneuver so dominant something was obliged to break. On the morning of the twenty-seventh Johnston noted that the Federals had again prolonged their line to the east, so he ordered Cleburne from Hardee's corps to the right to meet the Federal move. The Confederate right then rested on Little Pumpkin Vine Creek. Late that afternoon Sherman decided to smash through at that point and the Federals launched a furious assault in which close, desperate fighting continued until dark. Some Union troops found themselves left behind in a ravine when the main attacking body withdrew. The Confederates determined to dislodge

them in a night operation which furnished the climax of the day.
Over rocks, slopes and thickets three regiments charged in daring
recklessness and swept the position, taking prisoner all that were
left alive.[52]

Suspecting that the Federals by their constant extension of their
left had weakened their right, Johnston decided to see if an opportunity existed for Confederate offensive action there. On the next
morning, the twenty-ninth, he ordered Bate with his division to test
that portion of the Union line, but stiff opposition from the enemy
greeted the attacking Confederates who lost somewhat heavily in the
fighting and withdrew. Later in the day at a meeting of the corps
commanders with Johnston, Hood suggested that the next morning
they initiate a general engagement, to begin with an assault by his
corps on the Federal left with Polk and Hardee taking up the battle
in order. Johnston and the others accepted the idea and orders went
out accordingly. Hood was to move past Cleburne's division to the
extreme right of the Confederate line and to begin the attack at
dawn. All waited anxiously as day broke on the thirtieth for the
sound of Hood's firing, which the Confederates continued to use
as a battle signal despite its having failed them so frequently. About
ten o'clock word came from Hood that he had found the Union position to be changed, with an unexpected division entrenching farther
to the left and almost at right angles to the old line. He asked for
new instructions. Johnston, realizing that the opportunity for a surprise assault had passed, called off the action and the Confederates
resumed their defensive positions.[53]

Sherman daily continued to reach to the east toward the railroad,
amid constant skirmishing and frequent night attacks. A furious
cannonading kept up and some insisted that it was responsible for
the discomfort of the torrents which its roar veritably shook "out
of the clouds." The roads grew muddier and the going more difficult
by the rains which brought one blessing. "We see no one and get no
orders," wrote General French. It was a great relief for muscles tired
and aching from incessant marching and digging. Both commanders
kept their armies close in hand, constantly inviting and hoping for
the attack of the opponent.

On June 1 Federal cavalry entered Allatoona and with the railroad
in his possession Sherman ordered it repaired to that point. Although
Johnston tried to keep up with the steady Federal movement to the

east, "creeping around his right flank," as Sherman termed it, inferiority of numbers prevented it. He brought up cavalry to extend his line while the infantry skirmished to keep the Federals occupied. Despite all efforts the extension of the Northern line steadily continued. Finally the danger of having his right flank turned grew too great and Johnston pulled his army back on June 4 in a violent rainstorm. The next morning the Yankees cheered in relief the "nocturnal departure of the rebellious gentlemen," of whom they "had become heartily tired . . . as neighbors." Actually the men of neither army sufficiently enjoyed their stay along Little Pumpkin Vine Creek to recommend it as a resort.[54]

The Confederates' left flank in their new position rested on Lost Mountain. In the center a salient included Pine Mountain and the right, still manned by the cavalry, crossed the railroad slightly north of Kennesaw Mountain. Here on an arc about ten miles long Johnston awaited the Federals' next move. He had again given ground but he had prevented the accomplishment of Sherman's plan to reach the Chattahoochee River.

Sherman waited until June 9 to push his legions on, and in the period of inaction received the addition of 10,000 men, to bring the army to approximately the same strength as when it began to campaign. Repair crews hastened work on the bridge over the Etowah and on the eleventh the Confederates heard the whistles of Federal engines as they pulled trains to the front. Sherman was confident but cautious. In a letter to his brother, Senator John Sherman of Ohio, he said, "suffice it to say that General Grant and I had a perfect understanding, and all things are now as near our calculations as possible. . . ." More important to his particular army however was the fact that Johnston had drawn him so far into Georgia, and he explained its meaning in the same letter: "My long and single line of railroad to my rear, of limited capacity, is the delicate point of my game . . . It is a big Indian war; still thus far I have won four strong positions, advanced a hundred miles, and am in possession of a large wheat-growing region and all the iron mines and works of Georgia." But with all the Federals had accomplished, Johnston still had his army intact "and can fight or fall back, as he pleases. The future is uncertain, but I will do all that is possible," Sherman said in closing.[55]

Sherman apparently kept his misgivings for his family, for a few days later he optimistically wrote Halleck: "All well. There are troops enough in Kentucky to manage Morgan, and in Tennessee to watch Forrest, should he make his appearance, as Johnston doubtless calculates." But on the next day, June 14, when he heard of another victory of Forrest over the Federals in Mississippi, he was disturbed about the outcome and told Secretary of War Stanton, "Our troops must assume the offensive from Memphis" to keep Forrest busy. Again on the fifteenth he wrote Stanton on this pressing subject and told the Secretary of War there were two officers in Memphis whom he believed capable of the task. "I will order them to make up a force," he said, "and go out and follow Forrest to the death, if it costs 10,000 lives and breaks the Treasury. There will never be peace in Tennessee till Forrest is dead." For his own part Sherman promised that "General Grant may rest easy that Joe Johnston will not trouble him, if I can help it by labor or thought." [56]

While Sherman expressed his respect for Johnston in word and displayed it in his moves, and others of the Federal army marveled at the Confederate general's ability to forestall their every maneuver, some Southerners began to murmur about the steady retirement. Colonel Gorgas in Richmond wrote in his diary on May 21 that Johnston was at Allatoona and some thought "that he will reach Macon in a few days at the rate he is retreating. I trust the country will sooner or later find out what sort of general he is. I don't think he will suit the emergency." Mackall had in mind the combating of any such feeling when in his letter of May 29 he carefully explained the operations to his homefolks: "Nothing brilliant has been done, nothing of the kind may be done, but if under God we save the country, the General can certainly bear a temporary odium; this all must bear who do not succeed at once—a suffering people are always impatient, so is a sick man, but it is a poor physician who yields to his impatience and tries the most desperate remedies as soon as called in. . . ." [57]

General Polk apparently knew nothing about the grumbling. "It is very gratifying to find that the troops and the country appear to have undiminished confidence in the ability and skill of General Johnston," he told his wife. But it was the confident spirit of the soldiers which amazed Sherman every time he read captured Confederate mail. The soldiers consistently predicted victory. John Cotton insisted that if the Federals didn't attack "Johnston will go on them . . . and . . . we will whip them badly." Sid Champion was equally positive about his commander's merits.

That he is able—aye—one of the ablest Genls we have is beyond question and I thank God that I have so much confidence in him . . . When will the great "battle" come off, and where—is beyond my power to say—because no one here knows anything about Johnsons [sic] movements—"Old Fabius" as I have nicknamed him—keeps us completely in the dark—yet with him he is basking in the light—for instance by way of illustration—an absentee of [the] 28th arrived, when we were fighting along the whole line—who could not find his Brigade. He visited Genl. Johnsons [sic] Head Quarters—and reported to him—that he had been home on furlough—and was returning to his Regiment to report for duty but could not find it. What Regiment? says the Genl. 28th Miss, replied our comrade. You will find it on the extreme left, replied the Genl.—and there our comrade found us. Who would have thought that the Genl knew precisely where all his troops were precisely located. It shows that he is a great man—and is well posted relative to his army.[58]

Men came and went at headquarters as Johnston received information about Federal movements and directed efforts to counter them. The situation altered constantly and required a stream of couriers to carry changed orders. Far in the rear engineers and Negro laborers constructed works to protect the crossings of the Chattahoochee, which Johnston's old friend, Mansfield Lovell, had examined for him. At Dalton he had asked for Lovell as a corps commander only to be refused, but Lovell had joined him as a volunteer aide. To guard along the Chattahoochee, Johnston used 3,000 Georgia militia under another old associate, Gustavus W. Smith. Smith like Lovell was in Davis' disfavor and had resigned from the army in early 1863. He served for a time as a volunteer on Beauregard's staff and then moved to Georgia to manage an iron foundry on the Etowah. When Sherman's advance forced him away Governor Brown offered him the command of the state troops, with whom he took the field to assist Johnston.[59]

On June 2 a message offering belated help came from Bragg. He told Johnston that they had heard in Richmond of the addition of troops to the enemy and added, "I trust the assistance now on the way to you from S. D. Lee and Forrest will more than counterbalance." This was the first Johnston had heard of any such aid, and he asked eagerly about it. "I have no knowledge of any assistance now on way from S. D. Lee and Forrest," he advised Bragg. "Please inform me what movements of these forces are being made."

Johnston's plans for Forrest were not for the cavalry leader to join the army in Georgia. However helpful that might be, he preferred that the capable Tennesseean should take advantage of the opportunity Sherman's long line of communications afforded. For some weeks he had corresponded with S. D. Lee about it and on May 19 had pointed out that a successful raid by Forrest would be of inestimable assistance to the campaign in Georgia. Lee secured the approval of Richmond and made preparations for a prompt and vigorous effort by Forrest, but the threat of aggressive action by the Federals in Memphis caused him to call it off. Then Forrest, himself, recommended on May 29 that the time was opportune for a thrust into Middle Tennessee against the enemy's communications, but no authorization came for him to proceed.

In all these exchanges of ideas nothing passed between Richmond and Johnston about the use of Forrest or help from him to the Army of Tennessee. Now that Bragg gave him the opportunity Johnston said, "Cavalry on the rear of Sherman this side of the Tennessee, would do him much harm at present." On the same day he also attempted to persuade Lee to use cavalry, this time some troops which were reported near the Alabama-Georgia line, in a quick raid on the Western & Atlantic Railroad anywhere between Chattanooga and the Etowah. He predicted "great results" from it as the line was weakly protected and Sherman had insufficient supplies. But Lee again considered the movement risky and declined to order it.[60]

The failure of Bragg to reply to his earlier message did not deter Johnston from again trying and on June 12 he telegraphed: "I have urged General S. D. Lee to send his cavalry at once to break the railroad between Dalton and the Etowah. If you agree with me in the opinion that it can at this time render no service in Mississippi to be compared with this, I suggest that you give him orders." Bragg should have realized how acute the situation was, as on June 4 he had written the President a letter, a copy of which he sent to Johnston, in which he said, "The condition of affairs in Georgia is daily becoming more serious, and though the enemy there has for a few days been quiet, I fear it is only to avail himself of heavy re-inforcements." He went on to give the seven corps which composed Sherman's army, an enumeration in which he made only one slight error, a part of the Sixteenth corps was still in West Tennessee. In closing Bragg said: "Should all these forces concentrate on the Army of Tennessee we may well apprehend disaster. As the entire available force of the Confederacy is now concentrated with our two main armies, I see no solution of this difficulty but in victory over one of the enemy's armies before the combination can be fully perfected, etc." [61]

What Bragg could have meant by these last two sentences in view of the actual situation one cannot but wonder. Sherman had his army concentrated in front of the Army of Tennessee, so it would seem that Bragg's apprehension of danger did not permit of delay. But he must have forgotten his anxiety before he received Johnston's appeal for the use of some of S. D. Lee's cavalry, for on June 13 he turned it down. He explained his action by repeating the fears Lee had stated a month before of threatened Federal action from Memphis. Only when danger from that quarter no longer existed, Bragg said, could attention be given to Johnston's pleas for assistance.[62]

Nothing was said then or later by Bragg or anyone else about the positive statement of June 2 that help was on the way to Johnston from Lee and Forrest, but Johnston still did not give up hope. On June 13 before he received Bragg's message refusing his earlier request Johnston "earnestly" suggested that Forrest be ordered to "operate against the enemy's rear between his army and Dalton." On the same day, either by prompting from the army commander or by his own realization of the circumstances, Polk wrote the President a similar suggestion and secured the endorsement of Hardee on his communication. Only Hood of the major commanders of the Army of Tennessee remained aloof from these urgent pleas to use the great cavalry leader against the Federal's vulnerable line of communications. But Richmond still worried more about the possibility of action in Mississippi than it did its inevitability in Georgia. Bragg on June 18 seemed to dispose of the question when he told Johnston that S. D. Lee faced a superior opponent in his area, and said nothing about Forrest.[63]

Johnston had not ignored the possibility of his accomplishing something against Sherman's supply line while he attempted to persuade Richmond. He had to keep his own cavalry close at hand both to perform its tasks of observation and flank protection and because he had frequently to use it in the line when the Federals overlapped his positions. But he ordered small parties to slip past the enemy, and when well in the rear, to do all the damage they could to the railroad.[64]

Because of Sherman's consistent efforts to reach around the Army of Tennessee, Johnston's task continued to be one of keeping his men in position to confront any enemy move. On June 8 he concentrated his force in a shorter line north of Kennesaw Mountain, about twenty-five miles from Atlanta, to cover better the roads to that point, with Hardee's left at Gilgal Church, Polk in the center and Hood's right to the east of the road from Acworth to Marietta. Bate's division of Hardee's corps held Pine Mountain, a relatively low, detached hill in front of the general position. Wheeler's cavalry protected the right and Jackson's the left of the line.[65]

Hardee expressed some apprehension that Bate's division on Pine Mountain might be advanced too far from support for safety and asked Johnston to visit the position with him the next morning, the fourteenth. The weather had cleared and a cool wind was astir as the two generals rode to the front accompanied by Polk, who wished to study the topography from the height of the mountain. The examination convinced Johnston that Hardee's fear was well grounded and he instructed the corps commander to withdraw Bate after nightfall. The sight of the three generals as they looked carefully over the terrain and then discussed what they saw drew the attention of some of the enlisted men, who gathered close to watch them. The group grew to such proportions as to attract the interest of the enemy and a battery commander fired upon it. A cannonball struck a near-by tree and the men with their commanders sought the shelter of the trenches, but before he could reach them another shell struck Polk, killing him instantly. Johnston saw the bishop-general falling and hastened to him. While the cannonade continued he knelt beside his friend and colleague. Tears filled his eyes as he laid his hand upon Polk's head and said: "We have lost much! I would rather anything but this." [66]

CHAPTER XX

BACK TO THE CHATTAHOOCHEE

From signal stations high up on Kennesaw messages requested that Johnston's headquarters at Marietta send an ambulance for Polk's remains. When it arrived the sorrowful, silent cavalcade retraced its way with Polk's riderless horse accompanying the party. Johnston rode by the side of the ambulance with his head bare and his grief apparent in his face. At the Marietta depot the body was placed in a railroad car to continue the journey to Atlanta.

Johnston informed Davis of the calamitous loss to the army and the country, and appointed General Loring to be Polk's temporary successor. He then addressed the men in the ranks:

Comrades, you are called to mourn your first captain, your oldest companion in arms. Lieutenant-General Polk fell today at the outpost of the army, the army he raised and commanded, in all of whose trials he shared, to all of whose victories he contributed. In this distinguished leader we have lost the most courteous of gentlemen, the most gallant of soldiers. The Christian patriot soldier has neither lived nor died in vain. His example is before you; his mantle rests with you.[1]

On the next morning, the fifteenth, Sherman continued his creeping tactics by edging his troops forward to prevent the construction of a new Confederate line along Kennesaw and Lost mountains. The Federals found Pine Mountain deserted in accordance with Johnston's order, before Polk's death, to withdraw Bate's division. But wherever Sherman turned, strong Confederate defenses seemed to spring up. He rode the front constantly and studied Johnston's every move for the slightest mistake. The strength of the Confederate position impressed him, its only weakness being the Chattahoochee River so close to its rear. The Confederate commander covered all the roads so well and divined the Federal flanking moves so quickly that Sherman began to think about a change of tactics. On June 16 he divulged his new idea to Halleck. Although he continued to examine the enemy's position for any weakness, he said that he then "inclined to feign upon both flanks and assault the center. It may cost us dear but in results would surpass an attempt to pass around." [2]

Both commanders had conducted the campaign with the hope that the other would attack, except for Sherman's flanking move at Resaca and Johnston's first plan at Cassville. Sherman realized that if he changed his tactics he might be playing into Johnston's hands, but he hoped that it would be at a time and place where conditions would be more favorable to him than to his enemy. Confederate cavalry pestered him and caused him to worry about his long supply line. Rain was another problem as every small rivulet soon became another defense position for the enemy. Realistically he told Grant that the army could not keep pace "with my thoughts and wishes, but no impulse can be given it that I will not guide." [3]

Johnston was equally watchful in his efforts to correspond to enemy shifts or by anticipating them to throw the Northerners off balance. On the seventeenth he chose a new line and sent pioneers with axes and picks to prepare it. The Confederates withdrew to it on the dark, stormy night of the nineteenth. Its principal anchor was Kennesaw Mountain, some 700 feet above the surrounding countryside. Its height was not sufficient to offer protection against the power of the Federal cannon, the fire from which caused damage to Southern wagon trains and troops in the mountain's rear.

Loring's troops occupied the strong position along the mountain and from its slope and top could observe every movement of the enemy. Hood's men were in place on the right protecting the W. & A. railroad to the east with their flank resting on a small creek. To the west was Hardee's corps, stationed in an arcing line which bent back to the southwest of Marietta, with its left fixed on another of the numerous small streams which run through the area. The cavalry protected the flanks but moved from one threatened point to another if necessary to fight as infantry. All commands held themselves in readiness to shift at a moment's notice and working details used their strength sparingly to prevent any overfatigue of their members.[4]

When Johnston retired to the Kennesaw line, Sherman confidently told Washington that the Confederates had fled to the cover of the Chattahoochee but quickly admitted that he was wrong. It made no difference in the forward movement of the troops. Invariably they proceeded "on the principle of an advance against fortified positions," he told Halleck. "The whole country is one vast fort, and Johnston must have full fifty miles of connected trenches, with abatis and finished batteries." On the Federal right Sherman took advantage of a flooded creek to make another extension of his line toward the Chattahoochee, while over to the east on the other end of the long line Wheeler struck heavily against the Union left on the twentieth in an action which brought credit to the men and praise to their commander. All along the front skirmishing was heavy as the Union forces probed to find an enemy weak spot.[5]

Rain fell constantly and operations off the roads were impossible. Small cavalry parties worried Sherman, who grew more sensitive to the vulnerability of his line of communications, by their damage to the railroad and the telegraph lines. Johnston had a more pressing cause for alarm. Hardee said that he could no longer stretch his numbers safely to confront the shifting Federals. Again the Confederate commander had to make a quick decision. On the night of June 21 he moved Hood's corps from the right to the extreme left. He made Wheeler responsible for the eastern area Hood had occupied and extended Loring's front in that direction to the railroad to help.[6]

In their new position Hood's corps faced the enemy under Hooker. Before long the two commanders on their own initiative became engaged in an inconclusive action which brought upon them the reproach of their superiors. It began with a typical effort to extend and advance the Federal line. Hooker sent his men forward with the expectation of little resistance, but Johnston's anticipation of Sherman's intention brought Hood's Confederates straight in Hooker's path. The latter to his surprise found his men repulsed by an impetuous defense. Then Hood, deceived by the ease with which the divisions of Hindman and Stevenson threw back the Federals, determined to make an effort to push his line forward without any real idea of what lay in the way. It was a costly venture. Johnston estimated the loss at 1,000 and later exposed as untrue Hood's first report that it had been an exclusively defensive engagement on the part of the Confederates. Neither side gained anything by the fight, but Hood lost men whom the Confederates found impossible to replace.[7]

The details of cavalry operating behind the Federal front accomplished enough for Johnston to advise Wheeler to add to their number "under a commander capable of appreciating the importance of the service." And unknown to Johnston S. D. Lee had at long last decided to turn mounted troops loose to operate in the Federal rear. The venture proved less than fortunate when they met defeat near the Tennessee line. More and more it became clear that no help would come until an ably led, relatively large mounted force was assigned the task.[8]

The long delay in the Kennesaw area caused Sherman to grow more tense. He showed it in his attitude toward his subordinates whom he thought excessively cautious. "I suppose the enemy with his smaller force intends to surround us," he wrote to one with irritated sarcasm. Finally on June 24 he decided to put into practice the plan about which he had written Halleck. Monday, June 27, at 8:00 A.M. was to be the day and hour. Each commander should use the intervening time for probing reconnaissances to find soft spots in the opposing line but should attempt to give the impression of a general assault when the fighting began.[9]

Marching and countermarching, digging trenches, rifle pits and artillery replacements, such were the dominant activities of both Southerners and Northerners in the lines which stretched along the Kennesaw front. Rain seemed as unceasing as the "everlasting 'pop' 'pop' on the skirmish line." The positions of the two armies were so close to each other that about the only relief the men secured was by "jawing" or taunting one another. Those on picket duty arranged informal truces for ration time or as the mood might strike them, and whenever firing ceased the steady, rhythmic strokes of the woodchoppers took over. From his post high upon Kennesaw General French noted the difference between the two sides of the lines:

behind the enemy the vast panorama is ever changing. There are now large trains to the left of Lost Mountain and at Big Shanty, and the wagons are moving to and fro everywhere. Encampments of hospitals, quartermasters, commissaries, cavalry and infantry whiten the plain here and there as far as the eye can reach! Look at our side of the long line of battle! It is narrow, poor, and quiet, save at the front where the men are, and contrasts . . . strangely with that of the enemy.[10]

Army morale was high and Johnston moved to keep it so when he asked for a general, R. S. Ewell, whom he knew to be capable, to succeed to Polk's command. But Davis again made his own appointment without regard for Johnston's wishes, although the man he chose and promoted to lieutenant general, A. P. Stewart, had proved an effective division commander throughout the campaign.[11]

Helped by improved weather the Federals made their preparations and were ready when the appointed day arrived. Sherman with his telegraphers close at hand took station on a cleared hill, from which he could observe the action and guide the plan as it unfolded. To Sam Watkins that morning the "heavens seemed made of brass, and the earth of iron. . . . It seemed that the arch-angel of Death stood and looked on with outstretched wings, while all the earth was silent." The calm lasted for a few hours, broken only by the occasional sound of a picket's or sharpshooter's rifle. Then, with a crash like a dozen thunderstorms rolled into one, fire leaped from the Federal guns massed along the line, a mighty prelude for the assault to come. Solid shot, grape and shrapnel filled the air.[12]

As the roar of the cannon ceased men in blue massed in columns of brigades marched out of the veil of smoke toward the Confederate lines. Thomas chose as his target the divisions of Cheatham and Cleburne of Hardee's corps, while McPherson sent his men against the portion of Loring's command in position along that section of the mountain known as Little Kennesaw. A little more than a mile separated the two actions of the Battle of Kennesaw Mountain and neither was on the mountain proper.

Confederate skirmishers met the advancing columns with several rounds from rifle pits and then retired to the main positions. Onward the Federals came until within range of the men in the trenches. Then the shocking fury of the Confederate muskets and the enfilading fire of the batteries ground their efforts to a halt. Fieldpieces played upon them as fast as gunners could load, aim and fire. Amid the swelling din of explosions and yelling men, carnage and destruction took over; "Hell had broke loose in Georgia, sure enough," wrote one of the participants.

The Federals worked their way close to the Confederate trenches over fallen comrades, and when one group faltered more came on. Some staggered past the line to be captured and "company Aytch" soon had every " 'gopher hole' full of Yankee prisoners." Southern breastworks absorbed the Union lead but the continuous fire held the danger of death for defenders as well as attackers. Overhead a blazing sun brought the temperature well over 100° and added its discomfort to men already caught in the torment of the battle's fury. As General French watched and listened from his post on the top of Kennesaw, the fire of the batteries and the smaller arms of the men set up "a roar as constant as Niagara and as sharp as the crash of thunder with lightning in the eye. . . ."

At an angle in the line where Cheatham's men massed in defense, fighting reached its bloody zenith. There the courage and valor of the Federals could find no critic. "Dead Angle," they dubbed the spot where so many fell and where for a brief time the Union flag floated above the Confederate works. Prompt use of his reserves by Cheatham prevented a breach, but some Northerners reached so near the defenders' line that they remained in sheltered spots rather than hazard the return. Pat Cleburne's men also stood unflinching to receive the waves of the enemy. The effect of their accurate fire and the strength of their position is best shown in their commander's report, where he tabulated his own loss as only eleven, while that of the enemy in his front he estimated at 1,000.

As the Federal assaulting lines withdrew to re-form, the forest undergrowth blazed, set afire by the bursting shells, and endangered the wounded with the further threat of burning. Despite the fury of the fighting the Confederates signaled to their foes to carry off those stricken and vaulted their protective parapets to assist in the rescue. In this impromptu truce no breach of faith occurred; no man fired on or made another captive. When the field was clear of helpless men Federal officers tendered a brace of pistols to the Confederate colonel who arranged the truce and then withdrew to start again the duel of powder, iron and men.

Before noon Sherman realized that his change of tactics had failed.

He accepted full responsibility for it and justified the effort by the necessity to impress upon both his own troops and the Confederate command that he would order an assault against even such strong defensive works as those along the Kennesaw line. He wished all to know that he would fight as well as maneuver to gain his ends. That was the only result from the Union point of view. Most of the Federals returned to the lines from which they had launched the engagement, but "more of their best soldiers lay dead and wounded," said Johnston, "than the number of British veterans that fell in General Jackson's celebrated battle of New Orleans. . . ." Sherman reported his casualties as 3,000 dead and wounded, but Johnston maintained that was an understatement. From the number of dead who lay nearly covering the ground in some areas in front of the Confederate position he estimated the number at around 6,000, while his own losses were only 552.[13]

For Johnston and the Army of Tennessee Kennesaw had more important results than a victory over the attacking enemy. It was the conclusive evidence to convince Johnston that these men were in every way the equal of that great group of fighters whom he had led in Virginia. The enemy at Kennesaw, he said, "retired—unsuccessful—because they had encountered *entrenched* infantry unsurpassed by that of Napoleon's Old Guard, or that which followed Wellington into France, out of Spain." It was the first real Confederate achievement of the campaign and credit for it went to the men of the army although by emphasizing the word entrenched he undoubtedly claimed some portion for his foresight in preparing the position.[14]

But there was a further importance for Johnston in the action at Kennesaw. It gave him new insight into the man who opposed him. After Fredericksburg in a letter to Wigfall he had exclaimed that no one would ever attack him under such circumstances as Burnside had Lee on the December day in 1862. Here at Kennesaw he had what seemed to be exactly that good fortune. But Sherman proved to be no Burnside. He did not waste his army in repeated, futile efforts to storm a strongly held position. When it became apparent that assault was not the way, Sherman withdrew and closed the action before losses so weakened or disorganized his force that the Confederates could attempt a counterblow. For Johnston it was another evidence that his opponent was different from the other member of the Federal team, Grant, whose campaign against Lee Johnston watched with interest. Sherman had no intention of attempting to break his way through by sheer use of strength, as did Grant.

For the commander of the Army of Tennessee this obvious fact modified any exultant feeling. It meant that his inferior force must continue to stretch while he matched intelligence with intelligence in an attempt to forestall Sherman's every maneuver. Johnston understood from experience what Davis, Bragg, Seddon and Cooper never seemed to grasp: that the Confederates confronted no slow-moving, inexperienced, incapably led army in Georgia. This was an intelligently directed, hardened group of veterans who had to be met with somewhere near equal numbers if victory was to be gained.

In Richmond rumors had been current that the President was dissatisfied with Johnston's conduct of the campaign and was seriously considering the appointment of a new commander. From such sources as Hood's secret correspondence and his agent, Brewster, Davis and his associates secured the feeling that all was not well with the army in Georgia, that Johnston's conduct of the campaign was harmful to morale, both in the ranks of the army and in the public mind. Already they said he had lost the confidence of the authorities and people of Georgia. Should the campaign continue as it had—and it apparently would, as Johnston had reported no change of plans to the War Department—defeat was an inevitable end.[15]

Davis' adherents fed the stories. The more widespread the criticism of Johnston the more it removed the responsibility from the shoulders of Davis and indulged his antagonism for the army commander. In Columbia, South Carolina, Mrs. Chesnut and her set discussed the news and gossip about Georgia frequently because of their interest in Hood. They knew of the possibility of Johnston's removal, for Brewster told them that when he was in Richmond just after Cassville he heard of Davis' plan. Brewster continued, Mrs. Chesnut reported, by saying "that this blow at Joe Johnston, cutting off his head, ruins the schemes of the enemies of the government. Wigfall asked me to go at once, and get Hood to decline to take this command, for it will destroy him if he accepts it. He will have to fight under Jeff Davis' orders; no one can do that now and not lose caste in the Western Army." [16]

With such bitter comments prevalent among social and official groups some members of Congress began to wonder what the situation in Georgia actually was. It led two Alabamians, Representative Francis S. Lyon and Senator Richard M. Walker, into stopping at army headquarters for personal investigations on their way home. Lyon, a popular lawyer and planter with many years of public service, found many friends in Johnston's command and they gave convincing evidence that morale among the soldiers was undamaged. Walker investigated among the people of the area as well. Lyon was so pleased that as soon as he reached home he made a public statement of the excellent spirit in the army, while Walker sent his findings on to Richmond in a letter to his friend, Assistant Secretary of War John A. Campbell. ". . . I found on my return from Richmond no indication whatever that the popular confidence in General Johnston had been at all shaken by his retreating policy," he wrote in contradiction of the stories in circulation in the capital. "On the contrary, as far as I have been able to discover, the opinion is almost universal that the policy he adopted was judicious and necessary. As to the army itself, its confidence in Johnston seems unlimited." [17]

Of all of the visitors the most eagerly greeted by the Johnstons were the Wigfalls who were on their way to Texas, and stopped at Atlanta, not only to see and talk with their friends but to leave their two young daughters in acceptance of Mrs. Johnston's repeated invitations. While the ladies chattered away in the sparsely furnished small house in which Mrs. Johnston lived on the outskirts of Atlanta, the Senator hurried to Marietta to see the General. It was the day after the bloody repulse of Sherman at Kennesaw, but Wigfall brought Johnston news of greater import. On good authority he had learned that Davis had decided to remove Johnston from his command. The Senator had tried to use his knowledge of the situation to convince influential people that the rumor in Richmond about the feeling in the army and Georgia were not true and had promised to investigate both in his visit. To accomplish the purpose Wigfall talked with a number of friends in the army and sought among the people and officials of Georgia the real feeling toward Johnston. All that he heard proved that the stories in Richmond were untrue.

In the conversations between the two friends everything centered about the campaign. Wigfall had a number of questions about details on which he wished further information. As to the general conception they were in complete accord. Without the assistance of an extensive campaign against Sherman's communications Johnston would have to continue as he had from Dalton. He would meet stratagem with stratagem, inflicting all possible damage upon the enemy but not exposing his force, until Sherman chose to strike at a position Johnston selected or made some error of disposition which gave the Confederates an opportunity to meet the Federals with equal force. But when they reached Atlanta, Johnston said, they would man its defenses and hold it against any effort of Sherman. When Wigfall wondered if there might not be a possibility for a decisive battle before the army reached Atlanta and pointed to the Chattahoochee as a natural line, Johnston said that Peachtree Creek offered a better opportunity. There, if defeated, the Federals would have the Chattahoochee at their back, but if the result were otherwise, the Confederates could move into the fortifications of Atlanta.[18]

The day before the arrival of Wigfall Johnston had written another appeal to Bragg in which he estimated his losses for the campaign at 9,000 killed and wounded, and restated the situation. Johnston undoubtedly told Wigfall of this letter, and the Texan immediately went to work to secure support for Johnston and his request for a seriously conducted effort against Sherman's supply line. As soon as he reached Atlanta, after his talk with Johnston, Wigfall hurried to Governor Brown's office and at the Governor's suggestion wrote Senator B. H. Hill, then at his home in La Grange, to ask that he come to Atlanta for a meeting of the three of them on the approaching crisis.[19]

Instead of waiting for Hill in Atlanta, Wigfall traveled to Macon to call on Howell Cobb. He found Senator Henry of Tennessee there and enlisted the assistance of both of them. Brown also went to work at once, and at a late hour June 28 wrote Davis in an effort to persuade the President that the critical circumstances in Georgia demanded a revision of Richmond's attitude. "I need not call your attention to the fact that this place is to the Confederacy as important as the heart is to the body," he said with reference to Atlanta. "We must hold it." He had done all he could to help, but Johnston had to have more assistance. Brown asked specifically if Morgan or Forrest or both could not operate against the Federal communications. "I do not wish to volunteer advice," he wrote as though in an effort to prevent antagonizing the President, "but so great is my anxiety for success of our arms and the defense of the State that I trust you will excuse what may seem an intrusion." [20]

Hill reached Atlanta as quickly as he could after receiving the request of Brown and Wigfall. As Hill was a champion of Davis and at times a spokesman for him, the Governor and the Texan explained carefully the situation. After their discussion Hill decided against writing: "The matter is too important, time is too precious, and letters are too inadequate," he said. He would go himself to Richmond, but to be better posted he went to see Johnston, with whom he had a "free conversation" on July 1. With Hood present for at least a portion of the time, the Senator and the General reviewed the situation in detail. Johnston expressed the desire that the Federals might attack the Confederate entrenched lines but though they had given some indications that they might do so he did not seriously think that Sherman would order the attempt.

The General told his visitor that he would very willingly accept battle in the open field, but Sherman refused to move forward "except by entrenching as he advanced." Since to attack such strongly prepared Federal positions would be unwise, the Confederates would have to continue to fall back whenever Sherman threatened their flank and rear. Carefully and logically Johnston built an incontrovertible justification of his appeal that Richmond use Forrest or Morgan with 5,000 cavalry against the railroad which constituted Sherman's communications.

Hill questioned Johnston about his own source of supplies should he fall back of the Chattahoochee and thereby render bridges over the river from Alabama vulnerable to enemy attack. Johnston's answer to this vital query displays another weakness of the Confederate geographical command. The bridges were not in his department. All he could do was to rely upon reports that they were defended by works and by Alabama troops. But Hill said he had heard that not a "spade of dirt" had been turned or a pile driven in the construction of fortifications while the "militia called there to defend [the bridges] I understand, has been sent home." This surprised the army commander, but he only said that should the enemy cut that line he would use one farther south by way of Opelika, Columbus and Macon. Hill's better knowledge of the geography caused him to remark that if Sherman could burn the first bridges he could easily reach those at Columbus, which were only thirty-five miles away. As a possible greater danger, Hill suggested that should Johnston retire to or over the Chattahoochee Sherman would be free to cross the river below him and to pen the Confederates in Atlanta.

That would allow Sherman to cut Johnston's supply line from Alabama and Lee's from South Georgia. Thus he would force the fall of Richmond as well as Atlanta.

To this series of possible eventualities Johnston replied, according to the account Hill wrote two weeks later: " 'Well, before the enemy shall get the position you mention of course we shall have a bloody fight,' or words to that effect. This was the only point at which my mind received the impression that General Johnston would fight anyhow, or except under the conditions previously mentioned."

Johnston told Hill that his army was more nearly on numerical equality with that of Sherman than when the campaign began, but he explained as he had to Wigfall that he could not spare his cavalry for any extended effort against the enemy's rear. Everyone agreed about the total effect upon the Confederacy of the campaign in Georgia: "All, then is lost by Sherman's success, and all is gained by Sherman's defeat," as Hill summarized it. As though to make it as emphatic as possible Hill stated three times in his written account, which he prepared for the Richmond group after presenting orally his memory of his meeting with Johnston, that the best way to achieve a Confederate victory was by a campaign against Sherman's communications.

Hill wondered if there were still time for such an effort to be effective if he should win Richmond's approval of it. Johnston believed there was, but Hood thought the hour very late if it had not passed. Both generals agreed that action was imperative, that further delay would be dangerous. When Hill pressed for a definite answer as to how long the Confederates could remain north of the Chattahoochee, Johnston suggested the Senator himself make the calculation from the fact that the "enemy had been so many days (over thirty) advancing from New Hope to the present position, only a few miles." Hood again inclined to disagree with his superior. He said that the line they then held "was the strongest in that country; that the Kennesaw was the great military base in that region, and that when we left that line we should go back much more rapidly to the Chattahoochee River." But Johnston stated that he had other strong, prepared lines to his rear and apparently thinking that Sherman would continue his tactics of the previous month believed he could hold the "enemy for a long time." [21]

Whether or not Johnston was unduly optimistic about his ability to hold Sherman he felt sure of Atlanta, where few people had left and shops and plants were busy as usual turning out their wares of war. Gangs of slaves were at work strengthening the defensive positions around the town. But Sherman had already arrived at decisions which forced a change in the schedule Hill said that Johnston stated. In the evening hours of June 27 he kept his telegraphers busy as through their medium he discussed the next move with his principal subordinate, General Thomas. At 9:00 P.M. he asked if Thomas were willing to cut loose from the railroad for a return to the flanking movements of the earlier part of the campaign. Such a move Sherman predicted "would bring matters to a crisis. . . . " Thomas agreed as he considered "it decidedly better than butting against breastworks twelve feet thick and strongly abatised." [22]

By July 1, the day Senator Hill visited Johnston's headquarters, Sherman was ready to carry out his plan. Schofield was in position on the army's right for the first phase, which consisted of moving McPherson the night of the second from the extreme left to extend the line held by Schofield toward the Chattahoochee. If Johnston failed to detect the movement the Federals would soon be across the railroad between the Confederates and their base at Atlanta. Should he discover it, Sherman hoped that he might be tempted to attack the apparently weakened lines in his front, then held by Thomas; but if instead he abandoned his position at Kennesaw and gave up Marietta, Sherman had prepared to follow him closely to force him from the railroad or better to catch him in the confusion of the river crossing.

But Johnston was typically vigilant in observation and interpretation of Sherman's movements and was not without his own preparations. In his rear, he had constructed two lines, one about six miles from Kennesaw and the other along the Chattahoochee and covering the railroad crossing. The river line was more elaborate with fieldworks and a particularly strong fortification planned and prepared under the direction of General Shoup. Johnston called on Gustavus Smith to send forward to the main army some of the militia. Because they consisted mainly of young boys and old men he explained that he did not wish them to become involved in the actual fighting but only wanted to use them in conjunction with Jackson's cavalry "to show an infantry force" and to make the line seem longer. They were the only help available to him. Actually Johnston had to stop at this critical time and explain to Richmond why he had not sent some regiments as directed to the peace and quiet of Savannah. The reason was obvious: they, like all the army, were constantly within rifleshot of the enemy.[23]

From Kennesaw's top scouts noted a movement by McPherson the night of July 2 and reported it to Johnston. Ever since the action of June 27 cannon and small arms had roared and cracked along the line except when interrupted by formal truces to bury the dead or smaller arrangements devised by the men themselves. The General waited as long as he dared before he led his army, frayed and tattered by the long campaign in all but fighting spirit, southward. As the last man marched away details hauled down telegraph lines and destroyed sections of the railroad. Little was left behind for the Federals, who noted that the withdrawal was as usual "in good order and without loss." [24]

At daylight July 3 Federal soldiers peacefully climbed the scarred slopes of Kennesaw and by 8:30 occupied Marietta, which citizens as well as Confederates had virtually abandoned. Sherman urged his troops forward in a vigorous pursuit and by nightfall turned his energies against his subordinates for their slowness. But in a message to one of his cavalry leaders he explained failure in terms of praise of his opponent: "We ought to have caught Johnston in his retreat," he said, "but he had prepared the way too well." At the same time the Federal commander, secure in the belief that "no general, such as he, would invite battle with the Chattahoochee behind him," incorrectly interpreted Johnston's intentions, and was surprised to find the Confederates waiting for him in the first of their newly prepared positions.[25]

The Southerners, according to John Hagan's letter home, found their new line "tolerable good" and because it was the Fourth of July assumed they would have a "hopping time" with the Yankees, who instead kept their "proper distance" and exhibited their "fine Spirits playing their bands & hollering." Sherman reported that he kept up a "noisy but not a desperate battle" during the day as a cover for his efforts to discover good river crossings. Because of the threat in these movements Johnston abandoned this position for that Shoup had prepared on the Chattahoochee. Again he used night to cloak his marching columns and it was not until the morning of the fifth that the Federals discovered his departure. With the river directly in his rear Johnston seemed to defy military axiom by attempting there to hold up Sherman's drive. But he had six bridges at his back and he impressed upon all commanders the importance of keeping them free for emergency use. He sent all trains and wheeled vehicles to the south bank of the Chattahoochee and instructed his subordinates to send details there each morning to draw ammunition and other needed supplies. He used the cavalry to keep a vigilant watch at crossings up and down the river and assigned Wheeler the task of destroying boats as well as bridges in the area. He moved also to protect the valuable railroad trestle at West Point, which he had assumed to be adequately guarded until Senator Hill told him differently. He asked for State troops for the purpose, and the commander of the Alabama militia sent ten companies to West Point on July 7. But with the typical Confederate propensity to ignore the present danger in order to assuage fears at all places these "reserves," as they were called, proceeded within ten days to protect Mobile.[26]

Richmond gave new evidence of the same failure. When Davis received Brown's appeal of June 28 for assistance for Johnston he asked Bragg for information on which to base a reply. Bragg told the President that "every available man" had been sent. There was in Bragg's opinion no way further to reinforce Johnston, "and he had been informed so several times. Certainly not from Mississippi, where it would be more proper to return a part of what he had received than to remove more."[27]

Davis wrote his answer to Brown from Bragg's suggestions. His conclusion was that there could be no help. This summary dismissal which offered suppositional arguments instead of facts reached the governor on the day the army withdrew to the Chattahoochee line. It aroused his combative disposition and his reply displayed it.

Our people believe that Genl. Johnston is doing all in his power with the means at his command and all expect you to send the necessary force to cut off the enemy's subsistence. We do not see how Forrest's operations in Mississippi or Morgan's raids as conducted in Kentucky interfere with Sherman's plans in this State as his supplies continue to reach him. Destroy these and Atlanta is not only safe, but the destruction of the army under Sherman opens up Tennessee and Ky. to us. Your information as to the relative strength of the two armies in North Georgia cannot be from reliable sources. If your mistake should result in the loss of Atlanta and the occupation of other strong points in the State by the enemy, the blows may be fatal to our cause and remote posterity may have reason to mourn over the error.[28]

Brown's pointed criticism was not destined to be of assistance to Johnston, as it angered Davis. The President displayed his feeling in a sarcastic reply in which he typically indulged in personal reflections and ignored the grave and growing danger in the situation. Davis wrote:

I am surprised to learn from you that the basis of the comparison I made on official reports and estimates is unreliable. Until your better knowledge is communicated I shall have no means of correcting such errors, and your dicta cannot control the disposition of troops in different parts of the Confederate States. Most men in your position would not assume to decide on the value of the service to be rendered by troops in distant positions. When you give me your reliable statement of the comparative strength of the armies, I will be glad to know the source of your information as to what the whole country expects and posterity will judge.[29]

In his answer to this communication Brown began with an expression of regret over the President's "exhibition of temper," but his obligation as both a citizen of the Confederacy and Governor of Georgia forced him to hold his ground. With a sarcasm more direct than that used by Davis, he wrote:

If you continue to keep our forces divided and our cavalry raiding and meeting raids while the enemy's line of communication nearly 300 miles from his base is uninterrupted, I fear the result will be similar to those which followed a like policy of dividing our forces at Murfreesborough and Chattanooga. If Atlanta is sacrificed and Georgia overrun while our cavalry is engaged in distant raids, you will have no difficulty in ascertaining, from correct sources of information, what was expected of you by the whole people, and what verdict posterity will record from your statements as to the relative strength of the two armies. I venture, at the hazard of further rebuke, to predict that your official estimates of Sherman's numbers are as incorrect as your official calculations at Missionary Ridge were erroneous.[30]

By bringing in Murfreesboro, Chattanooga and Missionary Ridge Brown tied Bragg with Davis in his indictment of the misdirection of Confederate military policy, but he pointed his chief criticism at the President who prided himself above all else on his military acumen and ability. Davis could do no more officially than rebuke Brown, but the principal result was to harden the President's determination to follow his own path even though it led to destruction. As for

Johnston, he again suffered the consequences of having the support of the wrong people.

Brown waited for two days after his communication to the President of July 7 for evidence of a changed attitude in Richmond, but when none came he issued a proclamation in which he called upon virtually every man in the state who could bear arms to take a place in the line. In doing so he made Davis' position perfectly clear to the people:

A late correspondence with the President of the Confederate States satisfies my mind that Georgia is to be left to her own resources to supply the re-enforcements to General Johnston's army, which are indispensable to the protection of Atlanta, and to prevent the State from being overrun by the overwhelming numbers now under the command of the Federal general upon our soil. . . . If the Confederate Government will not send the large cavalry force now engaged in raiding and repelling raids to destroy the long line of railroad over which General Sherman brings his supplies from Nashville, and thus compel him to retreat with the loss of most of his army, the people of Georgia, who have already been drawn upon more heavily in proportion to population than any other state in the Confederacy, must at all hazards and at any sacrifice rush to the front and aid the great commander at the head of our glorious self-sacrificing army to drive him from the soil of the Empire State.[31]

Although Brown's interpretation was bitterly realistic and one not likely to help general Confederate morale, he made no claim for assistance from the army in Virginia where Grant pressed Lee ever closer to Richmond. He asked, as thoughtful men repeatedly had since the beginning of the war, for the abandonment of the policy which accomplished for the Federals the purpose of so dividing the Confederate forces that they might be easily conquered. It was obvious that Brown had no quarrel either with Johnston's conduct of the campaign or the army's spirit or ability to fight. His objections were to the strategic concepts of the Richmond authorities, with whom his proclamation created the further issue of whether he had the power to revoke exemptions granted by Confederate sources. Despite these differences Davis agreed to provide arms for the men Brown called into service.[32]

When Richmond heard that Johnston occupied the position with his back to the Chattahoochee on July 5, the news created different opinions. Jones in the War Office recorded that it caused "no uneasiness, for the destruction of Sherman's army is deemed the more certain the farther he penetrates," but Davis became "more apprehensive for the future." In his telegram to Johnston on July 7, his first communication containing instructions since the army left Dalton, the President appeared to be utterly confused and certainly left his general confounded. He said:

That river, if not fordable, should not be immediately in your rear, and if you cross, it will enable the enemy without danger to send a detachment to cut your communications with Alabama, and, in the absence of the troops of that department, to capture the cities, destroy the mines and manufactories, and separate the States by a new line of occupation. At this distance, I cannot judge of your condition or the best method of averting calamity. Hopeful of results in Northern Georgia, other places have been stripped to re-enforce your army until we are unable to make further additions, and we are dependent on your success.[33]

Johnston attempted at once to reassure Davis. The army was not dangerously exposed in its position on the Chattahoochee, he said, and as Sherman's interest concentrated on the capture of Atlanta, the cavalry in Mississippi and Alabama should be able to prevent damage by a Federal raiding detachment in that area. But he pointedly remarked, the pressure of Sherman's numbers had forced his retirement and again he asked if some of the cavalry reported to be in Alabama and Mississippi could not be used against Sherman's rear. This appeal proved as futile as those which preceded it and Davis' reply earned Mackall's description, "sneering." The President said that Johnston should know the conditions in Mississippi better than to think help could come from there. Although he must have known of Johnston's explanation given earlier to Bragg, Davis asked why he didn't use his own cavalry against Sherman's rear: "If it be practicable for distant cavalry, it must be more so for that which is near, and former experiences have taught you the difference there would be in time. . . ." But if Johnston felt any indignation similar to that of Mackall he kept it typically to himself. With his usual respect he carefully explained to the President his inability to use his own cavalry and that the source of his information about troops in Mississippi was General Polk. Surely Davis would believe him justified in accepting the "statement of such a soldier," who had just come from commanding the department.[34]

The presence of the fortified Confederate position at the Chatta-hoochee was a surprise to Sherman, who had believed that Johnston would not stop for battle with the river so close to his back. The Federal commander doubted the existence of the Chattahoochee stronghold until a personal reconnaissance convinced him that this *"tête-du-pont,"* as he called it, was as excellent a field fortification as he had ever seen. The sight of it satisfied him that Johnston had not foolishly chosen to stop there, and that it would be unnecessarily foolhardy for him to attempt to carry it. While Thomas held the attention of the Confederates at the fortified point Sherman sent other forces out both to discover possible crossings of the river and to confuse the enemy as to his intention. At the village of Roswell, about twenty miles up the river, cavalry found the bridge destroyed but several mills were in full operation, at least one of them under a French flag. The subterfuge infuriated the easily aroused Sherman, who ordered the plants burned and "the arrest for treason [of] all owners and employees," whom he sent to the North.[35]

As troopers applied the torch at Roswell and gathered the mill-workers others labored there and near by to prepare the way for crossing the river. All was activity within the Federal lines. Repair crews worked feverishly to get the railroad in full operating condition close to the front. McPherson and Stoneman busily engaged in creating the belief that Sherman planned to make the crossing down river while Thomas continued to give the impression of forcing the Confederate position. But Schofield had his men ready below Roswell and on July 8 began the crossing.

When Johnston confirmed this news he ordered the necessary retirement for the night of the ninth. In an easy, unhindered manner the troops withdrew with each corps having two bridges for its use. Rear guards removed the pontoons and destroyed the permanent structures while the main army encamped two to three miles south of the river in positions which had been under construction since mid-June, in preparation for the expected engagement at Peachtree Creek. Thus events began to move toward the crisis Johnston had foreseen, although with greater rapidity than he expected.[36]

CHAPTER XXI

REMOVAL FROM COMMAND

As the soldiers took positions north of Atlanta on July 10 to await Sherman's next move, Mrs. Johnston came out to field headquarters to be with her husband on their wedding anniversary. She was alone in her Atlanta home as she had sent the Wigfall girls to Macon. She had herself discarded all but "indispensable" baggage so she would be prepared to leave at once in an emergency, but devotion held her close despite the hardships and potential danger.[1]

Atlantans were divided in their feeling. Some decided that Johnston planned to give the place up without a fight and left at once when they heard that orders had gone out to move government stores, factory equipment, hospitals and all wounded capable of it farther south. Mackall noted some discontent among the citizens and occasional abuse of Johnston; but, he continued, "military commanders have a hard time of it; people are so fond of victories, that they expect one the moment that an army is out in the field."[2]

At Newnan, some miles away to the southwest, Kate Cumming said that everyone was "breathless with expectation, waiting to see what move [Johnston] will make next. There is much conjecture on the subject. Few seem to have lost confidence in General J.; they think he is acting as well as he can with his means." Farther away in

Richmond wider circulation was given similar views when the *Whig* said editorially, "It is true that . . . when General Johnston first began his retrograde movement, there was a disposition, not only among unmilitary critics, but in high official circles, to depreciate that commander's abilities, and to predict for him the most serious reverses." But the truth was, the editor remarked, that Johnston's reputation had "grown with every backward step." [3]

The same day, July 9, Davis ordered Bragg to Georgia, where he should "confer with General Johnston in relation to military affairs there, and then, as circumstances may indicate, [should] visit the country west or east of Atlanta with a view to such dispositions and preparations as may best promote the ends and objects which have been discussed between us." Johnston had no knowledge of this order and was not prepared to receive Bragg when he arrived. Bragg's lack of popularity among all ranks of the army would have made the assignment a difficult one for a more sensitive man, and he entered upon it in a manner typical of him. Without waiting to see Johnston he sent alarming word to Davis: "Our army all south of the Chatta-hoochee, and indications seem to favor an entire evacuation of this place." Not many hours later he emphasized his warning by tele-graphing Davis that some of the enemy had crossed the river and were advancing on Atlanta. "Our army is sadly depleted," he con-tinued, "and now reports 10,000 less than the return of 10th of June. I find but little encouraging." If Davis' intent had been to secure an emissary who would give him seemingly objective grounds for a decision already made, he chose properly.[4]

Bragg called upon Johnston only twice in the period of his stay and left the impression that his visit had no official purpose. The reason he gave for his journey was to visit commanders to the west to discover what reinforcements they could furnish the army in Georgia. Johnston recorded that he and Bragg

had no conversation concerning the Army of Tennessee than such as I introduced. He asked me no questions regarding its operations, past or future, made no comments upon the one, nor suggestions for the other, and, so far from having reason to suppose that Atlanta would not be defended, he saw the most vigorous preparations for its defense in progress. Supposing that he had been sent by the President to learn and report upon the condition of military affairs there, I described them to him briefly, when he visited me, and proposed to send for the lieutenant-generals, that he might obtain from them such minute information as he desired. He replied that he would be glad to see those officers as friends, but only in that way, as his visit was unofficial.[5]

Hood and Bragg met more as conspirators than friends. Even before Bragg called upon him for the conversation they held without the knowledge of Johnston, Hood wrote the visitor a long letter, which sounds as though it was a bid for the command for himself. In it Hood showed utter disregard for his superior in the army and for the facts. He estimated the army's losses at 20,000, double the number Johnston stated and insisted that opportunities to strike the enemy had been lost. He said:

I have, general, so often urged that we should force the enemy to give us battle as to almost be regarded reckless by the officers high in rank in this army, since their views have been so directly opposite. I regard it as a great misfortune to our country that we failed to give battle to the enemy many miles north of our present position. Please say to the President that I shall continue to do my duty cheerfully and faithfully, and strive to do what I think is best for our country, as my constant prayer is for our success.

Like everyone else, Hood felt that he had to say that the army needed reinforcements; but even here he made a less than practical suggestion when he recommended the transfer of the Trans-Mississippi command of Kirby Smith to Georgia. The movement would have required weeks to accomplish even if accepted and carried out with a degree of efficiency unknown before.[6]

Bragg made only a passing reference to his conversation with Hood in his communication to Davis, probably because the copy of Hood's letter which he enclosed contained its major points. He made two reports on his talks with Johnston and in the first stated a fundamental difference with Johnston's account of them. Where Johnston said there was no discussion of the army's operations except such as he introduced, Bragg left the impression that Johnston was the one who displayed reserve. The army commander received him "courteously and kindly," Bragg told the President; but he had not asked for advice so Bragg had volunteered none. The President's adviser reported:

I cannot learn that he has any more plan for the future than he has in the past. It is expected that he will await the enemy on a line some three miles from here and the impression prevails that he is now more inclined to fight. The enemy is very cautious, and intrenches immediately on taking a new position. His force, like our own, is greatly reduced by the hard campaign. His infantry is now very little over 60,000. The morale of our army is still reported good.[7]

In a fuller account, which he sent to Davis by courier the same day, Bragg again displayed his pique at Johnston. "As General J. has not sought my advice," he again told the President, "nor ever afforded me a fair opportunity of giving my opinion, I have obtruded neither upon him. Such will continue to be my course." Johnston apparently intended to continue to "await the enemy's approach and be governed, as heretofore, by the development in our front. All valuable stores and machinery have been removed, and most of the citizens able to go have left with their effects. Much disappointment and dissatisfaction prevails, but there is no open or imprudent expression." Bragg made no mention of the Atlanta defenses and the work to improve them but emphasized that only one course was practicable, offensive action. The enemy would hold the advantages of "position, numbers and morale," but as usual with Bragg when he was not the one directly responsible, he did not believe these were insurmountable. He gave the totals of Sherman's force, which he said had "always been overestimated," as being but 75,000.[8]

The real purpose of Bragg's trip to Atlanta was the appointment of the new commander. In this letter and in an exchange of telegrams which were so cryptic in their wording as almost to defy interpretation this becomes evident. Bragg pointed out that any change "would be attended by some serious evils. A general denunciation by the disorganizers, civil and military, will follow." But as the situation demanded aggressive, offensive action by the Confederates, a change had to be made. Johnston by his record would not attempt to fight on his own initiative, and Hardee disqualified himself by having "generally favored the retiring policy." Stewart since his appointment had "fairly and generally" showed an aggressive interest, but the man of Bragg's choice was Hood. Either Bragg based his opinion largely on conversations with Hood or he ignored the testimony of such informed officers as Hardee and Lieutenant Mackall, both of whom recorded that Hood consistently advocated retirement in councils; for he reported to Davis that Hood from Dalton to Atlanta had constantly "been in favor of giving battle." "If any change is made,"

Bragg advised, "Lieutenant-General Hood would give unlimited satisfaction, and my estimate of him, always high, has been raised by his conduct in this campaign." [9]

Events seemed to be approaching a crisis of some sort. On the fourteenth Johnston advised Richmond that the enemy had reached a point halfway between the Chattahoochee and the railroad which led east to Augusta from Atlanta. The next morning he reported the same information to Bragg and explained the delay by saying that he expected Bragg to come to see him at headquarters which he feared to leave. Then to add to those gathering troubles he received an important telegram from Senator Hill in Richmond. "You must do the work with your present force. For God's sake do it." On the next day, the sixteenth, a message came from Davis as though it were a follow-up to that of Hill. The President acknowledged the information about the enemy's extension to the east, but the more important content was "I wish to hear from you as to present situations, and your plan of operations so specifically as will enable me to anticipate events." [10]

Johnston did not know the full significance of Hill's message and Davis' request for his plans, but they probably added to his suspicion that Bragg's trip to Atlanta contained deeper implications than the one stated by the visitor. But whatever its purpose Bragg gave no evidence of an effort to understand and appreciate Johnston's problems as Johnston had his when on similar missions to Tullahoma. Johnston showed his usual self-control in all their relations but allowed himself more freedom in a conversation with another Congressional party who came to warn him that the President was dissatisfied with the campaign and was considering his removal. In the discussion the group stated Davis' conviction "as a military man . . . that if he were in your place he could whip Sherman now." Johnston said that he knew the President thought he could "do a great many things that other men would hesitate to attempt. For instance, he tried to do what God failed to do. He tried to make a soldier of Braxton Bragg and you know the result. It couldn't be done." [11]

Bragg's sycophancy in echoing Davis' every desire and his attitude in Atlanta caused Johnston to realize the error of assuming Bragg to be friendly to him. But the antagonism between the General and the President still originated with Davis, who viewed everything

Johnston did with a prejudiced critical eye. To justify himself the President consistently minimized the reports of enemy numbers, and insisted that "Almost all the available military strength of the south and west, in men and supplies, were pressed forward and placed at [Johnston's] disposal." Yet at Johnston's removal troops sat unoccupied in various sections of the Confederacy while a huge Federal army maneuvered its weaker foe out of the way.

As Johnston withdrew southward, his men battling at every turn "like Devils and Indians combined," as Sherman described them, Davis continued to fight his campaign of statistics, in which those he used consistently disagreed with reports from the scene. The figures as he gave them seemed in every detail to confirm his argument that only Johnston's lack of ability or fear of battle caused him to retreat all the way to the Chattahoochee instead of following the administration's wish for an offensive from Dalton. As Davis considered what he should do, according to his later testimony, "From many quarters, including such as had most urged his assignment, came delegations, petitions, and letters, urging me to remove General Johnston from the command of the army and assign that important trust to some officer who would resolutely hold and defend Atlanta." But despite his own apprehensions about the consequences of the campaign, Davis said that he resisted the pressure for fear a change of command might prove even more disastrous.[12]

From the existing records there is very little evidence which testifies to a clamor for Johnston's removal except among a limited group. It was Davis' own dissatisfaction with the army's retreat coupled with his dislike of Johnston that led to the crisis, not public demand, to which the Confederate President seldom made concessions. In June rumors of the extent of this dissatisfaction were at the base of Wigfall's conversations with Johnston and caused other members of Congress to visit him. All came with curiosity about the reported lack of confidence within the army in its leader, and left with the conviction of the opposite.

Then it was that the President sent Bragg to Atlanta, where Hood was ready to do what he could to feed Davis' feeling of dissatisfaction. Nor did the almost simultaneous arrival of letters from the governors of Georgia and Alabama, written to support Johnston, have any effect in stilling it. In fact, before Bragg arrived in Atlanta, the President revealed his intention to General Lee, who must have heard the rumors of a contemplated change of command in Georgia but was unacquainted with the immediate situation. "General Johnston has failed," Davis telegraphed in cipher to Lee on July 12, "and there are strong indications that he will abandon Atlanta. . . . It seems necessary to remove him at once. Who should succeed him? What think you of Hood for the position?" [13]

Lee discussed the matter with at least one of his subordinates, John B. Gordon, a native Georgian who had served with Johnston in Virginia. Gordon was certain that only Lee's transfer to Georgia could prevent a damaging shock to the morale of the Army if Davis removed Johnston. He disapproved a change of command particularly as Johnston held the confidence of his men and had not lost a battle or a campaign. Lee felt as Gordon did about Johnston and according to the Georgian's account said: "General Johnston is a patriot and an able soldier. He is upon the ground, and knows his army and its surroundings and how to use it better than any of us." [14]

Lee not only respected the ability of Johnston, but he had doubts about Hood as the commander of an army. He, too, questioned the wisdom of replacing a commander in the middle of a campaign. He accepted the American tradition of the subordination of the military to political authority, even in such a war as that in which he was engaged. But he could not resist the obligation to point out to the President the danger in the course suggested and said in his reply: "I regret the fact stated. It is a bad time to release [relieve] the commander of an army situated as that of Tenne. We may lose Atlanta and the army too. Hood is a bold fighter. I am doubtful as to other qualities necessary." [15]

Later that evening, July 12, Lee wrote in more detail about this situation which distressed him much. Actually his letter seems more the jotting of notes than a carefully written communication. He again told Davis that it was a "grievous thing" to relieve an army commander in such circumstances; but if it were necessary, a matter on which he was not informed, it ought to be done. But then he aligns himself fairly with Johnston. He had hoped that the Army of Tennessee would be made strong enough to give battle to Sherman. Alabama, Mobile and communication with the Trans-Mississippi were important but not sufficiently to endanger the rest of the country. He recommended that all the cavalry in Mississippi and Tennessee be concentrated on Sherman's communications; and in the event of further retirement by Johnston he assumed it would be to the east toward Augusta, not the west. As for Hood's capabilities, Lee repeated that he was a good fighter but what he might do with full responsibility, Lee could not judge.[16]

But Davis wished advice only if it affirmed the decision he had already made. The next day he again wrote Lee after receiving the first of Bragg's messages from Atlanta. The President used his adviser's hastily formed report of conditions to confirm that the "case seems hopeless in present hands," as he told Lee. "The measures are surely adequate if properly employed; especially the cavalry force is adequate." But letters were not sufficient to secure Lee's approval, so Seddon traveled to the headquarters of the Army of Northern Virginia and added his efforts in person to those of Davis. Lee again declined to make a recommendation; in fact, as he reported the interview later to Hampton, he urged the Secretary not to remove Johnston. If the latter "could not command the army we had no one who could." [17]

Senator Hill had arrived in Richmond by the time of this effort to get Lee's approval of a replacement for Johnston. After his hasty visit to Johnston, Hill for some reason failed to reach Richmond to make the General's views known for more than a week. The Senator undoubtedly had no inclination to promote Johnston's removal and undertook the journey only in the hope of informing the authorities in Richmond of the emergency in Georgia and of securing from them the amount of assistance which was necessary to avert a greater crisis. In his conference with Davis, Hill carefully presented the details of his conversation with Johnston and emphasized the latter's belief in an effort against Sherman's communications by cavalry from Mississippi and Tennessee.

But Davis impressed upon Hill that Mississippi and Tennessee were also under threat from the enemy, and therefore neither Forrest nor Morgan could be spared for the suggested campaign. He attacked Johnston's estimates of the number of troops in the different commands in his effort to show "how utterly General Johnston was at fault. . . . " But he held to the last the information which he thought would deliver the final blow to Hill's credence—how long, Davis asked, had Johnston said he could hold Sherman north of the Chattahoochee? Hill replied for forty-five to sixty days [this is the second Hill account of his conversation with Johnston; it was written more than twenty years after the event and differs from that written at the time]. Davis took a message from his desk and read it slowly. Johnston had already crossed the Chattahoochee! [18]

Senator Hill took no part in the decision for removal and forewarned Johnston that a crisis impended in his telegram of July 14. But the information he brought combined with that received from Bragg gave Davis what he sought as justification for his action. News that the Federals had crossed the Chattahoochee precipitated matters, coupled with Johnston's request for the removal of the prisoners from Andersonville about 100 miles in his rear. The latter was a natural military suggestion to protect against possible raids, but it lent itself to interpretation as a presage of further retreat. When the cabinet assembled to discuss the removal of Johnston, all favored it. Seddon, who had supported the General's appointment to command, according to postwar accounts played an unusually active role. He had the eager assistance of Benjamin whose antipathy for Johnston dated back to 1861. Davis was apparently able to dissemble his already expressed decision as all present had the feeling that he was loathe to act. [19]

On the sixteenth Davis called upon Johnston for specific plans for the future. Johnston's reply came the same day and realistically restated the situation. Even with his knowledge of Davis' intent to remove him he could not bring himself to a promise of any reckless effort to overcome the Federals. He still realized that the primary alternative to Confederate military chaos was to keep his army intact and before that of Sherman. The Federals could not afford side ventures with the Army of Tennessee undefeated in front of them. "As the enemy has double our number, we must be on the defensive," Johnston wired Davis. "My plan of operation must, therefore, depend upon that of the enemy. We are trying to put Atlanta in condition to be held for a day or two by the Georgia militia, that army movements may be freer and wider." [20]

The wording of the last sentence was unfortunate as it was open to the interpretation Davis made—that the task of guarding Atlanta would go to the weak state troops with the ensuing loss of that important point, while the retreat of the army might continue, to end no one knew where. As soon as Davis saw this reply, he gave the word that the order which directed Johnston to turn the command over to Hood could be sent. [21]

On Sunday night, July 17, Johnston held a conference with Colonel Presstman, his chief engineer, about the continuance of work on the fortifications of Atlanta. They comprised a strong line which excited the admiration of the Union soldiers when they saw them and gave evidence that no voluntary abandonment of the town was contemplated. "What tremendous defences of Atlanta the rebs had!" exclaimed one Federal officer. "Forts, breastworks, ditches, *chevaux-de-frise* (saw them) and stockade on flank, unapproachable by musketry, and protected by ground, etc., from artillery." They ran across the northern and eastern areas between Atlanta and Peachtree Creek, which entered the Chattahoochee just above the railroad bridge, and the latter's tributary, Peavine Creek, to the east. The line began on the Western & Atlantic northwest of Atlanta, about two miles from the river, followed an eastward direction six miles, and then turned southward to end at the Georgia Railroad, which ran east from Atlanta to Decatur and Augusta. It was a line well chosen for Johnston's purpose, which was to hit Sherman's force in detail as it crossed the creek and to hold the rest of it by the strength of the prepared positions.[22]

While Johnston talked with Presstman, the message which Davis had authorized earlier that day at Richmond was given to him. Signed by Cooper it read:

Lieutenant-General J. B. Hood has been commissioned to the temporary rank of general, under the late law of Congress. I am directed by the Secretary of War to inform you that, as you have failed to arrest the advance of the enemy to the vicinity of Atlanta, far in the interior of Georgia, and express no confidence that you can defeat or repel him, you are hereby relieved from the command of the Army and Department of Tennessee, which you will immediately turn over to General Hood.[23]

Before midnight Johnston prepared the orders by which he gave up the command, wrote a farewell address to the soldiers, and congratulated the new leader of the army. For the rest of the night headquarters teemed with activity, and about sunrise Stewart suggested that he, Hardee and Hood call on Johnston "in an effort to prevail on [him] to withhold the order, and retain command . . . until the impending battle should have been fought." Hood who had spent a night of sleepless anxiety, "overwhelmed . . . with a sense of the responsibility," readily agreed to the plan. They found Johnston in his tent. A candle burned flickeringly on the top of a barrel and the telegram lay beside it. The old and new commanders of the Army of Tennessee had a long conversation, in which Johnston said that he knew nothing of any immediate cause for the order which relieved him. Hood says that he "insisted" that Johnston "should pocket that dispatch, leave me in command of my corps and fight the battle for Atlanta. . . . " But Johnston replied that he was a soldier and as one his "first duty was to obey." As the President had thought it necessary to relieve him, he could not think of remaining in command unless the order was countermanded.[24]

Hardee, Hood and Stewart immediately formulated a telegram to Davis in which they pointed to the dangers and difficulties which attended a change of command at that moment and requested that it be delayed until the battle was over. But Davis proved adamant although he used the opportunity again to place the responsibility elsewhere. "A change of commanders, under existing circumstances, was regarded as so objectionable that I only accepted it as the alternative of continuing a policy which has proven disastrous," he said in his reply. "The order has been executed," he continued, placing his own interpretation of the situation before that of those actually on the ground, "and I cannot suspend it without making the case worse than it was before the order was issued." [25]

Hood upon receipt of this message returned to Johnston's headquarters to plead a second time that he "pocket the correspondence" and retain command, "as Sherman was at the very gates of the city." Johnston again wisely refused to become an object of additional hatred by Davis, who would have doubly resented a refusal to follow the order after it was repeated. He did explain his plans to Hood in detail and at the new commander's urgent request remained at headquarters to give orders placing the troops into position. Hood in his postwar writings denied recollection of all this and accused Johnston of "having deserted me in violation of his promises to remain and afford me the advantage of his counsel." But Hood's memory tricked him more than once, and Johnston would have been less than wise to remain long and thus to become a convenient target for responsibility for Hood's failure.[26]

On the morning of July 18 Johnston acknowledged to Richmond the receipt of the order of removal and advised that he had obeyed

it. Aroused as he was, he could not resist some defense of himself
and his campaign with a telling, sarcastic whiplash at the end. He
said:

As to the alleged causes of my removal, I assert that Sherman's
army is much stronger compared with that of the Tennessee than
Grant's compared with that of Northern Virginia. Yet the enemy has
been compelled to advance much more slowly to the vicinity of
Atlanta than to that of Richmond and Petersburg, and has penetrated much deeper into Virginia than into Georgia. Confident
language by a military commander is not usually regarded as evidence
of competency.

This defense of himself into which Richmond's message taunted
Johnston was unfortunately capable of distortion into an attack
upon Lee. Actually it was nothing more than a realistic statement
that he and Lee had perforce followed the same method and had
much to sustain it. From Dalton to the Chattahoochee in an airline
is but a few miles shorter in distance than that from the Rapidan to
Petersburg. Bragg had told Johnston that Sherman's army had a
greater superiority over his than Grant's over Lee's. In no degree did
Johnston intend a criticism of Lee by his statement, as some have
since interpreted it; but he attempted by it to emphasize that he had
done no worse than Lee, for whom all had nothing but praise. Whatever difference there was between the two campaigns was because of
Grant's aggressive willingness to accept battle, whatever the cost, and
Sherman's refusal to attack prepared positions and preference for
maneuver.[27]

The farewell address to the troops which Johnston prepared was
read to them on the morning of the eighteenth. It was for them the
first news of the change of commanders. To the men whose fate had
been so closely intertwined with his Johnston said:

In obedience to orders of the War Department, I turn over to
General Hood the command of the Army and Department of Tennessee. I cannot leave this noble army without expressing my admiration of the high military qualities it has displayed. A long and
arduous campaign has made conspicuous every soldierly virtue, endurance of toil, obedience to orders, brilliant courage. The enemy
has never attacked but to be repulsed and severly punished. You,
soldiers, have never argued but from your courage, and never counted
your foe. No longer your leader, I will still watch your career, and will

rejoice in your victories. To one and all I offer assurances of my friendship, and bid an affectionate farewell.[28]

"An universal gloom seemed cast over the army," Halsey Wigfall wrote his family, who he knew would be greatly interested. It was not because the men feared Hood's ability, in his opinion, but came from their "love for and confidence in Johnston. . . . " Halsey, an officer on Hood's staff, did not misread the last at least. As some units passed headquarters on their way to the lines after hearing the reading of the farewell message, they saw Johnston. "We lifted our hats," wrote Colonel J. C. Nisbet of the Sixty-sixth Georgia. "There was no cheering! We simply passed silently, with heads uncovered. Some of the officers broke ranks and grasped his hand, as the tears poured down their cheeks." [29]

Before Johnston left the army that day, he received a note from a brigade commander who said that his officers and men "in silence and deep sorrow" received news of the removal. "We feel that in parting with you as our commanding general our loss is irreparable, and that this army and our country loses one of its ablest, most zealous and patriotic defenders." In letters home and to friends barely literate and educated men alike poured out their indignation. Some like E. J. Harvie knew Old Joe well. Others like John W. Hagan had only seen him from afar. All were convinced that he "had been grievously wronged." So strong was the feeling that some observers feared the soldiers "would throw down their muskets and quit." In their opinion it was the General's leadership which had enabled them to withstand an enemy superior in all else but spirit. They wanted to keep him, secure in the belief that he would bring them successfully through "all their trials, dangers, and conflicts. . . ." [30]

Dissatisfaction over the removal of their commander reached to the ranking generals. Hardee and Mackall asked to be relieved. The former felt slighted when Hood, whom he ranked, was elevated above him and said the "President is attempting to create the impression that in declining the command at Dalton, I declined it for all future time." More important than being passed over was the fact that he had no faith in Hood's leadership and had observed his duplicity during the campaign. "You are entirely correct," Hardee wrote Mackall August 24, "in saying that Hood was, of all others, in favor of re-

treating. If General Johnston had followed his advice he would have
crossed the Chattahoochee two or three weeks before he did. This
can be proved beyond all controversy." The urgent plea of the
President held Hardee in his place, but Mackall received permission
to leave the army within a week after Johnston's departure.[31]

Stewart, "Old Straight," as his soldiers called him, made no protest
except for his participation in the effort to persuade Davis to hold up
the removal order; but more than once later he revealed his belief
that Johnston's removal was the clinching blow in the failure of the
Confederacy. Cleburne felt the change to be a disaster and expressed
his disbelief in Hood's ability this way: "we are going to carry the war
to Africa, but I fear we will not be as successful as Scipio was."
French assured Hood of his co-operation on the day that Johnston
left the army but with usual forthrightness said that he regretted
Johnston's removal. "Although he took my hand and thanked me,"
French says, "I was ever afterwards impressed with belief that he
never forgave me for what I said." [32]

Men who had served elsewhere with Johnston had no hesitancy in
expressing the opinion that "no more egregious blunder was
possible," as General "Dick" Taylor said, than the removal of Johnston before Atlanta. None of them was so well qualified to pass
judgment as Kirby Smith, who had been with Johnston at the
beginning of the war and had not only taught Hood at West Point
but had commanded him as a subordinate in the United States Army
before secession. In letters to his wife and his mother Kirby Smith
prophesied unhappy results from the substitution of Hood for
Johnston. "Hood is a soldier," he said, "Johnson [sic] the General—
Hood is bold, gallant, will always be ready to fight but will never
know when he should refuse an engagement. Hood is a man of
ordinary intellect, Johnson's [sic] brain soars above all that surrounds
him." [33]

The Union army soon knew of Davis' action and the general
feeling about it among the Confederates. By contrast that among
them was of great relief, particularly among the commanders, whose
responsibility it was to match wits with Old Joe. Each of them was
high in his praise of Johnston's ability, his "patient skill and watchful
intelligence and courage," to quote Cox, who interpreted the removal
"as equivalent to a victory for us." Hooker wrote an old Confederate
friend after the war, "The news that General Johnston had been

removed from the command of the army opposed to us was received by our officers with universal rejoicing." None of them was quite so pleased as Sherman, who in his *Memoirs* said that the Confederate government rendered him and his army "most valuable service" by its action. He exulted over what had happened in a letter home, for "Johnston had the most exalted reputation with our old army as a strategist." The campaign would take a different turn he believed. "The character of a leader is a large factor in the game of war," he told his wife, "and I confess I was pleased at the change." Not only did he get rid of a man whose reputation and ability overawed the Federal generals, but the one who took his place was easily understood. Howard, McPherson and Schofield had been at West Point with Hood, and Thomas had served with him before the war. All agreed about his courage and combativeness. He would prove rash where Johnston had been prudent. A story ran through the ranks that a Kentuckian had told Sherman, "I seed Hood bet $2,500 with nary a pair in his hand." Within a short while the belief was general that they should prepare for aggressive Confederate action.[34]

CHAPTER XXII

THE PUBLIC DEBATE

Sometime in the late morning or early afternoon of July 18 Old Joe told his staff good-by and mounted his horse to ride to his wife's home in Atlanta. The Johnstons gathered their personal belongings and left as quickly as they could, the General realizing that a supplanted commander had no place in the vicinity of his old army. They traveled in a freight car to Macon, which they chose "merely because it was the first stopping-place." There the General and his lady arrived about noon on July 20, to be greeted by an invitation to be the guests of Howell Cobb. Although Cobb had little chance for conversation with Johnston alone, he wrote his wife that day: "He evidently feels his present unpleasant situation of being relieved from the command of the army. Still he indulges in no spirit of complaint, speaks kindly of his successor and very hopefully of the prospect of holding Atlanta." Two days later Cobb, obviously much concerned over the course of events, wrote again and said, "I greatly fear that we shall have to regret too deeply the removal of Genl. Johnston. . . . " [1]

Johnston gave no public indication of his feelings, but some of his friends in Macon, incensed over Davis' treatment of him, had no hesitation about expressing their indignation and sympathy. The

323

most demonstrative of these was the impulsive Mrs. Clay, wife of the former senator from Alabama. Her first sight of the General after his arrival in Macon was as he left church on Sunday. She rushed to him and "rising on tiptoe imprinted on his bronze cheek a warm kiss of love and sympathy." Johnston blushed at her affectionate welcome but a murmur of approval arose among the onlookers." [2]

The Johnstons secured a house on the outskirts of the community to which they moved with Luly and Fanny Wigfall still their guests. Scarcely had they adjusted themselves when an alarm of a Federal raid urgently called all Macon to arms. Sherman had sent Stoneman out with two purposes, to break the railroad to Macon and then, in an effort Johnston had feared, to try to release the prisoners at Andersonville fifty miles to the southwest. His force of about 2,500 was rapidly nearing Macon when Georgia reserves and citizens moved out to meet it. Johnston offered his services at once and Cobb asked that he take over the command, but the General thought it better that he act only in an advisory capacity. Stoneman, whom the Confederate cavalry closely followed, turned away from Macon and its defenders to face his pursuers. In an action which was visible from the house in which the Johnstons lived, the Southerners defeated the Federals, who attempted to retire by the way they had come. But they were unable to escape and Stoneman with a large part of his command finally surrendered about twenty-eight miles northeast of Macon.[3]

After this exciting episode life in Macon settled to a comfortable, humdrum existence. When the expiration of the Johnstons' agreement for the house they had rented neared, the people of Macon offered it to them free for as long a period as they might desire. Although pleased by their generous interest, the General felt he could not accept. As they could not find another that he could secure for less than his pay, the Mackalls invited them to come with the two Wigfall girls and live with them. The Johnstons promptly accepted and moved to the little community of Vineville on the outskirts of Macon, where, in Luly Wigfall's words, they all "messed together in a snug house at the end of the village street." [4]

Food was very plain and there was fear of smallpox, then prevalent in the area. All took the precaution of vaccination and for additional protection wore a little bag of asafetida next to the skin. But the young spirits of the Mackall children and the Wigfalls prevailed over the depressing effects of war and other troubles. Neighbors opened their houses for hours of singing and dancing, and Mrs. Johnston, full of fun, led the way in a series of practical jokes. The General protested if they went too far, but his sense of humor and quick repartee added their share to the enjoyment of all.

The pleasure he experienced from these associations made a lasting impression upon the young people with whom he was thrown, but he could not long divert his mind from the great events of the moment and chafed at his inaction at such an important time. This strain added to that under which he had labored for months was displayed in an attack of shingles, "a complaint of which I had never heard before," he wrote Mansfield Lovell. But his humor asserted itself to turn even this affliction off, when he continued, "Such a covering, let me tell you is worse than none." [5]

Public feeling about his removal continued to hold attention in the press and is recorded in the letters and diaries of that period. Kate Cumming expressed one phase of it when she wrote, "There have been many conjectures as to this change of commanders, but no one can tell the why or the wherefore." Editors were not so noncommittal, and the Richmond press quickly offered its explanations. The *Whig* announced the news on July 19 and said only that there was a "good deal of comment in this city." The next day the paper said editorially that the placing of Hood in command was a great surprise and few believed that it would be permanent. The editor wrote:

The secret of this appointment is soon told. Our authorities are diseased in mind, and the craziest of their crazes is the fancied possession of an intuitive knowledge of men, especially military men. The success of the cause is subservient to the gratification of personal feelings, or else an army like that at Atlanta would not be entrusted to an untried General, made for the occasion. . . .

Hood's abilities may be adequate to the task assigned him. We trust so. He may possess the confidence of the army to a greater degree than Johnston. We doubt it. But the case does not admit experiments. Too much is at stake. It may be true, as the clerks who reflect the opinions entertained in high official circles declare, that the day for old fogies, like Lee, Beauregard and Johnston, is past, and the time has come for young men of the Dick Taylor, Hoke, and Hood stamp to lead our troops to Napoleonic victories. Nevertheless we hold to the belief that the situation in Georgia does not demand rash experiments, but, on the contrary, calls for an officer of proved ability of the first class.

Two days later the editor returned to the subject with a more specific charge: "But a cold snaky hate must be gratified at whatever cost to the country. To appease that hate, the people of Georgia must be sacrificed as cheerfully as were the people of Mississippi and Tennessee in the days of Pemberton and Bragg. . . . "[6]

The *Examiner* was no less critical and in reporting the removal said that everyone but the partisans of Bragg, to whom the news gave joy, considered the "change as a great calamity." Editorially the paper stated: "The reported removal of General Johnston is an act that may produce deplorable consequences. It was not, however, unexpected. For some time the wretched supplejacks of the Government have been busy in blackening him. They have talked about a letter from a young lieutenant [Hood] saying how he would not have retreated, disapproving the campaign, etc., etc. . . . " On the next day the editor included the same disturbing implication the *Whig* used: "However detestable it may be that the urgency of the country's situation should furnish the means and occasion for the gratification of the deliberate and long-abiding malignity—Johnston was not sustained by the Government, but nothing will be left undone to sustain Hood." The circumstances in 1864 were reminiscent of those in 1862 for the *Examiner*. Then the government had refused Johnston's requests for help against McClellan only to give them to Lee. In 1864 "Forrest's cavalry and reenforcements from Trans-Mississippi have been withheld." Later the editor said that Davis was willing to use Johnston to rebuild the efficiency of the Army of Tennessee, but everyone realized that the President would prevent the General's use of the army "to do anything effectual."[7]

The President also had his defenders, and in Richmond the *Despatch*, which the *Whig* called the "yelper in the administration kennel," the *Enquirer* and the *Sentinel* presented the case for him and at the same time for Hood. The editor of the *Enquirer* thought that Hood had "justified the confidence of the President" and deserved the appointment to army command. The *Despatch* was more insistent. Its editor described Hood as not only a "fighting man, but a man who knows how to fight," the very one "to infuse spirit into an army." He argued in addition that the "President was reduced to the alternative of retaining Johnston and losing Atlanta, or losing Johnston and the possibility of saving Atlanta."[8]

In Georgia and throughout the Confederacy newspapers divided similarly to present the pros and cons of the issue, a testimonial to freedom of the press in the Confederacy if nothing more. Private expression was just as heated and divided. Among the Chesnut group the conviction of Johnston's failure was so great that Sally (Buck) Preston, Hood's fiancée, deplored Hood's appointment to save Johnston "from the responsibility of his own blunders." A correspondent of Chaplain Quintard hoped Johnston could understand that he had carried his policy too far. Constance Cary, later to marry Burton Harrison, the President's secretary, knew of the "large faction" which supported the administration but recorded also, "People we met said outspokenly that the Executive's animus against Johnston was based upon a petty feud between their wives, who had been daily associates and friends in old Washington days." Another acute social observer states that the "people could not see the grounds for Johnston's removal." [9]

Among the group whom the President's action disturbed were some who made their analysis from other than social reasons and carried it further than a mere statement of approval or its opposite. Kenneth Rayner, a North Carolina politician, in a letter just four days after Johnston left the army at Atlanta, said that the removal was the consequence of the "President's long-cherished prejudice" and feared the result would be "very injurious to our cause." The army had been loyal to Johnston and "what is remarkable, the people of Georgia, in the very country which has been given up to the enemy, all believe that General Johnston has acted for the best." Rayner was troubled about eventualities. Hood knew that Davis removed Johnston for not fighting and might be tempted consequently to "precipitate his army of inferior numbers, on the strongly fortified lines of Sherman's and have his army cut to pieces." [10]

Rayner's fear was soon proved to be correct when Hood on July 20, 22 and 28 attacked the Federals and suffered losses he could not afford. These failures were enough for Colonel Ewell to record in his journal, "A more triumphal vindication of Genl. Johnston's policy could not be offered," and as an obvious postscript added, "Other things than kissing go by favor." Hood despite his denial of knowledge of Johnston's plans attempted to follow them in his first effort of July 20. Sherman divided his force as Johnston had expected and Hood tried to hit Thomas as the latter, separated from support, was in the midst of crossing Peachtree Creek. Whether Johnston would have been more successful none can do more than conjecture, but Hood failed and lashed at Hardee as the cause. For another scapegoat there was Johnston, whose policy of "timid defensive," Hood insisted, had so indoctrinated Hardee as to make him an ineffective commander. The army also received its share of criticism, as Hood insisted that these men, who others said were willing to "charge hell with a cornstalk," were affected by fear and timidity, although again he excused them to a degree by placing first responsibility on Johnston's policy of fieldworks and retreating.[11]

The administration had received the offensive effort it wanted, but the price, as Johnston had consistently foreseen, was one the Confederacy could not afford to pay. Though Hood continued to hold Atlanta the inevitable result only awaited Sherman's decision. In despair Hood called upon Richmond for reinforcements which failed to come. He made two glaring mistakes: one, when he sent Wheeler away to raid Sherman's communications; the other, his analysis of the situation at Jonesboro at the end of August, in which the absence of his cavalry was a potent factor. When on September 1 the Confederates moved out of Atlanta to begin the series of movements which would lead to disaster in Tennessee, they left behind them, on fields about the city, comrades they could not spare and had no prospect of replacing.[12]

The effect in the army of Hood's failures was even more distressing than it was among the civil population. General French twice in August requested Richmond to relieve him from service because of his resentment of Hood's actions, and in mid-September suggested to the President that it might be well to send some inspecting officers to investigate the spirit of the army. Instead, Davis decided to go himself, to see things at first hand and to try to restore morale. He feared the effect of such men as Brown, Stephens and Toombs, Georgians all, whom he considered highly susceptible to defeatism. He believed that he might overcome the public criticism of Hood and the growing support of Johnston.[13]

The President arrived unannounced at Macon on his long, roundabout trip to the army's position south of Atlanta on the day that a meeting was to be held for the relief of refugees gathered in the little community. Arrangements were immediately changed so that he might address the gathering. Johnston and Brown were the chief objects of his bitter, unrealistic speech. He said:

I know the deep disgrace felt by Georgia by our army falling back from Dalton to the interior of the State, but I was not of those who considered Atlanta lost when our army crossed the Chattahoochee. I resolved that it should not, and I then put a man in command who I knew would strike an honest and manly blow for the city, and many a Yankee's blood was made to nourish the soil before the prize was won.

There the secret was out: no Georgian, no official, no public voice had influence. Davis had changed commanders by his own resolution.

Although he used no names there is no difficulty in seeing just whom the speaker attacked. The Governor had accused the President of abandoning Georgia, a charge Davis mentioned and then described its author as "Miserable man. The man who uttered this was a scoundrel. He was not a man to save our country." Davis returned to a justification of Johnston's removal: "If I knew that a General did not possess the right qualities to command, would I not be wrong if he were not removed? Why, when our army was falling back from Northern Georgia, I even heard that I had sent Bragg with pontoons to cross it to Cuba. But we must be charitable."

The President was startlingly frank in telling his audience—and thereby the enemy, for it promptly reached them—that two out of every three soldiers of the Confederacy were absent from the army, most of them without leave. He exhorted all such to return and asserted his hope that the "limping soldier" would constitute the country's aristocracy, once independence was won. He prophesied for Sherman the same fate as that of Napoleon, and likened Atlanta to Moscow. Over it all he threw the glamorous name of Lee, with whom he said he had counseled "upon all these points," which was by implication a distortion of the truth as Lee had not approved of Johnston's removal. He called on his audience not to despond or distrust but to hope. "If one-half of the men now absent without leave will return to duty," he stated, "we can defeat the enemy." [14]

Davis arrived at Hood's headquarters late in the afternoon of September 25. The next morning he and Hood rode out to inspect the troops. It was then that the President found the attitude of the soldiers, one they expressed uninhibitedly despite the precautions which had been taken to prevent such a demonstration, in shouts of "We want Johnston," "Give us General Johnston." [15]

Davis held conferences with Hardee, Stewart and S. D. Lee, who succeeded to the command of Hood's corps after the removal of Johnston. In these discussions the command of the army held a large share of attention, with Stewart standing firmly for Johnston's return. According to the report of a newspaperman, a change was the unanimous recommendation of the three lieutenant generals with either Beauregard or Johnston as their suggestion. Hood says that he reminded the President that he "had accepted the assignment with reluctance," and was entirely willing to give it up if because of the "public outcry" against him Davis thought it expedient.[16]

Davis' only action was to accept Hardee's renewed request for a transfer. But the subject of the commander of the Army of Tennessee stayed with him as he traveled into Alabama. At Montgomery he addressed the legislature and a gathering of citizens, and conferred with military and political officers. Among them was his brother-in-law, Richard Taylor, who had succeeded S. D. Lee in command of the troops in Alabama and Mississippi. Davis conveniently forgot all that he had learned on his trip and informed Taylor that the officers and men of the Army of Tennessee were in "excellent spirits, not at all distressed by recent disasters." This surprised Taylor who had heard exactly the opposite from other sources. He told Davis so and warned him about listening to informants, "who were more disposed to tell what was agreeable than what was true." Davis still said nothing about the army's shouts for Johnston but agreed that anyone in such a position as his was likely to hear only the sort of opinion people believed he wished to hear.[17]

From Taylor's account he brought up the subject of the command in Georgia: "As Johnston had been so recently removed . . . I would not venture to recommend his return, but believed that our chances would be increased by the assignment of Beauregard to the army." Either because of his respect for Taylor's judgment or because he realized from the accumulating weight of opinion that some change was necessary, Davis agreed that "Beauregard should come, and, after consultation with Hood and myself," Taylor said, "decide the movements of the army." [18]

In this way the President deftly manipulated to accomplish his purpose of keeping Hood at the head of the Army of Tennessee while apparently acceding to the political necessity to do something about the command. He created a new department, the "Military Division of the West," of which Beauregard took charge with authority over the armies of Hood and Taylor. Thus with new players and a different title the President re-created the situation which had proved impossible to operate efficiently in 1863 with Johnston, Bragg and Pemberton. But the arrangement did save face for the administration by stilling ardent critics of Hood, who wanted him subordinated, and the friends of Beauregard who wished a larger opportunity for him.[19]

Everywhere he stopped, Davis continued his effort by speeches to influence the people and to encourage them to renewed confidence. He used much the same sort of method that he had at Macon, although he omitted direct personal attacks. He indiscreetly disclosed news of an intended campaign by Hood against Sherman's rear, information immediately noted by that astute commander, who was as interested in the Confederate President's tour as was any Southerner. From spies and newspapers he received accounts of Davis' addresses, which he carefully analyzed for their revelation of spirit and intention. Obviously Davis had "lost all sense and reason," Sherman said. He had denounced Brown and Johnston "as little better than traitors," but the most astounding thing to a military man was the frank disclosure of plans for the army. "He made no concealment of these vainglorious boasts [to invade Tennessee and Kentucky] and he gave us the full key to his future design." Sherman considered the speech so significantly revealing that he had a transcript sent on to Washington.[20]

As a soldier Johnston, like Sherman, probably marveled that Davis could be so indiscreet in his public statements, but he gave no indication of that or of resentment of the President's indictment of him. When Davis passed through Macon on his way back to Richmond the General called on him in what Mrs. Johnston described as "a friendly, almost cordial meeting—'velvet gloves upon the claws!' " Although willing to give a public appearance of friendly relations with the President out of deference to the latter's office and to be more charitable even in his references to Davis in letters than was Mrs. Johnston, the General had no illusions about the Chief Executive's intentions and attitude toward him. In a letter in early October he told Mansfield Lovell that not only was the information used by Davis about the Georgia campaign inaccurate, but there were indications that in matters of which Davis himself had knowledge he was "not being solicitous in regard to accuracy—or has a short memory." Gradually the convictions grew with Johnston that whatever the public clamor for his return to active service he should accept no appointment.[21]

However distorted his reasons for it or whatever its effect upon the country's fortunes, Davis' attitude toward Johnston was easily perceived. Bragg and Hood were more devious, but their activities gradually revealed themselves as reports reached Johnston from various sources. Bragg had deceived him about the reasons for his visit to Atlanta and then had done all he could on the rest of the trip to damage Johnston and to reconcile the people of the area to removal.[22]

Evidence of Hood's machinations became conclusive. "There is no doubt, I believe," Johnston wrote his brother, "that Hood, while spending several hours a day in my quarters, was writing to Richmond to my injury." From information that Hood's fiancée in Columbia had expected the removal for two weeks before it occurred and from the "loudness with which the gentleman volunteered to deny the having had any hand in my removal," Johnston had come to believe Hood "intrigued to bring it about." [23]

The willingness of Bragg and Hood to join in a plot against him was a surprise to Johnston. In similar circumstances the General had protected Bragg and he had welcomed Hood to his Army as a friend. Startled by the revelation of Hood's duplicity, he was amazed by the military movements which that general initiated. Blindly sure of himself and with the President's praise fresh in his ears, Hood turned the Army of Tennessee northward. When Johnston heard of it he said: "I fear that our commanders trust too much to Sherman's ignorance & hope he is not conscious that the sea furnishes him as good a base at Charleston, Savannah, Pensacola or Mobile as he can find at Chattanooga." [24]

Unwilling to engage in a public controversy with the President, Johnston saw but one opportunity to defend himself. In the approaching session of Congress he assumed that Davis would ask the Senate to confirm Hood's promotion to full general. In their consideration of the nomination Johnston hoped the senators would call for his report of the campaign, which he was preparing with difficulty as he had neither the reports of his subordinates nor other records to use. However he had but little hope that anything might result other than to bring the details of the report to public attention.[25]

In a bare, factual narration of the events of the campaign Johnston in his report effectively disproved one by one the arguments which had appeared in newspapers as the justification for his removal. In closing he made specific recognition of the charges against him and Bragg's part in them. Unequivocally he stated that Bragg had made no suggestions to him at Atlanta and emphasized that he had no intention of giving up the city to the enemy.[26]

In a letter to Beverley Johnston he went further than in the report by saying that had he been left in command "it is very unlikely that Atlanta would have been abandoned. At all events ten or twelve thousand soldiers whose lives have been thrown away would have been saved. Nor would I have left Sherman with a force about equal to my own in the heart of Georgia to make such an excursion as our army is now engaged in." He suggested for anyone interested a comparison of his campaign with such others "in this part of the world" as Pemberton's in 1862 and Bragg's in 1863. Both had retired and whether for good or bad reasons had received no criticism from Richmond. As for 1864, he and Lee had fought fairly well the same sort of campaign, faced by similar circumstances; in his opinion both retreats were necessary.[27]

The Johnstons still had Luly and Fanny Wigfall with them and planned to move from Vineville to Columbia, where Mrs. Johnston's sister lived, as soon as the elder Wigfalls returned from Texas. Should they find a proper house they hoped that Johnston's two brothers would join them for a visit. Sometime toward the end of November they made the move and in the South Carolina capital found themselves among a more active social group than had been their experience since leaving Richmond. Among them was Mrs. Chesnut, who reported that Hood's failures had made it a "day of . . . triumph" for Mrs. Johnston, but the observant diarist noted that "she was quiet and polite, and carefully avoided awkward topics. She said General Johnston took a gloomy view of affairs. Certainly he is not singular in that." [28]

Johnston had hardly adjusted himself to his new location when an urgent message came from Beverley that the War Department had in preparation "an attack upon [the] report which was to accompany it to Congress." Johnston should be on hand to defend himself in Beverley's opinion, a suggestion which the General accepted. Two years had passed since he had left Richmond to take the western command. As he walked the streets of the Confederacy's capital, Johnston found it dilapidated in appearance from the constant pounding of its streets by the passing of heavy equipment of war and thronged with people. Again as in the summer of 1862 the dull rumble of distant cannon rolled over the city periodically from the east.[29]

Although Johnston left no record of the impressions he gained on his visit, he must have noted the disheartenment on every side. Just a short while before Johnston's arrival in Richmond people knew of Lincoln's re-election and the consequent disillusion of any possibility of a real movement for peace in the North. To add to their dejection they knew also that Atlanta had not proved a Moscow for Sherman, nor had he been diverted by Hood's march to Tennessee. Farragut's ships had sealed the port of Mobile; Grant had the strength to hold Lee in Petersburg; Sherman hurried toward the hapless Savannah with nothing to hinder him.

As Johnston made his way about Richmond to see friends and to prepare his defense against whatever charges the War Department might state, it seemed to many observers that the decision had been rendered against the Confederacy. But the President still presented a defiant front. On the same day that he removed Johnston he told an unofficial delegation of two Northerners that the only possible peace was through the recognition by the United States of the Confederate States as an independent country. In November as the chill of winter began to add to the general gloom, Davis addressed the new session of Congress and assured its members that the "year's operations have not resulted in any disadvantage to us." The Confederacy, he maintained, would remain "as erect and defiant" after the fall of Richmond, should that occur, as it had after the loss of Atlanta.[30]

For the period of Johnston's stay both houses of Congress extended him "a privileged seat" on the floor. There and at various of the administrative departments he talked with friends. The result was to confirm his unhappy, depressed opinion. "It was painful . . . to observe the apathy in both branches of the Government," he wrote Mackall, "and still more the absolute subserviency of the Legislative to the Executive Branch. . . . Unless Congress takes some strong course, we cannot win; as Congress is not strong, that is unlikely." He was no less disturbed by his observation of the operation of the

War Department which was so ineffective that he gave up hope that the "many thousands of idlers [soldiers] it has scattered over the country could be brought back to their regiments."[31]

While in the War Department Johnston saw his report with Davis' endorsement, which with typical innuendo read: "The case as presented is very different from the impression created by other communications contemporaneous with the events referred to. The absence of the reports of subordinates suggests a reason for the want of fullness in many important points." The apparent generous acceptance of his excuse for the lack of details did not blind Johnston to the implication in the first sentence or the fact that it offered him an opportunity he had sought to secure absolute proof of what he had long believed, that Hood, while his subordinate, had corresponded surreptitiously with Richmond. On December 21 he consequently wrote Cooper: "I respectfully ask that His Excellency will permit the substance at least of those communications to be furnished to me, as well as the names of their authors. My object is to meet as fully as possible whatever in these letters differs from the statements in my report." [32]

Just a day or so before Johnston wrote the letter to Cooper, Hood again appeared tragically in the news when discouraging word of his crushing defeat by Thomas before Nashville reached Richmond. This renewed evidence of Hood's failure, which Davis could no longer explain away, brought public attention strongly upon Johnston. Papers which were friendly to him commented freely in editorials about their prophecies the preceding July. The editor of the *Whig* went on to point attention to the strange fact that under what he called the "royal decree" only Lee of the three "great generals of the highest rank" found favor. If by implication the editor wished to call for the employment of Johnston in some active capacity, the General himself was not altogether in agreement. He still held the opinion that it would be a mistake to place him in a crucial command as long as Davis was in power. His consistently realistic view caused him to subordinate his own desire to the country's good in this instance and for a similar reason he accepted an idea which others then promoted. "If there were any mode of doing it speedily," he wrote Mackall, "I think the people are now ready to make Lee dictator." [33]

Johnston knew Lee well enough to realize that he would not accept any such post as military dictator, but the times were growing desperate. On December 19 as the details of Hood's defeat emphasized its disastrous nature, word came from Wilmington, North Carolina, that Federal ships had arrived off that important outlet for the Confederacy. On the same day Beauregard telegraphed Richmond that Sherman neared Savannah and warned that Hardee would have to evacuate quickly. He asked for help from Lee until he could move the Army of Tennessee to oppose Sherman. Davis turned to Lee for advice but expressed his inability to realize that the situation in Georgia had become so acute. Lee wasted no time in that sort of quibble. If the circumstances at Savannah demanded evacuation it should be done to save the army. As for help, any that he had would have to go to Wilmington where the closer crisis existed.[34]

Lee had long confronted the effects of a degenerating cause. For months he had called for reinforcements and had prophesied the fall of Richmond without them. Rations were short and days without meat were common for his soldiers. Morale was low as the men began to speculate on how long the Confederacy could last. The number of deserters distressed Lee who suggested to Davis that a "rigid execution of the law is [best] in the end," only to have the President bark back in terms reminiscent of those he had used to Johnston: "When deserters are arrested they should be tried, and if the sentences are reviewed and remitted that is not a proper subject for the criticism of a military commander." Lee like others inevitably recognized the period as the twilight of the Confederacy, one in which there was obviously to be no help from the Executive.[35]

The disillusion and gloom which permeated Richmond added to Johnston's desire to return to South Carolina where he could be with his wife for whatever eventualities the military situation might develop and for the Christmas holidays. He had learned that the War Department would not send any comments with the copy of the report to the Senate, as Beverley had feared, so there was no longer any reason for him to remain in the capital. But he had to stay until December 28, caught in what he termed the "bad management" of the railroads as troops moved from Petersburg to reinforce Wilmington. When he finally reached Columbia he found the Wigfalls there on the way to Richmond. He discussed the general situation with the Senator, who, he told Mackall, was the "only one I have seen who appears to be disposed to take such measures as are necessary to redeem our affairs." [36]

Mrs. Chesnut was not so sure of Wigfall's contribution as she said he had only "been destructive," but she was wide of the mark when she construed his course as being "Make Joe Johnston dictator and all will be well." Whatever Wigfall planned he included nothing about a military dictatorship for Johnston. But the General was much in the mind of the diarist and her friends of Columbia. She wrote that there was much talk, "pro and con, of Joe Johnston." [37]

When Mrs. Chesnut met the General shortly after his return from Richmond they had a friendly chat. He surprisingly noted in one of his letters that he was delighted by the "comfort and pleasure . . . of perfect idleness." There were a number of people around whose company he enjoyed, among them Mansfield Lovell and ex-Governor John Manning. When Wade Hampton, sent to assist in the defense of his native state, arrived in Columbia and joined their group, he soon let Mrs. Chesnut know where his sympathies were by telling her that "Joe Johnston is equal if not superior to Lee as a commanding officer." Such an opinion astonished Mrs. Chesnut who welcomed about the same time one who held an opposite view, the crippled Hood, who had resigned his command of the Army of Tennessee.[38]

For a time Johnston visited in Charleston thus making the house even lonelier for his wife. She missed the company of the younger Wigfalls who had gone with their parents to Richmond where the family found quarters at the old Spotswood Hotel. The news aroused nostalgic memories in Lydia Johnston and bitter ones as well. She wrote Luly:

I have had some very pleasant days [at the Spotswood] in the infancy of our Confederacy, but its decaying old corridors now would be filled with ghosts. I'd almost be afraid of meeting the skeleton of "Varina" flourishing as of yore, carrying everything before her. She & her Jeff are certainly my skeletons. Would they were their own! I am longing to be in Richmond to see all things. I'd like to live there—or near, and am trying all my persuasion upon my better half . . . but so far he says nay.[39]

Had the Johnstons gone to Virginia to reside it would more likely have been to his childhood home at Abingdon where he heard a Federal raiding party had captured some valuable papers of his which they had scattered about the countryside. But costs had risen so that he found it difficult to live even in Columbia. He regretted that he had left Macon and thought of returning either to Georgia or Alabama. "We can't remain three months longer [in Columbia]," he wrote Mackall, "even with Sherman's consent." [40]

However Sherman may have felt about the Johnstons remaining in Columbia, he was not disposed to give anyone three months' time at that juncture. After presenting the capture of Savannah to Lincoln as a Christmas present he made plans to continue his march, which he had conceived with imagination and executed virtually unopposed. On February 1, after a month of rest and refitting, he again put his hardened veterans on the roads, this time toward the Carolinas and their goal in Virginia. The going was more difficult as they crossed the streams and swamps of South Carolina, but the Confederate command continued to assist him by keeping its troops scattered to defend every threatened point.

As Sherman neared Columbia, Johnston placed his wife aboard a departing train among a fearful group of refugees. She carried nothing with her but some clothes and after traveling for two days and nights reached Charlotte, where a family kindly took her in, ill and anxious about her husband, still in Columbia. "I'll never forget his pale face & moist eyes," she wrote to Luly, who more than her mother had become Mrs. Johnston's correspondent, "& never will I forgive the man that has crippled such a true soldier. God forgive me if I sin, but I felt so bitter when I heard him say, 'Oh for the right to lead these men.' And could you have seen his old soldiers meet him, you Luly, who love him would have felt as I did."

The General had remained behind to aid in the defense of South Carolina's capital. Governor McGrath asked him to take command of the troops but he refused as he had at Macon, "fearing that it would cause confusion among the officers & not result in harmony or good. . . ." On the eighteenth, the day after the fall of Columbia, Johnston rode to Chester and soon joined his wife in Charlotte. They traveled on to Lincolnton in the North Carolina Piedmont, where Johnston thought they would be safe, well outside the area of Sherman's march. There they found themselves in the company of other refugees, among them Mrs. Chesnut, who said with typical sarcasm when she heard of the Johnston's expected arrival, "I am in the regular line of strategic retreat." [41]

CHAPTER XXIII

RECALLED TO SERVICE

In Richmond, where gloom grew deeper as Sherman edged north-ward, Johnston was a central figure of one of the two major interests which kept echoing through official and unofficial consideration. The demand for his reinstatement to command and the appointment of Lee as commander-in-chief was almost universal, not only in the capital but throughout the country. The other dominant issue was not so widely discussed but its importance was not minimized. Since the suppression of Cleburne's plan to enroll slaves in the army and the failure to use Johnston's idea to substitute them in such capac-ities as cooks and teamsters, there had been a gradual realization that some extraordinary means to enlarge the dwindling source of Con-federate man power had to be found. In his address to Congress the preceding November the President threw out the hint that the government might have to turn to the use of Negro troops should insufficient whites respond to the call. On February 3 Johnston wrote Wigfall that he should do his best to pass a law which authorized the enlistment of Negroes for army tasks but not for fighting. Nine days later as Sherman bore down upon Columbia he suggested an even more drastic course when he wrote the Senator: "But don't let us be subjugated. Even should emancipation be necessary to prevent it." [1]

Such an idea was repugnant to the fiery Texan, but it made no difference in his relations with Johnston, for whose reappointment he worked steadily. He was but one of many, in office and out, who labored for that cause. From all over the South men wrote and advised Davis to return the General to command. There was growing need to do something. Discouraging evidence of failure in the conduct of the war increased public criticism of the administration and Congress alike. On January 9 the Senate had turned to consideration of the only seeming alternative to the growing military disintegration, a bill to authorize a "directing general of the armies of the Confederate States," even though its members knew that the idea would receive the bitter opposition of the President. [2]

In the course of their debate senators naturally brought in the name of Johnston, not only as an unemployed ranking general of the army but because of the widespread belief that his great abilities were unused as a consequence of a prejudice the President held for him. Senator Henry offered a resolution on January 13 which stated that it was the "deliberate judgment" of the Congress that the appointment of Lee as general-in-chief and Johnston to the command of the Army of Tennessee would have a happy effect upon the spirit of the troops and country and would be "highly conducive to the success of the great cause in which we are engaged." Three days later Senator Caperton offered another resolution that the assignment of Johnston to the command of the Army of Tennessee would "be hailed with joy by the Army, and will restore confidence to the country." Both the Senate and the House passed it but the latter changed the wording to read that the appointment would "receive the approval of the country." [3]

Johnston had no knowledge of these efforts and had they accomplished their purpose would have regretted them. As he wrote Wigfall, it was the President's prerogative to assign generals to armies "and Congress has no more to do with the manner in which he performs this duty than any other citizen, barring the process of impeachment." The realization of that fact may have been behind the deletion of the name of Lee from the resolution creating a general-in-chief which passed at the same time as that requesting the reappointment of Johnston, both with large majorities in House and

Senate. Davis accepted the bill for a general-in-chief but ignored the appeal to reappoint Johnston.[4]

Davis did not make the obvious appointment of Lee as general-in-chief at once. In fact he was closer to a breaking point with the commander of the Army of Northern Virginia than at any other time. Shortly before, he asked Lee for a consultation about impending matters only to have the General request that the material be sent to him for consideration. Resenting what he conceived to be a slight, the President replied in a letter which ended: "Rest assured I will not ask your views in answer to measures. Your counsels are no longer wanted in this matter." But the demand was too insistent to be long denied, both for Lee as general-in-chief and the return of Johnston to active command. Longstreet lost no time in advising Lee:

> I learn from friends at the South that nothing but the restoration of General Johnston to the command of the Army of Tennessee will restore that army to organization, morale, and efficiency. This is my opinion also. I hope, therefore, that you will not think it improper in me to beg that this may be one of your first acts as commander-in-chief. . . . I have served under General Johnston, and, so far as I am capable of judging, I am satisfied that he is one of the ablest and best generals. He has not been successful, but you can readily see that no general can be successful if he does not receive the support of the authorities above.[5]

Fifteen senators signed a letter to Lee in early February "earnestly but respectfully" urging him to return Johnston to the command of the troops "lately composing the Army of Tennessee." Those troops under Hood's leadership had become "seriously disorganized" and the population of the general area entrusted to that army to defend was despondent. Johnston's reappointment in the opinion of the senators would correct not only these unfortunate consequences of Hood's failures but would "do much towards restoring public confidence and reanimating the hopes and courage of the people." The letter also bore the signature of Vice President Stephens and two other senators, although each had objections to some of the statements it contained.[6]

Actually the hour for soldiers had passed. Richard Taylor had seen it the summer before and had told Davis in their conversation in Montgomery "that the best we could hope for was to protract the struggle until spring. It was for statesmen, not soldiers to deal with the future." But neither then nor later could the President bring himself to this realistic appraisal of the Confederacy's condition. More and more it seemed evident that the only possibility of peace was the re-entry of the Southern states into the Federal Union under Lincoln's plan of reconstruction. But when Davis authorized a group to meet with a Union delegation in Hampton Roads he based negotiations on a recognition of Confederate independence. Under such a condition there was no possible hope for a successful conclusion to the meeting, a fact which he undoubtedly understood. In its failure, though, he thought he saw a strong propaganda weapon to inspire the Southern people to continue the struggle. When the Confederate commissioners returned with no hope of peace with recognition, Davis and a few adherents attempted unrealistically to whip up a fighting crusade which neither Southern spirit nor resources could then sustain. Enthusiasm spread but it was blind though stout-hearted. Statesmanship in the South was as bankrupt as military resources were exhausted, but the President was fully committed to carry on the war, however extreme and dismal the end.[7]

The growing chasm between the Executive and the Congress was an obvious indication of the political discontent which had begun to engulf the Confederacy. To prevent a public disclosure of the crisis the members of the Virginia delegation met on January 16. Some of them later conferred with the President and advised him that there was talk of a resolution, which if offered would pass by a vote of three to one, "that the country wants confidence in the cabinet as an administration." To prevent such an unpleasant outcome they asked that he anticipate it. But Davis only grew indignant at this invasion of his prerogatives. Seddon learned of the meeting of the Virginia group and the conference with Davis and consequently offered his resignation. The President delayed acceptance for two weeks, hopeful that Seddon might reconsider, but on February 1 the scholarly Secretary of War, who seemed so ill at ease and subservient at times in his office, retired. In his place Davis appointed General John Cabell Breckinridge, who had strong Congressional support. The forty-five-year-old Kentuckian was cordial and impressive in appearance, and brought to the war office personal experience in the field.[8]

Breckinridge soon discovered the deplorable condition of the bureaus under his administration and told the President with particular regard to relations with the Treasury, "It is plainly impracticable for this Department to carry on any of its operations under such a condition of things." He corrected quickly one shortcoming which had hampered every army commander of the Confederacy when he relieved the unpopular Colonel Northrop from his post as Commissary-General. Other than that there was little Breckinridge could do. He soon came to accept the fact that the Confederacy was doomed and hoped that there might be a complete capitulation rather than a piecemeal collapse by the surrender of the individual armies.[9]

On the same day, February 6, that Davis sent Breckinridge's name to the Senate for confirmation he appointed Lee to the position of general-in-chief. He continued to give no public indication of his intention about the request from Congress that he reappoint Johnston. Nor did Lee do anything. As he explained to the senators who requested him to act, he held a "high opinion of Gen Johnston's capacity," but his position did not give him the right to use men not in active service: "I can only employ such troops and officers as may be placed at my disposal by the War Dpt." [10]

Although Lee's view of his power obviously was not that of the men who had written the law which created his new authority, it confirmed Johnston's belief that Congressional action was not an effective solution of the crisis. "I think that you will be disappointed in the appointment of a commander-in-chief of the armies," he wrote Wigfall February 12. "Genl. Lee will probably have less influence than his predecessor, Genl. Bragg. He cannot relinquish command of the Army of Northn Va. without dropping into a comparatively insignificant official. Nor can he command that army & at the same time exercise an impartial supervision of the whole service." It was but natural in such circumstances for matters affecting Virginia to appear much greater than those which "at the same time threaten South Carolina." [11]

On the Senate floor Wigfall resumed his active defense of Johnston in all discussions of the conduct of the campaigns and supported those who asked that the General be returned to command. While that issue remained undecided the melancholy Hood arrived at the capital. Although Wigfall and the other members of his family felt a great sympathy for their fellow Texan, the Senator was not diverted from his greater feeling for the unjustly treated Johnston, particularly when Hood's report gave new impetus to the controversy which raged among adherents of the President and the General.

This document, though Hood stated it to be a report of the

"operations of the Army of Tennessee, while commanded by me," was much more than that indicates. Hood undertook to support the President by bluntly charging Johnston with having disastrously conducted the campaign from Dalton to the Chattahoochee, something entirely without the limits of his own military report. In doing so he badly misrepresented facts and included illogical generalizations. He stated that Johnston had 70,000 men at Dalton, a total which demonstrated the "extraordinary efforts" the administration had made to reinforce Johnston so he could "secure an easy victory." He argued that the "South had been denuded of troops to fill the strength of the Army of Tennessee," while that under Sherman was "but little superior in numbers, none in organization and discipline, inferior in spirit and confidence." The only drawback was the commander whose proclivity to retreat "soon became a routine of the army, and was substituted for the hope and confidence with which the campaign opened. . . . Thus for seventy-four days and nights that noble army, if ordered to resist, no force that the enemy could assemble could dislodge from a battle field, continued to abandon their country, to see their strength departing, and their flag waving only in retreat or in partial engagements." Hood claimed that nearly one third of the army was lost before he took command, something which was inevitable he said because of the methods of Johnston. As for his own defeats around Atlanta, Hood placed the responsibility on the shoulders of his subordinates.[12]

Hood submitted his report on February 15 and both branches of Congress quickly asked for copies, which they received in open session within two weeks. The House ordered that it be printed, to which the Senate agreed because as Wigfall pointed out there was no way to prevent its reaching the public. The whole circumstance aroused the indignation of the Texan who fulminated against Hood, the report and the manner with which the administration had handled it. He pointed out the contrast in the delay in Davis' compliance with Congress' request for Johnston's report with his promptness in acceding to that for Hood's. In addition he had sent Johnston's to a secret session of the Senate "with a protest against publication." Nor was Hood's report what the Senate wanted. It was little more than a rehash of charges made earlier against Johnston which if it were possible to sustain them, the Senator ironically stated, made manifest "that our present disasters are not to be attributed to

General Johnston's removal, but to his ever having been appointed."
With that introduction Wigfall developed a masterly refutation one
by one of the charges against Johnston and drew the inevitable conclusion, "From the evidence before me, I think that General Hood
has failed to make out his case." [13]

Johnston himself didn't see the report for some weeks, but when
he read it he advised Cooper and Hood that he would prefer charges
against his successor as soon as he found time. Hood in turn requested a court of inquiry, but in the Confederacy's extremity there
was no opportunity to thresh out a family quarrel even of the
proportions of this one. Cooper advised Hood to proceed to Texas in
accordance with instructions previously issued, and as Johnston made
no formal demand there was no Richmond recognition of his communication.[14]

All the while Davis ignored or failed to see the irresistible course of
events. Appeals for the reappointment of Johnston to command
came from all directions, but the only impression they made upon
the President was to create a more unyielding attitude. To justify
his position he prepared for Congress a statement of around 4,500
words in which he attempted to give the reasons for his lack of confidence in Johnston. His bitterness caused him to distort fact
repeatedly and to demonstrate anew his lack of the qualities which
are most necessary to the successful revolutionary leader. He reviewed Johnston's career from Harper's Ferry to Atlanta only to find
in it consistent evidence of abysmal failure. Having thus demonstrated conclusively as he thought Johnston's overwhelming shortcomings, Davis stated his conviction that as long as he was President
Johnston should never again hold command of Confederate troops.[15]

Having prepared this statement, Davis for some reason decided
not to send it to Congress as had been his original intention. This
was not because of a decrease in the appeals for Johnston. They continued to come and the refusal of the issue to die down caused some
who had previously upheld the President to change their minds. Lee
consistently remained aloof from all such matters as long as his advice was not specifically requested, but the situation in February 1865
grew steadily too pressing for him to continue. On the nineteenth,
the day after Davis signed his long, unsent message to Congress, Lee
wrote to Breckinridge and tactfully pointed out that Beauregard's
health was "indifferent" and should he become incapacitated there

was no one to replace him. "General Johnston is the only officer," Lee continued, "whom I know who has the confidence of the army and people, and if he was ordered to report to me I would place him there on duty." Because of the round-about approach the Secretary of War was not sure that Lee wished Johnston's assignment at once and consequently asked for clarification of the request. On February 21 Lee asked specifically that Johnston be recalled to duty. Davis had no way to avoid a request from such a source and agreed, explaining to a correspondent that he complied "in the hope that General Johnston's soldierly qualities may be made serviceable to his country when acting under General Lee's orders. . . . " [16]

Pleased by the President's apparent co-operation Lee thanked him and in his letter repeated what he had told Breckinridge, "I know of no one who had so much the confidence of the troops and people as General Johnston, and believe he has capacity for the command." But Lee said nothing about supervision of Johnston or in any way upholding the arguments Davis had used to justify his failure to bring Johnston back into service. The result was an increase of the President's bitterness. Wigfall reported to Johnston in a letter on February 27:

Lee I believe fully sustains you & is now I understand hated by Davis as much as you are. Mrs. Jeff is open in her denunciations. They all feel that the attempt to supercede you with Hood has resulted in Jeff's being superceded by you. Lee's support of you too has given great offense. He does not hesitate to speak of your removal as unfortunate and having caused all our present difficulties. Lee assumes to be the commander of the armies. . . . His asking that you should be ordered to report to him and immediately assigning you to the command of the forces in front of Sherman is spoken of in official circles as "indelicate" to say the least of it. Lee does not hesitate to say that he was consulted and disapproved of your removal.[17]

An evidence that Wigfall correctly reported the situation between Davis and Lee is the curt note which the President wrote Lee February 25. "Rumors assuming to be based on your views have affected the public mind, and it is reported obstructs needful legislation. A little further progress will produce panic. If you can spare the time I wish you to come here." When Lee returned to Petersburg after a hurried trip to Richmond a few days later he remarked to Gordon about the President's determination, and "his remarkable faith in the possibility of our still winning our independence." But whatever direction future events might take Davis wished to make his position permanent. He did not destroy the "unsent message," which after Johnston's reassignment could serve no purpose except as a justification for Davis' failure to act, but sent it March 1 to his friend, ex-Senator Phelan of Mississippi.[18]

If Lee and the President were somewhat at odds the two old companions, Lee and Johnston, for the first time in the war had an opportunity to work together as field commanders. Wigfall expressed the hope that they would co-operate in complete harmony and told Johnston of Lee's continued friendship. It brought from Johnston one of his warmest letters. He wrote the Texan:

In youth & early manhood I loved & admired him more than any man in the world. Since then we have had little intercourse & have become formal in our personal intercourse: a good deal, I think, for change of taste & habits in one or the other. When we are together former feelings always return. I have long thought that he had forgotten our early friendship. To be convinced that I was mistaken in so thinking would give me inexpressible pleasure. Be assured, however, that knight of old never fought under his king more loyally than I'll serve under General Lee.

He enjoyed hearing of the distress his reappointment gave the Davises. "I have a most unchristian satisfaction," he told Wigfall, "in what you say of the state of mind in the leading occupants of the presidential mansion. To me it is sufficient revenge." [19]

Cooper's order to Johnston to report to Lee for assignment had reached him on February 23, the same day that he received Lee's instructions to assume command of all the troops in the Department of South Carolina, Georgia and Florida, as well as of the Army of Tennessee, then under Beauregard. Knowing what Johnston's reply to Cooper's call to service would be Lee had not waited for it. It had created a tremendous decision for Johnston, for as he told Wigfall the command offered little chance of success. "Not exactly no hope, but only a faint hope." The task assigned him by Lee was to "concentrate all available forces and drive back Sherman," but the prospect of stopping the Federals who had by then forced the Confederates to retire into North Carolina was not bright. Men with experience of the tide of Northerners from Dalton to Atlanta to Savannah and on knew its power, but neither Davis nor Lee seemed to comprehend it. In his reply to Lee's telegram of assignment Johnston was forced to use somewhat the same wording that he had used from Mississippi in 1863. "It is too late," he advised the general-in-chief, "to expect me to concentrate troops capable of driving back Sherman. The remnant of the Army of Tennessee is much divided. So are other troops." [20]

His new duties placed Johnston in a position with relation to Beauregard somewhat similar to that he had avoided with Bragg at Tullahoma in 1863. One difference was that this time the order was definite; nevertheless before executing it Johnston traveled to Charlotte to learn from Beauregard himself whether or not the subordinate's place was acceptable. The hero of Sumter courteously affirmed that the change of status was agreeable because of the condition of his health although inwardly he regretted being again cast in a secondary role. With that knowledge Johnston assumed command on February 25, but "with a full consciousness . . . that we could have no other object, in continuing the war, than to obtain fair terms of peace; for the Southern cause must have appeared hopeless then, to all intelligent and dispassionate Southern men." [21]

At Charlotte where he set up his first headquarters Johnston had neither a staff nor an assembled army, but he immediately issued a general order in which he exhorted all absent soldiers to rejoin their regiments. To his comrades-in-arms he stated that the "confidence in their discipline and valor which he has publicly expressed is undiminished." But his letter of the same day to Lee was far from sanguine. He had little if any hope that he could stop the powerful columns of Sherman with the small, scattered army available to him. But he not only faced that seemingly impossible task; he had to reckon as well with another strong Union force which under Schofield had disembarked in North Carolina after the fall of Fort Fisher.[22]

By that time the Federal strategy was crystal clear—to brush out of the way the troops in North Carolina and to unite Grant and Sherman for a fatal blow at Lee. In twin columns with flanking parties of foragers the men of Sherman threatened both Raleigh and Goldsboro. Concentrated as he was on the direction of rapidly moving, separated forces, Sherman was not aware of the Confederate situation, although within a few days he heard that Johnston was again his opponent. It had no effect upon his general plans but it did upon the details of the campaign. He knew from experience that he could not mislead his adversary by feints and false reports, and would have to operate with greater caution and to hold his army more compactly than he hitherto had done.[23]

The men whom Johnston could bring against Sherman were widely separated and had never worked together as a fighting team. Before any action could be attempted it was necessary to concentrate them. Hardee with some 11,000 men was on the way via Florence and

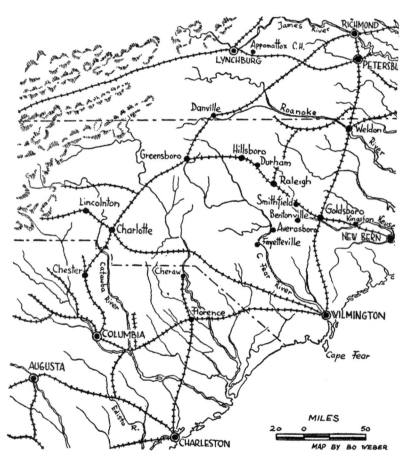

THE LAST CAMPAIGN

Cheraw. They included the Charleston garrison who found active campaigning a grueling experience. Johnston was not certain that such soft troops could outrace Sherman northward, nor was he sure that the South Carolina militia, which comprised about one tenth of Hardee's little army, would leave their state. Cheatham and Stewart were moving toward a concentration point at Fayetteville with fragments of the Army of Tennessee, which Thomas had so nearly destroyed under Hood in Tennessee. Different from Hardee's troops, they still possessed the durability which they had consistently displayed. In front of Sherman was S. D. Lee with about 3,000 other veterans from Johnston's old command, assisted by about 6,000 cavalry led by Hampton. The only other available troops were the 5,500 under Bragg whom the Federals had forced to abandon Wilmington but a short time before. Johnston asked Lee to assign them to him, which the general-in-chief promptly did, thus adding not only a division of infantry to Johnston's force but a sadly needed battalion of artillery.[24]

Bragg, troubled by memories of the part he had played in the removal of Johnston, was most uncomfortable in his new situation. On March 5 he wrote to Davis: "This military department having been merged by the general-in-chief, as a natural consequence of the present condition, in the command of General Johnston, it fairly terminates the temporary command to which you assigned me. For this and other reasons which present themselves to your mind as forcibly as I could express them, I beg that you will relieve me from the embarrassing position." Bragg's appeal came too late. Davis, having secured what he wanted from his onetime faithful servant, made no reply to the request, and Bragg went on to suffer with his conscience as Johnston's subordinate.[25]

Johnston moved his headquarters on March 4 to Fayetteville where he would be nearer the gathering troops and could better supervise their movements. Although speed was of the essence, many of the units were almost destitute of transportation. Another pressing matter, because of its effect upon morale, was the fact that the men had been without pay for months. Some were discouraged, among them John Cotton who confided in a letter to his wife:

It don't look to me like thers any use of fiting any longer I think they had better make peace now than to wate till we are subjugated it looks like we can't whip no where they whip us at every point here is shermans hole armey and nobody to fite them only a few cavalry and a few militia and it takes the cavalry all the time to watch the movement of the army. . . . [26]

Johnston appealed to the new Secretary of War for four months' pay for the troops and suggested that each one receive at least part of it in specie, only to have Breckinridge make the startling admission that the Treasury was out of funds. The General then asked that some coffee, then being held in Charlotte as the property of the Navy Department which had no ships on which to use it, be released to him, but to no avail. Instead he received the old instructions that he should subsist his men from the surrounding country except in circumstances of absolute necessity as Lee's army was "in a great strait for provisions." Because the transport of supplies to the Army of Northern Virginia required most of the railroad resources, Johnston turned to the Governor of North Carolina for wagons and teams, and worked strenuously to improve the dilapidated rail service.[27]

Only one of the old problems did not arise. Left to his own devices Johnston might have made different choices but there was no dearth of general officers in North Carolina. Besides the two full generals under him, he had four lieutenant generals, fourteen major generals and innumerable brigadiers. The personal differences in which the individualistic Southerners had indulged so frequently required that he use tact in making assignments of this array to commands. When on March 6 Bragg advised Johnston that Schofield's Federals were approaching Kingston, the nearest troops were under D. H. Hill, whom Bragg had removed from command after Chickamauga. In ordering Hill to Bragg's assistance Johnston said, "I beg you to forget the past in this emergency." However the doughty Hill may have felt about Bragg as a superior he co-operated to deliver a minor but relatively successful blow which halted the Federals at least momentarily with losses estimated at 1,257 as compared to the Confederates' 134. Johnston immediately congratulated Bragg on a victory "which this army and the country will appreciate." [28]

As the troops trudged onward toward a concentration Johnston urged Hampton and Hardee to try all possible means to impede the forward progress of the Federals. In Lee's instructions of February 23 he had told Johnston that if Sherman continued his northward course "it will become necessary for this army to change its position.

I am endeavoring to hold General Grant in check as long as possible and resist any attempt he may make to co-operate with the Federal forces in North Carolina. At this time nothing can be sent from here to your assistance, but should the enemy reach the Roanoke, I should endeavor to unite with you to strike him, or if opportunity occurred, to attack General Grant if he follows me rapidly." At the same time Lee gave the President similar information with its disturbing implication of the abandonment of Richmond.[29]

Johnston realized Lee's situation both as to Petersburg and Richmond and suggested an alternative. "Would it be possible," he asked the general-in-chief, "to hold Richmond itself with half your army, while the other half joined us near [the] Roanoke to crush Sherman? We might then turn upon Grant." Again on March 11, as Sherman's force moved toward Fayetteville, Johnston wrote to Lee. He gave details about his troops, still widely dispersed and, he feared, poorly organized. Johnston praised his cavalry as better, more ably led and more numerous than that of the enemy, but they could not overcome the superiority otherwise of the Federals. Obviously the Confederates in North Carolina could not alone stop Sherman, so Johnston again spoke of the possibility of uniting with half of Lee's army while the other held Richmond.[30]

There is no reply to Johnston to indicate Lee's acceptance or rejection of the plan, but Gordon reports a conversation in which Lee said that even should the President agree to the movement and Grant refrain from interfering with it the condition of the Army of Northern Virginia would prevent it. Lee and Johnston faced a mutual dilemma, which both recognized. The need for co-operation between their armies grew with the passing hours, but there seemed no way to effect it in view of the overwhelming force which confronted each of them. But both commanders were ready to meet whatever developed. On the twelfth Johnston asked if the road from Raleigh to Virginia was sufficiently important to risk battle against Sherman. Two days later Lee said that it was, as he could not hold his position without it, but Johnston should be the judge of the probabilities. "A bold and unexpected attack might relieve us." [31]

By the fifteenth Lee had changed his mind. On that day he wrote to Johnston:

You are right in supposing that the course you may be able to pursue will materially affect mine. If you are forced back from Raleigh, and we be deprived of the supplies from East North Carolina, I do not know how this army can be supported. Yet a disaster to your army will not improve my condition, and while I would urge upon you to neglect no opportunity of delivering the enemy a successful blow, I would not recommend you to engage in a general battle without a prospect of success.

In any event Lee could give no help as he would be unable to hold his position should he further reduce his force. He wished to remain at Petersburg "as long as it appears advisable, both from the moral and material advantages of holding Richmond and Virginia." But should he have to abandon the Petersburg lines, the sooner the two armies joined to strike one of the enemy's columns the better.[32]

Johnston had stayed in Fayetteville until March 10 while Hampton's cavalry and Hardee's infantry skirmished frequently with front and flank units of Sherman's advancing columns in efforts to hold up the progress of the Federals. All were of no avail, as onward the blue-clad soldiers rolled, impeded more by swollen streams and muddy roads than by the Confederates.

Uncertain whether Sherman would take the road to Goldsboro, where he could make an earlier junction with Schofield, or the one to Raleigh, Johnston moved his headquarters to the latter point and directed the troops to Smithfield, about halfway between Sherman's possible targets. Messages went to all the elements in the scattered Confederate command as Old Joe worked to bring them together for an attack upon Sherman before the latter could join Schofield. Bragg held on at Kinston with a rear guard while his main body moved to the concentration point, and Beauregard hurried the gathering fragments of the Army of Tennessee. Quartermaster and commissary officers moved stores and supplies to safer places and thus gave Davis a new opportunity to complain. He told Lee his fears that it presaged a retirement, and volunteered the advice that if true, "the region of supplies will be lost, and we cannot maintain our position in Virginia and North Carolina." His next sentence is a typical one, for he expressed the hope that Lee, "by specific instructions," would be able to prevent it. Davis seemed even then to think that to issue an order was enough. How Johnston could hold the Federals with his small army and what Sherman might do with his large one were questions the Confederate President failed to consider.[33]

With the troops moving toward their junction and the North Carolina reservists called out for service under General T. H. Holmes,

Johnston went to Smithfield, where his old comrades of the Army of Tennessee greeted him with cheers. They had made a long journey in difficult circumstances across much of the South, via Mobile, Montgomery and Augusta by rail, by road from Augusta to Edgefield, South Carolina, then again by train to Raleigh. One of the General's first acts after arriving at Smithfield was to place A. P. Stewart in command of the infantry and artillery remnants of the Army of Tennessee, and on the next day he made a visit to Stewart's headquarters, escorted by Captain Bromfield L. Ridley of Stewart's staff. The young officer was charmed by the older man, who he said was "surprisingly social, and endeavors to conceal his greatness rather than to impress you with it. I expressed to him the joy the Army of Tennessee manifested, on hearing of his restoration to command. He said that he was equally as much gratified to be with them as they were at his coming but he feared it 'too late to make it the same army.' " [34]

Johnston had no time to spare as he and Sherman engaged in a duel of wits to unite their forces and to take advantage of any slip the other might make. After a brief pause at Fayetteville, where they destroyed the arsenal with its machinery, some of which had come from Harper's Ferry in 1861, the Federals again began to move. Sherman worked in close co-operation with Schofield to achieve their junction before Johnston could bring his force together for battle. Hardee in Sherman's front used every opportunity to retard the progress of the Federals and on the sixteenth in a strong position near Averasboro held the enemy until Sherman made a typical flanking movement to force the Confederates to retire. After Averasboro Sherman turned his left wing under Slocum toward Goldsboro, where he planned to meet Schofield. Sherman accompanied these troops for a while, but then went to join the right, to be closer to Schofield. The next day—the nineteenth—he heard firing from the left but assumed it was but another minor delaying action until a courier arrived with a message that Slocum had encountered the whole of Johnston's army near Bentonville. [35]

Johnston had accomplished the remarkable feat of uniting his army, but before attempting its reorganization he chose to strike. The risk was great but the need required bold action. The two Federal columns were approximately a day's march apart, when Johnston on the seventeenth asked Hampton for information about their positions and a recommendation as to where the closer might be met. Hampton suggested a spot near Bentonville, a small village about sixteen miles from Confederate headquarters at Smithfield. Johnston ordered Hampton to hold the position and directed Hardee, Stewart and Bragg to gather there as quickly as they could. While the infantry moved to the battle site, Hampton's cavalry skirmished with the advanced units of Slocum and gradually fell back to the crest of a wooded hill overlooking a large field, the spot he had chosen for the action. The 14th Union Corps demonstrated briefly against the Confederates and then withdrew out of range, while Hampton dismounted his men to hold on until the arrival of the rest of the Southern army.[36]

Johnston advised Lee that all his troops would join that day except for two divisions of Cheatham's corps, still on the way. Most of them reached Bentonville as expected and bivouacked for the night in high spirits despite their hard day of marching. The maps proved wrong as to the distance of Hardee from Bentonville and he had to stop about five miles away, although he issued orders for an early march so that his troops could take their place in the morning. Johnston arrived after dark and immediately conferred with Hampton, who briefed him on the terrain and suggested troop dispositions which the army commander approved. Because of the expected delay in Hardee's arrival the Confederates could not gain the advantage of an attack against the head of the enemy column, so Hampton threw up entrenchments in the night to hold the enemy until Hardee did reach the battlefield.[37]

The plan called for the infantry to form with Bragg on the left across the road and Hardee and Stewart extending the line in that order obliquely to the right, while Hampton's cavalry covered their front. With these troops in place Hampton was to take a position on the extreme right. This placed Hardee, Stewart and Hampton roughly parallel to the road along which the enemy marched. If all went well, the Federals would come unexpectedly upon Bragg's roadblock and before they could recover from their surprise Stewart and Hampton would hit their flank with Hardee holding the hinge at first and then joining the attack as the Union troops faltered. As the dawn of the third Sunday in March broke, the Confederates began moving out of Bentonville to their appointed places at Cole's farm, about three miles away. Spring was in the air as the men forced their way through the dense undergrowth of stubborn blackjack, which made their deployment a slow, weary business. Johnston rode along the forming

lines offering words of encouragement, to which officers added the
welcome news that "Old Joe" had caught one of Sherman's wings
beyond the reach of support, that he intended to smash that wing
and then go for the other.[38]

As the leading Federal corps under Slocum took the road again
about six on the morning of the nineteenth, Hardee had not reached
his position but Hampton placed two batteries and some of his
cavalry in the vacancy. When the Union column encountered the
Confederates, Slocum assumed that he had met only a rear guard
of cavalry with some artillery and sent word to Sherman that he
needed no assistance to clear it out of the way. Almost immediately
he discovered that instead he had run square into Johnston's whole
army and a second courier hurried to contradict the impression carried by the first. On the Confederate side of the line Bragg, fearful
that he could not hold, sought assistance also. Hardee's column
neared the field at about the same time and Johnston had to make
a quick decision: whether to allow Bragg to be driven from his position or to send troops from Hardee to aid the left. Either eventuality
meant virtual abandonment of the original plan. "Most injudiciously,"
he said in writing about it later, Johnston decided to help Bragg, for
the latter's troops repulsed the enemy after a spirited, half hour's
fight at short range in the dense undergrowth. The Federals next
threw an assault against Stewart, but again the Southerners repelled
their assailants.[39]

The unnecessary change of position of Hardee's troops held up the
Confederate counterattack until mid-afternoon, when with piercing
Rebel yells the whole Confederate army moved forward. On Bragg's
end of the line the Federals held, but the Army of Tennessee swept
the foe back with old-time fury across two series of entrenchments and
into a heavy pine woods. There, though the Union troops attempted
to regroup, the Confederates continued to drive them, only to have
the thick forest and undergrowth so disturb their own alignment that
Johnston issued orders to halt and restore organization. This required
time and the Federals used it to attempt another offensive effort but
again had no success. Because of the lateness of the hour and the
difficulty of directing the troops in such circumstances Johnston
called off the action. After details carried the wounded to safety and
secured the three pieces of artillery captured, the men withdrew
wearily to the positions from which they had started the day's
fighting.[40]

When Sherman heard that Johnston had brought the Confederates together he immediately turned the second Union column in the direction of the fighting, hoping that it could come up on the enemy's rear. Early the next morning—the twentieth—leading elements of these troops pressed down on Bentonville but Johnston discovered their approach and rearranged his little army as best he could to meet this new threat. Skirmishing—at times heavy in character— occupied the day but Sherman did not offer general battle.

Rain fell the morning of the twenty-first and Sherman, although he had with him around 56,000 infantry, still did not push the attack. In the afternoon one of the Federal divisions broke through the thin line on the extreme Confederate left and made straight for Bentonville and the bridge over a creek in the rear of the Southern army. Hardee and Hampton gathered up the few men available and led them in a sudden, furious charge which turned the Federals back. "That was Nip and Tuck," Hardee explained when the action had closed, "and for a time I thought Tuck had it," but his heart was heavy as his son of sixteen ,who had that day joined one of the cavalry troops, lay dead on the field.[41]

Johnston held to his precarious position until night when he withdrew safely to the other side of the creek and bivouacked two miles past it. What is reputed to be the greatest battle ever fought on North Carolina soil was over, with losses to the Federals of around 1,300 killed and wounded and slightly more than 1,900 Confederates. In view of the great disparity between his numbers and those of his stronger enemy Johnston planned the engagement at Bentonville boldly and capably, and except for the mistake of accepting Bragg's judgment of the situation on the left, the execution was equal to the conception. But the Confederates lacked the strength for conclusive action so the result was little more than a temporary delay to the Federals. Lee congratulated Johnston when he heard the news but in the same dispatch returned to the important question, "Where, in your opinion, can we best meet Sherman?" [42]

CHAPTER XXIV

SURRENDER

The General was well pleased with the way the men had fought at Bentonville, particularly those of the Army of Tennessee who in his opinion "fully disproved slanders that have been published against them." But he had no illusions about the possibilities. "Sherman's force cannot be hindered by the small force I have," he informed Lee. "I can do no more than annoy him. I respectfully suggest that it is no longer a question whether you leave present position; you have only to decide where to meet Sherman. I will be near him." [1]

With the junction with Schofield, which Sherman reported to Grant March 24, the Federals numbered over 80,000 men. But they had been on the march for six weeks, and their commander thought that they needed to take time for "rest and to fix up a little." While the men relaxed and refreshed, Sherman traveled to City Point for a conference with other Union military and political leaders. Johnston had withdrawn his army toward Smithfield and camped near that town. The need of the Northerners for a respite offered an even more welcome opportunity to the Confederates. Many were without weapons and shoes. What clothes they had hung upon them in rags. This pitiful semblance of a once great army was nowhere more evident than in a review in early April which Ridley described as the "saddest spectacle of my life." The ranks were so depleted that each regiment contained only thirty or forty men. "Oh, what a contrast between the Dalton review and this one! . . . The countenance of every spectator who saw both reviews was depressed and dejected, and the solemn, stern look of the soldiery was so impressive—Oh! it is beginning to look dark in the east, gloomy in the west, and like almost a lost hope when we reflect upon the review of today!" [2]

At the end of March the still gathering Confederates numbered less than 29,000, while Sherman's totals caused Beauregard to wonder gloomily "if Minerva has stamped upon the earth for our foes." Johnston had somewhat similar thoughts when hard-pressed as he was he had to detach troops to try to check a Federal cavalry raid from Tennessee into the western part of the state. More and more the conviction grew that the chief hope lay in bringing the armies in North Carolina and Virginia together. With that in mind Johnston wrote for a conference with Lee and then sent Holmes to see the general-in-chief. [3]

In the midst of these difficulties Wigfall, who with his family was on the way home after the adjournment of Congress, reached Johnston's headquarters with the disquieting news that even at this late date Johnston's enemies in Richmond continued to circulate rumors and statements intended to harm his reputation. Johnston denounced all the accusations as false in a letter he wrote Wigfall:

I resigned my commission in the U. S. Army on the Monday following the secession of Virginia. Let me remind you & inform my assailants that I was the only general officer in that army who did so. I think that you know that I left behind me, at the same time, my only source of income. On the next day I left Washington for Richmond with my family. On my arrival, knowing General Lee to be commander-in-chief, I offered my services to the state—& was, I believe, by his influence appointed major-general.

Only the fact that the Confederacy, not Virginia, would fight the war caused him to give up the state's commission. [4]

The General sent this letter to Wigfall for use in answering the charges but even as he wrote he must have realized that its only purpose was to clear the record for future examination. Within two days, the morning of April 5, he learned from unofficial sources that the government had evacuated Richmond and was at Danville. He at once telegraphed for information to Breckinridge, who he assumed

would be with the President. The reply came from Davis as Breckinridge had ridden to Lee's headquarters. The President had no late
news from the Army of Northern Virginia but advised Johnston to
move in accordance with his earlier understanding of Lee's intentions.
No one told Johnston that Grant had driven Lee from the lines
around Petersburg so he assumed that the Virginia commander
sought to bring the two armies together. To accomplish it Johnston
had to have accurate information of Lee's direction, before Sherman
resumed the march. Davis promised to pass on all communications
as he received them but none came. Finally on April 8 word came
from Breckinridge that he did not believe the enemy to be pressing
Lee, who still planned to move toward North Carolina.[5]

Breckinridge's message arrived on the ninth as Johnston with the
last of the Army of Tennessee at hand set about reorganizing his
force into three corps under Hardee, Stewart and S. D. Lee. But
the readjustment on that level did not complete the task. From
divisions down to companies consolidations had to be effected. In
the process numbers of officers of lower grades lost their posts but
they patriotically accepted the new conditions, "even down to enlist-
ing, as many of them had done at the beginning of the war, as
privates in their companies." [6]

Some must have wondered if at that late date all the effort was
necessary, and Johnston himself displayed that he suspected that
hostilities were about over when he told Stewart to suspend all execu-
tions. But still hopeful of joining Lee he continued to keep alert
watch on enemy movements, and when early on March 10 he heard
that the Federals had resumed their march he started his troops
toward Raleigh. He rode with Stewart and S. D. Lee, and bivouacked
that night near Battle's bridge over the Neuse River. About one
o'clock he was awakened to receive a code dispatch from the President. The ominous news it contained was somewhat garbled so
Johnston asked that it be repeated. According to a scout Lee had
surrendered Sunday the ninth. Although he had no official confirmation Davis told Johnston that he had little doubt as to the truth of
the report.[7]

The next morning the army took up the march again as though
nothing had occurred to affect the war's direction. Governor Vance
rode out as the troops neared the capital to talk as quickly as he could
with Johnston about the new turn of events. The General said that
he would be unable to defend the city and caused Vance to approach

Sherman to secure the best terms he could. But Davis, when he heard of it, charged the effort to "disaffection." [8]

With the surrender of Lee, Davis again became the director of military matters. When Johnston reached Raleigh he reported to the President who ordered him to come to Greensboro. As soon as Johnston reached town he joined Beauregard with whom he went to the President's quarters. They found Davis with three Cabinet members. Without asking a question or making any effort to secure information about the military situation the President addressed the two generals optimistically about recruiting a large army to carry on the war by bringing back into service men who had deserted and by conscripting those who were previously exempted. Nothing was said of the weighty immediate problems. The generals attempted to evaluate the possibilities more realistically but accomplished nothing. Finally Davis adjourned the conference until Breckinridge arrived from Virginia with more definite information about the situation there.

Johnston and Beauregard agreed that the war had to be stopped. Johnston called on Breckinridge when the Secretary reached Greensboro that night and informed him of their belief that the end should not be delayed. He told Breckinridge that he was willing to tell Davis so if the opportunity availed, whereupon the Secretary undertook to provide it. Later Mallory came to Johnston and made the suggestion that the General advise the President to open negotiations.

On the next day, April 13, Davis again called Beauregard and Johnston for a conference. The Cabinet had just concluded a session in which Breckinridge gave his report, and the atmosphere was solemn. Although the President this time called for the two generals to give their evaluation of the military situation, he proceeded first to state again his own. Breckinridge's news had not changed it. "Our last disasters are terrible, but I do not think we should regard them as fatal," the President said. "I think we can whip the enemy yet, if our people will turn out."

When Davis finished he called on Johnston as the senior officer. The General compared the military resources of the Confederacy with those of the Union. He remarked upon the fact that the South was "without money, or credit, or arms, or ammunition, or means of procuring them." Any effort to continue the war "would be the greatest of human crimes"; negotiations for peace were inevitable.

The President listened quietly as Johnston spoke, but the nervous way with which he folded and unfolded a newspaper displayed his annoyance. When Johnston finished Davis asked Beauregard for his opinion. Without hesitation the Louisianian stated his complete agreement with all his colleague had said. Breckinridge, Mallory and Reagan supported the two generals. Only Benjamin accepted the judgment of the President.

Davis remarked that previous experience disclosed that the Federals would not accept any effort of his toward negotiation, but Johnston said that he would be willing to approach Sherman. There was little Davis could do in the face of the opposition of the group. Although he said that he was "not sanguine as to ultimate results," he dictated a letter for Johnston to sign and send to the Federal commander. In it he asked for an armistice "to permit the civil authorities to enter into the needful arrangements to terminate the existing war." [9]

With the conclusion of the conference Johnston left to meet the army, then on its way toward Greensboro, and reached the advancing columns of Stewart's corps near Hillsboro as they started the day's march the morning of April 14. Two days later as the troops neared Greensboro he received Sherman's reply to the message Davis had dictated. "I am fully empowered," the Federal commander said, "to arrange with you any terms for the suspension of further hostilities as between the armies commanded by you and those commanded by myself, and will be willing to confer with you to that end." He stated his intention to hold his position and his expectation that Johnston would do the same, and suggested the same terms of surrender as those agreed on by Lee and Grant at Appomattox. [10]

Johnston requested Hampton to arrange the time and place of meeting while he rode as quickly as possible to inform the President of developments. But Davis, having no faith in the possibility of successful negotiations, had not stayed to see the outcome. Still unable to accept the idea of surrender he left for Charlotte with his party on the fifteenth, escorted by a small band of cavalry. As soon as he ascertained this, Johnston telegraphed to Breckinridge, "Your immediate presence is necessary, in order that I should be able to confer with you." Johnston followed the advice of Beauregard in this instance, as the Louisianian saw trouble if a Cabinet member were not present to shield Johnston "from the invidious & ungenerous remarks which would certainly be made, otherwise" by the President and his followers, regardless of the terms agreed on. [11]

The time of the meeting with Sherman was noon April 17 at a point near Durham, about halfway between the pickets of the two armies. With Hampton and several of the latter's staff Johnston rode silently, deep in contemplation of the drama in which he was engaged. No particular meeting place had been named, so the little party continued until it encountered General Sherman, coming from the opposite direction. There were no dramatics, no assertion of the victor over the vanquished, no indication of resentment over defeat. As Sherman said, their mutual service in the army before the war caused them to meet almost as friends, although they had never known each other. Quietly and casually, they shook hands and started an immediate conversation.[12]

The two parties turned their horses to a near-by house with Johnston and Sherman riding side by side and leading the way. The generals asked the permission of the owner, James Bennett, to use it for their conference. He readily granted their request, amazed at the direction events had taken to catapult his home into history. The Federals eagerly observed their adversary, "Old Joe," whom they viewed with the same respect for his ability that their commander did. "He was dressed in a neat, gray uniform, which harmonized gracefully with a full beard and mustache of silvery whiteness, partly concealing a genial and generous mouth . . . " one of them recorded. "His eyes, dark brown in color, varied in expression—now intense and sparkling, and then soft with tenderness, or twinkling with humor. The nose was Roman, and the forehead full and prominent. The general cast of the features was an expression of goodness and manliness, mingling a fine nature with the decision and energy of the capable soldier." [13]

Still talking, the two army leaders entered the house. As soon as they were out of sight of the others Sherman took a paper from his pocket and handed it to Johnston. It was a telegram from Stanton with the tragic word of Lincoln's assassination. Sherman had received it shortly before he left Raleigh but had concealed the news from everyone and had ordered the telegrapher to do the same. As Johnston read, Sherman watched him closely to see how he would receive the momentous content. Obviously shaken Johnston exclaimed that he hoped Sherman did not connect the Confederate government with such an infamous act. Sherman was unwilling to go quite so far. "I told him," Sherman wrote, "I could not believe that he or General Lee, or the officers of the Confederate army, could possibly be privy to acts of assassination; but I would not say as much for Jeff. Davis, George Sanders, and men of that stripe." [14]

In their discussion of the possible effect of the tragedy upon the people and the armies Johnston stated his conviction that the "event was the worst possible calamity to the South." Then they turned to the important matter they met to discuss. Both were convinced that further fighting between their armies "would be 'murder,' " and both desired the return of general peace. But there was an essential difference in their methods to accomplish it. Sherman rejected the idea of a negotiation between civil authorities, as Washington refused to look upon the Confederacy as a legitimate government. He had advised Grant and Stanton a few days before, "I will accept the same terms as General Grant gave General Lee and be careful not to complicate any points of civil policy." But Johnston's hope was to do more than to surrender his single army. Insofar as he could, he wished to bring permanent peace to all the war-torn country. Sherman questioned Johnston's ability to control the forces of the other commanders, but the Southerner stated his belief that he could secure such authority. The major point of difference continued to be Sherman's refusal to include Davis and the members of the Cabinet in a general amnesty.[15]

Day drew to a close without the two having reached a conclusive agreement, so they adjourned the conference till the next morning. Sherman hastened off to Raleigh with his escort as he feared that news of the assassination might leak out when he was not present to control the situation. After issuing a proclamation on that tragic matter, he telegraphed his superiors about the day's developments. His chief fear, he said, and he thought it Johnston's also, was that the Confederate army might break up into small units and carry greater chaos to the Southern countryside.[16]

Johnston was no less eager to get away. Early in the afternoon he had interrupted the conversation with Sherman to send an imperative telegram to the Secretary of War to join him that evening, but it was not until shortly before dawn that Breckinridge arrived, along with Postmaster General Reagan, whom Davis had sent to help with the negotiations. Johnston explained to them what he had discussed with Sherman and the difficulties which prevented a final understanding. Among them they arrived at a series of agreeable terms which

Reagan set about to write, but before he completed his task Johnston had to leave to meet his appointment with Sherman.[17]

Breckinridge rode with Johnston until they neared the Bennett house when he joined the escort. In the conference room Johnston told Sherman that he had authority to surrender all the Confederate armies but asked that Sherman give some assurance of the political rights of men and officers as an aid to securing their compliance with the terms. In the midst of this discussion Johnston suggested bringing in Breckinridge but Sherman disagreed, insisting that theirs had to be a military convention. Johnston was persuasive and pointed out that Breckinridge was a major general in the army as well as a member of the Cabinet. This placed a different light on the matter, and the Federal gave permission for Breckinridge to join the conference.

Breckinridge, who was large in size, was "rather dull and heavy" because of the lack of his customary supply of bourbon. As the best alternative he turned to chewing tobacco which he did with vigor. Shortly after he entered the conference room Sherman stepped to the door, called for his saddlebags, and invited the two Southerners to have a drink. In an account he gave later to a friend Johnston described Breckinridge's expression when he heard Sherman's invitation as "beatific." The Kentuckian tossed his worn quid into the fire, washed out his mouth and "poured out a tremendous drink, which he swallowed with great satisfaction. With an air of content, he stroked his mustache and took a fresh chew of tobacco."

The conference then continued. Breckinridge was completely relaxed and Johnston marveled at his ability to quote constitutional and international law, the rules of war and of rebellion. He was "so resourceful, cogent, persuasive, learned, that at one stage of the proceedings, General Sherman, when confronted by the authority, but not convinced by the eloquence or learning of Breckinridge, pushed back his chair and exclaimed: 'See here, gentlemen, who is doing the surrendering anyhow? If this thing goes on, you'll have me sending a letter of apology to Jeff Davis.' "

As the three men carried on their discussion, a courier arrived with the memorandum Reagan had prepared. Johnston read it to Sherman and remarked that it contained nothing they had not agreed on except that the terms of amnesty did not exclude Davis and the members of his Cabinet. But Sherman objected to the statement as too general and wordy, and sat down to write a version of his own.

As he worked to prepare it, he grew more and more absorbed. Suddenly he arose from his chair and walked over to his saddlebags where he fumbled in an abstract sort of way for the bottle. Breckinridge watched with intense interest and prepared himself for another treat by tossing his second quid away. But Sherman in his preoccupation poured himself a drink and without thought of the others corked the bottle and replaced it. When he went back to his writing, Breckinridge's face fell. The Kentuckian found what solace he could in a new chew of tobacco.

When Sherman finished he handed the paper to Johnston to read. It provided for a continuation of the armistice while superior authorities gave consideration to the terms. The Confederate armies everywhere were to be disbanded and conducted to the state capitals where arms and stores were to be deposited. The United States President was obligated to accept the existing state governments in the Confederacy when state officials took an oath of loyalty. Civilians were to be guaranteed, "so far as the Executive can," full political and property rights, immune from punishment for their participation in the war.[18]

When the copies were ready the generals signed. It was about dark as they came from the house and walked to their horses. Johnston courteously raised his hat to the Union officers, but Breckinridge strode along, looking neither to the right nor left. As they prepared to mount Johnston asked his companion how Sherman had impressed him. "Sherman is a bright man, and a man of great force," replied Breckinridge, speaking with deliberation, "but," raising his voice and with a look of great intensity, "General Johnston, General Sherman is a hog. Yes, sir, a *hog*. Did you see him take that drink by himself?" Johnston tried to explain that Sherman had been merely absent-minded, actually a tribute to Breckinridge's "masterly arguments." But Breckinridge was not satisfied. He assured Johnston that "no Kentucky gentleman would ever have taken away that bottle. He knew we needed it, and needed it badly." Sherman's neglect in that matter disturbed the Confederate Secretary of War far more than the Federal's warning that he had best get out of the country as speedily as possible.[19]

As quickly as they could, the two generals sent copies of the agreement to the heads of their governments. Sherman explained in an accompanying letter that he agreed to the Confederate proposal about arms as it gave the states the "means of repressing guerrillas, which we could not expect them to do if we stripped them of all [weapons]. . . . I know that all the men of substance South sincerely want peace, and I do not believe they will resort to war again during this century." He urged the speedy acceptance of the agreement "as it is important to get the Confederate armies to their homes as well as our own." [20]

When Johnston returned to the army he found that the truce and the news of the conference with Sherman had caused the belief to spread that the war was over. The soldiers had denounced the first rumors of the surrender of Lee as lies, but as men from the Army of Northern Virginia drifted through the area with paroles in their pockets, the fact had to be accepted. The orders to hold their positions added to the speculation which ran back and forth through the camps with amazing speed. Hardee confessed, "We are all agog," and lesser officers sought information frantically with which to ease the men, many of whom slipped away at night on artillery horses ladened with whatever a last-minute raid on a depot might yield. [21]

Johnston immediately issued a general order to explain that he and Sherman had agreed only to a "suspension of arms" under which the two armies should hold their positions. But before the day was over he saw the necessity to add to that statement a circular in which he appealed more strongly to the men and attempted to relieve the widespread rumors. "General Johnston learns with pain," the circular read, "that an impression that negotiations were pending for the capitulation of this army has extensively prevailed and produced much desertion. He begs that you will instantly make it known that the general order this day published discloses the whole object of the recent conferences under flag of truce." [22]

In the period of waiting which followed suspense hung over the Confederates. To most of them the result was inevitable, whether fighting was resumed or not. Large numbers continued to desert, some to go home, while others, swearing eternal warfare against the North, were off for new adventures in the Trans-Mississippi area. Those who remained displayed their depth of depression in a chaos of drunkenness, fighting and gambling. The roadsides were lined with groups of men who played the variety of games known to soldiers. Confederate paper money seemed too worthless to preserve and poured in surprising amounts from haversacks. Johnny Reb seemed much more capable of finding applejack and corn whisky than Breckinridge had been in his search for bourbon. Captain Ridley watched unhappily the disintegration of the army as it waited for what might come. News of Lincoln's assassination greatly distressed him as did the fact that his fellow Tennesseean, Andrew Johnson, was President of the United States. "What! O, what will become of us all?" he confided to his journal.[23]

Turmoil created an opportunity for gangs of men, some who had been soldiers and others from the countryside, to rob and to destroy. They plundered the property of the state of North Carolina, stopped and pillaged trains of supplies on the way to Johnston's army, and created general havoc. The situation deeply perturbed Governor Vance, whose complaints to Johnston reflected not only the collapse of military and civil authority in the area but also his chagrin at not having been invited to be present at the meeting with Sherman. Johnson tried to pacify the governor by telling him that the conference had been strictly military, and asked that he give details of the plundered state properties. Vance wanted to send the archives and treasury of the state to Sherman for protection, but Johnston thought it best that the North Carolina governor have no communication with the Federal commander in the period of the armistice. With their authority in the twilight zone between peace and war neither Johnston nor Vance could completely cope with the rapidly deteriorating situation.[24]

The confusion produced another problem whose complexity is representative of the hour and created postwar disagreement. When Davis left Greensboro he gave orders for the Confederate Treasurer, John N. Hendren, to "report to General Beauregard with the treasure in your possession that he may give it due protection as a military chest to be moved with his army train. For further instructions, you will report to the Secretary of the Treasury." Hendren attempted to get Beauregard to designate an officer to receive what he estimated to be $39,000 in silver coin. Beauregard quite properly sent the message to his superior, with the additional information that Breckinridge had authorized the use of the money by the army for urgent needs. Armed with this knowledge Johnston planned to divide the amount among his men as the most urgent use he could imagine.[25]

While they awaited news from Washington as to official action on their agreement Johnston and Sherman fully co-operated. Both insisted on a strict observance of the suspension of fighting. Johnston used the Southern telegraph lines to deliver messages for Sherman halting Federal cavalry operations under Stoneman in western North Carolina and Wilson in central Georgia. Sherman was disturbed about Wilson in particular and wrote Johnston, "I have almost exceeded the bounds of prudence in checking him without the means of direct communication, and only did so on my absolute faith in your personal character."[26]

As newspapers began to arrive from the North Sherman grew apprehensive about the reception of the agreement between him and Johnston. On April 23 he sent the Confederate commander a bundle of the papers and an unofficial communication in which he said that the assassination had aroused a most intense feeling among Union people. Already permission for a meeting of the Virginia legislature had been withdrawn. He feared that the "bias of the popular mind" and the "desire of our politicians" might combine to make it impossible to carry out his and Johnston's intention to recognize "existing local governments." That evening Sherman wrote again. The courier from Washington would arrive the next day and he advised Johnston to be ready to resume negotiations at once.[27]

While Johnston waited he received a message from Davis in Charlotte, in which the Confederate President stated his opinion of the negotiations. Davis' bitter feeling about surrender was strengthened when Hampton in a letter expressed his entire disapproval and his conviction that nothing could be so bad as returning to the Union. On the twenty-second Hampton again encouraged Davis to resist and stated his determination to go to Texas with all the men he could secure to continue the war. On the same day Davis wrote his wife of a similar intention, "and if nothing can be done there which it will be proper to do, then I can go to Mexico, and have the world from which to choose a location." [28]

But when the President asked the members of the Cabinet for their opinions he found that their decision was unanimous against him. Even Benjamin was by then convinced that the Confederacy could no longer continue the struggle and that Davis should approve the agreement between Johnston and Sherman. So the message Johnston received as he awaited the arrival of Sherman's courier contained authorization to continue negotiations "on the basis adopted," if it were also acceptable to Washington. Almost immediately Johnston discovered that Washington did not approve. Within an hour of his receipt of Davis' message, he had word from Sherman that the Union government had rejected the peace proposal. Sherman notified Johnston that he would resume hostilities at eleven on the morning of the twenty-sixth unless the Confederates surrendered "on the same terms as were given General Lee . . . . purely and simply." [29]

Discouraged over his failure to bring an end to all fighting, Johnston sent out orders advising the army of the termination of the armistice and the resumption of active operations. The response to the news was everywhere much the same. When a courier reached the 24th Tennessee Cavalry after dark someone stirred the fire so the message could be read. The truce was over and patrols had again to be established. Talk of home changed to questions of what might be next. Some found the news more saddening than the earlier intimations of probable surrender. The same was true in Stewart's corps to whom the major general personally explained the changed orders. "The eagerness of the men to get to their homes now is beyond picture," said Stewart's aide, Captain Ridley.[30]

Troubled about what his next move should be Johnston advised the Secretary of War, then in Charlotte with Davis, of Washington's rejection of the agreement and asked for instructions. At the same time he suggested, "We had better disband this small force to prevent devastation to the country." The reply which came from Breckinridge reflected Davis' hope of continuing the war. He asked if Johnston could not use transportation animals to mount some of the infantry, who with the cavalry "could march away from Sherman and be strong enough to encounter anything between us and the Southwest." [31]

Every implication in this suggestion was repugnant to Johnston's moral sense and his training as a professional soldier. From any logical point of view the South had lost the war. To attempt to continue it in the fashion Breckinridge suggested could only result in meaningless fighting and ensuing chaotic devastation. In his reply to the Secretary of War Johnston emphatically expressed his position: "We ought to prevent invasion, make terms for our troops, and give an escort of cavalry for the President, who ought to move without the loss of a moment. Commanders think troops will not fight again. We think your plan impracticable." He then waited to hear no more from the civil government but approached Sherman for a new conference and notified Breckinridge of his action.[32]

Sherman was no less interested than Johnston in bringing an end to the difficult circumstances into which the situation had degenerated, and suggested that they meet at noon the next day, the twenty-sixth. The Federal commander knew from Grant, who had brought the news of Washington's disapproval of the first agreement, that he must confine himself to military matters in the territory of his own command and that he should offer the same terms to Johnston that Grant had extended to Lee. Johnston realized that Sherman's message of the twenty-fourth amounted to an ultimatum. Nevertheless he hoped to be able to avoid one result of the surrender of Lee's army, and asked Sherman to meet him for a "further armistice and conference" so they might arrive at a satisfactory agreement about the manner in which the surrendered men could proceed to their homes. "The disbanding of General Lee's army has afflicted this country with numerous bands having no means of subsistence but robbery, a knowledge of which would, I am sure, induce you to agree to other conditions," he wrote.[33]

On the twenty-sixth Johnston and Sherman again closeted themselves in the plainly furnished room of the Bennett house. This time Sherman was the one who brought a third conferee, Major General John M. Schofield, his second in command. Schofield says that both were "discouraged at the failure of the arrangement to which they had attached so much importance" and feared that Washington would again disapprove whatever they might arrange except the surrender of the troops. Schofield suggested that they agree on general terms which he would prepare, and leave details until later. This proved satisfactory and Schofield turned to write the original draft as the two former antagonists paced the floor nervously. When he completed it Schofield handed the paper to Sherman, who read it and passed it to Johnston. It was simply stated:

1. All acts of war on the part of the troops under General Johnston's command to cease from this date.

2. All arms and public property to be deposited at Greensborough, and delivered to an ordnance officer of the United States Army.

3. Rolls of the officers and men to be made in duplicate, one copy to be retained by the commander of the troops, and the other to be given to an officer to be designated by General Sherman, each officer and man to give his individual obligation in writing not to take up arms against the Government of the United States until properly released from this obligation.

4. The side-arms of the officers and their private horses to be retained by them.

5. This being done, all the officers and men will be permitted to
return to their homes, not to be disturbed by the United States
Authorities so long as they observe their obligation and the laws in
force where they may reside.

As the generals found nothing in the document to which they
had objection they signed it. Except for a few minor activities the
war which had started with the firing on Sumter four years and fourteen days before was at an end.[34]

Johnston returned to his army then gathered near Greensboro to
await news of the Federal government's attitude toward the new
convention. It came the next day in a communication from Sherman,
who had taken a copy of the agreement to Grant for approval. The
Federal general-in-chief accepted it for the government, as he did the
informal arrangements which Johnston and Sherman had orally
agreed upon for getting the Confederate troops home. Sherman
accompanied his letter with copies of two General Orders. One explained to his troops that a final suspension of hostilities in his
theater was in effect and named the officers who would be responsible
for carrying out the details. The other displayed Sherman's conviction that the war was over, for it started a large portion of his men
on the road home. The letter itself was frank and genuine. The
Federal general offered ten days' rations from his stores for 25,000
Confederates, in an effort "to facilitate what you and I and all good
men desire, the return to their homes of the officers and men composing your army." In conclusion he wrote:

Now that war is over, I am as willing to risk my person and reputation as heretofore to heal the wounds made by the past war, and
I think that my feeling is shared by the whole army. I also think that
a similar feeling actuates the mass of your army; but there are some
unthinking young men, who have no sense or experience, that unless
controlled may embroil their neighbors. If we are forced to deal with
them, it must be with severity, but I hope they will be managed by
the people of the South.[35]

Johnston also issued a General Order on the end of fighting. "The
object of this convention," he explained to his veterans, "is pacification to the extent of the authority of the commanders who made it.
Events in Virginia, which broke every hope of success by war, im-

posed on its general the duty of sparing the blood of this gallant army and saving our country from further devastation and our people from ruin." He then wrote, both for his own records and those of the Federals, a draft of the supplementary terms which the generals had discussed the day before. Its most important items were the retention of wagons, horses and a portion of their arms by the Confederates, and the inclusion of the naval officers in the department in those covered by the convention.[36]

Sherman designated Schofield to command the delicate operation of ending hostilities and in his letter to Johnston stated the hope that his subordinate had demonstrated "his ability and kind disposition toward the inhabitants of North Carolina" in their conference the day before. Schofield would have "full and ample power" to carry the convention into effect, Sherman assured Johnston. Having completed these necessary arrangements, the Federal commander left for Savannah to ascertain for himself the circumstances of his cavalry leader, Wilson, who was deep in the heart of Georgia.

Moved by Sherman's sincerity and obvious magnanimity Johnston's reply was relaxed and heartfelt. He stated that the "enlarged patriotism," which Sherman evidenced in his letter and the accompanying General Orders reconciled him to what he had come to regard as the misfortune of his life, "that of having had you to encounter in the field." Such an "enlightened and humane policy" as Sherman had adopted could not fail. Johnston agreed with Sherman that the men who had fought the war were ready for peace.[37]

Johnston's conviction was somewhat too inclusive as almost immediately he began to have difficulties with portions of his force. Hampton and Wheeler and many like them preferred almost any alternative to surrender. The South Carolinian insisted that as he had not been present with the army at the time of the convention he was not bound by it. Wheeler made no argument but moved off with any troops who wished to go with him. While the two cavalry leaders attempted to avoid surrender and parole, Cooper and his staff in contrast asked if they might be included in the terms of the convention. Cooper had been left in Charlotte because of his health when the Presidential party resumed its flight April 26, the day the original truce expired.[38]

Johnston had no further communication with Davis who later was very critical of the surrender. He argued that Johnston could have withdrawn his army, joined with units farther west and thus changed the course of history. The way was open, Davis insisted, supplies were available and the Confederate cavalry superior to the Federal. In an illusion of wishful thinking the Confederate President wrote in *Rise and Fall*:

The show of continued resistance, I then believed, as I still do, would have overcome the depression which was spreading like a starless night over the country, and that the exhibition of a determination not to leave our political future at the mercy of an enemy which had for four years been striving to subjugate the States would have led the United States authorities to do, as Mr. Lincoln had indicated—give any terms which might be found necessary speedily to terminate the existing war.

Where Davis got the idea that Lincoln, after earlier refusals, or his successors would treat with a Confederate civil government much less end the war on any terms but Confederate capitulation, one can hazard no opinion. Nothing in the record justifies it and even Davis himself in a letter to his wife in April 1865 described the country as in a state of panic, with neither arms nor troops in sufficient number to defend itself.[39]

Despite the chaos which accompanied the discontinuance of fighting and the preparations to disband the army, Johnston continued work with customary efficiency. He ordered the return of Federal prisoners to their commands and placed strong guards about all stores. At last he had time to dispose of the coin from the Confederate Treasury. He directed that it be divided equally among the men of all ranks, and a supply of cotton yarn and cloth distributed among the subsistence officers to use for bartering as the troops made their way home.[40]

With the immediate military details out of the way there was still the obligation to inform the state authorities and the people as to what had occurred and why, inasmuch as the Confederate government no longer existed to perform that duty. First Johnston sent a succinct statement of explanation to the governors of Florida, Georgia and South Carolina, which with North Carolina comprised the area of his military authority. A few days later he prepared a longer account for newspaper publication. In all he analyzed the hopelessness of the situation and stated the fact of his convention with Sherman. "The consequences of prolonging the struggle," he pointed out in his letter to the papers, "would only have been the destruction or dispersion of our bravest men, and great suffering of women and children . . . ." [41]

The General and his staff signed their paroles on May 2, but it took another day to accomplish the task of paroling the whole army. As part of the effort to keep the men together for the march home, the officers held the individual papers for distribution at the place of actual disbandment. On May 3 the Army of Tennessee started its last march and its commander, reluctant to bid his comrades farewell until the final moment, went with them to Salisbury, where the army separated into three columns to go in different directions. [42]

While on this last journey with the army Johnston discovered two details of unfinished business which demanded attention. One was of major importance, as his sense of history told him. He heard that the archives of the Confederate War Department were in the area and immediately advised Schofield to secure them. The other was exceedingly minor but displays his determination scrupulously to carry out his agreement. He discovered that one of his staff officers had a small United States flag, which had been taken from a surrendered cavalry unit and the officer planned to keep as a souvenir. Johnston claimed it but apologized to the officer, to whom he explained that he had pledged to Sherman the return of all captured flags. [43]

The time had arrived for the final division of the army which had fought so long, faithfully and well for the Confederacy. Unquestionably its commander would have preferred to bid each individual in it a personal good-by, but that was impossible. All he could do was to address them in an order of farewell. At the end of the last day in which the troops marched in their usual corps organization, officers read this final message. Many of the men were veterans of campaigns which had covered every Confederate state east of the Mississippi but Florida and Virginia. As they stood under the trees that spring evening in North Carolina their memories could go back to days and nights of marching and fighting in Kentucky and Tennessee under Albert Sydney Johnston, to the long journey from Mississippi to Kentucky to Tennessee under Bragg, to the campaign in Georgia under "Old Joe" and the disheartening experience around Atlanta and in Tennessee under "Sam" Hood. Then came the long march to North Carolina and the tragic end, which, had they known, was in reality a beginning.

Only one man among their army commanders had won their complete confidence, admiration and affection. He now addressed them in a farewell order, which though reticent displayed that he held the same feelings for them that they did for him:

Comrades: In terminating our official relations I most earnestly exhort you to observe faithfully the terms of pacification agreed upon, and to discharge the obligations of good and peaceful citizens at your homes as well as you have performed the duties of thorough soldiers in the field. By such a course you will best secure the comfort of your families and kindred and restore tranquility to your country. You will return to your homes with the admiration of our people, won by the courage and noble devotion you have displayed in this long war. I shall always remember with pride the loyal support and generous confidence you have given me. I now part with you with deep regret, and bid you farewell with feelings of cordial friendship and with earnest wishes that you may have hereafter all the prosperity and happiness to be found in the world.[44]

CHAPTER XXV

AFTER THE CONFLICT

As the veterans of the Army of Tennessee began the long march home only one thing seemed sure. They had lost the war. Old Joe's words of advice were wise but whether the morrow would allow their accomplishment none could foresee. As for the General himself, the future seemed unpromising. About all he had were good health and the conviction that he had done his best for the Southern cause. Faced with the uncertainty of the period he first decided to go to Canada and received the permission of the Federal authorities to do so. But Mrs. Johnston's illness and the discovery that he would be unable to return to the United States without first obtaining the consent of the government caused him to give up the venture. He did not wish to run the risk of becoming a permanent exile.[1]

The Johnstons left North Carolina in early June. Lack of funds and difficulties of transportation prevented a visit to Abingdon or rest at the Sulphur Springs, which Mrs. Johnston's physician recommended. Instead they found accommodations at another resort a few miles from Danville. For a while the General enjoyed the quiet but it was not long until he began to find things dull. He worried about employment and Mrs. Johnston inquired of Colonel Ewell about prospects in Richmond. "Engineering he rather prides himself upon,

377

but would take anything that would keep the kettle boiling," she wrote their friend.[2]

The stay at Buffalo Springs brought no improvement in the health of Mrs. Johnston, so with Grant's permission they went to Maryland for their first stay with her family since the start of the war. About the same time the General appealed for amnesty to President Johnson but without success. "I regret to be unable to advance any special claim for indulgence," he said in his petition. "Perhaps, however, Your Excellency may think it worth consideration that while an officer of the United States Army I served faithfully for many years & gave my blood & offered my life in that service many times." [3]

Search for a livelihood held the General's primary attention and Richmond offered his first opportunity. There with other ex-Confederates he joined in the organization of the National Express and Transportation Company, which began business in November 1865. It was an ambitious undertaking which included operations in the North and South, and Johnston as its president had to do much traveling. Everywhere the war was still a subject of great interest and Johnston as one of the foremost Confederate commanders attracted constant attention. One man on a trip on a Chesapeake Bay steamer insisted that the South "was conquered but not subdued." The General immediately asked with what command the speaker had served. "Unfortunately circumstances made it impossible for me to be in the army," the reply came. Johnston cut him off abruptly: "Well, Sir, I was. You may not be subdued, but I am." [4]

On another occasion Bradley Johnson accompanied the General on a visit to Grant's headquarters in Washington, where Johnston complained of the failure of Federal authorities consistently to honor the paroles which had been issued at the surrender of the army in North Carolina. After he and Grant conferred and the Federal general promised to act to correct the error, Johnston rose to leave. Grant asked that he wait to meet the members of the official staff who had gathered, eager to pay their respects to so great a soldier, and an orderly "ushered in a procession of general officers," whom Grant individually presented to his visitor.[5]

The position with the express company began to get on Johnston's nerves within a few months. For one thing expected financial support failed to materialize, a fact which handicapped operations and presaged failure. But the details of his duties irritated the General who wrote Ewell that his soul "abhorred" them as "that of Achilles had duplicity." He grew even more restive when first his wife and then he became seriously ill in the summer of 1866, and began to negotiate for another position. Friends suggested him for the presidency of the Mobile & Ohio, a post for which he felt qualified by his experience in engineering. He failed to secure that appointment but within a few weeks was named to the same office with the Alabama & Tennessee River Rail Road Company.[6]

The Johnstons anticipated their move to Alabama with much pleasure. It was an area in which they had made friends in the dreary, frustrated months of 1863, and they hoped that its climate would prove beneficial to Mrs. Johnston's health. The little town of Selma was the headquarters of the company and there they established residence. It still showed the destructive results of Wilson's raid near the end of the war, but in 1867 it was active with railroading interest. While there the General renewed the interest in the church which had led to his baptism by Bishop Polk, and on Good Friday 1867 Bishop Wilmer of Alabama confirmed him in a ceremony at St. Paul's Church, of which he became a communicant.[7]

Despite the implications of its title the Alabama & Tennessee River railroad was of but local importance. It ran from Selma to the village of Blue Mountain, which it had reached when the war caused the stop of construction. Its directors sought to continue it to meet the Western & Atlantic and in August 1867 reorganized it as the Selma, Rome & Dalton. In the effort to secure funds for the resumption of construction Johnston became discouragingly conscious of the economic consequences of the war and Reconstruction. The financial difficulty which they brought to the Selma, Rome & Dalton created difficulties as to policy. One result was the resignation of Johnston as president.[8]

In the summer months before his resignation the General and Mrs. Johnston visited Virginia. He had begun to think seriously about writing an account of his campaigns which in his opinion both the "northern generals & Confederate Government" had misrepresented. In preparation for the task he corresponded with army colleagues and other friends. He sought permission from Wigfall to use information reported in confidence in the war years and asked the Texan, who was then living in England, if the book would pay the cost of publication in that country. Wigfall encouraged Johnston in every way he could but the impropriety of publishing such a volume while Davis was a prisoner of the Federal government and unable to answer caused the General to put it to one side. From Mrs. Johnston's point of view the decision was difficult to accept, as Davis through his sympathizers continued freely to spread "false statements far and wide." [9]

But the postponement of the book meant no cessation of the General's interest in collecting material for it. Usually in his discussions with comrades he continued to give Davis the same deference he had extended in the war, but occasionally his memories would carry him away. One such circumstance occurred in a conversation with Dr. Pendleton, who had visited him twice at Dalton and knew enough to cause Johnston to speak frankly in criticism of their wartime commander-in-chief. It troubled the General to such an extent that he wrote a letter of apology to Pendleton. "I wish very much that I could make you forget our conversation in relation to Mr. Davis," he said. "It is very pleasant to think well of people, and much the reverse to think unfavorably of them. Therefore there was something very like malice on my part in saying anything calculated to shake your belief in the good qualities of our late President. Selfishness made me, in love for my own opinion, forget you." [10]

After giving up the railroad presidency the General was again troubled about a vocation. He lamented to Wigfall that his "personal prosperity" was commensurate with that of any of the Southern states. The only pleasure in his freedom from business responsibilities was that it gave him more time for his wife, whose poor health worried him. It was probably because she was not well enough to accompany him that he went alone to Europe in the fall of 1868 on a hasty journey on which he visited London, Liverpool and Paris. It was more of a business than a pleasure trip but he saw a number of friends among the expatriated ex-Confederates, particularly in Paris, for which he said "Americans seem to have a great fancy." Shortly after his return, with B. G. Humphreys and Livingston Mims as partners, he organized Joseph E. Johnston and Company to act as General Agents for the Liverpool and London and Globe Insurance Company and the New York Life Insurance Company in several of the Southern states. Humphreys, who had served actively throughout the war as an officer and had been the first governor of Mississippi upon the return of peace, was in charge of the Jackson office, and Mims, whom Johnston knew as the Chief Quartermaster for Mississippi in the war, was in Atlanta. Johnston, himself, was responsible for the business in Savannah. The love of the Southern veterans for Old Joe was important in securing the services of good local agents and in making the venture a success.[11]

General and Mrs. Johnston established themselves in a comfortable home and for the first time since the days in Washington felt secure and fixed. He took part quietly in civic affairs and served as a trustee for the Savannah Medical College. They found a warm circle of friends including the Mackalls and frequently attended social affairs. At one an inquisitive lady inquired of the General in which of his battles he acquired the scar on his face. With the humor he so frequently displayed he explained: "The wound, my dear madame, is the result of too much cherry bounce, for when I was a small boy, I was up a cherry tree engaged in the delectable occupation of stuffing myself with cherries, when the limb on which I sat gave way and precipitated me to the ground; you see it was a veritable cherry bounce." [12]

The General continued to collect material and to work on the preparation of his book but it was for personal reasons that he welcomed the visit of R. E. Lee to Savannah in the spring of 1870. It was the first opportunity since the end of the war for a meeting of the two old friends. Unquestionably they talked about the great struggle and Johnston's projected volume. One of the most touching of the postwar photographs is that which shows these two great Southerners as they sit in obvious discussion of a paper which lies on the table in front of them. An eavesdropper that day might have heard valuable reflections on matters of Confederate success and failure, but equally interesting would have been the remarks out of their long friendship, comments upon mutual experiences in more fortunate and doubtless humorous adventures.

It was their last meeting, as within a few months Lee lay dead in Lexington. When word came of Lee's death, Johnston, who was unable to go to the funeral, wrote Mrs. Lee to express his sympathy and his own sense of loss. Out of his feeling of loyalty and friendship he made plans to raise a fund for her assistance, but Mrs. Lee, writing with great difficulty because of her own ill-health, said in a touching response:

I hasten to reply to your kind letter my dear Genl & assure you how deeply I appreciated your warm sympathy. Long before I had seen you I felt quite familiar with your name & qualities having heard my husband so often speak of you as one of his favorite friends & always considered you equally mine. Now. Genl, knowing Robert as you did, I was surprised that you had made a proposition that the poor Confederates who lost all in the war but their honor should raise a hundred thousand dollars for my benefit. I fear they will tax themselves too severely for the monument & I could never consent to receive aught from them but a small portion of the love & veneration they bear to the memory of their chieftain.

After expressing regret that Mrs. Johnston had been unable to pay her an expected visit at Lexington and the wish that the "charming climate of Savannah" would improve her health, Mrs. Lee closed the letter with the kindest regards of herself and her daughter.[13]

The General gave up the idea of a fund for Mrs. Lee and devoted his efforts to assisting in the creation of the memorial at Lexington. But this and the requirements of business did not divert his attention from his research and writing. He requested accounts of their experiences from generals who served under him in the Georgia campaign, but only Stevenson wrote in sufficient detail to be of real assistance. He talked with onetime associates of the Confederacy when he could and corresponded with them and others including Sherman, who helped by sending him such publications as the reports of the Committee on the Conduct of the War.[14]

In his effort to secure all possible evidence Johnston sought most pertinaciously for Davis' "unsent message" of February 1865, about which he heard when on a visit to Jackson in the winter of 1866-1867. Ethelbert Barksdale, who had represented Mississippi in the Confederate Congress, had lent it to another prominent Mississippian, T. J. Wharton. The latter considered it a "most triumphal defense of [Davis'] conduct in the removal of Genl. Johnston, and only regretted that considerations of policy made it imprudent to publish it from the housetops." He decided to do as much as he could to overcome that shortcoming by reading the document to a group of friends, who included Governor Humphreys, and lending it to others, among them the governor's official secretary, James M. Kennard, for more extended examination.[15]

Johnston heard of the existence of the document from Kennard, whom he questioned closely about it as he could not believe that

Davis could be the author of it. Kennard described the paper as being very unfair to Johnston but was unwilling to allow the use of his version as he did not want his name to appear "as inimical to Mr. Davis" in any association. Because of Kennard's reluctance the General turned to other friends in an effort to secure a copy of the document but with no success. But from their evidence he could have no doubt Davis had himself written the "message" as they called it.[16]

Knowledge that such a document was in existence strengthened Johnston's conviction that he should publish an accurate account of his campaigns. Should he fail to do it, this and other similar efforts to distort the truth about his career might be held and published after his death without the possibility of reply. To avert such an eventuality in this instance he made redoubled efforts to secure a copy. With usual directness he wrote to Davis, then in Canada, and requested that Wharton be authorized to give it to him. He described the paper in the terms he had received, that it was a message which contained attacks on all his actions as a Confederate commander up to the time of his removal before Atlanta. He explained that Davis' friends had circulated the document and that in ordinary decency he should have knowledge of its allegations "that I may have the opportunity to defend myself." [17]

Davis' reply was exasperatingly equivocal, resting upon Johnston's statement that it was an official document. He admonished Johnston that the latter's "recital [was] certainly inaccurate both as to the address and purpose of anything I may have written regarding you. That your conduct as a military commander did on various occasions seriously disappoint me cannot have been new to you; but that my disapproval was made the subject of a message or a circular is not possible." Then after thus virtually denying the authorship of any such communication Davis continued: "Though your application is for a copy of such a public paper, yet the last paragraph of your letter implies something more. I will therefore write by this mail to my friend Genl. Wharton and authorize him if he has any letter of mine affecting you and 'circulated' as you suppose, to send to you a copy of it." [18]

In the letter to Wharton which he wrote the same day Davis made no similar effort to deny the possibility of his having written such a document as Johnston described. "I do not know to what he refers,"

Davis told Wharton after explaining the source of the request, "but from the date Feby. 1865 can imagine it to be an explanation of the considerations which led me to remove him from command in Georgia." Although he recognized that the circulation of the letter might entitle Johnston to a copy, Davis did not directly tell Wharton to give the General one. Instead he wrote: "You will judge according to your knowledge of the facts, and you are authorized, if you warrant the application, to send to Genl. Johnston the copy he requests." [19]

As soon as Johnston received Davis' letter that he would write Wharton the General asked Kennard in Mississippi to secure the copy for him. But Wharton who was entirely agreeable to releasing the paper to Johnston because of his belief that it justified Davis' action explained that it was not in his possession. It belonged to Barksdale, whom Kennard then approached for a copy. But Barksdale, who in Johnston's phrase "understood the correspondence better" than Wharton, refused. Undaunted Johnston again addressed Davis. He said that he had been mistaken about Wharton's possession of the original and asked that Davis instruct Barksdale to give him the desired document. Davis had gone to Mississippi in the meanwhile so Johnston instead of mailing his letter of request sent it to a friend in Jackson to deliver. Although by this maneuver Johnston was sure that Davis received it the latter made no acknowledgment. Barksdale remained steady in his refusal to furnish the copy and Davis' friends began to refer to the original as a private letter rather than a message.[20]

Having exhausted all possible efforts to secure an actual copy of the document, Johnston was without resource until Kennard, disgusted by Davis' evasive tactics, changed his attitude and gave the General a synopsis of it. Johnston took precautions to assure himself of its accuracy by sending it to Humphreys and Mims, who were among those who had either heard the original read or had an opportunity to examine it. Both reported it to be substantially correct.[21]

Johnston contracted with D. Appleton and Company of New York to publish his book. Early in 1874 he was struggling with the last phases of its preparation and like many another author engaged in certain differences with his publisher. He complained about charges for correcting the text in proof and insisted that the contract called for the publisher to bear them. He argued that the arrangement called for Appleton's "printing what I wrote," while the copyreader had made material changes in the text, "doing me wrong thereby." He grumbled most because " 'your reader' has invariably dropped the s from my generally used 'towards,' and Mr. Irwin objects to replace it on the ground that *toward* is, according to Webster, as good as *towards*. If it were so your reader had no right capriciously to make the change. But Webster does *not* sanction toward. On the contrary he says: 'The original form was towards . . . . ' " [22]

In April 1874 Appleton released the volume with the title, *Narrative of Military Operations Directed During the Late War between the States*. Instead of an introduction Johnston made a simple statement of purpose: "I offer these pages as my contribution of materials for the use of the future historian of the War between the States." The *Narrative* is written as concisely as a military report, a number of which do appear in the text. So calm and objective is it that Johnston the man, the "Old Joe" who won and held the soldiers' affections, is completely obscured. For the future historian he did bring out of the murky dust of the official archives for open scrutiny the evidence which lay behind the involved movements and the confused actions of the war as he experienced it. But the biographer goes in vain to this source for the self-revelation which displays the man or for explanation of such a thing as the original reason for his differences with Davis. Instead he seems as remote as he must have appeared when on a round of inspection to the eye of a lowly recruit.

Johnston having presented the evidence left the task of evaluating the record to whoever might peruse the volume. But the objective reader can hardly miss in this clear statement the obvious weaknesses of the Confederacy, particularly the failures of Davis, his insistence upon handling trifling details, his domineering personality, his preference for sycophancy above independent judgment, his unfortunate tendency to express himself so badly that his meaning was open to question.

Yet little of this is more than implicit in the book. Johnston made his points of argument with almost the impersonality of a lawyer writing a brief. In the last two chapters he departed from his theme of history to argue specifically. In one he ventured an analysis of the causes of the failure of the Confederacy. He insisted that the South's lack of success could not be charged to an inferiority of man power and material resources, nor to want of loyalty, unanimity and perserverance among the people. Instead it was because the government had failed to use cotton to create a strong financial structure in the early period of the war.

In his final chapter Johnston printed Kennard's synopsis of the "unsent message" and answered it point by point, thus in essence summarizing a major portion of the book. In every instance Davis' conclusions seem reasonable to anyone who does not pursue the circumstances as far as possible, and as a consequence some historians have used them without question.

Once Johnston finished his manuscript and sent it to the publishers, he busied himself in another phase of the book business. He not only had a contract with Appleton for a royalty of ten per cent, but agreed to act as their agent for Southern sales of his book for a commission of fifty per cent. Like most authors he was optimistic about the possibilities. But the South was not a good market nor were adequate methods of distribution easily secured. At first there seemed an opportunity when he reported in mid-March that he had over 1,800 subscribers, but sales began to dwindle in the depression which covered the country. He persisted in the effort until June 1875 when he signed a supplement to his contract and turned the rights to Southern sales over to the publishers.[23]

The reception of the *Narrative* was mixed. The stanch friends of Johnston were pleased by it, but the majority of Southerners under the harsh rule of military reconstruction had come to see a necessity for a unity and harmony which had not previously existed among these highly individualistic people. Davis offered the most easily recognized rallying point. For two years after the close of the war he was in prison and for almost an equal period he was at liberty under bail while awaiting trial for treason. The Federal government seemed determined to make him the scapegoat for the participation of the South in the war, and Southerners followed the Northern lead in making him the personification of the defeated cause. To him the growing legend attributed all the virtues of the Old South, enshrouding him in a cloak of chivalry as well as a mantle of martyrdom. Suppressed if possible was any echo of the dissension or criticism which had crowded the days of the government in Richmond.

The fact of the differences between Davis and Johnston was common knowledge among Southerners. Some criticised the General for publishing the book at all to reopen old wounds and bitter memories, while others took issue with him over particular portions. The ex-Secretary of the Treasury, C. G. Memminger, published a rebuttal to Johnston's argument that misuse of the opportunity cotton offered was the primary cause of the loss of the war. Beauregard and his friends grew angry over the account of the First Manassas. The Louisianian forgot his earlier enthusiasm for Johnston and termed him in private correspondence a "dissatisfied and disappointed officer." [24]

Wigfall did not live long enough to appraise the *Narrative* or to lend his support in the controversies which it brought forth. In February 1874, just two months before the volume appeared, he died in Texas at the age of fifty-seven. General and Mrs. Johnston were deeply grieved by the news of his death. "I dearly loved & admired your noble, generous, fearless father," Lydia Johnston wrote Luly, "my husband's true, faithful friend, & we have wept many tears over his loss." As one by one his wartime friends and colleagues departed, the scenes and associations of Virginia grew closer to the General. He was in Richmond in May 1874 as the speaker at a celebration of Queen Victoria's birthday by the British Association and in October 1875 served as marshal of the parade which preceded the unveiling of a monument to Stonewall Jackson. That same year he was a Virginia delegate to the National Railroad Convention in St. Louis, despite his residence in Georgia. Among his old friends at the convention he found Sherman, and their presence caused a delegate to propose that "any Commanding General on either side in the late war will be requested to take a seat upon the platform." The suggestion was withdrawn when it was discovered that there "wouldn't be room enough on the platform to accommodate all the Generals present." [25]

At the beginning of 1877 the Johnstons moved to Richmond, where the General busied himself as Virginia agent for the Home Insurance Company. They welcomed the return to his home state for sentimental reasons as well as their belief that Mrs. Johnston's health would be helped by the cooler climate. Not long after they had settled themselves some of his army associates began to think of the General as the proper man to represent the Richmond area in Congress. They selected Colonel Archer Anderson, who was a member of Johnston's staff at the surrender in North Carolina, to sound him out. Anderson reported that he believed the General would be

agreeable to the nomination which he would interpret as a testimonial of respect and affection.[26]

Like most professional army officers Johnston had displayed little
interest in politics, but his moderate attitude and judgment won
the attention of leaders in the North as early as 1865. As the Nation
entered the presidential campaign of 1876 some of both parties
sought his views and political aid. Early that year he received an inquiry as to his opinion about a Republican ticket of Grant and
Fitzhugh Lee. In a typically reticent reply he made no reference to
a possible controversy over a third term for Grant and refused to
commit himself about Lee. If the Republican leaders wished the
assent of Lee, they should approach him directly. But Johnston was
somewhat warmer in his reception later in the year of correspondence
with Montgomery Blair about Democratic possibilities. Blair was
convinced that a reform candidate was necessary and urged support for
Samuel Tilden. Johnston replied that he felt certain that the "South
wanted new leaders" and began to work for Tilden, although he felt
that his influence would prove of little value.[27]

In December as the contest over the presidential election remained
undecided, Johnston made a second effort to have his political disabili-
ties as a general of the Confederacy removed. A bill to that purpose
passed both houses of Congress and President Grant approved it
February 23, 1877. It fortuitously made Johnston eligible for the
consideration which Hayes, who wanted a Southerner in his Cabinet,
gave him for membership in that body. But when the President-elect
asked Sherman, then the commanding general of the Army, about
Johnston's appointment, Sherman advised against it while stating
that he had no personal objection. The position most natural to
Johnston's abilities was Secretary of War, and Sherman felt that his
appointment to it would be "distasteful to the ex-soldiers of the
Union Army and to the public." Reluctantly Hayes gave up the idea
and turned to a less well-known Southerner to take a place in his plan
of reconciliation of the sections.[28]

The prominence given to Johnston in the national scene caused
his Richmond friends to become even more eager to push their plans
for his election to Congress. Astutely they maneuvered other aspirants
out of the contest by drawing up a petition in which they requested
Johnston to be a candidate. They carried it to those interested in the
race for their signatures. Secure in their belief that it was only a

gesture and that Johnston would not accept, all signed it, each hoping thereby to use it as an argument for his support. When the General instead agreed to run, the others had committed themselves to him and he was without Democratic opposition.[29]

Major Robert Stiles and Captain Louis F. Bossieux conducted the campaign for the General and received the eager assistance of a number of other veterans. Johnston, as some of his supporters had feared, proved not to be a good campaigner. He disliked the noise and bustle of the rallies, and refused to accept political maneuvering which savored in any way of duplicity. One day after seeing a banner, rich in catchwords which implied that he might be a supporter of a protective tariff, he burst into his headquarters and insisted upon meeting with the campaign committee. When they assembled, he hotly laid down an ultimatum: "Gentlemen, this is a matter about which I do not propose to ask your advice, because it involves my conscience and my personal honor. I spoke yesterday at Louisa Court House under a 'free-trade' flag. I have never ridden 'both sides of the sapling,' and I don't propose to learn how at this late day. That banner in Clay Ward comes down to-day or I retire from the canvass by published card tomorrow." [30]

The spirited race caused Johnston's supporters to worry about finances. They were reluctant to discuss the problem with him for fear that he would believe the expenditure of any sizable sum implied the purchase of the seat, and would resign his candidacy. Having failed in efforts to secure additional funds, a close friend went to call upon Mrs. Johnston. His report aroused her and she scolded her visitor for having put "Johnston," as she frequently referred to her husband in conversation, in such an embarrassing position. "It's all your fault," she exclaimed. "It's all your fault. You got him into this thing, and it's shameful, a man of his age and reputation, going around to your cross roads, like a common member of Congress. I do hope he'll be beat. That'll serve you right."

Upset, the visitor attempted to agree. "Well, Mrs. Johnston," he said, "you will certainly be gratified, for the General is beat now!" This response was a bit more than she had expected. "What's that you say?" she queried her caller and her indignant anxiety brought out all her vivacious charm. "If he's beat it will be simply disgraceful and shameful! It will kill him. He shan't be beat; you must not allow it. I will not permit it."

Her visitor again explained the need for funds and that all were afraid to approach her husband about it. As the only person able to win his approval, they sought her assistance. "Oh, that's it, is it?" she responded. "I'll see you get the money in the morning."

The next day she turned over two of her own securities to the committee, whose members found inspiration in her action. They quickly raised additional funds and after the results, which showed the General's election, were in, returned her bonds to her. But none of them had the courage to discuss the incident with him.[31]

When he took his seat in the 46th Congress March 4, 1879, Johnston found among its members a number with whom he had been associated in one way or another in the Confederacy. John B. Gordon and B. H. Hill of Georgia, George Vest of Missouri, Matthew C. Butler and Wade Hampton of South Carolina, Zebulon Vance of North Carolina, and Isham G. Harris of Tennessee were senators, while Alexander H. Stephens of Georgia, James R. Chalmers of Mississippi, and John H. Reagan of Texas sat with him in the House. More important to him was the presence of two kinsmen. His nephew, John Warfield Johnston of Abingdon, had been one of Virginia's senators since 1870, and his brother-in-law, Robert M. McLane, had a desk not far away in the House.[32]

As a member of the House, Johnston served on the Military Affairs Committee and the Committee on Levees and Improvements of the Mississippi River, posts for which his experience particularly fitted him. He held appointments as Regent of the Smithsonian Institution and Visitor to the Military Academy at West Point. He was conscientious in his attention to committee duties, but his limitations as a speaker caused him to take little part in debate. His chief interest seems to have been in matters affecting local Virginia problems or in the administration and efficiency of the Army. As a member of the Military Affairs Committee he joined with a majority of his colleagues in a report which recommended the reversal of a court-martial's decision against Major General Fitz-John Porter and his restoration to his rank of a colonel in the active Army or his retirement with his wartime status. A board of army officers had reviewed the case with a decision in Porter's favor in 1879, and Johnston wanted to correct what he knew to be an injustice. "You may be sure," he wrote Porter, "that I will leave nothing undone. I had rather lose an arm than see your enemies succeed in preventing the righting of your grievous wrongs." [33]

Invitations to participate in civic and commemorative activities came to Johnston from far and wide. He declined regretfully an appointment as commissioner from Virginia to the Paris Exposition but delightedly became a member of the Board of Visitors of the College of William and Mary, of which Colonel B. S. Ewell was again president. In 1880 he visited Nashville for the city's centennial celebration and the unveiling of a statue to Andrew Jackson, and while there was the object of many testimonials of the affection and loyalty which the Johnny Rebs of the Army of Tennessee continued to feel for their Old Joe.[34]

Such demonstrations touched Johnston, a typical Victorian, deeply. There was a strong strain of sentiment under his inherent dignity and apparent reserve. He was always at ease, genial and confiding, particularly among the friends—frequently younger than he—with whom he had so many ties of kindred experience. It was to a gathering of some of them that Mackall invited him in rhymed humor in the period of his Congressional experience.

> On Tuesday, my friend, I invite you to dine,
> If you fear not to feast on cabbage and chine.
> I'll expect you at eight, but will await you 'till nine.
> Whiskey I'll furnish, Bourbon or Rye,
> Stilled in Kentucky and of strength for Bill Nye.
> If better you'll want ye'll fetch it, I say,
> Perhaps 'twill enliven the very rough way.
> Congress adjourned, you're out of employment,
> So give a *long night* to fun and enjoyment. . . . [35]

Johnston did not consider a campaign for re-election to Congress, but he and his wife decided to keep their home in Washington, although he maintained legal residence in Richmond and regularly voted there. Before the year's end after the expiration of his term in Congress he became involved in a controversy which spread quickly over the whole of the South. Usually discreet to an extreme he engaged in a long conversation which he assumed to be private with a reporter, Frank A. Burr, whom he knew. Shortly after the *Philadelphia Press* carried what purported to be an interview by Burr with Johnston. In it Burr said that Johnston charged Davis with having failed to account for $2,000,000 in gold which the government carried from Richmond in April 1865. Johnston immediately wrote a disclaimer, but it was neither firm nor explicit. He said that the article was filled with inaccuracies and that he never intended the conversation for publication. If the General actually said the things attributed to him he was obviously in error. Davis had no association with the funds of the Treasury, which were nowhere near the amount named.

Why Johnston did not more vigorously deny and denounce Burr's story one cannot say. Journals throughout the South reprinted the piece and resentment grew rapidly. Men who had gathered around Davis as the living embodiment of the Confederacy kept the episode alive to degrade Johnston in every way they could. B. H. Hill, whose own role in the war's post-mortems had led him to write a second account, contradictory of his first, of his conversation with Johnston before removal, was in communication with Burr, who offered his columns to Davis to reply. In writing to Davis, Hill condemned Johnston but was pleased by the effect of the incident on the growing Davis tradition. "Poor Johnston has ruined himself," Hill told Davis, "unless he can save his character by a retreat. If he can do anything at all he can retreat, though I think that even that oft practised habit will fail him this time. . . . In truth I am sorry for him though he does not deserve pity. . . . The whole Southern people are your defenders, and the calumny has only served to show once more how devotedly they love you. I think that Johnston will spend the remnant of his days without character." [36]

Although others with experience with Burr did not hesitate to accuse him of "incredible fabrications, falsehoods without the shadow of truth to sustain them" in other published accounts of supposed interviews, Johnston's failure to make a denial of the reported accusation left him under a new onus of ill-will. While discussion of the interview raged, the committee in charge of the dedication of the Lee Memorial at Lexington invited Davis to give the principal address which he consented to do. When further correspondence revealed that Johnston as president of the association would preside, Davis curtly wrote the committee, "That fact not previously communicated or anticipated causes me promptly . . . to withdraw my consent heretofore given to deliver an address on that occasion." [37]

It was against this background of increased bitterness that Johnston agreed to contribute to a project of the *Century Magazine*, whose editors planned an extensive series of articles on the war from participants on both sides. Johnston's contributions gave him an opportunity to state his side in such debates as that with Beauregard over the command at the First Manassas, but more importantly to analyze publicly Davis' *The Rise and Fall of the Confederacy*, which had appeared in 1881. He gave his four articles the titles, "Responsibilities of the First Bull Run," "Manassas to Seven Pines," "Jefferson Davis and the Mississippi Campaign," and "Opposing Sherman's Advance to Atlanta." In them he dealt largely with the differences between him and the Confederacy's President. Although he was never more forthright as with steady, direct strokes he disposed of each of Davis' arguments, the amount of controversy leads the reader frequently to wonder, as in many other of the articles in this enlightening series, who the greater enemy of the Confederates actually was, the Federal opponent or they themselves.[38]

Another corporative venture, this time as president of the Pan-Electric Company, which was to engage in the manufacture and distribution of telegraphic and other electrical inventions, proved no more fortunate than the express company or the railroad. It soon became involved in patent disputes and other troubles, and disappeared. Uncomfortable in the legal tangles and with much free time on his hands the General found his usual solace in his books. Even in his campaigns he kept favorite volumes at hand, particularly military history. He received with great pleasure a copy of Lyman Draper's *King's Mountain and Its Heroes* from its author. "I find it the most interesting American historical work I have read," he wrote in acknowledgment. "For the battle described was the most important in the Revolutionary War, and you describe it like the ancient historians—circumstantially and with excellent choice of circumstances." [39]

He loved to discuss either in conversation or correspondence his campaigns or those of others in the war. He disliked the comparison of himself with Fabius, the Roman commander in the Second Punic War. Fabius had deliberately chosen his retiring, delaying tactics before Hannibal, whereas Johnston had no alternative in the Georgia campaign. Sherman's superior force required him to conduct the sort of campaign he did. He had great admiration for Sherman's ability. "McClellan was the best organizer in the Federal army," he told a young South Carolinian who queried him on the relative merits of the Federal commanders and never forgot the courtesy the distinguished old gentleman showed an inquisitive youngster. "Grant was

the best fighter, but Sherman was the genius of the Federal army."
Then as though to impress it on his young listener he said more
slowly, "But, young man, never forget that Robert E. Lee was their
superior in any capacity." [40]

When the Virginia legislature commissioned the painting of the
General's portrait to hang in the Capitol building in Richmond it
became Dabney Maury's responsibility to keep the talk going so
that the artist, Jack Elder, could watch the animated play of expression in Johnston's face. Military history and figures held the major
share of their attention. In ranking the great commanders Johnston
placed Napoleon above all after Julius Caesar and stated that Marl-
borough was England's best soldier and statesman. When talk
turned to the Confederacy the General gave full credit to Lee and
Jackson for the reputations they had won, but stated the firm opinion
that Forrest was the greatest soldier of the war. He expressed regret
that Virginians had known so little in the period of the conflict of
the ability and the exploits of the great cavalry leader. [41]

When Grover Cleveland became the first Democratic President
since the outbreak of the war he appointed the aging General commissioner of railroads, a position which required that he travel considerably to all parts of the country. While in Portland, Oregon, in
July 1885 he received word to return east at once to act as one of the
pallbearers at Grant's funeral. It was a fitting assignment as each
man held great respect for the other. Grant had singled Johnston
out as the ablest of the Confederate commanders and the one who
had given him the most anxiety. Shortly before his death Grant had
written of the campaign in Georgia that neither the great defensive
soldier, Thomas, nor the ingenious Sherman, "nor any other soldier
could have done it better" than Old Joe. [42]

As the nation stopped to mourn Grant's passing, the errors of his
Presidential career were forgotten and writers and orators paid tribute
to his military achievements. In New York around the first small
tomb in Riverside Park a great crowd gathered. Among them four
men stood erect as the personification of the growing spirit of reunion. Simon Buckner and Philip Sheridan stood arm in arm along
with Sherman and Johnston. Their appearance together, a reporter
for *Harper's Weekly* wrote, "gives a picture of American fraternity
astonishing almost to ourselves who remember terrible conflict within
the present generation. . . . " [43]

But a few months passed before Johnston stood at the graveside of another of his wartime opponents. Early in November he traveled to Trenton in New Jersey to participate in the funeral of his dear associate of prewar days who became his adversary in the Peninsula campaign, George B. McClellan. The passing of "Beloved Mac" was a heavy blow to Johnston who wrote a mutual friend: "This death has been to me like the loss of my brother. That of no other man could have been so afflicting to me. . . . He will appear in history as an exemplary Christian, noble gentleman, valiant soldier and wise leader." [44]

Johnston mourned the death of these friends, but on February 22, 1887, he received a crushing blow from which he never recovered. Although his wife had suffered for years from poor health, her death in their Washington home was sudden and its shock left him a lonely old man. For more than forty years their devotion made life together idyllic for them. Without children they drew more closely to each other, and he "worshipped her as her knight and hero." Lydia Johnston was a graceful, delightful person who knew her husband's every mood, but who never attempted to force her will upon him in vital decisions. In the war years she mirrored the effect of Davis' attitude toward and treatment of him much more openly than he. She spoke freely and frankly about both in her letters to friends, while he took each reverse with stoic, outward calm.

Mrs. Johnston's humor, which she frequently displayed in banter and little jokes at his expense, delighted him. Maury tells of one example, when he and the General sat upon the upper porch of the Johnston's cottage on one of their stays at Sweet Chalybeate Springs. As the General was talking, a shriek came from the walkway below. He looked over the banister and then resumed his conversation. Quickly, a second and then a third shrill cry echoed in the air. The General called down to a young lady who confronted a turkey gobbler, "Why don't you run away?" Maury turned to his older friend and chided, "That is fine advice to come from a great commander." Always realistic the General said, "Well, sir, if she won't fight, the best she can do is to run away, isn't it?" Mrs. Johnston could not resist pushing the point and with an infectious chuckle exclaimed, "That used to be your plan, I know, sir," which sent all three off into bursts of laughter. [45]

After her burial in Baltimore Johnston never trusted himself to mention her name. He kept the house exactly as she had left it and lived alone, enjoying the company of the dwindling circle of old friends. Members of the McLane family were steadfast in their devotion to him and assisted to keep him active and entertained. Bradley Johnson stirred an old interest when he asked the General to assist him in the preparation of a biography. Johnston offered to help but expressed fear "that the difficulty of finding data will make you drop the enterprize." Later he promised Johnson to correct some errors of fact about his prewar career in the article on him in Pollard's *Lee and His Lieutenants*. He worked periodically otherwise with Johnson, who completed his manuscript in time for publication the year of the General's death.[46]

As time passed and bitter memories began to blend into a general feeling of comradeship, even the steady growth of the Davis tradition had little if any effect upon the affectionate regard of the veterans of the Army of Tennessee for their Old Joe. It brought to him a warm invitation to attend memorial exercises in Atlanta in the spring of 1890, an invitation he promptly accepted. His army and business associate, Livingston Mims, who was then mayor of Atlanta, met and entertained him for the period of his stay. Although the trip tired him greatly newspaper reporters found him to have "all the old-time grace and dignity." Such general officers as E. P. Alexander and Kirby Smith called upon him and reminisced about army days. But it was the demonstrative actions of the veterans and citizens which made him realize that the events of the intervening years since 1864 had not influenced their real admiration and affection for him. His visit was an almost continuous ovation of which the climax came in the parade.

For his part in that momentous affair he rode with Kirby Smith in a flower-bedecked carriage drawn by a pair of coal-black horses, with the Governor's Horse Guard as an escort. As they moved to take their place in the procession, a shout went up from the crowd: "That's Johnston! That's Joe Johnston!" Men who had served under him pushed forward and surrounded the carriage. Amid shouts and yells they lifted the vehicle and its occupants from the ground, and extended their hands to Old Joe's or to touch him. Troopers of the Horse Guard tried to push the eager crowd aside but to no avail. Police stormed down to assist, but devotion and sentiment took precedence over pleas to let the parade proceed. Finally as the way cleared someone shouted, "Take the horses away!" In a moment the team was out of the traces and the carriage moved forward, drawn by the veterans.

"Up Marietta Street it went," a reporter wrote, "to the Custom-house, then it was turned, and back toward the opera house it rolled. The rattle of the drums and the roll of the music were drowned by yells of the old soldiers; they were wild, mad with joy; their long pent-up love for the old soldier had broken loose." When the carriage drew up in front of the opera house where the speaking was to be, only the knowledge of the General's infirmities kept the crowd from carrying him on their shoulders into the building. The overwhelming demonstration of devotion brought tears from the usually controlled Johnston and again disproved the statements of his critics that these soldiers had lost confidence in him in their great campaign together.[47]

Gratifying too was the warm, appreciative reception which Richmond gave him just a month later when veterans from all corners of the country gathered for the unveiling of Mercie's equestrian statue of Lee. But more than the pleasure which the greeting of his comrades produced shone in Johnston's face as he pulled the cord to display the beloved figure of Lee. Across his mind there must have flashed memories of West Point and of early service in the Peninsula of Virginia, of the war in Mexico and of their final great joint experience in the tragic years of 1861-1865.

While in Richmond the General visited with friends and particularly enjoyed the company of Maury's little granddaughter for whom he stood as godfather, holding her in his arms throughout the ceremony. At a party given by Archer Anderson he met and talked at length with the Comte de Paris, who had served with the Federal army and had written a lengthy history of the war. But old associates noticed that the General tired easily and that his age in other ways grew more noticeable. In mid-February 1891 he nevertheless journeyed to New York to take his place as an honorary pallbearer for his oldtime opponent and friend, Sherman. The day was raw and cool following a winter rain, but the General stood bareheaded with the other pallbearers, as the flag-draped coffin was carried from the Sherman residence to the waiting caisson. A spectator leaned forward and suggested, "General, please put on your hat; you might get sick." Without hesitation the eighty-four-year-old Johnston replied, "If I were in his place and he were standing here in mine, he would not put on his hat." [48]

He did take a severe cold which aggravated an already bad heart condition. Steadily he grew worse despite all that could be done.

Calmly he received his last communion and on Saturday, March 21, 1891, died quietly, with his brother-in-law, Robert McLane, at his bedside. His funeral in accordance with his wish was conducted with the same simplicity which distinguished his life. Attired in a black suit with no indication of military rank his body rested in a plain casket. Veteran groups asked the postponement of the ceremony and offered a military escort, but the McLane family declined. After a short service at St. John's Episcopal Church the body was taken to Baltimore for interment. Veterans of both blue and gray gathered to pay respect by their presence as the remains of Joseph Eggleston Johnston were placed in Greenmount Cemetery beside those of his wife and his nephew, Preston Johnston, whose body he had brought from Mexico some years before.[49]

As the news of his death spread through the country editorial writers, veterans' groups and others paid tribute to him. Individuals in isolated country cabins, hamlets and metropolitan centers recalled incidents in which they and he had a common participation. They thought of Kennesaw and Seven Pines, of First Manassas and Dalton, of the removal before Atlanta and even of Bentonville, always in terms of admiration for a revered leader. Others remembered only the controversies and the stories that Johnston was a general who chose to retire when another would have stood or even have advanced.

What is the truth? Can it at this date be determined or even estimated? No one can say what results might have been had a different course been adopted. But from an objective point of view the evidence seems to justify Johnston's actions.

Had he waited in the Manassas-Centerville line McClellan could have driven him back by sheer weight of numbers or got in his rear by using the Potomac and Chesapeake Bay.

In the early part of 1863 the effect of every effort to exchange troops between Tennessee and Mississippi proved inconsequential and dangerous. Later in Mississippi, alone Johnston could have achieved success only had Pemberton worked energetically and co-operatively as a subordinate.

In the Georgia campaign Richmond failed to correct handicaps which cause the historian to marvel that for more than sixty days and over a hundred miles Johnston kept Sherman from destroying the Confederate army. At the end of this phase there is the only opportunity to contrast what Richmond wanted with what Johnston did. Hood gave Davis, Bragg and Seddon what they had demanded all year—offensive action against Sherman—and the result was as Johnston feared, the end of the Army of Tennessee as a vital force.

Could the result have been different with Johnston in command? Who can say? That Johnston was a far abler commander than Hood a comparison of the campaign of the Army of Tennessee in the few weeks of late July and August with that of May, June and early July easily demonstrates. But even Johnston did not fully comprehend the strength of the Federal potential in 1864. He interpreted Sherman's long line of communications as a seeming source of weakness, but had Forrest been able to interrupt it, who can believe it would have been more than a temporary inconvenience? Before too long Sherman was to demonstrate that he needed no communications when he went from Atlanta to the sea. Had Johnston been able to keep his army intact before Sherman the aspect would have been different, but what the eventuality might have been one can only conjecture. Yet whatever the answer about all these questions, it favors Johnston more than Davis.

What sort of man was he? Some qualities are easily seen. He was uniformly courteous; even in his military relations he could not be brusque or rude. He realized the importance of his position, yet his dignity was never oppressive. A typical Southerner, he was a strong individualist and his sense of propriety caused him to defend himself even against the weight of the administration when he knew himself right. He was modest and without any semblance of vainglory, reserved yet friendly, and possessed a sense of humor which charmed everyone.

Almost a century has passed since this war was fought. In those years many Southern leaders have emerged not only as Confederate heroes but as exemplars of the enduring American tradition. Joseph Eggleston Johnston is one of them. Ironically much of his recognition has come to him because of the campaign in which his commander in chief most doubted him, that against Sherman from Dalton to Atlanta. Although overshadowed by the postwar Davis legend and overlooked by biographers since 1893, Johnston is accepted as one of America's great commanders. With his love of his profession that would have satisfied him.

NOTES

NOTES

NOTES FOR CHAPTER 1
(Pages 11-28)

[1] R. M. Hughes, *General Johnston*, 36-37.

[2] A. L. Long, *Memoirs of Robert E. Lee*, 71.

[3] W. L. Fleming, "Jefferson Davis at West Point," *Publications of the Mississippi Historical Society*, X, 247-287; Robert McElroy, *Jefferson Davis: The Unreal and the Real*, I, 19. McElroy used the story of a fight between Johnston and Davis and cited a letter to Fleming from Augustus Bethune, June 12, 1908, but Fleming, who published his article in 1909, ignored Bethune's letter and merely said that a "tradition" existed of such an occurrence.

[4] G. W. Cullum, *Biographical Register of the Officers and Graduates of the U. S. Military Academy at West Point, N. Y., from Its Establishment in 1802 to 1890, with the Early History of the United States Military Academy*, 343-344.

[5] Long, *Memoirs of Lee*, 35-37; D. S. Freeman, *R. E. Lee*, I, 115, 132, R. E. Lee to John Mackay, Feb. 18, 1833.

[6] J. R. Motte, *Journey into Wilderness: An Army Surgeon's Account of Life in Camp and Field During the Creek and Seminole Wars, 1836-1838*, 168, 170, 182-183.

[7] R. M. McLane, *Reminiscences, 1827-1897*, 65, 71; Joseph E. Johnston to Preston Johnston, March 16, 1840, May 13, Nov. 27, 1842, Apr. 14, 1843, College of William and Mary Library.

[8] G. G. Meade, *The Life and Letters of George Gordon Meade*, I, 187, George Gordon Meade to wife, March 8, 1847; Freeman, *Lee*, I, 219, 221, 226.

[9] D. H. Maury, *Recollections of a Virginian in The Mexican, Indian and Civil Wars*, 38-41.

[10] *Ibid.*, 40-41; Long, *Memoirs of Lee*, 71; Freeman, *Lee*, I, 260-266; Hughes, *Johnston*, 28-29. In a note, Hughes says

that Johnston fell prostrate when he heard the news. Lt. Johnston had been an orphan to whom Johnston felt much like a father. Through the rest of his life, Hughes says, Johnston kept a photograph of this favorite nephew in his room.

[11] Hughes, *Johnston*, 29-32; J. H. Smith, *The War with Mexico*, II, 154; R. S. Henry, *The Story of the Mexican War*, 359 ff.; Winfield Scott, *Memoirs of Lt. Gen. Scott, LL.D.*, II, 184.

[12] C. W. Elliott, *Winfield Scott: Soldier and Man*, 555: W. W. Mackall, *A Son's Recollections of His Father*, 120, W. W. Mackall to wife, Oct. 18, 1847.

[13] Maury, *Recollections*, 154.

[14] J. E. Johnston to Samuel Cooper, Feb. 24, 1855, Duke University Library.

[15] J. E. Johnston to L. T. Wigfall, March 14, 1865, Library of Congress.

[16] J. E. Johnston to G. B. McClellan, Dec. 2, 1855; March 30, 1856; Oct. 25, 1856; Nov. 18, 1856; June 4, 1857; Sept. 15, 1857, Library of Congress.

[17] J. E. Johnston to G. B. McClellan, Jan. 2, 1857, Library of Congress.

[18] Jefferson Davis, *Constitutionalist, His Letters, Papers and Speeches*, collected and edited by Dunbar Rowland (hereafter, Rowland, *Jefferson Davis*), VIII, 370-371, R. A. Ransom to W. T. Walthall, March 23, 1879.

[19] Mary Boykin Chesnut, *A Diary from Dixie*, (Appleton) 351-352. "Mrs. Davis," is Mrs. Jefferson Davis, whose husband was then a senator from Mississippi.

[20] J. E. Johnston to G. B. McClellan, Jan. 31, 1859, Library of Congress; Maury, *Recollections*, 107: Freeman, *Lee*, I, 388.

[21] Ibid., I, 411, R. E. Lee to John Mackay, Feb. 3, 1846, R. E. Lee to Custis Lee, Apr. 16, 1860.

[22] J. E. Johnston to G. B. McClellan, March 28, 1859, Apr. 7, 1859, Apr. 29, 1859, Library of Congress; W. S. Myers, *General George Brinton McClellan*, 114-116; Ralph Roeder, *Juarez and His Mex-*

ico, I, 161 ff. The reference to "our respectable quartette" includes McClellan, G. W. Smith and A. P. Hill, according to Myers. It is possible that some other than Hill might have been the fourth member.

[23] Hughes, *Johnston*, 33-35; *Journal of the Executive Proceedings of the Senate of the United States*, 229-230; Varina Davis, *Jefferson Davis, Ex-President of the Confederate States of America* (hereafter Mrs. Davis, *Jefferson Davis*), II, 150, 157-158. The letter which is quoted in part by Mrs. Davis, was written to James Lyons and can be found complete in Rowland, *Jefferson Davis*, VIII, 257-258. In the vote on confirmation, Davis was for J. E. Johnston.

[24] Hughes, *Johnston*, 34, R. E. Lee to J. E. Johnston, July 30, 1860.

[25] J. E. Johnston to "My dear friends," July 3, 1860, Library of Congress.

[26] United States War Department, *The War of the Rebellion: A Compilation of the Official Records of the Union and Confederate Armies*, #122, 2 ff. (hereafter O.R., with serial number).

[27] O.R., # 122, 18.

[28] Ibid., #127, 165-166; Chesnut, *Diary* (Houghton), 133. Later Mrs. Chesnut wrote, "And did not Mrs. Johnston tell us how General Scott thought to save the melancholy, reluctant, slow Joe for the Yankees; but he came to us." *Ibid.*, 344.

[29] Mrs. Johnston to Mrs. Wigfall, Aug. 2, 1863, Library of Congress; J. E. Johnston to Andrew Johnson, July 1, 1865, Amnesty Papers, File 67, National Archives; Hughes, *Johnston*, 36; E. A. Pollard, *Lee and His Lieutenants*, 344-345 (the section on Johnston in Pollard's book was prepared by Judge R. W. Hughes, a nephew by marriage of Johnston, and father of R. M. Hughes, who said that Pollard freely edited it); Elliott, *Winfield Scott*, 714; Freeman, *Lee*, I, 439 ff.

NOTES FOR CHAPTER 2
(Pages 29-41)

[1] O. R., #108, 60, 69; #111, 167. Joseph E. Johnston to L. T. Wigfall, Apr. 3, 1865, Library of Congress.
[2] W. H. Russell, *My Diary North and South*, 173.
[3] O. R., #127, 117, 127-131, 163-164, 326-327.
[4] Ellsworth Eliot, Jr., *West Point in the Confederacy*, 318, 402, 403.
[5] O. R., #2, 872; J. E. Johnston, *Narrative of Military Operations . . .*, 14; A. H. Noll, *General Kirby Smith*, 172-173.
[6] O. R., #2, 871, 872, 877.
[7] Chesnut, *Diary* (Houghton) 50, 65 ff.; A. H. Bill, *The Beleaguered City: Richmond*, 53-55; Mrs. Johnston to Louise Wigfall, July 15, 1864, Library of Congress.
[8] O. R., #2, 959-960.
[9] D. H. Strother, "Personal Recollections of the War," *Harper's New Monthly Magazine*, XXXIII, 24.
[10] O. R., #2, 880-881, 890, 895-896, 897, 901, 907-908; Johnston, *Narrative*, 17-21.
[11] O. R. #2, 889, 897-898, 901, 929-930.
[12] *Ibid.*, 471: Johnston, *Narrative*, 22-23; *Southern Historical Society Papers* (hereafter *S.H.S.P.*) IX, 93.
[13] O. R., #2, 472; Strother, "Personal Recollections," 142-143; Johnston, *Narrative*, 23-24, *S.H.S.P.*, IX, 351.
[14] O. R., #2, 691, 698, 934, 935, 937, 940; Pollard, *Lee and His Lieutenants*, 348; J. B. Jones, *A Rebel War Clerk's Diary* (hereafter Jones, *War Clerk*), I, 52-53.

NOTES FOR CHAPTER 3
(Pages 42-58)

[1] O. R., #2, 187, 470.
[2] *Ibid.*, 158. He estimated Johnston's force as being from 15,000 to 18,000 infantry. The respect which the Federal officers had for Johnston's ability is shown by Strother, who says that he heard West Pointers in the Federal Army say: "Joe Johnston is considered the foremost man among the Southern leaders in point of general ability and military genius. A man eminently brave, energetic, and ambitious; capable of enlarged views in war or politics, and one who will take the highest position in case the rebellion succeeds. Cold and concentrated in manner, of immovable self-possession, he will exhibit great vigor in the field, but will probably lack confidence and steadfastness under reverses." Strother, "Personal Recollections," 549.
[3] Noll, *Kirby Smith*, 182-184, E. Kirby Smith to mother, July 4, 1861.
[4] Chesnut, *Diary* (Appleton), 68-69; G. F. R. Henderson, *Stonewall Jackson and the American Civil War*, 98; O. R., #2, 963, 973-974; Johnston, *Narrative*, 30-31.
[5] English Combatant, *Battle-Fields of the South from Bull Run to Fredericksburgh*, 32; Johnston, *Narrative*, 21; Pollard, *Lee and His Lieutenants*, 350; Alfred Roman, *Military Operations of General Beauregard*, I, 87, 436-437.
[6] O. R., #2, 806, 894.
[7] *Ibid.*, 967; Johnston, *Narrative*, 19, 32; Hughes, *Johnston*, 50. Although Roman claims (Roman, *Military Operations*, I, 76) that Beauregard originated the idea of concentrating the armies, Lee and Johnston were in correspondence about such a move as early as May 30, before the arrival of Beauregard. O. R., #2, 894, 897.
[8] *Ibid.*, 473; Roman, *Military Operations*, I, 438. This single request by Johnston for a clarification of the cir-

cumstances was later enlarged by Jefferson Davis, in a letter he wrote Feb. 18, 1865, one in which he was attempting to justify his refusal to reappoint Johnston to the command of the Army of Tennessee, as follows: "When General Beauregard was threatened at Manassas by a large column of the enemy, his numerical inferiority and the inactivity of the enemy in the Valley, under General Patterson evinced the necessity, propriety and practicability of a prompt march of our Valley Army to his aid. General Johnston made serious objections to, and expressed doubts as to the practicability of such a move; and only after repeated and urgent instructions, did he move to make the junction proposed. The delay thus occasioned retarded the arrival of the head of his column until after the first conflict had occurred, and prevented a part of his troops from getting into position until the victory had been won. Indeed, we were saved from a fatal defeat at the battle of Manassas by the promptness of General E. Kirby Smith, who, acting without orders, and moving by a change of direction, succeeded in reaching the battlefield in time to avert disaster." Rowland, *Jefferson Davis*, VI, 493, Jefferson Davis to James Phelan, Feb. 18, 1865. This statement, as anyone who reads an account of the battle of Manassas will perceive, is startlingly distorted and erroneous.

⁹ O. R., #2, 470-479: Johnston, *Narrative*, 33; Jefferson Davis, *The Rise and Fall of the Confederate Government*, I, 346-347. This message led to later controversy between Davis and Johnston. It began as soon as Davis read Johnston's report and continued at intervals after the war. Johnston interpreted the order roughly in his report as advising him to move at his discretion to the assistance of Beauregard "after" sending his sick to Culpeper Court-House. Davis argued that the word "after" was not in the original order. As Johnston left his sick where they were at Winchester, this point is wholly academic. David also said that the words, "if practicable," did not

imply that Johnston was to use his discretion. The expression meant only that if Johnston were engaged in battle, as some of his letters had seemed to predict he might be, he need not break the engagement and move; if not, he was to move at once. All this seems mere quibbling. Whatever Davis may have had in mind, the order to a reader today stands as Johnston interpreted it.

¹⁰ O. R., #2, 982, 983; Roman, *Military Operations*, I, 94-95; R. U. Johnson and C. C. Buel, *Battles and Leaders of the Civil War* (hereafter *B. & L.*), I, 229; Mackall, *A Son's Recollections*, 189, letter of Johnston to Mackall, Aug. 18, 1863.

¹¹ Mary Anna Jackson, *Memoirs of Stonewall Jackson*, 175, T. J. Jackson to wife, undated.

¹² Johnston, *Narrative*, 37-38.

¹³ *Ibid.*, 38; R. M. Johnston, *Bull Run, Its Strategy and Tactics*, 152-153.

¹⁴ O. R., #2, 473, 985; *B. & L.*, I, 245; Johnston, *Narrative*, 38, 39; J. E. Johnston to B. T. Johnson, Sept. 30, 1887, Duke University Library. In this letter Johnston asserts that Beauregard was not in tactical command at Manassas. It is true that Beauregard issued all orders, but only after consultation and approval by Johnston. Because Beauregard's commission was in the Provisional Army he had not received automatic elevation to a full general.

¹⁵ O. R., #2, 479-480; Johnston, *Narrative*, 41; Johnston, *Bull Run*, 159-163; D. S. Freeman, *Lee's Lieutenants*, I, 50-52, *B. & L.*, I, 246.

¹⁶ O. R., #2, 558-559: E. P. Alexander, *Military Memoirs of a Confederate*, 3-4, 30-31.

¹⁷ O. R., #2, 474; Alexander, *Military Memoirs*, 32.

¹⁸ O. R., #2, 395; Alexander, *Military Memoirs*, 33; Johnston, *Bull Run*, 190.

¹⁹ Alexander, *Military Memoirs*, 34; Freeman, *Lee's Lieutenants*, I, 60-61. Freeman observes that Johnston "meticulously had respected his assignment to Beauregard of the conduct of the battle"

to this moment. Hughes, *Johnston*, 61-63; *O. R. #2*, 491. Alexander's account of the departure of Johnston and Beauregard from Lookout Hill is slightly different from that given by Beauregard in his report and from that by Col. Thomas L. Preston, used by Hughes, but the difference is in minor details.

[20] *O. R. #2*, 475, 492.

[21] *S.H.S.P.*, IX, 130-131; Freeman, *Lee's Lieutenants*, I, 52 n; Noll, *Kirby Smith*, 189; McHenry Howard, *Recollections of a Maryland Confederate Soldier and Staff Officer under Johnston, Jackson and Lee*, 34.

Only four regiments arrived at Manassas Junction with Kirby Smith. One of them was left there, while the other three went with him into action.

[22] *O. R., #2*, 476, 496, 557; Noll, *Kirby Smith*, 186-187; Johnston, *Narrative*, 51-52; *B. & L.*, I, 215, 249; Johnston, *Bull Run*, 229-231; R. S. Henry, *The Story of the Confederacy*, 59.

[23] Davis, *Rise and Fall*, I, 349-350; Alexander, *Military Memoirs*, 41-42, 49; Johnston, *Narrative*, 53-54; Jones, *War Clerk*, I, 65-66. There is disagreement among sources as to when Davis arrived on the field and what he did.

NOTES FOR CHAPTER 4
(Pages 59-71)

[1] *O. R., #2*, 986; Alexander, *Military Memoirs*, 49-50; Davis, *Rise and Fall*, I, 352-356; Johnston, *Narrative*, 59-65; Roman, *Military Operations*, I, 114-119. In these accounts of the conference, the positions of the conferees is not always clear. However, all were written many years after the event, when fact had changed to argument. Davis insisted that he was all the while for pursuit. If so, it seems strange that he gave up so easily his order for it on the conflicting evidence about Hill's report. He remained at Manassas all the next day and could have easily determined, it would seem, whether or not pursuit was in progress. Moreover, he said in his history of the Confederacy (*Rise and Fall*, 360), "The generals, like myself, were well content with what had been done." Johnston, as usual, is very reticent about his participation in the conference, but from other comments by him it would seem that he held to his realistic belief as a practical soldier that pursuit should not be attempted, even though he apparently agreed, or did not object, to the writing of the unsent Davis order.

[2] J. E. Johnston to Jefferson Davis, July 24, 1861, Duke University Library.

[3] *O. R., #2*, 327, 570; Johnston, *Bull Run*, 252-261.

[4] Richard Taylor, *Destruction and Reconstruction*, p. 18; Pollard, *Lee and His Lieutenants*, 359-360; Johnston, *Narrative*, 60-61; Davis, *Rise and Fall*, I, 353-355.

[5] *O. R., #2*, 508.

[6] J. E. Johnston to Jefferson Davis, July 24, 1861, Duke University Library; Johnston, *Narrative*, 59; *B. & L.*, I, 259, R. E. Lee to J. E. Johnston, July 24, 1861.

[7] *O. R., #2*, 168, 171.

[8] *Ibid.*, 511-512; *#108*, 374.

[9] Roman, *Military Operations*, 136; Johnston, *Narrative*, 66-67.

[10] *S.H.S.P.*, IX, 483; *O. R., #2*, 507-508; Roman, *Military Operations*, I, 120-130.

[11] J. E. Johnston to Jefferson Davis, Aug. 3, 23, 1861, Duke University Library; Johnston, *Narrative*, 67-68; Roman, *Military Operations*, I, 121-130; Davis, *Rise and Fall*, I, 303, 315; *O. R., #2*, 507-508, 789, 790; Charles Marshall, *An Aide-de-Camp of Lee*, 44-47; G. C. Eggleston, *A Rebel's Recollections*, 43-44, gives a good idea of what a lesser soldier thought of the Confederate service of supply. In Freeman, *Lee*, II, 494-495, there is a good display of Northrop's lack of consistency, for there he is in an argument with Lee because Lee

wanted to draw supplies from Richmond, while Northrop insisted that he feed his army off the country. It was then in the dead of winter.

[12] J. E. Johnston to Jefferson Davis, Aug. 3, 1861, Duke University Library.

[13] Maury, *Recollections*, 144-145.

[14] *O. R.*, #2, 1007; Mrs. Davis, *Jefferson Davis*, II, 138-140. The orders Johnston objected to came from Lee.

[15] Freeman, *Lee*, I, 527 ff.

[16] *Journal of the Congress of the Confederate States of America, 1861-1865*, (hereafter *Jour. of Cong.*), I, 461.

[17] *O. R.*, #127, 605-608.

[18] *Ibid.*, 511.

[19] Johnston, *Narrative*, 73; Rowland, *Jefferson Davis*, VIII, 257, Jefferson Davis to James Lyons, Aug. 30, 1878; Taylor, *Destruction*, 27; Mrs. Davis, *Jefferson Davis*, II, 150 n.

[20] Hughes, *Johnston*, 89-90; W. P. Johnston, *Life of General A. S. Johnston*, 275 ff.

[21] Chesnut, *Diary* (Appleton), 101-102, 318; J. S. Wise, *The End of an Era*, 401. Wise says, "Among us 'Irreverents,' it was believed that Mrs. Davis possessed great influence over her husband, even to the point that she could secure promotion for us, if she liked." Mrs. Chesnut described Gen. Mansfield Lovell's experience with Davis, after he had inadvertently failed to speak to Mrs. Davis on entering a room. When he heard of Davis' indignation, Lovell called on him to apologize and explain, "but the President was inexorable, and would not receive his overtures. . . . "

[22] *O. R.*, #5, 1060. In this connection, a letter written by Davis to Judge W. M. Brooks of Alabama on March 13, 1862 (*O. R.*, #127, 998-1000; Rowland, *Jefferson Davis*, V, 216-217) is interesting. In it Davis explains that Johnston, though offended by the ranking of the generals, "certainly never thought of resigning. . . . "

[23] *O. R.*, #5, 833-834, 944. The first of these is a letter of Sept. 8, 1861, which closes, "Ever, truly, your friend"; the second was written Nov. 9, and closes, "Very respectfully, etc."

[24] Eliot, *West Point*, 84-85, A. H. Cole to General R. S. Ripley, Oct. 10, 1861.

NOTES FOR CHAPTER 5
(Pages 72-81)

[1] Joseph E. Johnston to Jefferson Davis, Sept. 3, 1861, Duke University Library.

[2] Mackall, *A Son's Recollections*, 170, J. E. Johnston to W. W. Mackall, July ——, 1861; *O. R.*, #5, 777, 797, 829; #108, 325. Stuart received his promotion Sept. 24, 1861. He had just as high praise for Johnston as the latter for him. In one of his letters he said, "Johnston is in capacity head and shoulders above every other general in the Southern Confederacy," and in another he spoke of his affection for his leader, "General Johnston is the dearest friend I have on earth. . . . " Quoted in J. W. Thomason, Jr., *Jeb Stuart*, 131.

[3] *O. R.*, #5, 829-830.

[4] *Ibid.*, 881-882.

[5] *Ibid.*, 883.

[6] *Ibid.*, 884-887; Davis, *Rise and Fall*, I, 448-453; Johnston, *Narrative*, 75-77; Roman, *Military Operations*, I, 137-151; Gustavus W. Smith, *Confederate War Papers*, (hereafter Smith, *War Papers*), 13-20. Postwar argument raged over this conference as over so many other matters. Davis maintained that the paper prepared by Smith did not agree with his memory (he wrote years after the event, while the memorandum was written and agreed to by all the other principals within a few months), that it argued with itself and that it was surreptitiously drawn up. Smith, in turn, answered Davis by refuting some of the latter's claims and insisting that irrelevant argument was introduced to confuse the

issues. All this was undoubtedly a result of the popular view that the army was chained to immobility for the fall and winter by the President. But it does not touch the more important matter of the large difference in strategic conception between the generals and Davis. Interestingly enough, from correspondence which passed between Senator Louis T. Wigfall and General Beauregard in March 1864, it appears that Davis at that time denied that any proposal for an offensive was made at the conference. O. R., #108, 839-840, 843.

[7] *Ibid.*, #5, 834.

[8] *Ibid.*, 850-851, 877-878, 892, 896, 897, 904-905, 906-908, 945-947; #108, 359; Smith, *War Papers*, 311; Freeman, *Lee's Lieutenants*, I, 118. Davis told Beauregard he should hold himself in readiness to take over command in the event anything happened to Johnston.

[9] O. R., #5, 913-914.

[10] Hughes, *Johnston*, 98; O. R., #5, 913-914, 922, 934-935.

[11] Roman, *Military Operations*, I, 170-171, 188-189, 488-489.

[12] O. R., #2, 485, 505-515, 903; #5, 1048; Roman, *Military Operations*, I,

85-87, 163-169, 189, 492. When Johnston heard of Beauregard's new place, he wrote: "Your transfer from this army is a great loss to it—a very great loss to me. The troops you have formed regard you as their general, and my confidence in you makes me feel weakened by our separation. You will take with you my best wishes. The best is that you may have fair opportunities; you know how to use them." From this it seems apparent that Johnston was not troubled in his relations with Beauregard by the circumstances after Manassas.

[13] O. R., #5, 947; Johnston, *Narrative*, 77-78; Roman, *Military Operations*, I, 133-134, 153; James Longstreet, *From Manassas to Appomattox*, 60-61.

[14] Joseph Howard Parks, *General Edmund Kirby Smith, C. S. A.*, 144-145, E. K. Smith to wife, Nov. 1, 1861.

[15] English Combatant, *Battle-Fields of the South*, 112; Eggleston, *A Rebel's Recollections*, 40; W. M. Owen, *In Camp and Battle with the Washington Artillery of New Orleans*, 63.

[16] J. E. Johnston to "Dear General," Dec. 24, 1861, Duke University Library.

NOTES FOR CHAPTER 6
(Pages 82-97)

[1] U. B. Phillips, ed., "The Correspondence of Robert Toombs, Alexander H. Stephens, and Howell Cobb," *The Annual Report of the American Historical Association for the Year 1911*, II, 580, 586, T. W. Thomas to A. H. Stephens, Oct. 5, 1861, Dec. 31, 1861.

[2] O. R., #5, 913-914, 960-961, 979, 985; #108, 402.

[3] *Ibid.*, #5, 987, 993-994. In the Huntington Library collection of Johnston papers, there is a draft of this letter with corrections. It indicates an angry note which is not evident in the letter which was sent. In the draft, Johnston says, "I am not obnoxious to the reproof which runs thro' your letter."

[4] Taylor, *Destruction*, 26-27. Taylor,

who wrote after the full enactment of the drama, continued: "Time but served to widen the breach. Without the knowledge and despite the wishes of General Johnston, the descendants of the ancient dwellers of the cave of Abdullum gathered themselves behind his shield, and shot their arrows at President Davis and his advisors, weakening the influence of the head of the cause for which all were struggling." This refers to the use of the estrangement between Johnston and Davis by the many opponents of the President, whose common interest existed only in their attacks upon him. As Taylor viewed the circumstances, Johnston never aided them by making popular cause out of Davis' treatment of him.

[5] Freeman, *Lee's Lieutenants*, I, 119; *S.H.S.P.*, XXVI, 150-151.

[6] *O. R.*, #5, 1011-1012.

[7] *Ibid.*, 1015-1016.

[8] *Ibid.*, 1028, 1035; #14, 547.

[9] *Ibid.*, #5, 1023, 1028.

[10] *Ibid.*, 974; Johnston, *Narrative*. 477.

[11] *O. R.*, #5, 1016-1017; #18, 832-833; #127, 825-827. At the same time, the Virginia Legislature had passed a bill which complicated procedures further. For an interesting contemporary analysis of the difficulties the bills presented to commanders, there is a letter written March 21, 1862, by Col. J. M. Brockenbrough, 40th Virginia Volunteers, to Gen. T. H. Holmes: "I desire to call your attention to the demoralized and disorganized condition of our Virginia troops, and to suggest that some plan should be immediately adopted to reorganize them upon permanent basis.

"The action of our Confederate and State Legislatures have been conflicting, fickle and almost incomprehensible. The constructions placed upon the different bills by our officers have alike been unsatisfactory."

[12] *S.H.S.P.*, XXVI, 360; *O. R.*, #5, 1001-1002.

[13] Roman, *Military Operations*, I, 488; *O. R.*, #5, 1036-1037, 1045-1046, 1075.

[14] *Ibid.*, 1057-1058; Johnston, *Narrative*, 91-94.

[15] *O. R.*, #5, 1086-1087.

[16] *Ibid.*, 1089. There is an interesting comparison of this reply of Davis to Johnston and his answer to Beauregard's similar remonstrance about Benjamin's activities. In both instances Davis starts in an apparent effort to smoothe his correspondent's feelings and then, having disarmed him, supports the Secretary of War by advancing other, unrelated matters in justification of Benjamin. *O. R.*, #5, 920.

[17] *Ibid.*, 1060-1061.

[18] *Ibid.*, 1064-1065, 1069; Johnston, *Narrative*, 91. A number of the subordinates in the Department of Northern Virginia commented then and later on the damage done the army, both by the law and Benjamin's effort to administer it. One of the best is from a letter by Richard S. Ewell, then a newly commissioned major general, on March 7, 1862, in which he said that if Benjamin's orders had been carried out the "whole army would have been broken up except for those two branches (cavalry and artillery)." In addition, he said, "You would be surprised to see the amount of weakness, favoring and the time serving exhibited towards favorites to the injury of any part of the service. . . . " P. G. Hamlin, *Old Bald Head (General R. S. Ewell)*, 78.

[19] *O. R.*, #5, 1049, 1051.

[20] *Ibid.*, 1053.

[21] Jackson, *Memoirs*, 233-234.

[22] *O. R.*, #5, 1056.

[23] *Ibid.*, 1059-1060.

[24] *Ibid.*, 1062.

[25] *Ibid.*, 1059, 1065.

[26] *Ibid.*, 1071.

[27] *Ibid.*, 1073, 1074.

[28] *Ibid.*, 1077; Johnston, *Narrative*, 96. It will be remembered that no official record was preserved of the Fairfax council. Nor at first did officials always feel it necessary to preserve correspondence. On Nov. 9, 1861, Davis wrote Beauregard, Johnston and G. W. Smith, saying that he had neglected to keep copies of his correspondence and orders, and asked that they assist him to secure them. *O. R.*, #5, 944.

[29] Rowland, *Jefferson Davis*, VI, 493-494, Jefferson Davis to James Phelan, Feb. 18, 1865; Davis, *Rise and Fall*, I, 464-465.

[30] *O. R.*, #5, 1079, 1083.

[31] *Ibid.*, 1079; Johnston, *Narrative*, 97; Jones, *War Clerk*, I, 112; *Rebellion Record*, IV, ("Diary of Events"), 37. Jones on Feb. 26 recorded the prospective move in his diary. Moore, under the date of Feb. 21, says, "Rumors of the partial evacuation of Manassas, Va., by the rebels, were prevalent in Washington today, but they were not generally credited."

[32] R. W. Patrick, *Jefferson Davis and His Cabinet*, 53-55, 169 ff.; H. S. Foote,

War of the Rebellion, 352-353; "Pro-
ceedings of First Confederate Congress,"
S.H.S.P., XLIV, 177; "A Richmond
Lady," *Richmond During the War,* 101;
L. A. White, *Robert Barnwell Rhett,*
207 ff.

³³ Foote, *War,* 356-357.

³⁴ Jones, *War Clerk,* I, 116.

³⁵ Foote, *War,* 356-357; Jones, War
Clerk, I, 117; Patrick, *Davis and His
Cabinet,* 175-177; Johnston, *Narrative,*
108.

³⁶ *O. R.,* #5, 1099; #127, 997-998;
S.H.S.P., XLIV, 53, 67-68, 69, 80; Freeman, *Lee,* II, 4-7.

³⁷ *O. R.,* #5, 1086.

NOTES FOR CHAPTER 7
(Pages 98-113)

¹ *O. R.,* #5, 1079, 1081, 1083, 1085,
1092; Johnston, *Narrative,* 102.

² *O. R.,* #5, 1079, 1081, 1083; Johnston, *Narrative,* 98-99; Marshall, *An
Aide-de-Camp,* 44-45; Northrop attempted to justify the selection of
Thoroughfare Gap as the site for the
packing plant by saying it was well
located "to support a threatening army"
and had good railroad connections. The
army was not a "threatening" one and
the railroad connections failed when
needed. Nothing in Northrop's statement explained the holding of huge
quantities of processed meat so near the
enemy's lines. *O. R.,* #127, 1036, 1039.

³ *Ibid.,* #5, 1088.

⁴ *Ibid.,* 1088, 1093.

⁵ *Ibid.,* 1083-1084.

⁶ *Ibid.,* 1079, 1082-1083, 1085, 1087-
1088, 1090-1092, 1093; #108, 487-488;
Johnston, *Narrative,* 106.

⁷ *O. R.,* #108, 1087; Johnston, *Narrative,* 101-103.

⁸ *O. R.,* #108, 496, 497, 498.

⁹ *Ibid.,* #5, 525-526; #108, 1073-
1074; #127, 1039.

¹⁰ *Ibid.,* #108, 1073-1074. Johnston
had reported to Cooper the day before
(*Ibid.,* #5, 26-27) about the retirement.

¹¹ *Ibid.,* #5, 527-528, 1096.

¹² *Ibid.,* 1097; #108, 495; #127,
965, 970, 971.

¹³ *Ibid.,* #5, 527-528.

¹⁴ Rowland, *Jefferson Davis,* VI, 494,
Jefferson Davis to James Phelan, Feb. 18,
1865; VIII, 7; VIII, 187, Jefferson Davis

to L. B. Northrop, Apr.29, 1878; Davis,
Rise and Fall, 468.

¹⁵ *S.H.S.P.,* IX, 516; Taylor, *Destruction,* 35; English Combatant, *Battle-
Fields of the South,* 163. Another soldier
from the other side of the Atlantic but
serving with McClellan added his voice
to the chorus of praise of Johnston for
this movement. The Comte de Paris said
that the timely evacuation of the Manassas positions should "not be attributed to
indiscretions following the councils of
war in Washington," as some assumed.
"I prefer . . . to ascribe it to the military sagacity of the great soldier who
commanded the Army of Northern Virginia." *B. & L.,* II, 121.

¹⁶ Johnston, *Narrative,* 101, 108.

¹⁷ S. G. French, *Two Wars,* 134;
Phillips, "Correspondence of Toombs,
Stephens, and Cobb," *loc. cit.* 591-592,
Robert Toombs to A. H. Stephens,
March 24, 1862; Johnston, *Narrative,*
109.

¹⁸ Davis, *Rise and Fall,* I, 464.

¹⁹ *O. R.,* #15, 379-384.

²⁰ *B. & L.* I, 692-711.

²¹ *O. R.,* #14, 392, 393, 394.

²² *Ibid.,* 397.

²³ *Ibid.,* 405-406.

²⁴ *Ibid.,* 405-407, 408, 409. Johnston
gave information about the size of his
army. At the Rapidan he had about
23,000; at Fredericksburg about 12,000.
Jackson had about 5,000, as of February
1. *Ibid.,* 400-401.

²⁵ *Ibid.,* 419.

[26] Ibid., 64, 66, 67-68.
[27] Ibid., #127, 420, 429; Johnston, Narrative, 109-110.
[28] O. R., #14, 412, 413, 426, 436.
[29] Johnston, Narrative, 111.
[30] Ibid., 111-112.
[31] O. R., #12, 19.
[32] Johnston, Narrative, 112-116; L. T. Wigfall to J. E. Johnston, undated, Library of Congress; Longstreet, Manassas to Appomattox, 66; Smith, War Papers, 41-44; Davis, Rise and Fall, II, 87-88. Davis wrote, "Though General J. E. Johnston did not agree with this decision, he did not ask to be relieved,

and I had no wish to separate him from the troops with whom he was so intimately acquainted, and whose confidence I believed he deservedly possessed." In Lee, II, 21-23, Freeman calls the decision of Davis "sound" and is very critical of Johnston for remaining in command although convinced that he would be unable to carry it out and would fall back. From a tactical point of view it is difficult to agree that the Peninsula was defensible. The time gained seems to have been more a matter of time lost by McClellan.

NOTES FOR CHAPTER 8
(Pages 114-128)

[1] O. R., #14, 455-456, 456-457, 465; Susan P. Lee, Memoirs of William Nelson Pendleton, D.D., 180-181, W. N. Pendleton to wife, Apr. 23, 1862.
[2] O. R., #9, 36; #14, 431, 434, 456, 465, 475, 478; #108, 2, 252, 456-457.
[3] Robert Stiles, Four Years Under Marse Robert, 77.
[4] English Combatant, Battle-Fields of the South, 197-198; S.H.S.P. XXI, 105.
[5] English Combatant, Battle-Fields of the South, 171-172.
[6] O. R., #127, 1095-1100; B. I. Wiley, The Life of Johnny Reb, 130, quoting a South Carolinian; Smith, War Papers, 44.
[7] O. R., #14, 503, 507-508.
[8] Ibid., 3, 17-19, 65, 79, 86, 97-98, 130.
[9] Ibid., 456, 461.
[10] Ibid., 452, 458.
[11] L. T. Wigfall to J. E. Johnston, May 2, 1862, Huntington Library.
[12] O. R., #14, 469-470.
[13] Ibid., 473.
[14] Ibid., 474-475, 476-477.
[15] Ibid., 477, 485.
[16] Ibid., 484-485; B. & L., II, 204.
[17] O. R., #14, 485, 486, 491, 492.

[18] Alexander, Military Memoirs, 66; Johnston, Narrative, 119; English Combatant, Battle-Fields of the South, 197-198.
[19] O. R., #12, 18, 348. As in other instances, there was much long argument over the Confederate loss of supplies, despite Cole's statement. See Davis, Rise and Fall, II, 94; Rowland, Jefferson Davis, VIII, 16-17; B. & L., II, 204-205. Cole's statement is found in Johnston, Narrative, 484; S. P. Lee, Memoirs of Pendleton, 182, says that the guns left at Yorktown could not be moved.
[20] O. R., #14, 135, 509 510; B. & L., II, 201.
[21] Johnston, Narrative, 119.
[22] Ibid., 119-120; O. R., #12, 275, 441-443.
[23] Johnston, Narrative, 120.
[24] O. R., #12, 565; S. H. S. P., XXXVIII, 341.
[25] O. R., #12, 23; G. B. McClellan, McClellan's Own Story; The War for the Union, 337-338.
[26] B. & L., II, 275-276.
[27] O. R., #12, 614.
[28] Ibid., 276, 627.
[29] Ibid., 627, 629; #108, 552-553.
[30] Ibid., #14, 500.

[31] *Ibid.*, #5, 986-987, 1030, 1058; #14, 500; M. W. Wellman, *Giant in Gray*, 68-72.

[32] J. B. Hood, *Advance and Retreat*, 16; *B. & L.*, II, 276

[33] Johnston, *Narrative*, 126.

[34] *O. R.*, #14, 462, 488, 490. Davis, *Rise and Fall*, II, 92-93.

[35] *Rebellion Record*, V ("Documents and Narratives"), 46-48; *B. & L.*, I, 709-710.

[36] *O. R.*, #14, 164, 518.

[37] *Ibid.*, #12, 276; Johnston, *Narrative*, 128; *B. & L.*, II, 207-208.

NOTES FOR CHAPTER 9
(Pages 129-140)

[1] *O. R.*, #14, 495-496, 501-502, 512-513, 557.

[2] Chesnut, *Diary* (Houghton), 219, 229; "A Richmond Lady," *Richmond*, 129-130; Mrs. Davis, *Jefferson Davis*, II, 269; Mrs. Clement C. Clay-Clopton, *A Belle of the Fifties*, 178-179; *O. R.*, #14, 496, 518. Davis' baptism was by the Reverend Charles Minnigerode. He was confirmed shortly after by Bishop John Johns.

[3] *Ibid.*, 499-500, 506.

[4] *Ibid.*, 500-501, 505.

[5] *Ibid.*, #18, 845, 848, 852; Johnston, *Narrative*, 110.

[6] *O. R.*, #18, 859, 862.

[7] *Ibid.*, 888; Taylor, *Destruction*, 38; J. E. Johnston to T. J. Jackson, May 12, 1862, from D. S. Freeman.

[8] R. S. Ewell to T. J. Jackson, May 13, 1862, from D. S. Freeman; *O. R.*, #14, 519; #18, 890, 892.

[9] *Ibid.*, 892-893.

[10] *Ibid.*, 894-895.

[11] *Ibid.*, 896-897.

[12] R. L. Dabney, *Life and Campaigns of Lieut.-Gen. Thomas J. Jackson*, 358-359.

[13] *Ibid.*, 359-360; *O.R.*, #18, 892-893, 897.

[14] J. E. Johnston to R. S. Ewell, May 18, 1862, from D. S. Freeman.

[15] *O. R.*, #18, 897, 898.

[16] *New York Times*, June 16, 1861, quoted in Louis M. Starr, *Bohemian Brigade*, 121-122.

[17] *S.H.S.P.*, XXXVIII, 346.

[18] Meade, *Life and Letters*, I, 276.

[19] *O. R.*, #18, 219, 220-221.

[20] *Ibid.*, #15, 710; H. K. Douglas, *I Rode with Stonewall*, 65, J. E. Johnston to T. J. Jackson, May 27, 1862. A postscript to this letter reads, "Time will be gained and saved by addressing me always instead of the government."

[21] *O. R.*, #13, 511; Davis, *Rise and Fall*, II, 101-102.

[22] *B. & L.*, II, 206-207; *O. R.*, #14, 524. This meeting was held apparently on May 12, as Davis referred to it in a letter written to his wife the next day. Mrs. Davis, *Jefferson Davis*, II, 270.

[23] J. E. Johnston to L. T. Wigfall, Nov. 12, 1863, Library of Congress.

[24] *O. R.*, #14, 523-524. Davis wrote after the war that it "had not occurred to me that he [Johnston] meditated a retreat which would uncover the Capital, nor was it ever suspected until, in reading General Hood's book, published in 1880, the evidence was found that General Johnston when retreating from Yorktown, told his volunteer aide, Mr. McFarland, that 'he [Johnston] expected or intended to give up Richmond.'" Davis, *Rise and Fall*, II, 120. The quotation which Davis used is from Hood, *Advance*, 153-155. Hood quotes at second hand from a man who wished to withdraw the information when he found that Hood planned to use it. Johnston completely discredits every fragment of the story in *B. & L.*, II, 209-210, and is supported by letters from members of his staff, who say also that McFarland never served as Johnston's aide, either voluntary or otherwise.

[25] *O. R.*, #14, 526, 530; Rowland,

Jefferson Davis, V, 248; Davis, *Rise and Fall*, II, 103. Davis said that he rode out to Johnston's headquarters some time after Col. Lee reported to him and was surprised to find that the army was across the Chickahominy and that some of the troops were in the suburbs of the city itself. Although Reagan would seem to confirm this (John H. Reagan, *Memoirs*, 137-138), a letter from Gen. Lee, written at Davis' direction apparently, (O. R., #14, 526) on May 18, and Col. Lee's visit on May 19, after the move across the Chickahominy, are evidence that Davis' memory must have confused him about the sequence of events. Davis also said that Johnston explained that he retired close to Richmond, as the water of the Chickahominy was unhealthy and he preferred to have the stream in his front instead of his rear. Johnston (*B. & L.*, II, 207-208) denied that either was a factor in his reasoning. He said that the reason for his movement was that the activity of the Federals on the James caused him to think they might change their base to that river from the York and he wanted to be in position to meet them, whether they did or still continued to use the York.

NOTES FOR CHAPTER 10
(Pages 141-157)

[1] O. R., #12, 25, 32.
[2] *Ibid.*, 51; #14, 176-177; #15, 281; Hughes, *Johnston*, 139.
[3] O. R., #14, 536.
[4] *Ibid.*, 533-534, 535, 537; Johnston, *Narrative*, 130.
[5] Davis, *Rise and Fall*, II, 120.
[6] Johnston, *Narrative*, 130-131; *B. & L.*, II, 211, 224-225; Longstreet, *Manassas to Appomattox*, 85-86; G. W. Smith, *The Battle of Seven Pines* (hereafter Smith, *Seven Pines*), 12-15; Smith, *War Papers*, 147-150; J. E. Johnston to L. T. Wigfall, Nov. 12, 1863, Library of Congress.
[7] Davis, *Rise and Fall*, II, 121-122. Davis' account of this whole episode is filled with confusion, and some of his references possibly relate to other incidents. Johnston says nothing in his writing on Seven Pines and the preliminary movements about the visit of Lee, described by Davis, or a promise to fight on May 29. It is quite possible, even probable, that with the army so close to Richmond, Lee did ride out and talk to Johnston, and did secure the information which the President states he brought. But the ride must have taken place on Wednesday, May 28, whereas Davis indicates that he had the report several days in advance. Further confusion is created by the republication in Rowland, *Jefferson Davis*, V, 252-254, of what appears to be a letter from Davis to his wife dated May 28, 1862, which is taken from Mrs. Davis' biography of her husband. Actually a comparison reveals that only a paragraph from the letter is cited, while the remaining portion of the quotation is directly from *Rise and Fall*, which was written many years later. Smith, *Seven Pines*, 9-11; Smith, *War Papers*, 153-158; Freeman, *Lee's Lieutenants*, I, 214 n, 222 n.
[8] O. R., #15, 78, 95, 281-282.
[9] *Ibid.*, #12, 30-31, 943; #14, 559; Long, *Memoirs of Lee*, 158-159.
[10] Nowhere is the plan given in exactly this detail, which is a compilation of the communications, reports and later writings of the generals who participated in the battle.
[11] O. R., #12, 933, 938, 943; #14, 563; Johnston, *Narrative*, 132-133; Longstreet, *Manassas to Appomattox*, 87-90; Smith, *Seven Pines*, 18-33. These references apply to various phases of Johnston's plan for Seven Pines.
[12] O. R., #12, 938.
[13] *Ibid.*, 986. The brigades reached

the Williamsburg Road about 5:00 P.M. and got into action before the close of the day.

[14] *Ibid.*, 924.

[15] Smith, *Seven Pines*, 22. No copy of this communication from Longstreet has been found. The above is a summary made by Smith in his report of the battle, dated June 23, 1862. At Johnston's request Smith deleted this and other portions of the report before he filed it. Longstreet, writing from memory in 1883, gives a different idea of its contents. See Freeman, *Lee's Lieutenants*, I, 237 n.

[16] Mrs. Davis, *Jefferson Davis*, II, 292; Hughes, *Johnston*, 153; *S.H.S.P.*, XVIII, 187-188. The last is Armistead's own account of the wounding of Johnston and the succeeding events.

[17] O. R., #14, 569. Citations of sources have been included in this account of the Battle of Seven Pines only where direct quotations of controversial materials have been used. In making this reconstruction a large number of sources have been consulted. The best secondary account is in Freeman, *Lee's Lieutenants*, I, 225-263. Reports of the participants are in O. R., #12, with correspondence and orders in #14. In addition to those already cited, accounts of the battle by Confederate participants are: Johnston, *Narrative*, 132-146; Davis, *Rise and Fall*, II, 122-129; Smith, *War Papers*, 144-251; Smith, *Seven Pines*; Alexander, *Military Memoirs*, 75-93; Longstreet, *Manassas to Appomattox*, 87-102; *B. & L.*, II, 202-262; J. B. Gordon, *Reminiscences of the Civil War*, 54-59.

NOTES FOR CHAPTER 11
(Pages 158-165)

[1] Mrs. Davis, *Jefferson Davis* II, 292.

[2] Pollard, *Lee and His Lieutenants*, 374.

[3] Hughes, *Johnston*, 154-155, R. E. Lee to Mrs. Johnston, June 2, 1862. McClellan apparently learned quickly of Johnston's mishap, despite the effort to keep it quiet. On June 9, he wrote his wife, "I had another letter from our friend A. P. H. yesterday in reply to mine to Joe Johnston; so I am now confident Joe is badly wounded." Myers, *McClellan*, 294.

[4] Pollard, *Lee and His Lieutenants*, 373. Somewhat different versions of this story are found in Mrs. Roger A. Pryor, *Reminiscences of Peace and War*, 169-170, and Maury, *Recollections*, 150-151. Maury reports it as told to him years later by Dr. Fauntleroy, who was Johnston's medical aide and chief surgeon of his army. See Johnston, *Narrative*, 145-146, about the reinforcements for Lee's army.

[5] Jones, *War Clerk*, I, 135; Rowland, *Jefferson Davis*, V, 284, Jefferson Davis to wife, June 23, 1862; Mrs. Davis, *Jefferson Davis*, II, 314; Hughes, *Johnston*, 155 n. Hughes uses this letter to discredit those who hold that the Davis-Johnston antipathy antedated this time.

[6] O. R., #25, 641-642.

[7] *Ibid.*, #12, 939-941; #14, 580; Smith, *Seven Pines*, 19.

[8] O. R., #12, 933-939.

[9] Although at *Seven Pines* Huger was the victim of Longstreet's shortcomings, his conduct in the Seven Days leads one to believe that he might well have blundered in the earlier engagement, had he been given the opportunity. He was relieved by Lee of field command after the Seven Days and made an inspector of artillery and ordnance; he never held a field command again in the war.

[10] T. C. DeLeon, *Belles, Beaux and Brains of the 60's* (hereafter DeLeon, *Belles*), 153; Mrs. D. G. Wright, *A Southern Girl in '61*, 90.

[11] Mrs. Chesnut, *Diary* (Houghton), 75, 84, 85, 106, 107, 144; Mrs. Pryor, *Reminiscences*, 173; Mrs. Burton Harrison, *Recollections Grave and Gay*, 154.

[12] Hughes, *Johnston*, 156, R. E. Lee

to J. E. Johnston, November 11, 1862.
[13] *O. R.,* #19, 788-789, 898-899; #110, 386. The reply of Davis to some Mississippians who asked for Johnston's assignment to the West is also in #25, 727, but incorrectly dated.
[14] J. C. Pemberton, *Pemberton, Defender of Vicksburg,* 48; Johnston, *Narrative,* 148-149; *O. R.,* #19, 906-907.
[15] *Ibid.,* 914-915; #128, 178; Johnston, *Narrative,* 148-149; Jones, *War Clerk,* I, 188, 190-191; Patrick, *Davis and His Cabinet,* 128-131; Rowland, *Jefferson Davis,* V, 371, 374, Jefferson Davis to G. W. Randolph, Nov. 14, 15, 1862.
[16] *O. R.,* #30, 423-424, 432.
[17] *Ibid.,* #110, 496-497.
[18] J. E. Johnston to L. T. Wigfall, Dec. 3, 1863, Library of Congress.
[19] *O. R.,* #25, 758; #30, 439; Johnston, *Narrative,* 149-150; Mrs. Wright, *Southern Girl,* 98, Mrs. Wigfall to Luly, Dec. 5, 1862. Ewell was president of the College of William and Mary in 1861, and though he opposed secession went into the army when Virginia seceded.
[20] DeLeon, *Belles,* 400-402.
[21] Mrs. Wright, *Southern Girl,* 96, 98-100, Luly to Halsey Wigfall, Dec. 5, 1862, J. E. Johnston to L. T. Wigfall, Dec. 4, 1862; *O. R.* #30, 436; Mrs. Johnston to Mrs. Wigfall, Dec. 12, 1862, Library of Congress.
[22] *O. R.,* #30, 439.

NOTES FOR CHAPTER 12
(Pages 166-174)

[1] J. E. Cooke, *Wearing of the Gray* (hereafter Cooke, *Wearing*), 195; *O. R.,* #38, 948; Mrs. Wright, *Southern Girl,* 98-100, J. E. Johnston to L. T. Wigfall, Dec. 4, 1862; Parks, *Kirby Smith,* 248, E. Kirby Smith to wife, Nov. 20, 1863.
[2] *O. R.,* #25, 765-766, 767, 768, 777, 780, 781; #30, 435, 436, 437, 438.
[3] Mrs. Wright, *Southern Girl,* 98-100, 101-103, J. E. Johnston to L. T. Wigfall, Dec. 4, 1862, L. T. Wigfall to James Seddon, Dec. 8, 1862. Johnston's letter to Wigfall was apparently shown in the War Department, as Jones (*War Clerk,* I, 209) speaks of it in his entry for Dec. 10.
[4] *O. R.,* #30, 441, 444, 445.
[5] Davis, *Rise and Fall,* II, 399-400; *O. R.,* #25, 721-723; #26, 847.
[6] Mrs. Johnston to Mrs. Wigfall, Dec. 12, 1862, Library of Congress.
[7] Johnston, *Narrative,* 151; D. C. Seitz, *Braxton Bragg, General of the Confederacy,* 254-255, Braxton Bragg to J. E. Johnston, Jan. 11, 1863.
[8] Rowland, *Jefferson Davis,* V, 294-295, 384-386, Jefferson Davis to wife, Dec. 15, 1862, Jefferson Davis to R. E. Lee, Dec. 8, 1862; *O. R.,* #30, 449-450;
#110, 397; Johnston, *Narrative,* 151; T. B. Wilson, *Reminiscences,* 29.
[9] *O. R.,* #25, 788-792.
[10] J. E. Johnston to L. T. Wigfall, Dec. 15, 1862, Library of Congress. The information from Davis about Holmes not having had orders, a word which Johnston underscored in his letter, contradicted all the advice to Johnston from Cooper. It demonstrates also that in spite of the latter's message to Holmes of December 6, "The President reiterates his orders that you send without delay sufficient forces from your command to General Pemberton," Richmond did not intend the interpretation of a positive command. Actually, Cooper said five days later in a telegram to Holmes that he should use his own judgment as it was "impossible at this distance to judge of your necessities," but the hope was that he would assist Pemberton if he could. *O. R.,* #25, 786, 793.
[11] J. E. Johnston to L. T. Wigfall, Dec. 15, 1862, Library of Congress.
[12] J. K. Bettersworth, *Confederate Mississippi,* 271-272; *B. & L.,* III, 482-484; Johnston, *Narrative,* 152; *O. R.,* #25, 800, 802; #30, 424.

[13] *Ibid.*, #25, 800-801; #30, 459-460. By Jan. 11, 1863 the strength of the Confederates in Mississippi was as follows: field army, 15,000; Vicksburg, 18,000; Port Hudson, 10,000; in reserve at Jackson and Columbus, 3,600, #25, 833.

[14] Sarah A. Dorsey, *Recollections of Henry Watkins Allen*, 173, quotes a letter from Johnston to Pemberton, Dec. 31, 1862, in which he makes these points, with application to Vicksburg and Port Hudson.

[15] Johnston, *Narrative*, 153; *B. & L.* III, 474; *O. R.* #110, 397-399; Rowland, *Jefferson Davis*, V, 386-388.

[16] *O. R.*, #25, 784-785; #30, 440-441; Johnston, *Narrative*, 153.

[17] Dunbar Rowland, *History of Mississippi*, I, 804; Johnston, *Narrative*, 154.

[18] *Ibid.*, 154-155. In commenting upon this circumstance Richard Taylor said that the result was Johnston "commanded nobody." Taylor, *Destruction*, 207.

[19] *O. R.*, #25, 823, 826.

[20] *Ibid.*, 800, 808-811, 813, 822; #30, 469, 482. In his *Narrative*, 154, Johnston says that the time consumed for this transfer was not unusual, as the "management of the railroad was at least as good as usual in such cases."

Stevenson's movement was reported in the *Chattanooga Rebel*, which caused Johnston to write Ewell to "urge upon the editors . . . the importance of not making such publications in the future." *O. R.*, # 30, 479.

[21] *Ibid.*, 463; Mrs. Johnston to Mrs. Wigfall, Dec. 25, 1862, Library of Congress.

[22] *O. R.*, #30, 476; #110, 402.

[23] *B. & L.*, III, 611, 612.

[24] *O. R.*, #25, 827; #110, 404.

NOTES FOR CHAPTER 13
(Pages 175-182)

[1] *O. R.*, #25, 834; Mrs. Wright, *Southern Girl*, 106-108, J. E. Johnston to L. T. Wigfall, Jan. 8, 1863; Mrs. Johnston to Mrs. Wigfall, Jan. 19 [1863], Library of Congress.

[2] *O. R.*, #110, 410.

[3] *Ibid.*, #38, 599-600, 602.

[4] Mrs. Wright, *Southern Girl*, 121-123, J. E. Johnston to L. T. Wigfall, Jan. 26, 1863.

[5] *O. R.*, #35, 626-627.

[6] Mrs. Johnston to Mrs. Wigfall, Jan. 19 [1863], Library of Congress.

[7] *O. R.*, #35, 613-614.

[8] Mackall, *A Son's Recollections*, 194-196, B. Bragg to W. W. Mackall, Feb. 14, 1863; *O. R.*, #29, 699.

[9] *Ibid.*, 699. Bragg was wrong about Kirby Smith, who was in Richmond to receive instructions about his new command west of the Mississippi.

[10] *Ibid.*, #35, 613-614.

[11] *Ibid.*, #29, 682, 683, 684, 701, 702; William M. Polk, *Leonidas Polk, Bishop and General*, II, 198-204.

[12] *O. R.*, #29, 698-699; Polk, *Polk*, II, 205; J. E. Johnston to L. T. Wigfall, Dec. 15, 1862, Feb. 14, 1863, Library of Congress; Mrs. Johnston to Mrs. Wigfall, March 16, 1863, Library of Congress; Mrs. Wright, *Southern Girl*, 121-123, J. E. Johnston to L. T. Wigfall, Jan. 26, 1863.

[13] *O. R.*, #35, 624.

[14] *Ibid.*, 632-633.

[15] *Ibid.*, 640-641; Hughes, *Johnston*, 167 n-169 n, J. E. Johnston to Jefferson Davis, March 2, 1863. This letter does not appear in O. R. Johnston was not alone among the Confederate generals in feeling as he did. General Richard Taylor for example wrote that no officer should have the responsibility of removing another under such conditions, as it "should be assumed by the government, not left to an individual." Taylor, *Destruction*, 207.

[16] J. E. Johnston to L. T. Wigfall, Dec. 27, 1863, Library of Congress; *O. R.*, #35, 658-659.

[17] J. E. Johnston to L. T. Wigfall, Feb. 14, 1863, Library of Congress.
[18] L. T. Wigfall to J. E. Johnston, Feb. 28, 1863, Huntington Library.

[19] J. E. Johnston to L. T. Wigfall, March 4, 8, 1863, Library of Congress.

NOTES FOR CHAPTER 14
(Pages 183-197)

[1] O. R., #35, 652-653; Mackall, A Son's Recollections, 194-196, Braxton Bragg to W. W. Mackall, February 14, 1863.

[2] Chattanooga Rebel, Dec. 14, 1862, March 4, 1863. This reference to Johnston is part of a column which ran unsigned in the Rebel. It was written by Henry Watterson, who for several months had been the Rebel's editor.

[3] Chattanooga Rebel, March 15, 1863; "Personne," Marginalia, 39. Johnston's absence and the heavy rain which fell on the scheduled evening did not deter the merrymakers in Chattanooga. The dance went on and the gentlemen rolled up their trousers and carried the ladies from the vehicles in which they rode over the muddy roads to the dance floor, which was decorated with cedar boughs and Confederate colors.

[4] Augusta Jane Evans to P. G. T. Beauregard, March 17, 1863, Duke University Library.

[5] O. R., #35, 674, 684-685, 698; #110, 432.

[6] Ibid., #35, 708; Johnston, Narrative, 163.

[7] Arthur Howard Noll, ed., Doctor Quintard, Chaplain C. S. A and Second Bishop of Tennessee, 69-70.

[8] O. R., #35, 729-730.

[9] Ibid., 745-746.

[10] Ibid., 757-758.

[11] Ibid., #34, 629, 635, 636-637, 747.

[12] Ibid., #30, 496; #128, 405-406.

[13] A. B. Moore, Conscription and Conflict in the Confederacy, 191-197; O. R., #35, 642, 651, 758, 762-763; #128, 442-445, 463.

[14] Ibid., #35, 759, 771-772.

[15] Ibid., 618-619, 647, 648-649; J. E. Johnston to L. T. Wigfall, March 24, 1863, Library of Congress.

[16] O. R., #21, 1055-1056; #35, 621, 626, 628, 631, 637, 713, 726, 727, 744-745, 752, 753, 773, 791, 800, 803, 822, 826, 833. As commanders of the Department of East Tennessee, Brig. Gen. Henry Heth followed Kirby Smith, but on Jan. 30 Brig. Gen. D. S. Donelson took over. He served until taken ill in early April, when Maj. Gen. D. H. Maury assumed command, to serve but a few days when he exchanged posts under Richmond's orders with Maj. Gen. S. B. Buckner, who commanded at Mobile.

[17] Ibid., 833-834.

[18] Ibid., 761.

[19] Ibid., 674; #38, 608, 615, 649, 657, 659-660, 672, 729-730; Pemberton, Pemberton, 92, 291-314, which is a long, unfinished letter by General Pemberton; O. R., #36, 238, Johnston says mistakenly that from the time of his arrival at Tullahoma to Apr. 14, all of Pemberton's communications were by telegraph.

[20] Mrs. Johnston to Mrs. Wigfall, March 16, 1863, Library of Congress.

[21] O. R., #38, 599, 600, 603, 611, 615, 618.

[22] Ibid., #36, 9.

[23] Ibid., #35, 727; #38, 632, 664, 665, 668, 670, 681, 685-686, 709, 712.

[24] Ibid., 712, 714.

[25] Ibid., 712, 714; #40, 713-714.

[26] Ibid., #38, 738, 740, 745, 747, 752-753. Pemberton had dispatched only one brigade, 4,065 men, under Buford.

[27] Ibid., 778, 786, 787, 789, 791.

[28] Ibid., #36, 241, 252, 255; #38, 797, 801, 802, 803, 811.

[29] Ibid., 797, 807, 808, 811; Johnston, Narrative, 170.

[30] *O. R.*, #38, 808, 815.

[31] *Ibid.*, 826; Pemberton, *Pemberton*, 296.

[32] U. S. Grant, *Personal Memoirs*, I, 490-495.

[33] *O. R.*, #38, 836, 837, 838, 839, 845, 846, 935-936. On May 29, Kirby Smith wrote Pemberton, "I have the honor to acknowledge the receipt today of your communication of April 22, from Jackson." Dispatches took two to five weeks to deliver.

[34] *Ibid.*, 844, 846.

[35] *Ibid.*, 842.

[36] R. M. Hughes, "Some War Letters of General Joseph E. Johnston," *Journal*

of the *Military Institution of the United States*, L, 319-320, J. E. Johnston to Beverley Johnston, May 7, 1863.

[37] *O. R.*, #38, 838, 845.

[38] *Ibid.*, #110, 468, 469.

[39] Jones, *War Clerk*, I, 299; *Annals of the War*, 415-416; Longstreet, *Manassas to Appomattox*, 327-328, 331; *O. R.*, #40, 790; #110, 469.

[40] *Ibid.*, #35, 825-826; Hughes, "Some War Letters," *loc. cit.*, J. E. Johnston to Beverley Johnston, May 7, 1863; J. E. Johnston to L. T. Wigfall, May 7, 1863, Dec. 27, 1863, Library of Congress; Noll, *Quintard*, 70.

NOTES FOR CHAPTER 15
(Pages 198-208)

[1] *O. R.*, #36, 215; #38, 870.

[2] *Ibid.*, 877-878.

[3] Grant, *Personal Memoirs*, I, 492-500; *O. R.*, #36, 50-51.

[4] Grant, *Personal Memoirs*, I, 507-511; W. T. Sherman, *Memoirs*, I, 349; Rowland, *History of Mississippi*, I, 804; Johnston, *Narrative*, 567-568, quoting letter from Livingston Mims, July 27, 1871; J. E. Johnston to L. T. Wigfall, Dec. 3, 1863, Library of Congress.

[5] *O. R.*, #38, 877.

[6] *Ibid.*, #36, 261-262, 322-325. On Nov. 10, in answer to a query from Seddon, Pemberton explained his disobedience of Johnston's orders by saying that he knew that the holding of Vicksburg was the object of the campaign.

[7] *Ibid.*, 262.

[8] *Ibid.*, #38, 882.

[9] *Ibid.*, #36, 241, 269; #38, 884.

[10] *Ibid.*, 884.

[11] *Ibid.*, #36, 216; #38, 886-887. Davis endorsed the communication to Seddon: "Do not perceive why a junction was not attempted, which would have made our force nearly equal in number to the estimated strength of the enemy, and might have resulted in his total defeat under circumstances

which rendered retreat or re-enforcement to him scarcely practicable." The endorsement reveals a virtually complete misunderstanding of the circumstances if directed at Johnston as one suspects.

[12] *Ibid.*, #36, 217-218. Grant says in his *Memoirs*, I, 523, that Pemberton might have escaped him by crossing the Big Black and moving north on the west side. It would have exposed Vicksburg but the Federal commander interpreted it as Pemberton's "proper move—and the one Johnston would have made had he been in Pemberton's place. In fact it would have been in conformity with Johnston's orders to Pemberton."

[13] *O. R.*, #36, 216-217, 266-269; #38, 888; Johnston, *Narrative*, 186-187.

[14] *Ibid.*, 187; *O. R.*, #38, 887.

[15] *Ibid.*, #36, 216-218. Johnston, *Narrative*, 187.

[16] *O. R.*, #38, 889-890. In his report Pemberton justified his action by enlarging upon the ideas in his letter to Johnston. He stated his belief that he could hold Vicksburg and that "every effort would be made" by Davis and Johnston to help him. *Ibid.*, #36, 272.

[17] Johnston, *Narrative*, 189; *O. R.*, #38, 896, 897.

[18] A. J. L. Fremantle, *Three Months in the Southern States*, 111-126; O. R., #36, 242.

[19] Fremantle, *Three Months*, 126; O. R., #38, 901-902; Johnston, *Narrative*, 190.

[20] O. R., #38, 899, 902-903; #36, 191; Johnston, *Narrative*, 191.

[21] O. R., #36, 242; Johnston, *Narrative*, 191.

[22] O. R., #35, 836-838; #36, 190, 191, 192, 193, 194, 195, 219, 222, 223-224; #40, 842; #110, 472, 473, 475-476, 482, 489-490; Jones, *War Clerk*, I, 325, 326, 327, 333; Reagan, *Memoirs*, 121, 151-152.

[23] O. R., #38, 971; French, *Two Wars*, 180-181; Grant, *Personal Memoirs*, I, 535; J. M. Schofield, *Forty-Six Years in the Army*, 69-71; W. T. Sherman, *Home Letters of General Sherman*, 262, W. T. Sherman to wife, May 25, 1863. Lincoln later wrote: "Few things have been so grateful to my anxious feelings as when, in June last, the local force in Missouri aided General Schofield to so promptly send a large general force to the relief of General Grant, then investing Vicksburg and menaced from without by General Johnston. . . . " Quoted in Schofield, *Forty-Six Years*, 94-99.

NOTES FOR CHAPTER 16
(Pages 209-222)

[1] O. R., #38, 899, 929, 930; #110, 486-487, 489-490, 493-494; Mackall, *A Son's Recollections*, 187-188, J. E. Johnston to W. W. Mackall, June 7, 1863.

[2] O. R., #110, 499-500.

[3] Josiah Gorgas, *The Civil War Diary of General Josiah Gorgas*, 42-43; L. T. Wigfall to C. C. Clay, June 12, 1863, Duke University Library; L. T. Wigfall to J. E. Johnston, June 8, 15, 1863, Huntington Library.

[4] O. R., #36, 219, 227, 228.

[5] *Ibid.*, 224-225, 226; #38, 969-971.

[6] *Ibid.*, #36, 226-227; #38, 970.

[7] *Ibid.*, #36, 193, 196, 197, 198, 224; #38, 974; #110, 495, 496-497. Davis' message said, "We have withheld nothing which it is practicable to give." Seddon's stated that they "had drained resources even to the danger of several points."

[8] *Ibid.*, #26, 1084; #38, 963, 965, 969, 971-972; Johnston, *Narrative*, 195; Parks, *Kirby Smith*, 268-277; Pemberton, *Pemberton*, 214, 215, 216-217; Taylor, *Destruction*, 137-139.

[9] O. R., #38, 974, 980.

[10] *Ibid.*, #47, 162, 163; #110, 501-502, 503. Although Davis did not request Lee, then involved in the Gettysburg campaign, to send reinforcements to Johnston, he wrote him a letter on June 28, in which he said that "General Johnston continues to call for reinforcements, though his first requisition was more than filled by withdrawing troops from Generals Beauregard and Bragg." It is difficult to explain this statement as Davis had known by the correspondence with Johnston and Seddon that the troops which reached Johnston were less in number than the requests made by Richmond. *Ibid.*, #43, 76.

[11] *Ibid.*, #38, 978; Johnston, *Narrative*, 202-203; S. D. Lee, "The Campaigns of Vicksburg, Mississippi, in 1863, from April 15 to and including the Battle of Champion Hills, or Baker's Creek, May 16, 1863," *Publications of the Mississippi Historical Society*, III, 27-28.

[12] Johnston, *Narrative*, 202-205; French, *Two Wars*, 182; O. R., #36, 244-245; #38, 989-990; #110, 503. Grant supports Johnston's interpretation fully in his *Memoirs*, I, 549: "We were now looking west, besieging Pemberton, while we were also looking east to defend ourselves against an expected siege by Johnston. But as against the garrison of Vicksburg we were as substantially protected as they were against us. Where

we were looking east and north we were strongly fortified, and on the defensive. Johnston evidently took in the situation and wisely, I think, abstained from making an assault on us because it would simply have inflicted loss on both sides without accomplishing any result. We were strong enough to have taken the offensive against him; but I did not feel disposed to take any risk of losing our hold upon Pemberton's army, while I would have rejoiced at the opportunity of defending ourselves against an attack by Johnston."

Sherman was in command of the shield to the east from June 22 on, which assured Grant that Johnston would be unable to cross the Big Black. The Federals kept a constant vigil against an attempt by Johnston in all sectors. O. R., #38, 428, 449, 458.

[13] *Ibid.*, 439, 982-983; Pemberton, *Pemberton*, 219.

[14] O. R., #38, 987.

[15] French, *Two Wars*, 182; Johnston, *Narrative*, 204; O. R., #36, 199, 245, 285. In his report Johnston says he heard of the surrender of Vicksburg July 5, which French confirms. In the *Narrative* he says that he heard it on the evening of the fourth. Pemberton's explanation of his choice of that day was that he could obtain better terms by capitulating on a national holiday.

[16] Sherman, *Memoirs*, I, 359.

[17] Johnston, *Narrative*, 205; French, *Two Wars*, 182; O. R., #37, 521-522; Sherman reported on July 12 that his chief difficulty was the shortage of water, O. R., #36, 245.

[18] *Ibid.*, #38, 460, 461.

[19] *Ibid.*, 157, 309.

[20] *Ibid.*, 472, 475-476; Sherman, *Home Letters*, 269-273, W. T. Sherman to wife, July 5, 1863; Johnston, *Narrative*, 205.

[21] O. R., #37, 522, 524, 527; #38, 506, 508, 509.

[22] *Ibid.*, #35, 199, 230. It was not until July 13 that Johnston received official confirmation of the terms, *Narrative*, 207-208.

[23] O. R., #36, 230.

[24] *Ibid.*, 198.

[25] *Ibid.*, 199.

[26] *Ibid.*, 199, 200.

[27] *Ibid.*, 230, 231; #38, 994, 1000, 1001, 1002, 1005, 1006, 1007, 1010, 1014, 1015. Davis advised Pemberton on July 16 that he and the other general officers who had surrendered at Vicksburg had been exchanged.

[28] J. E. Johnston to L. T. Wigfall, Dec. 3, 1863, Library of Congress; O. R., #110, 507; Pemberton, *Pemberton*, 241. The latter quotes a report by an eyewitness of the meeting between Pemberton and Johnston. According to this unnamed person, Johnston came forward to greet Pemberton but the latter refused his hand and after formally reporting turned away, never to see Johnston again. This would seem to be contradicted by Johnston's letter to Wigfall and by the letter to Pemberton from Ewell, written the next day. O. R., #38, 1002. On June 28 Pemberton wrote a message to Johnston in which he said, "I am surprised that you have so small a force," but for some reason did not send it. *Ibid.*, 981.

[29] *Ibid.*, #36, 200-201; #110, 507.

[30] *Ibid.*, #36, 201; French, *Two Wars*, 183.

[31] O. R., #36, 201; #39, 624.

[32] Johnston, *Narrative*, 208-209; O. R., #36, 207, 246.

[33] Johnston, *Narrative*, 208-209; O. R., #36, 207; #38, 1007; #110, 508.

[34] Johnston, *Narrative*, 209; O. R., #36, 246; #38, 1008.

[35] Johnston, *Narrative*, 209; O. R., #37, 522, 536; #38, 1008; Jones, *War Clerk*, II, 8.

[36] O. R., #37, 522; #38, 1018; Johnston, *Narrative*, 567-568, quoting a letter of Livingston Mims, under whose direction the work of repairing the bridge was attempted, July 27, 1871; Rowland, *Jefferson Davis*, VI, 498, Jefferson Davis to J. Phelan, Feb. 18, 1865; VIII, 375, Jefferson Davis to L. B. Northrop, Apr. 19, 1879.

[37] J. E. Johnston to wife, June 12,

1863, Johnston Letterbook, College of William and Mary Library.

[88] Jones, *War Clerk*, I, 380; Gorgas, *Civil War Diary*, 50; T. R. Hay, "Confederate Leadership at Vicksburg," *Mississippi Valley Historical Review*, XI, 559 n. In his report Pemberton denied that the surrender had been caused by a shortage of rations. O. R., #36, 285.

NOTES FOR CHAPTER 17
(Pages 223-239)

[1] O. R., #36, 208; #38, 1018, 1026, 1029, 1036-1037, 1049; #53, 493-494, 720; #110, 509-510, 512-513; J. E. Johnston to L. T. Wigfall, Dec. 3, 1863, Library of Congress.

[2] O. R., #35, 912-913; #128, 636, 637-638, 675-678, 868-869.

[3] *Ibid.*, #128, 742, 748-749, 749-750, 759-761, 781-785, 797, 869, 911; Jones, *War Clerk*, II, 42. Both Johnston and Seddon accepted the responsibility for Pillow's appointment.

[4] O. R., #128, 681, 693, 715, 717, 761, 799, 847-852, 859.

[5] S. S. Scott, "Some Account of Confederate Indian Affairs," *The Gulf States Historical Magazine*, II, 144-148.

[6] J. E. Johnston to wife, June 12, 25, 28, 1863, College of William and Mary Library.

[7] Mrs. Johnston to Mrs. Wigfall, July 5, 1863, Library of Congress.

[8] L. T. Wigfall to C. C. Clay, July 13, 1863, Duke University Library; Mrs. Wright, *Southern Girl*, 143-144, Mrs. Wigfall to Halsey Wigfall, July 22, 1863. Clay wrote Yancey May 2, 1863, in somewhat the same vein as Wigfall's letter to him: "He [Davis] is a strange compound which I cannot analyze, although I thought I knew him well before he was President. He will not ask or receive counsel, and, indeed, seems predisposed to go exactly the way his friends advise him not to go. I have tried harder than I ever did with any other man to be his friend and to prevent his alienating me or other friends. I have kept my temper and good will towards him longer than I could with any other than an old and cherished friend. If he survives this war and does not alter his course, he will

find himself in a small minority party." J. W. DuBose, *The Life and Times of William Lowndes Yancey* (hereafter DuBose, *Yancey*), 743-744.

[9] *Richmond Examiner*, July 9, 10, 1863.

[10] O. R., #36, 202-207; #47, 173-174; Johnston, *Narrative*, 229, 230-241; Mrs. Davis, *Jefferson Davis*, II, 425-438. Mrs. Davis did not include Johnston's reply; J. E. Johnston to Beverley Johnston, Feb. 14, 1864, Huntington Library; L. T. Wigfall to J. E. Johnston, Aug. 9, 1863, Library of Congress. In this letter Wigfall said that he had heard in Richmond "about three weeks" before that Benjamin ("Jerusalem") was preparing the material for Davis to use.

[11] Johnston, *Narrative*, 229.

[12] Mrs. Johnston to Mrs. Wigfall, Aug. 2, 1863, Library of Congress.

[13] Undated memo by Ewell, College of William and Mary Library; O. R., #36, 209-213; Johnston, *Narrative*, 244-252; J. E. Johnston to L. T. Wigfall, Aug. 12, 1863, Library of Congress. Johnston said in his answer that the necessity to secure some papers delayed it.

[14] J. E. Johnston to L. T. Wigfall, Aug. 12, 1863, Library of Congress.

[15] O. R., #53, 490-491.

[16] Taylor, *Destruction*, 26.

[17] O. R., #38, 1033, 1034, 1057, 1070; #53, 625; #110, 515; Rowland, *Jefferson Davis*, VI, 1, Jefferson Davis to J. E. Johnston, Aug. 24, 1863; 2-13, D. W. Yandell to John M. Johnston, June 17, 1863; VII, 408, Jefferson Davis to W. T. Walthall, Nov. 23, 1874.

[18] O. R., #38, 1045, 1058; Johnston, *Narrative*, 253; Mackall, *A Son's Recol-*

lections, 189-191, J. E. Johnston to W. W. Mackall, July 18, 1863; L. T. Wigfall to J. E. Johnston, Aug. 9, 1863, Huntington Library.

[19] O. R., #38, 1045 n; #42, 201-202; #53, 572-573; #110, 524; Johnston, *Narrative*, 255; J. E. Johnston to L. T. Wigfall, Sept. 15, 1863, Library of Congress.

[20] O. R., #53, 618-619.

[21] *Ibid.*, #38, 1061, 1064-1065; #110, 496-497; J. E. Johnston to L. T. Wigfall, Sept. 15, 1863, Library of Congress.

[22] L. T. Wigfall to J. E. Johnston, Sept. 11, Oct. 6, 1863, Huntington Library.

[23] O. R., #35, 592-593; #110, 514. Bragg told Johnston that had the operation been ordered he planned to ask Johnston to take command. Bragg also wrote a letter of explanation to Richmond. He was not as frank in it as he was to Johnston, but the meaning is largely the same. When Davis read it he returned it to Seddon with the endorsement, "However desirable a movement may be, it is never safe to do more than suggest to a commanding general, and it would be unwise to order its execution by one who foretold failure." The attitude of Davis toward Bragg in his retirement from Middle Tennessee is in marked contrast with that he evinced under similar circumstances toward Johnston.

[24] *Ibid.*, #53, 529-530, 540-541, 607-608, 635; #110, 522; Johnston, *Narrative*, 253-254.

[25] J. E. Johnston to L. T. Wigfall, Sept. 15, 1863, Library of Congress.

[26] O. R., #51, 757-763; #53, 707, 713, 717, 724; #54, 738; Johnston, *Narrative*, 256, 259-260; S. D. Lee, "The War in Mississippi after the Fall of Vicksburg, July 4, 1863," *Publications of the Mississippi Historical Society*, X, 49; Sherman, *Memoirs*, 1, 379-381, 385.

[27] Longstreet, *Manassas to Appomattox*, 465-466, 468.

[28] Mackall, *A Son's Recollections*, 177-179, 181-182, 183, 185, W. W. Mackall

to wife, Sept. 27, 29, Oct. 5, 9, 10, 12, 1863; O. R., #53, 742-743. On his trip Davis traveled with Johnston for part of the way, but neither man made any record of what occurred and no other source gives information about it.

[29] *Ibid.*, #56, 809; J. E. Johnston to L. T. Wigfall, Nov. 12, 1863, Library of Congress; Mrs. Johnston to Mrs. Wigfall, Nov. 22, Dec. 8, 1863, Library of Congress.

[30] O. R., #36, 238-249.

[31] *Ibid.*, #55, 666, 681, 682.

[32] *Ibid.*, 683; #56, 771, 776.

[33] Jones, *War Clerk*, II, 104-106.

[34] O. R., #56, 764-765, 779-780, 785-792.

[35] Chesnut, *Diary* (Appleton), 248-249.

[36] "Proceedings of the First Confederate Congress," S.H.S.P., L, 21, 22, 23, 37; O. R., #56, 796-797, 800-801.

[37] "Proceedings of the First Confederate Congress," L, 37; Mrs. Wright, *Southern Girl*, 161-162, J. E. Johnston to L. T. Wigfall, Dec. 14, 1863. When the correspondence was published by order of the Congress in February, Johnston complained in a letter to his brother Beverley and asked that Beverley see a number of senators to try to have all the material given to the public. "I don't perceive," he said, "that our cause will be benefitted by my being thought worse than I am." J. E. Johnston to Beverley Johnston, Feb. 14, 1864, Huntington Library.

On Apr. 30, 1864, Lee complained of the publication for the information it gave the enemy and said that he had "no doubt" but that it had been helpful in the Federals' "subsequent expedition" into Mississippi. O. R., #60, 1330-1331.

[38] L. T. Wigfall to J. E. Johnston, Aug. 9, 1863, Huntington Library. Mrs. Wigfall wrote her daughter July 22 that the supporters of the President attacked Johnston bitterly, but she believed the public supported him and it was unlikely that he would lose his post. Mrs. Wright, *Southern Girl*, 144.

[39] "Proceedings of the First Confederate Congress," *loc. cit.* 55-60.

[40] L. T. Wigfall to J. E. Johnston, Dec. 18, 1863, Huntington Library.

[41] *O. R.,* #56, 843-844.

[42] *Ibid.,* #128, 991, 993. For some reason, either lack of information or misunderstanding, Johnston incorrectly interpreted Seddon's questioning of Pemberton about his report. In the *Narrative,* 215, 216, he accused Seddon of attempting to coach Pemberton in the improvement of his report by allowing him to submit a supplement. The supplementary report is found in *O. R.,* #36, 322-325. Rowland, *Jefferson Davis,* VIII, 351, J. A. Seddon to W. T. Walthall, Feb. 10, 1879. Jones in his diary recorded that the President sent to the War Office on Dec. 24, 1863, for some reason the war clerk did not understand, a copy of an Alabama newspaper with an article in which Davis "was very severely castigated for hesitating to appoint General J. E. Johnston to command the western army." Jones, *War Clerk,* II, 119.

[43] Chesnut, *Diary* (Appleton), 265; L. T. Wigfall to J. E. Johnston, March 17, 1864, Huntington Library. *O. R.,* #56, 835-836; #110, 579-580; Mrs. Johnston to Mrs. Wigfall, Dec. 18, 1863, Library of Congress.

[44] J. E. Johnston to L. T. Wigfall, Dec. 27, 1863, Library of Congress; Chesnut, *Diary* (Houghton), 343.

NOTES FOR CHAPTER 18
(Pages 240-260)

[1] *O. R.,* #56, 828, 850, 873, 883, 887-888; #58, 2, 510. It is impossible to determine accurately the number of men then with the Army of Tennessee as three differing returns were filed in the last weeks of December.

[2] J. E. Johnston to L. T. Wigfall, Dec. 27, 1863, Library of Congress.

[3] *O. R.,* #38, 1065-1066; #56, 877-879; #58, 543; J. E. Johnston to J. E. B. Stuart, Jan. 31, 1864, Huntington Library; L. T. Wigfall to J. E. Johnston, Dec. 18, 1863, Huntington Library.

[4] *O. R.,* #56, 839-840, 842-843, 856-857, 860. The optimistic report of the President's aide was based on conversations with Hardee. Hardee confirmed it on Dec. 24 in a letter which contrasts with another he had written Cooper a week before, in which he said, "But in our present condition it is necessary to avoid a general action; and should the enemy, uniting his scattered columns, advance, a retrograde movement becomes inevitable." Davis said that he was quoting Bragg in his statement of confidence in the morale of the troops. The statement contained a double contradiction, one of the opinions expressed by the President to the Congress on the reasons for defeat at Missionary Ridge, and the other of that written by Bragg to Johnston after that failure.

[5] *Ibid.,* 873-874; #58, 510-511, 644-645; Johnston, *Narrative,* 260-270.

[6] *O. R.,* #58, 530-535, 644.

[7] *Ibid.,* 630; S. R. Watkins, "Company Aytch," 132, S.H.S.P., XXXVIII, 344-345.

[8] Watkins, "Company Aytch," 132; S.H.S.P., XXVI, 158-159; J. E. Johnston to L. T. Wigfall, Jan. 5, 1864, Library of Congress; J. E. Johnston to J. E. B. Stuart, Jan. 21, 1864, Huntington Library.

[9] *O. R.,* #58, 564, 697, 699, 763; #110, 624, 628-629.

[10] *Ibid.,* #56, 780, 873-874; #58, 510, 539, 573, 604, 645; #110, 585-588.

[11] *Ibid.,* #38, 510; #58, 522, 528, 537, 548, 552, 557, 564-566, 591-592, 612, 707-708, 775; #110, 596, 601, 607-608, 616-617, 621-622; R. C. Black, III, *The Railroads of the Confederacy,* 173, 195-197; Rowland, *Jefferson Davis,* VI, 149, Jefferson Davis to J. E. Johnston, Jan. 16, 1864; Phillips, "Correspondence of Toombs, Stephens, and

Cobb," 632, J. E. Brown to A. H. Stephens, Jan. 4, 1864; J. E. Johnston to L. T. Wigfall, Jan. 5, 1864, Library of Congress.

[12] O. R., #110, 586-599, 606-609.

[13] *Ibid.*, #48, 511, 565. J. E. Johnston to L. T. Wigfall, Jan. 4, 5, 1864, Library of Congress. Johnston also wrote to Governor Brown about this use of slaves. Brown stated his full sympathy with the idea in his reply and said that if the Congress authorized it by legislation he felt sure that the planters of Georgia would fill their quota.

[14] O. R., #59, 740, 853; #74, 614; #128, 897-898; #129, 207-209; S.H.S.P., II, 184.

[15] O. R., #58, 553, 554, 555, 716.

[16] *Ibid.*, 716, 726, 729, 730, 751-752; #110, 619-620.

[17] *Ibid.*, #58, 763, 772, 775; #110, 621, 626, 627.

[18] *Ibid.*, 627.

[19] *Ibid.*, #58, 193-194, 198-199, 207, 245, 254, 255.

[20] *Ibid.*, #359, 365, 367, 373, 375, 383, 444, 445.

[21] *Ibid.*, #57, 351-355; #58, 113-114, 798; #110, 627; Sherman, *Memoirs*, I, 420-422; Sherman, *Home Letters*, 285, W. T. Sherman to wife, March 10, 1864.

[22] O. R., #57, 9-11, 476-477; #58, 482, 714; #74, 613.

[23] Hood, *Advance*, 89-92; Johnston, *Narrative*, 277-278; O. R., #58, 697-698, 804. Hood arrived Feb. 24, not Feb. 4 as he says in his book.

[24] O. R., #58, 799, 808-809; Bill, *Beleaguered City*, 208; Mackall, *A Son's Recollections*, 207-208, W. W. Mackall to wife, April 30, 1864; J. E. Johnston to L. T. Wigfall, Dec. 27, 1863. Davis called Bragg to Richmond after some discussion of him as chief of staff to Johnston. Ewell and Mackall had no optimism about Bragg's helping Johnston. "He can only record the President's edicts," Mackall said, "and grant small favors to persons not disliked by the President."

[25] O. R., #59, 584-585, 592.

[26] *Ibid.*, #58, 808, 812, J. E. Johnston to L. T. Wigfall, March 6, Apr. 1, 1864, Library of Congress.

[27] O.R., #59, 606-607; Hood, *Advance*, 92-93. It is interesting to compare the version of this letter as it was sent by Hood and is printed in the O. R. with that he used in *Advance and Retreat*. In the latter he carefully edited the comment about taking the initiative to read, "but fear we will not be able to do so unless our Army is increased," which removes the implied criticism of Johnston. He dropped the paragraph in which he said that his corps included the "untried men" of the army, which with an impartial audience does not stand up. A more serious indictment of his writing in *Advance and Retreat* is that he leaves the impression by his introduction to the two letters of this correspondence which he includes that they were all of it. At least six letters are known, five of which are found in O. R., #59, 606-608, 781; #76, 879, and one other is quoted by Eliot, *West Point*, 101. None of them actually is in "furtherance of General Johnston's wishes."

[28] O. R., #59, 606-608.

[29] *Ibid.*, #56, 813-816; #58, 541-542, 653-654; #59, 586, 587; #110, 596-597, 634.

[30] *Ibid.*, #59, 618.

[31] *Ibid.*

[32] Longstreet, *Manassas to Appomattox*, 544-546. For section of Bragg's report to which Longstreet referred, see O. R., #50, 37.

[33] *Ibid.*, #59, 614-615.

[34] *Ibid.*, #39, 614-615, 649, 653-654; #110, 642-643.

[35] *Ibid.*, #59, 666.

[36] *Ibid.*, 584-589, 684-709; S. P. Lee, *Memoirs of Pendleton*, 314-318, W. N. Pendleton to wife, March 11, 19, 20, 1864.

[37] O. R., #59, 736-737; #110, 648-649; S. P. Lee, *Memoirs of Pendleton*, 318.

[38] O. R., #59, 207-208, 720, 753, 794. Among the most difficult problems in a study of the war is the effort to

reconcile totals. On March 31, 1864, Johnston reported: "Effective total present, 42,125; Aggregate present, 55,113; Aggregate present and absent, 85,973." The last figure is obviously of no moment. The "effective total" does not actually represent the potential strength of the army as it excludes all commissioned officers and men detailed for any reason. Johnston in his letter advocating the use of Negroes on details estimated that 10,000 to 12,000 men were held out of the fighting force for such duties (O. R., #58, 511). In an effort to make the figures represent more accurately the comparative strength of the two armies the authors use the "aggregate present" from the Confederate returns. This will make the figures different from those given by Johnston, who followed the usual Confederate custom of citing the effective total.

[39] Ibid., #49, 772-774.

[40] J. E. Johnston to L. T. Wigfall, Apr. 1, 1864, Library of Congress.

[41] O. R., #59, 781, 839, 840, 841-842; #110, 657. Johnston's reply was sent Apr. 14 and restated his belief that offensive operations depended on "relative forces" and adequate preparations. "I shall be ready to do it whenever they warrant it. . . . No one is more anxious than I for offensive operations by this army."

[42] Ibid., #74, 622-624.

[43] Ibid., #59, 781.

[44] Ibid., 207-210, 781; #74, 624-625, 627. On Apr. 1, Thomas reported that the Army of the Cumberland had approximately 90,000 effectives in the proximity

of Chattanooga. Schofield's Army of the Ohio had around 20,000 near Knoxville, and McPherson's Army of the Tennessee had 30,000 in North Alabama. All of these could be easily concentrated if the Federals wished to initiate a campaign.

[45] J. E. Johnston to L. T. Wigfall, Apr. ———, 1864, Library of Congress.

[46] J. E. Johnston to L. T. Wigfall, March 6, Apr. 23, 30, 1864, Library of Congress.

[47] J. E. Johnston to L. T. Wigfall, Apr. 30, 1864, Library of Congress; S.H.S.P., XXVI, 159. J. E. Johnston to W. H. C. Whiting, March 7, 1864; Mackall, A Son's Recollections, 203, 205, 209, W. W. Mackall to wife, Jan. 31, Feb. 27, May 12, 1864; Sid A. Champion to wife, June 5, 1864, Duke University Library; John W. Cotton, Yours Till Death: Civil War Letters of John W. Cotton, 103; J. W. DuBose, General Joseph Wheeler and the Army of Tennessee, 274.

[48] Watkins, "Company Aytch," 132-133; B. L. Ridley, Battles and Sketches of the Army of Tennessee, 282; Mary A. H. Gay, Life in Dixie During the War, 66-67, Tom Stokes to sister, March 15, 1864.

[49] O. R., #58, 245-246, 836, 839; #75, 654, 656, 657; #110, 660.

[50] Ibid., #59, 434.

[51] Ibid., #75, 20; J. D. Cox, Atlanta, 61-63; Lloyd Lewis, Sherman, the Fighting Prophet, 350-355; G. E. Turner, Victory Rode the Rails, 322-327.

[52] Lewis, Sherman, 351; O. R., #59, 531.

NOTES FOR CHAPTER 19
(Pages 261-288)

[1] O. R., #59, 816; #75, 91; J. C. Nisbet, Four Years on the Firing Line, 270; Cotton, Yours Till Death, 105-108; W. A. Cate, ed., Two Soldiers: The Campaign Diaries of Thomas J. Key, C. S. A., and Robert J. Campbell, U. S. A., 73; B. F. Scribner, How

Soldiers Were Made or the War As I Saw It, 223.

[2] O. R., #75, 11, 25, 42-43.

[3] Ibid., 668, 669; #110, 666-667. In conformity with Cooper's instructions Polk moved with 10,000 infantry and 4,000 cavalry to assist Johnston. The

number exceeded that authorized by Bragg and led to a controversy between Bragg and Polk which lasted until late June, when Davis after Polk's death acknowledged that he gave Polk the authority but denied that it was for more than his infantry. Polk, *Leonidas Polk*, II, 348-349; Seitz, *Bragg*, 434-435; *O. R.*, #78, 658.

⁴ *Ibid.*, #75, 663, 664, 665; Johnston, *Narrative*, 304.

⁵ *O. R.*, #75, 56, 83-84, 670, 675.

⁶ *Ibid.*, 664, 678, 681-682.

⁷ *Ibid.*, 682, 683, 684. From the scanty records it seems that 4,000 is an overestimate of the Confederates at Resaca; 2,000 might be a better number.

⁸ *Ibid.*, 39-40, 88, 111; T. B. Van Horne, *The Life of Major-General George H. Thomas*, 210, 220-221.

⁹ *O. R.*, #72, 63-64; #75, 105, 106; Lewis, *Sherman*, 357.

¹⁰ *O. R.*, #74, 614; #75, 677; *B. & L.*, IV, 277-281. In his *B. & L.* article Col. W. T. C. Breckinridge, who commanded at Dug Gap, leaves the impression that his messages read more clearly about McPherson's movements than they actually did. Johnston in his *B. & L.* account, IV, 266, said that he knew of McPherson's being in Snake Creek Gap May 8 but in his report gave it as May 9.

¹¹ Johnston, *Narrative*, 315-316; *Annals of the War*, 332. The only explanation of the contemporary use of "defile," which has led other writers since to assume Snake Creek Gap is narrow and has steep, unscalable walls, is that the forest shut in tightly the road through it. This was wild, sparsely settled country, which had been the possession of the Cherokee Indians but a few decades before and closed to white men. In the 1860's it was heavily forested with an untouched, luxuriant undergrowth, which gave it the "wild, picturesque" appearance recorded by Cox. It would be a fine place for delaying action, as Johnston obviously planned from his orders to his cavalry as soon as he heard that McPherson was in the gap, but to hold

it he would have needed to detach more of his troops than he could spare from the defense of Dalton. Cox, *Atlanta*, 31-32.

¹² Mackall, *A Son's Recollections*, 205, W. W. Mackall to wife, March 4, 1864; *O. R.*, #74, 721.

¹³ *Ibid.*, #75, 686, 687, 688; Johnston, *Narrative*, 307-308.

¹⁴ *O. R.*, #75, 106, 111, 114, 124, 125; #126, 951; Sherman, *Home Letters*, 292, W. T. Sherman to wife, May 22, 1864.

¹⁵ *O. R.*, #75, 689, 692, 693, 694, 696.

¹⁶ Polk, *Leonidas Polk*, II, 349, 351, 353-354.

¹⁷ *O. R.*, #75, 163, 698; Johnston, *Narrative*, 309; Watkins, "Company Aytch," 148; *B. & L.*, IV, 299.

¹⁸ *O. R.*, #74, 161, 163, 172.

¹⁹ *Ibid.*, 615.

²⁰ *S.H.S.P.*, XXXVIII, 342; Watkins, "Company Aytch," 148.

²¹ *O. R.*, #74, 615, 979; Johnston, *Narrative*, 311.

²² *O. R.*, #74, 979-980; #75, 615, 709, 711; Johnston, *Narrative*, 311-312.

²³ *Ibid.*, 313-314; *O. R.*, #74, 615.

²⁴ *Ibid.*, 981; W. F. Hinman, *The Story of the Sherman Brigade*, 529.

²⁵ *O. R.*, #75, 201; Nisbet, *Four Years*, 281; Watkins, "Company Aytch," 149-150.

²⁶ *O. R.*, #74, p. 615.

²⁷ Johnston, *Narrative*, 319; J. P. Austin, *The Blue and the Gray*, 124-125; French, *Two Wars*, 193-195; *O. R.*, #74, 704, 982; #75, 723.

²⁸ Johnston, *Narrative*, 320; *O. R.*, #74, 615, 982.

²⁹ Polk, *Leonidas Polk*, II, 354-355.

³⁰ Mackall, *A Son's Recollections*, 210, W. W. Mackall to wife, May 18, 1864; *O. R.*, #74, 982-983; #75, 723, 726.

³¹ *Ibid.*, 201, 214.

³² *Ibid.*, 219.

³³ *Ibid.*, 242, 260. The Federals had possession of Rome May 19.

³⁴ *Ibid.*, 615, 704, 982-983. *B. & L.*, IV, 268.

³⁵ Johnston, *Narrative*, 321; *O. R.*,

#74, 616, 705, 983; #75, 728; Wat-kins, "Company Aytch," 166; G. B. Guild, A Brief Narrative of the Fourth Tennessee Cavalry Regiment, 61-62.

[36] O. R., #74, 622, 983.

[37] Ibid., #73, 751-752; #74, 616, 635, 985. Hood in Advance and Retreat, 96 ff., says that he saw the enemy and called Mackall's attention to them, but Mackall in a memorandum written at the time says that he did not see any. Hood also says that he had been told by a Federal officer that they were a part of Gen. Butterfield's command, which cannot be true as Butterfield's communications display that he was west of the Adairsville-Kingston road. More important, Hood claims that he had no orders to do anything but was "merely granted the privilege of doing what I requested. . . ." This belated account differs widely from contemporary messages and reports and cannot be credited as a true description of events.

[38] Johnston, Narrative, 322; Sherman, Memoirs, II, 88; O. R., #74, 983-984.

[39] Johnston, Narrative, 323; B. & L., IV, 268; O. R., #74, 984.

[40] Ibid., 616, 635; B. & L., IV, 268-269; Johnston, Narrative, 323-324; Polk, Leonidas Polk, II, 355-357, 376-382; French, Two Wars, 186-198, 367-382; Hood, Advance, 104-109; S.H.S.P., XXI, 314-321. The detail of this conference follows fundamentally the accounts of it given by Mackall, Hardee, Johnston and French. They make no reference to any suggestion by Hood that the position was a good one for launching an attack, something he years later claimed to have said. Capt. W. J. Morris, Polk's engineer officer, who was present, said that both Polk and Hood advocated an offensive move the morning of the twentieth. Nisbet, Four Years, 290, says, "All the way from Dalton to Atlanta Hood complained about his part of the line we would form as being enfiladed, flanked, untenable," and Watkins, "Company Aytch," 166, reports similarly.

[41] O. R., #75, 728.

[42] Mackall, A Son's Recollections, 211,

W. W. Mackall to wife, May 21, 1864; O. R., #74, 991.

[43] Eliot, West Point, 100-101.

[44] Chesnut, Diary (Houghton), 410, 411, 416.

[45] Mackall, A Son's Recollections, 213, W. W. Mackall to wife, June 3, 1864.

[46] O. R., #75, 736.

[47] Ibid., 732; #110, 670, 671-672, 673-674.

[48] Ibid., #75, 260, 299.

[49] Johnston, Narrative, 325-326; O. R., #72, 65, 143.

[50] Sherman, Memoirs, II, 44; Johnston, Narrative, 327-328; O. R., #73, 14; #74, 818. Hooker reported his losses in the action at 1,665 but the Confederates said they were higher.

[51] Ibid., #75, 331.

[52] Gay, Life in Dixie, 77; Johnston, Narrative, 329-331.

[53] O. R., #74, 616, 635-636. Johnston, Narrative, 333-334; Hood, Advance, 119-123; B. & L., IV, 270. In later writing Hood and Johnston disagreed over this operation but added no enlightenment as to what happened and why. Johnston argued that Hood failed to reach his proper position but does not dispute Hood's testimony about the change of the Federal line.

[54] O. R., #75, 385, 400-401; Johnston, Narrative, 334-335; French, Two Wars, 144; Tuttle mss.; Guild, Brief Narrative, 63; Mackall, A Son's Recollections, 213, W. W. Mackall to wife, June 5, 1864.

[55] O. R., #75, 433, 448-449, 454-455; Johnston, Narrative, 335; W. T. Sherman, The Sherman Letters, 235-236, W. T. Sherman to John Sherman, June 9, 1864.

[56] O. R., #75, 46, 474, 480, 492.

[57] Scribner, How Soldiers Were Made, 303; Gorgas, Civil War Diary, 106-107; Mackall, A Son's Recollections, 211-212, W. W. Mackall to wife, May 28, 1864.

[58] Polk, Leonidas Polk, II, 366, L. Polk to wife, June 11, 1864; Sherman, Home Letters, 294-295, W. T. Sherman to wife, June 9, 1864; Cotton, Yours Till Death, 111, John Cotton to wife, June 1,

1864; Sid S. Champion to wife, June 9, 1864, Duke University Library. That not all the Army of Tennessee thought Johnston a great general almost goes without saying. In any army one finds disgruntled, unhappy individuals. Three officers and 27 enlisted men deserted to the Federals, for example, on June 14. They were Alabamians and reported that Johnston had so lost the confidence of the army that desertions would be frequent if the Confederates felt sure of amnesty. *O. R.,* #75, 479.

⁵⁹ Mackall, *A Son's Recollections,* 215, W. W. Mackall to wife, June 18, 1864; Johnston, *Narrative,* 332; Phillips, "Correspondence of Toombs, Stephens, and Cobb," 664. J. E. Brown to A. H. Stephens, June 6, 1864; *O. R.,* #75, 749, 758, 767, 770-771. In describing the conditions at headquarters Mackall said, "Now let me give an idea of how I am writing: a little room, Johnston, Hood, Hardee, Hindman, Lovell, all talking, and every now and then talking to me."

⁶⁰ *O. R.,* #75, 689, 719, 723, 736, 747, 755, 756; #110, 672-673. Others than Johnston had attempted to have Forrest turned loose on Sherman's communications, as on May 25, when Senator G. A. Henry suggested to Seddon that it be done. Bragg in an endorsement

on Henry's note said, "The movement has not escaped notice and it is hoped that we shall soon hear of good results." No orders then or at any other time in this period went to S. D. Lee to turn Forrest loose upon Sherman's communications. Sherman, who feared greatly the results of a raid by Forrest, did not understand how effectively the Confederate high command worked to his advantage at this time.

⁶¹ *Ibid.,* #75, 762, 770.

⁶² *Ibid.,* #110, 678.

⁶³ *Ibid.,* #75, 772, 774; #110, 679.

⁶⁴ *Ibid.,* #75, 473, 479, 507-508, 775-776; Cox, *Atlanta,* 116; Austin, *Blue and Gray,* 126-127; G. W. Pepper, *Personal Recollections of Sherman's Campaigns in Georgia and the Carolinas,* 119.

⁶⁵ *O. R.,* #75, 466, 763, 772-773; Johnston, *Narrative,* 336; French, *Two Wars,* 201.

⁶⁶ *O. R.,* #75, 775, 776; Polk, *Leonidas Polk,* II, 372-375; Johnston, *Narrative,* 337; Sherman, *Memoirs,* II, 53-54; J. E. Johnston to C. T. Quintard, October 9, 1885, University of the South Library. Sherman says that he saw the group on Pine Mountain and suggested to the battery commander that he fire on it to force its members to take cover. He then rode away without waiting to see the result of the firing.

NOTES FOR CHAPTER 20
(Pages 289-307)

¹ *O. R.,* #75, 775, 776-777; Polk, *Leonidas Polk,* II, 374-375.

² *O. R.,* #75, 479, 492; Johnston, *Narrative,* 337.

³ *O. R.,* #75, 498, 507-508.

⁴ *Ibid.,* 777, 781.

⁵ *Ibid.,* 519, 572-573, 783.

⁶ Johnston, *Narrative,* 339; *O. R.,* #75, 546, 557, 581, 775, 784.

⁷ *Ibid.,* 558, 562-563, 788; Johnston, *Narrative,* 339-340; Sherman, *Memoirs,* II, 58-59, 86. There is nothing in *O. R.* to explain the report from Hood "soon after the firing ceased," of which John-

ston speaks in the *Narrative.* Like many similar lacunae in the Confederate record it is probably attributable to the habit of the generals to communicate orally reports and orders.

⁸ *O. R.,* #75, 535, 581-582, 586, 775, 789, 792; #78, 657-658.

⁹ *Ibid.,* #75, 582, 583; Sherman, *Home Letters,* 298, W. T. Sherman to wife, June 26, 1864.

¹⁰ Watkins, "Company Aytch," 152-153; Nisbet, *Four Years,* 302; French, *Two Wars,* 205-206.

¹¹ *O. R.,* #75, 785, 787. Stewart

assumed command of the Army of
Mississippi July 7, O.R., #110, 687-688.
[12] *Ibid.*, #75, 607; Watkins, "Company Aytch," 156.
[13] *Ibid.*, 156-157; French, *Two Wars*,
207-208; Johnston, *Narrative*, 341-344;
Sherman, *Memoirs*, II, 60-61. Sherman
in *B. & L.*, IV, 252, puts Johnston's
losses as 630 but in his *Memoirs* by
erroneously adding the figures in the
Narrative states them as 808. T. L. Livermore, *Numbers and Losses in the Civil
War in America, 1861-1865*, 120-121,
gives the Federal losses as 2,051 and the
Confederate as 432 but in a footnote says
that he used the figures only of the
troops engaged in the assault. The total
Union losses that day he gives as 3,000.
[14] Johnston, *Narrative*, 343.
[15] Jones, *War Clerk*, II, 229; Gorgas,
Civil War Diary, 108; DuBose, *Wheeler*,
344.
[16] Chesnut, *Diary* (Appleton), 320.
[17] DuBose, *Wheeler*, 344-345; O. R.,
#110, 685-686.
[18] L. T. Wigfall to J. E. Johnston,
undated, Library of Congress. This is
a memorandum obviously prepared by
Wigfall to help Johnston in writing an
account of the war, as it covers the whole
period.
[19] O. R., #75, 795-796; L. T. Wigfall to Johnston, undated memo., Library
of Congress. Johnston's communication
to Bragg was the seventeenth of the
campaign.
[20] O. R., #110, 680-681; L. T. Wigfall to J. E. Johnston, undated memo.,
Library of Congress. Wigfall secured the
help of Governor Watts of Alabama,
although the latter's letter is not printed
in the O. R. Wigfall said that Watts had
just returned from a visit to the army at
Kennesaw when they conferred. Watts
was so impressed by the need to operate
on Sherman's communications that he
expressed a willingness to strip his state
of mounted troops if Forrest's force was
insufficient. In the letter he wrote Cobb
said: "It is proper that I should say that
our people are in the best spirits, hopeful and confident. They have the utmost

confidence in General Johnston, which
has not been shaken by his falling back,
and they believe that the President will
do all that any man can do." O. R.,
#76, 858.
[21] *Ibid.*, #110, 693-695, 704-707. On
July 13 Seddon wrote an official account
of Hill's oral report of his conversation
with Johnston and Hood. The Secretary
of War submitted it to Hill for his
approval. In it Seddon says that Johnston
believed he could hold the enemy from
the Chattahoochee for at least a month.
Hill accepted Seddon's version on July
14 and at the same time made his own
written record of the conversation which
he sent to Seddon. In it he used the
phrase "for a long time" as the period
Johnston estimated he could hold Sherman. On Oct. 12, 1878, at the request
of Maj. W. T. Walthall, Hill wrote a
somewhat different account in which he
quoted Johnston as stating a belief he
could hold the Federals north of the
river for perhaps 45 to 60 days. This is
the letter Davis used in *Rise and Fall*,
II, 557-561 (see also Rowland, *Jefferson
Davis*, VIII, 284-285, B. H. Hill to
Jefferson Davis, Oct. 12, 1878). Just
what these discrepancies indicate it is
difficult to say, but it seems strange that
Johnston should have thought he could
hold Sherman, even with his prepared
positions, if the Federal commander returned to his turning maneuvers.
[22] O. R., #75, 611, 612.
[23] *Ibid.*, O. R., #75, 497, 584, 802;
Johnston, *Narrative*, 344, 345; *Confederate Veteran*, III, 262-265.
[24] O. R., #75, 651-654; #76, 15, 29,
41-42, 859, 860.
[25] Sherman, *Memoirs*, II, 65; O. R.,
#76, 29, 30, 33, 36-37, 50, 61, 860.
[26] J. W. Hagan, *Confederate Letters
of John W. Hagan*, 46-48, J. W. Hagan
to wife, July 4, 1864; O. R., #76, 65,
67, 862, 879; #110, 687.
[27] *Ibid.*, #75, 795-796. Bragg gave
the latest returns from the army in
Georgia, those of June 10, as 45,282
infantry, 12,231 cavalry, 4,259 artillery,
a total of 61,772, and said that the dis-

parity between the armies was no more than was true of those in other areas.

[28] *Ibid.*, 805; #78, 688.

[29] *Ibid.*, 688.

[30] *Ibid.*, #110, 687.

[31] *Ibid.*, 688-691.

[32] *Ibid.*, 691, 702, 710-711, 712.

[33] Jones, *War Clerk*, II, 246; O. R., #76, 867.

[34] *Ibid.*, 868-869; #110, 692; Mackall, *A Son's Recollections*, 219-220, W. W. Mackall to wife, July 12, 1864.

[35] Sherman, *Memoirs*, II, 66; O. R., #76, 73, 76-77, 92; Pepper, *Personal Recollections*, 95; Cox, *Atlanta*, 137. Sherman said that both British and French flags were used in the effort to protect the mills. As most of the workers were women the incident created a feeling of outrage among Southerners.

[36] Johnston, *Narrative*, 347; B. & L., IV, 274; French, *Two Wars*, 216; O. R., #76, 92, 108, 872, 873.

NOTES FOR CHAPTER 21
(Pages 308-322)

[1] Louise Wigfall to Mrs. C. C. Clay, July 6, 1864, Duke University Library; Mrs. Johnston to Mrs. Wigfall, June 16, 1864, Library of Congress; Mrs. Wright, *Southern Girl*, 177-179; Mackall, *A Son's Recollections*, 218-219, W. W. Mackall to wife, July 10, 1864. On the next day a spy informed Sherman that he had seen Mrs. Johnston at the Confederate headquarters where they seemed to be having a "jollification." O. R., #76, 115-116.

[2] Mackall, *A Son's Recollections*, 218, 219, 220, W. W. Mackall to wife, July 7, 12, 1864. On the seventh Mackall wrote, "I suppose that there is great excitement in Atlanta, as I ordered the hospitals removed; people will never think that it would be well to get sick and wounded out of the way if it was decided to fight near the town, they will only listen to their fears and conclude that we will not fight at all . . . ." This situation was noted in an Atlanta paper for July 6 by Sherman, who said, "It's tone is changed and it apologizes for the necessity of civilians quitting the place." O. R., #76, 86.

[3] K. Cumming, *A Journal of Hospital Life in the Confederate Army of Tennessee*, 134; *Richmond Whig*, July 9, 1864.

[4] O. R., #76, 878; #78, 695-696.

[5] *Ibid.*, 712; Johnston, *Narrative*, 364; Maury, *Recollections*, 146, J. E. Johnston to D. H. Maury, Sept. 1, 1864; Hughes, "Some War Letters," *loc. cit.*, 320-321, J. E. Johnston to Beverley Johnston, Aug. 28, 1864. In both the letters to his brother Beverley and to Maury, Johnston says more concisely what he states in the *Narrative* but in the one to Maury also says that Bragg told him that Sherman's army was larger than Grant's. Mackall received the same impression of Bragg's visit. In a letter home at the time he said: "Bragg arrived, seemed a little disposed to be civil to me, that was all; it looked a good deal as if he thought he was magnanimous. I don't think he has any special mission, but is just sent because Mr. Davis is uneasy about things generally." Mackall, *A Son's Recollections*, 217, W. W. Mackall to wife, July ——, 1864.

[6] O. R., #76, 879-880.

[7] *Ibid.*, 881. Where Bragg got his figures about the Federal infantry, he does not say. The returns of the three armies under Sherman for June 30 show almost 111,000 in the field in Georgia with the cavalry totals separate. *Ibid.*, #75, 650-654.

[8] *Ibid.*, #78, 712-714. A little later in July Thomas alone reported 65,000 men. *Ibid.*, #76, 256-259.

[9] *Ibid.*, #74, 991; #76, 987; #78, 712-714. On July 14, Davis wired Bragg, "The selection of a place must depend upon military considerations so mainly that I can only say if C. is thus indicated

adopt advice and execute as proposed."
Bragg's reply was: "I am decidedly
opposed, as it would perpetuate the past
and present policy which he has advised
and now sustains. Any change will be
attended with some objections. This one
could produce no good." *Ibid.*, #110,
705, 707.

The content of these communications
between Bragg and Davis disturbed Col.
John B. Sale, Bragg's military secretary,
to such a degree that when Davis asked
to keep Bragg's books and papers, Sale
advised against it. As he told Bragg in a
letter, "your correspondence about Johnston and the appointment of Hood, is
there recorded, and make it look as if
you originated that programme. This
might become unsafe." Seitz, *Bragg*, 505,
J. B. Sale to B. Bragg, Feb. 4, 1865.

    ¹⁰ *O. R.*, #76, 879, 881, 882.
    ¹¹ Seitz, *Bragg*, 444-445. Seitz attri-
buted this story to G. G. Vest, member
of Congress from Missouri, who told it
to a New York newspaperman.
    ¹² Sherman, *Home Letters*, 302, W.
T. Sherman to wife, July 26, 1864; Davis,
Rise and Fall, II, 547-551; French, *Two
Wars*, 218.
    ¹³ Freeman, *Lee*, III, 461; *O. R.*,
#110, 692.
    ¹⁴ Gordon, *Reminiscences*, 131-132.
    ¹⁵ R. E. Lee, *Lee's Dispatches* (here-
after *Lee's Dispatches*), 282.
    ¹⁶ *Ibid.*, 283-284.
    ¹⁷ *O. R.*, #110, 692; *B. & L.*, IV,
277, quoting letter of Hampton to Johnston, date not given. Hampton's letter
caused Davis to write to the South Carolinian and say he considered it an "endorsement of complaints" against him.
In Hampton's reply he repeated Lee's
expression of regret at Johnston's removal. But he reported it not to sustain
any attacks on Davis, whom he pointed
out he had consistently supported. "I
felt that it was due to Gen. Johnston
and to truth," Hampton wrote Davis,
"to give so much of Gen. Lee's conversation on that occasion as would do away
with the charge that he had advised the
removal of Gen. Johnston." Rowland,

Jefferson Davis, VII, 399-400, Wade
Hampton to Jefferson Davis, Sept. 5,
1874.
    ¹⁸ Davis, *Rise and Fall*, II, 472-474;
H. J. Pearce, Jr., *Benjamin H. Hill*, 101.
In 1874 Hill took the opportunity in a
speech in Atlanta to denounce reports
that he advised removal, but he attempted to defend Davis by saying that
the latter relieved Johnston not because
of personal hostility but with great reluctance on the basis of the military situation. In doing so he left the false impression that Lee agreed with Davis' action
by saying, "I know he consulted with
General Lee fully, earnestly and anxiously
before this removal."

Undoubtedly Davis did leave the impression with Hill and others by his
references to consultation with Lee that
the latter approved the removal of Johnston. But it was Hill's appearance of
agreement with Davis that beclouded his
own part in the matter. Davis also had
a role here, as in 1878 James Lyons in
a letter to W. T. Walthall says flatly that
Davis told him on the evening of removal
that he could not resist the pressure for
it. "Hill urged it on behalf of the people
of Georgia and Benjamin and Seddon
were so violent they would listen to
nothing—." Rowland, *Jefferson Davis*,
VIII, 215-216. James Lyons to W. T.
Walthall, July 31, 1878.
    ¹⁹ *O. R.*, #76, 876. All the reports of
this meeting of the cabinet were written
years after the event and display in many
statements the failure of the memory of
their writers. For example, Postmaster
General Reagan reported that Lee and
Beauregard as well as Bragg suggested
independently the appointment of Hood
in Johnston's place. Rowland, *Jefferson
Davis*, VIII, 78-79, J. H. Reagan to
Jefferson Davis, Feb. 7, 1878, 349-354;
J. A. Seddon to W. T. Walthall, Feb.
10, 1879; Davis, *Rise and Fall*, II, 472-
474, B. H. Hill to W. T. Walthall, Oct.
12, 1878; W. C. Oates, *The War Between the Union and the Confederacy*,
331-333; Thomas R. Hay, "The Davis-
Hood-Johnston Controversy of 1864,"

Mississippi Valley Historical Review, XI, 64.

²⁰ *O. R.*, #76, 883. Davis was able to create a belief in his reluctance to remove Johnston, despite the widespread rumors of his desire to do so. Gorgas noted in his diary, "It is a pity President Davis did not act earlier on his own judgment, which has been adverse to Johnston." Gorgas was among those who believed that Hill finally induced Davis' tardy action. Gorgas, *Civil War Diary*, 127-128. Davis tried publicly and privately to appear unwilling to remove Johnston. Rowland, *Jefferson Davis*, VI, 336.

²¹ Davis, *Rise and Fall*, II, 557.

²² Johnston, *Narrative*, 348; Henry Hitchcock, *Marching with Sherman*, 55; Lindsley, *The Military Annals of Tennessee. Confederate*, 94.

²³ *O. R.*, #76, 885. Hood received a message from Seddon about an hour later. It said: "You are charged with a great trust. You will, I know, test to the utmost your capacities to discharge it. Be wary no less than bold. It may yet be practicable to cut the communication of the enemy or find or make an opportunity of equal encounter whether he moves east or west. God be with you."

²⁴ *Ibid.*, 887, 888, 889; Hood, *Advance*, 126-127, quotes A. P. Stewart to J. B. Hood, Aug. 7, 1872; Hay, "Davis-Hood-Johnston Controversy," 66, quotes letter of J. P. Young to T. R. Hay, March 26, 1921.

²⁵ *O. R.*, #76, 888; #110, 708-709. Hood also expressed the danger in making a change of commanders at that time in his telegram to Cooper acknowledging the receipt of the order with his appointment.

²⁶ Johnston, *Narrative*, 349-350; *O. R.*, #74, 618; Hood, *Advance*, 127, 141, 143, 162. In the *Narrative* Johnston says he stayed at headquarters until sundown but in his report says it was until afternoon, which is more accurate.

²⁷ *O. R.*, #76, 888; Hughes, "Some War Letters," 320-323, J. E. Johnston to Beverley Johnston, Aug. 28, 1864. In this letter as in a number of others written about the same time Johnston develops somewhat more fully the arguments in the dispatch to Cooper July 18. "After his experience in the Wilderness," Johnston said to his brother, "Lee adopted as thoro' a defensive as mine & added by it to his great fame. The only other difference between our operations is due to Grant's aggressiveness and Sherman's extreme caution, which carried the armies in Va. to Petersburg in less than half the time in which Sherman reached the vicinity of Atlanta." In commenting upon Bragg's visit Johnston said that he "left me in the belief that his visit was casual & that he was gratified with the state of things. He spoke in a different tone of affairs in Va. & assured me that he had always maintained that Sherman's army was stronger than Grant's which I never doubted."

²⁸ *O. R.*, #76, 887.

²⁹ Mrs. Wright, *Southern Girl*, 181-185, Halsey Wigfall to parents, July 31, 1864; Nisbet, *Four Years*, 305; *O. R.*, #74, 717.

³⁰ Wilson, *Reminiscences*, 33; Cate, *Two Soldiers*, 89; Ridley, *Battles and Sketches*, 483; Austin, *Blue and Gray*, 130; DuBose, *Wheeler*, 362; Watkins, "Company Aytch," 168-170; Guild, *Brief Narrative*, 66; Hagan, *Confederate Letters*, 51-52, J. W. Hagan to wife, July 19, 1864; J. E. Dooley, *John Dooley: Confederate Soldier. His Journal*, 162; unknown writer to C. T. Quintard, July 22, 1864, Duke University Library; Mrs. George E. Purvis to ———, Duke University Library; E. J. Harvie to B. S. Ewell, Nov. 12, 1864, Ewell papers, kindness Dr. T. G. Hamlin; W. L. Nugent to wife, Aug. 15, 1864, Nugent Letters, typescript in possession Lucy Somerville Howorth, kindness of Bell I. Wiley. This list could be extended to include virtually all the writing, either for publication or in private correspondence, the authors have seen from soldiers of the army under Johnston. As Hagan told his wife, "he . . . was loved by all who ever Sirved under him. . . .'"

[31] O. R., #74, 697; #76, 987-988; Johnston, *Narrative*, 365-367, W. J. Hardee to J. E. Johnston, Apr. 20, 1868. Bragg was against the retention of either Hardee or Mackall. He blamed Mackall's "want of administration" for many of the woes of the Army of Tennessee and advised the transfer of Hardee on July 27. He recommended Dick Taylor to Davis as a replacement for Hardee and said that with him the Army of Tennessee "would be invincible." When Davis visited the army in late September, Hardee renewed his plea and received assignment as commander of the Department of South Carolina, Georgia and Florida. Cheatham succeeded to the command of Hardee's corps., O. R., #78, 880; #110, 713.

[32] S. F. Horn, *Army of Tennessee*, 345, quoting a letter from Stewart in the author's possession; T. R. Hay, "The Atlanta Campaign," *Georgia Historical Quarterly*, VII, 29-30; French, *Two Wars*, 216-217. In a letter to Johnston four years later, Stewart interpreted the spirit of the army in this way: "The army had confidence *in itself*, and had long been wanting a commander in whom they could place reliance. The consequence was, that army *surrendered to you;* they gave you their *love* and *unlimited confidence*, were willing to follow you, advancing or retreating, and you could lead them wherever you chose. . . . The Army of Tennessee *loved* you and *confided in you implicitly*, as an army of brave men will love and confide in *skill, pluck*, and *honor*." John-

ston, *Narrative*, 637-639, A. P. Stewart to J. E. Johnston, Feb. 11, 1868.

[33] Taylor, *Destruction*, 44; Parks, *Kirby Smith*, 428-429, quoting letters of E. Kirby Smith to wife, Aug. 10, 1864, and to mother, Aug. 17, 1864.

[34] B. & L., IV, 253; Sherman, *Home Letters*, 304, W. T. Sherman to wife, July 29, 1864; Sherman, *Memoirs*, II, 72, 75; Lewis, *Sherman*, 383; Cox, *Atlanta*, 148; J. D. Cox, *Military Reminiscences of the Civil War*, II, 277; Oates, *War Between*, 461, quotes Joseph Hooker to Mansfield Lovell, ——, 1873. In this letter Hooker states high praise of Johnston's ability. After remarking that the strength of the Federal Army was so superior that they could "turn all his positions without risk from any quarter," Hooker wrote that all considered Johnston's retreat "the cleanest and best-conducted . . . that we had seen or read of." He called it the "most prominent feature of the war" and suggested that "all persons who may hereafter elect for their calling the profession of arms" should study it.

Grant was no less pleased by the news of Johnston's removal than the generals in his front. "When I heard your Government had removed Johnston from command," he told an ex-Confederate friend, "I was as happy as if I had reenforced Sherman with a large army corps. Joe Johnston gave more anxiety than any of the others." Grant, *Personal Memoirs*, II, 167, 344-345; McElroy, *Jefferson Davis*, 416.

NOTES FOR CHAPTER 22
(Pages 323-338)

[1] Mrs. Wright, *Southern Girl*, 181-187, Halsey Wigfall to parents, July 31, 1864; Maury, *Recollections*, 146, J. E. Johnston to D. H. Maury, Sept. 1, 1864; Phillips, "Correspondence of Toombs, Stephens, and Cobb," *loc. cit.*, 647, 648, Howell Cobb to wife, July 20, 22, 1864.

[2] Mrs. Wright, *Southern Girl*, 185-186.

[3] *Ibid.*, 186-187; O. R., #73, 914, 925-930; #74, 972; #76, 350, 940; Austin, *Blue and Gray*, 132; Cate, *Two Soldiers*, 106; J. A. Cobb, "Civil War Incidents in Macon," *Georgia Historical Quarterly*, VII, 282.

[4] Mrs. Wright, *Southern Girl*, 193-194; J. E. Johnston to Mansfield Lovell, Oct. 3, 1864, Library of Congress. The

house in Vineville belonged to Mrs. Mackall's brother, then a captain in the Trans-Mississippi army. Mackall, *A Son's Recollections*, 221.

⁵ Mrs. Wright, *Southern Girl*, 193-200; Mackall, *A Son's Recollections*, 221-222; J. E. Johnston to Mansfield Lovell, Oct. 3, 1864, Library of Congress.

⁶ *Richmond Whig*, July 19, 20, 22, 1864.

⁷ *Richmond Examiner*, July 19, 20, 25, 1864; Hay, "Davis-Hood-Johnston Controversy," p. 72.

⁸ *Ibid.*, 71-72; *Richmond Dispatch*, July 21, 25, Aug. 3, 1864; *Richmond Enquirer*, July 19, 25, 1864; *Richmond Sentinel*, July 20, 23, 1864.

⁹ Chesnut, *Diary* (Houghton), 420; John M. Mitchell to C. T. Quintard, July 29, 1864, Duke University Library; Harrison, *Recollections*, 192; T. C. DeLeon, *Four Years in Rebel Capitols*, 343.

¹⁰ Hay, "Davis-Hood-Johnston Controversy," 78 n, quotes Kenneth Rayner to Thomas Ruffin, July 22, 1864; H. Gourdin to "Dear Robert," July ——, 1864, Duke University Library.

¹¹ B. S. Ewell, manuscript journal, Aug. 8, 1864, College of William and Mary Library; Hood, *Advance*, 184; Cox, *Atlanta*, 186-187.

¹² *Richmond Examiner*, Sept. 5, 1864, quoted in Eliot, *West Point*, 108; Hay, "Davis - Hood - Johnston Controversy," 78 n, quotes Kenneth Rayner to Thomas Ruffin, Sept. 29, 1864.

¹³ French, *Two Wars*, 219, 220, 222; O. R., #78, 448, 836. When Lincoln heard that Davis was with Hood's army in Georgia, he wrote Sherman, "I judge that Brown and Stephens are the objects of his visit."

¹⁴ Rowland, *Jefferson Davis*, VI, 341-344, quoting *Richmond Enquirer*, Sept. 29, 1864. From the *Enquirer's* account it would appear that Davis arrived in Macon Sept. 28, obviously an error. A dispatch from Sherman to Grant says that Davis was there Sept. 23, which is probably the correct date. O. R., #78, 488.

¹⁵ Hood, *Advance*, 253; undated memo by B. S. Ewell of conversation with Custis Lee, who was with Davis as an aide. College of William and Mary Library.

¹⁶ Hood, *Advance*, 254-255; Horn, *Army of Tennessee*, 372, quoting *Augusta Chronicle*, Sept. 26, 1864; O. R., #78, 660; Johnston, *Narrative*, 367-369, A. P. Stewart to J. E. Johnston, Feb. 11, 1868. S. D. Lee was promoted to lieutenant general in June.

¹⁷ O. R., #78, 880; Taylor, *Destruction*, 204-206.

¹⁸ *Ibid.*

¹⁹ T. H. Williams, *P. G. T. Beauregard*, 240, 242. The fortunes of Beauregard, whom Hardee replaced as head of the Department of South Carolina, Georgia and Florida, in this geographical command were no happier than Johnston's had been.

²⁰ O. R., #78, 464, 479, 488, 501; Sherman, *Memoirs*, II, 141-142; Rowland, *Jefferson Davis*, VI, 345-347, quoting the account of the Montgomery speech as reported in the *Charleston Daily Courier*, Oct. 3, 1864; 349-356, quoting the talk at Charleston as reported in the same paper, Oct. 6, 1864; 356-361, quoting the *Richmond Dispatch*, Oct. 10, 1864, on the speech at Augusta. Davis later denied that he had anything to do with Hood's Tennessee campaign, which he attributed to Beauregard despite Hood's acceptance of responsibility for it. *Ibid.*, VIII, 374-377, 415-419, Jefferson Davis to L. B. Northrop, Apr. 9, Sept. 25, 1879. These two letters are interesting for another reason. In them Davis flatly contradicts the opinion he gave Taylor and expressed publicly in speeches when he implies or states that the spirit of Hood's army was not good.

²¹ Hughes, "Some War Letters," 320-322, J. E. Johnston to Beverley Johnston, Aug. 28, 1864; J. E. Johnston to Mansfield Lovell, Oct. 3, 1864, Library of Congress; Mackall, *A Son's Recollections*, 225-228, J. E. Johnston to W. W. Mackall, Dec. 31, 1864, Jan. 26, 1865;

Mrs. Johnston to B. S. Ewell, Oct 15, 1864, Library of Congress.

[22] Maury, *Recollections*, 146, J. E. Johnston to D. H. Maury, Sept. 1, 1864; Hughes, "Some War Letters," 320-322, J. E. Johnston to Beverley Johnston, Aug. 28, 1864; J. E. Johnston to L. T. Wigfall, Aug. 27, 1864, Library of Congress.

[23] Hughes, "Some War Letters," 320-322, 326-327, J. E. Johnston, to Beverley Johnston, Aug. 28, Nov. 15, 1864.

[24] J. E. Johnston to Mansfield Lovell, Oct. 3, 1864, Library of Congress.

[25] Hughes, "Some War Letters," 322-326, Joseph E. Johnston to Beverley Johnston, Oct. 6, Nov. 8, 1864. Hood failed to receive the Senate's confirmation of his elevation to full general, inasmuch as when it came up for final action he was out of service. *Jour. of Cong.* IV, 733.

[26] O. R., #74, 621.

[27] Hughes, "Some War Letters," 324-326, J. E. Johnston to Beverley Johnston, Nov. 8, 1864.

[28] O. R., #92, 589; Chesnut, *Diary* (Houghton), 452, 463.

[29] Mackall, *A Son's Recollections*, 225-226, J. E. Johnston to W. W. Mackall, Dec. 31, 1864; Jones, *War Clerk*, II, 342. Jones reported Johnston at the War Office, where he "was warmly greeted by his friends," on Nov. 29. Johnston did not see Bragg who had been in active command at Wilmington, N. C., since Oct. 15, nor did he apparently see Davis.

[30] McElroy, *Jefferson Davis*, 411-414; J. D. Richardson, comp. & ed., *A Compilation of the Messages and Papers of the Confederacy*, 1, 482-498.

[31] Jones, *War Clerk*, II, 342; Gorgas, *Civil War Diary*, 156; Mackall, *A Son's Recollections*, 225-226, J. E. Johnston to W. W. Mackall, Jan. 31, 1864; *Jour. of Cong.*, IV, 326, VII, 309. Among those with whom Johnston talked was Representative Henry S. Foote of Tennessee. Foote asked the General about the possibilities of continuing the war "under the disadvantageous circumstances then existing." Foote says that Johnston "with

the utmost frankness" said it depended on stopping Sherman, about which he had no optimistic opinion. The conversation so convinced Foote of the futility of further fighting that he tried to get Congress to appeal for peace. H. S. Foote, *Casket of Reminiscences*, 302-303.

[32] O. R., #74, 621; Mackall, *A Son's Recollections*, 225-226, J. E. Johnston to W. W. Mackall, Dec. 31, 1864. The report finally reached the Senate on Jan. 9, almost two months after that body had requested it on Nov. 14. On Jan. 12 the Senate asked for the "contemporaneous correspondence and documents," without which the Administration suggested it was inadvisable to publish the report. Again the Executive Department delayed. Wigfall moved that the "injunction of secrecy" be removed from the report and accompanying documents on Feb. 18, but it was not until March 1 that Davis sent the material and only included the communications which passed between Johnston and the Department of War and between Johnston and Davis. There was none of the secret correspondence from Hood. Again on March 18, the last session of the Senate, Wigfall moved that the material be printed, but that ended the matter. *Jour. of Cong.* IV, 432, 448, 573, 620, 740.

On Jan. 20 the House called for all correspondence between Davis and Johnston, Hood and Beauregard which touched on the command of the Army of Tennessee up to the recent disastrous retreat from Nashville. Davis delayed his reply for a little more than a month and included copies of all the correspondence between Richmond and Johnston "in relation to the conduct of the war in the valley of the Mississippi," which the House had asked him to send May 16, 1864! He explained that the delay was because "an important paper, which had been handed to me by General Johnston in person at Chattanooga, and in which he objected to sending re-enforcements from the Army of Tennessee to that in Mississippi, had been mislaid and seemed necessary to the completeness of the correspondence." Davis said that he was still unable to find the statement but sent the rest without it as he did not want to delay the matter longer. The House ordered the printing of all the matter it received. *Jour. of Cong.* VII, 472, 654-655.

According to Johnston in the *Narrative*, 151, this mysterious document was no more than a copy of his communication to Cooper of Dec. 6, 1862, in which he presented the arguments against sending troops from Bragg to Pemberton, arguments Davis overlooked to weaken Bragg just before the battle of Murfreesboro. *O. R.,* #30, 441.

[83] *Richmond Examiner,* Dec. 19, 1864; *Richmond Whig,* Dec. 20, 1864; Mackall, *A Son's Recollections,* 225-226, J. E. Johnston to W. W. Mackall, Dec, 31, 1864. Longstreet hinted at this idea on Dec. 21 to Lee himself, but no one ever addressed him forthrightly on the subject. Gorgas about the same time noted a strong feeling in Congress for making Lee "Generalissimo to command all our armies—not constructively and 'under the President'" but with "full control of all military operations" and responsibility for the results. *O. R.,* #89, 1286-1287; Gorgas, *Civil War Diary,* 158; Jones, *War Clerk,* II, 364-365.

[84] *O. R.,* #89, 1278-1279, 1280, 1283; #92, 966, 969.

[85] *Ibid.,* #89, 1134, 1213; *Lee's Dispatches,* 305; Freeman, *Lee,* III, 517-545. Lee was equally despondent about Congress.

[86] Mackall, *A Son's Recollections,* 225-226, J. E. Johnston to W. W. Mackall, Dec. 31, 1864.

[87] Chesnut, *Diary* (Houghton), 467, 469-470.

[88] J. E. Johnston to B. S. Ewell, Jan. 23, 1865, Library of Congress; J. E. Johnston to L. T. Wigfall, Feb. 12, 1865, Library of Congress; Chesnut, *Diary* (Appleton), 343. When Hood resigned Davis gave the command of the Army of Tennessee to General Taylor.

[89] Mrs. J. E. Johnston to Louise Wigfall, Jan. 23, 1865, Library of Congress.

[40] Hughes, "Some War Letters," 327-328, J. E. Johnston to Beverley Johnston, Feb. 13, 1865; Mackall, *A Son's Recollections,* 226-228, J. E. Johnston to W. W. Mackall, Jan. 26, 1865; J. E. Johnston to B. S. Ewell, Jan. 23, 26, 1865, Duke University Library.

[41] Mrs. J. E. Johnston to Louise Wigfall, Feb. 19, 1865, Library of Congress; Chesnut, *Diary* (Houghton), 481, 485, 486.

NOTES FOR CHAPTER 23
(Pages 339-357)

[1] J. E. Johnston to L. T. Wigfall, Feb. 3, 12, 1865, Library of Congress.

[2] *O. R.,* #94, 784; #103, 966-967; #111, 388, 393-394; Mrs. Wright, *Southern Girl,* 223, Wade Hampton to L. T. Wigfall, Jan. 20, 1865; *Jour. of Cong.,* IV, 432, 671. Debate in Congress on the use of Negroes as soldiers continued until March, when it was authorized. Wigfall opposed it until the end.

[3] *Jour. of Cong.,* IV, 453-454, 458; VII, 463-464.

[4] J. E. Johnston to B. S. Ewell, Jan. 23, 1865, Duke University Library; J. E.

Johnston to L. T. Wigfall, Feb. 3, 1865, Library of Congress; Mackall, *A Son's Recollections,* 226-228, J. E. Johnston to W. W. Mackall, Jan. 26, 1865; *O. R.,* #96, 1205; *Jour. of Cong.,* IV, 457-458; VII, 463-464, 496. The vote in the Senate on the bill creating a general-in-chief was 20-2, in the House, 63-14; requesting the reappointment of Johnston, Senate, 16-5; in the House totals of the vote were not recorded.

[5] *O. R.,* #99, 1078-1079. Interestingly Beauregard describes the Army of Tennessee at around the end of January as

"If not, in the strict sense of the word a disorganized mob, it was no longer an army." Roman, *Military Operations*, II, 332.

⁶ Mrs. Wright, *Southern Girl*, 235-238, R. H. Walker *et al* to R. E. Lee, Feb. 4, 1865. Senator R. T. M. Hunter of Virginia did not sign the letter although he approved the reappointment of Johnston. Writing to Davis about a week later, Hunter said: "I did not sign because I did not want to embarrass you. But my opinion is, that such an assignment would have a most beneficial effect. If I am to trust the manifestations which I have witnessed from certain members of Congress, there is nothing which could be done, which would so much revive hope, as the assignment of Genl. Joseph E. Johnston to the command of that Army." Mrs. Wright, *Southern Girl*, 239-240, R. M. T. Hunter to Jefferson Davis, Feb. 10, 1865.

⁷ Taylor, *Destruction*, 206.

⁸ O. R., #96, 1118; #129, 1046-1048; Gorgas, *Civil War Diary*, 165.

⁹ O. R., #129, 1094, 1183; Jones, *War Clerk*, II, 395; Patrick, *Davis and His Cabinet*, 146-154; Gorgas, *Civil War Diary*, 165. Northrop's successor was Col. I. M. St. John.

¹⁰ O. R., #108, 1082-1083; Mrs. Wright, *Southern Girl*, 238-239, R. E. Lee to A. H. Stephens, A. E. Maxwell *et al*, Feb. 13, 1865.

¹¹ J. E. Johnston to L. T. Wigfall, Feb. 12, 1865, Library of Congress.

¹² Hood, *Advance*, 317-337, where the complete report is found. Divided into sections, it is also in O. R., #74, 628-636; #77, 801-803; #93, 652-658.

¹³ *Jour. of Congress*, IV, 582, 664, 740; VII, 640, 708, 732, 744; Johnston, *Narrative*, 588-602, where Wigfall's speech, which he delivered March 18, 1865, is printed in full.

¹⁴ O. R., #74, 637-638.

¹⁵ *Ibid.*, #99, 1304-1311.

¹⁶ *Ibid.*, #96, 1242, 1244-1245; #98, 1044; #99, 1313; Davis, *Rise and Fall*, II, 536. Eliot, *West Point*, 255, H. D. Clayton to Jefferson Davis, Feb. 15, 1865.

¹⁷ O. R., #111, 413; L. T. Wigfall to J. E. Johnston, Feb. 27, 1865, Huntington Library.

¹⁸ O. R., #96, 1256; #99, 1303; Gordon, *Reminiscences*, 393. Lee said nothing to Gordon apparently about the reason behind Davis' request for the visit. In addition to the copy sent Phelan the President's secretary delivered two copies of the "unsent message" to Congressman Barksdale of Mississippi. Rowland, *Jefferson Davis*, VII, 381, E. Barksdale to Jefferson Davis, Jan. 7, 1874.

¹⁹ J. E. Johnston to L. T. Wigfall, March 14, 1865, Library of Congress.

²⁰ O. R., #99, 1247; J. E. Johnston to L. T. Wigfall, March 14, 1865, Library of Congress.

²¹ Williams, *Beauregard*, 252-253; Johnston, *Narrative*, 371-372; Roman, *Military Operations*, II, 361; O. R., #99, 1248. Beauregard told Lee, "I will at all times be happy to serve with or under so gallant and patriotic a soldier as General Johnston." But in the account of his career by Roman his disappointment is obvious. Roman states that Beauregard's health was never better in the war than at this time in North Carolina. Johnston in the *Narrative* states that Beauregard described the condition of his health as "feeble and precarious." Johnston received Lee's order Feb. 23 and took his place at Charlotte on Feb. 25, after visiting Beauregard.

²² O. R., #99, 1271, 1274; Johnston, *Narrative*, 376.

²³ O. R., #99, 536, 595, 612, 628; Sherman, *Memoirs*, II, 292, 297-299; George W. Nichols, *The Story of the Great March*, 197, 201, 217. Although Sherman says in his *Memoirs* that he didn't know of Johnston's reassignment until after March 2, his subordinates knew of it by Feb. 28. Grant had the news on Feb. 23 and sent it to Washington on the twenty-seventh. Sherman's casual references to Johnston in his message would indicate that the fact of his being in command was general knowledge. Nichols said that the news was general

among the people of North Carolina, who, he noted, "are delighted with Johnston's restoration for they profess to think him the greatest general in the country. I have never heard but one expression of opinion among the Southerners relative to the respective merits of Johnston and Lee. Johnston is regarded as much superior to Lee, especially as a genius for strategy."

[24] O. R., #98, 1050; #99, 1257, 1271, 1316, 1320, 1334, 1424; Johnston, *Narrative*, 377.

[25] O. R., #99, 1328.

[26] Cotton, *Yours Till Death*, 126.

[27] O. R., #99, 1290, 1296-1297, 1311, 1312, 1316, 1324, 1330, 1372, 1373-1374.

[28] Henry, *Confederacy*, 455; B. & L., IV, 698-700; O. R., #99, 1338. Under Johnston there were: Generals: Beauregard and Bragg; lieutenant generals: Hampton, Hardee, S. D. Lee, A. P. Stewart; major generals: Patton Anderson, W. B. Bate, J. C. Brown, M. C. Butler, B. F. Cheatham, H. D. Clayton, D. H. Hill, R. F. Hoke, W. W. Loring, L. McLaws, C. L. Stevenson, W. B. Taliaferro, E. C. Walthall, Joseph Wheeler.

[29] Ibid., 1257; #111, 413.

[30] Ibid., #99, 1297-1298, 1372-1373.

[31] Freeman, *Lee*, IV, 8-13; Gordon, *Reminiscences*, 389-394; *Lee's Dispatches*, 342-346; O. R., #96, 1295; #99, 1372, 1380. The dispatch from Lee is dated March 11 with a question mark in O. R., but the copy in the *Johnston Papers*, Huntington Library, carries the date March 14. As it logically follows Johnston's query of the twelfth

the fourteenth is used above.

[32] O. R., #99, 1395-1396.

[33] Ibid., 1347, 1353, 1361, 1364, 1375, 1377, 1384.

[34] Ibid., 1382, 1399; Ridley, *Battles and Sketches*, 452, 455; Wilson, *Reminiscences*, 41; Guild, *Brief Narrative*, 126-127.

[35] Johnston, *Narrative*, 382-383; O. R., #99, 822, 829, 1402; Sherman, *Memoirs*, II, 300-303.

[36] Johnston, *Narrative*, 385; B. & L., IV, 701, 702; O. R., #99, 1415, 1428, 1429.

[37] Ibid., 1426; B. & L., IV, 702; Johnston, *Narrative*, 385. In his message to Lee Johnston estimated his numbers as follows: Bragg, 6,500; Hardee, 7,500; Army of Tennessee, 4,000. According to the returns of March 17 the totals exclusive of Hardee were 9,513. Hardee as of March 23 had 6,255, a total of 15,768. The cavalry, which were not included in either of the above, numbered 4,093 in returns for March 25. O. R., #98, 1058, 1060; #99, 1426.

[38] B. & L., IV, 692, 703.

[39] Ibid., 692-693, 703-704; Johnston, *Narrative*, 386-387.

[40] Ibid., 388-389.

[41] B. & L., IV, 704-705; Sherman, *Memoirs*, II, 304. Sherman says that the attack occurred without his orders and that he ordered it recalled. Hampton says that if the incident was as Sherman reported, "the order was obeyed with wonderful promptness and alacrity."

[42] B. & L., IV, 705; Johnston, *Narrative*, 392; O. R., #98, 76, 1060; #99, 1454.

NOTES FOR CHAPTER 24
(Pages 358-376)

[1] O. R., #98, 1055.

[2] Ibid., 43, 1476; #99, 689, 716, 950; #100, 3-4; Ridley, *Battles and Sketches*, 453, 456.

[3] O. R., #100, 713, 731, 737; Johnston, *Narrative*, 395.

[4] Ridley, *Battles and Sketches*, 455; J. E. Johnston to L. T. Wigfall, Apr. 3, 1865, Library of Congress.

[5] Johnston, *Narrative*, 395; O. R., #100, 755, 765, 767.

[6] Ibid., 770, 773-774; Guild, *Brief*

Narrative, 136; Ridley, *Battles and Sketches,* 457.

⁷ *O. R.,* #100, 776, 777, 780, 782, 783, 787.

⁸ Ridley, *Battles and Sketches,* 454; Pepper, *Personal Recollections,* 387; O. R., #100, 791-792; R. E. Yates, "Zebulon B. Vance as War Governor of North Carolina, 1862-1865," *Journal of Southern History,* III, 73-74.

⁹ J. E. Johnston to A. H. Stephens, Apr. 28, 1868, Library of Congress; Johnston, *Narrative,* 396-400; Roman, *Military Operation,* II, 394-395; Reagan, *Memoirs,* 199-200; S. R. Mallory, "Last Days of the Confederacy," *McClure's Magazine,* XVI, 240-242; J. T. Durkin, *Stephen R. Mallory: Confederate Navy Chief,* 339-340, quoting from Mallory's manuscript diary.

¹⁰ Johnston, *Narrative,* 400-401; O. R., #100, 207, 798.

¹¹ Johnston, *Narrative,* 401; O. R., #100, 803, 805; J. E. Johnston to P. G. T. Beauregard, March 30, 1868, with an endorsement by Beauregard of Apr. 10, 1868, Huntington Library.

¹² Pepper, *Personal Recollections,* 409; Sherman, *Memoirs,* II, 348.

¹³ Pepper, *Personal Recollections,* 412; Nichols, *Great March,* 311-312; Sherman, *Memoirs,* II, 348.

¹⁴ *Ibid.,* 348-349. When Davis read Sherman's account of this incident he grew indignant that Johnston had not resented the implication against him. But Johnston had a larger responsibility, that of the army. He could not endanger it by antagonizing Sherman. Sanders was a diplomatic agent for the Confederacy. Davis, *Rise and Fall,* II, 686; Rowland, *Jefferson Davis,* VII, 251 n-252 n.

¹⁵ O. R., #100, 221; Sherman, *Memoirs,* II, 349-350; Johnston, *Narrative,* 402-404; J. E. Johnston to A. H. Stevens, Apr. 29, 1868, Library of Congress; Sherman, *Home Letters,* 344-345, W. T. Sherman to wife, Apr. 18, 1865.

¹⁶ Sherman, *Memoirs,* II, 350-351; O. R., #100, 237.

¹⁷ *Ibid.,* 806; Johnston, *Narrative,* 404-405.

¹⁸ *O. R.,* #100, 243-244. The full text of the first Sherman-Johnston agreement will be found here.

¹⁹ Johnston, *Narrative,* 404-407; Sherman, *Memoirs,* II, 352-354; Pepper, *Personal Reminiscences,* 417-420; Wise, *End of Era,* 449-453; O. R., #100, 243-245; J. E. Johnston to A. H. Stephens, Apr. 29, 1868, Library of Congress.

²⁰ *O. R.,* #100, 243; Sherman, *Memoirs,* II, 354.

²¹ Ridley, *Battles and Sketches,* 457; O. R., #100, 807, 808, 809, 810; J. E. Johnston to A. H. Stephens, Apr. 29, 1868, Library of Congress. Johnston told Stephens that Mallory in an article in a Florida newspaper had confused what he heard of this phase of the disintegration of the army with what Johnston told Davis at their meeting in Greensboro. He denied also another Mallory statement that he had said the Southern people felt "whipped." Mallory restated these remarks in an article he published in 1902.

²² O. R., #100, 810, 813.

²³ Wise, *End of Era,* 453-454; Wilson, *Reminiscences,* 42-43; Guild, *Brief Narrative,* 146; Ridley, *Battles and Sketches,* 459; Johnston, *Narrative,* 410.

²⁴ *O. R.,* #100, 810-811, 812, 815, 819, 828-829.

²⁵ *Ibid.,* 801, 803-804. Rumors were widely afloat as to the amount of money the government carried with it from Richmond, and the incomplete contemporary records leave many questions unanswered. Naval officers asked Johnston to assist them to secure funds for themselves only to be told that he did not have enough to pay his men and had no control over any funds, if there were such, at Charlotte. But he wasted no time to put in his claim. On the day before, Apr. 21, he wrote Breckinridge that he had heard there were additional funds. If so he respectfully urged "the appropriation of a portion of that sum to the payment of the army, as a matter of policy and justice." Even in the instance of the $39,000 the record is not clear. Johnston said after the war that he had two messages from Davis

about it. The first directed him to get it and to use it as a military chest. The second told him to send it on to Charlotte where the President's party was. Johnston says that he did not obey the second, as only the "military part of our Government had then any existence," and determined to divide it among the soldiers. Davis also writing after the war denied that he sent any message but that containing the instructions to Hendren. O. R., #100, 830; Johnston, *Narrative*, 408-409; Davis, *Rise and Fall*, II, 691-692; S.H.S.P., IX, 542-566, letter of Captain M. H. Clark, Jan. 10, 1882.

²⁶ O. R., #100, 249, 257, 264, 266, 268, 286, 810, 814, 817, 818.

²⁷ *Ibid.*, 287.

²⁸ *Ibid.*, 813-814, 829-830; Rowland, *Jefferson Davis*, VI, 559-562, Jefferson Davis to wife, Apr. 22, 1865.

²⁹ O. R., #100, 293, 294, 821-826, 827-828, 830-831, 832-834, 835; Johnston, *Narrative*, 410-411.

³⁰ O. R., #100, 837-838; Ridley, *Battles and Sketches*, 464; Guild, *Brief Narrative*, 147.

³¹ O. R., #100, 835, 837.

³² *Ibid.*, 836.

³³ *Ibid.*, 303, 304.

³⁴ Schofield, *Forty-Six Years*, 351-352; Johnston, *Narrative*, 412-413; Sherman,

Memoirs, II, 362-363; O. R., #100, 313.

³⁵ *Ibid.*, 320, 322, 323.

³⁶ *Ibid.*, 321, 843-844.

³⁷ *Ibid.*, 336-337.

³⁸ *Ibid.*, 349, 392, 842, 848, 853.

³⁹ Davis, *Rise and Fall*, II, 682, 689, 692-693; Rowland, *Jefferson Davis*, VI, 559-562, Jefferson Davis to wife, Apr. 23, 1865.

⁴⁰ O. R., #100, 848, 849, 850, 854; Johnston, *Narrative*, 419. Actually the division of the money was impossible by the mathematical allocation named. Ridley, *Battles and Sketches*, 460, says he received $1.15—"four quarters, one dime and a five cent piece"—and Wise, *End of Era*, 455, also reports $1.15. Wise says that one of his coins was a Mexican dollar on which he cut his initials, but it was stolen the next day from his pocket.

⁴¹ O. R., #100, 855, 872-873, 874.

⁴² *Ibid.*, 379-380, 483, 858, 865, 872. When the columns separated at Salisbury one went via Morganton, the second and largest group by Spartanburg and Abbeville, and the third by Chester and Newberry.

⁴³ *Ibid.*, 443, 520; Cox, *Military Reminiscences*, II, 533-534. Schofield secured the archives and sent them to Washington.

⁴⁴ O. R., #98, 1061.

NOTES FOR CHAPTER 25
(Pages 377-399)

¹ O. R., #100, 560, 564, 675; Pollard, *Lee and His Lieutenants*, 410, quoting a letter of Johnston, Aug. 17, 1865. In the letter Johnston enlarged on the ideas in his farewell to the soldiers and emphasized that as the South had referred the issue to the "arbitrament of the sword," there was an obligation to accept the decision.

² O. R., #100, 615; Mrs. Johnston to B. S. Ewell, June 8, 1865, Library of Congress.

³ O. R., #100, 675; Amnesty papers, File 67, National Archives. The Johnston file bears the number 1330 and contains

no evidence of any action. Johnston's appeal was for the removal of restrictions placed on those who held higher than colonel's rank and had resigned from the United States Army. An interesting sequel to this application of Johnston for relief is given in Maury, *Recollections*, 240. Maury had heard from Admiral Buchanan who said that he had not asked amnesty because he could not express regret for what he had done. "I showed the letter to General Joe Johnston," Maury wrote, "who said, in his terse way: 'You don't have to express any regret. I have asked pardon and have expressed no regret. Oh, yes, I did, too. I requested that His Excellency would grant me a pardon, and expressed regret that I could offer no reason why he should.'"

[4] J. E. Johnston to B. S. Ewell, May 16, 1866, Library of Congress; J. E. Johnston to L. T. Wigfall, June 1, 1866, Library of Congress; J. H. Wilson, Under the Old Flag, II, 381; R. S. Henry, Story of Reconstruction, 28.

[5] O. R., #121, 814-815, 842; Johnson, A Memoir, 265.

[6] J. H. Wilson, Under the Old Flag, II, 382-383; J. E. Johnston to B. S. Ewell, May 16, 1866, Library of Congress; J. E. Johnston to Duff Green, June 28, 1867, Library of Congress.

[7] J. E. Johnston to L. T. Wigfall, June 1, 1866, Library of Congress; St. Paul's Episcopal Church, Parish Record, 76.

[8] J. E. Johnston to L. T. Wigfall, Nov. 24, 1866, June 27, 1868, Library of Congress.

[9] Mrs. J. E. Johnston to B. S. Ewell, June 8, 1865, Library of Congress; Mrs. J. E. Johnston to L. T. Wigfall, July 26, 1866, Library of Congress; J. E. Johnston to L. T. Wigfall, Nov. 24, 1866, Library of Congress; J. W. Jones, Personal Reminiscences, Anecdotes, and Letters of Gen. Robert E. Lee, 207-208, Oct. 3, 1865. "I hope both you and Johnston," Lee wrote Beauregard, "will write the history of your campaigns. Every one should do all in his power to collect and disseminate the truth, in the hope that it may find a place in history, and descend to posterity."

[10] S. P. Lee, Memoirs of Pendleton, 440, J. E. Johnston to W. N. Pendleton, Aug. 7, 1867.

[11] J. E. Johnston to L. T. Wigfall, June 27, Sept. 29, 1868, undated letter, "Ship Hansa, Southampton, Tuesday morning," Library of Congress; National Cyclopedia American Biography, II, 58; C. M. Thompson, Reconstruction in Georgia, 330-331; J. E. Johnston to Bradley T. Johnson, Aug. 2, 1887, Duke

University Library. The partners represented the two companies with which they started until 1873, when they gave up the English firm for the Home Insurance Company of New York.

[12] Mackall, A Son's Recollections, 221-222.

[13] Mary Custis Lee to J. E. Johnston, Nov. 14, 1870, Library of Congress.

[14] S. P. Lee, Memoirs of Pendleton, 460, J. E. Johnston to W. N. Pendleton, Jan. 25, 1871; Hughes, Johnston, 283; Sherman, Letters, 330, W. T. Sherman to John Sherman, March 21, 1871. Johnston succeeded John C. Breckinridge as president of the Lee Memorial Association when the Kentuckian died in 1875. Rowland, Jefferson Davis, IX, 203-204, J. J. White to Jefferson Davis, March 13, 1883.

[15] Johnston, Narrative, 430; Rowland, Jefferson Davis, VII, 234-236, T. J. Wharton to Jefferson Davis, Jan. 24, 1868. This was the paper which Davis wrote to send to Congress but instead mailed it to James Phelan of Mississippi.

[16] Johnston, Narrative, 430; J. M. Kennard to J. E. Johnston, Sept. 1, 1874, College of William and Mary Library.

[17] Rowland, Jefferson Davis, VII, 129-130, J. E. Johnston to Jefferson Davis, Sept. 30, 1867.

[18] Rowland, Jefferson Davis, VII, 131, Jefferson Davis to J. E. Johnston, Oct. 23, 1867.

[19] Rowland, Jefferson Davis, VII, 132, Jefferson Davis to T. J. Wharton, Oct. 23, 1867.

[20] J. E. Johnston to L. T. Wigfall, June 27, 1868, Library of Congress; J. M. Kennard to J. E. Johnston, Sept. 1, 1874, College of William and Mary Library. Kennard wrote for Johnston at this time a full history of the efforts to secure a copy of Davis' letter or message.

[21] Johnston, Narrative, 431-433, N. G. Humphreys to J. E. Johnston, Jan. 10, 1870, L. Mims to J. E. Johnston, Oct. 8, 1873. For a comparison of Kennard's

synopsis of the "unsent message" with the original, see Johnston, *Narrative*, 433 ff. and Rowland, *Jefferson Davis*, VI, 491 ff.

[22] J. E. Johnston to D. Appleton and Company, Apr. 1, [1874], College of William and Mary Library.

[23] J. E. Johnston to D. Appleton and Company, Apr. 2, 1874, College of William and Mary Library; J. E. Johnston to J. C. Darby [Appleton and Co.], March 17, 1874, College of William and Mary Library; J. E. Johnston to A. D. Banks, June 29, 1875, College of William and Mary Library.

[24] McElroy, *Jefferson Davis*, 643; Rowland, *Jefferson Davis*, VIII, 42-44, C. G. Memminger to Editor, *Charleston News and Courier*, March 27, 1874; T. H. Williams, *Beauregard*, 307-308; *B. & L.*, I, 226-227.

[25] W. A. Christian, *Richmond, Her Past and Present*, 344, 349; C. V. Woodward, *Reunion and Reaction*, 91; J. E. Johnston to J. M. Smith, Nov. 8, 1875, College of William and Mary Library.

[26] Hughes, *Johnson*, 283; B. T. Johnson, *A Memoir of the Life and Public Service of Joseph E. Johnston*, 243, 246. Hughes uses 1877 as the date the Johnstons moved to Richmond while Bradley Johnson says that it was 1876. From his letter books in the College of William and Mary Library it appears that the Johnstons left Savannah late in December 1876 and that the General opened his office in Richmond early in 1877.

[27] J. E. Johnston to A. H. Dogenne, Feb. 7, 1876, College of William and Mary Library; W. E. Smith, *The Francis Preston Blair Family in Politics*, II, 473-474.

[28] *United States of America Statutes at Large*, XIX (1877), 511; C. R. Williams, *The Life of Rutherford Birchard Hayes*, II, 18-20.

[29] B. T. Johnson, *A Memoir*, 246-247.

[30] Stiles, *Four Years*, 90.

[31] B. T. Johnson, *A Memoir*, 248-250.

[32] U. S. Congress, *Biographical Directory of the American Congress, 1774-1927*, 352-361, 1158, 1271. J. E. Brown

also was a member of the Senate after the resignation of Gordon in 1880.

[33] Hughes, *Johnston*, 284; Otto Eisenschiml, *The Celebrated Case of Fitz John Porter*, 256, 266. After Second Manassas General Pope, the Federal commander, brought accusations of failure to obey orders and misconduct in the face of the enemy against Porter, who was cashiered. The case became a *cause celebre* involving the political attitudes of the postwar years. Porter's innocence of Pope's charges is now generally accepted, but it was not until 1886 that his name was cleared.

[34] J. E. Johnston to Governor F. W. M. Holliday, March 5, 1878, College of William and Mary Library; Hughes, *Johnston*, 285; *Confederate Veteran*, XIV, 467.

[35] Mackall, *A Son's Recollections*, 69-70. Mackall sent a copy of the invitation, which is about twice as long as given here, with the remark that he got the idea from Horace's fifth epistle and considered his an improvement on the original.

[36] Rowland, *Jefferson Davis*, IX, 24, 29-30, 37-38, B. H. Hill to Jefferson Davis, Dec. 27, 1881; *ibid.*, 40-43, 66, 142.

[37] Rowland, *Jefferson Davis*, IX, 30-31, S. K. Phillips to W. T. Walthall, Dec. 22, 1881; 150-151, J. F. Wheless to Jefferson Davis, Feb. 10, 1882; 177-178, W. N. Pendleton to Jefferson Davis, July 15, 1882; 203-204, J. J. White to Jefferson Davis, March 13, 1883; 205, Jefferson Davis to J. J. White, March [1883]; 260-262, Mrs. W. H. Felton to Jefferson Davis, Sept. 17, 1883.

[38] Johnston also contributed an article to the *Philadelphia Weekly Times*, later published in the volume, *Annals of the War*. The *Century* series was collected in *Battles and Leaders of the Civil War*.

[39] *New York Daily Tribune*, Apr. 8, 1886; W. B. Hesseltine, *Pioneer's Mission*, 281, J. E. Johnston to Lyman Draper.

[40] J. E. Johnston to Captain Robert Hunter, Dec. 8, 1875, Duke University

Library. The conversation was with Thomas Clarkson Thompson, Sr., who reported it to G. E. Govan.

[41] B. T. Johnson, *A Memoir*, 299-300; Maury, *Recollections*, 150.

[42] Hughes, *Johnston*, 291; Grant, *Personal Memoirs*, II, 525.

[43] *Harper's Weekly*, XXIX, 538.

[44] Myers, *McClellan*, 510 n, quotes letter of Johnston to Gen. R. B. Marcy, Nov. 5, 1885; Douglas, *I Rode With Stonewall*, 178.

[45] Maury, *Recollections*, 152-154; B.

T. Johnson, *A Memoir*, 262, 263, 298.

[46] J. E. Johnston to B. T. Johnson, July 27, 1887, Aug. 1, 1887, Duke University Library.

[47] *Atlanta Constitution*, Apr. 25, 26, 27, 1890.

[48] Hughes, *Johnston*, 287; Maury, *Recollections*, 154; *Harper's Weekly*, XXXV, 154, Lewis, *Sherman*, 652.

[49] Maury, *Recollections*, 155; Hughes, *Johnston*, 288; B. T. Johnson, *A Memoir*, 270-290.

ACKNOWLEDGMENTS AND BIBLIOGRAPHY

ACKNOWLEDGMENTS

Like all writers on historical subjects the authors are indebted to many persons. The bibliography of sources used is an acknowledgment of obligation to those who have published, but in addition there are those who have generously helped to bring this project to completion. Sometimes the debt is to an institution, first among them the University of Chattanooga, whose administration and staff encouraged the writers and gave material assistance by a grant-in-aid. Particular recognition among individuals should go to Dr. Robert S. Henry, among the foremost scholars on the Confederacy, who suggested this biography, and D. Laurance Chambers, then president of the Bobbs-Merrill Company, who made the idea possible.

It is impossible to list all who have aided, but in one way or another the following, some of them now deceased, contributed so valuably that the authors wish publicly to make this recognition: Albert Banton, Yorktown, Virginia; Dewey Carroll, Atlanta, Georgia; Chattanooga Public Library Staff; Confederate Memorial Literary Society (The Confederate Museum) Richmond; Dr. E. M. Coulter, University of Georgia; Mrs. R. M. Crawford, Croton-on-Hudson, New York; Duke University Library, Manuscripts Department; Dr. D. S. Freeman, Richmond; Mrs. Frances Stone Friedman, Chattanooga; Dr. Thomas P. Govan, New York; Dr. P. G. Hamlin, Williamsburg; W. G. Harkins, College of William and Mary Library; Cecil F. Holland, Washington; Capt. R. M. Hughes, Norfolk; Henry E. Huntington Library and Art Gallery, San Marino; Mrs. Charles R. Hyde, Chattanooga; Col. Allen P. Julian, Atlanta; Bettie Keith, Selma Public Library, Selma; James H. Latimer, Richmond; Library of the Boston Athenaeum, Boston; Library of Congress, Washington; Dr. David A. Lockmiller, Chattanooga; David C. Mearns, Library of Congress; John R. Peacock, High Point; Major Thomas Price, Chattanooga; Dr. C. H. Smith, Chattanooga; J. R. Sullivan, Chickamauga-Chattanooga National Military Park; University of Chattanooga Library Staff; Bodo Weber, Chattanooga; Bertie Wenning, Chattanooga; Dr. Bell I. Wiley, Emory University; Dr. Owen H. Wilson, Nashville; Ola M. Wyeth, Savannah Public Library; B. C. Yates, Kennesaw Mountain National Battlefield Park; and Dr. Edward Younger, University of Virginia.

BIBLIOGRAPHY

Alexander, E. P. *Military Memoirs of a Confederate*. New York: Charles Scribner's Sons, 1907.

Annals of the War. Philadelphia: Times Publishing Company, 1878.

Austin, J. P. *The Blue and the Gray*. Atlanta: Franklin Printing and Publishing Company, 1899.

Beauregard, P. G. T. *With Beauregard in Mexico*. Edited by T. Harry Williams. Baton Rouge: Louisiana State University Press, 1956.

Bettersworth, J. K. *Confederate Mississippi*. Baton Rouge: Louisiana State University Press, 1943.

Bill, A. H. *The Beleaguered City: Richmond, 1861-1865*. New York: Alfred A. Knopf, 1946.

Black, III, R. C. *The Railroads of the Confederacy*. Chapel Hill: University of North Carolina Press, 1952.

Buck, I. B. *Cleburne and His Command*. New York: Neale Publishing Company, 1908.

Burne, A. H. *Lee, Grant and Sherman*. New York: Charles Scribner's Sons, 1929.

Cate, W. A. (ed.) *Two Soldiers: The Campaign Diaries of Thomas J. Key, C.S.A., and Robert J. Campbell, U.S.A.* Chapel Hill: University of North Carolina Press, 1938.

Chesnut, M. B. *A Diary from Dixie*. Edited by Ben Ames Williams. Boston: Houghton Mifflin Company, 1949.

————. *A Diary from Dixie*. Edited by Isabella D. Martin and Myrta Lockett Avary. New York: D. Appleton and Company, 1905.

Christian, W. A. *Richmond, Her Past and Present*. Richmond: L. H. Jenkins, 1912.

Clay-Clopton, Mrs. C. C. *A Belle of the Fifties*. Edited by Ada Sterling. New York: Doubleday, Page and Company, 1905.

Cobb, J. A. "Civil War Incidents in Macon," *Georgia Historical Quarterly, VII*.

Confederate Veteran. Nashville, 1893-1932.

Cooke, J. E. *A Life of Gen. Robert E. Lee.* New York: D. Appleton and Company, 1871.

———. *Wearing of the Gray.* New York: E. B. Treat and Company, 1867.

Cotton, J. W. *Yours Till Death: Civil War Letters of John W. Cotton.* Edited by Lucille Griffith. University, Alabama: University of Alabama Press, 1951.

Coulter, E. M. *The Confederate States of America 1861-1865.* Baton Rouge: Louisiana State University Press. Dallas: The Littlefield Fund for Southern History of the University of Texas, 1950.

Cox, J. D. *Atlanta.* New York: Charles Scribner's Sons, 1882.

———. *Military Reminiscences of the Civil War.* New York: Charles Scribner's Sons, 1900.

Crawford, J. M. *Mosby and His Men.* New York: G. W. Carleton and Company, 1867.

Cullum, G. W. *Biographical Register of the Officers and Graduates of the U. S. Military Academy at West Point, N. Y., from Its Establishment in 1802 to 1890, with the Early History of the United States Military Academy.* Boston: Houghton Mifflin Company, 1891.

Cumming, K. *A Journal of Hospital Life in the Confederate Army of Tennessee.* Louisville: John P. Morton and Company, 1866.

Dabney, R. L. *Life and Campaigns of Lieut.-Gen. Thomas J. Jackson.* New York: Blelock and Company, 1865.

Davis, J. *Jefferson Davis, Constitutionalist: Letters, Papers and Speeches.* Collected and edited by Dunbar Rowland. Jackson, Miss.: Mississippi Department of Archives and History, 1923.

———. *The Rise and Fall of the Confederate Government.* New York: D. Appleton and Company, 1881.

Davis, V. *Jefferson Davis, Ex-President of the Confederate States of America.* New York: Belford Company, 1890.

[DeFontaine, F. G.], *Marginalia.* By "Personne." Columbia, S. C.: F. G. DeFontaine and Company, 1864.

DeLeon, T. C. *Belles, Beaux and Brains of the 60's.* New York: G. W. Dillingham Company, 1907.

———. *Four Years in Rebel Capitals.* Mobile: Gossip Printing Company, 1890.

Dictionary of American Biography. New York: Charles Scribner's Sons, 1928-1936.

Dooley, J. E. *John Dooley: Confederate Soldier. His Journal.* Edited by J. T. Durkin. Washington: Georgetown University Press, 1945.

Dorsey, S. A. *Recollections of Henry Watkins Allen.* New York: M. Doolady, 1866.

Douglas, H. K. *I Rode with Stonewall.* Chapel Hill: University of North Carolina Press, 1940.

Dubose, J. W. *General Joseph Wheeler and the Army of Tennessee.* New York: Neale Publishing Company, 1912.

———. *The Life and Times of William Lowndes Yancey.* Birmingham: Roberts and Son, 1892.

Durkin, J. T. *Stephen R. Mallory: Confederate Navy Chief.* Chapel Hill: University of North Carolina Press, 1954.

Dyer, J. P. *The Gallant Hood.* Indianapolis: The Bobbs-Merrill Company, 1950.

Eckenrode, H. J. *Jefferson Davis, President of the South.* New York: The Macmillan Company, 1923.

Eckenrode, H. J. and Conrad, B. *James Longstreet*. Chapel Hill: University of North Carolina Press, 1936.

Eggleston, G. C. *A Rebel's Recollections*, New York: Hurd and Houghton, 1874.

Eisenschiml, O. *The Celebrated Case of Fitz John Porter*. Indianapolis: The Bobbs-Merrill Company, 1950.

Eliot, E., Jr. *West Point in the Confederacy*. New York: G. A. Baker and Company, 1941.

Elliott, C. W. *Winfield Scott: Soldier and Man*. New York: The Macmillan Company, 1937.

English Combatant. *Battle-Fields of the South from Bull Run to Fredericksburgh*. New York: John Bradburn, 1864.

Estes, C. (comp.). *List of Field Officers, Regiments and Battalions in the Confederate States Army 1861-1865*. Macon, Ga.: J. W. Burke Company, 1912.

Ewell, R. S. *The Making of a Soldier*. Edited by P. G. Hamlin. Richmond: Whittet and Shepperson, 1935.

Fleming, W. L. "Jefferson Davis at West Point," *Publications of the Mississippi Historical Society*, X.

Foote, H. S. *Casket of Reminiscences*. Washington: Chronicle Publishing Company, 1874.

——. *War of the Rebellion*. New York: Harper and Brothers, 1866.

Freeman, D. S. *R. E. Lee*. New York: Charles Scribner's Sons, 1934-1935.

——. *Lee's Lieutenants*. New York: Charles Scribner's Sons, 1942-1944.

Fremantle, A. J. L. *Three Months in the Southern States*. New York: John Bradburn, 1864.

French, S. G. *Two Wars*. Nashville: The Confederate Veteran, 1901.

Gay, M. A. H. *Life in Dixie During the War*. Atlanta: Foote and Davies Company, 1894.

Geer, W. *Campaigns of the Civil War*. New York: Brentano's, 1926.

Gordon. J. B. *Reminiscences of the Civil War*. New York: Charles Scribner's Sons, 1903.

Gorgas, J. *The Civil War Diary of General Josiah Gorgas*. Edited by Frank E. Vandiver. University, Alabama: University of Alabama Press, 1947.

Grant, U. S. *Personal Memoirs*. New York: Charles L. Webster and Company, 1885.

Guild, G. B. *A Brief Narrative of the Fourth Tennessee Cavalry Regiment*, Nashville: n.p., 1913.

Hagan, J. W. *Confederate Letters of John W. Hagan*. Edited by Bell I. Wiley. Athens: University of Georgia Press, 1954.

Hamlin, P. G. *Old Bald Head (General R. S. Ewell)*. Strasburg, Virginia: Shenandoah Publishing House, 1940.

Hanna, A. J. *Flight into Oblivion*. Richmond: Johnson Publishing Company, 1938. *Harper's Weekly*, 1857-1916.

Harrison, Mrs. Burton. *Recollections Grave and Gay*. New York: Charles Scribner's Sons, 1911.

Hay, T. R. "The Atlanta Campaign," *Georgia Historical Quarterly*, VII.

——. "Confederate Leadership at Vicksburg," *Mississippi Valley Historical Review*, XI.

——. "Davis-Hood-Johnston Controversy of 1864," *Mississippi Valley Historical Review* XI.

Henderson, G. F. R. *Stonewall Jackson and the American Civil War.* New York: Longmans, Green and Company, 1936.

Hendrick, B. J. *Statesmen of the Lost Cause.* Boston: Little, Brown and Company, 1939.

Henry, R. S. *"First with the Most" Forrest.* Indianapolis: The Bobbs-Merrill Company, 1944.

———. *Story of the Confederacy.* Indianapolis: The Bobbs-Merrill Company, 1931.

———. *The Story of the Mexican War.* Indianapolis: The Bobbs-Merrill Company, 1950.

———. *Story of Reconstruction.* Indianapolis: The Bobbs-Merrill Company, 1938.

Hesseltine, W. B. *Pioneer's Mission.* Madison, Wisconsin: State Historical Society of Wisconsin, 1954.

Hill, L. B. *Joseph E. Brown and the Confederacy.* Chapel Hill: University of North Carolina Press, 1939.

Hinman, W. F. *The Story of the Sherman Brigade.* Alliance, Ohio: Author, 1897.

Hitchcock, H. *Marching with Sherman.* Edited by M. A. DeW. Howe. New Haven: Yale University Press, 1927.

Hood, J. B. *Advance and Retreat.* New Orleans: Hood Orphan Memorial Fund, 1879.

Horn, S. F. *Army of Tennessee.* Indianapolis: The Bobbs-Merrill Company, 1941.

Howard, McH. *Recollections of a Maryland Confederate Soldier and Staff Officer under Johnston, Jackson and Lee.* Baltimore: Williams and Wilkins Company, 1914.

Hughes, R. M. *General Johnston.* New York: D. Appleton and Company, 1897.

———. "Some War Letters of General Joseph E. Johnston," *Journal of the Military Service Institution of the United States,* L.

Hungerford, E. *The Story of the Baltimore & Ohio Railroad, 1827-1927.* New York: G. P. Putnam Sons, 1928.

Jackson, M. A. *Memoirs of Stonewall Jackson.* Louisville: Prentice Press, 1895.

Johnson, B. T. (ed.). *A Memoir of the Life and Public Service of Joseph E. Johnston.* Baltimore: R. H. Woodward and Company, 1891.

Johnson, R. U., and Buel, C. C. (eds.). *Battles and Leaders of the Civil War.* New York: Century Company, 1887-1888.

Johnston, J. E. *Narrative of Military Operations, Directed, During the Late War between the States.* New York: D. Appleton and Company, 1874.

Johnston, R. M. *Bull Run: Its Strategy and Tactics.* Boston: Houghton Mifflin Company, 1913.

Johnston, W. P. *Life of General Albert Sidney Johnston.* New York: D. Appleton and Company, 1878.

Jones, J. B. *A Rebel War Clerk's Diary.* Philadelphia: J. B. Lippincott and Company, 1866.

Jones, J. W. *Personal Reminiscences, Anecdotes, and Letters of Gen. Robert E. Lee.* New York: D. Appleton and Company, 1874.

Lee, R. E. *Lee's Dispatches.* Edited by D. S. Freeman. New York: G. P. Putnam's Sons, 1915.

Lee, R. E. Jr. *Recollections and Letters of General Robert E. Lee.* New York: Doubleday, Page and Company, 1904.

Lee, S. D. "The Campaigns of Vicksburg, Mississippi, in 1863, from April 15 to and including the Battle of Champion Hills, or Baker's Creek, May 16, 1863," *Publications of the Mississippi Historical Society*, III.

———. "Siege of Vicksburg," *Publications of the Mississippi Historical Society*, III.

———. "The War in Mississippi after the Fall of Vicksburg, July 4, 1863," *Publications of the Mississippi Historical Society*, X.

Lee, S. P. *Memoirs of William Nelson Pendleton, D.D.* Philadelphia: J. B. Lippincott Company, 1893.

Leech, M. *Reveille in Washington, 1860-1865.* New York: Harper and Brothers, 1941.

Lewis, L. *Sherman, the Fighting Prophet.* New York: Harcourt, Brace and Company, 1932.

Lindsley, J. B. *The Military Annals of Tennessee. Confederate.* Nashville: J. M. Lindsley and Company, 1886.

Livermore, T. L. *Numbers and Losses in the Civil War in America, 1861-1865.* Boston: Houghton Mifflin Company, 1900.

Long, A. L. *Memoirs of Robert E. Lee.* New York: J. M. Stoddart and Company, 1886.

Longstreet, J. *From Manassas to Appomattox.* Philadelphia: J. B. Lippincott Company, 1895.

Lonn, E. *Desertion during the Civil War.* New York: Century Company, 1928.

McClellan, G. B. *McClellan's Own Story; The War for the Union.* New York: Charles L. Webster and Company, 1886.

McElroy, R. *Jefferson Davis: The Unreal and the Real.* New York: Harper and Brothers, 1937.

Mackall, W. W. *A Son's Recollections of His Father.* New York: E. P. Dutton and Company, 1930.

McKim, R. H. *A Soldier's Recollections.* New York: Longmans, Green and Company, 1910.

McLane, R. M. *Reminiscences, 1827-1897.* Privately printed, 1903.

Mallory, S. R. "Last Days of the Confederacy," *McClure's Magazine*, XVI.

Marshall, C. *An Aide-de-Camp of Lee.* Edited by Maj. Gen. Sir Frederick Maurice. Boston: Little, Brown and Company 1927.

Maury, D. H. *Recollections of a Virginian in the Mexican, Indian and Civil Wars.* New York: Charles Scribner's Sons, 1894.

Meade, G. G. *The Life and Letters of George Gordon Meade.* Edited by George Gordon Meade. New York: Charles Scribner's Sons, 1913.

Moore, A. B. *Conscription and Conflict in the Confederacy.* New York: The Macmillan Company, 1924.

Motte, J. R. *Journey into Wilderness: An Army Surgeon's Account of Life in Camp and Field During the Creek and Seminole Wars, 1836-1838.* Edited by James F. Sunderman. Gainesville, Fla.: University of Florida Press, 1953.

Myers, W. S. *General George Brinton McClellan.* New York: D. Appleton-Century Company, 1934.

National Cyclopedia of American Biography. New York: J. T. White Company, 1893-1919.

Nichols, G. W. *The Story of the Great March.* New York: Harper and Brothers, 1865.

Nisbet, J. C. *Four Years on the Firing Line.* Chattanooga: Imperial Press, n.d.

Noll, A. H. *General Kirby Smith.* Sewanee, Tenn.: University of the South Press, 1907.

———. (ed.). *Doctor Quintard, Chaplain C. S. A. and Second Bishop of Tennessee.* Sewanee, Tenn.: University of the South Press, 1905.

Oates, W. C. *The War Between the Union and the Confederacy.* New York: Neale Publishing Company, 1905.

Owen, T. McA. *History of Alabama and Dictionary of Alabama Biography.* Chicago: S. J. Clarke Publishing Company, 1921.

Owen, W. M. *In Camp and Battle with the Washington Artillery of New Orleans.* Boston: Ticknor and Company, 1885.

Paris, Comte de. *History of the Civil War in America.* Philadelphia: Porter and Coates, 1876.

Parks, J. H. *General Edmund Kirby Smith, C. S. A.* Baton Rouge: Louisiana State University Press, 1954.

Patrick, R. W. *Jefferson Davis and His Cabinet.* Baton Rouge: Louisiana State University Press, 1944.

Pearce, H. J., Jr. *Benjamin H. Hill.* Chicago: University of Chicago Press, 1928.

Pemberton, J. C. *Pemberton, Defender of Vicksburg.* Chapel Hill: University of North Carolina Press, 1942.

Pepper, G. W. *Personal Recollections of Sherman's Campaigns in Georgia and the Carolinas.* Zanesville, Ohio: Hugh Dunne, 1866.

Phillips, U. B. (ed.). "The Correspondence of Robert Toombs, Alexander H. Stephens, and Howell Cobb," *The Annual Report of the American Historical Association for the Year 1911*, II. Washington: Government Printing Office, 1913.

Polk, W. M. *Leonidas Polk, Bishop and General.* New York: Longmans, Green and Company, 1915.

Pollard, E. A. *Lee and His Lieutenants.* New York: E. B. Treat and Company, 1867.

Pressly, T. J. *Americans Interpret Their Civil War.* Princeton: Princeton University Press, 1954.

Pryor, Mrs. R. A. *Reminiscences of Peace and War.* New York: The Macmillan Company, 1904.

Reagan, J. H. *Memoirs.* Edited by W. F. McCaleb. New York: Neale Publishing Company, 1906.

Rebellion Record. Edited by Frank Moore. New York: G. P. Putnam's Sons, 1864-1868.

Richardson, J. D. (comp. and ed.). *A Compilation of the Messages and Papers of the Confederacy.* Nashville: United States Publishing Company, 1904.

"A Richmond Lady" [Mrs. S. A. B. Putnam]. *Richmond During the War.* New York: G. W. Carleton and Company, 1867.

Ridley, B. L. *Battles and Sketches of the Army of Tennessee.* Mexico, Mo.: Missouri Printing & Publishing Company, 1906.

Roeder, R. *Juarez and His Mexico.* New York: Viking Press, 1947.

Roman, A. *Military Operations of General Beauregard.* New York: Harper and Brothers, 1883.

Rowland, D. *History of Mississippi.* Chicago-Jackson: S. J. Clarke Publishing Company, 1925.

Russell, W. H. *My Diary North and South.* Boston: T. O. H. P. Burnham, 1863.

Schofield, J. M. *Forty-Six Years in the Army*. New York: Century Company, 1897.

Scott, S. S. "Some Account of Confederate Indian Affairs," *The Gulf States Historical Magazine*, II.

Scott, Winfield. *Memoirs of Lt. Gen. Scott, Ll. D.* New York: Sheldon and Company, 1864.

Scribner, B. F. *How Soldiers Were Made, or the War as I Saw It*. [Chicago: Donahue & Henneberry], 1887.

Seitz, D. C. *Braxton Bragg, General of the Confederacy*. Columbia, S.C.: State Company, 1924.

Shanks, H. T. *The Secession Movement in Virginia, 1847-1861*. Richmond: Garrett and Massie, 1934.

Sherman, W. T. *Home Letters of General Sherman*. Edited by M. A. DeWolfe Howe. New York: Charles Scribner's Sons, 1909.

————. *Memoirs*. New York: Charles L. Webster and Company, 1891.

————. *The Sherman Letters*. Edited by R. S. Thorndike. New York: Charles Scribner's Sons, 1894.

Smith, G. W. *The Battle of Seven Pines*, New York: C. G. Crawford, 1891.

————. *Confederate War Papers*. New York: Atlantic Publishing and Engraving Company, 1883.

Smith, J. H. *The War with Mexico*. New York: The Macmillan Company, 1919.

Smith, W. E. *The Francis Preston Blair Family in Politics*. New York: The Macmillan Company 1933.

Southern Historical Society Papers. 1876-

Squires, J. D. "Aeronautics in the Civil War," *American Historical Review*, XLII.

Starr, L. M. *Bohemian Brigade*. New York: Alfred A. Knopf, 1954.

Steele, M. F. *American Campaigns*. Washington: Bryan S. Adams, 1909.

Stiles, R. *Four Years Under Marse Robert*. New York: Neale Publishing Company, 1903.

Strother, D. H. "Personal Recollections of the War," *Harper's New Monthly Magazine*, XXXIII.

Taylor, R. *Destruction and Reconstruction*. New York: D. Appleton and Company, 1879.

Thomason, J. W., Jr. *Jeb Stuart*. New York: Charles Scribner's Sons, 1930.

Thompson, C. M. *Reconstruction in Georgia*. New York: Columbia University Press, 1915.

Turner, G. E. *Victory Rode the Rails*. Indianapolis: The Bobbs-Merrill Company, 1953.

United States Congress. *American State Papers. Military Affairs*, III. Washington: Gales and Seaton, 1860.

————. *Biographical Directory of the American Congress, 1774-1927*. Washington: Government Printing Office, 1928.

United States Senate. *Journal of the Congress of the Confederate States of America, 1861-1865*. Washington: Government Printing Office, 1904.

————. *Journal of the Executive Proceedings of the Senate of the United States*, XI. Washington: Government Printing Office, 1887.

United States War Department. *The War of the Rebellion: A Compilation of the Official Records of the Union and Confederate Armies*. Washington: Government Printing Office, 1880-1901.

Van Horne, T. B. *History of the Army of the Cumberland*. Cincinnati: Robert Clarke & Company, 1875.

———. *The Life of Major-General George H. Thomas*. New York: Charles Scribner's Sons, 1882.

Watkins, S. R. *"Company Aytch."* Jackson, Tenn.: McCowat-Mercer Press, 1952.

Wellman, M. W. *Giant in Gray*. New York: Charles Scribner's Sons, 1949.

White, L. A. *Robert Barnwell Rhett*. New York: Century Company, 1931.

Wiley, B. I. *The Life of Johnny Reb*. Indianapolis: The Bobbs-Merrill Company, 1943.

Williams, C. R. *Life of Rutherford Birchard Hayes*. Boston: Houghton Mifflin Company, 1914.

Williams, T. H. *P. G. T. Beauregard*. Baton Rouge: Louisiana State University Press, 1954.

Wilson, J. H. *Under the Old Flag*. New York: D. Appleton and Company, 1912.

Wilson, T. B. *Reminiscences*. (Nashville: Owen H. Wilson), n.d.

Wise, J. S. *The End of an Era*. Boston: Houghton Mifflin Company, 1899.

Woodward, C. Vann. *Reunion and Reaction*. Boston: Little, Brown and Company, 1954.

Wright, Mrs. D. G. *A Southern Girl in '61*. New York: Doubleday, Page and Company, 1905.

Wright, M. J. *General Officers of the Confederate Army*. New York: Neale Publishing Company, 1911.

Yates, R. E. *"Zebulon B. Vance as War Governor of North Carolina, 1862-1865," Journal of Southern History*, III.

NEWSPAPERS:

Atlanta Constitution
Chattanooga Daily Rebel
Richmond Dispatch
Richmond Enquirer
Richmond Daily Examiner
Richmond Sentinel
Richmond Daily Whig

MANUSCRIPTS:

Chickamauga-Chattanooga National Military Park Library
  J. W. Tuttle, Extracts from diary. Typescript
  Anonymous, Atlanta campaign diary. Typescript
Duke University Library:
  P. G. T. Beauregard papers
  S. Champion papers
  Georgia portfolio
  R. N. Gourdin papers
  F. W. M. Holliday collection
  B. T. Johnson papers
  J. E. Johnston papers
  C. T. Quintard papers

A. H. Stephens papers
Miscellaneous items
Henry E. Huntington Library and Art Gallery:
R. A. Brock papers
J. W. Eldridge papers
J. E. Johnston papers
J. P. Nicholson papers
J. E. B. Stuart papers
Miscellaneous items
Library of Congress:
Barton-Jenofer papers
A. T. Bledsoe papers
G. W. Campbell collection
Jefferson Davis collection
B. S. Ewell collection
Duff Green papers
G. F. Holmes collection
T. J. Jackson collection
Mansfield Lovell papers
G. B. McClellan papers
Alfred Roman collection
Wigfall family papers
Miscellaneous items
National Archives:
Amnesty papers
University of North Carolina Library: .
S. R. Mallory, Diary, typescript
St. Paul's Episcopal Church, Selma, Alabama:
Parish record
College of William and Mary:
J. E. Johnston collection

INDEX

INDEX